THE WHOLE LIBRARY HANDBOOK

CURRENT DATA, PROFESSIONAL ADVICE, AND CURIOSA ABOUT LIBRARIES AND LIBRARY SERVICES

compiled by

George M. Eberhart

AMERICAN LIBRARY ASSOCIATION

Chicago and London 1991

Cover designed by Jim Lange

Text and graphics designed by Priority Publishing

Composition by Priority Publishing using Aldus PageMaker and Corel Draw!
   with a Canon LBP-8 III laser printer and a LaserMaster LX6S Professional
   controller card

Printed on 50-pound Glatfelter, a pH-neutral stock, and bound in 10-point
   Carolina cover stock by Edwards Brothers, Inc., Ann Arbor

The paper used in this publication meets the minimum requirements of American
National Standard for Information Sciences—Permanence of Paper for Printed
Library Materials, ANSI Z39.48-1984. ∞

Library of Congress Cataloging-in-Publication Data

Eberhart, George M.
     The whole library handbook : current data, professional advice,
   and curiosa about libraries and library services / compiled by George
   M. Eberhart.
          p.   cm.
     Includes index.
     ISBN 0-8389-0573-0
     1. Library science—United States—Handbooks, manuals, etc.
   2. Libraries—United States—Handbooks, manuals, etc.   I. American
   Library Association.   II. Title.
   Z665.2.U6E24 1991
   020'.973—dc20   91-17311

Printed in the United States of America.

95 94 93 92   5 4 3

CONTENTS

    Statistics • Users • Services • Types of libraries •
    Bookmobiles • The Library of Congress • Trends

    Events • Conferences • Grants • Scholarships •
    Awards • Library education • Research tips

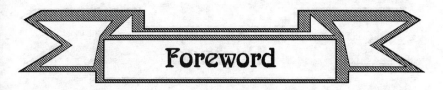

The Whole Library Handbook:
A new product for whole library people

Art Plotnik
Associate Publisher, ALA Publishing

THE WHOLE LIBRARY HANDBOOK began as a concept at American Library Association Publishing, where, like other professional publishers, we seek to develop certain products that everyone in our special universe needs desperately and will use and cherish forever. A general handbook came to mind because many professions have just such a compact reference—a first-stop sampler of the most common information, with a quick referral to more detailed sources. Why should the library community not have its *vade mecum?*

Because, argued the devil's advocates, the library community has twigged into a thousand specialized interests, and no compact, eclectic volume could capture that special energy at the roots—that general enthusiasm experienced during the early days at library school or when we walk into a library building.

No one knows better than a library publisher how fragmented the field has become; reader passions run from subject authorities in an online environment to storytelling with flannel boards. Yet, we believe that within each library specialist resides the *whole* library person; someone whose overall passion for libraries piques an interest in all aspects of this delightfully variegated realm.

And so we pursued the concept of a compact, affordable compendium of useful and engaging library-related information directed at the *whole* community of library workers, educators, friends, trustees, and users. Much of the information would be extracted from current ALA sources—including many elusive and unpublished documents—and other major sources willing to share their bounty.

All we needed now was a very special compiler: A unifier, not only knowledgeable in library matters and editorial techniques, but someone of whole library passion, who could impart the delights as well as the data of our world.

We found that person in George M. Eberhart. Or did George find us? Somehow we converged, and the result of much synergistic interplay is before you. George, as noted on page 484, is an experienced librarian and library-journal editor. He is also an enthusiast of librariana—that body of wit, lore, and curiosa never so ably represented as in Chapter 10 of this handbook. He is a respected author and bibliographer of the scientific study of the UFO phenomenon—one of many diverse interests that have led him to use, revere, and, yes, love libraries.

"This is the book I've always wanted to do," he told me when we first talked about it. He not only did it to our high expectations—he also set the type and designed the pages on his personal desktop publishing system, helping to make the book timely and affordable.

The Whole Library Handbook is a book we very much wanted to do at ALA Publishing, too. We hope it's one you've always wanted to own.

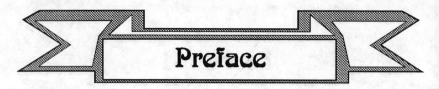

Preface

The Whole Library Handbook

George M. Eberhart

MANY TIMES AS A LIBRARIAN, as well as an editor of an ALA library journal, I found myself racking my brains, trying to remember where I had seen that handy checklist or apt summary, that clever diagram or unforgettable table, that concise lexicon or enlightening chronology . . . and wishing I had had the foresight to secure a permanent copy for my bookshelf or desk drawer. Quite often these sources were in magazines I had scanned quickly, or small booklets sent as review copies, or articles I had even edited and published in *College & Research Libraries News* (what issue *was* that in? the green or the blue one?).

To a large extent, *The Whole Library Handbook* is a solution to my dilemma. I will consult it when I want to alphabetize Portuguese surnames; I will browse through the notable book lists the next time I can't decide on something to read; I will point out the relevant chapters to friends who ask me what they should do with their old books or how to write their legislators. Perhaps you, as library staff or users, will find many similar applications.

The Whole Library Handbook is also an attempt to gently remind those of us who have become overspecialized that others in this protean profession have generated some excellent literature. It's easy, as a reference librarian, to forget the brilliant concepts originated by catalogers; academic librarians may often be unaware of the pioneering projects of public or school librarians; and we sometimes undervalue the work of those on the periphery of our profession—the indexers, the freedom of information activists, the archivists, the collectors of popular culture.

Looking back on this project, I note many topics that because of lack of space, or unconscious editorial preference, are missing or underrepresented. This one volume was not intended to be the "compleat" library handbook, but to be a tantalizing sampler with many suggestions on where to look further.

Please keep in mind that some of the guidelines reprinted here have been slightly edited in format, though not in content; others are only excerpts from a much larger document. You should consult the original source before quoting chapter and verse.

Finally, I hope you will find herein an interesting fact or humorous statement that will brighten an otherwise boring or gloomy day!

How you can help shape future editions

When it's time to update this book I will need your help. If you know of a checklist, a glossary, a how-to guide that you find indispensible, or interesting facts and concepts of the kind presented here, please write and tell me about it so that it can be shared with other librarians. Or, if your committee has been working on standards or guidelines, or collecting interesting data that somehow I missed this first time around, please send a memo about that, too. Send it all to: *The Whole Library Handbook*, c/o ALA Publishing, 50 E. Huron St., Chicago, IL 60611-2795.

If you do, you will ensure that this book remains what I hope it already is for you now: one of the first things you reach for when you have a question about libraries.

LIBRARIES

Some basic figures

by Mary Jo Lynch

MOST OF THE FIGURES given here are from surveys published by the National Center for Education Statistics (NCES): *Academic Libraries 1988* (1990), *Public Libraries 1989* (1991), and *Statistics of Public and Private School Library Media Centers 1985* (1987). Additional sources are cited where appropriate.

How many libraries are there?

Libraries of various types exist in all parts of the United States, and there is no official source that counts them every year. The following count is based on the three surveys cited above, except for special library figures and Canadian data, which come from the 1990–91 *American Library Directory* compiled by the R. R. Bowker Company.

Libraries in the United States		
College and university libraries		3,438
Public libraries		8,968*
Branches	6,513	
Buildings	15,481	
School library media centers		92,538
Public schools	73,352	
Private schools	19,186	
Special libraries		11,275
Armed forces	489	
Government	1,735	
Other special	9,051	
TOTAL		116,219

* This is the number of administrative units. Many libraries have one or more branches, totalling 6,513 nationally. Thus, the total number of buildings is 15,480.

These libraries are often involved in cooperative organizations through which they share collections, technology, and staff expertise. The most recent figures available indicate that approximately 760 networks and cooperatives exist in the United States (*Survey of Library Networks and Cooperative Library Organizations, 1985–1986*, NCES, 1987). Most college, university, and public libraries and many school libraries belong to at least one and many participate in more than one.

Libraries in Canada		
College and university libraries		502
Public libraries		756
Branches	965	
Buildings	1,721	
Special libraries		1,519
Government	360	
Other special	1,159	
TOTAL		2,777

Who uses libraries?

Libraries serve many different kinds of people. The 3,058 **academic libraries** submitting "attendance" figures to the National Center for Education Statistics in 1988 reported that more than 14,235,000 people visited these libraries in a typical week. NCES reported that 2,870 academic libraries in 1985 served student populations as shown below (*Library Statistics of Colleges and Universities 1985*, ALA/ACRL).

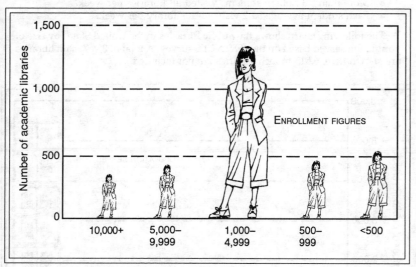

Ninety-three percent of **public schools** had school library media centers in 1985. Distribution of those libraries by size of enrollment in the school is shown below.

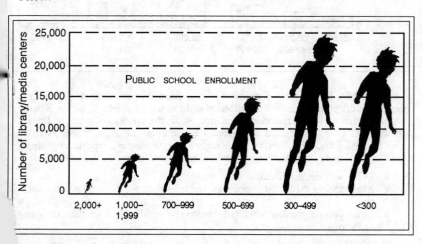

The 1985 survey estimated that for public school library media centers in the United States:

- More than 42.4 million students visited all libraries per week.
- Each student averaged 1.2 visits to the library per week.

Most **private schools** have small enrollments and are less likely to have a library. The 1985 NCES survey estimated that:

- Of the 19,197 private schools with less than 300 students, 69% had libraries.
- Of the 6,418 private schools with 300 or more students, 93% had libraries.

The same survey showed that for private school library media centers in the United States:

- More than 5.3 million students visited all libraries per week.
- Each student averaged 1.2 visits to the library per week.

The following chart shows the **public libraries** in the United States by size of population served based on the 1989 NCES survey. A total of 8,967 main libraries are shown here; 6,513 branch libraries are not included.

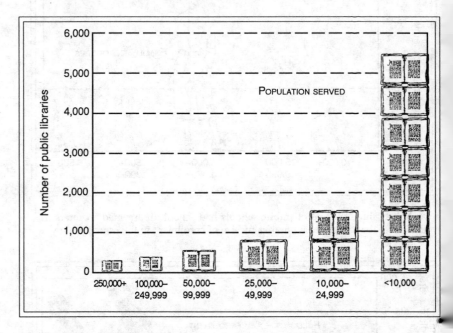

In 1990 the Louis Harris Organization and Alan Westin conducted a national sample survey that included questions about the use of public libraries. Results revealed that 66% of respondents reported using the services of a public library in the past year (*Using the Public Library in the Computer Age: Present Patterns, Future Possibilities*, ALA, 1991). This is higher than the figures reported by earlier studies. However, detailed demographics confirmed many earlier results:

- More women use libraries than men.
- More college-educated people use libraries than do those with less education.
- More people earning $35,000 or more use public libraries than do those with lower incomes.

Public library users share several interesting characteristics. Compared to those who do not use public libraries, they are much more likely to:

- Attend an opera, ballet, or concert.
- Have a personal computer at home.
- Belong to a voluntary association.

What do libraries provide?

From the vast number of resources available, librarians:

- Select those most likely to be needed by users of a particular library
- Purchase and organize them
- Manage systems to keep track of where things are and what users borrow
- Arrange interlibrary loans when an item is not available locally
- Help users to find what they need.

Resources to use in the library

The most visible and familiar resource of a library is a collection of printed materials. The 3,438 college and university libraries reporting collection statistics to the Department of Education in the fall of 1988 had collections of from less than 5,000 (106 libraries) to 1,000,000 or more (57 libraries). Of the 8,967 public libraries in the United States included in the 1989 NCES report, more than half had collections of less than 25,000, but more than 50 had collections of 500,000 or more.

Book collections in public school library media centers range from less than 2,000 in 3% of the public schools to over 30,000 in one percent. The average public school library in 1985 had:

- 8,466 volumes
- 20.3 volumes per pupil
- 921 audiovisual titles
- 34 periodical subscriptions.

Each private school library in 1985 had an average of:

- 5,615 books
- 869 items of audiovisual and other materials
- 19 periodical subscriptions.

Resources to borrow

Although many people use materials in libraries, most people probably think of a library as a source for materials that circulate outside the building. Public librarians often speak of their circulation in terms of "per capita" figures, i.e., items borrowed per person in the population that the library is legally established to serve. In 1989, the average per capita circulation for **public libraries** was 5.39 items. The total number of items circulated nationally from public libraries in 1989 was over 1,328,726,000, an increase of more than 13% from 1982, when the previous national data were gathered.

In addition to books, a 1986 survey found that the following items circulate in more than 50% of public libraries serving populations of 25,000 or more (*ALA Survey of Public Library Services*, ALA Office for Research, 1987, unpublished):

- art prints
- videocassettes (educational)
- videocassettes (entertainment)
- 16mm films
- books-on-tape
- records, tapes, or compact disks (music).

During 1987–1988, more than 154,414,100 items circulated from **college and university libraries**.

During the 1984–1985 school year, all **public school libraries** in the U.S.:

- circulated a total of more than 38,300 items per week
- circulated an average of 523 items per school per week.

Resources not available in the local library

Libraries of all types borrow material for their clients from other libraries through a cooperative arrangement known as interlibrary loan. Guidelines and forms have been devised by ALA to facilitate this service. In 1989, **public libraries** in the United States:

- provided more than 4,109,036 loans to other libraries
- received more than 4,754,857 loans from other libraries.

During the 1985 school year, **public school libraries**:

- provided 639,540 loans to other libraries with an average number of 9 loans per school
- received 2,235,042 items from other libraries with an average number of 30 loans per school.

During the academic year 1987–1988, **academic libraries** in the United States:

- provided a total of 5,390,301 items and
- received 3,672,852 items.

In the figures just given, the number of items provided is not equal to the number received for each type of library. This is due to several factors such as lending across library types (including types for which no statistics are available).

Answers to questions

Librarians find answers to questions or help library users do so. During 1989, the 6,733 **public libraries** in the U.S. reporting on this topic answered more than 196,281,600 reference questions. The 3,438 **academic libraries** reporting in the fall of 1988 answered a total of 1,625,465 reference questions in a typical week.

The 143 **medical school libraries** in the U.S. and Canada reported a total of 2,802,193 reference questions answered in 1988–1989. Each medical school library averaged 20,306 questions.

Database searching

The last 15 years have seen the rapid growth of computer-readable collections of data available for interactive access by library users from computer terminals in the library. Usually the data file is either on a remote computer contacted via telephone or on a CD-ROM disk that the library owns. Reference databases provide bibliographic citations to published literature or referrals to non-published information. Source databases contain numerical data, textual-numeric records, or the full text of documents. More than 6,000 databases and unique subfiles are listed in the 1990 edition of *Computer-Readable Data Bases* (Gale Research). Most are available from remote computers, but many are on CD-ROM or other formats that allow local ownership. The latest edition of the *Directory of Portable Databases* lists 951 such products, 534 on CD-ROM.

The 1986 survey of **public libraries** serving populations greater than 25,000 cited earlier found that more than 34% offered database searching. The number is much higher today.

Virtually all doctorate-granting **university libraries** offer searching from remote databases and from CD-ROMs (*Alternative Sources of Revenue in Academic Libraries*, ALA, 1991). The number is not so high in other types of academic libraries, but well over half of all others offer either or both types of searching.

During the academic year 1988–1989, the 143 **medical school libraries** in the United States and Canada reported that librarians used online databases 278,519 times on behalf of clients (*Annual Statistics of Medical School Libraries in the United States and Canada*, Houston Academy of Medicine-Texas Medical Center Library, 1990). During the academic year 1988–1989, each of 172 **law school libraries** in the U.S. spent an average of $39,002 to search databases ("1988–89 Statistical Survey of ABA Law School Libraries and Librarians," *Law Library Journal*, Summer 1990).

Online searching is also available in and through a few **school libraries**. The 1985 NCES survey showed that for public school libraries:

- 4% have database search services in-house for students
- 5% make database searches available off-site for students
- 7% have database search services in-house for teachers
- 11% make searches available off-site for teachers.

The figures are slightly lower for private schools.

Microcomputers

Besides using microcomputers to access databases online or on CD-ROM, libraries are making microcomputers available for the public to use for their own programs or for library-owned software. An ALA survey found that, as of the fall of 1986, more than 43% of **public libraries** serving populations of over 25,000 had microcomputers for public use. By the spring of 1989, 50% of all **college and university libraries** also made micros available (*Alternative Sources of Revenue in Academic Libraries*, ALA, 1991).

In the fall of 1985:

- 39% of **public school library** media centers had microcomputers for the use of students
- 42% had microcomputers for the use of teachers
- 29% of private school library media centers had microcomputers for the use of teachers and students.

Instructional services in school libraries

The 1985–86 NCES survey found that professionals in more than 50% of public school library media centers offer the following services:

- assist students in locating information and resources valuable to their educational needs and to the growth of their personal interests and abilities
- provide reference assistance to teachers
- offer a sequential program of library skills instruction
- informally instruct students in the use of various types of materials and equipment
- provide reading/listening/viewing guidance to students
- provide teachers with information about new educational and media developments.

The same source found that over 15,500,000 students in public schools participate in library skills instruction each week. In private schools more than 1,375,000 participate in such instruction each week.

Source: ALA Office for Research

The biggest university research libraries, 1989–1990

THE FOLLOWING FIGURES are based on an index developed by the Association of Research Libraries (ARL) to measure the relative size of its university library members. The five categories used in the rankings were determined by factor analysis of 22 categories of quantitative data and represent the elements in which ARL university libraries most resemble one another. The index does not attempt to measure a library's services, quality of collections, or success in meeting the needs of users. The five data elements are: number of volumes held, number of volumes added (gross), number of current serials received, total operating expenditures, and number of professional and support staff.

This rank order table is only for 107 university library members of ARL, which has 12 non-university library members. Non-university libraries are not gauged by the same index formula as the universities, and are sufficiently different that it would be misleading to incorporate them into the table.

ARL does not claim that this ranking incorporates all the factors necessary to give a complete picture of research library quality. However, it is a measuring device that has proven reliable over the years for specific internal and comparative purposes.

Volumes in library does not include microforms, manuscripts, audiovisual and computer resources, maps, or certain other items central to research library collections and services. It includes government documents in some (but not all) cases. It is thus not a complete indicator of library resources.

Total staff includes professional, nonprofessional, and student assistants; however, only the first two groups are used to calculate the rank score.

Total expenditures include money spent on materials purchases, salaries, and general operations, but does not include capital expenditures for buildings, expenditures for plant maintenance, and some kinds of computing and administrative services; these are often part of the main university budget and not directly allocated to the library. However, such additional expenditures are crucial to an effective library and reflect the total commitment of an institution to providing and preserving research information.

	Rank	Volumes in library	Volumes added	Current serials	Total staff	Total expenditures[1]
Harvard University	1	11,874,148	261,846	103,075	1,095	$45,703,359
University of California at Los Angeles	2	6,156,761	246,737	96,676	686	32,653,412
University of California at Berkeley	3	7,540,234	202,202	92,978	788	31,399,069
Yale University	4	8,862,768	147,841	51,985	704	28,709,200
University of Illinois at Urbana-Champaign	5	7,748,736	187,489	92,077	532	18,520,182
University of Toronto	6	5,951,752	174,598	38,063	701	27,138,651
Stanford University	7	5,871,063	144,450	49,673	596	31,326,296
University of Texas	8	6,265,236	202,338	50,506	608	19,191,606
Columbia University	9	6,032,545	148,872	59,044	644	23,417,989
University of Michigan	10	6,639,490	141,606	69,937	583	22,394,006
Cornell University	11	5,216,501	189,070	59,801	551	21,055,340
University of Wisconsin	12	5,036,144	139,194	49,553	528	21,844,945
University of Minnesota	13	4,651,111	105,357	47,491	484	21,836,149
University of Washington	14	4,908,988	102,887	50,215	486	18,111,845

[1]Figures for Canadian libraries are expressed in U.S. dollars.

	Rank	Volumes in library	Volumes added	Current serials	Total staff	Total expenditures
University of Chicago	15	5,191,998	132,437	48,925	370	$14,922,568
Indiana University	16	4,133,331	103,279	38,430	475	18,376,165
Rutgers University	17	3,219,823	102,635	30,097	519	21,880,472
Princeton University	18	4,276,086	105,659	32,037	396	17,038,820
Ohio State University	19	4,430,132	101,714	32,870	473	16,813,196
University of North Carolina	19	3,751,660	123,899	39,998	405	14,402,816
Arizona State University	21	2,599,701	138,242	34,844	388	14,948,385
University of Florida	22	2,892,301	127,167	27,999	441	16,122,500
University of Pennsylvania	23	3,665,786	98,659	31,887	372	16,495,798
University of Arizona	24	3,549,281	128,634	28,620	390	13,662,887
University of Georgia	24	2,889,108	101,285	55,954	351	12,883,133
University of British Columbia	26	2,918,279	106,091	22,151	407	17,120,088
Pennsylvania State University	26	3,095,863	64,286	31,846	472	17,243,989
University of Virginia	28	3,193,260	106,577	26,268	370	15,921,187
Duke University	29	3,846,295	95,633	30,364	312	14,523,509
University of California at Davis	29	2,376,157	80,900	51,604	335	16,203,556
Northwestern University	31	3,474,423	80,284	36,696	342	13,586,594
University of Alberta	32	2,956,553	99,331	18,823	396	14,841,362
New York University	33	3,092,620	73,877	23,474	408	17,045,841
Michigan State University	34	3,417,388	114,116	28,910	329	12,481,402
University of Pittsburgh	35	2,878,713	96,693	22,403	358	13,026,194
University of California at San Diego	36	1,949,397	72,815	32,551	364	16,735,467
University of Kansas	36	2,868,223	80,443	28,431	333	14,767,353
Johns Hopkins University	38	2,835,664	77,339	20,531	339	15,214,302
University of Southern Calif.	39	2,626,271	54,528	33,805	350	14,892,419
University of Iowa	40	3,104,621	91,083	24,176	273	11,613,626
University of Maryland	41	2,055,403	67,348	23,018	345	15,121,610
McGill University	42	2,509,979	64,930	17,516	326	13,667,722
State University of New York at Buffalo	43	2,591,006	64,787	23,507	289	12,113,946
University of Hawaii	44	2,385,601	74,381	32,265	232	9,754,608
University of California at Santa Barbara	45	1,996,662	77,487	21,242	250	11,680,964
Wayne State University	46	2,374,831	66,286	24,173	238	11,457,301
Georgetown University	47	1,802,242	64,921	22,799	295	12,070,953
University of Western Ontario	47	1,961,386	68,930	17,995	287	11,557,572
University of Connecticut	49	2,271,849	79,837	17,620	230	11,968,917
University of Laval	50	1,793,368	72,682	15,847	267	11,246,268
Texas A&M University	51	1,892,454	55,037	25,378	309	11,008,870
Boston University	52	1,761,954	58,075	29,540	274	10,054,921
Washington University (Mo.)	52	2,277,203	59,093	18,387	258	11,403,738
Vanderbilt University	54	1,873,598	68,622	16,448	303	11,476,698
Howard University	55	1,783,876	55,294	26,300	283	10,618,060
Massachusetts Institute of Technology	56	2,180,873	55,710	21,313	245	9,718,298
Purdue University	57	1,924,982	61,606	21,505	266	9,691,456
Emory University	57	1,872,313	59,399	16,623	264	11,969,585
York University (Ontario)	59	1,845,478	64,633	19,641	250	10,385,556
University of Illinois at Chicago	60	1,656,307	52,924	17,652	298	11,365,864
University of New Mexico	61	1,711,771	56,303	16,169	337	11,241,022
Florida State University	62	1,829,826	68,447	18,843	249	10,234,935
University of Cincinnati	62	1,746,857	59,686	19,642	302	10,718,338
Syracuse University	64	2,332,676	50,126	18,044	267	9,457,422
University of South Carolina	65	2,431,129	64,735	20,552	198	8,170,685
University of Delaware	65	1,953,028	55,097	24,202	225	9,228,202

	Rank	Volumes in library	Volumes added	Current serials	Total staff	Total expenditures
Brown University	67	2,227,301	55,392	13,510	277	$10,603,303
University of Colorado	68	2,286,736	60,149	15,588	223	10,225,273
Louisiana State University	68	2,460,219	52,689	19,573	252	8,263,718
University of Rochester	70	2,686,996	54,792	14,214	244	8,908,321
Brigham Young University	71	2,063,384	70,162	18,582	335	9,533,011
University of Massachusetts	72	2,409,946	67,670	15,267	202	8,311,979
University of Notre Dame	73	1,996,606	76,518	17,513	191	7,183,272
University of Missouri	74	2,486,014	43,872	17,766	235	8,388,702
University of Tennessee	75	1,874,535	42,491	21,606	259	8,249,066
University of Kentucky	76	2,154,837	39,591	19,819	250	8,908,340
University of California at Irvine	77	1,449,246	54,097	16,346	250	11,266,455
University of Miami	77	1,697,581	48,714	16,717	249	9,628,243
Southern Illinois University	79	2,082,358	50,074	19,842	245	8,796,210
Queen's University at Kingston	79	1,796,893	48,481	15,982	227	8,849,728
University of Nebraska	81	2,013,548	51,485	18,041	214	8,131,992
Virginia Polytechnic Institute and State University	82	1,710,202	53,286	17,746	204	8,730,428
Temple University	83	2,071,461	44,852	15,474	226	8,396,512
Iowa State University	83	1,830,214	43,204	18,557	222	9,218,296
Dartmouth College	83	1,824,377	51,846	20,788	175	7,838,950
Washington State University	86	1,606,851	47,300	22,573	211	8,136,463
University of Oregon	87	1,844,996	41,880	21,187	217	8,394,719
North Carolina State University	88	1,375,049	48,917	18,401	217	8,414,798
Tulane University	89	1,802,910	47,767	17,091	187	7,585,533
State University of New York at Stony Brook	90	1,701,101	47,355	11,239	220	9,800,376
University of Utah	91	1,813,560	58,137	12,144	230	7,429,915
University of Guelph	92	1,900,416	63,252	13,600	159	6,456,800
University of Manitoba	93	1,520,920	38,260	12,578	228	9,140,214
McMaster University	94	1,377,237	47,111	11,549	203	9,336,427
University of Alabama	94	1,814,178	48,149	17,603	178	7,070,586
University of Oklahoma	96	2,297,087	39,412	17,783	185	7,082,575
University of Saskatchewan	97	1,404,391	60,519	10,689	179	7,847,548
Kent State University	98	2,041,567	35,321	10,692	238	9,278,896
University of Waterloo	99	1,566,042	24,941	15,150	206	8,437,553
University of California at Riverside	100	1,461,147	47,604	13,901	177	7,422,888
Georgia Institute of Technology	101	1,648,178	52,015	23,438	113	5,196,995
State University of New York at Albany	102	1,278,657	38,231	14,534	174	7,697,389
Case Western Reserve University	103	1,584,782	31,990	13,033	175	7,305,047
University of Houston	104	1,622,189	28,681	15,103	192	6,723,883
Oklahoma State University	105	1,543,356	31,284	11,482	177	6,942,329
Colorado State University	106	1,220,897	39,596	11,720	143	6,856,673
Rice University	107	1,441,470	39,034	12,413	145	5,098,528

Source: Association of Research Libraries, *ARL Statistics 1989–1990* (Washington, D.C.: ARL, 1991)

Data from non-ARL university libraries, 1989

THE FOLLOWING STATISTICS are from North American research universities and doctorate-granting institutions that are not members of the Association of Research Libraries. Data were compiled by the ALA Association of College and Research Libraries. Institutions are arranged by number of volumes in the library and not by a ranking similar to the ARL list.

	Volumes in library	Volumes added	Current serials	Total staff	Total expenditures
Southern Methodist University	2,028,059	50,878	6,494	136	$5,069,024
University of Ottawa	1,900,943	45,159	11,932	212	7,876,523
University of Calgary	1,781,651	N/A	13,319	246	8,520,304
University of Wisconsin-Milwaukee	1,684,181	34,220	10,356	132	5,282,848
Claremont Colleges	1,680,881	31,646	6,042	86	3,236,637
Auburn University	1,582,126	65,204	14,720	193	7,668,733
George Washington University	1,571,751	39,943	18,260	249	8,447,017
Bowling Green State University	1,557,668	50,713	8,020	149	5,527,560
Georgia State University	1,535,309	46,577	12,251	168	5,904,738
Fordham University	1,466,695	29,386	9,180	122	4,397,673
Ohio University	1,430,939	51,443	15,945	144	5,108,600
University of Windsor	1,392,187	N/A	9,130	123	4,722,000
State University of New York at Binghamton	1,368,368	41,320	11,094	134	6,004,181
West Virginia University	1,350,616	17,825	8,932	167	4,182,941
Baylor University	1,312,995	N/A	6,445	139	4,360,717
Miami University	1,312,101	33,636	7,244	152	5,231,481
University of Arkansas, Fayetteville	1,274,232	31,891	15,467	170	4,702,046
Northern Illinois University	1,246,648	39,019	14,832	178	5,516,634
University of South Florida	1,246,567	56,039	5,308	222	7,952,934
Boston College	1,144,959	53,014	12,500	184	7,516,497
Texas Tech University	1,296,659	32,386	11,637	152	4,959,380
Illinois State University	1,137,121	32,260	9,123	149	4,797,833
Kansas State University	1,130,522	33,170	7,469	148	5,136,149
Oregon State University	1,122,248	22,022	19,034	135	4,570,806
University of Denver	1,120,055	30,195	4,774	71	2,097,485
Catholic University	1,106,675	12,534	5,707	101	2,681,794
College of William and Mary	1,088,471	30,809	10,365	110	5,419,629
Memphis State University	1,086,155	19,960	11,611	138	4,715,017
North Texas State University	1,072,076	27,289	4,990	171	3,849,256
Indiana State University	1,070,350	30,150	6,067	108	2,916,476
University of Louisville	1,062,064	32,060	11,770	204	7,355,737
Loyola University, Chicago	1,030,953	41,493	11,115	150	5,851,999
University of Vermont	999,740	33,760	10,133	133	5,328,660
Hofstra University	989,913	24,287	5,618	128	4,095,590
Western Michigan University	988,752	29,397	10,061	142	4,279,653
University of Wyoming	978,388	42,515	13,344	118	4,982,642
Ball State University	967,393	31,317	5,988	194	5,146,382
St. John's University	966,558	25,636	8,305	170	4,844,244
University of New Brunswick	960,316	23,176	6,420	110	3,702,763
University of New Hampshire	940,684	19,987	8,626	111	3,027,033
Lehigh University	937,807	31,228	9,500	91	3,705,926
University of California, Santa Cruz	934,527	43,400	13,190	121	6,056,573
University of Rhode Island	902,706	31,193	9,767	111	4,270,900
Yeshiva University	874,421	25,873	7,574	78	3,476,443
University of Missouri, Kansas City	868,231	24,205	9,701	113	3,111,024
University of Alabama, Birmingham	865,308	33,039	5,910	140	4,443,386

	Volumes in library	Volumes added	Current serials	Total staff	Total expenditures
Virginia Commonwealth University	860,013	38,242	9,667	182	$7,342,961
Brandeis University	846,510	30,574	7,596	101	3,651,945
Portland State University	826,411	27,429	10,873	120	4,381,695
University of Southern Mississippi	824,402	29,511	5,305	88	4,077,608
New Mexico State University	807,375	19,906	7,242	98	2,951,140
Utah State University	801,067	29,365	5,837	68	2,799,383
University of Mississippi	793,688	30,224	11,244	92	3,920,166
University of Tulsa	793,348	40,078	7,226	81	4,599,917
Mississippi State University	788,747	21,766	7,396	98	2,954,050
University of Akron	786,075	26,266	6,369	112	4,372,573
University of Nevada, Reno	781,102	21,010	7,568	88	3,477,459
St. Louis University	759,478	13,304	3,909	80	2,417,548
Cleveland State University	755,382	29,070	9,886	113	3,391,078
Texas Woman's University	754,206	13,383	3,329	66	1,652,281
University of North Carolina at Greensboro	747,673	24,847	6,331	93	3,809,608
University of Toledo	744,560	26,777	6,625	115	4,506,425
Marquette University	743,097	27,040	5,657	102	3,440,772
Carnegie-Mellon University	740,482	25,503	5,215	94	3,651,874
Idaho State University	740,252	17,225	3,043	52	1,806,603
University of Maine at Orono	716,790	26,140	6,700	86	3,622,507
University of Idaho	715,103	23,265	10,503	72	2,622,306
Clemson University	689,467	22,349	6,956	107	4,377,362
Texas Christian University	684,099	10,784	4,609	67	2,458,115
University of Texas at Arlington	680,383	19,845	5,492	98	2,466,388
University of Alaska	652,408	21,592	6,719	87	4,098,123
East Texas State University	648,052	11,481	2,283	60	1,430,597
University of Montana	609,931	13,101	4,720	93	1,989,145
Northeastern University	595,263	22,082	6,454	162	4,522,113
Old Dominion University	584,580	16,103	4,596	89	3,640,048
University of New Orleans	542,063	14,994	5,017	76	2,273,631
University of North Dakota	541,004	14,880	3,844	59	1,821,000
University of Missouri, St. Louis	529,697	16,259	3,703	70	2,171,981
University of San Francisco	522,967	16,598	2,229	34	1,605,468
Middle Tennessee State University	518,096	18,854	3,593	61	2,590,782
American University	515,853	13,819	5,932	99	3,090,949
Andrews University	511,648	15,497	3,062	50	1,427,222
University of Northern Colorado	506,730	17,728	3,592	75	2,755,421
Florida Atlantic University	494,776	20,804	4,433	85	3,017,356
Montana State University	494,738	7,243	4,483	64	2,197,650
University of Maryland, Baltimore Co.	479,703	20,190	4,196	64	2,667,331
Drexel University	478,396	10,487	6,928	76	2,211,456
Clark University	475,021	10,672	2,068	50	1,576,688
University of Texas, Dallas	457,812	12,848	3,885	79	3,290,657
California Institute of Technology	455,561	14,832	6,368	60	3,211,086
Drake University	440,752	8,270	2,200	42	1,206,310
Adelphi University	439,768	8,872	5,082	88	2,429,713
Northern Arizona University	435,136	26,571	5,100	98	3,870,492
South Dakota State University	422,093	13,968	5,548	38	1,635,599
University of Missouri, Rolla	417,864	8,407	1,570	29	983,937
North Dakota State University	417,776	8,843	4,240	63	1,655,078
University of South Dakota	406,350	9,884	3,099	37	1,372,519
University of the Pacific	401,879	7,650	3,070	46	1,420,664
Duquesne University	380,244	10,798	1,810	55	879,623
Rensselaer Polytechnic Institute	378,488	11,676	3,670	61	2,578,977
Illinois Institute of Technology	369,436	7.073	2,472	50	1,387,446
Tennessee Technical University	340,978	9,097	3,205	58	1,552,934
Louisiana Technical University	322,003	8,621	2,571	57	1,243,150

Source: Denise Bedford, comp., *ACRL University Library Statistics, 1988–1989* (Chicago: ALA Association of College and Research Libraries, 1990)

Learning resources programs in two-year colleges: Basic and special services

Basic library services and activities

Listed below are specific services that are considered to be normal and basic services in learning resources program budgets in two-year colleges. Inclusion does not mean that an institution must or should have every activity or service listed.

Acquisition of computer software.
Acquisition of microforms.
Acquisition of non-print materials.
Acquisition of print materials.
Automated online catalog.
Bibliographic instruction.
Circulation of non-print materials.
Circulation of print materials.
Collection management.
Computer reference searching.
Government document borrowing.
Government document selective
    depository.
Independent study guidance.
Institutional publications reference
    collection.
Instructional television individualized
    access.
Interlibrary borrowing.
Interlibrary lending.
Laser optical/reference searches.
Literacy training materials.
Local history collection.

Machine-assisted AV cataloging.
Machine-assisted cataloging of books.
Microcomputers for public use.
Microform cataloging.
Microform print service.
Online public access catalog.
Participation in bibliographic
    networks.
Physical access to materials.
Preparation of bibliographies.
Processing of audiovisuals.
Processing of microforms.
Processing of print materials.
Reference services.
Reserve book service.
Selection of materials.
Self-service copy machine.
Special collections services.
Telefacsimile service.
Telephone reference service.
Term paper counseling.
Union card catalog.
User-available typewriters.

Basic instructional media activities and services

Listed below are services that are considered to be normal and basic services in two-year college learning resources program budgets. This list may not include future technologies and services. Inclusion does not mean that an institution should have every activity or service listed.

Adult literacy laboratory.
Audiocassette duplication.
Audiocassette editing.
Audiocassette recording.
Audiovisual equipment distribution.
Audiovisual equipment maintenance.
Closed circuit television.
Copyright consultation.
Darkroom services.
Equipment distribution.
Equipment maintenance.

Equipment repair.
Equipment specifications.
Graphic art layouts.
Group presentations.
Group television viewing
Identification photography.
Instructional design and development
    counseling.
Instructional film and video renting
    and borrowing for classroom use.
Instructional materials scheduling.

Interactive television.
Inventory of audiovisual equipment.
Listening services.
Media orientation and instruction.
Microcomputer literacy.
Motion picture photography.
News photography.
Photography for slides.
Preview services for faculty.
Production of instructional materials.
Production of sound slide programs.

Satellite communication downlink.
Scripting of audiovisual presentations.
Scripting of television modules.
Self-paced learning assistance.
Telecourse availability information.
Television off-air video recording.
Television off-site video recording.
Videotape editing.
Videotape multi-camera production.
Videotape one-camera production.

Special services components

This list includes technologies and roles which, if assigned to the learning resources program, will require capital funds, space, personnel, and operational budgets in excess of those recommended in the ACRL *Standards for Community, Junior and Technical College Leaning Resources Programs*. Inclusion of programs in this list is not advocacy for these services as part of the learning sources program but recognition that some institutions have included them in the supervisory responsibilities of the chief administrator.

Adult literacy program direction.
Auto-tutorial laboratory.
Career counseling.
College catalog production.
College press.
Community cable televised instruction.
Computer center.
Copy shop (not self-service).
Cross-divisional programs.
Government document full depository.
Institutional records center and archives.
Instructional design office.
Library technician curricular program.
Materials preservation laboratory.

Media technician curricular program.
Print shop.
Public library branch services.
Public museum.
Radio on-air broadcasting station.
Records management.
Satellite communications uplink.
Special learning laboratory operation.
Teleconference and distant learning.
Telecourse administration.
Television course broadcast-level production.
Television on-air broadcasting.
Television station maintenance.
Testing.
Text-book rental service.
Tutoring program supervision.

Source: Standards for Community, Junior and Technical College Learning Resources Programs
(Chicago: ALA Association of College and Research Libraries, 1990)

On Norm's Library Levity

Good library humor does more than amuse us. It allows us to express a point of view, especially a critical or unconventional point of view, in an indirect fashion that may be regarded as more harmless than it really is. My initial article, "Humor and Creativity," in *College & Research Libraries News*, March 1988, which somehow turned into a continuing series, suggests some of the pleasures and purposes of library laffs. "Laughing together," it concludes, "is an ideal way to foster an atmosphere in which creativity and innovation, and even risk-taking, may stand a chance of emerging, surviving, and perhaps flourishing."—*Norman D. Stevens, The Molesworth Institute.*

Public library governance

by James Scheppke

HOW ARE PUBLIC libraries in the United States governed? Are there any significant trends taking place? In 1989 the ALA Public Library Association's Governance of Public Libraries Committee surveyed state library agencies in all 50 states and asked them these questions. Here are some of their most important findings:

• Well over half (55%) of the libraries in the 50 states are municipal libraries. After municipal libraries the most common types are nonprofit corporation libraries (12%) and county libraries (11%).

• The amount of consolidation of public libraries that has occurred varies greatly from state to state. There are five states in which the average service area population exceeds 100,000, but there are also 10 states in which the average service area population is less than 10,000.

• Over three-fourths (76%) of the libraries in the U.S. have governing library boards. Only 13% have advisory library boards.

• While the pace of change in public library governance is slow, many states are experiencing important changes. The most commonly reported new governance trends are the formation of library taxing districts, changes in the responsibilities of library boards, and various kinds of consolidation of public library services.

Governance types in the 50 states

According to the results of the committee survey, in the fall of 1989 there was a total of 9,019 public libraries in the 50 states (the Public Library of the District of Columbia would make a total of 9,020 for the U.S.). Of these libraries, the breakdown by type is shown below:

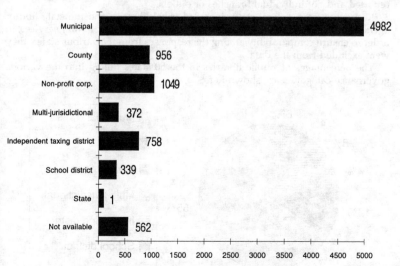

Number of public libraries in 50 states by governance type, 1989

The committee used the following definitions of library governance types:

Municipal. Libraries administered as a department of municipal government (cities, townships, etc.).

County. Libraries administered as a department of county (parish, etc.) government.

Non-profit corporation. Libraries administered by a private non-profit corporation, typically under contract to one or more units of local government.

Multi-jurisdictional. Libraries operated jointly by two or more units of local government under an intergovernmental agreement which creates a jointly appointed board or similar means of joint governance.

Independent taxing district. Libraries governed by units of local government separate from cities or counties. They typically have their own elected citizen governing board and are established solely for the purpose of providing public library services.

School district. Libraries administered by local public school districts.

State. Libraries administered by the state.

The governance type defined as multi-jurisdictional was not part of the survey questionnaire. The questionnaire provided a number of "other" categories for the states to indicate libraries that did not, in their judgment, fall in the governance types listed. It became apparent that a number of states have libraries falling into the multi-jurisdictional category as defined above. Multi-jurisdictional libraries are to be distinguished from city, county, or other libraries having contracts to serve other jurisdictions, and also from independent taxing districts that are independent of other local governments.

The questionnaire requested information only on those libraries which satisfied the requirements for legal establishment in a given state. "Community libraries" or "club" libraries that do not meet a given state's requirements were to be excluded. The survey asked respondents to exclude cooperative library systems or other library entities that do not directly serve the public. The survey also made clear that only administrative units of public libraries were to be reported and not individual branches or outlets.

Responses from several states included tribal libraries and the state library agency. While it is true that these libraries may provide public library services, in order to ensure comparability among the responses from the various states, they were excluded from the data.

The percentages of public libraries in the 50 states falling into the various governance categories are shown here:

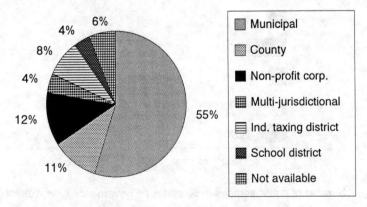

Percentage of public libraries in 50 states by type of governance, 1989

By far the predominant form of public library governance in the 50 states is the municipal library, representing over half (55%) of the total. Next come county libraries and nonprofit corporations, each representing about one-eighth of the total. Independent taxing districts make up only 8% of the total and school district and multi-jurisdictional libraries each make up only 4% of the total. Information on governance type was not provided for about 6% of the libraries.

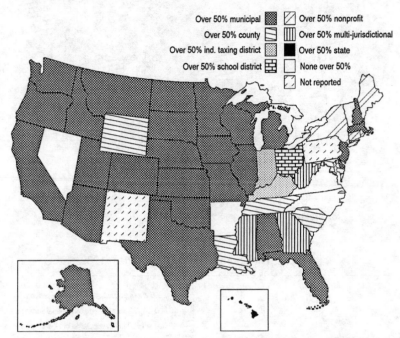

Map 1. Predominant form of public library governance, 1989

Map 1 illustrates the predominant form of public library governance in 48 of the 50 states for which sufficient data were available. The predominant form of governance is defined here as one which encompasses more than 50% of the libraries in a given state. In 26 states municipal libraries predominate, in five states county libraries predominate, in four states nonprofit corporation libraries predominate, in three states multi-jurisdictional libraries predominate, in two states independent taxing district libraries predominate, and in one state school district libraries predominate.

Consolidation of public library services

Another aspect of public library governance is the degree to which public library services are consolidated in the various states. One indicator of the degree of consolidation is the total number of public libraries. Map 2, showing the number of public libraries in the 50 states, tells us that the number of public libraries varies a great deal. The statistics range from only one public library in Hawaii (administered by the state) to well over 700 public libraries in New York. Interestingly, this statistic does not appear to vary with population size. For example, the most populous state in the country, California, has only 169 public libraries, while relatively small states may have many more libraries, such as Iowa with 520. Because the survey also gathered data on the total population served by

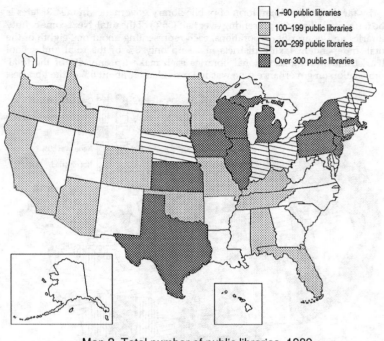

Map 2. Total number of public libraries, 1989

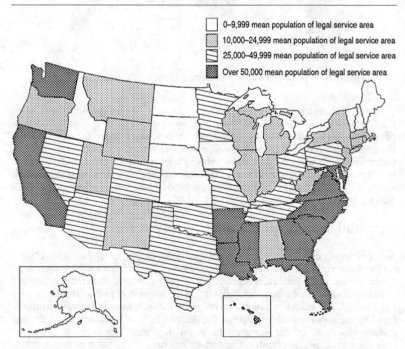

Map 3. Consolidation of public library services as measured by mean population of legal service area in 50 states, 1989

public libraries in each state, it was possible to compute the average (mean) population served by dividing this figure by the total number of libraries in each state. Map 3 illustrates this statistic for the 50 states. Again the statistics here show a great deal of variation. After Hawaii, which as noted above has only one library to serve the entire state population, there are four states in which the average population of the library service area is greater than 100,000. On the other hand, there are 10 states in which the average is less than 10,000 population served.

Public library boards

Another very important aspect of public library governance is the prevalence and characteristics of public library boards. Map 4 shows the predominance of governing or advisory boards by state. Here predominance is defined by 60% or more of the public libraries in a given state having a governing or advisory board. Note the 24 states in which all of the public libraries have governing boards. In only six states do advisory boards predominate.

Trends in public library governance

The survey asked for a brief description of any important governance trends that library development officers have seen in theirs states in the past ten years or so. These important trends were reported:

Reorganization or consolidation into independent taxing district libraries. Five states reported significant district formation in recent years. In Illinois the number of library districts has increased from 99 in 1981 to 202 in 1988. In Oregon, nine library taxing districts have formed since permissive legislation was enacted in 1981. Five states reported efforts to enact library district legislation or to begin formation of districts under existing legislation.

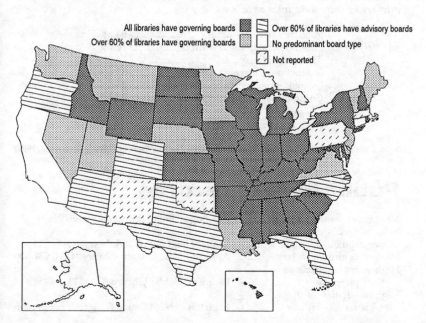

Map 4. Predominant type of library board in public libraries, 1989

Changes in library board responsibilities. Three states reported a trend from governing library boards to advisory library boards. Indiana reported attempts in their legislature to curtail the powers of governing library boards and to force direct election of board members. Louisiana reported a trend in the opposite direction—nine library boards have recently taken over financial management of the library from local governments.

Other consolidation activity. Some states reported other library consolidation activity, aside from the formation of districts. California noted that some smaller city libraries are merging into county library systems as branches of the larger system. However, they also noted some larger city libraries leaving county library systems to become independent. Florida noted that 63 of its 67 counties are now providing county-wide library service. Kansas and South Dakota both reported increased interest in forming combined school/public libraries. Washington reported work on permissive legislation to allow city/county libraries.

While some states experienced a number of important changes in public library governance in recent years, the overall impression that emerges is that the pace of change is very slow in most states. Only 27 out of the 49 states responding to the survey provided an answer to the questions about recent governance trends. Of these 27, most reported relatively few changes in public library governance in recent years.

Source: Report of the ALA Public Library Association's Governance of Public Libraries Committee, Fall 1990

The role of public libraries

MOST PUBLIC LIBRARIANS consider their libraries to be repositories of popular materials, according to a 1990 survey. A total of 210 libraries listed their primary or secondary roles as follows:

Popular materials library	94.3%
Preschoolers' door to learning	76.7%
Reference library	76.2%
Independent learning center	37.6%
Formal education support center	35.2%
Community information center	30.5%
Community and activity center	13.3%
Research center	2.4%

Source: Statistical Report '90: Public Library Data Service (Chicago: ALA Public Library Association, 1990)

Public library records

Most expenditures per capita	Cutchogue Free Library (NY), $87.35
Most materials expenditures per capita	Shaker Heights Public Library (OH), $15.69
Highest beginning salary	Auburn-Placer County Library (CA), $37,800
Highest registrations as % of population	Pasadena Public Library (CA), 111.5%
Highest circulation per registered borrower	Houston Public Library (TX), 65.8 per person

Source: Statistical Report '90: Public Library Data Service (Chicago: ALA Public Library Association, 1990)

Public library use today

by Alan F. Westin and Anne L. Finger

THE FOLLOWING OBSERVATIONS are from a 1991 report by the Reference Point Foundation in cooperation with the American Library Association. The data are based on a 1990 survey by Louis Harris and Associates, "The Consumer in the Information Age," sponsored by Equifax, Inc.

1. **Public library use has substantially increased in recent years.** Sixty-six percent of Americans, more than 122 million people, reported using the public library in 1989.

Public library users are more likely to reside in the East and West (70% and 69%, respectively), than in the Midwest or South (63% each.) They are also more likely to live in suburban areas: 71% of suburbanites use the public library, whereas 58% of people in rural areas do so.

The frequency of public library use has also increased. Although Equifax/ Harris found a 16% decline in the lightest use since 1978, it found a 9% increase in moderate library use, and a 7% increase in heavy use. This total increase in public library use is striking, particularly when compared with newspaper readership, which has substantially declined over the past twenty years.

2. **Public libraries continue to attract the most well-educated, culturally active, civically involved people.** The highest level of public library use was among those with the most formal education: 90% of respondents with postgraduate education reported use, as did 83% of college graduates. Those with less than a high school education were least likely to be public library users (48%).

Public library users are far more likely to engage in cultural activity than nonusers: 89% of those who attended an opera, ballet, or symphony in the past year have used the public library, compared with only 11% who did not attend such events.

3. **Use of the public library largely decreases with age.** Among American adults, use of the public library is most prevalent between the ages of 18 and 24 (78%). After a 10% drop between 25–29, there is a rise to 73% among ages 30–39. Thereafter, there is a steady decline, until only 51% of the American public over age 65 use the public library.

4. **There has been a substantial increase in use of almost all library services.** Since the Gallup survey in 1978, use of nearly every library service listed has increased. "Took out a book" continues to be most popular, with 91% of library users.

5. **Minorities are among the heaviest users of specific library services.** Hispanics are heavily represented among those who took out a book (96%, compared with 91% of the public). Blacks are well represented among those who read a newspaper or magazine (56%), and took out records, tapes, or films (40%). Blacks are also the only distinguishing demographic group among moderate library users (30%, compared with 24% of the public).

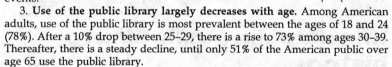

Low-income people (earning $7,500 or less) are well represented among those who read newspapers and magazines (54%, compared with 49% of the public—a 5% difference).

6. **Public library users seem to feel more in control of their lives than nonusers do.** Although both public library users and nonusers express concern about threats to privacy and distrust of established institutions, library users are less likely to think that technology is out of control: 58% of them disagreed with that statement, com-

pared with only 45% of nonusers. They indicate a willingness to control abuses: roughly one-third said they had not applied for a job, credit, or insurance because they did not want to provide certain personal information.

Public library users are more likely than nonusers to believe matters of private morality should be left to the individual: 69% felt private homosexual acts between consenting adults should be treated that way, compared with 53% of nonusers.

7. **There is broad interest in the future possibilities of a library connection via home computer, with minorities showing particular interest.** More than two-thirds of the American public—68% (representing over 125 million Americans)—feels that if they had a home computer, it would be either "very valuable" or "somewhat valuable" for them to be able to obtain online information from the public library or a non-profit organization.

Hispanics and blacks showed greater interest in the service than whites. Blacks, at 47%, had the highest percentages responding "very valuable." Taking "very valuable" and "somewhat valuable" together, Hispanics showed the highest interest, with 78%, followed by blacks, with 75%. Sixty-seven percent of whites were also interested.

8. **The leaders of America's voluntary associations, who are heavy public library users, are ready to use technology to increase their civic involvement.** The 12% of the American public—twenty-two million people—who are leaders of our nation's voluntary associations are both more likely to use the public library than the general public (75%, compared with 66%), and are among the heaviest users (50%, compared with 42%).

These organizational leaders are eager to use online connections that are meaningful to them: 72% of them think it would be valuable to be able to dial up the public library or nonprofit service for experts or publications, and 41% think it would be very valuable. This compares with 34% of the public would think it would be very valuable. The public library would be one major point of entry for such online connections.

Source: Alan F. Westin and Anne L. Finger,
Using the Public Library in the Computer Age (Chicago: ALA, 1991)

Key dates in public library history

1656—Boston, Mass., and New Haven, Conn., started their public libraries from collections bequeathed to them by prominent citizens.

1731—Benjamin Franklin founded the Library Company of Philadelphia as a subscription library.

1774—The Library Company of Philadelphia made its resources available to the members of the First Continental Congress.

1787—The first free public library was founded in Newington, Conn.

1800—One of the first endowed town libraries, the Hale Donation Library, was established in Coventry, Conn.

1827—A municipally supported juvenile library was established in Lexington, Mass.

1834—The first general library in Chicago, the Chicago Lyceum, was established.

1849—The first public library in California was organized in Monterey.

1890—Cleveland PL became the first large public library to adopt an unrestricted open access policy.

Source: Elizabeth W. Stone, *American Library Development, 1600–1899* (N.Y.: H.W. Wilson, 1977)

The 15 largest public libraries

1

THE NUMBER OF VOLUMES a library owns is not a measure of the quality of library service. However, volume counts do have a certain fascination. The following are the largest public libraries in the United States, according to 1989 data. (The Library of Congress, though technically a public library, was not included.)

New York (N.Y.) Public Library (The Branch Libraries) 9,662,225
Chicago (Ill.) Public Library 8,037,705
Houston (Tex.) Public Library 7,023,475
Boston (Mass.) Public Library 6,141,482
Queens Borough (N.Y.) Public Library..6,130,738
Los Angeles (Calif.) Public Library 5,460,170
Free Library of Philadelphia (Penna.) 4,916,380
Brooklyn (N.Y.) Public Library 4,829,764
Los Angeles County (Calif.) Public Library 4,549,575
Public Library of Cincinnati and Hamilton County (Ohio) 4,007,040
Memphis/Shelby County (Tenn.) Public Library 3,459,059
Cleveland (Ohio) Public Library 2,996,237
Detroit (Mich.) Public Library 2,746,021
Milwaukee (Wisc.) Public Library 2,581,474
Miami-Dade (Fla.) Public Library System 2,483,184

More public library records

Highest director's salary ....Los Angeles Public Library,
$103,272
Most reference transactions ....Los Angeles County Public Library,
9,656,224
Most interlibrary loans to others ....Enoch Pratt Free Library (Md.),
138,787
Most interlibrary loans from others ....Lake Lanier (Ga.) Regional Library,
74,714

Source: Statistical Report '90: Public Library Data Service (Chicago: ALA Public Library Association, 1990)

Books and public libraries in the Western United States

PUBLIC LIBRARIES ARE an exceptional value, providing virtually unlimited access to information for one-twelfth to one-twenty-fifth of what the average person spends for a handful of books or magazines each year.

The average person in the West spent an estimated $187 on reading materials in 1988. (The U.S. Bureau of the Census *Statistical Abstract* for 1987 gives a figure of $140 per capita expenditures for reading materials for 1984; this amount was adjusted to $187 for 1988 by indexing average book and periodicals prices from the *Bowker Annual*.)

Per capita expenditures for public libraries in the Western states (excluding Alaska, Hawaii, and Nevada) averaged $15.40 in 1988, ranging from $7.59 in Montana to $18.40 in Washington.

Source: Fast Facts (Colorado State Library), April 12, 1990

School library media centers

Why are school library media centers important?

Senator Claiborne Pell in the January 21, 1987, *Congressional Record* stated, "Libraries obviously play a most central role in developing and extending literacy. Studies have shown that reading skills and verbal expression have increased dramatically in elementary schools simply by adding or extending library activities." Research shows that quality library media programs have a direct positive relationship upon student achievement.

How many are there?

According to the 1985–86 U.S. Department of Education survey, 73,352 (93%) of the nation's public schools have a library media center.

What kinds of services do they provide?

No two library media programs are exactly alike because each reflects the particular emphases and needs of the school of which they are a part; however, certain basic services are provided through most programs:

- Assistance to students and staff in locating, evaluating, and using information and resources
- Reference assistance and information concerning new educational and media developments
- Informal instruction in the use of materials and equipment
- Guidance in reading, listening, and viewing materials
- Coordination of library media program activities and resources with subject areas, units, and textbooks

How are school library media centers staffed?

The ALA guidelines for school library media programs recommend that every school building, regardless of size or level, employ at least one certified library media professional full-time, with appropriate support staff, and note that many programs will require additional professional and support personnel.

Most library media centers are staffed at least part-time by a certified library media specialist who holds a teaching degree and a master's degree or additional course work in library and information science, management, education, media, communications, and technology. Unfortunately, in many school districts, library media specialists are responsible for more than one school building, thus significantly limiting the program that can be offered in those schools.

What kinds of materials are in the centers?

Information today is available in many formats—print, video, cassette, disk. The school library media specialist tries to match the learner's needs with information in the appropriate format to match his or her learning style.

Are the collections in these centers growing?

Yes, but not as fast as the increase in the cost of materials. In 1985, $4,743 was spent on the collection for the average school library media center. This expenditure level was a *decrease* from $6,384 in 1978, and $7,667 in 1974 (expressed in 1985 dollars). Yet the price of these materials has *increased* nearly 95% since 1974. The data in the following table are also from the 1985–86 survey.

The School Library Media Center Dollar		
School	Collection Budget per Pupil	Total Budget per Pupil
Elementary schools with less than 500 students	$19.46	$33.22
Elementary schools with more than 500 students	14.93	27.26
Middle/junior high schools with less than 500 students	28.42	44.34
Middle/junior high schools with more than 500 students	17.27	30.68
High schools with less than 500 students	44.58	72.21
High schools with 500–1,000 students	23.71	34.16
High schools with more than 1,000 students	19.71	27.45

Sources: CEMA Update, May 1989; and *Information Power: Guidelines for School Library Media Programs* (Chicago: American Library Association; Washington: Association for Educational Communications and Technology, 1988)

The school library media program

THE SCHOOL LIBRARY media program is an integral part of the school curriculum and provides a wide range of resources and information that satisfy the educational needs and interests of students. Materials are selected to meet the wide range of students' individual learning styles. The school library media center is a place where students may explore more fully classroom subjects that interest them, expand their imagination, delve into areas of personal interest, and develop the ability to think clearly, critically, and creatively about the resources they have chosen to read, hear, or view.

The school library media center provides a setting where students develop skills they will need as adults to locate, analyze, evaluate, interpret, and communicate information and ideas in an information-rich world. Students are encouraged to realize their potential as informed citizens who think critically and solve problems, to observe rights and responsibilities relating to the generation and flow of information and ideas, and to appreciate the value of literature in an educated society.

The school library media program serves *all* of the students of the community—not only the children of the most powerful, the most vocal or even the majority, but all of the students who attend the school. The collection includes materials to meet the needs of all learners, including the gifted, the mentally, physically, and emotionally impaired, and those who are culturally disadvantaged. The school library media program strives to maintain a diverse collection that represents various points of view on current and historical issues, as well as a wide variety of areas of interest to all students served. Though one parent or number of the school community may feel a particular title in the

school library media center's collection is inappropriate, others will feel the title is not only appropriate but desirable.

The school library media center is the symbol to students of our most cherished freedom as Americans—the freedom to speak our minds and hear what others have to say. School boards are urged to reaffirm the importance and the value of the freedom to read, view, and listen. Students have the right to develop the ability to think clearly, critically, and creatively about what they have chosen to read, hear, or view.

Source: Sample Statement on the Role of the School Library Media Program
(ALA American Association of School Librarians)

How do the states rank?

by Howard D. White

THE CHART ON THE FOLLOWING PAGE shows the state scores for the total collection efforts of 3,527 public school library media centers. The scores for elementary, junior high, and high school levels have been combined into a single aggregate measure of collection effort, which reveals "the best and the worst" states in the United States (along with the many in between). Though rough, these scores should tell library media specialists something about how their states compare with others when identical criteria are applied to each and how their own data compare with state averages. The figures are based on 1985 and 1986 surveys by Westat, Inc., under contract to the U.S. Department of Education's Center for Education Statistics.

Highest place goes to Oregon, with the greatest number of high or medium high means across all measures of collection size and expenditure. The top twelve states are all Northern, and eight of them are contiguous across the northern Midwest and Great Plains: Wisconsin, Minnesota, North Dakota, South Dakota, Nebraska, Kansas, Montana, and Wyoming.

Alaska and Vermont are similar to this group in having relatively low population densities and nonindustrial economies. New Jersey, on the other hand, is both highly industrial and densely populated. Washington state, often thought to be economically and environmentally similar to neighboring Oregon, is by this measure very dissimilar. Thus economics and populations fail as easy explanations of the rankings. There may be a Midwestern "school library culture" that promotes above-average performance on collection measures.

One thing is clear: none of the Sun Belt states are shown to do well in overall collection effort as of 1985. Since most Southern states have long histories of substandard funding of school and public libraries, perhaps the new shocker is California. America's richest state, post-Proposition 13, is very close to the bottom of the rankings. Michigan and Massachusetts fare little better. The position of the nation's capital, at the very bottom without a single point, calls for exploration beyond the scope of this study. There has to be a bottom to every ranking, of course, but one would not expect the federally funded capital of the United States to occupy it.

Source: Howard D. White, "School Library Collections and Services: Ranking the States," *School Library Media Quarterly* 19 (Fall 1990): 13–26

State collection effort scores, public school library media centers

State (Total)	Score	State (Elementary)	Score	State (Junior High)	Score	State (High School)	Score
Ore.	67	Mont.	26	Ore.	22	Ore.	23
Wisc.	65	Minn.	26	Kan.	22	Wisc.	21
Wyo.	64	Wyo.	24	Wyo.	21	Vt.	21
Alask.	62	Wisc.	23	Wisc.	21	N.J.	21
Vt.	60	Alask.	23	N.J.	21	Conn.	21
Minn.	59	Vt.	22	S.D.	20	Wyo.	19
Mont.	58	Ore.	22	Alask.	20	N.D.	19
Nebr.	57	Nebr.	21	N.H.	18	Minn.	19
Kan.	56	Mo.	19	Nebr.	18	Ia.	19
N.J.	55	N.D.	18	N.C.	18	Alask.	19
N.D.	51	N.C.	18	Vt.	17	Nebr.	18
S.D.	48	Kan.	18	Mont.	17	Kan.	16
N.C.	45	Ind.	17	N.D.	14	S.D.	15
Ia.	44	S.D.	13	Minn.	14	Mont.	15
Mo.	42	N.J.	13	Ia.	14	N.Mex.	14
Conn.	38	Conn.	12	Penna.	12	Colo.	14
Ind.	34	Ala.	12	Mo.	12	Tex.	12
Fla.	31	Va.	11	Fla.	12	N.Y.	12
Colo.	31	Ia.	11	Ga.	11	Ill.	12
Tex.	30	Fla.	11	Colo.	11	Va.	11
N.H.	30	Okla.	9	Tex.	10	Mo.	11
Va.	29	N.Y.	9	Ark.	9	Me.	11
Penna.	26	Ga.	9	Ohio	8	Ariz.	11
N.Y.	26	Ut.	8	Ill.	8	N.H.	10
Ga.	26	Tex.	8	Va.	7	Ky.	10
Me.	25	Me.	8	Ky.	7	Ind.	10
Ill.	24	Haw.	8	Ind.	7	N.C.	9
Ky.	23	S.C.	7	Wash.	6	Haw.	9
Ariz.	23	Ariz.	7	Ut.	6	Penna.	8
N.Mex.	22	Penna.	6	S.C.	6	Ohio	8
Ohio	21	La.	6	Okla.	6	Fla.	8
Haw.	21	Ky.	6	Me.	6	Del.	7
Ala.	21	Colo.	6	Md.	6	Tenn.	6
Okla.	20	Ark.	6	Ala.	6	Md.	6
Ut.	19	Ohio	5	Tenn.	5	Ga.	6
Ark.	18	Wash.	4	N.Y.	5	Ut.	5
Md.	16	Tenn.	4	N.Mex.	5	Okla.	5
Tenn.	15	Md.	4	Mass.	5	Nev.	5
S.C.	15	Ill.	4	Colo.	5	Ida.	5
Wash.	14	Nev.	3	Ariz.	5	Calif.	5
La.	14	N.Mex.	3	La.	4	Wash.	4
Del.	13	Del.	3	Haw.	4	Mich.	4
Nev.	11	N.H.	2	Nev.	3	Mass.	4
Mass.	11	Mich.	2	Mich.	3	La.	4
Mich.	9	Mass.	2	Del.	3	Ark.	3
Ida.	6	Miss.	1	Miss.	2	Ala.	3
Calif.	5	W.Va.	0	W.Va.	1	S.C.	2
Miss.	4	R.I.	0	R.I.	1	W.Va.	1
W.Va.	2	Ida.	0	Ida.	1	R.I.	1
R.I.	2	D.C.	0	D.C.	0	Miss.	1
D.C.	0	Calif.	0	Calif.	0	D.C.	0

U.S. Mean 29.6   Std. Dev. 19.3

School library media centers: Space considerations

AMONG THE SPECIFIC variables to be considered in the design of facilities are the differences between elementary and secondary schools, the differences in school populations and community involvement, the total amount of space available, and the extent of centralized district services. Both the present situation and future technological changes must be taken into account in analyzing these variables. The following specifications should be incorporated into planning or reviewing library media program facilities at the building level:

1. Reading, listening, viewing, and computing areas for independent study, with ready access to collections and equipment. Considerations include:
   a. individual study spaces provided by carrels or study tables
   b. tables, counters, carrels, or carts to accommodate a variety of electronic equipment
   c. informal seating or an informal area with comfortable chairs
   d. special carrels and equipment for users with physical or sensory impairments.

2. Space for small and medium-sized group activities, either as conference rooms or as specially organized and acoustically treated areas within the general seating space, for viewing, discussing, and working on projects. Considerations include:
   a. in elementary school library media centers, the incorporation of a storytelling area equipped for dramatizations and electronic presentations
   b. adequate space and appropriate furnishings for small group work with newer technologies, such as computers and interactive video.

3. A large multipurpose area off the main area of the library media center, serving as a viewing room, lecture hall, classroom, or meeting area. Considerations include:
   a. a control room to provide special lighting and sound
   b. convenient access to audiovisual equipment and technical support
   c. movable seating to provide flexibility
   d. floor coverings appropriate to multipurpose activities.

4. Space to house and display the collections of library media materials, provide a supervised entry-exit area, organize reference materials and index tools for easy access, and carry out circulation and reserve activities. Considerations include:
   a. the changing nature of collections, such as the increased packaging of information in electronic or audiovisual formats, the storage of periodicals on microfiche or microfilm instead of paper copy, the distribution of films on videocassettes, and the acquisition of computer disks and other software
   b. the need for electronic access to information within and outside the center through online services, CD-ROM capability, and computerized catalogs
   c. dedicated telephone and data lines for access to information sources and television outside the school building
   d. space for the storage of hard copy made from electronic sources and the copy equipment to transfer information from nonprint to print media

e. the space required for physical access to and control or distribution of special technologies, such as CD-ROM, optical laser disks, hard disks, satellite systems, magnetic storage, electronic distribution systems, and other emerging technologies

f. space and raceways to allow use of electrical and electronic technologies for security systems, automated circulation systems, and computerized catalogs

g. well-placed and secure space for displays and promotional materials

h. fireproof space with compact shelving and adequate theft protection for storage of archives and important school records.

5. Facilities for the organization, maintenance, and control of equipment in the center, for the preparation and maintenance of all materials in the collection, for the production of materials by teachers, students, production specialist, and staff, and for the delivery of information within the school. Considerations include:

a. areas for consultation with teachers and students

b. work areas where library media personnel carry out technical processes and support activities

c. facilities for the production of materials, including graphics, photography, videotaping, audio production, computer programming

d. a secure equipment area from which distribution, repair, and maintenance of equipment can be carried out, with convenient access to hallway, elevator, loading dock

e. spaces where students and teachers have ready access to equipment to view, listen, read, and compute, using media in all formats

f. space for the distribution systems, which capture and rebroadcast instructional television, radio, computer programs, and audio and video teleconferencing or distance learning.

6. Facilities for computers for both administrative and teaching or learning applications, within the library media center. Space requirements vary with the nature of computer use and its relation to the school program. Considerations include:

a. the number of computer laboratories in the building and the nature of their use

b. the flexibility demanded by services such as database searching, dial access, computerized catalog, automated circulation systems, interactive video

c. the relationship of the library media center to other learning areas, such as distance learning labs and satellite resource centers.

7. Space where faculty and media professionals can work without student interruption, where professional materials can be housed and displayed, and where general-purpose equipment, such as typewriters, computers, and copiers, is available for teacher use.

Source: Information Power: Guidelines for School Library Media Programs (Chicago: American Library Association; Washington: Association for Educational Communications and Technology, 1988)

Architect Frank Lloyd Wright (1869–1959) was responsible for a design proposal (never realized) for the Milwaukee (Wisc.) Public Library (right). The proposal was submitted in 1898. One library he was responsible for, however, was the library in the Marin County (Calif.) Civic Center, San Rafael.

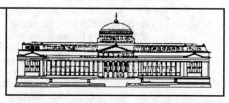

Planning a new building

by William W. Sannwald

HERE ARE SOME KEY POINTS to consider in planning a new library building.

1. Does the building fit into the site and neighborhood?
2. Is the building visually satisfying to look at?
3. Does the building look like an inviting building to enter?
4. Is there a large, exterior, well-lighted sign identifying the library that is visible from passing cars and not accessible from the ground to protect it from vandalism?
5. Is the entrance identifiable to people in cars as well as to pedestrians?
6. Are the library's hours of service prominently displayed on a sign at the entrance? Are the library's hours also visible from a car?
7. Is there sufficient parking for staff as well as patrons meeting local codes?
8. Is parking convenient to the entrance, and is the parking area lit at night?
9. Are parking spaces easy to get into and out of for larger cars?
10. If there is a parking garage, is it easily located, well lighted, and well identified from the street?
11. Is the library near mass transportation?
12. Are public telephones available outside?
13. Is the entrance sheltered from weather and well lit?
14. Is the building lit and inviting at night?
15. Can the exterior be easily maintained?
16. Is there an after-hours book return sheltered from the weather?
17. Is the bookdrop separate from the building or located in a fireproof area?
18. Are bicycle racks clearly visible from the street and/or interior?
19. Is there an entrance for deliveries?
    a. Has a buzzer been included in the delivery entrance?
    b. Is the entrance secure from theft and vandalism?
20. Can trucks easily unload?
21. Is there adequate provision for storing of trash, and is it accessible from the building and for pick-up?
22. Can landscaping be easily maintained?
    a. Does the landscaping enhance or limit building or personal security?
    b. Is the landscaping drought tolerant?
23. Is there provision for storage of lawnmowers, snowblowers, and other equipment?
24. Is there provision for outside faucets and electrical outlets? Are they vandal proof?
25. Are all walkways and ramps leading into the building well lighted?
    a. In Northern areas do sidewalk lamps give off heat to help melt snow?
    b. Are there curb cutouts for wheelchairs?
26. Is the fenestration arranged to take maximum advantage of the best views and allow maximum use of floor and wall space?
27. Will sunlight, glare, and ultraviolet rays be controlled architecturally?
28. Is the loading dock detailed for vehicles using it and detailed for vehicular variance in floor height?
29. Is there space for a bookmobile, van, or library employee of the year very near the staff or receiving entrance?
    a. Are exhaust fumes accommodated in the design?
    b. Is the entrance convenient for staff and movement of materials?
30. Is the building's skin and roof easily maintained and energy-efficient?

Source: William W. Sannwald, *Checklist of Library Building Design Considerations* (Chicago: ALA Library Administration and Management Association, 1991)

Carnegie libraries

by George Bobinski

BETWEEN 1889 AND the mid-1920s American steel magnate Andrew Carnegie built 1,679 public library buildings in 1,412 U.S. communities. This had a great impact on public library development. Free public libraries supported by local taxation had begun in Boston in 1849 and were slowly spreading through the country. Carnegie's benefactions made them leap forward.

He attached two conditions to his offer of money for a public library building: the local community had to provide a suitable site and formally agree to continuous support for the library through local tax funds. The latter solidified acceptance of the concept of tax support for libraries.

Carnegie also provided funds for 108 academic library buildings in the U.S. Indeed, his library philanthropy was international; he donated $56,162,622 for a total of 2,509 library buildings throughout the English-speaking world.

With the financial assistance of the H.W. Wilson Foundation, George Bobinski conducted a survey of the status of public library buildings built with Carnegie funds. Here are the preliminary results based on responses from 1,315 of the 1,679 Carnegie libraries.

- 204 buildings have been demolished.
- 337 have been converted to other uses.
- 744 remain as libraries.
- About 250 remain unchanged from the time of original construction.
- 22 reported restorations or planned restoration projects.
- More than 130 indicated that the building had been extensively remodeled.
- Just over 200 reported an expansion of the original building.
- Plans for expansion, remodeling or replacement were indicated by 127 Carnegie library communities.

Source: George Bobinski, "Carnegies," *American Libraries,* April 1990, pp. 296–301

Bookmobiles

by Bert R. Boyce and Judith I. Boyce

SINCE 1905 WHEN Mary Titcomb originated the idea of a wagon designed to provide direct book service to rural areas, the bookmobile has been the only available mechanism for moving a collection rather than duplicating it to expand service. In 1965 there were nearly 2,000 bookmobiles in service in the United States. It is likely that the height of bookmobile service came in the early 1970s. The dramatic increase in gasoline prices later in this decade undoubtedly caused many libraries to reconsider the cost of the service and to drop it.

There were between 1,130 and 1,200 bookmobiles in the United States in 1988. More than one-third of major public library systems are providing bookmobile service. Seventy-two percent of the bookmobiles in use were purchased for less than $45,000, and 75% of them cost less than $2,000 annually to maintain. Forty-eight percent of the libraries surveyed in 1988 were then in the market for a new bookmobile and 90% expected to continue to provide bookmobile service.

About 6% of the circulation of the libraries in the survey came from bookmobiles. One-third of the operating vehicles had some form of two-way mobile communication, and 17% had an automated circulation system or catalog (although the Gaylord charge machine remains the most popular item of on-board technology).

It is common for libraries offering bookmobile service to offer other outreach services as well. Shut-in service was provided by 59% of the libraries, deposit collections were kept by 43%, and a books-by-mail service was maintained by more than 25%.

The most frequent service provided by bookmobiles was interlibrary loan, with 82% of the libraries reporting this feature. Other bookmobile services recorded by the 1988 survey are listed on the following graph.

Bookmobile Services Offered, 1988

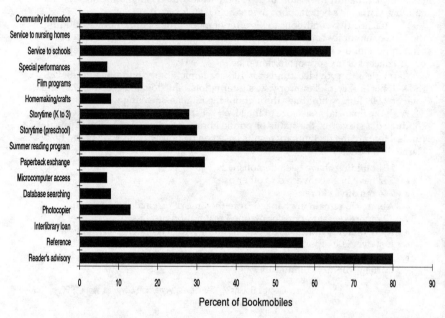

Percent of Bookmobiles

Source: Bert R. Boyce and Judith I. Boyce, *The Bookmobile: A Service Mechanism for the Nineties?* (Baton Rouge: Louisiana State University School of Library and Information Science, 1989)

Bookmobiles have long been a familiar sight in remote areas.

1

The Library of Congress:
The nation's library

THE LIBRARY OF CONGRESS is the nation's library. Its services extend not only to members and committees of the Congress but to the executive and judicial branches of government, to libraries throughout the Nation and the world, and to the scholars and researchers and artists and scientists who use its resources. This was not always the case. When President John Adams signed the bill that provided for the removal of the seat of government to the new capital city of Washington in 1800, he created a reference library for Congress only. The bill provided, among other items, $5,000 "for the purchase of such books as may be necessary for the use of Congress—and for putting up a suitable apartment for containing them therein."

The first books were ordered from England and shipped across the Atlantic in 11 hair trunks and a map case. The Library was housed in the new Capitol until August 1814, when British troops invaded Washington and put the torch to the Capitol Building, and the small collection was lost. Within a month former President Thomas Jefferson, living in retirement at Monticello, offered as a replacement his personal library, accumulated over a span of 50 years. As Minister to France, Jefferson had spent many afternoons at bookstalls in Paris, "turning over every book with my own hands, putting by every everything which related to America, and indeed whatever was rare and valuable in every science." His library was considered one of the finest in the United States.

In offering his library to the Congress Jefferson wrote, "I do not know that it contains any branch of science which Congress would wish to exclude from their collection; there is, in fact, no subject to which a Member of Congress may not have occasion to refer." After considerable debate Congress in January 1815 accepted Jefferson's offer, appropriating $23,950 for the collection of 6,487 books. Thus the foundation was laid for a great national library.

Buildings and facilities

The Library of Congress complex on Capitol Hill includes three buildings. The Thomas Jefferson Building, executed in Italian Renaissance style, is the oldest of these. Heralded as the largest and costliest library structure in the world when it was completed in 1897, it is elaborately decorated with splendid sculpture, murals, and mosaics created by 50 American artists. The building's Great Hall includes towering marble columns, murals and mosaics, statuary, and stained glass, portraying themes relating to learning, knowledge, and the many pursuits of civilization. The Main Reading Room, reopening in late 1990 following extensive renovation, soars 160 feet from floor to dome. The room houses a collection of 45,000 reference books and desks for 250 readers. The adjacent Computer Catalog Center provides public access to the Library's automated catalog files through computer terminals.

The simply designed, dignified John Adams Building, faced with white Georgia marble, was opened in 1939. Bas relief sculptures on its large bronze doors represent 12 historic figures credited with giving the art of writing to their people. They include Ts'ang Chieh, Chinese patron saint of pictographic letters; Cadmus, honored in Greek legend as the inventor of the alphabet; and Sequoyah, the renowned American Indian who invented an alphabet for the Cherokee language and taught his people to read. Ezra Winter's murals of the *Canterbury Tales* decorate the building's fifth-floor reading room.

The white marble James Madison Memorial Building, dedicated on April 24, 1980, more than doubled the Library's available Capitol Hill space. The building houses the official memorial to the nation's fourth president, James Madison Memorial Hall, as well as eight reading rooms, offices, and storage areas for the Library's special-format collections, which number over 70 million items.

From papyrus to lasers

Collections of the Library include more than 86 million items covering virtually every subject in formats that vary from papyrus to optical disks. These materials stretch along 535 miles of shelves and are being acquired at a rate of 10 items a minute. The Library has 27 million books and pamphlets in 60 languages and more than 39 million manuscripts, among them such treasures of American history and culture as the papers of presidents, notable families, writers, artists, and scientists. The Library has the world's largest and most comprehensive cartographic collection—almost 4 million maps and atlases, dating back to the middle of the 14th century—and a 7-million-piece music collection that includes autograph scores, correspondence of composers and musicians, flutes from throughout the world, and rare Stradivarius instruments, with Tourte bows.

The Library's 10 million prints and photographs provide a visual record of people, places, and events in the United States and in many foreign countries. Master photos, fine prints, works of popular and applied graphic arts, and documentary photographs are included. Approximately 75,000 serial titles are received annually; 1,200 newspapers are held in the Library's permanent collections, with some dating back to the 17th century. There are also

RUBY MAGIC LANTERN

80,000 motion picture titles, 50,000 television broadcasts, 350,000 radio transcriptions, and over one million other sound recordings, as well as about seven million microforms.

Throughout the Library buildings manuscripts, rare books, prints, and maps from collections are exhibited. On permanent display are such priceless treasures as the Library's copy of the Gutenberg Bible, one of three surviving examples printed on vellum and perfect in all respects, and the Giant Bible of Mainz, an illuminated manuscript executed by hand at about the time the Gutenberg Bible was printed. Also on permanent display is a copyright exhibit with such familiar items as Ken and Barbie dolls, a speech by Martin Luther King, Jr., and a copy of the movie "Gone With the Wind," which trace the history of copyright through landmark cases.

In 1982 the Library began a pilot program in image preservation and retrieval using state-of-the-art optical disk technology. The pilot program evaluated the use of optical disk technology for information preservation, improved access, compact storage, and determination of the costs and benefits of the technology in a library setting. Two types of disk storage are now being used. High resolution images of print materials are being stored on digital optical disks, while lower resolution images of non-print materials are stored on analog videodisks. Several user stations are in place in selected reading rooms so readers may gain access to certain articles, journals, maps, music, manuscripts, motion picture stills, drawings, and photographs. Some of the earliest motion pictures produced, as well as samples of color film segments and television broadcasts, are a part of the one program.

Services to Congress

The Library of Congress provides numerous services which directly or indirectly benefit all Americans. A primary role is to serve as the research and reference arm of the Congress. Through the Congressional Research Service (CRS), a department established over 60 years ago, the Library provides legislators with the information they need to govern wisely and effectively. The staff of CRS answers about 450,000 inquiries a year, ranging from simple requests for data to highly complex in-depth studies. In addition, CRS prepares bill digests, summaries of major legislation, and other reference tools to help members and their committees stay abreast of the daily flow of legislation.

The CRS staff of 860 ranges from civil engineers and oceanographers to labor arbitrators and experts on Soviet rocketry. Their most important function is to provide objective, unbiased information to the Congress, presenting the pros and cons of each issue so that members can make their own decisions on the basis of complete knowledge of the problems involved.

The staff of the Law Library, a department created by an Act of Congress more than 150 years ago, is the research arm of the Congress for questions regarding foreign law. The Law Library answers congressional requests for analyses of foreign legislation and legal developments. Translations of foreign laws are handled by the Law Library's legal specialists, who are proficient in 50 different languages.

Scholarly resources

As its most important service to the scholarly community the Library of Congress makes its vast resources available to the public. Scholars, writers, teachers, artists, journalists, students—anyone over the age of 18 pursuing serious research—may use the Library's reading rooms, each of which has a catalog, reference collection, and reference librarians to guide the way. Readers may use computer terminals to search the Library's databases for new titles, for sources of information on a variety of subjects, and for legislative histories.

The uses of the Library's resources are as varied as its collections. For example, a graduate student doing a comparative study of American writers may go to the Manuscript Reading Room to examine the papers of Walt Whitman and Archibald MacLeish. A violinist may use the Music Reading Room to study the notations on an original score of a Mozart string quartet. An attorney may use the Law Library's comprehensive collection of foreign law materials. To gather background material for a spy story set in Eastern Europe, a novelist may refer to the extensive reference collections of the Main Reading Room, the European Division, and the Government Publications, Newspaper, and Current Periodical Reading Room.

For those who are not able to visit the Library a number of special services are available. Through its interlibrary loan program the Library extends the use of its books and other research materials to scholars working at academic, public, or other libraries across the country. The service is intended to aid scholarly research by making available unusual materials not readily accessible elsewhere. Through the Library's Photoduplication Service the public may purchase photographs, photostats, facsimile prints, and microfilms of research materials by mall (subject to copyright or other restrictions).

In 1980 the Library established the Council of Scholars, a group of 22 distinguished individuals representing a wide spectrum of academic fields and disciplines. These men and women are charged with examining the state of knowledge in their subject fields and exploring the extent to which the Library's collections effectively support active research in these areas.

Cultural programs

Chamber music concerts, poetry readings, films, lectures, and symposia are presented throughout the year in the Library's 500-seat Coolidge Auditorium, the adjacent Whittall Pavilion, the Mary Pickford Theater, and the Mumford Room. Live broadcasts of many of the concerts are carried by radio stations throughout the country. Many lectures given at the Library are published. (The Coolidge Auditorium will be closed for renovation until 1992.)

Through its exhibits program, the Library displays examples of the treasures in its collections, including prints and photographs, maps, musical scores, rare books, and manuscripts. Many of the exhibits travel to libraries and museums across the nation.

Especially popular is the lunchtime concert series sponsored by the Library's American Folklife Center. Once a month, from May through October, musical groups representing a variety of folk traditions perform on the Neptune Plaza in front of the Library's Jefferson Building.

The Center for the Book in the Library of Congress is a catalyst for stimulating public interest in books, reading, and the printed word. Its symposia, exhibits, and publications are supported by tax-deductible contributions from individuals and corporations. "A Nation of Readers," "Books Make a Difference," and "Year of the Young Reader," are reading promotion themes used nationally and by affiliated Centers for the Book in a number of states.

Source: Library of Congress

Library of Congress 1990 fact sheet

IN FISCAL YEAR 1990, the Library of Congress—

Welcomed 1,719,522 users and visitors.

Held 97,505,044 items, including:

15,095,645 books in the classified collections.

82,409,399 items in the nonclassified collections. These included

12,501,998 books in large type and raised characters, incunabula, monographs and serials, music, bound newspapers, pamphlets, technical reports, and other printed material.

2,050,490 audio materials, such as disks, tapes, and other recorded formats.

39,413,936 manuscripts.

3,976,778 maps.

8,160,285 microforms.

16,305,912 visual materials, including 525,589 motion pictures, 13,987,367 photographs, 78,910 posters, 347,448 prints and drawings, 115,210 videotapes and videodisks, and 1,251,388 other visual materials.

Completed full-level cataloging of 198,222 titles.

Processed 686,854 copyright claims, registered 642,604 claims to copyright, and answered 424,285 inquiries through the Copyright Office.

Completed 508,887 research assignments for the Congress through the Congressional Research Service.

Conducted public tours for 24,142 visitors and special tours (available in 25 languages) for 5,737 visitors. Visitor Services staff and Information Desk volunteers answered 120,790 inquiries.

Coordinated 230 special events through the Special Events Office.

Circulated more than 20,500,000 disk, cassette, and braille items to more than 693,920 blind and physically handicapped persons.

Had more than 11,928,747 records in its computer database.

Employed a staff of 4,632 employees.

Operated with a total fiscal 1990 appropriation of $266,720,000.

Source: Library of Congress

Main entry for oracle bones?

The National Library of China's 13 million holdings include 35,000 pieces of oracle bones with inscriptions carved during the 16th century B.C.; more than 250,000 rubbings from inscriptions on bronze vessels, lutes, and stone tablets, some dating from the 10th century B.C.; 2.3 million documents handwritten after the invention of papermaking in the first century A.D.; and woodblock and movable-type documents produced after the invention of printing in the 6th and 7th centuries A.D.

Source: American Libraries, May 1987, p. 330

BIG ideas for small libraries

by Jan Feye-Stukas

MOST PEOPLE WHO work in small libraries have entirely too much to do. They are expected to perform all the tasks involved in running a successful library operation: reference and reader's advisory, collection development and maintenance, circulation and overdues, as well as administration, public relations, and programming. Impossible? Probably. But there are things that can be done and resources available to help a beleaguered staff person in the small library cope.

Here are some basic suggestions and innovative ideas that may help the librarian get the job done, even with too little time and money.

1. Signs to help people help themselves. We are a do-it-yourself society. The discount-store chains are a testament to our ability to help ourselves without staff assistance. Most people would prefer to try to find what they want or need on their own. In addition, there are those who would like a little privacy while using the library.

Signs are necessary even in the smallest physical facility to make a library user feel welcome and comfortable. Inexpensive materials are available at art supply stores to help staff or artistic volunteers make handsome, professional-looking signs that are in everyday language (see *A Sign System for Libraries,* by Mary S. Mallery and Ralph E. DeVore, ALA, 1982, for the basics). Libraries should avoid hand-lettered signs, which give the impression of impermanence and nonprofessionalism.

2. Get a telephone answering machine. It will save having to answer many of the what-are-your-hours questions when the library is open. People can call in and make their requests even when the library is closed. The staff can then respond to the questions more efficiently before the library opens.

3. Weed. This is not, of course, a new idea. But most libraries, big and small, could use more than a little help in carrying out what many view as an onerous task. Weeding is absolutely essential for the small library, which by its very size cannot be all things to all people; it must target its collection to those items its patrons want and use most.

Crowded shelves make reshelving materials much more time-consuming and tedious; overcrowding is also hard on the materials. If regular staff members cannot find the time or cannot bear to throw anything away, volunteers may be able to at least begin the job. Using the "CREW method" (see *Evaluating and Weeding Collections in Small and Medium-sized Public Libraries: The CREW Method,* by Joseph P. Segal, ALA, 1980), a volunteer could do the initial selecting, and a trained staff member could go through the potential discards a second time to either approve the decision to discard or "save" the item.

Discards may be put on a permanent "for sale" shelf, or be given to a Friends of the Library group for a once- or twice-a-year sale. If an item is extremely difficult to part with, it may be donated to a nearby university, a large public library, or the state library; any of these choices makes the item available for interlibrary loan, thus making the discarding much easier on the staff and the occasional patron that may want noncurrent materials.

4. Lengthen the loan period. Statistics show that many libraries, particularly small public libraries, have a standard loan period of only two weeks. This requires patrons to make frequent trips to the library and increases the work load in renewals. A three- or four-week loan period could make life much easier for all involved.

5. Get a coin-operated photocopier. As many as half the very small public libraries still do not have photocopiers. Coin-operated photocopiers let patrons do their own photocopying, saving the overworked staff from another time-consuming task. Even if a library cannot afford to buy a machine, there may be businesses in the community that would supply the equipment. The benefits in time saved, goodwill generated, and improved service will please everyone. Photocopiers have come down in size so even the tiniest library can find the space for one.

6. Cooperate. Join with nearby large and small libraries to perform various tasks cooperatively. Acquisitions (this does not mean selection), cataloging, and processing can all be done jointly and economically by groups of libraries banded together.

7. Interfile juvenile and adult nonfiction. Again, this saves staff time and makes library use easier for the patrons. Juvenile items at a third-grade-or-below level can be shelved separately on lower shelves, but anything on a fourth-grade-or-above level can be interfiled. This saves staff from having to run between two areas, even if they are only a few feet apart, and removes the stigma of age in library use. Interfiling also allows more efficient use of the collection and saves on duplication of materials.

8. Do not send overdue notices; after four weeks, send a bill. Small, unautomated libraries cannot afford the staff time involved in sending out numerous notices. If the overdue policy regarding fines and billing is clearly spelled out in signs, on the library card, or on special small flyers inserted in the materials as they are checked out, there should be no cause for surprise on the part of users.

9. Prepare a "wishbook" that includes pictures of equipment or furniture needed. This can be used to motivate and inform organizations or individuals in the community that may be looking for a worthy service project.

10. Professionalize the staff. This does not necessarily mean sending them off to library school. Professionalism is a state of mind as much as anything. It means: looking and performing the part of a leader in the community; being open to new ideas and using every opportunity to go to workshops and conferences; spending some time working in other libraries at least once a year; keeping up with library literature, even if the library must share subscriptions to professional journals with several other libraries; and performing at all times in a businesslike fashion.

The staff personifies the institution and projects an image to the community. Even if they have no formal training in library science (and most staff in small libraries do not) and are grossly underpaid (all staff in small libraries are), they have been hired to do an extremely important job. If they can see themselves as competent, important professionals performing a valuable service to their community, their ability to cope and succeed on the job will be greatly enhanced.

Source: Jan Feye-Stukas, "Ten Big Ideas for Small Libraries," *American Libraries,* December 1986, pp. 835–36

The five laws of library science

by S. R. Ranganathan

1. Books are for use.
2. Every reader his book.
3. Every book its reader.
4. Save the time of the reader.
5. The library is a growing organism.

Source: S. R. Ranganathan, *The Five Laws of Library Science* (Bombay: Asia Publishing House, 1963)

Hopes, fears, trends

by Thomas J. Hennen, Jr.

AT THE END of the OCLC Conference on the Future of the Public Library in March 1988, futurist Robert Olson asked library leaders participating to list their greatest hopes, worst fears for the future, and anticipated trends:

Worst fears

1. Librarians' leadership will be inadequate to the challenges of the future.
2. Fee-setting and privatization will get out of control and overwhelm libraries.
3. The gap between society's haves and have-nots will widen.
4. Public libraries, especially rural ones, will disappear and be replaced by fee-based services—or, the worse for the poor, will not be replaced at all.
5. Libraries will become a small part of the creeping authoritarianism of Big Brother government.
6. Public libraries will no longer provide humane community centers in urban neighborhoods and small towns.
7. Libraries will cease to share resources with one another.

Greatest hopes

1. Libraries will adapt to the future successfully through creative leadership and excellence in staff development.
2. Libraries will finally become identified by the public as the "information hub" of society because they are gateways to electronic data as well as storehouses of printed materials.
3. Usage will increase dramatically owing to library responsiveness to public needs.
4. A creative society will successfully shift to lifelong learning and library use.
5. Libraries will greatly increase efforts to reach society's have-nots.
6. New governance and funding structures will allow libraries to respond to public needs.

Trends

1. Even as our bibliographic and other networks expand from a national to an international scale, technology is paradoxically allowing bibliographic and full-text data transfer to move from highly centralized time-sharing on mainframes to decentralized systems on microcomputers.
2. Future library circulation and other services will be almost totally automated and self-service provided, as in today's automated teller machines.
3. Technology application will be increasingly focused on the library user rather than on technical processing or circulation.
4. Fee-based providers will replace reference delivery, unless libraries stay in the forefront.
5. Libraries will shift focus from container (book, film, etc.) to content.
6. Librarians will focus on selecting, judging, advising, and interpreting increasing amounts of information.
7. Libraries will integrate incompatible technologies and create user-oriented standards for information handling.
8. Public libraries will employ market research to make the best use of limited resources and learn to get closer to their clients in order to understand their needs.

Source: Thomas J. Hennen, Jr., "Public Librarians Take Cool View of Future," *American Libraries*, May 1988, p. 390

PEOPLE

Librarians

Who works in libraries?

by Mary Jo Lynch

LIBRARIES HIRE LIBRARIANS and other professionals, paraprofessionals, clerical and technical personnel. The 3,438 college and university libraries responding to a 1988 survey reported a total of 99,669 paid staff (full-time and full-time equivalent of part-time) for the academic year 1987–1988.

A total of 105,408 persons were employed in public libraries in 1989, including full-time staff and full-time equivalent of part-time staff.

Public and private school library media centers reported a total of 112,952 employees for 1985–1986. Both full-time and full-time equivalent of part-time are included.

Student volunteers are used in 44% of public schools and 27% of private schools.

Adult volunteers are used in 29% of public schools and 54% of private schools.

A 1982 National Center for Education Statistics (NCES) study of the library labor market (*Library Human Resources: A Study of Supply and Demand,* ALA, 1983) estimated employment in special libraries as follows:

- 18,600 librarians
- 6,280 other professionals
- 22,530 support staff

The following figures provide an estimate of employment in libraries as of 1989:

151,554	Librarians and other professionals
212,831	Support staff
364,385	Total persons employed in libraries

Source: Mary Jo Lynch, ALA Office for Research; NCES, *Academic Libraries 1988* (1990); NCES, *Public Libraries in the United States 1989* (1991); NCES, *Statistics of Public and Private School Library Media Centers 1985* (1987)

What job categories are there?

IN ADDITION TO FORMAL TRAINING and education, skills other than those of librarianship may have an important contribution to make to the achievement of superior library service. There should be equal recognition in both the professional and support ranks for those individuals whose expertise contributes to the effective performance of the library.

The tables on the next page suggest a set of categories and define basic requirements and responsibilities for professional and support staff.

The titles recommended here represent categories or broad classifications, within which it is assumed that there will be several levels of promotional steps.

Categories of library personnel—Professional

Senior Librarian/Senior Specialist
Requirements: In addition to relevant experience, education beyond the M.A.
   (i.e., a master's degree in any of its variant designations: M.A., M.L.S.,
   M.S.L.S., M.Ed., etc.) as: post-master's degree; Ph.D.; relevant continuing
   education in many forms.
Responsibility: Top-level responsibilities, including but not limited to administration; superior knowledge of some aspect of librarianship, or of other subject
   fields of value to the library.

Librarian/Specialist
Requirements: Master's degree
Responsibility: Professional responsibilities including those of management,
   which require independent judgment, interpretation of rules and procedures,
   analysis of library problems, and formulation of original and creative solutions
   for them (normally utilizing knowledge of the subject field represented by the
   academic degree).

Categories of library personnel—Support staff

Library Associate/Associate Specialist
Requirements: Bachelor's degree (with or without course work in library science);
   or bachelor's degree, plus additional academic work short of the master's
   degree (in librarianship for the Library Associate; in other relevant subject
   fields for the Associate Specialist).
Responsibility: Support responsibilities at a high level, normally working within
   the established procedures and techniques, and with some supervision by a
   professional, but requiring judgment, and subject knowledge such as is
   represented by a full, four-year college education culminating in the bachelor's degree.
Library Technical Assistant/Technical Assistant
Requirements: At least two years of college-level study; *or* A.A. degree, with or
   without Library Technical Assistant training; *or* post-secondary school training
   in relevant skills.
Responsibility : Tasks performed as support staff to Associates and higher ranks,
   following established rules and procedures, and including, at the top level,
   supervision of such tasks.
Clerk
Requirements: Business school or commercial courses, supplemented by in-
   service training or on-the-job experience.
Responsibility: Clerical assignments as required by the individual library.

Specific job titles may be used within any category: for example, catalogers,
reference librarians, children's librarians would be included in either the "Librarian" or (depending upon the level of their responsibilities and qualifications)
"Senior Librarian" categories; department heads, the director of the library, and
certain specialists would presumably have the additional qualifications and responsibilities that place them in the "Senior Librarian" category.

The title "Librarian" carries with it the connotation of "professional" in the
sense that professional tasks are those which require a special background and
education. This is the basis by which the librarian identifies library needs,
analyzes problems, sets goals, and formulates original and creative solutions,
integrating theory into practice, and planning, organizing, communicating, and

administering successful programs of service to users of the library's materials and services. In defining services to users, the professional recognizes potential users as well as current ones, and designs services that will reach all who might benefit from them.

"Librarian" therefore should be used only to designate positions in libraries that utilize the qualifications and impose the responsibilities suggested above. Positions that are primarily devoted to the routine application of established rules and techniques, however useful and essential to the effective operation of a library's ongoing services, should not carry the word "Librarian" in the job title.

The salaries for each category should offer a range of promotional steps sufficient to permit a career-in-rank. The top salary in any category should overlap the beginning salary in the next higher category, in order to give recognition to the value of experience and knowledge gained on the job.

Inadequately supported libraries or libraries too small to be able to afford professional staff should nevertheless have access to the services and supervision of a librarian. To obtain the professional guidance that they themselves cannot supply, such libraries should promote cooperative arrangements or join larger systems of cooperating libraries through which supervisory personnel can be supported. Smaller libraries that are part of such a system can often maintain the local service with building staff at the Associate level.

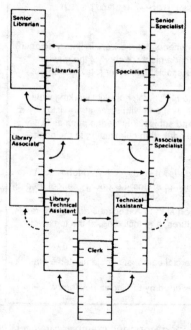

Career Lattice: The movement among staff responsibilities is not necessarily directly up, but often may be lateral to increased responsibilities of equal importance. Each category embodies a number of promotional steps within it, as indicated by the gradation markings on each bar. The top of any category overlaps in responsibility and salary the next higher category.

The *Clerk* classifications do not require formal academic training in library subjects. The assignments in these categories are based upon general clerical and secretarial proficiencies. Familiarity with basic library terminology and routines necessary to adapt clerical skills to the library's needs is best learned on the job.

The *Technical Assistant* categories assume certain kinds of specific "technical" skills; they are not meant simply to accommodate advanced clerks. While clerical skills might well be part of a Technical Assistant's equipment, the emphasis in an assignment should be on the special technical skill. For example, someone who is skilled in handling audiovisual equipment, or at introductory data processing, or in making posters and other displays might well be hired in the Technical

Assistant category for these skills, related to librarianship only to the extent that they are employed in a library. A *Library Technical Assistant* is a person with certain specific library-related skills—in preliminary bibliographic searching for example, or utilization of certain mechanical equipment—the performance of whose duties seldom requires a background in general education.

The *Associate* categories assume a need for an educational background like that represented by a bachelor's degree from a good four-year institution of higher education in the United States. Assignments may be such that library knowledge is less important than general education, and whether the title is *Library Associate* or *Associate Specialist* depends upon the nature of the tasks and responsibilities assigned. Persons holding the B.A. degree, with or without a library science minor or practical experience in libraries, are eligible for employment in this category. Titles within the Associate category that are assigned to individuals will depend upon the relevance of their training and background to their specific assignments.

The Associate category also provides the opportunity for persons of promise and exceptional talent to begin library employment below the level of professional (as defined in this statement) and thus to combine employment in a library with course work at the graduate level. Where this kind of work/study arrangement is made, the combination of work and formal study should provide 1) increasing responsibility within the Associate ranks as the individual moves through the academic program, and 2) eligibility for promotion, upon completion of the master's degree, to positions of professional responsibility and attendant reclassification to the professional category.

The first professional category—*Librarian*, or *Specialist*—assumes responsibilities that are professional in the sense described above. A good liberal education plus graduate-level study in the field of specialization (either in librarianship or in a relevant field) are seen as the minimum preparation for the kinds of assignments implied. The title, however, is given for a position entailing professional responsibilities and not automatically upon achievement of the academic degree.

The *Senior* categories assume relevant professional experience as well as qualifications beyond those required for admission to the first professional ranks. Normally it is assumed that such advanced qualifications shall be held in some specialty, either in a particular aspect of librarianship or some relevant subject field. Subject specializations are as applicable in the *Senior Librarian* category as they are in the *Senior Specialist* category.

Administrative responsibilities entail advanced knowledge and skills comparable to those represented by any other high-level specialty, and appointment to positions in top administration should normally require the qualifications of a *Senior Librarian* with a specialization in administration. This category, however, is not limited to administrators, whose specialty is only one of several specializations of value to the library service. There are many areas of special knowledge within librarianship that are equally important and to which equal recognition in prestige and salary should be given. Highly qualified persons with specialized responsibilities in some aspects of librarianship—archives, bibliography, reference, for example—should be eligible for advanced status and financial rewards without being forced to abandon for administrative responsibilities their areas of major competence.

Source: Library Education and Personnel Utilization (Chicago: ALA, 1976)

Writing a job description

by Jeniece Guy

WHETHER YOU ARE WRITING job descriptions for the first time, or updating existing ones, there are some preliminary steps. You should first decide on the objectives of the program. Will the job descriptions be used for compensation, training, general management, or recruitment? You should then enlist support from both the managers and supervisors and from the library employees. The best way to accomplish this is by clear communication of the purposes of the program and by allowing input from both employees and supervisors.

Who will write the actual job descriptions? While nearly all personnel professionals believe that input from the employees and supervisors is necessary in order to produce good job descriptions, the experts are divided on who should actually do the writing. Some feel that it is best to let either the employee or supervisor do the writing. Proponents of this view feel that if done by the employee or the supervisor, the person who wrote the description will identify with the description and thus be more supportive of the program. Others feel that the employee and the supervisor are not likely to be objective enough about the job description, and in fact may try to exaggerate or "pad" it. Proponents of this view feel that the job description should be written by a trained job analyst, with the employee and the supervisor having input either through questionnaires or structured interviews. Some who feel this way also would allow the employee and the supervisor to review the job description and make suggestions for changes before it is considered final.

While library administrators will want to be aware of the considerations described above, the library's resources will also play a key role in the consideration of whether to use an outside job analyst. In some cases, such assistance may be available from the personnel department of the parent institution (i.e., city or campus personnel); however, unless this is the case, the use of an outside job analyst can be costly.

Approaches

There are as many different approaches to job descriptions as there are employing organizations utilizing this personnel management tool. The publication *How to Write Job Descriptions—the Easy Way* (Stamford, Conn.: Bureau of Law and Business, 1982) suggests that these approaches tend to fall into three categories, the workflow-oriented job description, the goals or standards-oriented job description, and the duties and responsibilities-oriented job description.

The workflow-oriented job description is usually a long narrative description, emphasizing not only the tasks and duties of the position but the larger environment. This type tends to be quite detailed, often describing work samples and including some procedures. The results-oriented job description emphasizes performance standards—what the job is expected to achieve. They are often used in management by objectives programs. The third approach, the responsibilities-oriented job description, is probably the most common approach. This approach emphasizes the tasks and functions of the job.

Which approach is best for your library? The answer is, of course, that it depends on the needs of your particular institution. A workflow-oriented job description may be best if its main use is the training and orientation of new employees. The results-oriented job description works well with performance appraisal programs and is useful in recruitment and training of new employees. The responsibilities-oriented job description provides a good, concise documentary record of the job and can be useful for personnel administration and recordkeeping. It also can provide the new employee with an introduction to the actual duties and responsibilities of the position. Before selecting a particular approach to job descriptions, it is a good idea to analyze the uses the job descriptions will have in your library as well as the goals and objectives of this particular personnel program.

Another issue to consider before embarking on a job description program is whether to write generic or specific job descriptions. Specific job descriptions are written for each job in the library. Generic job descriptions cover all the jobs in a given class (e.g., Librarian I or Library Assistant I).

One can extend the concept even further and consider whether to write an individual position description for each incumbent in a specific job. The specific job description will provide more information about each job and the position description is a further refinement. The advantages to the more generic class approach is that it saves time and it helps to categorize jobs into class groups. Some job evaluation methods such as position classification ranking may require this type of job description.

Elements of a job description

Just as there is no one approach for job descriptions, there is also no definitive format for a job description. Some job evaluation systems which use the job description as a basis for evaluating the job incorporate the factors used in the evaluation into the job description. If, for example, job evaluation factors are "knowledge required to do the job, kind and complexity of the problems to be solved, and the decision making authority," the job descriptions form may ask questions about these factors.

If your library is not using a job evaluation system that requires a particular job description format, then the choice of the elements to include is up to the library. As with the format, the uses of the job description and the preferences of staff should play an important role. A format that libraries might wish to use consists of the following elements: Job Title, Summary Statement, Duties and Responsibilities, and Accountabilities.

Summary Statement: This section should provide a brief (two or three sentences) summary of the position, including the major purpose.

Duties and Responsibilities: This section lists the major tasks (for lower-level jobs) and the responsibilities and assignments (for higher-level jobs).

Job Specifications: This section lists the qualifications required of the position. Although it is appropriate to list educational or experience requirements, writers of job descriptions should also remember to list actual skills and abilities required in the position as well. Examples of skills and abilities are: "Type 50 words per minute," "Ability to make presentations before community groups," "Ability to supervise." Any special requirements such as "Requires valid state driver's license," or "Requires at least 20% travel" should also be listed in the job specifications. Whenever possible, specific terms should be listed. "Job requires lifting heavy packages" is not as meaningful as "must be able to lift 50 lbs."

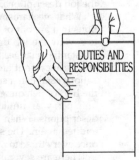

Accountabilities: The accountabilities section describes the end results of the job, and can also include how success or failure is measured on the job. If this is included, it incorporates some elements of the results-oriented job description. Examples are: "Accountable for children's book selection, developing children's programs and staffing the children's room."

A question that is often asked when discussing job descriptions is "What about the phrase: Other duties as assigned?" Some have criticized this phrase as being too vague and wide-open. On the other hand, a job description program must communicate to employees that the job descriptions are not intended to be restrictive and cannot contain everything an employee may be required to do. Emergency circumstances may require an employee to do things other than those specified in the job description. Employees do, however, sometimes object to the phrase "other duties as assigned," so perhaps a more tactful way is to indicate the job description is not intended to cover every circumstance that can be found. A statement such as "job descriptions are meant to be general guides to the duties and responsibilities of the job and are not intended to list every possible task an employee may be called upon to perform" may be more acceptable.

Writing style

In general, job descriptions should be succinct both in the style of writing and in content. A job description is not a procedure manual; therefore, it should not reflect a detailed statement on how each task is carried out. Much more effective is a brief listing of the major duties and responsibilities of the job. Specific recommendations on writing style include:

1. Keep the style terse and direct.
2. Omit all unnecessary words. Often adjectives and articles can be omitted.
3. Begin each sentence with an active verb.
4. Use nontechnical language whenever possible. The job description should be understandable to people from another department or division of the library and to employees on the first day of the job.
5. Avoid vague words and terminology. It may be desirable to establish a working definition of certain terms. The Bureau of Law and Business gives the following suggestion for two troublesome terms. "May" should be used to describe tasks that only some employees in a particular job perform. "Occasionally" should be used to describe tasks performed once in a while but not by any particular employee on a job.

When is the library administrator justified in a complete overhaul of the existing job descriptions? Developing new job descriptions is time-consuming and can be expensive if a consultant is used. How do you determine if the costs are justified? If the library is embarking on a new personnel program in which the job descriptions are an important element, new ones may be in order. Before embarking on the project, however, consider whether they will be used or just filed in a drawer. If managers, supervisors, and employees are unlikely to consult the job descriptions, it may be better to spend staff time on other projects.

What mechanism will you use for updating the job descriptions? Job descriptions that are out of date are also useless. Encourage supervisors and employees to review the job descriptions periodically and revise them if there have been substantial changes. Logical times to review the job descriptions are when there is a vacancy or at annual performance appraisal time. In addition, many organizations establish a schedule for reviewing and updating job descriptions. Often, the library personnel staff will attempt to audit at least one department or work unit per year until each department has undergone an audit of its position descriptions. When the cycle is completed, the first department on the list is audited again. The schedule can be set so that each department will be audited once every three to five years or whatever seems appropriate for the organization.

There are several basic reasons why job descriptions are important in organizations. They help clarify the responsibilities of the position. They also help employees define relationships between positions and departments. Job descriptions are essential for many personnel programs, including recruitment, equal employment opportunity (EEO), training and development, job evaluation, compensation and performance appraisals. A good, accurate job description is the foundation for all of these personnel activities.

Source: Jeniece Guy, "Writing Library Job Descriptions," *Topics in Personnel, no. 7*
(Chicago: ALA Office for Library Personnel Resources, 1985)

Guide to library placement sources

by Margaret Myers

General sources of library jobs

2

Classified ads are regularly found in *American Libraries, Chronicle of Higher Education, College & Research Libraries News, Library Journal,* and *Library Hotline.* State and regional library association newsletters, state library journals, and foreign library periodicals are other sources.

The *New York Times* Sunday "Week in Review" section carries a special section of ads for librarian jobs in addition to the regular classifieds. Local newspapers, particularly the larger city Sunday editions, often carry job vacancy listings in libraries for both professional and support staff.

Specialized library associations and groups

Other organizations assist library job seekers with advertisements or placement services. Only a short listing with address and phone number is found here; further information may be obtained from the organization itself, or from a more complete listing available from ALA's Office for Library Personnel Resources.

Advanced Information Management, 444 Castro St., Suite 320, Mountain View, CA 94041; (415) 965-7799.

Affirmative Action Register, 8356 Olive Blvd., St. Louis, MO 63132.

American Association of Law Libraries, 53 W. Jackson Blvd., Suite 940, Chicago, IL 60604; (312) 939-4764.

American Libraries, "Career LEADS," 50 E. Huron St., Chicago, IL 60611; (312) 280-4211.

ALA/Office for Library Personnel Resources, 50 E. Huron St., Chicago, IL 60611; (312) 280-4277.

American Society for Information Science, 8720 Georgia Ave., #501, Silver Spring, MD 20910-3602; (301) 495-0900.

Art Libraries Society/North America, c/o Executive Director, 3900 E. Timrod St., Tucson, AZ 85711; (602) 881-8479.

Association for Educational Communications and Technology, Placement and Referral Service, 1126 16th St., N.W., Washington, DC 20036; (202) 347-7834.

Association for Information Management, c/o Paul Oyer, Executive Director, 2026C Opitz Blvd., Woodbridge, VA 22191; (703) 490-4246.

Black Caucus Newsletter, c/o George C. Grant, Editor, Rollins College, Campus Box 2654, Winter Park, FL 32789; (407) 646-2676.

C. Berger and Company, 327 E. Gundersen Dr., Carol Stream, IL 60188; (708) 653-1115.

Canadian Association of Special Libraries and Information Services, Job Bank Coordinator, 707 Boulevard St.-Joseph, Apt. 406A, Hull, PQ J8Y 4B5, Canada.

Catholic Library World, 461 W. Lancaster Ave., Haverford, PA 19041; (215) 649-5250.

Chronicle of Higher Education, 1255 23d St., N.W., Suite 700, Washington, DC 20037; (202) 466-1000.

College & Research Libraries News, ALA/Association of College & Research Libraries, 50 E. Huron St., Chicago, IL 60611; (312) 280-2510.

Council for International Exchange of Scholars, 3007 Tilden St., N.W., Suite 5M, Washington, DC 20008-3097; (202) 686-4000.

Council on Library/Media Technicians, c/o Membership Chair, Ruth A. Tolbert, Central Indiana ALSA, 1100 W. 42d St., #305, Indianapolis, IN 46208.

Education Information Service, P.O. Box 662, Newton Lower Falls, MA 02162.

Gossage Regan Associates, Inc., 25 W. 43d St., New York, NY 10036; (212) 997-1127.

Grapevine, c/o *American Libraries,* 50 E. Huron St., Chicago, IL 60611; (312) 280-4211.

HBW Library Recruiters Associates, Inc., 419 S. Carroll, Denton, TX 76201-5928; (817) 566-0417.

Indiana Jobline, Central Indiana Area Library Services Authority, c/o Publications Coordinator, 1100 W. 42d St., Suite 305, Indianapolis, IN 46208; (317) 926-6561.

Information Exchange System for Minority Personnel, P.O. Box 90216, Washington, DC 20090.

Institutional Library Jobline, c/o S. Carlson, R.I. Department of State Library Services, 300 Richmond St., Providence, RI 02903; (401) 277-2726.

International Association of School Librarianship, P.O. Box 1486, Kalamazoo, MI 49005.

International Schools Services, P.O. Box 5910, Princeton, NJ 08543; (609) 452-0990.

Library Associates, 8845 W. Olympic Blvd., Suite 205, Beverly Hills, CA 90211; (213) 289-1067.

Library Journal, R.R. Bowker Co., 245 W. 17th St., New York, NY 10011.

Library Management Systems, 4730 Woodman Ave., Suite 330, Sherman Oaks, CA 91423; (818) 789-3141; and 1201 Dove St., Suite 600, Newport Beach, CA 92660; (714) 251-1020.

Library Mosaics, P.O. Box 5171, Culver City, CA 90231; (213) 715-3525.

Medical Library Association, 6 N. Michigan Ave., Suite 300, Chicago, IL 60602; (312) 419-9094.

National Faculty Exchange, 4656 W. Jefferson, Suite 140, Fort Wayne, IN 46804.

Online, Inc., c/o June Thompson, 11 Tannery Lane, Weston, CT 06883; (203) 227-8466.

Pro Libra Associates, Inc., 6 Inwood Place, Maplewood, NJ 07040; (201) 762-0070; (800) 262-0070.

Rhode Island Library Association, c/o Pamela Stoddard, Government Publications Office, University of Rhode Island Library, Kingston, RI 02881; (401) 792-2606.

Rural Libraries Jobline, Dept. of Library Science, Clarion University of Pennsylvania, Clarion, PA 16214; (814) 226-2383.

School Library Career Awareness Network, School of Information Studies, Syracuse, NY 13244; (315) 443-2740.

Society of American Archivists, 600 S. Federal, Suite 504, Chicago, IL 60605; (312) 922-0140.

Special Libraries Association, 1700 18th St., N.W., Washington, DC 20009; (202) 234-4700.

Theresa M. Burke Employment Agency, 60 E. 42d St., Suite 1333, New York, NY 10165-1333; (212) 986-4050.

U.S. Information Agency, Special Services Branch, 301 4th St., S.W., Washington, DC 20547.

Source: Margaret Myers, *Guide to Library Placement Sources* (Chicago: ALA Office for Library Personnel Resources, 1991)

Library joblines

LIBRARY JOBLINES GIVE recorded telephone messages of job openings. Most tapes are changed once a week, although individual listings may be repeated. The majority are for professional jobs only.

Jobline sponsor	Job-seekers call	
American Association of Law Libraries	(312) 939-7877	
American Library Association	(312) 280-2464	(ALA staff positions)
Arizona Dept. of Library, Archives & Public Records	(602) 275-2325	(Arizona only)
Association of College & Research Libraries	(312) 944-6795	
British Columbia Library Association	(604) 430-6411	(B.C. only)
California Library Association	(916) 443-1222	(in north)
	(818) 797-4602	(in south)
California Media & Library Educators Association	(415) 697-8832	
Colorado State Library	(303) 866-6741	(Colorado only)
Connecticut Library Association Jobline	(203) 645-8090	(Connecticut only)
Delaware Division of Libraries	(800) 282-8696	(in-state)
	(302) 736-4748	(out-of-state)
Drexel University College of Information Studies	(215) 895-1672	
State Library of Florida	(904) 488-5232	(Florida only)
Library Jobline of Illinois	(312) 828-0930	(professional)
	(312) 828-9198	(support)
Indiana Statewide Library Jobline	(317) 926-6561	
Kansas State Library Jobline	(913) 296-3296	
Maryland Library Association	(301) 685-5760	
Metropolitan Washington Council of Governments	(202) 962-3712	
Michigan Library Association	(517) 694-7440	
Midwest Federation of Library Associations	(317) 926-8770	(regional only)
Missouri Library Association Jobline	(314) 442-6590	
Mountain Plains Library Association	(800) 356-7820	(regional only)
	(605) 677-5757	
Nebraska	(402) 471-2045	
New England Library Jobline	(617) 738-3148	(regional only)
New Jersey Library Association	(609) 695-2121	
New York Library Association	(800) 252-6952	(in New York)
	(518) 432-6952	
North Carolina State Library	(919) 733-6410	(North Carolina only)
Oklahoma Jobline	(405) 521-4202	
Oregon Library Association	(503) 585-2232	(regional only)
Pacific Northwest Library Association	(206) 543-2890	(regional only)
Pennsylvania Jobline	(717) 234-4646	
Pratt Institute GLS Job Hotline	(718) 636-3742	
Special Libraries Association	(202) 234-3632	
Special Libraries Association, N.Y. Chapter	(212) 214-4226	
Special Libraries Association, San Andreas-San Francisco Bay Chapter	(408) 378-8854 (415) 391-7441	
Special Libraries Association, S.Calif. Chapter	(818) 795-2145	
Texas Library Association Job Hotline	(512) 328-1518	
Texas State Library Jobline	(512) 463-5470	
University of South Carolina College of Library and Information Science	(803) 777-8443	
Virginia Library Association	(703) 370-7267	(Virginia only)
University of Western Ontario	(519) 661-3543	

Source: ALA Office for Library Personnel Resources, 1991

Academic status

IN 1971 THE ALA Association of College and Research Libraries (ACRL) adopted *Standards for Faculty Status for College and University Librarians* that specify faculty rank, status, and tenure for academic librarians. A 1990 survey of academic libraries of all types by ACRL's Academic Status Committee showed that librarians in 67% of all the institutions surveyed had full faculty status. For those institutions that do not yet have faculty status, ACRL has developed the following guidelines for academic status.—*GME.*

1. Professional responsibilities. Librarians should be assigned general responsibilities within their particular area of competence. They should have maximum latitude in fulfilling these responsibilities. Their performance should be regularly and vigorously reviewed by committees of their peers as well as by supervisory personnel. Review standards should be published and uniformly applied; reviewing bodies should have access to all appropriate documentation.

2. Governance. Librarians should participate in the development of policies and procedures for the library, and in the hiring, review, retention, and continuing appointment processes for their peers. Because the library exists to support

the teaching and research functions of the institution, librarians should participate in the development of the institution's educational policy, have a role in curricular planning, and be a part of the institution's governance structure.

3. Contracts. A librarian's appointment should be by written contract, agreement, or letter of appointment of no less than one year in duration. The appointment document should state the terms and conditions of service and grant security of employment for the contractual period. After a probationary period of no longer than 7 years and through a process that includes peer review, librarians should be granted continuing employment if they have met the appropriate conditions and standards.

4. Compensation. The salary scale and benefits for librarians should be the same as for other academic categories with equivalent education, experience, or responsibility.

5. Promotion and salary increases. Librarians should be promoted through ranks on the basis of their professional proficiency and effectiveness. A peer review system should be an integral part of procedures for promotion and decisions on salary increases. The librarians' promotion ladder should have equivalent titles and ranks as that of the faculty.

6. Leaves and research funds. Librarians should be eligible for research funds within the university and encouraged to apply for such funds from sources outside the university. University and library administrators should provide leaves of absence, sabbaticals, and other means of administrative support to promote the active participation of librarians in research and other professional activities.

7. Academic freedom. Librarians are entitled to the protection of academic freedom as set forth in the 1940 Statement of Principles on Academic Freedom and Tenure of the American Association of University Professors.

8. Dismissal or nonreappointment. Dismissal of librarians during the terms of appointment may be effected by the institution only for just cause and through academic due process. Nonreappointment should involve adequate notice, peer review, and access to a grievance procedure.

9. Grievance. Grievance procedures should be accessible to librarians and should include steps to be completed within specified time limits, effective safeguards against reprisal by the institution, or abuse of the procedures by the grievant, and must be consistent with applicable institutional regulations and contracts.

Source: ALA Association of College & Research Libraries, Academic Status Committee, *Guidelines for Academic Status for College and University Libraries,* 1990

2

The acting position

by Claire-Lise Benaud and David G. Null

WHAT FOLLOWS IS a word of advice from two former acting librarians. If asked to assume an acting position, one should put aside one's initial reaction ("Yeah, sure" or "No way!") and examine the benefits and drawbacks—personal, professional, and institutional. The potential acting librarian should discuss with the library management the expectations for the acting position, including a specified time period. Any acting position should have a set length of time; a six-month period seems reasonable. At the very least, the position should be reviewed at an agreed-upon date.

It should also be possible for either the acting librarian or the library administration to call off the arrangement without bad feelings from either party. Furthermore, the librarian's new status, however short-lived it might be, should be officially announced along with its duration and the stated objectives. Once the expectations are clearly known, one can accept the position with some confidence of success. Even if these conditions are met, however, it is often difficult to "just say no."

Source: Claire-Lise Benaud and David G. Null, "Acting Positions: The Good, the Bad, and the Ugly," *College & Research Libraries News,* January 1991, pp. 30-33

Outreach: Young factory workers take a break to browse through books provided by their public library, ca. 1920

The job interview

THESE GUIDELINES ARE designed for librarians interviewing for an entry-level position, but may also prove useful for more experienced librarians. They provide suggestions for preparation, interviewing, and follow-up. Throughout the interview process it is helpful to remember that an interview is a two-way street: you are interviewing the library as well as being interviewed by them.

Preparing for the interview

Learn as much as you can about the library and its parent organization before the interview. Read the library's annual report, the *American Library Directory*, and state library annual reports on public libraries. Many libraries send interview candidates a packet of information; study this information carefully and make a list of questions as you read.

Learn the names of the key library personnel and find out about their background and publications.

Be prepared for some hard questions, such as "tell me about yourself"; formulate your answers to these questions in advance so that you can easily respond.

Be prepared to discuss current issues of concern to libraries; be conversant with several major issues facing your potential employer.

Be prepared and rested for the interview. Know the time and place for the interview as well as the interviewer's name. Remember to ask about where you should park. Plan to arrive at least fifteen minutes early so that you won't feel rushed.

Look professional. Usually conservative clothes are most appropriate, but wear something that makes you feel comfortable and confident.

Carry a small briefcase for interview materials, including a pad of paper, a pen, and the packet of materials received from the library. Do not carry any more items with you than necessary, as this presents an unprofessional impression.

Be prepared to be assertive and prepare yourself to engage in a few minutes of appropriate small talk.

During the interview

Introduce yourself to the interviewer or search committee and listen carefully when people are introduced to you. Try to repeat the person's name several times to yourself so that you remember it. Do not use a person's first name unless invited to do so.

Use simple, correct etiquette. Don't smoke or chew gum during the interview.

Act naturally, and show enthusiasm, sincerity, and tact during the interview.

Sell yourself. You have made it through the first step in the selection process by obtaining the interview. Now sell your experience, skills, and personality.

Focus on what you can do for the library rather than what the library can do for you.

Try to treat the interview as an expanded conversation. Usually the interviewer is not looking for the "right" answer to questions; they want to hear your opinion.

Listen carefully to each question and answer accordingly. Ask for clarification of the question if you are unclear. Take a few minutes to collect your thoughts about an issue.

If you are faced with an interview conducted by a search committee, concentrate on each individual member's question and respond directly to that person.

If you are interviewed throughout the day by different individuals, remain consistent with your responses.

If you are asked a personal or illegal question such as your age or marital status, pause before you answer. The most appropriate response to these types of questions is, "I don't believe that information affects my ability to perform the job well."

Pace yourself throughout the interview; some interviews may be lengthy and include lunch or dinner.

Do not initiate discussion regarding salary. Salary is usually discussed by employers after they have made a job offer. At many libraries the salary may be predetermined based on your experience and budgetary constraints.

At the conclusion of your interview find out when the library will be making a decision on the position; in some institutions this process can take several weeks.

After the interview

Relax, then write a short thank-you note to the interviewer or chair of the search committee.

If you are offered the job, never accept or reject it immediately. Give yourself time to review your options; make arrangements to call the appropriate administrator with your decision a few days later.

Be prepared at this point to discuss salary. Find out in advance what is an appropriate salary for that position, type of library, and geographic location. The *ALA Survey of Librarian Salaries* may be useful for this information.

Bibliography

ALA Survey of Librarian Salaries. Chicago: ALA Office for Research and Office for Library Personnel Resources, 1988.

Allen, Jeffrey G., *The Complete Q & A Job Interview Book.* New York: Wiley, 1988.

A Discussion and Annotated Bibliography on the Selection Interview for Interviewers and Interviewees. Chicago: ALA Library Administration and Management Association, n.d.

Medley, H. Anthony. *Sweaty Palms: The Neglected Art of Being Interviewed.* Berkeley: Ten Speed Press, 1984.

Krannich, Caryl Rae, and Ronald L. Krannich. *Interview for Success.* Manassas, Va.: Impact Publications, 1988.

Source: Guidelines for Interviewing for the Entry-Level Position
(Chicago: ALA Library Administration and Management Association, 1991)

Job contracts

EVERY INSTITUTION THAT employs librarians is strongly urged to put into writing, in the form of a contract, the specific terms of employment. These guidelines are to aid those institutions that have no formal written agreement in which all basic employment terms are specified.

Every contract should include the following items:

Legal and functional employer. The contract should specify the name of the employing institution (e.g., Cole Public Library) and in which particular unit the librarian will have the initial appointment (e.g., Reference Dept., Essex Branch).

Title. The specific title and/or rank of the position should be stated (e.g., Assistant to the Director).

Salary. A statement concerning salary should include a minimum of the total annual salary for the position. Employers may wish to include frequency of payment or other related items.

Term of employment. Every contract should include the specific period of time covered by the contract (1 year, 2 years, etc.)

Probationary period. Any probationary period (3 months, 6 months, 1 year, etc.) should be stated, together with action and criteria for termination of probationary status and future advancement.

Notice of termination. The contract should include reasons that could result in the termination of employment and the amount of notice which *each* party to the contract must give to terminate the contract (2 weeks, 60 days, 6 months, etc.).

Source: Guidelines for Professional Contracts,
(Chicago: ALA Library Administration and Management Association, 1978)

Librarians: Racial, ethnic, and gender statistics

by Jeniece Guy

A 1985 SURVEY by the American Library Association revealed the following ethnic and racial profile of American librarians:

Number and percentage of public and academic librarians by race and ethnic group		
Native American	42	0.2%
Asian/Pacific Islander	639	3.4
Black	1,149	6.1
Hispanic	337	1.8
White	16,715	88.5
TOTAL	18,882	100.0

Women made up three-quarters of all public and academic librarians in 1985:

Number and percentage of librarians by gender		
Female	14,171	75.1%
Male	4,711	24.9
TOTAL	18,882	100.0

Women constitute a higher percentage of public librarians than academic librarians (80.2% to 65.9%). Conversely, males are found to a greater extent in academic libraries than in public libraries (34.1% to 19.8%).

A higher percentage of public librarians are black (7.2%) than academic librarians (4.1%). A higher percentage of the academic librarians are Asian/Pacific Islander (4.5% as compared to 2.8% in public libraries). There is less difference in the percentage of Hispanic librarians in academic and public libraries (1.5% in academic and 2.0% in public). There is a sizable difference between male and female whites working in academic libraries—58.4% white females to 31.3% white males—while public libraries are made up of 70.1% white females and 17.7% white males.

The distribution of men and women in the various racial and ethnic groups parallels the overall distribution of men and women in the total sample, except for a larger percentage of Hispanic males and a smaller percentage of black males. The minority group with the largest percentage of women is black—84.8%. The minority group with the smallest percentage of females is Hispanic—66.2%.

Female librarians are 87.8% white, 0.2% American Indian/Alaskan Native, 3.5% Asian/Pacific Islander, 6.9% black, and 1.6% Hispanic. Male librarians are 90.6% white, 2.4% Hispanic, 3.7% black, 3.0% Asian/Pacific Islander and 0.3% American Indian/Alaskan Native.

The percentage of females in top management in public libraries is higher than that of males (67.3% to 32.7%). In academic libraries, the distribution of top management reverses the distribution. Males have a slight majority in top management (51.8% to 48.2%).

The racial and ethnic distribution of top management shows a greater percentage of whites than among librarians as a whole (93.5% of upper level managers are white vs. 88.5% overall).

Within each racial and ethnic group, except Hispanic, females constitute a larger percentage than males of public library top managers. In academic libraries, female top managers are found to a greater extent than male top managers in the Hispanic, American Indian/Alaskan Native, and black minority groups. Males constitute 57.1% of the Asian/Pacific Islanders and 53.5% of whites in top management in academic libraries.

The percentage of blacks who are branch and department heads is slightly larger than their representation in the total work force, while the percentage of American Indian/Alaskan Natives is the same. The percentage of Asian/Pacific Islanders and Hispanics is slightly smaller than their representation in the profession at large. These figures would suggest that most minority groups have made progress in moving into middle management.

At the branch and department head level, the distribution of males and females is almost the same as the total work force: 75.7% of branch and department heads are female compared with their 75.1% overall representation, and 24.3% percent are males, compared with a 24.9% overall distribution. This is considerably higher than the percentage of female top managers and raises questions as to what happens to the females who are in middle management positions but do not move to the top management positions. Female branch and department heads are found in a greater percentage in public libraries than in academic libraries—80.5% in public libraries are female compared to 66.4% in academic libraries.

At the entry level, there is a higher percentage of females (81.7%) compared to the overall distribution of females in the profession (75.1%). The percentage is closer for academic libraries (75.3% entry level vs. 75.1% of all librarians).

There is a higher percentage of minorities at the entry level than in the total work force, with the exception of American Indian/Alaskan Natives, which is the same. The percentage of minorities in the entry-level category is 1.9% more than the percentage of minorities in the overall population.

Entry level librarians were 77.8% female in 1980, compared to 75.3% in 1985. With the exception of blacks, all minority groups in the entry-level category remained almost constant, showing less than 1% change. Black entry-level librarians, however, declined from 11.8% in the 1980 study to 6.9% in 1985.

Source: Jeniece Guy, *Academic and Public Librarians: Data by Race, Ethnicity and Sex* (Chicago: ALA Office for Library Personnel Resources, 1986)

Working at home

TELECOMMUTING AND AT-HOME WORK are not common library staffing practices. Sixty libraries responded to a 1989 ALA survey on work-at-home policies. Only 20% of the libraries had employees who sometimes worked at home during regular work hours. Academic libraries were somewhat more likely (24%) to allow at-home work than public libraries (17%).

The professional staff works at home more frequently (18%) than support staff (2%). The majority of libraries that allow work at home do so to accommodate the needs of the employee rather than the needs of the library. One library specifically cited the needs of new parents as a reason for allowing at-home work.

Writing is the most common task done at home (13%). Other tasks include word processing (3%), with 2% for each of the following: cataloging, computer data entry, research, collection development, ordering, reviewing journals, program planning, and scheduling.

Source: Library Personnel News, Winter 1990, p. 2

Age data: librarians in Colorado

A 1988 SURVEY of public librarians in Colorado by the Colorado State Library uncovered some interesting facts.

Predictably, librarians ages 25–34 are most likely to be line librarians rather than directors or branch and department heads. But, somewhat curiously, they are more likely to be directors than branch and department heads. Most likely, this finding is attributable to the fact that Colorado has a substantial number of public libraries which employ only one or a very few people. Although not investigated, it seems a strong possibility that these younger directors are employed by those libraries, rather than libraries with larger staffs.

By far the most surprising finding of this study is the extent to which public librarians tend to be older than the general population ages 25 and over. Public librarians fall in the 35–49 and 50–64 age groups at over twice their proportions of the general population. Thus, public librarians fall in the 25–34 age group at less than one-third of their proportion of the general population.

What factors might explain this "aging" of public librarians in Colorado? The following factors may explain this phenomenon:

- the impact of Colorado's recent economic malaise, trapping more experienced librarians in lower-paying jobs and preventing regular turnover of lower-level jobs to new and less experienced members of the profession.
- limited access to library education in Colorado in recent years and/or poor recruitment by library schools in this region of the country.
- the inability of librarianship to compete with other career options, particularly for women, due to low salaries and inadequate career ladders.
- the possibility that public librarianship may be a "second career" or, considering the predominance of female librarians, a career choice preferred by women returning to the labor force after beginning families.

Source: "Who Are We?" First Facts (Colorado State Library), August 20, 1990

How to avoid sex discrimination

by Sandra K. Peterson, Mary I. Vera-Creixell, and Glen A. Zimmerman

Equal pay

2

OF ALL FEMINIST DEMANDS, equal pay for equal work is the most universally accepted, and of all federal sex discrimination laws, the Equal Pay Act is the easiest to understand and enforce. (Equal pay is also guaranteed by Title VII of the Civil Rights Act of 1964, but with a complaint filed under the Equal Pay Act, the monetary award may be higher.) Under the Equal Pay Act, jobs must be "substantially equal," not absolutely identical. Jobs are considered substantially equal if they have similar job content; if they are performed under similar conditions; and if they involve equal skill, effort, and responsibility. They may have different titles as well as some variation in duties and still qualify for equal pay under the law. If, for example, a female "librarian" does essentially the same job as a male "information specialist," but is paid less, she can file a complaint under the Equal Pay Act. To make pay scales equal, employers must raise the wages of women, not reduce the wages of men. Employers may pay differential wages based on bona fide systems of seniority, merit, or piecework. Under the provisions of the Equal Pay Act, "wages" refers to all aspects of compensation, including overtime, commissions, bonuses, vacation and sick leave, and health benefits.

The Equal Pay Act has been amended several times over the years to expand the number and types of employees covered. The 1972 and 1974 amendments extended coverage to executive, administrative, and professional workers and employees of federal, state, and local governments. All librarians should therefore be covered.

What can I do? The Equal Pay Act is enforced by the Equal Employment Opportunity Commission (EEOC). You can file a complaint with EEOC if your employer pays you less than men are paid for the same work. When you file, EEOC will investigate your complaint without revealing your name and will negotiate with your employer on your behalf. If no settlement or an unacceptable settlement is reached, you can sue your employer directly. However, you must file suit within two years of receipt of the last unequal paycheck. If you win, your employer can be forced to pay back wages for no more than two years prior to the filing date of the suit, unless the violation is found to be "willful," in which case the payment may be extended to three years. In either case, it is essential to act quickly. The decision to accept the EEOC-negotiated settlement or to press the case yourself should be made only after consulting an experienced attorney. You may be awarded more money by the courts, but legal suits can be long and expensive, and they are always a risk.

What resources are available?

Laws Enforced by the U.S. Equal Employment Opportunity Commission. Washington, D.C.: EEOC, 1987. (Order from: EEOC, 2401 E Street, N.W., Washington, DC 20507; free.)

Hiring and promotion

Sex discrimination in hiring and promotion is prohibited both by federal law and by executive order (presidential decree). Title VII of the Civil Rights Act of 1964 prohibits employers from basing hiring or promotion decisions on sex (or on race, color, religion, or national origin). If you are turned down for a job or are passed over for a promotion in favor of a less qualified man, you have the right under Title VII to file a complaint with the Equal Employment Opportunity Commission.

In 1965, Executive Order 11246 established affirmative action regulations that require employers to go a step beyond the simple nondiscrimination demanded by Title VII. Not only must all discrimination cease, but employers must make an extra effort to place women and minority workers into jobs at all levels and in all occupations to a degree that is consistent with their numbers in the work force. The order requires employers to set hiring and promotion goals along with procedures and timetables to meet them. Affirmative action can have the greatest impact for women librarians in hiring for and promotion to high level and prestigious positions. In order to comply with affirmative action regulations, employers must make a "good faith" effort to recruit both women and minorities for all available jobs. Employers are not barred from hiring white males, but they must be able to demonstrate that they attempted to find qualified female and minority candidates and that the chosen candidate is the most qualified. Affirmative action is meant to prevent the discrimination that results from hiring through informal, behind-the-scenes channels in which "who you know" matters more than "what you can do."

Under Executive Order 11246, affirmative action plans are required of employers who receive federal government contracts in excess of $10,000; this regulation is monitored and enforced by the Office of Federal Contract Compliance Programs (OFCCP). OFCCP is also authorized to receive and investigate individual complaints of sex discrimination. You should be aware, however, that affirmative action requirements are subject to review and are currently being studied.

Not all libraries will be covered under Executive Order 11246, but your library may have affirmative action obligations that arise from other federal, state, or municipal sources. The courts also have the authority to require the development of affirmative action plans as part of the settlement in discrimination cases. Employers may, of course, establish such plans voluntarily and are urged to do so by both the American Library Association and the Special Libraries Association.

What can I do?

- If you have lost a job or promotion to a less qualified man, you can file charges with the EEOC. You should file immediately.
- Contact the nearest Office of Federal Contract Compliance Programs to find out if your employer is required to have an affirmative action plan under Executive Order 11246. If so, ask to see the plan. Is it adequate? Suggest ways to strengthen it.
- If your library has no affirmative action plan, ask your employer to designate a committee to draft one. Volunteer to work on it.
- If you belong to a union, make your library's affirmative action plan part of your union contract.
- Monitor the hiring and promotion decisions in your library to insure compliance with affirmative action goals.
- Develop your own networks to keep qualified women and minorities informed of job openings at all levels.
- For those of you who have no recourse but to litigate the matter it should be noted that in *Price Waterhouse v. Hopkins,* 109 S.Ct. 1775, 104 L.Ed. 2d 268 (1989), the Rehnquist Court rendered a decision holding that when a plaintiff in a Title VII case proves that gender played a motivating part in an employment decision, the defendant may avoid liability only by proving that it would have made the same decision despite taking the plaintiff's gender into account. However, the defendant need make proof only by a preponderance of the evidence rather than by clear and convincing evidence. The judgment was reversed and the case was remanded.

What resources are available?

The ALA Office for Library Personnel Resources (OLPR), 50 East Huron Street, Chicago, IL 60611. ALA passed a comprehensive equal employment opportunity resolution in 1974, urging libraries to adopt affirmative action plans—voluntarily if necessary.

OFCCP: Making EEO and Affirmative Action Work. (OFCCP-28) Washington, D.C.: Office of Federal Contract Compliance Programs, U.S. Department of Labor, 1987. (Order from: OFCCP, 200 Constitution Avenue, N.W., Washington, DC 20001; free.)

Pay equity

2

In 1980 women earned approximately sixty cents to every dollar earned by men. This disparity in wages is not explained by violations of the Equal Pay Act, but by the ghettoization of women workers which has a long history in the United States. Most women (and men) work in occupations populated primarily by their own sex. Furthermore, the number of occupations open to women is very small, and these are mostly low-status, poorly paid jobs with little or no promotion potential. As more and more women enter the labor force and compete for the few positions available, the wages for those jobs are driven down even further, and the earnings gap widens, as indeed it has over the past twenty-five years.

To close the earnings gap, proponents of pay equity would take this definition of sex discrimination in wages a step beyond the simple concept of equal pay for equal work to include equal pay for work of comparable value. To achieve real equity in wages, comparisons must be drawn not between individual men and women workers, but between men's occupations and women's occupations. Studies comparing the salaries of librarians with those of men's occupations requiring comparable education and experience show pay disparities as high as 30%.

Unlike equal pay or pregnancy discrimination, there is no specific legislation or clear-cut legal injunction against pay inequity; protection under Title VII of the Civil Rights Act of 1964 will have to be developed case by case. Early pay equity suits were completely unsuccessful because the courts limited Title VII coverage of wage discrimination to the narrow equal pay for equal work standard set by the Equal Pay Act. Subsequent lower court decisions have accepted the argument that Title VII coverage is broader than the Equal Pay Act—including the theory of equal pay for work of comparable value—but have given no guidance as to what evidence would be required in pursuing a comparable worth case. In its only pay equity decision to date (June 1981), the Supreme Court ruled in *Gunther v. County of Washington* that Title VII coverage is not limited to cases based on equal pay for equal work. However, the Court did not in any way endorse the comparable worth theory. This important but narrow legal victory gives women the right to pursue pay equity cases under Title VII, but nothing more. Until a clear precedent is set through case law and until final guidelines are issued by the EEOC, the fate of pay equity suits will remain in doubt.

What can I do? Until the legal issues are clear, librarians can fight for pay equity on the local level by organizing and negotiating directly with their employers and by working with departments or agencies that have responsibility for job classification and salary structure. These guidelines are limited; see the following section, "What Resources Are Available?" for additional assistance.

- Raise the issue of pay equity in your union, faculty organization, employee association, and local or state professional association. Work to pass a resolution in favor of comparable pay.
- Sponsor a program on pay equity at union or association meetings to educate others.
- Find out when the last full-scale review of job and wage classifications at your place of employment was done. Ask for a new one, and press for upgrading of librarians' salaries based on comparable worth arguments.
- Urge your faculty, employee, or professional association or your union to

sponsor a pay equity study of your library, school district, university, or city system.
- Organize your own committee if your union or association will not take the lead. Make every effort to get their support and assistance.
- Contact other women's groups concerned with employment issues—especially the professional associations of other predominantly female occupations.
- File a complaint with the EEOC, but only after exhausting all other avenues and only with the advice of experts.

What resources are available?

National Committee on Pay Equity, 1201 Sixteenth Street, N.W., Suite 420, Washington, DC 20036. A national coalition of organizations and individuals committed to eliminating race and sex discrimination from wage setting systems and achieving pay equity. The committee provides leadership, coordination, information, and strategy direction to pay equity advocates, public officials, and the general public.

Fact Sheet on Pay Equity. Women's Bureau, 1984. (Order from: Women's Bureau, Department P, U.S. Department of Labor, 200 Constitution Avenue, N.W., Washington, DC 20210; free.)

Pay Equity: Issues and Strategies (TIP Kit No. 9). Chicago, Illinois: ALA, Office for Library Personnel Resources, 1987. (Order from: American Library Association, 50 East Huron Street, Chicago, IL 60611; $10.00.)

Pay Equity: An Action Manual for Library Workers. Chicago, Illinois: American Library Association, 1989. (Order from: ALA, 50 East Huron Street, Chicago, IL 60611; $24.95.)

Questions and Answers on Pay Equity: A Fact Sheet. Washington, D.C.: National Committee on Pay Equity, 1988. (Order from: National Committee on Pay Equity, 1201 Sixteenth Street, N.W., Suite 420, Washington, DC 20036; $.50.)

Pregnancy discrimination

In 1978 Congress passed the Pregnancy Discrimination Act as an amendment to Title VII of the Civil Rights Act of 1964. The basic concept of the amendment is that the pregnant employee must be treated like all other employees: if a pregnant worker is able to do her job, she must be treated like any other healthy worker; if a pregnant worker is unable to do her job for health reasons, she must be treated like any other disabled worker. What this means in practice is that an employer may not refuse to hire or promote an employee who is or might become pregnant and may not fire or underpay her because of an actual or possible pregnancy.

Disability leave and medical benefits are prime concerns of the Pregnancy Discrimination Act. It is important to understand that the Act does not require employers to institute leave programs or medical coverage; it does insure that existing benefits are offered equally for pregnancy, childbirth, and related conditions. A pregnant worker may not be forced to take a leave of absence at some arbitrary point in her pregnancy. The librarian who works with the public or with small children, for example, cannot be forced to take leave because her pregnancy has become visible. On the other hand, when she is unable to work because of childbirth, recuperation, or other related conditions, she must he offered leave on the same terms as other, similarly disabled employees. When she returns to work, the woman must be reinstated in her previous position, or one of equal status, seniority, and salary, if other disabled workers are so reinstated. And if medical coverage is offered for other disabilities, it must be made available on the same terms for childbirth.

One exception to the requirements for medical coverage is that employers may exclude abortion from health insurance plans unless the life of the mother would be endangered by delivery. Any complications arising from abortion must be covered, however, and all other provisions (such as job security and leave) apply. Note that employers are not required to exclude abortion from medical coverage, but they may exclude it and still be in compliance with the law.

What can I do? If you are discriminated against because of pregnancy in any of the ways described above, you can file a complaint with the Equal Employment Opportunity Commission.

What resources are available?

Legislative Fact Sheet: Pregnancy Discrimination. New York: Women's Rights Project, American Civil Liberties Union Foundation, 1984. (Order from: ACLU Women's Rights Foundation, 132 West 43 Street, New York, NY 10036; single copies free with self-addressed stamped envelope.)

Pregnancy and Employment: Federal and State Legal Requirements. Washington, D.C.: Women's Bureau, 1988. (Order from: Women's Bureau, Dept. P, U.S. Department of Labor, 200 Constitution Avenue, N.W., Washington, DC 20210; free.)

The Pregnancy Discrimination Act of 1978 and Its Impact on Educational Institutions. Washington, D.C.: Project on the Status and Education of Women, Association of American Colleges, 1979. (Order from: Project, Association of American Colleges, 1818 R Street, N.W., Washington, DC 20009; single copies free.)

Pregnant and Working? Washington, D.C.: Women's Legal Defense Fund. (Order from: Women's Legal Defense Fund, 2000 P Street, N.W., Suite 400, Washington, DC 20036; free.)

Sexual harassment

Sexual harassment can be verbal or physical and ranges from leering looks to repeated requests for dates, to "accidental" or purposeful touching, to actual or attempted assault. Often, sexual harassment carries an implied or articulated threat: "Give in or lose your job (promotion, raise, etc.)." In other instances, while the harassment may not constitute a specific quid pro quo, its relentlessness creates an intolerable and debilitating atmosphere for the victim. Only recently has sexual harassment come out of the closets and into the courts. A series of cases dating back to 1975 has firmly established that sexual harassment constitutes sex discrimination under Title VII of the Civil Rights Act of 1964. A 1981 U.S. Court of Appeals decision provides the broadest protection against sexual harassment to date. In previous cases, unless there was proof that the female employee had been threatened with loss of a promotion, job, or raise as part of the harassment, the courts did not consider it illegal under Title VII. In *Bundy v. Jackson,* the court said that unless the "discriminatory environment" created by sexual harassment is considered illegal, men will continue to harass their women employees "with impunity by carefully stopping short of firing the employee or taking any other tangible actions against her." In effect, this decision makes sexual harassment of any kind illegal. This definition follows the EEOC 1980 guidelines on sexual harassment.

In a recent court action, *Meritor Savings Bank FSB v. Vinson,* 44 U.S. 57 (1986), a 9-0 opinion rendered by Justice Rehnquist, the court identified two types of harassment as sex discrimination under Title VII: making sexual favors a condition of employment and creating a hostile environment.

- Always begin by firmly rejecting any unwanted advance; sexual harassment should never be mutely accepted. Put your demand in writing if your verbal request is ignored.
- Keep a diary of incidents if it becomes clear that the harassment is not going to stop. Note date, time, place, and any witnesses. You will need a body of evidence should you later file a grievance or complaint.
- Do you have a sympathetic superior or personnel officer? He or she may be able to advise you or to put pressure on the harasser from above.

- Do your library's personnel policies or your union contract include a procedure for filing an internal grievance? Use it if you think you can win. If sexual harassment is specifically prohibited by your employer, you will be on much firmer ground.
- Organize. Talk to other women and enlist their support.
- Encourage your library to adopt a policy on prevention of sexual harassment.
- If all your efforts fail and the harassment continues, you can file a complaint with the EEOC. If you have been fired or are denied some other deserved job benefit because you have refused a superior's sexual demands, you should file immediately.

What resources are available?

Legal Remedies for Sexual Harassment. Washington, D.C.: Project on the Status and Education of Women, Association of American Colleges, 1983. (Order from: Project on the Status and Education of Women, Association of American Colleges, 1818 R Street, N.W., Washington, DC 20009; $5.00 prepaid.)

Mary Beth Minick and Sarah B. Watstein, *Sexual Harassment in the Workplace.* Chicago: Committee on the Status of Women in Librarianship, American Library Association, 1989. (Order from: OLPR, American Library Association, 50 East Huron Street, Chicago, IL 60611; free.)

Sexual Harassment Packet. Washington, D.C.: Project on the Status and Education of Women, Association of American Colleges, 1987. (Order from: Project on the Status and Education of Women, Association of American Colleges, 1818 R Street, N.W., Washington, DC 20009; $5.00 prepaid.)

Stopping Sexual Harassment; an AFSCME Guide. Washington, D.C.: American Federation of State, County and Municipal Employees, 1988. (Order from: AFSCME, 1625 L Street, N.W., Washington, DC 20036; free.)

Procedure for filing a Title VII complaint

Title VII of the Civil Rights Act of 1964 covers all establishments with fifteen or more employees and all federal, state, and local governments. Unless you work for a very small company or in a small private library, you can file charges with the EEOC. (If you are not covered by Title VII, see the next section on state and local remedies.) The steps in filing a Title VII complaint with EEOC are the same regardless of the type of discrimination suffered. If you have been sexually harassed, passed over for a job or promotion, denied pregnancy leave or benefits, or have experienced any of the other discriminations described in the preceding sections, the following guidelines apply.

If you live in a state and/or city governed by fair employment practice laws, you may be required to file with the state and/or city-level enforcement agency first, but you retain your right to file with EEOC later if you choose. When you call your regional EEOC office, they will inform you if you need to file with the state and/or city agency first. Once you have filed with a state or local agency, EEOC *cannot* take up your case for 60 days or until the other agency has completed its work, whichever comes first. Where there is no state or city fair employment practices agency recognized by EEOC as a "deferral" agency, you must file within 180 days after the discriminatory act occurred. Where there is a state or city agency, you can file with EEOC at a later date but this cannot exceed 300 days after the discriminatory act took place. The safest course is to file with the EEOC and the state or local agency immediately and simultaneously.

In order to conduct its investigation, EEOC must reveal your name to your employer, but the law specifically prohibits retaliation against employees who file charges. If some punitive action is taken against you, you can immediately file another complaint which will be treated completely independently of your first one. That is, even if you lose on your original charge, it is possible to be reinstated and awarded back pay for the retaliation.

After listening to you and your employer, EEOC will attempt to negotiate a settlement. If the reconciliation efforts fail, or if you are dissatisfied with the results, you may take your case to court. (In rare instances, EEOC itself will go to court on behalf of the complainant.) In order to proceed with a suit, you must get a "right to sue" letter from EEOC and you must file within 90 days of the receipt of the letter. If EEOC holds your complaint for 180 days, you may request a right-to-sue letter whether or not they have acted on your case. The decision to sue should be made carefully and with the advice of an attorney experienced in sex discrimination suits. Court battles can be long and expensive and are difficult to win.

What can I win? If EEOC negotiates successfully in your behalf or if the court decides in your favor, what do you get? First, the employer will be required to end the discriminatory behavior; this is called "injunctive relief." "Make whole" relief may be part of the settlement as well. In order to "make you whole," your employer must put you in the position or situation you would have been in had the discrimination never taken place. While settlements will vary depending on the case, you may be reinstated, promoted, given a raise, provided with maternity leave and/or benefits, and/or awarded appropriate back pay depending on the requirements of the case. Back pay will not be awarded for more than two years prior to the date of filing with EEOC, however, so take action promptly. If you were part of a class action suit, your employer may be required to develop a comprehensive affirmative action plan as part of the settlement. Finally, if you have gone to court and won, your employer may be required to pay your attorney's fees and other legal costs.

Remedies through the workplace, state law, and professional associations

Seeking redress for sex discrimination under federal law has always been a slow process. The EEOC was substantially reorganized in 1978 in response to this problem, and complaints began to move more quickly. With the new conservative mood in the White House and in Congress, however, any progress made in the efficiency of processing complaints may be eroded. Therefore, it will become more and more important to seek alternative avenues of relief. Title VII complaints should still be filed with the EEOC, but that should not necessarily be your only or your primary effort. You should use every procedure available to securing your job rights.

State and local antidiscrimination legislation. Most states and some cities have fair employment practice laws (FEP) laws, which are similar to federal antidiscrimination statutes. These laws prohibit discrimination based on sex, race, color, religion, national origin, and handicap. State FEP laws are sometimes preferable to federal laws because they offer broader coverage. If your library is too small to be covered by Title VII, your state FEP laws may be your only protection; many cover employers who have as few as two or three workers. In some instances, state laws offer better or more specific protections than federal laws. California and New York laws, for example, provide protection superior to federal law in the area of pregnancy discrimination. Some state and local laws also prohibit additional forms of discrimination, including those based on lifestyle, marital status, and sexual or affectional preference. Finally, state or local enforcement commissions may act faster. Filing on the state or local level does not prevent you from going to EEOC later but may make it unnecessary. Nevertheless, simultaneous filing is recommended. Contact your state department of labor or employment rights commission to find out what protection your state offers and what filing procedures are required.

Redress at the workplace. It is usually wise to begin by demanding your job rights from your employer directly. If your rights have been specifically guaranteed through contracts, affirmative action plans, or personnel policies, you can build a much stronger case. Since employers are not generally inclined to extend certain protections to their workers voluntarily, you may have an organizing job ahead of you before you can make demands successfully. It you have no organization that represents employees, form one. Whether it is a union or an employee association, you will need a body with the force of numbers to negotiate with your employer. Attempt to incorporate all the protections guaranteed by law into your union contract or library personnel policies. Taking your employer to court should be a last resort; the more avenues available to you before you reach that point, the better your chances for successful redress. If you can secure your rights by filing a grievance through your union or employee association, you will be spared time, aggravation, and money. But do not neglect other procedures—file simultaneously a workplace grievance, a complaint with your state fair employment practice commission, and a complaint with EEOC. Accept the settlement that comes soonest or provides the greatest relief.

ALA Standing Committee on Review, Inquiry, and Mediation. The librarian who is unprotected by grievance procedures at the workplace may contact the American Library Association's Standing Committee on Review, Inquiry, and Mediation for assistance. The Committee can mediate or make inquiries into situations involving tenure, status, fair employment practices (including discrimination and sexual harassment), due process, ethical practices, and intellectual freedom as set forth in ALA policies. The librarian-complainant contacts the Committee and completes the "Request for Action" form. If Committee members decide that the complaint comes within the purview of ALA policy, they can attempt to mediate between employer and employee. If mediation is unsuccessful, a full-scale inquiry may be mounted. Where circumstances warrant, ALA may impose sanctions as a result of an inquiry. Many state library associations offer similar services, so contact them for information as well.

Source: Sandra K. Peterson, Mary I. Vera-Creixell, and Glen A. Zimmerman,
Equality in Librarianship: A Guide to Sex Discrimination Laws
(Chicago: ALA Committee on the Status of Women in Librarianship, 1990)

What should be included in a personnel manual?

WRITTEN PERSONNEL POLICIES are an expression of an organization's desire to provide fair and equitable treatment of all employees. A personnel policies manual is a comprehensive collection of the organization's policies, which should be up-to-date and compatible with one another. The manual provides a reference guide for the personnel function, as well as all levels of staff. The manual helps communicate expectations, procedures, and systems throughout the organization, helps with training, and reduces the risk of lawsuits and unnecessary conflict between management and employees. Policies development is an ongoing process because of changing government regulations and legislation, changes in organizational structure or union composition, and other factors.

The content and organization of the manual may vary depending on the size and type of organization. *The Personnel Manual: An Outline for Libraries* (Chicago: ALA, 1977) presents recommended topics to include in a manual, as follows:

- Policies that affect employment and working conditions (e.g., affirmative action, state and federal fair employment practices laws, union contract)
- Organization of the library (organization chart, classification of positions, responsibilities of management and supervisors)

- Employment practices (recruitment, requirements for employment, selection and appointment)
- Personnel actions (placement within classification, probation, performance evaluations, tenure, promotions, resolution of grievances, disciplinary actions, personnel records, separation from service, death of an employee)
- Salary administration (procedures for determining salaries, factors related to take-home pay, schedule of paydays, premium pay)
- Employee benefits (health, insurance, retirement)
- Work conditions (work hours, special scheduling, overtime, disciplinary action)
- Leaves of absence (sick leave, paternity/maternity leave, vacation, holidays, personal leave, funeral leave, leave without pay, attendance at conferences, meetings, sabbatical leave).

The *Personnel Policies Workbook* by Richard H. Wexler (Paramus, N.J.: Prentice Hall, 1987) suggests the following topics and organization:

- Letter from the president or director of the organization
- Human resources philosophy
  Use and revision of the manual
  Philosophy and role of the personnel department
  EEO/Affirmative Action
  Drug-free workplace
  Sexual harassment
  Handicapped employees
  Authorized alien status and citizenship
  Employer/employee relations
  Labor relations
  Nature of supervision
  Staff development and training
- Employment policies
  Hiring procedures
  Special employment conditions
  Promotions/internal transfers
  Layoff and recall
  Termination
  Retirement
  Death of an employee
  Outside employment
  Personnel records
- Salary administration
  Work hours
  Overtime
  Exempt/nonexempt employees
  Performance appraisals
  Salary changes
  Severance pay
- Employee benefits
  Vacations, holidays, personal days, flexible time from work, leaves of absence, sabbatical leave, family leave, jury duty, funeral leave
  Group insurance, workers' compensation
  Employee assistance programs
  Pension plan, tuition assistance
  Service awards
  Recreational facilities, wellness programs, discounts
  Child care, adoption assistance, eldercare benefits
- Personal conduct
  Attendance and punctuality, personal appearance

The Work Ethic.

Personal use of organization facilities
Security, safety
Ethics, employee theft, solicitation
Smoking, substance abuse
- Problem resolution
Corrective action/involuntary termination, problem resolution
- Miscellaneous
Reimbursement of expenses, travel and entertainment
Vehicle policy, parking
Video display terminals
AIDS

Source: Library Personnel News, Summer 1990, pp. 47–48

Why they chose to be librarians

IN 1988 THE ALA Office for Library Personnel Resources and the Louisiana State University School of Library and Information Science conducted a survey of library school students. Among the questions asked were reasons they chose the profession and reasons they would give to others to become librarians. Several themes were recurrent. The service aspect of librarianship, the opportunity to work with both people and information, the social role of librarianship, and the rewards offered are a few of the themes. Quotes below from library school students illustrate these and other themes.

What library school students say

Many chose librarianship because it provides a service.
"Provides a truly needed service to others."
"I wanted to work in a helping profession."

The combination of working with both people and information appealed to some.
"Working with and giving information to people is fun."
"I wanted a job where I could work with both people and information but neither exclusively."
"I like working with and helping people. I enjoy tracking down information with patrons and seeing their excitement."

The importance of information in our society intrigued others.
"I felt, and still do, that information management was the key to the future."
"I wanted to master the ability to find any kind of information anywhere and help [users] recognize the wealth of resources that our field represents and to gain access more easily to those resources."
"I believe that to a great extent, knowledge, i.e., information, is power, and I would like to help organize and disseminate that knowledge."
"I chose this profession because I believe it is a vital one in a changing society. Information production, diffusion and dissemination are of paramount importance in the times in which we live."

The intrinsic rewards of the profession appealed to others.
"The independence, flexibility, and rapid development in this field should be appealing."
"It is a very creative field; intellectually challenging."
"There is a feeling of professionalism, or of a mission in what we're doing."
"Satisfaction of helping others and having a rewarding career—not just a job."
"I want to be part of the excitement of librarianship."

"I wanted a career where I could be intellectually challenged and more in charge."

The variety and multiple options accounted for the career choice.

"From this job I can teach, manage, do my own research, or do research for others. That is what I want for my work—options."

"Librarianship offers many job options, work settings, type of work, geographical mobility."

"We need specialists in business, marketing, computers, public relations, communication, political science—all sorts of things..."

Librarians had provided positive role models for some students.

"As a child I found librarians to be helpful. They also seemed to know everything and I wanted to be like them."

"Greatly admired librarians I had encountered."

For some librarianship was a second career or career change.

"I wanted an alternative career to teaching—Research was a major enjoyment. I would have the opportunity to continue working with materials that helped research."

"It is similar to my former profession (social work) in that it is a helping profession, but does not involve crisis situations to the same degree."

What experienced librarians say

Librarianship is a profession in which the reality bears out the expectations according to experienced librarians who were asked why they liked their jobs.

Provide a service.

"I feel that I am of use to the community where I live and I improve the quality of life of the people in it."

"I enjoy working with the public and helping people do research."

Working with people and information.

"I like helping faculty and students discover how to discover new knowledge."

"It's interesting! I like working with people. I like doing reference work, searching for that one fact."

Role of information in society.

"I truly do believe that it enables me to make a worthwhile contribution to society. In the Information Age, it is terribly important that access to information be promoted, defended, and increased for the good of both individuals and society."

"The importance of free access to information in a democracy."

Intrinsic rewards.

"It provides virtually unlimited challenge."

"I feel what I do is worthwhile and valuable."

Variety and multiple options.

"One can switch careers without switching fields. I have been a children's librarian, library educator, library consultant, and academic librarian. All had appeal at the time and I can still see exciting things that could be done in any one of these specialties."

"I wear many hats: manager, acquisitions, reference, cataloging."

Source: ALA Office for Library Personnel Resources, *Each One Reach One: Recruiting for the Profession* (1989)

Librarians in the year 2000

TO LOOK AHEAD to the year 2000, ALA library leaders were queried on their thoughts about the coming decade and possible changes in librarian skills and jobs. Those asked were Richard M. Dougherty, University of Michigan School of Information and Library Studies; Nancy John, University of Illinois at Chicago; Norman Kelinson, Trustee, Bettendorf (Iowa) Public Library; Sarah Long, North Suburban Library System (Ill.); William A. Moffett, Huntington Library; and Dallas Y. Shaffer, Monterey County (Calif.) Free Libraries.

What will the librarian's job look like in the year 2000?
- It will be as varied as it is today but have a stronger emphasis on the manipulation of technology to provide access to increasingly complex information. It is important to remember there will still be one- and two-person libraries, and the demands on them will be awesome (Shaffer).
- Librarians will be more active as information intermediaries, working with users who seek information from the rich, yet complex array of electronic sources (Dougherty).
- Persons seeking information will become more dependent than ever on the librarian's expertise in accessing information (Kelinson).
- The current trend toward CD-ROM and optical media will continue, and audiovisual media will be important. Control over this more complex information environment will require new bibliographic and information processing skills (John).
- Librarians at all levels will be more concerned with planning and management. There will be more women in top library jobs (Long).

How will the prevalence of personal computers change librarians' roles?
- Libraries will become nodes in a national system of electronic networks. While many users will access information directly from home and office, there will still be many who will seek the assistance of librarians serving as gateways to and interpreters of specialized databases (Dougherty).
- The information-broker role will become more important and the need to communicate effectively and personably via computers will become more important. Librarians will need to find access many more hours a day (Shaffer).
- As our patrons are enabled to access both traditional and new sources of information through electronic means, librarians will have to anticipate and respond accordingly. In academic libraries, especially, their teaching role will be enhanced (Moffett).
- Librarians' contact with their patrons will lessen (Kelinson).
- Librarians will need to develop improved methods of guiding the user to information. While computers are becoming more commonplace, a goodly number of users will either be unable to afford access to this equipment or will be unwilling to use it; these users will need special care so we do not contribute unknowingly to an information elite (John).
- Librarians will be involved in building databases of local information. There will be a much greater demand for interpretation of data. There will be great pressure to provide such value-added services—for a fee (Long).

What major competencies will be important for librarians in the 1990s?
- Skills to understand and articulate librarian roles in the organizations in which they function. Articulation will come from understanding differences between the library profession and various information industries

2

and the nature of the value librarians add to lifelong learning and the process of discovering knowledge (John).

- Synthesizing and communicating skills after the computer has provided the information. Management skills. Fund-raising skills (Long).
- Skills and sensitivity to work effectively with diverse cultural and ethnic groups. Ability to market the library's services and build constituent groups. Skills to learn and use ever-changing technologies (Shaffer).
- Facility with the information technologies and ability to work in such environments. Greater stress on skills and techniques associated with management as librarians assume responsibility for managing information-oriented organizations (Dougherty).
- The same skills that are important now; especially communication and interpersonal skills (Moffett).
- Technological skills to compete and ability to access information in all formats (Kelinson).

What education and staff development programs will be most effective in preparing librarians for the coming decade?
- Computer training, CD-ROM use, networking (Kelinson).
- Awareness of changes in our society and means to change our organizations constantly (Shaffer).
- Programs to teach information technologies, refresh information retrieval skills, design retrieval systems. Preservation of information, both preventive and diagnostic. Programs that lead to furthering the role of the librarian in the educational process (John).
- Personnel skills. Political and fund-raising programs. Dealing with multi-cultural groups. Information handling (Long).
- Electronic techniques such as computer conferencing and satellite TV will play central roles as vehicles for delivering educational programs to groups widely dispersed geographically (Dougherty).
- Undergraduate education to provide a rich generalist base. Staff development to help secure a genuine expertise in specialized, applied knowledge (Moffett).

Source: Library Personnel News, Spring 1990, pp. 18–19

Librarian salaries in 1990

by Mary Jo Lynch

BETWEEN JANUARY 1989 and January 1990, the average salary for librarians increased 4.3%—slightly below the increase in comparable occupations reported by the U.S. Bureau of Labor Statistics in the April 1990 *Monthly Labor Review.* Civilian workers in private industry, state and local government received an average 4.4% increase in 1989. White collar workers received an average increase of 4.9% in 1989.

The percentage increases for 1990 librarian salaries shown in the table on the next page were less than in 1989, when they varied from 9 to 15%, which were unusual. Increases from 1989 to 1990 may be more realistic, especially since the average—4.3%—is only slightly below the 4.6% cost of living increase for the period.

The 1990 survey showed that the mean of salaries paid is highest in large public libraries for director and lowest in medium-sized public libraries. For deputy, associate, or assistant director and department head or branch head, the mean is highest in university libraries. For deputy, associate, or assistant director, the mean is lowest in four-year colleges. Medium-sized public libraries showed the lowest mean salaries for department/branch heads. For the

Rank order of position titles by mean salary, 1989–1990

Title	1990 Salary	1989 Salary	%
Director	$44,495	$43,623	2.0
Deputy/Associate/Assistant Director	41,445	40,054	3.5
Department Head/Branch Head	34,248	32,780	4.5
Collection Development Librarian/ Subject Bibliographer	33,357	32,853	1.5
Cataloger and/or Classifier	30,268	28,577	5.9
Reference/Information Librarian	29,999	28,227	6.2
Children's/Young Adult Librarian	27,669	26,008	6.4

other three common positions, the mean is highest in 2-year colleges, lowest in medium-sized public libraries for catalogers, and lowest in four-year colleges for the other two positions. For the position found only in public libraries—children's and/or young adult services librarian—the mean is higher in large public libraries. In most cases, salaries are highest in the West and Southwest, followed by the North Atlantic region. For most positions, the lowest salaries are paid in the Southeast.

Source: Mary Jo Lynch, Margaret Myers, and Jeniece Guy, *ALA Survey of Librarian Salaries, 1990* (Chicago: ALA, 1990)

Median salaries for academic library positions,1990–1991

Dean, library and information sciences	$68,000
Director, library services	46,480
Director, learning resources center	38,500
Director, educational/media services	35,900
Public services librarian	34,080
Technical services librarian	32,700
Acquisitions librarian	31,922
Reference librarian	30,428
Circulation librarian	28,000

Source: College and University Personnel Association

Mean salaries of special librarians by region, 1989–1990

Census Division	1990 Salary	1989 Salary	%
Middle Atlantic	$40,694	$38,891	4.6
Pacific	39,519	37,071	6.6
New England	38,775	40,226	–3.7
South Atlantic	37,833	35,881	5.4
East North Central	36,072	33,908	6.3
West South Central	34,382	35,920	–4.4
West North Central	33,628	32,040	4.9
Mountain	32,558	31,088	4.7
East South Central	32,084	28,405	12.9
Total U.S.	37,761	36,212	4.2

Source: Tobi A. Brimsek, "SLA Biennial Salary Survey," *Special Libraries,* Fall 1990

ALA presidents

Justin Winsor	1876–1885	Milton James Ferguson	1938–1939
William Frederick Poole	1885–1887	Ralph Munn	1939–1940
Charles Ammi Cutter	1887–1889	Essae Martha Culver	1940–1941
Frederick Morgan Crunden	1889–1890	Charles Harvey Brown	1941–1942
Melvil Dewey	1890–July 1891	Keyes D. Metcalf	1942–1943
Samuel Swett Green	July–Nov. 1891	Althea H. Warren	1943–1944
William Isaac Fletcher*	1891–1892	Carl Vitz	1944–1945
Melvil Dewey	1892–1893	Ralph A. Ulveling	1945–1946
Josephus Nelson Larned	1893–1894	Mary U. Rothrock	1946–1947
Henry Munson Utley	1894–1895	Paul North Rice	1947–1948
John Cotton Dana	1895–1896	Errett Weir McDiarmid	1948–1949
William Howard Brett	1896–1897	Milton E. Lord	1949–1950
Justin Winsor	July–Oct. 1897	Clarence R. Graham	1950–1951
Herbert Putnam	Jan.–Aug. 1898	Loleta Dawson Fyan	1951–1952
William Coolidge Lane	1898–1899	Robert Bingham Downs	1952–1953
Reuben Gold Thwaites	1899–1900	Flora Belle Ludington	1953–1954
Henry James Carr	1900–1901	L. Quincy Mumford	1954–1955
John Shaw Billings	1901–1902	John S. Richards	1955–1956
James Kendall Hosmer	1902–1903	Ralph R. Shaw	1956–1957
Herbert Putnam	1903–1904	Lucile M. Morsch	1957–1958
Ernest Cushing Richardson	1904–1905	Emerson Greenaway	1958–1959
Frank Pierce Hill	1905–1906	Benjamin E. Powell	1959–1960
Clement Walker Andrews	1906–1907	Frances Lander Spain	1960–1961
Arthur Elmore Bostwick	1907–1908	Florrinell F. Morton	1961–1962
Charles Henry Gould	1908–1909	James E. Bryan	1962–1963
Nathaniel Hodges	1909–1910	Frederick H. Wagman	1963–1964
James Ingersoll Wyer	1910–1911	Edwin Castagna	1964–1965
Theresa West Elmendorf	1911–1912	Robert Vosper	1965–1966
Henry Eduard Legler	1912–1913	Mary V. Gaver	1966–1967
Edwin Hatfield Anderson	1913–1914	Foster E. Mohrhardt	1967–1968
Hiller Crowell Wellman	1914–1915	Roger McDonough	1968–1969
Mary Wright Plummer	1915–1916	William S. Dix	1969–1970
Walter Lewis Brown	1916–1917	Lillian M. Bradshaw	1970–1971
Thomas Lynch Montgomery	1917–1918	Keith Doms	1971–1972
William Warner Bishop	1918–1919	Katherine Laich	1972–1973
Chalmers Hadley	1919–1920	Jean E. Lowrie	1973–1974
Alice S. Tyler	1920–1921	Edward G. Holley	1974–1975
Azariah Smith Root	1921–1922	Allie Beth Martin	1975–April 1976
George Burwell Utley	1922–1923	Clara Stanton Jones	July 1976–1977
Judson Toll Jennings	1923–1924	Eric Moon	1977–1978
Herman H. B. Meyer	1924–1925	Russell Shank	1978–1979
Charles F. D. Belden	1925–1926	Thomas J. Galvin	1979–1980
George H. Locke	1926–1927	Peggy A. Sullivan	1980–1981
Carl B. Roden	1927–1928	Elizabeth W. (Betty) Stone	1981–1982
Linda A. Eastman	1928–1929	Carol A. Nemeyer	1982–1983
Andrew Keogh	1929–1930	Brooke E. Sheldon	1983–1984
Adam Strohm	1930–1931	E. J. Josey	1984–1985
Josephine Adams Rathbone	1931–1932	Beverly P. Lynch	1985–1986
Harry Miller Lydenberg	1932–1933	Regina Minudri	1986–1987
Gratia A. Countryman	1933–1934	Margaret E. Chisholm	1987–1988
Charles H. Compton	1934–1935	F. William Summers	1988–1989
Louis Round Wilson	1935–1936	Patricia Wilson Berger	1989–1990
Malcolm Glenn Wyer	1936–1937	Richard M. Dougherty	1990–1991
Harrison Warwick Craver	1937–1938	Patricia G. Schuman	1991–1992

ALA treasurers

Melvil Dewey	1876–1877	Carl B. Roden	1910–1920
Charles Evans	1877–1878	Edward D. Tweedell	1920–1927
Melvil Dewey	1878–1879	Matthew S. Dudgeon	1927–1941
Frederick Jackson	1879–1880	Rudolph H. Gjelness	1941–1947
Melvil Dewey	1880–1881	Harold F. Brigham	1947–1949
Frederick Jackson	1881–1882	R. Russell Munn	1949–1952
James Lyman Whitney	1882–1886	Raymond C. Lindquist	1952–1956
Henry James Carr	1886–1893	Richard B. Sealock	1956–1960
George Watson Cole	1893–1895	Arthur Yabroff	1960–1964
Edwin Hatfield Anderson	1895–1896	Ralph Blasingame	1964–1968
George Watson Cole	1896	Robert B. McClarren	1968–1972
Charles Knowles Bolton	1896–1897	Frank B. Sessa	1972–1976
Gardner Maynard Jones	1897–1906	William Chait	1976–1980
George Franklin Bowerman	1906–1907	Herbert Biblo	1980–1984
Anderson Hoyt Hopkins	1907–1908	Patricia Glass Schuman	1984–1988
Purd B. Wright	1908–1910	Carla J. Stoffle	1988–

ALA executive secretaries

Melvil Dewey	1879–1890	(Edward C. Hovey, executive officer)	
William E. Parker and			1905–1907
Mary Salome Cutler	1890–July 1891	Chalmers Hadley	1909–1911
Frank Pierce Hill	1891–1895	George Burwell Utley	1911–1920
Henry Livingston Elmendorf	1895–1896	Carl H. Milam	1920–1948
Rutherford Platt Hayes	1896–1897	Harold F. Brigham (interim)	
Melvil Dewey	1897–1898		July–Aug. 1948
Henry James Carr	1898–1900	John MacKenzie Cory	1948–1951
Frederick Winthrop Faxon	1900–1902	David H. Clift	1951–1958
James Ingersoll Wyer	1902–1909		

ALA executive directors

David H. Clift	1958–1972	Thomas J. Galvin	1985–1989
Robert Wedgeworth	1972–1985	Linda F. Crismond	1989–

Justin Winsor

Melvil Dewey

Mary W. Plummer

Linda A. Eastman

101 library leaders

IN 1988 A GROUP of 600 librarians was asked to name individuals perceived to be leaders in the field of librarianship in the United States. Here is the list of 101 librarians most frequently nominated by that group.

Millicent Abell
Lester Asheim
William Asp
Pauline Atherton
Hugh Atkinson
Henriette Avram
Augusta Baker
Tom Ballard
Patricia Battin
Toni Carbo Bearman
Sanford Berman
John Berry
Nancy Bolt
Daniel Boorstin
Richard Boss
Lillian Bradshaw
Rowland Brown
Michael Buckland
Ching-chih Chen
Morris Cohen
Eileen Cooke
Linda Crismond
Carlos Cuadra
Arthur Curley
Evelyn Daniel
Dennis Day
Richard DeGennaro
Keith Doms
Richard Dougherty
Ken Dowlin
Robert Downs
Ron Dubberly
Leigh Estabrook
Evan Farber
Hardy Franklin
Thomas Galvin
Kaye Gapen
Eugene Garfield
Fred Glazer
Herbert Goldhor
Michael Gorman
Vartan Gregorian
Warren Haas
Robert Hayes
Kathleen Heim
Irene Hoadley
Edward Holley
Norman Horrocks
E. J. Josey
David Kaser
William Katz

Fred Kilgour
Judith Krug
F. W. Lancaster
Mary Lankford
Ronald Leach
David Loertscher
Helen Lyman
Beverly Lynch
Charles McClure
Rob McGee
Will Manley
Lowell Martin
Marilyn Gell Mason
James Matarazzo
Regina Minudri
Patricia Molholt
Eric Moon
Stefan Moses
Paul Mosher
Patrick O'Brien
Major Owens
Arthur Plotnik
Lawrence C. Powell
Jane Robbins-Carter
Charles Robinson
Eleanor Jo Rodger
Robert Rohlf
Donald Sager
Patricia Schuman
Marvin Scilken
Russell Shank
Brooke Sheldon
Elliott Shelkrot
Joseph Shubert
Elizabeth Stone
Gary Strong
Robert Stueart
Peggy Sullivan
William Summers
Roger Summit
Nettie Taylor
Robert Taylor
Lucille Thomas
Alphonse Trezza
Duane Webster
Robert Wedgeworth
William Welsh
Herbert White
Martha Williams
Douglas Zweizig

2

Hugh Atkinson

Henriette Avram

Fred Glazer

E. J. Josey

Source: Alice Gertzog

Most prolific library authors

THE FOLLOWING ACADEMIC librarians were found to be the most prolific authors of journal articles in 1983–1987.

William Studwell	Bruce Morton	Ruth B. McBride
Tony Stankus	Marcia Tuttle	Lawrence J. McCrank
Bruce Connolly	Henry N. Mendelsohn	Evelyn S. Meyer
Michael Gorman	Marcia Pankake	John Rutledge
Norman Stevens	Steven D. Zink	Karen A. Schmidt
Bill Bailey	Hugh Atkinson	Robert G. Sewell
Robert H. Burger	Joe Crotts	Frederick E. Smith
Larry Cruse	Donna M. Goehner	John Swan
Richard DeGennaro	Joe A. Hewitt	Paula D. Watson
Richard M. Dougherty	Emerson Hilker	James W. Williams
Susan K. Martin	David Isaacson	

Source: John M. Budd & Charles A. Seavey, "Characteristics of Journal Authorship," *College & Research Libraries,* September 1990, pp. 463–470

The library hall of fame

WILLIAM E. STUDWELL and Byron P. Anderson have suggested the following 15 inductees into a proposed American Library Hall of Fame.

Hugh Atkinson (1933–1986). One of the outstanding academic librarians of his era. A visionary and innovator, he promoted networking.

Henriette D. Avram (1919–   ). Developer of the MARC system at the Library of Congress during the 1960s and 1970s.

Verner W. Clapp (1901–1972). Multifaceted leader of such projects as *Index Medicus, Choice,* and Cataloging in Publication.

Benjamin A. Custer (1912–   ). Long-time editor of the *Dewey Decimal Classification.* Custer did more for DDC than anyone except Melvil Dewey.

Charles Ammi Cutter (1837–1903). Early library innovator. Pioneer in subject cataloging and the development of cataloging rules, and the father of LC classification.

John Cotton Dana (1856–1929). Eminent public librarian and innovator. Organized the Special Libraries Association.

Melvil Dewey (1851–1931). Great library pioneer who devised the Dewey Decimal Classification, established the first library school, and founded the American Library Association.

Robert B. Downs (1903–1991). Library administrator and educator with a vast publication record. Noted for his interest in library resources.

Charles Evans (1850–1935). Noted compiler of *American Bibliography,* the primary source for early American imprints.

Charles Coffin Jewett (1816–1868). Early leader in American librarianship who promoted standardization of cataloging rules and centralized cataloging. His shared cataloging idea was adopted by the Library of Congress 50 years after being proposed.

Margaret Mann (1873–1960). Creative instructor who revolutionized cataloging instruction. Author of the noted treatise, *Introduction to Cataloging and the Classification of Books.*

William Frederick Poole (1821–1894). Exceptional library administrator and creator of the indexing project that culminated in the famous *Poole's Index to Periodical Literature.*

Minnie E. Sears (1873–1933). Developer of the Sears subject heading list, a leading alternative to LC subject headings.

William J. Welsh (1919–   ). Distinguished Library of Congress administrator during the 1960s, 1970s, and 1980s. A key player during this active period of growth.

H. W. Wilson (1868–1954). Bookseller and publisher associated with the standard indexes and bibliographies issued by the company that bears his name.

Source: William E. Studwell and Byron P. Anderson, "Why Not a Library Hall of Fame?" *American Libraries,* March 1990, pp. 202–203

Directors

Finding a new library director

by Andrew Geddes and James A. Hess

THE EMPLOYMENT OF a competent director is the most important single responsibility of a library board. In approaching the task of selection, trustees should make use of their accumulated experience, do their homework, and chart a course which will assure them of the best possible chance for success. The following guidelines should be helpful to a board in its efforts to secure the right administrator.

Preliminary assessment

Before thinking about a new director, a board should take a hard look at the current status of the library. This might well begin with an exit interview with the present director. What does this session reveal that needs immediate attention? Are the personnel policies adequate? Will the transition be smooth? Are changes indicated? If so, now is the time to make the necessary decisions.

At this time of self-examination, the board may be wise to address itself to such fundamental questions as: What is the role of this library in the community today? Have library needs changed in the community? Has our library kept pace? What do we want in our next director? Will this person be willing and able to implement the board's goals and objectives for the library? What does the community want?

Homework before you advertise

After this preliminary assessment, the board should take several steps which will enable it to meet candidates for the directorship with confidence.

1. **Develop or obtain an existing up-to-date description of the community.** Along with geographic and demographic information, this should include facts about the economy, government, education, recreation, and cultural activity. It should note any important trends or changes underway.

2. **Prepare or obtain an up-to-date description of the public library program in the community and its relationship to other library programs in the area.** For the public library, this should include a history of the institution, its board composition, its articles of incorporation and bylaws, together with facts on staffing, collection, programs, and budget. For the schools, information should be provided on the number and location of each, the kinds of library service offered, methods of staffing, collections, and how they are housed. For the colleges and universities and for special libraries, the same information will be needed as for schools. A summary of existing cooperation among all the types of libraries listed should be added.

3. **Write or update a detailed job description for the position.** Include data on specific duties, salary, fringe benefits, hours, civil service requirements, period of probation, etc. (You may need professional guidance on this one.)

4. **Review civil service regulations which might affect your library.** Answer the following questions:
   a. Is the director's position included?
   b. If so, what are the civil service requirements?
   c. Has a board member met with civil service personnel to learn necessary procedure?
   d. What forms must be completed?
   e. Must one follow civil service regulations absolutely?
   f. How does the board get a civil service list to canvass?
   g. What can we do if there is no civil service list?
   h. What are the board's prerogatives?

5. **Create or adopt a standard reference form.** This will be sent with a return-addressed, stamped envelope to former employers and others whose names are given as references on applications. If at all possible visit or at least telephone and talk to one or more references in person.

6. **Agree upon a fairly standard series of questions to be posed to each candidate.** This will insure that each candidate is asked to respond to the same questions and therefore the same basis for evaluation will exist; and that the interview proceeds smoothly without nonproductive lulls. (Some of the topics which might be dealt with in interviews are: What are the candidate's goals? How interested is the person in your position and on what terms? What questions does the candidate have for the board? What are this individual's strengths? What should be the relationship between the library director and the board?)

7. **Make up a standardized evaluation sheet.** Then, during interviews, the interviewing committee can be evaluating the same characteristics—within a flexible interview format, of course.

8. **Consider whether outside assistance should be secured to assist in interview sessions.** This might be a library consultant, a member of the system  staff if your library is part of a system, one or more other librarians from the community, librarians within your own library, or a member of a lay group such as Friends of the Library. Initial screening may be done by one or more of these groups, but final screening by the board or a subcommittee of it is essential to the process. Consider the participation of a delegated staff member in the search process up to but not including the voting decision.

9. **Decide whether the director will be offered a contract, a schedule, or an open-ended agreement.**

10. **Make provision for costs of interviews and moving.** What expenses will the board reimburse for those coming for interviews? What costs of relocation will the board pay? Inform all candidates invited for interviews of the board's policy on these expenses.

11. **Take a good look at your present staff.** Now that you know what you want and are ready for interviews, one of them might be eligible. However, don't select such a person—just because he or she is on the scene. You are looking for the best person for the job, who may or may not be one of your own. If the assistant librarian or another staff member is expecting to be offered the job, explore possible reactions if the local person is not hired.

12. **Give consideration to eligible persons from nearby libraries.** Nevertheless, keep in mind your continuing relations with people from those libraries who might resent what they would describe as raiding. If your screening produces a candidate on the local scene, proceed with the interview process.

Source: Andrew Geddes and James A. Hess, *Securing a New Library Director*
(Chicago: ALA American Library Trustee Association, 1979)

Evaluating the library director: Public libraries

by Nancy M. Bolt

Methods of evaluation

There are three methods of evaluation that surface in a study of the literature on evaluating a library director (brief though that may be).

1. Evaluation based on personality and behavior traits.
2. Evaluation based on the job description.
3. Evaluation based on negotiated objectives.

Evaluation based on personality and behavior

This method has more disadvantages than advantages. It is normally used on a very brief evaluation form with the opportunity for the evaluators to rank the evaluatee on a scale. The following personality and behavior traits were taken from actual evaluation forms:

Has cooperative attitude
Organizes work well
Takes initiative
Demonstrates creativity
Meets deadlines
Shows tact
Communicates well
Shows enthusiasm for work
Sets a professional example
Motivates staff
Is receptive to new ideas and suggestions
Makes good decisions

While all of the above traits do contribute to the successful management of the library, they are not helpful to the board or the director as the only basis for evaluation. The traits are presented out of any context and without definition. Each board member and the library director could and, in fact, probably would, have a different interpretation of the meaning of each of the traits and what behavior would elicit a positive evaluation For example, while a cooperative attitude is desirable in most instances, a board would not want the director to be cooperative with requests to remove controversial material from library shelves or with suggestions from a funding body that the budget be cut 30 percent. What are "good" decisions and how can the board know which ones should be made?

Some behavior or personality traits can be part of the evaluation of a library director, but when they are used, they need to be carefully defined so that both the board and the director have a clear understanding of what is expected.

A word about short evaluation forms should be added here. Many sources recommend that the evaluation form be short and easy to complete. A library, however, is a complex entity to manage and the successful operation of a library is not something that can be easily summed up on a short form. Trustees, in accepting appointment to the board, pledge themselves to allocate the time necessary to do the job. Evaluation of the library director requires thought in the development of the criteria, time to discuss the criteria with the director, effort to review progress, and energy to summarize this year's evaluation and plan for the next year. The more time and care spent in evaluation, the more benefit will accrue to both the board and the director.

Evaluation based on the job description

A job description is essential to the process of hiring a library director and is certainly an excellent place to start in developing criteria for evaluation. The job description should clearly indicate the major areas of responsibility of the library director and can be used to develop more specific criteria for evaluation.

Ken Ragland, in his trustee workshop for the Washington State Library, proposed detailed evaluation criteria that could be used with the Prince George's County library director job description. Many of these criteria pertain to what most boards require of their library director. If used, however, they should be adapted to the local library situation. Some of the factors listed will not be relevant to your situation. Other factors that you feel to be important may be missing.

Evaluation criteria

1. Preparing and managing the budget. To what degree:
   a. Is all the necessary staff work completed in a timely manner prior to presentation to the board?
   b. Does the budget cover all necessary expenses?
   c. Are funds allocated or reserved for unanticipated contingencies?
   d. Are funds effectively allocated?
   e. Are mid-course corrections minimized?

2. Managing the staff. To what degree:
   a. Are positive management/staff relations maintained?
   b. Are fair and equitable policies proposed for board adoption and then fairly administered?
   c. Are grievances filed? If so, what is their nature?

3. Professional state-of-the-art awareness. To what degree?
   a. Are innovative methods of service delivery, technical processes, etc., studied thoroughly and implemented only after they fit the needs of the institution and are proven to be cost effective?
   b. Does the director maintain an adequate knowledge of the current state of the art?

c. Is the staff encouraged and aided in maintaining an awareness of technological advances in the profession?
d. Conversely, does the director adopt change only for change's sake?

4. Collection development.
   a. How adequate is the library's program of determining user needs/wants and translating these into acquisitions and services?
   b. Has a plan been established to enable the library to respond to materials budget cuts?

5. Implementation of board decisions.
   a. Are board decisions implemented on a timely basis?
   b. Once a decision has been made does the director fully and enthusiastically back it (to what extent?) or are they sometimes presented to the staff in an apologetic or deprecatory manner?

6. Use of the library.
   a. How effectively are the services of the library communicated to the public?
   b. Is a proper and realistic balance established between promotion of services and budget constraints?
   c. Are circulation trends and in-house use adequately analyzed and are there appropriate reactions to the results of such analyses?

7. Development of staff.
   a. Are potential managers identified, encouraged to develop, and assisted in their development?
   b. Are internal candidates for promotion competitive with outside candidates for management positions?
   c. Does the director adequately justify the need for staff development funds, actively campaign for such funds, and adequately account for the use of such funds?

8. Utilization of staff.
   a. Is there a clear separation of professional and clerical tasks for staff guidance?
   b. Have peak service hours been identified and staff deployed accordingly?
   c. Are functions analyzed periodically with the objectives of combining, eliminating, and/or creating new positions?

9. Community involvement.
   a. How active is the director in the community?
   b. Is the director "visible" to large segments of the population?
   c. Is the director available for speaking engagements in the community?

10. Activity in professional organizations.
    a. Is the library represented and does the director actively participate in the American Library Association, state, and regional library associations?
    b. Does the director hold office in professional organizations?
    c. Do the staff and the director have articles published in professional journals?

11. Policy recommendations to board.
    a. Is adequate staff work completed prior to presentation to the board?
    b. Are reasonable alternatives recommended?
    c. Are policy recommendations generally made in advance rather than reactive?
    d. Are policy recommendations necessary and appropriate to the efficient operation of the library?

12. Maintenance and construction of physical plants.
    a. Are the buildings and grounds adequately maintained?
    b. Does the director have an ongoing program that provides adequate information on the need for new and/or remodeled facilities?
    c. Are new and/or remodeled facilities functionally appropriate and aesthetically pleasing?
    d. Are new and/or remodeled facilities constructed within budget allocations?

13. Established priorities.
    a. Do the director's recommended priorities implement the library's mission as defined by the board?
    b. Do these priorities appropriately reflect community needs?
    c. Are priorities established in advance or reactively?

14. Staff selection.
    a. Is staff selection accomplished at appropriate supervisory levels?
    b. Is adequate emphasis placed on Equal Opportunity Employer/Affirmative Action and is the director's commitment to these principles communicated to the staff?
    c. Is the selection process designed to insure the selection of the most qualified person for the job?

15. Short- and long-range planning.
    a. To what degree do the director's short- and long-range plans reflect board priorities?
    b. Are the short- and long-range plans updated on a continuous basis to reflect changing circumstances?
    c. Do the director's accomplishments reflect and relate to the short- and long-range plans?
    d. Are the short- and long-range plans flexible enough to allow for unforeseen circumstances?
    e. Does the director provide adequate information to the board on the implementation, revision, etc., of short- and long-range planning?

16. Union/Management relations.
    a. How positive are union/management relations?
    b. Assuming that some dissension is unavoidable, does it exist to a degree that it has an adverse effect on the institution's mission or charter?
    c. Is the disruption attributable to contract negotiations kept at a reasonable level?

17. Friends of the Library.
    a. Has the director actively promoted the formation and/or maintenance of a Friends group?
    b. Do the director and staff provide adequate support to the Friends organization?
    c. Has the director delineated and/or helped define the role of the Friends group?
    d. Has the Friends group had adequate explanation of its role in relationship to the role of the board?

18. Miscellaneous rating factors.
    a. Are difficult decisions made and implemented or are they deferred or ignored?
    b. Does the director display adequate initiative or rather merely react to problems as they arise?
    c. Is the director objective in making the necessary decisions or do personal prejudices intrude too often?

d. Is the director consistent in decisions that affect the staff and/or public?

e. Is the director open with the board or does a "hidden agenda" intrude too often in the relationship?

f. Does the director set an example for the staff through professional conduct, high principles, and business-like approach?

Evaluation based on negotiated objectives

2

Using this method, the board and the library director agree together on specific objectives to be accomplished during a specific period of time and how both will know that those objectives have been met. This setting of measurable objectives is part of a planning process. Using this method of evaluation will involve the board and the library director in planning library objectives and the responsibilities of the library director in implementing those plans.

Seymour Nordenberg, in his address at the 1983 Public Library Association meeting in Baltimore, put it this way: "A successful evaluation is better based on evaluating preset objectives than people. The evaluations are clearly spelled out in terms of objectives, time frames, and responsibilities. Successful evaluations are those that have a direct line back to a well-defined job description and objective setting. In other words, if the planning, the thought, and the work are each seriously approached through the job description and negotiated objectives, the work of evaluation will be simplified and will become much more palatable and sometimes, a pleasant duty. Directors must be aware of what the evaluation will include. There should be no surprises."

Nordenberg and Ragland both suggest steps that would be used in an evaluation by negotiated objectives.

1. The board and the director jointly determine the mission of the library and the goals necessary to fulfill that mission and develop a long-range plan to achieve these goals.

2. The board and director identify specific areas that need attention during the coming year—the annual program.

3. The director prepares a budget designed to implement the annual program.

4. The director prepares a list of measurable objectives including a time line for implementation and the resources needed to achieve the objective. The objectives should be based on the annual program and budget.

5. The board reviews the objectives and negotiates with the director the final objectives and measurable targets.

6. The objectives are published.

7. The director is responsible for the implementation of the objectives including the delegation of tasks to library staff.

8. The director reports back to the board at interim periods on progress toward meeting objectives. This could be monthly or as appropriate.

9. The board and director jointly revise the objectives as necessary.

10. At the end of the year, the director prepares a report on the status of each objective to be reviewed by the library board.

11. The evaluation of the library director is conducted based on the agreed-upon objectives.

12. The process is repeated.

Source: Nancy M. Bolt, *Evaluating the Library Director*
(Chicago: ALA American Library Trustee Association, 1983)

Evaluating the library director: Academic libraries

by Mike Simons and Anne Amaral

THE FOLLOWING CRITERIA are used by the staff at the University of Nevada Library, Reno, to evaluate the library director.

Leadership in library operations

The director:

1. Sees that library work is delegated to appropriate department heads.
2. Supports supervisors in the administration of their departments.
3. Requires that supervisors be fair and equitable in the administration of their departments. (Give examples of support or lack of support.)
4. Regularly checks with supervisors and staff to see that library work is progressing smoothly.
5. Provides recognition for outstanding individual accomplishments.
6. Provides constructive criticism when and where appropriate.
7. Acknowledges exemplary performance of library units.
8. Respects Library Faculty Bylaws and encourages collegiality in the operations of the library.
9. Performs duties in a timely manner.
10. Acts quickly and decisively in resolving problems.
11. Sees that funds are fairly distributed and wisely spent.
12. Works to acquire additional funding through gifts, grants, etc.
13. Makes good decisions in the selection of new library faculty.
14. Successfully mediates conflicts and disputes within the library.
15. Sees that library disciplinary matters are handled fairly.
16. Handles merit raises fairly and equitably.
17. Handles promotion and tenure fairly and equitably.
18. Promotes staff development.
19. Commands respect and confidence of the library staff.

Communication

The director:

1. Maintains an environment in which faculty and staff are encouraged to make suggestions for improving library operations.
2. Is available and cooperative when faculty have questions or problems to discuss.
3. Promotes candor and openness which allows free exchange of ideas (philosophy, professional issues, etc.) within the library.
4. Clearly delineates areas of responsibility to department heads.
5. Ensures that existing channels of communication are used to transmit information from the administrative levels to library staff.

6. Ensures that existing channels of communication are used to transmit information from library staff to appropriate administrative levels.

7. Ensures that channels exist for sharing information between various library units.

Leadership in identifying and achieving goals

The director:

1. Is successful in maintaining a staff and budget proportionate in size to the library's mission.

2. Produces and implements coherent plans which make the most efficient use of the library's personnel and material resources.

3. Effectively represents the needs, concerns, and interests of the University Libraries to the UNR administration and other organizations that influence the library's development.

4. Has effectively involved library faculty committees in the strategic planning process.

5. Has successfully directed the planning and development of the University Libraries to meet the challenges of growing enrollment and an increased university emphasis on research.

Professional development

The director:

1. Contributes to the growth of knowledge through publication, professional papers, or other accepted vehicles.

2. Demonstrates awareness and understanding of current developments in librarianship and library management.

3. Is appropriately active in university and community service.

4. Is appropriately active in statewide library activities.

Source: Mike Simons and Anne Amaral, "Evaluating the Library Director," *College & Research Libraries News,* May 1989, pp. 360–63

John Cotton Dana's rules

1. Read.
2. Read.
3. Read some more.
4. Read anything.
5. Read about everything.
6. Read enjoyable things.
7. Read things you yourself enjoy.
8. Read, and talk about it.
9. Read very carefully, some things.
10. Read on the run, most things.
11. Don't think about reading, but
12. Just read.

Trustees

Who are library trustees?

by Mary Arney

THE COMPOSITION OF public library boards across the nation and Canada was surveyed during the 1987 Annual Conference of the American Library Association. At this conference questionnaire forms were distributed to attendees at nine of the programs, meetings, and functions of the American Library Trustee Association. Of the distributed forms, 169 forms were returned, representing 144 different public library systems.

The results

The questionnaire yielded the following information:

Number of trustees on boards. Board sizes varied from three members to 21 members, with the majority having seven members (41%) or five members (25%).

Most respondents commenting on the size of the board felt that boards should have at least seven or nine members in order to have more input and ideas and to ensure a true representation of the area.

Membership. Demographic characteristics of board members in relation to board size were as follows:

Board Size	Percent Female	Percent Black	Percent Other Minority
5	58%	7%	4%
7	57%	4%	5%
9	58%	9%	5%
Average of all boards	57%	6%	4%

Although women and men on the average are represented equitably, some individual boards have many more of one sex. Those surveyed indicated that fewer minority members than the national average population are represented on library boards.

Length of trustee's term of office. The number of years for a term of office ranged from one year to life as follows:

Length of Term	Percent of Boards	Length of Term	Percent of Boards
1 year	2%	5 years	25%
2 years	7%	6 years	14%
3 years	22%	7+ years	2%
4 years	27%		

Most respondent boards have three- to five-year terms.

Although the questionnaire did not ask about possible multiple terms, respondents noted this possibility and recommended limiting the number of consecutive terms, urging for periodic board membership turnover.

Other concerns were: the definition of a "full term" when filling vacancies and attendance policies (such as if a member misses four consecutive meetings and automatic resignation is constituted). Some boards have had trouble getting a quorum for their regular meetings.

Trustee selection. Most of the trustees were appointed (73.2%), while 26.8% of trustees were elected. Arguments for election as the method of selection included:

- political party appointments are not the best way to always get good and active board members
- election works better in terms of building a board that is more representative of and to the community at large
- an elected board can take an independent stand where appropriate, yet work with other elected officers, as peers, when appropriate.

Those who favored appointing boards cited the lack of voter interest as well as the lack of well-qualified candidate interest in conducting a campaign.

Several respondents commented on the kinds of people they felt should be on a library board. Library board members should be interested, capable, not the "Lady Bountiful" type, politically and organizationally savvy, and current library patrons. They should be a group that represents a cross-section of the community with varying income levels (not an elitist board), is able to disagree civilly, is a mixture of Republicans and Democrats, and is appointed by multiple entities.

Some stated current library boards should actively recruit well-qualified, capable candidates, and should be "ruthless and aggressive in recruiting trustees with the competencies your board requires." Boards try to secure capable and interested board members by seeking applications, using an assessment system, or making recommendations (formal and informal) to the appointing body. One method was described as follows:

"Notice of vacancy is advertised, interested persons are invited to apply. The application form asks for age, address, occupation, previous community involvement, interest in and activities for the library. Staff are given copies of the applications and invited to recommend. Choices are made with age and geographic distribution in mind, for as broad representation as possible. We have found some excellent board members by this method, people we didn't know or wouldn't have thought of."

Area of selection. Whether appointed or elected, 56% of all boards were selected from the service area at large; and 16% were selected from a combination of at-large and geographic areas. Elected boards more frequently represented the entire service area than did appointed boards.

Feelings about ethnic representation. Roughly two-thirds of the respondents indicated they felt that the composition of their boards reflected the ethnic composition of their service population.

Some comments regarding ethnic equity were explanations for low minority membership. Most respondents who felt their boards did not reflect the service population indicated in writing their regret of a lopsided, male/female representation or the lack of minority representation.

Conclusions. The survey suggests the following:

1. Blacks and other minorities are not represented on library boards in proportion to their percentage in the national population. Women and men on the whole are represented equitably.

2. Elected board members tend to be selected from the service area at large.

Source: Mary Arney, *Library Boards: Who Are They and How Do They Get There?* (Chicago: ALA American Library Trustee Association, 1988)

What library trustees do

by Jeanne Davies

1. Attend Board meetings.
2. Employ a competent and qualified librarian at an adequate salary. Prepare and sign a contract for the librarian (director).
3. Provide an adequate and qualified staff to work with the librarian.
4. Assist in the preparation of an annual budget.
5. Establish conditions of employment and provide for the staff's welfare.
6. Establish policies (including personnel) to govern the operation and programs of the library and assign their execution to the librarian and the staff, in compliance with federal, state, and local laws.
7. Approve bylaws for the board.
8. Provide for building and space needs and maintain library property.
9. Determine short-range and long-range goals and objectives of the library and reexamine them regularly. Study the programs and needs of the library in relation to the community by keeping informed on community changes, trends, needs, and interests.
10. Adopt clear-cut policies and procedures in the area of collection management and censorship.
11. Establish rules and regulations governing the use of the library, upon the recommendation of the librarian.
12. Provide for accurate record keeping for the library and the library board.
13. Help secure adequate funds from appropriating agencies and from new sources, if necessary, to carry out the library's programs and to make the objectives for updated and improved services a reality.
14. Establish, support, and participate in a vital public relations program for the library.
15. Report regularly to the governing officials and to the general public and establish an annual reporting procedure.

16. Acquire knowledge about state and national library laws. Actively support state and national library legislation which would improve and extend library service.
17. Acquire an awareness of public library standards and library trends.
18. Attend and participate in regional, state, and national trustee meetings and workshops for a fuller understanding and utilization of trustee talent, knowledge, and experience.
19. Affiliate with professional organizations and provide funds through the budgeting process for involvement by trustees and staff.

Source: Jeanne Davies, *Major Duties, Functions and Responsibilities of Public Library Trustees* (Chicago: ALA American Library Trustee Association, 1988)

Friends

Friends of the library

by Sandy Dolnick

FRIENDS ARE A NECESSARY part of life for institutions as well as for people. Support and recognition are important elements of any friendship. Friends of the Library groups can and should supply these elements to all libraries while they represent the library to the community. The potential effectiveness of a group of citizens with no vested interest cannot be overestimated. The library, which is often taken for granted, can multiply its support by the community if it is willing to establish and perpetuate a Friends organization.

Inflation and changes in public attitudes toward government spending have brought intense pressures to bear upon library budgets. In many cases, Friends of the Library groups, by raising funds from private sources or by providing volunteer labor, have made it possible for the library to continue services that would otherwise have been terminated.

Friends
of
Libraries
U.S.A.

The initial reasons for having a support group differ among libraries and communities but generally include:

Money. Friends groups have traditionally raised funds for projects or acquisitions in excess of the general library budget.

Services. There is no limit to the services that a dedicated volunteer group can provide, short of substituting members for specialized staff.

Public relations. Each Friend is a walking public relations vehicle for the library.

Advocacy. An informed, active citizen lobby can be the strongest weapon the library has.

Community involvement. An organized Friends group is living proof of the library's value to the community.

The rationale for a Friends group may change over time. A group that begins as a purely social organization, for example, may shift its orientation as the library's needs grow.

Friends of Libraries, therefore, are many different things to many different communities. They all may be defined as groups of citizens that are associated on behalf of libraries.

The interest in Friends groups grows steadily. Every year the American Library Association receives more queries about them. Friends of Libraries U.S.A., a national organization, was formed to further the growth of new groups and to exchange information among existing ones.

The ten commandments

Certain principles, if adhered to and reviewed annually, will develop a nurturing atmosphere and pleasant environment for Friends and library staff. These ten commandments were learned through the combined experiences of hundreds of groups.

1. The library director must want a Friends group. If this is not the case, do not proceed any further. There is no use in continuing.
2. The library staff must be willing to work with Friends—at least that part of the staff—that must come into contact with the Friends.
3. All parties involved must realize that a time commitment is involved, and that a successful group is no accident. The activity level of the group will determine the amount of time involved; if there is only one book sale a year to worry about, for example, there will be minimal time involved *once the group is organized.*
4. The library must agree which of its resources (e.g., space, staff time, paper, and telephone) will be used by the Friends.
5. A committed core group must exist. This core group may be only two or three people.
6. The authority to which the library director reports must be aware of the Friends group.
7. Communication must be open to all groups involved in the use of the library; the Friends should not have an exclusionist policy.
8. All those involved in the Friends must realize that the Friends group does not make library policy, which is the function of the trustees.
9. The library must decide, in discussion with the Friends, the roles it wishes the group to play: advocates, social, fundraising, volunteers or a combination. These roles change as needs change, so they should be reviewed annually.
10. All those involved must understand that trustees and Friends have separate functions, and liaisons should be developed between the two groups. Money raised by the Friends should be disbursed by them as they see fit according to information on the library's needs.

Groups being organized should be able to check off each item listed above; established groups will find this list a good yearly evaluation. By renewing its goals each year, a group can retain the vitality of a new organization and reap the benefits of experience.

Services to the community

Literacy program newsletter
Christmas open house
Produce and host television series or radio show
Book sales
Exhibit booth at county fair
Volunteers for the blind
High school essay contest
Parade float
Outreach program at retirement center
Film program for elderly in public housing
Oral history
Teachers' tea
Newcomers' day
Survey on library use
Shut-ins brought to the library for National Library Week lunch to meet staff
     and the mayor
Librarian sent to ALA conference
Help for "mother's morning out"

Storyphone
Rare book appraisals
Community calendar

Services to the library

Legislative Day
Clerical help
Coffee and refreshments at programs
Christmas decorations
Tours of library
Clipping and setting up magazine file
Displays
Grounds and shrubs maintenance
Painting shelving
Mailings assistance
Piano tuning
Memorial gift procedure maintenance
Article clipping for vertical file
Free paperback book exchange
Typing
Book mending
Library switchboard operation
Newspaper indexing
Microfilm indexing
Telephoning
Bags to carry art reproductions

Purchases for the library

Videotapes, audiotapes
Film programs
Special audiovisual equipment
Matching funds for Reading Is Fundamental grant
Books

Funds to increase endowment

Special furnishings
Rare books
Printing
Hospital book carts
Repair of rare books
Elevator for handicapped
Fiscal agent for humanities grant
Building repair
Security system
Rental book collection
Copy machine
Large-print books
Landscaping
Shades
Computer hardware and software
Magazine subscriptions
Compact disks
Laser printer

Source: Sandy Dolnick, *Friends of Libraries*
Sourcebook (Chicago: ALA, 1990)

Rew staff

Orienting new employees

by Edward Garten and Joan Giesecke

MANY SUPERVISORS BREATHE a sigh of relief once they have made a hiring decision; however, even greater time and work should be devoted to *orienting* the new employee. New employees often lack a sense of belonging, which results in high turnover in the early weeks of employment. The new employee needs to be recognized as a person and feel that the job is important. The first day on the job can influence the way the new employee feels about the library throughout his or her employment. In addition, an organized plan for orientation that ensures that employees know where to go for help can increase morale and productivity.

Before the employee arrives

Find out whether there are standard orientation procedures within the library. If there are not, consider asking that procedures be developed. Volunteer to work on a draft of the procedures, form a committee to address the issue, or discuss it with your personnel librarian. Also, see what your parent institution provides as orientation information. Many universities, government agencies, and corporations provide in-depth orientation sessions or packets.

Preparation for the employee's first day at work is essential. Ask other employees about their orientation experience and needs. Listen for gaps in their orientation and determine how those gaps affected their performance.

Second, sit down with the job description for the new employee and analyze the job duties. Decide how the employee should be oriented so that she or he has an understanding of how his or her duties fit into the library's mission and relate to the duties of others in the library.

Third, decide who in the library is best suited to orient the new employee to specific types of information. As the supervisor, you should not do the entire orientation yourself. It is important that the new employee get to know his or her coworkers and their areas of expertise. However, you should retain responsibility for the orientation because you have a vested interest in being sure that the employee is well-oriented. In addition, the employee is motivated to learn from you since you will be evaluating his or her performance. Because you want to transmit the codes of conduct important to you, you should not delegate discussions of conduct or behavior to others.

Fourth, try to schedule a variety of orientation activities, since people have different methods of learning. Some alternatives to one-on-one discussions include written exercises, workbooks, audiovisual "tours," computer-assisted instruction, small group sessions, and written orientation, policy, and procedure materials.

Fifth, determine the time frame for the orientation period. A part-time shelving job may require a shorter orientation period than a professional reference or cataloging job. When deciding on the length of the orientation period, be sure to allow time for independent exploration by the employee, time for formation of on-the-job friendships, and time for beginning actual job duties. If new employees do not begin to do some work shortly after

their first day, they can feel as though they are not making a contribution to the library. They may feel as though others are judging them and wondering why they are not beginning to do "real work." Remember that new employees are anxious and eager to begin work. Capitalize on this enthusiasm!

After completing the orientation plan, you should arrange for the new employee's desk or office space so that it is ready before she or he arrives.

Another essential step in making the new employee feel welcome is to prepare other staff members prior to the new employee's first day. This can help prevent unintentional (or intentional) "hazing." Hazing can occur when current employees feel threatened by the eagerness and enthusiasm of a new employee. Occasionally a new employee unwittingly encourages hazing by referring to how things were done in other libraries where she or he worked. To current employees, these references can imply a negative judgment about their library. To minimize or preclude this, be sure to define the role of the new employee, being clear about the authority and autonomy the new employee will have.

Another step is to assign a "buddy" or "guide" to the new employee—someone from a different department who is friendly and knowledgeable about the library. A staff member from a different department can provide a link for the new employee in knowing how things are done outside his or her department. The guide might undergo training so that she or he knows what is expected in orienting the new employee.

The first day

The first day is crucial and can have a significant impact on reducing the new employee's anxiety and encouraging a positive attitude. Perhaps the most important aspect of the first day's orientation is attending to (and being aware of) the new employee's social needs.

First, you should tell the new employee how you and others in the library prefer to be addressed. (Be sure the new employee knows how to pronounce difficult names correctly. There is nothing more embarrassing for a new employee than mispronouncing a name!)

Second, she or he should be introduced to coworkers and others with whom he or she will have frequent contact. Schedule time so that the new employee can get to know coworkers. Stress teamwork in your discussions.

Third, the employee should have an introduction to the layout of the building so she or he feels comfortable about being there. Safety and security information should be covered, particularly in a library prone to theft or personal threats.

Fourth, give the employee a general outline of the job so that she or he is fully aware of and comfortable with his or her duties. Provide an orientation packet and discuss particularly important information in the packet.

Orientation duties on the first day might be divided in the following manner. The supervisor welcomes the new employee as the new employee arrives and briefly discusses general issues, such as the employee's hours, breaks, conduct, library philosophy, and procedures for reporting absences. The supervisor then introduces the new employee to coworkers. A coworker within the department gives the new employee a tour of the department. Depending on the size of the library, the coworker (or an assigned "buddy" or "guide" from another area of the library) gives the new employee a tour of the entire library. Be sure that lunch arrangements with yourself, the new employee's guide, or a group of coworkers are made in advance. The library's administrator or personnel librarian should discuss benefits,

Orientation checklist

Before the employee arrives

The library director (or designee) should send a letter specifying conditions of employment, such as salary, hours of work, job title.
Equip employee's desk or work area with basic supplies:

stapler	ruler	staff directory
cellophane tape	pens, pencils	phone books
stationery	paper	keys
scissors	note pads	procedure manuals

Prepare an orientation packet, including:

    history and philosophy of the library
    organization chart
    descriptions of the functions of each library department
    library staff directory
    library or institution's newsletter
    library's annual report
    map of the institution, campus, or agency
    if the employee is from out of town, information on the locale

Order nameplate (pin, badge, etc.) and business cards.
Update staff directory to include new employee.
Put new employee on mailing list for library and institutional newsletters.
Notify coworkers of new employee's name, duties, and start date.
Provide employee with parking information.

First day

Introduce employee to coworkers.
Library tour, focusing on restrooms, cafeteria or lounge, location of supplies, photocopy machines, and telephones.
Cover safety and security issues, such as emergency procedures and personal safety.
Discuss hours, breaks, payday, and procedures for reporting absences.
Make lunch arrangements for new employee with yourself, the new employee's guide, or a group of coworkers.
Inform employee how you, coworkers, and administrators prefer to be addressed (i.e., by first name, last name, or title).
Discuss the philosophy of the library and its commitment to service.
Discuss standards of conduct and formal or informal dress codes.
Be sure all personnel paperwork is completed.

Second day

Discuss telephone procedures and policies.
Tour entire institution or agency, pointing out credit union, cafeteria(s), and post office.
Explain timekeeping procedures, including overtime and compensatory time.

Orientation checklist (continued)

By end of first week

Review library's organizational chart and reporting structure.
Arrange for employee to get ID and library card.
Explain library policies on office collections, soliciting, confidentiality of library records, smoking, alcohol, and drugs.
Arrange for explanation of benefits, such as insurance, vacation, leave policies, retirement, disability, credit union, tuition coverage, holidays, jury duty, bereavement leave, and travel policy.
Explain safety procedures.
Explain procedures for communicating problems or concerns.
Cover department-specific plans, policies, and procedures.
Cover housekeeping responsibilities.
Explain operation of employee's union (if applicable).

By end of second week

Discuss probationary period.
Discuss performance standards and appraisal.
Discuss library's tenure or salary review program.
Cover long-range plans of the library.
Cover grievance procedures.

By end of first month

Set appointment with library director and your supervisor.
Arrange for orientation to other departments with whom employee frequently interacts.
Ask for employee's feedback on orientation.
Discuss opportunities for advancement.

---

safety, and grievance procedures. Time should be scheduled so that the employee can read policies, get accustomed to his or her work area, and think about what has been learned so far.

The first week

By the end of the first week, the new employee should understand the functions of other departments within the library and how the employee and his or her department interact with other departments. The new employee should be familiar with the library's organizational chart and how the library fits into its parent institution's goals and plans. He or she should know how performance will be evaluated and be aware of acceptable and unacceptable behavior. He or she should know where to go for help and how to contact resource people within the library and institution. Other important topics are included in the checklist.

The first month

In the first month, discuss opportunities for advancement and career development. By the end of the first month, schedule time for formal feedback about the new employee's orientation period. This meeting provides an opportunity to fill any gaps in the orientation and can help you in planning for the next new employee.

In general, be nonthreatening and observant during the orientation period. Communicate your concerns and be open to the concerns, however trivial-sounding, of your new employee. Small concerns, if neglected, can be blown out of proportion. By thoroughly preparing for the orientation period, you can do much to guarantee that your new employee adjusts easily to his or her new environment and becomes a productive employee.

Source: Edward Garten & Joan Giesecke, eds., *Practical Help for New Supervisors,*
(Chicago: ALA Library Administration and Management Association, 1990)

Support staff networks

MANY ASSOCIATIONS EXIST for library support staff. The following list appears courtesy of *Library Mosaics: The Magazine for Support Staff.*

Alabama Library Association, Paraprofessional Roundtable, Angelene Kelly, Moderator, 11146 Longbow Dr., Tuscaloosa, AL 35404; (205) 262-5210.

Arizona State Library Association, Arizona Library Technicians and Paraprofessionals, John Charles, Scottsdale Public Library, 3839 Civic Center Plaza, Scottsdale, AZ 85251-4434; (602) 994-2476.

California Library Association, California Library Employees Association, Janet Arenberg, President, Santa Monica Public Library, 1343 6th St., Santa Monica, CA 90406-1610; (213) 458-8603.

Colorado Library Association, Paralibrarian Division, Gwen Jones, Chair, Pikes Peak Library District, P.O. Box 1579, Colorado Springs, CO 80901; (719) 473-2080, x255.

Connecticut Library Association, Library Technical Assistants, Carol A. Stepas, LTA Section Chair, Executive Board, 97 Hollister Way North, Glastonbury, CT 06033.

Council on Library Media Technicians, Bettye Smith, President, Covington & Burling Law Library, 1201 Pennsylvania Ave., N.W., Washington, DC 20004; (202) 662-6156.

Florida Library Association, Virginia Gerster, 1133 W. Morse Blvd., Suite 201, Winter Park, FL 32789; (407) 647-8839.

Illinois Library Association, Library Assistants Section, Debbie Rodgers, Shawnee Library System, RR#2 Greenbriar Rd., Carterville, IL 62918; (618) 985-3711.

Indiana Library Association, Library Assistants and Technicians, Gloria Grooms, Chair, Brownsburg Public Library, 450 S. Jefferson St., Brownsburg, IN 46112; (317) 852-7734.

Central Indiana Library Services Support Staff Committee, Ruth Tolbert, 1100 W. 42d St., Indianapolis, IN 46208; (317) 926-6561.

Kentucky Library Association, Continuing Education & Staff Development Committee, Jebb Mathias, Chair, 3033 Shagbark Trail, Sellersburg, IN 47172; (502) 935-9840.

Maine Library Association, Standing Advisory Committee on Continuing Education Development, Sylvia K. Norton, Regional Memorial Hospital, 58 Baribeau Dr., Brunswick, ME 04011; (207) 729-0181, x365.

Maryland Library Association, Paraprofessionals and Library Support Staff, Nisa Merritt, Potomac Community Library, 10101 Glenolden Rd., Potomac, MD 20854; (301) 365-0662.

Minnesota Library Association, Support Staff Roundtable, Deborah Struzyk, President, Minneapolis Public Library, 300 Nicollet Mall, Minneapolis, MN 55401; (612) 372-6507.

Missouri Library Association, Technical Services Council, Joyce Howells, Chair, 1015 E. Broadway, Suite 21, Columbia, MO 65201; (704) 983-7322.

Nebraska Library Association, Paraprofessional Roundtable, Marie Rasmussen, Chair, Von Tiesen Library, McCook Community College, 1205 E. 5th, McCook, NE 69001; (800) 658-4348.

New Jersey Association of Library Assistants, Martha Harris, President, East Orange Public Library, 21 S. Arlington Ave., East Orange, NJ 07018; (201) 266-5613.

New York Library Association, Administrative, Clerical and Support Staff Roundtable, Esther Schecter, President, Yonkers Public Library, 7 Main St., Yonkers, NY 10701; (914) 337-1500, x425.

New York State Library Assistants Association, Judith Andrew, President, Ithaca College Library, Danby Rd., Ithaca, NY 14850; (607) 274-3182.

North Carolina Library Association, Paraprofessional Association, Meralyn Meadows, Chair, Stanly County Public Library, 133 E. Main St., Albemarle, NC 28001; (704) 983-7322.

Ohio Library Association, Supportive Staff Division, Sheila Boren, Coordinator, Findlay-Hancock Public Library, 206 Broadway, Findlay, OH 4584 0; (419) 422-0881.

Academic Library Association of Ohio, Support Staff Interest Group, Julianne Houston, Chair, P.O. Box 3082 University Station, Columbus, OH 43210-0082; (614) 368-3255.

Oklahoma Library Association, Support Staff Roundtable, Jean Bowers, Chair, Public Library of Enid & Garfield County, P.O. Box 8002, Enid, OK 73702; (405) 234-6313.

Utah Library Association, Library Assistants Roundtable, Kent Slade, President, 2150 S. 300 West, Suite 16, Salt Lake City, UT 84115; (801) 392-7113.

Virginia Library Association, Paraprofessional Forum, Susan McFaden, Chair, Fairfax County Public Library, Technical Operations Center, 13135 Lee-Jackson Highway, Suite 115-B, Fairfax, VA 22033; (703) 222-3119.

Washington Library Association, Association of Library Employees, Ruth A. Poynter, Chair, 300 8th Ave., North, King County Library System, Seattle, WA 98109; (206) 684-6635.

Wisconsin Library Association, Support Staff Roundtable, Jeanne Eloranta, Chair, University of Wisconsin-Madison, White Hall, 600 N. Park St., Madison, WI 53706.

Wyoming Library Association, Technical Services Interest Group, Donna Kolarich, Acting Chair, Casper College Library, 125 College Dr., Casper, WY 82601; (307) 362-2665.

Source: "Networking: The Net That Works for You," Library Mosaics, January/February 1991, pp. 8–10

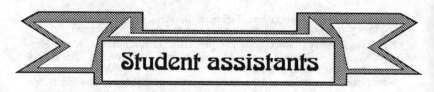

Student assistants

Evaluating student assistants

by F. Jay Fuller

EVALUATING LIBRARY STAFF can be a time-consuming and frustrating process. In the case of library student assistant employees, the problems associated with evaluation are compounded; although student assistant job descriptions are usually clear and concise (even restrictive), the circumstances and pressures under which these individuals work are quite different from those of other library employees.

The foundation of any evaluative process is the attitude of the individual doing the appraising. When evaluating regular staff, many aspects may be taken for granted; however, with student employees there are a few pivotal points that need to be considered closely.

First, the evaluator should remember that the document used for formal, written student evaluations is simply a reference tool, and not an end product in itself. Evaluation for this class of employee is an ongoing, daily process, and not something which is only done at the conclusion of library employment.

Second, one should always take into consideration that the student assistant is just that, a student, in the academic setting to learn, grow, and develop, and that students have substantial commitments in addition to their library work.

Third, student assistants are temporary, but not inferior, employees. If the evaluating staff perceives student workers as an expendable commodity, whose worth can be measured solely in terms of how much labor can be acquired for nominal costs in both time and money, then student employees simply function as cogs in the great library machine, and one's formal evaluation may consist of an elementary mathematical formula designed to rank performance on an absolute and immutable scale. Although this enormously simplifies the evaluation process, it leaves much to be desired in terms of providing a positive work environment or for giving student employees valuable feedback on their work.

In the Meriam Library at California State University, Chico, we formally evaluate each of our student assistants at least twice a year, usually at the end of each semester. Our forms divide the criteria for our student assistant evaluations into four broad categories: operational, personal, interpersonal, and leadership. All student workers know from the first day of employment what is expected of them, and what will be the criteria for their formal, written evaluation.

Operational aspects deal with how well student assistants grasp the policies and procedures of their unit, and put them into daily practice. Here the key points we emphasize are: grasp of the department's routines, the ability to carry out verbal and/or written instructions, and the accuracy, thoroughness, and neatness of work produced. Because many of our student employees must carry out their jobs away from the close scrutiny of a staff supervisor, we also include in this category the ability to work without immediate supervision.

In the *personal* category, we have found it helpful to remember that most students employed by the academic library come to their jobs as unskilled labor, and generally have little or no knowledge of library operations or procedures, except for that which they may have managed to incidentally acquire as patrons using the facility. For many, their jobs with the library may be their very first employment experience. Not only are the supervisors of new student assistants going to need to train and evaluate student employees in the daily routine of the unit's operation, but supervisors will need to encourage in these young adults personal habits appropriate to the work environment.

The obvious personal commodity that a new or continuing student employee must have or acquire is a sense of appearance appropriate to the workplace. We find that it proves quite effective to simply remind each student worker at the beginning of employment that the library is a public place where common decency prevails.

A far more important part of learning good personal work habits, which we especially emphasize, is the development of personal time management. Student assistants are students first and foremost. Course loads can be substantial, demanding an enormous amount of effort and requiring meticulous scheduling of each day's activities. If students are made aware that employment in the library requires the same sense of responsibility that they bring to their college coursework, and that a balance between class, study, and work is expected, many problems concerning time management, particularly attendance, may be avoided. There must be a clear and uniform provision for occasional changes in schedule, consistently and equitably applied.

The *interpersonal* aspects of evaluation involve assessing the student assistant's ability to interact with fellow employees, and with the public, in a reasonable, mature fashion. Tact, manners, and the capacity to listen are all paramount when dealing with the public. This is especially important when student workers are confronted with patrons who adamantly believe they have been wronged in some way by the library or the system, and express their displeasure in no uncertain terms. Responding to such situations is never easy, even for those of us who must do so every day, but it is important for staff to allow student assistants to handle problem patrons on their own as much as possible, while being ready to quickly intercede if the situation gets out of hand. Later, after the situation has been rectified, it has proven quite beneficial to review the entire incident with the students involved, making suggestions and allowing the students to express concerns about their performance.

In the Meriam Library, we have a Student Supervisor program which promotes individuals who have shown a marked ability for *leadership*. For these student assistants, a special set of criteria are utilized to evaluate their abilities in special areas. As supervisors themselves, it is essential that these workers are self-motivating and capable of working without themselves being closely supervised. This means that their commitment to the job must approximate that of regular library staff.

Finally, the evaluator must take into consideration that student workers can only be as good as their training. Training techniques and manuals should be renewed or rewritten at least annually, especially in academic libraries where changing priorities and the influx of new technologies have become the norm rather than the exception. It is our responsibility to make sure that every effort is made by us to allow our student employees their best chance at doing their best for us. It is their performance on the job, good or bad, which serves as our evaluation as their supervisors and mentors.

Source: F. Jay Fuller, "Evaluating Student Assistants as Library Employees," *College & Research Libraries News*, January 1990, pp. 11–13

Where to find volunteers

by Robert A. Berk

IN ADDITION TO other efforts to conserve the precious time of the librarian, there is at least one way that has proven effective for many libraries to actually increase the size of their staffs without spending additional funds. This method is the effective use of volunteers. Volunteers can be taught to perform a variety of library functions, and those who are motivated can be of great help to the librarian. Some of the negative factors associated with volunteer help have to do with lack of dependability, frequent turnover, and selective motivation for only certain types of library work. If volunteers are used they must be recruited, trained, supervised, and evaluated, and it is perhaps best for the librarian to consider volunteers as regular library staff with regard to any management problems that may arise.

In most libraries, the use of a volunteer program is probably worth investigating, particularly for the very small public library. Such a program can be initiated on a very limited basis and, if successful, continued and improved as a means of conserving the librarian's time for other more demanding functions.

The source for volunteers will depend upon the type of small library. In a library for an art museum or an art school, a friends of the museum group may be a ready source. In the case of a hospital library, the institution may already have a volunteer program, such as an auxiliary group, that can be approached. In a for-profit organization such as an insurance agency, community job training agencies for young people or the underemployed may be a source for volunteers. Other job training agencies associated with local government may be seeking temporary placements where on-the-job experience can be acquired. There is always the chance that someone is interested in being active in an organization or institution and is willing to contribute some time to the library. A notice in the organization's newsletter may reach friends and relatives of those already employed.

In selecting volunteers, one should consider skills needed by the library and the ability of the individual to work independently with a minimum of training. Typing and keyboarding skills are always useful. The ability to interact in a personable and effective manner with library users may be essential. Answering the telephone may have a high priority. Accuracy and attention to detail are critical for the consistency required in many library operations. The volunteer may represent the library to many of the users and should convey the image that the library hopes to project; flexibility is important in a volunteer. Frequently volunteers are pleased to perform only certain tasks, but the librarian must determine what needs to be accomplished and use volunteers that can accommodate these needs. For these reasons, volunteers should be carefully interviewed before being accepted by the library.

Occasionally, the librarian in the very small library may be asked to accept a library school student intern. This is not a way for the librarian to get rid of some of the drudgery of library work. In fact taking on an intern implies an educational commitment that will take a considerable amount of the librarian's time. The time spent meeting the educational needs of the intern will certainly exceed time saved with this additional staff member.

Source: Robert A. Berk, *Starting, Managing, and Promoting the Small Library* (Armonk, N.Y.: M.E. Sharpe, 1989)

How to use volunteers

THE USE OF VOLUNTEERS in public services is traditional. Social services, health, and welfare activities are well known for their extensive utilization of voluntary manpower. Volunteer programs in libraries are less well developed, and have been somewhat limited in size and scope.

Volunteer workers are unpaid staff; they give of their time and energy to assist an organization or institution to conduct certain kinds of programs or specific services. Volunteers are generally part-time workers, giving time over periods of short or long duration.

Volunteers often bring to an activity and an organization a new outlook, a different perspective, added talents, a fresh approach, and a stimulating concept. They also bring a different motivation.

In considering the direct services gained by an institution from its volunteers, a library also needs to give cognizance to two other benefits often derived from volunteer assistance. First, community support, community utilization, and public relations are immeasurably enhanced by the direct and personal involvement of large numbers of persons in the activity. Volunteer workers are personally involved; they are a community liaison par excellence. Second, work experience is a major source of potential recruitment into occupations and professions. Many persons who do begin work on volunteer projects continue their education and training for careers in the same kind of work.

The use of volunteers in many types of services and programs may expand in the foreseeable future. The trend toward earlier retirement by professional and skilled workers, the increased need for wider public services, the earlier maturity of young people, the time and labor saving devices which bring more leisure, and the limited financial support of many agencies or institutions, all suggest an increased use of volunteers.

Principles for success

The following principles should be borne in mind by libraries in using volunteers:

1. Basic to the success of a volunteer program are prior planning and approval on the part of the staff and the governing body of the library.

2. All the principles and good practices that relate to sound manpower administration, such as planning, training, evaluation, and development, must be applied to volunteer workers.

3. Planning for the use of library volunteers must include clarification of their status regarding such items as compensation for work-related injuries, insurance coverage when operating a library vehicle, and related benefits.

4. Library volunteers may have work-related expenses which are to be paid for or reimbursed by the library. The library's policies and procedures regarding such expenses should be established and made known to the volunteers before they begin library service.

5. If it is essential that a minimum or basic library program be initiated or developed by volunteers, this use of voluntary persons should be considered as a temporary measure pending the employment of staff.

6. Volunteers should not supplant or displace established staff position spaces.

7. Recognition and appreciation of every volunteer and of all voluntary assistance is imperative. As volunteers receive no salary, other forms of appreciation and recognition are essential.

8. Volunteers should be assigned to meaningful work which makes use of their own talents, experience, training, and interests.

9. Volunteers should be assigned to those jobs which they feel competent to do and for which they have been trained and given orientation.

10. Volunteer assignments should generally be for specific time periods to enable the library and the volunteer to review, evaluate, and reassign duties.

11. There should be a staff coordinator of volunteers.

12. Continued orientation and training is essential for volunteers to keep them informed of procedures, policies, etc., just as is the continued training of regular staff members.

13. The staff should have training on the use of volunteers and should share responsibility for the success of the volunteer program.

14. Written, detailed job descriptions for volunteers are necessary.

15. Realistic scheduling of volunteers is essential; this may mean some overlapping or duplication of personnel schedule, to cover emergencies and absences.

16. Programs and services must be planned bearing in mind the possible termination or unavailability of volunteer help.

17. Friends of Libraries, parent-teacher associations, and other groups occasionally provide volunteer services and programs. Some kinds of volunteer assistance may best be provided through such organizations.

Types of work

These are some of the kinds of work which have been done by library volunteers:

- sharing of books with children in Head Start and day-care groups
- preparation of picture files
- presenting film programs
- making of braille, talking books, and tapes
- making deliveries to homebound borrowers
- storytelling to children in libraries and other locations
- teaching in literacy classes
- conducting discussion groups inside and outside the library
- mending library materials
- shelving returned materials
- making publicity materials for the library
- planning exhibits in the library
- preparation of oral history collection
- collection of historical and archival materials
- preparation of a clipping and vertical file
- inspecting and repairing audiovisual materials
- staffing a circulation desk
- staffing a book cart in a hospital or home for the aged
- working with outreach programs.

Source: Guidelines for Using Volunteers in Libraries
(Chicago: ALA Library Administration and Management Association, 1971)

Library media specialists

School library staff

2

THE SUCCESS OF ANY school library media program, no matter how well designed, depends ultimately on the quality and number of the personnel responsible for the program. A well-educated and highly motivated professional staff, adequately supported by technical and clerical staff, is critical to the endeavor.

Although staffing patterns are developed to meet local needs, certain basic staffing requirements can be identified. Staffing patterns must reflect the following principles:

1. All students, teachers, and administrators in each school building at all grade levels must have access to a library media program provided by one or more certificated library media specialists working full-time in the school's library media center.

2. Both professional personnel and support staff are necessary for all library media programs at all grade levels. Each school must employ at least one full-time technical assistant or clerk for each library media specialist. Some programs, facilities, and levels of service will require more than one support staff member for each professional.

3. More than one library media professional is required in many schools. The specific number of additional professional staff is determined by the school's size, number of students and of teachers, facilities, specific library media program components, and other features of the school's instructional program. A reasonable ratio of professional staff to teacher and student populations is required in order to provide for the levels of service and library media program development described in *Information Power: Guidelines for School Library Media Programs*.

All school systems must employ a district library media director to provide leadership and direction to the overall library media program. The district director is a member of the administrative staff and serves on committees that determine the criteria and policies for the district's curriculum and instructional programs. The director communicates the goals and needs of both the school and district library media programs to the superintendent, board of education, other district-level personnel, and the community. In this advocacy role, the district library media director advances the concept of the school library media specialist as a partner with teachers and promotes a staffing level that allows the partnership to flourish.

Source: Position Statement on Appropriate Staffing for School Library Media Centers (Chicago: ALA American Association of School Librarians, 1990)

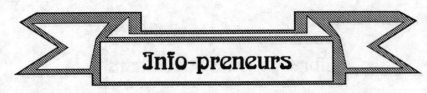

Info-preneurs

What does it take to consult?

by Alice Sizer Warner

MANY LIBRARIANS NOW earn their livings nontraditionally. Some work as *intrapreneurs*—those employed by an organization to manage libraries as businesses-within-businesses. Others work as *entrepreneurs,* that is, as self-employed people who work for an organization only when that organization becomes their client.

What does it take to be a successful information entrepreneur?

1. You've got to like money, you've got to be up-front about money, you've got to like talking about it, charging it, chasing it if people are slow in paying it to you.

2. You have to like selling. You have to sell all the time, think about it all the time.

3. You must learn very quickly to seek out the kinds of customers who will become repeaters. You want 75% of your business to be repeat business.

4. You must learn to look for, and to use, referrals to new clients. It's a lot easier to sell your services when you've been referred than when you haven't.

5. When you're selling, you must learn how to describe your service to clients in very simple, nonlibrary terms. I'm serious about this. We librarians are very bad at simplifying what we do.

6. You must learn to look for customers who can afford to pay you. Go where the money is and that doesn't mean simply avoiding small, cash-poor customers. Some of the biggest companies in the world are slow to pay, so check each potential client's paying habits before accepting an assignment. Money doesn't count until you get it, and you cannot afford to wait.

7. You must learn to sell what people want to buy, not what you are convinced they need to buy.

Only a small percentage of those in librarianship will be happy and successful as either intrapreneurs or entrepreneurs. Overall, our biggest stumbling block is that most of us aren't tough enough in the for-profit sense. We are more interested in the quality of our work than we are in chasing customers. Fee-based information providers must strike a good balance between the two, and this is very hard to do.

If you can follow the seven suggestions listed above, you just might make it. You should know, though, that the vast majority decide that entrepreneuring is not for them. They didn't realize that entrepreneuring meant liking money.

Liability

Protect yourself against the possibility that you may give a client a bad answer. Talk to an attorney before you start your fee-based service. You will probably be provided with a disclaimer statement declaring that you are to be "held harmless" and that you have used your "best efforts" in serving your customers.

Source: Alice Sizer Warner, "Librarians as Money Makers," *American Libraries,* November 1990, pp. 946–48 ©1990 Alice Sizer Warner. Used by permission.

THE PROFESSION 3

Calendar to 1994

1991

September

23–29	Society of American Archivists	Philadelphia, Pa.
25–28	Florida Assoc. for Media in Education	Tampa, Fla.
26–28	North Dakota Library Assoc.	Jamestown, N.D.
28–Oct. 5	Banned Books Week	
29–Oct. 1	Arkansas Library Assoc.	Little Rock, Ark.
29–Oct. 1	New England Library Assoc.	Hyannis, Mass.

October

2–4	Kentucky Library Assoc.	Louisville, Ky.
2–4	Missouri Library Assoc.	St. Louis, Mo.
2–5	Nevada Library Assoc.	Reno, Nev.
2–5	South Dakota Library Assoc.	Huron, S.D.
2–5	Idaho Library Assoc.	Nampa, Ida.
2–6	Pennsylvania Library Assoc.	The Poconos
3–5	Wyoming Library Assoc.	Casper, Wyo.
4–8	Colorado Library Assoc.	Vail, Colo.
9–11	Nebraska Library Assoc.	Omaha, Nebr.
9–11	Washington Library Media Assoc.	
10–12	Oregon Educational Media Assoc.	Bend, Ore.
15–16	Connecticut Educational Media Assoc.	Stamford, Conn.
15–18	Michigan Library Assoc.	Lansing, Mich.
16–18	Wisconsin Library Assoc.	Milwaukee, Wisc.
16–19	EDUCOM '91	San Diego, Calif.
17–19	Ohio Educational Library/Media Assoc.	Cincinnati, Ohio
22–25	Mississippi Library Assoc.	Biloxi, Miss.
23–25	Assoc. of Research Libraries	Washington, D.C.
23–27	Michigan Assoc. for Media in Education	Dearborn, Mich.
25–29	Georgia Library Assoc.	Savannah, Ga.
27–31	American Society for Information Science	Washington, D.C.
29–Nov. 2	Mountain Plains Library Assoc. / Arizona Library Assoc.	Phoenix, Ariz.
30–Nov. 2	Ohio Library Assoc./Minnesota Library Assoc. Midwest Federation of Library Associations	Minneapolis. Minn.
30–Nov. 3	Virginia Educational Media Assoc.	Roanoke, Va.
31–Nov. 2	Illinois School Library Media Assoc.	Decatur, Ill.

November

	AMIGOS Bibliographic Council	Dallas, Tex.
3–4	Massachusetts Assoc. for Educational Media	Sturbridge, Mass.
4	Rhode Island Library Assoc.	Providence, R.I.
4–6	Canadian Assoc. of Research Libraries	Halifax, N.S.
5–8	South Carolina Library Assoc.	Greenville, S.C.
6–9	School Libraries (Mississippi Library Assoc.)	Jackson, Miss.
7–9	West Virginia Library Assoc.	White Sulphur Springs, W.Va.
8–9	Illinois School Library Media Assoc.	Decatur, Ill.
12–15	North Carolina Library Assoc.	High Point, N.C.
12–18	Book Week	
13–15	Virginia Library Assoc.	Hot Springs, Va.

13–16	Literacy Volunteers of America Week	
14–16	California Media & Library Educators Assoc.	Palm Springs, Calif.
15–17	Theatre Library Assoc.	New York, N.Y.
16–20	California Library Assoc.	Oakland, Calif.
17–19	Educational Media Assoc. of New Jersey	New Brunswick, N.J.
20–24	New York Library Assoc.	New York, N.Y.

1992

January

| 21–24 | Assoc. for Library & Information Science Educ. | San Antonio, Tex. |
| 25–30 | American Library Assoc. (Midwinter) | San Antonio, Tex. |

February

5–9	Assoc. for Educational Communications & Technology	Washington, D.C.
6–13	Art Libraries Society of North America	Chicago, Ill.
19–22	Music Library Assoc.	Baltimore, Md.
28–Mar. 3	Alaska Library Assoc.	Fairbanks, Alaska

March

14–15	Utah Educational Media Assoc.	Ogden, Utah
15	Hawaii Library Assoc.	Honolulu, Haw.
17–22	Southeastern Library Assoc. / Louisiana Library Assoc.	New Orleans, La.
18–20	Illinois Library Assoc.	Chicago, Ill.
27–29	Michigan Assoc. for Media in Education	Port Huron, Mich.

April

5–11	National Library Week	
7–11	Texas Library Assoc.	Houston, Tex.
8–11	Oregon Library Assoc. / Washington Library Assoc.	Portland, Ore.
9–11	Missouri Assoc. of School Librarians	Springfield, Mo.
12–14	ALA Assoc. of College & Research Libraries	Salt Lake City, Utah
15–17	Utah Library Assoc.	Salt Lake City, Utah
20–23	Catholic Library Assoc. / National Catholic Education Assoc.	St. Louis, Mo.
26–27	Wisconsin Educational Media Assoc.	Eau Claire, Wisc.
27–28	Massachusetts Library Assoc.	N. Falmouth, Mass.
29–May 2	Montana Library Assoc.	Bozeman, Mont.

May

	Assoc. of Research Libraries	Charleston, S.C.
7–8	SOLINET	Atlanta, Ga.
9–13	Council of Planning Librarians / American Planning Assoc.	Washington, D.C.
15–21	Medical Library Assoc.	Washington, D.C.
20–21	Vermont Library Assoc.	Fairlee, Vt.

June

| | American Theological Library Assoc. | Dallas, Tex. |
| | Rhode Island Library Assoc. | |

6–11	Special Libraries Assoc.	San Francisco, Calif.
10–14	Canadian Library Assoc.	Winnipeg, Man.
25–July 2	American Library Assoc. (Annual)	San Francisco, Calif.
29	Theatre Library Assoc.	San Francisco, Calif.

July

| 12–14 | Church & Synagogue Library Assoc. | Lansing, Mich. |
| 18–23 | American Assoc. of Law Libraries | San Francisco, Calif. |

August

| 11–15 | Pacific Northwest Library Assoc. | Seattle, Wash. |
| 30–Sep. 5 | International Federation of Library Associations | New Delhi, India |

September

2–6	Black Caucus of ALA Nat'l Conference	Columbus, Ohio
13–17	ALA Library & Info. Technology Assoc.	Denver, Colo.
14–18	Society of American Archivists	Montreal, Que.
24–26	School Library Media Section (North Dakota Library Assoc.)	Fargo, N.D.
29–Oct. 3	Mountain Plains Library Assoc. / Wyoming Library Assoc.	Cheyenne, Wyo.

October

	Assoc. of Research Libraries	Washington, D.C.
4–6	New England Library Assoc.	Sturbridge, Mass.
7–9	Iowa Library Assoc.	Waterloo, Ia.
7–10	South Dakota Library Assoc.	Pierre, S.D.
8–10	Nevada Library Assoc.	Las Vegas, Nev.
10–12	Colorado Library Assoc.	
15–17	West Virginia Library Assoc.	Parkersburg, W.Va.
21–25	ALA American Assoc. of School Librarians	Baltimore, Md.
23–26	Michigan Library Assoc.	Traverse City, Mich.
25–29	American Society for Information Science	Pittsburgh, Pa.
27–30	Mississippi Library Assoc.	Jackson, Miss.
28–30	Wisconsin Library Assoc.	La Crosse, Wisc.
28–31	Michigan Assoc. for Media in Education	Lansing, Mich.
31–Nov. 4	Pennsylvania Library Assoc.	Pittsburgh, Pa.

November

4–7	Ohio Library Assoc. / Ohio Education/Library Media Assoc.	Columbus, Ohio
11–15	New York Library Assoc.	Syracuse, N.Y.
14–18	California Library Assoc.	Long Beach, Calif.
18–21	California Media & Library Educators Assoc.	Sacramento, Calif.

1993

January

| 14–18 | Assoc. for Educational Communications & Technology | New Orleans, La. |
| 22–28 | American Library Assoc. (Midwinter) | Denver, Colo. |

| 28–Feb. 3 | Art Libraries Society of North America | San Francisco, Calif. |

March

| 9–13 | Texas Library Assoc. | San Antonio, Tex. |
| 11–13 | Middle Atlantic Regional Library Federation | White Sulphur Springs, W.Va. |

April

| 12–15 | Catholic Library Assoc. / National Catholic Education Assoc. | New Orleans, La. |
| 18–24 | National Library Week | |

May

1–5	Council of Planning Librarians / American Planning Assoc.	Chicago, Ill.
6–7	SOLINET	Atlanta, Ga.
11–15	Pacific Northwest Library Assoc. / Montana Library Assoc.	Kalispell, Mont.
14–20	Medical Library Assoc.	Chicago, Ill.

June

5–10	Special Libraries Assoc.	Cincinnati, Ohio
24–July 1	American Library Assoc. (Annual)	New Orleans, La.
24–July 1	Theatre Library Assoc.	New Orleans, La.

July

8–11	Canadian Library Assoc.	Toronto, Ont.
11–13	Church & Synagogue Library Assoc.	Houston, Tex.
17–22	American Assoc. of Law Libraries	Boston, Mass.

August

| 15–21 | International Federation of Library Associations | Barcelona, Spain |

September

2–5	Society of American Archivists	New Orleans, La.
23–25	School Library Media Section (North Dakota Library Assoc.)	Williston, N.D.
26–28	New England Library Assoc.	Burlington, Vt.
30–Oct. 2	Nevada Library Assoc.	Elko, Nev.
30–Oct. 4	Mountain Plains Library Assoc. / Colorado Library Assoc.	Aspen, Colo.

October

6–9	South Dakota Library Assoc.	Brookings, S.D.
13–15	Iowa Library Assoc.	Ames, Ia.
14–16	West Virginia Library Assoc.	Huntington, W.Va.
28–30	Ohio Library Assoc. / Ohio Education/ Library Media Assoc.	Cleveland, O.

November

| 3–5 | Wisconsin Library Assoc. | Green Bay, Wisc. |

3–7	New York Library Assoc. / Ontario Library	
	Assoc.	Niagara Falls, N.Y.
19–23	California Library Assoc.	San Francisco, Calif.

1994

January

| 14–20 | American Library Assoc. (Midwinter) | Los Angeles, Calif. |
| 20–27 | Art Libraries Society of North America | Providence, R.I. |

February

| 9–13 | Assoc. for Educational Communications | |
| | & Technology | Anaheim, Calif. |

Norm's Library Levity

There is—woe is me—no true library holiday on which colleagues, friends, relatives, and users send us Hallmark cards created especially to reward the dedication and virtues of librarians. National Book Week and National Library Week are, at best, pale imitations of what a true celebration of librarianship ought to be.

Many libraries celebrate holidays in their own fashion. It is traditional in many libraries to hold some kind of library-wide staff feast to mark Christmas, Hannukah, Kwanza, and the winter solstice. A few libraries celebrate Halloween with costume parties or pumpkin-carving contests. For the most part, holidays come and go in libraries unobserved by the staff, even though book exhibits are often built around a library theme.

For the library humorist, April Fool's Day is the best library holiday of all. It somehow serves in many libraries as an opportunity for the local humorist(s) to assemble and distribute a parody of the ubiquitous staff newsletter. Although the jokes are often too parochial to be readily understood outside the individual library, those special creations contain what may be the best and truest library humor of all.

Rather than a small sample of the best of that foolery—a selection that cannot be made judiciously—a sampling of titles may be set forth to suggest the imagination that lurks in those creative ventures. *News Notes* (Ohio State) becomes *News Nosey*, hinting at the personal news found in both; *The Innocent Bystander* (University of Connecticut) appears as—what else—*The Guilty Participant*; *Update* (Capitol Regional Library Council) reverses itself to become *Downdate*; *Southeastern Newsline* (Southeastern New York Library Resources Council) is transformed to *Southeastern Gnusline*; *Level Talk* (Johns Hopkins) has appeared as *Libel Talk*, hinting at the sharp barbs it distributes; the *Weekly Agenda*'s (Rutgers University) strength is sapped as it becomes *Weakly Agenda*; *Library Line* (University of Richmond) drops a single letter to aptly become *Library Lie*; *Torn Sheet* (University of Wyoming) carefully is revealed as *No Sheeet*; *The Bibliophile* naturally turns upside down into *The Biblio-Fobe*; and at several libraries, including Colgate University and the Library of Congress, issues of the *National Library Enquirer* have been known to make an appearance on or about April 1.

—*Norman D. Stevens, The Molesworth Institute*

March

	Southeastern Library Assoc.	Charlotte, N.C.

April

4–7	Catholic Library Assoc. / National Catholic Education Assoc.	Anaheim, Calif.
12–16	Texas Library Assoc.	Corpus Christi, Tex.
16–20	Council of Planning Librarians / American Planning Assoc.	San Francisco, Calif.
17–23	National Library Week	
24–27	Montana Library Assoc.	Butte, Mont.

May

3–7	School & Children's Division, Southeastern Library Assoc.	Orlando, Fla.
3–7	Florida Library Assoc.	Orlando, Fla.
19–26	Medical Library Assoc.	San Antonio, Tex.

June

11–16	Special Libraries Assoc.	Atlanta, Ga.
16–19	Canadian Library Assoc.	Quebec City, Que.
23–30	American Library Assoc. (Annual)	Miami, Fla.
23–30	Theatre Library Assoc.	Miami, Fla.

3

Past ALA annual conferences

A LIST OF ALL ALA annual conference dates and locations, with attendance figures, contrasted with total ALA membership (from 1900).

Date	Place	Attendance	Membership
1876, Oct. 4–6	Philadelphia	103	[not available
1877, Sept. 4–6	New York	66	for 1876–1899]
1877, Oct. 2–5	London, England	21*	
1878	[No meeting]		
1879, June 30–July 2	Boston	162	
1880	[No meeting]		
1881, Feb. 9–12	Washington, D.C.	70	
1882, May 24–27	Cincinnati	47	
1883, Aug. 14–17	Buffalo, N.Y.	72	
1884	[No meeting]		
1885, Sept. 8–11	Lake George, N.Y.	87	
1886, July 7–10	Milwaukee, Wisc.	133	
1887, Aug. 30–Sept. 2	Thousand Island, N.Y.	186	
1888, Sept. 25–28	Catskill Mountains, N.Y.	32	
1889, May 8–11	St. Louis, Mo.	106	
1890, Sept. 9–13	Fabyans (White Mts.), N.H.	242	
1891, Oct. 12–16	San Francisco	83	
1892, May 6–21	Lakewood, N.Y., Baltimore, Washington	260	

* U.S. attendance.

Date	Place	Attendance	Membership
1893, July 13–22	Chicago	311	
1894, Sept. 17–22	Lake Placid, N.Y.	205	
1895, Aug. 13–21	Denver & Colorado Springs	147	
1896, Sept. 1–8	Cleveland	363	
1897, June 21–25	Philadelphia	315	
1897, July 13–16	London, England	94*	
1898, July 5–9	Lakewood, N.Y.	494	
1899, May 9–13	Atlanta	215	
1900, June 6–12	Montreal, Quebec	452	874
1901, July 3–10	Waukesha, Wisc.	460	980
1902, June 14–20	Boston & Magnolia, Mass.	1,018	1,152
1903, June 22–27	Niagara Falls, N.Y.	684	1,200
1904, Oct. 17–22	St. Louis, Mo.	577	1,228
1905, July 4–8	Portland, Me.	359	1,253
1906, June 29–July 6	Narragansett Pier, R.I.	891	1,844
1907, May 23–29	Asheville, N.C.	478	1,808
1908, June 22–27	Lake Minnetonka, Minn.	658	1,907
1909, June 28–July 3	Bretton Woods, N.H.	620	1,835
1910, June 20–July 6	Mackinac Island, Mich.	533	2,005
1910, Aug. 28–31	Brussels, Belgium	46*	
1911, May 18–24	Pasadena, Calif.	582	2,046
1912, June 26–July 2	Ottawa, Ontario	704	2,365
1913, June 23–28	Kaaterskill, N.Y.	892	2,563
1914, May 25–29	Washington, D.C.	1,366	2,905
1915, June 3–9	Berkeley, Calif.	779	3,024
1916, June 26–July 1	Asbury Park, N.J.	1,386	3,188
1917, June 21–27	Louisville, Ky.	824	3,346
1918, July 1–6	Saratoga Springs, N.Y.	620	3,380
1919, June 23–27	Asbury Park, N.J.	1,168	4,178
1920, June 2–7	Colorado Springs	553	4,464
1921, June 20–25	Swampscott, Mass.	1,899	5,307
1922, June 26–July 1	Detroit	1,839	5,684
1923, April 23–28	Hot Springs, Ark.	693	5,669
1924, June 30–July 5	Saratoga Springs, N.Y.	1,188	6,055
1925, July 6–11	Seattle, Wash.	1,066	6,745
1926, Oct. 4–9	Atlantic City, N.J.	2,224	8,848
1927, June 20–27	Toronto, Ontario	1,964	10,056
1927, Sept. 26–Oct. 1	Edinburgh, Scotland	82*	
1928, May 28–June 2	West Baden, Ind.	1,204	10,526
1929, May 13–18	Washington, D.C.	2,743	11,833
1929, June 15–30	Rome and Venice, Italy	70*	
1930, June 23–28	Los Angeles	2,023	12,713
1931, June 22–27	New Haven, Conn.	3,241	14,815
1932, April 25–30	New Orleans	1,306	13,021
1933, Oct. 16–21	Chicago	2,986	11,880
1934, June 25–30	Montreal, Quebec	1,904	11,731
1935, May 20–30	Madrid, Seville & Barcelona, Spain	42*	
1935, June 24–29	Denver	1,503	12,241
1936, May 11–16	Richmond, Va.	2,834	13,057
1937, June 21–26	New York	5,312	14,204
1938, June 13–18	Kansas City, Mo.	1,900	14,626
1939, June 18–24	San Francisco	2,869	15,568
1940, May 26–June 1	Cincinnati	3,056	15,808

* U.S. attendance.

Date	Place	Attendance	Membership
1941, June 19–25	Boston	4,266	16,015
1942, June 22–27	Milwaukee	2,342	15,328
1943	[No meeting]		14,546
1944	[No meeting]		14,799
1945	[No meeting]		15,118
1946, June 16–22	Buffalo, N.Y.	2,327	15,800
1947, June 29–July 5	San Francisco	2,534	17,107
1948, June 13–19	Atlantic City, N.J.	3,752	18,283
1949:	Regional conferences	[not recorded]	19,324
Aug. 22–25	(Far West) Vancouver, B.C.		
Sept. 2–5	(Trans-Miss.) Fort Collins, Colo.		
Oct. 3–6	(Middle Atlantic) Atlantic City, N.J.		
Oct. 12–15	(New England) Swampscott, Mass.		
Oct. 26–29	(Southeastern) Miami Beach, Fla.		
Nov. 9–12	(Midwest) Grand Rapids, Mich.		
Nov. 20–23	(Southwestern) Fort Worth, Tex.		
1950, July 16–22	Cleveland	3,436	19,689
1951, July 8–14	Chicago	3,612	19,701
1952, June 29–July 5	New York	5,212	18,925
1953, June 21–27	Los Angeles	3,258	19,551
1954, June 20–26	Minneapolis	3,230	20,177
1955, July 3–9	Philadelphia	4,412	20,293
1956, June 17–23	Miami Beach, Fla.	2,866	20,285
1957, June 23–30	Kansas City, Mo.	2,953	20,326
1958, July 13–19	San Francisco	4,400	21,716
1959, June 21–27	Washington, D.C.	5,346	23,230
1960, June 19–24	Montreal, Quebec	4,648	24,690
1961, July 9–15	Cleveland	4,757	25,860
1962, June 17–23	Miami Beach, Fla.	3,527	24,879
1963, July 14–20	Chicago	5,753	25,502
1964, June 28–July 4	St. Louis	4,623	26,015
1965, July 3–10	Detroit	5,818	27,526
1966, July 10–16	New York	9,342	31,885
1967, June 25–July 1	San Francisco	8,116	35,289
1968, June 23–29	Kansas City, Mo.	6,849	35,666
1969, June 22–28	Atlantic City, N.J.	10,399	36,865
1970, June 28–July 4	Detroit	8,965	30,394
1971, June 20–26	Dallas	8,087	29,740
1972, June 24–30	Chicago	9,700	29,610
1973, June 24–30	Las Vegas	8,539	30,172
1974, July 5–13	New York	14,382	34,010
1975, June 29–July 5	San Francisco	11,606	33,208
1976, July 18–24	Chicago (Centennial)	12,015	33,560
1977, June 17–23	Detroit	9,667	33,767
1978, June 25–30	Chicago	11,768	35,096
1979, June 24–30	Dallas	10,650	35,524
1980, June 29–July 4	New York	14,566	35,257
1981, June 26–July 2	San Francisco	12,555	37,954
1982, July 10–15	Philadelphia	12,819	38,050
1983, June 25–30	Los Angeles	11,005	38,862
1984, June 23–28	Dallas	11,443	39,290
1985, July 6–11	Chicago	14,160	40,761
1986, June 26–July 3	New York	16,530	42,361
1987, June 27–July 2	San Francisco	17,844	45,145
1988, July 9–14	New Orleans	16,530	47,249

Date	Place	Attendance	Membership
1989, June 24–29	Dallas	17,592	49,483
1990, June 23–28	Chicago	19,982	50,509
1991, June 29–July 4	Atlanta	17,764	52,920

Who gets to go to conference?

by Dan Clemmer

ONE OF THE KNOTTIEST PROBLEMS you head librarians and would-be heads must confront sooner or later is this: What is the best way to decide which staff members get to go to library conferences? And once you have decided who *does* get to go, how do you deal with those who *don't* get to go? The following scene is all too common:

Head Librarian: "Hi, Bob, what's up?"

Bob: "I bust my butt for this library, attend all the piddly-poo professional development workshops on my own time, and you let Milt Wembley, the biggest airhead in the public service division, go to ALA while I take his 2-to-10 shift for a whole week! That's what's up!"

Head Librarian: "Umm, well, I'm sorry, Bob, but, you know, with all our, umm, budget and staffing problems—but I don't have to tell *you* about *that*—I mean it looks all right now, umm, but who knows what might happen any day, that we won't be able to, umm, send as many people to ALA as we'd like this year. You know, of course, Bob, that we'd like to let, umm, *everybody* go who wants to go. But, I'm afraid, this year, Bob, you won't be able to, umm, go."

Bob: "Sheesh."

Wouldn't it be better to use some unchallengeable yardstick to help you make your decision? To an irate employee, wouldn't you rather tender a decision based on quantitative techniques, demonstrating conclusively, with objective criteria, why he or she can't go?

Utter cutter

Quantitative techniques? You probably thought those things were the domain of library science Ph.Ds and professors, who were careful to make them incompre-

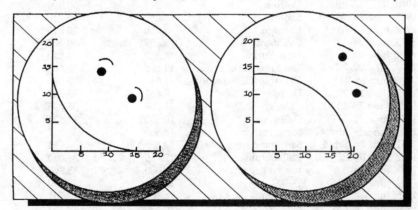

Fig. 1A. Staff member can go to conference.   Fig. 1B. Staff member cannot go to conference.

hensible to the ordinary librarian. In general, I agree with you. I'm not sure, for instance, that the Cutter Scree Test for Estimating the Number of Meaningful Factors in Determining Who Can Go to Library Conferences (see Figs. 1A and 1B) is at all conclusive. Though it is a favorite of ARL and ASIS, a number of questions about this test—sampling frame, coding scheme, statistical assumptions, etc.— have yet to be resolved.

The most useful quantitative techniques are the most accessible ones, the ones that are immediately understood by both employee and decision maker. If you can add and subtract, you can use the Library Conference Decision Module, first developed by a joint ARL/ASIS task force and then discarded when it became clear that it was effective and easy to use.

Lies don't figure

The beauty of the Library Conference Decision Module is its simplicity. Just fill in the blanks of the data sheet (see Fig. 2) and add up the scores. The employees with the highest positive scores win. I believe you will find that the most deserving employees get the highest scores. The undeserving will be so stunned by your rationale they will be unable to question the fairness of your procedure. Contrast the following conversation with the one above:

Head Librarian: "Hi, Bob, what's up?"

Bob: "Don't 'Hi, Bob' me! I want to know why you're letting that twirp Milt Wembley and not me go to ALA!"

Head Librarian: "Bob, I'm sorry, but your numbers just don't support a trip to ALA this year."

Bob: "My numbers?"

Head Librarian: "Yes, Bob. Milt came in with a 260 to your 30 on the Library Conference Decision Module. Maybe your numbers will be better next year, Bob."

Bob: "Well, I'm disappointed, of course, but if that's what the numbers say, I really don't have much of a case. Thanks for your time and have a nice day."

Now, isn't that better?

Fig. 2. Library Conference Decision Module

Name of Supplicant: _____

1. Has Supplicant (hereafter referred to as S.) been to a conference in the last two years? Yes (–10) No (+10)
2. Has S. ever failed to turn in a written report after attending a conference? Yes (–10) No (+10)
3. If S. has ever done a conference report, has it been lifted directly from the conference program? Yes (–15) No (+10)
4. Has there ever been any suggestion that S. spends all his/her conference time in bars, ball parks, or at the beach? Yes (–30) No (+10)
5. Does S. request to go to conferences only when they are in San Francisco, New Orleans, or Honolulu? Yes (–20) No (+20)
6. Is S. willing to go to ALA Midwinter Meetings in Chicago? Yes (+40) No (–30)
7. Is S. presenting a paper at the conference? Yes (+30) No (0) If yes, will S. be reading the paper (–30) or speaking from notes (+30)?
8. Would it be a relief to have S. gone for awhile? Yes (+10) No (–10)
9. Is S. a hard worker who does whatever you ask without question and laughs at your jokes? Yes (+150) No (–150)
10. Or is S. a general pain in the butt and you'll be damned if you'll reward him/her with a conference trip? Yes (–150) No (0)

Source: Dan Clemmer, "Let the Numbers Decide!" *American Libraries,* December 1988, pp. 990–91

Grants, scholarships, and awards

MANY OPPORTUNITIES EXIST in the field of library and information science for its practitioners to obtain assistance for their research and to gain recognition for their achievements. The following list provides information on grants, scholarships, and awards given by ALA and other national associations. While 1991–1992 deadlines are given, most of these programs are ongoing.

The list could be expanded substantially, especially in the grant area, by taking into consideration the offerings of state and regional library associations, private companies, and the public sector—e.g., OCLC, the Council on Library Resources, HEA and LSCA government grants, and many commercial organizations provide funds for research. The arrangement is topical under two major headings: **grants and scholarships** (money awarded for things you are going to do); and **awards** (honors and honoraria awarded for things you have already done).

Considered topically, this list can also be viewed as a measure of what we value most in our profession. Under grants and scholarships the subheads are: **for education; for programs;** and **for publications, research, and travel.** Under awards the subheads are: **for intellectual freedom; for professional achievement; for publications and research; for service in general; for service to children and young adults; for service to special populations; for social responsibility; for special libraries;** and **for technology.**—*GME.*

Grants and scholarships

For education

AJL May K. Simon Scholarship. A $500 award for a student who intends to become a Judaica librarian. Administered by the Association of Jewish Libraries. *For more information:* AJL, 330 Seventh Ave., 21st Fl., New York, NY 10001. *Deadline for applications:* January 31, 1992. *1990 winners:* Laura Wolfson, Bat-Ami Sofer.

ALA David H. Clift Scholarship. Scholarship in the amount of $3,000 given annually to a worthy student to begin a program of library education at the graduate level. Funded by individual contributions and proceeds from the ALA President's Dance, as many scholarships as possible will be awarded, depending upon the total amount of contributed funds. Administered by the ALA Awards Committee and the ALA Office for Library Personnel Resources. *For more information:* ALA Office for Library Personnel Resources, 50 E. Huron St., Chicago, IL 60611-2795. *Deadline for applications:* December 30, 1991. *1991 winners:* Anne Marie Hudson, Margaret Mary Kulis.

ALA Louise Giles Minority Scholarship. Cash awards in the amount of $3,000 made to a worthy student who is a U.S. or Canadian citizen and is also a member of a principal minority group. Funded by individual contributions and proceeds from the ALA President's Dance, as many scholarships as possible will be awarded, depending upon the total amount of contributed funds. Administered by the ALA Awards Committee and the ALA Office for Library Personnel Resources. *For more information:* ALA Office for Library Personnel Resources, 50 E. Huron St., Chicago, IL 60611-2795. *Deadline for applications:* December 30, 1991. *1990 winners:* Judith A. Bruce, Ngoc-My Guidarelli.

ALA NMRT EBSCO Scholarship. A cash award of $1,000 for the following academic year. Applicants must be enrolled in an ALA-accredited library school and be a member of NMRT. Administered by the New Members Round Table. *For more information:* ALA Communications, 50 E. Huron St., Chicago, IL 60611-2795. *Donated by:* EBSCO Subscription Services. *Deadline for applications:* December 16, 1991. *1991 winner:* Margaret Kulis.

ALA/AASL Information Plus Continuing Education Scholarship. This scholarship provides financial assistance for the continuing education and professional development of a school library media specialist, supervisor, or educator. The $500 grant will enable an AASL member to attend an ALA or AASL pre- or postconference or an ALA- or AASL-sponsored regional workshop. Administered by the ALA American Association of School Librarians. *For more information:* ALA/ AASL, 50 E. Huron St., Chicago, IL 60611-2795. *Donated by:* Information Plus. *Deadline for applications:* February 1, 1992. *1991 winner:* Elinor Maureen White.

ALA/AASL *School Librarian's Workshop* Scholarship. An annual grant of $2,500 to provide financial assistance for the education of persons who plan to become school library media specialists working at the preschool, elementary, or secondary levels in public or private educational settings. Administered by the ALA American Association of School Librarians. *For more information:* ALA/AASL, 50 E. Huron St., Chicago, IL 60611-2795. *Donated by:* Library Learning Resources Co. *Deadline for applications:* February 1, 1992. *1991 winner:* Brian P. Stafford.

ALA/ACRL Doctoral Dissertation Fellowship. An annual award of $1,000 presented to a doctoral student in the field of academic librarianship whose research indicates originality, creativity, and interest in scholarship. Administered by the ALA Association of College and Research Libraries. *For more information:* ALA/ACRL, 50 E. Huron St., Chicago, IL 60611-2795. *Donated by:* Institute for Scientific Information. *Deadline for applications:* December 2, 1991. *1991 winner:* Kamala Balaraman.

ALA/ALSC Book Wholesalers Summer Reading Grant Program. An annual award of $3,000. *For more information:* ALA/ALSC, 50 E. Huron St., Chicago, IL 60611-2795. *Deadline for applications:* December 1, 1991.

ALA/ALSC Bound to Stay Bound Books Scholarship. Two annual $3,500 scholarships established to assist individuals who wish to work in the field of library service to children. Administered by the ALA Association for Library Service to Children. *For more information:* ALA/ ALSC, 50 E. Huron St., Chicago, IL 60611-2795. *Donated by:* Bound to Stay Bound Books, Inc. *Deadline for applications:* March 1, 1992. *1990 winners:* Sara Gilbert, Karen Guma.

ALA/ALSC Frederic G. Melcher Scholarship. Two annual $5,000 scholarships established to encourage and assist people who wish to enter the field of library service to children. Administered by the ALA Association for Library Service to Children. *For more information:* ALA/ ALSC, 50 E. Huron St., Chicago, IL 60611-2795. *1990 winners:* Margaret Lynn Leach Sartin, Nancy Silverrod.

ALA/LITA CLSI Scholarship in Library and Information Technology. A cash award of $2,500 to a beginning student at the master's degree level in an ALA-accredited program in library and information science with an emphasis on library automation. Administered by the ALA Library and Information Technology Association. *For more information:* ALA/LITA, 50 E. Huron St., Chicago, IL 60611-2795. *Donated by:* CLSI, Inc. *Deadline for applications:* April 1, 1992. *1990 winner:* Susan Saul.

ALA/LITA OCLC Minority Scholarship in Library and Information Technology. A cash award of $2,500 to a student to begin or continue a master's level ALA-accredited program in library automation and the information sciences. Its purpose is to encourage a qualified member of a principal minority group with a strong commitment to the use of automation in libraries to follow a career in that field. Administered by the ALA Library and Information Technology Association. *For more information:* ALA/LITA, 50 E. Huron St., Chicago, IL 60611-2795. *Donated by:* OCLC, Inc. *Deadline for applications:* April 1, 1992.

ALISE Doctoral Students Dissertation Awards. Awards in the amount of $400 to promote the exchange of research ideas between doctoral students and established researchers. Administered by the Association for Library and Information Science Education. *For more information:* Ilse Moon, ALISE, 5623 Palm Aire Dr., Sarasota, FL 34243. *Deadline for applications:* October 1, 1991. *1991 winners:* Ruth Palmquist, Nancy Everhart.

ARMA International Scholarships. Four awards, two in the amount of $1,500 for undergraduates enrolled in a business or records information management program, and two in the amount of $750 for students working toward an associate's degree. Administered by the Association of Records Managers and Administrators. *For more information:* ARMA International, 4200 Somerset Dr., Suite 215, Prairie Village, KS 66208. *Deadline for applications:* April 1, 1992. *1991 winners:* Michele L. St. Peter, Barbara Nixon, Janet Nelson, and Yu Kong Chow.

ASIS ISI Information Science Doctoral Dissertation Scholarship. To support dissertation research in information science. Administered by the American Society for Information Science. *For more information:* ASIS, 8720 Georgia Ave., Suite 501, Silver Spring, MD 20910. *Deadline for applications:* July 1, 1992. *1990 winner:* Cynthia Lopata.

Beta Phi Mu Frank B. Sessa Scholarship. Award in the amount of $750 for continuing education for a Beta Phi Mu member. Administered by the Beta Phi Mu International Library Science Honor Society. *For more information:* Beta Phi Mu, School of Library and Information Science, University of Pittsburgh, Pittsburgh, PA 15260. *Deadline for applications:* March 1, 1992. *1989 winner:* Marion T. Reid.

Beta Phi Mu Harold Lancour Scholarship. An award of $1,000 for graduate study in a foreign country related to the applicant's work or schooling. Administered by Beta Phi Mu International Library Science Honor Society. *For more information:* Beta Phi Mu, University of Pittsburgh SLIS, Pittsburgh, PA 15260. *Deadline for applications:* March 1, 1992. *1990 winner:* Maureen White.

Beta Phi Mu Sarah Rebecca Reed Scholarship. Award in the amount of $1,500 for study at an ALA-accredited library school. Administered by the Beta Phi Mu International Library Science Honor Society. *For more information:* Beta Phi Mu, School of Library and Information Science, University of Pittsburgh, Pittsburgh, PA 15260. *Deadline for applications:* March 1, 1992. *1990 winner:* Mary Colleen Deigman.

CALA Sheila Suen Lai Scholarship of Library and Information Science. An award of $500 for students of Chinese heritage to promote graduate studies in library and information science. Administered by the Chinese-American Librarians Association. *For more information:* CALA, Auraria Library, Lawrence at 11 St., Denver, CO 80204. *1990 winner:* Jan Elmer.

CLA Dafoe Scholarship. An award of $1,750 (Can.) for a Canadian citizen or landed immigrant to attend an accredited Canadian library school. Administered by the Canadian Library Association. *For more information:* CLA, 200 Elgin St., Ottawa, Ontario K2P 1L5, Canada. *Deadline for applications:* May 1, 1992. *1990 winner:* Mary Boldrini.

CLA H.W. Wilson Company Scholarship. An award in the amount of $2,000 (Can.) available to a Canadian citizen or landed immigrant for pursuit of studies at an accredited Canadian library school. Administered by the Canadian Library Association. *For more information:* CLA, 200 Elgin St., Ottawa, Ontario K2P 1L5, Canada. *Donated by:* H.W. Wilson Co. *Deadline for applications:* May 1, 1992. *1990 winner:* Janice Laduke.

CLA Howard V. Phalin-World Book Graduate Scholarship in Library Science. A scholarship in the amount of $2,500 (Can.) for a Canadian citizen or landed immigrant to attend an accredited library school in Canada or the United States. Administered by the Canadian Library Association. *For more information:* CLA, 200 Elgin St., Ottawa, Ontario K2P 1L5, Canada. *Donated by:* World Book, Inc. *Deadline for applications:* May 1, 1992. *1990 winner:* Lis Nygaard.

CLA Rev. Andrew L. Bouwhuis Scholarship. A cash award of $1,500 for a student with a B.A. degree who has been accepted in an accredited library school. The award is granted on a basis of financial need. Administered by the Catholic Library Association. *For more information:* CLA, 461 W. Lancaster Ave., Haverford, PA 19041. *Deadline for applications:* February 1, 1992. *1990 winner:* Joseph Holterman.

CLA World Book Inc. Grant. An award of $1,500 for added proficiency in school or children's librarianship through a workshop or seminar, distributed among no more than four members of the Catholic Library Association. Administered by the Catholic Library Association. *For more information:* CLA, 461 W. Lancaster Ave., Haverford, PA 19041. *Donated by:* World Book, Inc. *Deadline for applications:* February 1, 1992. *1991 winner:* Sr. Mary Elizabeth Gallagher.

MLA Continuing Education Awards. Awards of $100–$500 for MLA members to develop a knowledge of the theoretical, administrative, or technical aspects of librarianship. More than one may be offered in a year, and they may be used either for MLA courses or for other CE activities. Administered by the Medical Library Association. *For more information:* MLA, 6 N. Michigan Ave., Suite 300, Chicago, IL 60602. *Deadline for applications:* February 1 and October 1, 1992. *1990 winner:* Sandra K. Parker.

MLA Doctoral Fellowship. A fellowship in the amount of $1,000 to foster and encourage superior students to conduct doctoral work in an area of medical librarianship and to provide support to individuals who have been admitted to a candidacy. The award may not be used for tuition. Administered by the Medical Library Association. *For more information:* MLA, 6 N. Michigan Ave., Suite 300, Chicago, IL 60602. *Donated by:* Institute for Scientific Information. *Deadline for applications:* February 1, 1992. *1990 winner:* Cheryl Dee.

MLA Scholarship. A $2,000 award for graduate study in medical librarianship. Administered by the Medical Library Association. *For more information:* MLA, 6 N. Michigan Ave., Suite 300, Chicago, IL 60602. *Deadline for applications:* February 1, 1992. *1990 winner:* Reeta Sinha.

MLA Scholarship for Minority Students. A $2,000 award for a minority student intending to study medical librarianship and who is entering an ALA-accredited library school. Administered by the Medical Library Association. *For more information:* MLA, 6 N. Michigan Ave., Suite 300, Chicago, IL 60602. *Deadline for applications:* February 1, 1992. *1990 winner:* Judith V. Rogers.

SLA Affirmative Action Scholarship. A $6,000 scholarship for a member of a minority group pursuing graduate study leading to an MLS in the United States or Canada. Administered by the Special Libraries Association. *For more information:* SLA, 1700 18th St., N.W., Washington, DC 20009. *Deadline for applications:* October 31, 1991. *1990 winner:* Lilia Fernandez.

SLA ISI Scholarship. A $1,000 award for beginning doctoral candidates in library or information science. Administered by the Special Libraries Association. *For more information:* SLA, 1700 18th St., N.W., Washington, DC 20009. *Donated by:* Institute for Scientific Information. *Deadline for applications:* October 31, 1991.

SLA Mary Adeline Connor Professional Development Scholarship. One or more awards, not to exceed $6,000, for mid-career special librarians to assist with a post-MLS certificate or degree programs in any subject area, technological skills, or managerial expertise relevant to the applicant's career needs and goals in special librarianship. May include travel assistance. *For more information:* SLA, 1700 18th St., N.W., Washington, DC 20009. *Donated by:* Mary Adeline Connor. *Deadline for applications:* October 31, 1991.

SLA Plenum Scholarship. An award in the amount of $1,000 for graduate study leading to a doctorate in library and information science. Administered by the Special Libraries Association. *For more information:* SLA, 1700 18th St., N.W., Washington, DC 20009. *Donated by:* Plenum Publishing Corp. *Deadline for applications:* October 31, 1991. *1990 winner:* Kathleen Eisenbeis.

SLA Scholarships. A total of $6,000 for students with financial need who show potential for special librarianship. Administered by the Special Libraries Association. *For more information:* SLA, 1700 18th St., N.W., Washington, DC 20009. *Deadline for applications:* October 31, 1991. *1990 winners:* Laura Lennertz, Nancy Poppleton, Edward Surges.

For programs

ALA Grolier National Library Week Grant. An annual $2,000 cash award presented for a cooperative project among libraries of any type and a local or state organization for a public relations program supporting the goals of National Library Week to be conducted in the year in which the grant is presented. Administered by the ALA National Library Week Committee. *For more information:* ALA Public Information Office, 50 E. Huron St., Chicago, IL 60611. *Donated by:* Grolier Educational Corporation. *Deadline for applications:* December 1, 1991. *1990 winners:* Colorado Educational Media Association, Colorado Library Association, and Colorado State Library.

ALA H.W. Wilson Library Staff Development Grant. A cash grant of $2,500 awarded to a library organization to assist it in a current or proposed program designed to further the goals and objectives of the library organization. The criteria for selection of a grant winner include: clearly defined documentation of need in relation to staff development, a well-defined program to meet the organization's needs, and the commitment and demonstrated ability to implement the program. Administered by the American Library Association Awards Committee. *For more information:* JoAn S. Segal, ALA, 50 E. Huron St., Chicago, IL 60611-2795. *Donated by:* H.W. Wilson Co. *Deadline for applications:* 1991. *1991 winner:* Janet Steiner, South Central Research Library Council, for *Good Supervisors, Good Employees: Training for Teamwork.*

ALA World Book-ALA Goal Awards. Two annual grants of $5,000 to encourage and advance the development of public, academic, and/or school library service and librarianship through recognition and support of programs that implement the goals and objectives of ALA. Units of the American Library Association eligible for grants under the award are: ALA committees, ALA joint committees, ALA divisions, ALA round tables, and ALA chapters. Applications for grants from units within a division must be approved by the governing board of the division. The proposals are judged by a jury of the American Library Association Awards Committee. *For more information:* JoAn S. Segal, ALA, 50 E. Huron St., Chicago, IL 60611-2795. *Donated by:* World Book, Inc. *Deadline for applications:* 1992. *1991 winners:* ALA PIO/Chapter Relations Committee/ALA President-Elect Proposal, "The Right to Know: A United Voice."

ALA/AASL ABC/CLIO Leadership Development Award. An annual grant of $1,750 to enable an AASL Affiliate Organization to plan and implement a leadership development program.

3

Administered by the ALA American Association of School Librarians. *For more information:* ALA/ AASL, 50 E. Huron St., Chicago, IL 60611-2795. *Donated by:* ABC/CLIO, Inc. *Deadline for applications:* February 1, 1992. *1991 winner:* South Dakota School Library Media Association.

ALA/RASD Facts on File Grant. A cash grant of up to $1,000 awarded to a library for imaginative programming that would make current affairs more meaningful to an adult audience. Programs, bibliographies, pamphlets, and innovative approaches of all types and in all media qualify. Administered by the ALA Reference and Adult Services Division. *For more information:* ALA/RASD, 50 E. Huron St., Chicago, IL 60611-2795. *Donated by:* Facts on File, Inc. *Deadline for applications:* December 15, 1991. *1991 winner:* Gale Borden PL District, Elgin, Ill.

ALA/YASD Frances Henne *Voice of Youth Advocates* Research Grant. An annual grant of $500 to provide seed money for small-scale projects encouraging significant research that will have an influence on library service to young adults. Applicants must be a member of YASD. Grants will not be given for research leading to a degree. Administered by the ALA Young Adult Services Division. *For more information:* ALA/YASD, 50 E. Huron St., Chicago, IL 60611-2795. *Donated by: Voice of Youth Advocates (VOYA). Deadline for applications:* December 14, 1991. *1990 winners:* Lesley S.J. Farmer, Marilyn Kay Maynard.

ARLIS/NA Chadwyck-Healey Professional Development Award. A grant of $500 for session moderators, speakers, and panelists at the ARLIS/NA annual conference. Administered by the Art Libraries Society of North America. *For more information:* ARLIS/NA, 3900 E. Timrod St., Tucson, AZ 85711. *Donated by:* Chadwyck-Healey. *Deadline for applications:* December 15, 1991.

CLA John T. Corrigan Memorial Award. A $1,000 stipend for programs initiated by CLA chapters to encourage and foster the work of the chapter. Administered by the Catholic Library Association. *For more information:* CLA, 461 W. Lancaster Ave., Haverford, PA 19041. *Deadline for applications:* February 1, 1992. *1991 winners:* Bishop Bryne Chapter, New England Chapter.

MLA Janet Doe Lectureship. An award of $250 to support a lecture in either the history or the philosophy of medical librarianship presented at the MLA annual meeting. Administered by the Medical Library Association. *For more information:* MLA, 6 N. Michigan Ave., Suite 300, Chicago, IL 60602. *Deadline for applications:* October 1, 1992. *1990 winner:* Ruth Holst.

MLA John P. McGovern Award Lectureship. For a significant national or international figure to speak on a topic of importance to health sciences librarianship at the MLA annual meeting. Administered by the Medical Library Association. *For more information:* MLA, 6 N. Michigan Ave., Suite 300, Chicago, IL 60602. *1990 winner:* Nicholas Negroponte.

MLA NLM Joseph Leiter Lectureship. For a lecture on biomedical communications presented every other year at the MLA annual meeting and in alternate years at the National Library of Medicine. Administered by the Medical Library Association. *For more information:* MLA, 6 N. Michigan Ave., Suite 300, Chicago, IL 60602. *1990 winner:* Michael E. DeBakey, NLM.

For publications, research, and travel

AJL Doris Orenstein Memorial Fund. For first-time attendees at the AJL conference. Administered by the Association of Jewish Libraries. *For more information:* AJL, 330 Seventh Ave., 21st Fl., New York, NY 10001. *Deadline for applications:* February 28, 1992. *1990 winner:* Marina Lasch.

ALA 3M/NMRT Professional Development Grant. This grant is intended to encourage professional development and participation by new librarians in national ALA and NMRT activities. Cash awards are presented to librarians to attend an ALA Annual Conference. The recipients must be current members of ALA and the New Members Round Table. Administered by the ALA New Members Round Table. *For more information:* ALA Communications, 50 E. Huron St., Chicago, IL 60611-2795. *Deadline for applications:* November 15, 1991. *1991 winners:* Joni Gomez, Glendora Johnson-Cooper, Ann L. Pinnack.

ALA Bogle International Library Travel Fund. A $500 award to assist ALA members to attend their first international library conference. Administered by the ALA International Relations Committee. *For more information:* Robert P. Doyle, ALA, 50 E. Huron St., Chicago, IL 60611-2795. *Deadline for applications:* December 1, 1991. *1991 winner:* Connie Wu.

ALA Carnegie Reading List Awards. These awards are granted to official units of the American Library Association, such as divisions, committees, or round tables. They are based on a special fund established by Andrew Carnegie in 1902 and are "to be applied to the preparation and publication of such reading lists, indexes, and other bibliographical and library aids as will be especially useful in the circulating libraries of this country." Administered by the ALA Publications Committee. *Deadline for applications:* Accepted throughout the year. *Send nominations to:* ALA Publishing, 50 E. Huron St., Chicago, IL 60611-2795. *1991 winners:* Coretta Scott King Award Task Force, for *Coretta Scott King Awards, 1969-1991*; Association for Library Service to Children, for *How to Raise a Reader*.

ALA Carroll Preston Baber Research Grant. An annual cash reward of up to $10,000 and a citation presented to one or more librarians or library educators who will conduct innovative research that could lead to an improvement in services to any specified group(s) of people. Administered by a jury of the American Library Association Awards Committee. *For more information:* Mary Jo Lynch, ALA Office for Research, 50 E. Huron St., Chicago, IL 60611-2795. *Donated by:* Eric R. Baber. *Deadline for applications:* March 1, 1991. *1991 winner:* Delia Neuman.

ALA Herbert W. Putnam Honor Award. An award of $500 presented as a grant-in-aid to an American librarian of outstanding ability for travel, writing, or any other use that might improve his or her service to the library profession or to society. Administered by a jury of the American Library Association Awards Committee. *Made possible by:* Herbert W. Putnam Honor Fund. *Send nominations to:* JoAn S. Segal, ALA, 50 E. Huron St., Chicago, IL 60611-2795.

ALA Readex/GODORT Catharine J. Reynolds Grant. An annual award of $2,000 for grants to documents librarians to travel and/or study in the field of documents librarianship or in an area of study that will directly benefit their performance as a documents librarian. Administered by the ALA Government Documents Round Table. *For more information:* ALA, 50 E. Huron St., Chicago, IL 60611-2795. *Donated by:* Readex Corporation. *Deadline for applications:* December 15, 1991. *1991 winners:* Suzanne Clark, John Shuler, Laura Lee Carter, and Daniel O'Mahony.

ALA Shirley Olofson Memorial Award. An annual cash award made to individuals to attend their second ALA Annual Conference. Recipients must be members of ALA and be potential or current members of NMRT. Administered by the ALA New Members Round Table. *For more information:* ALA Communications, 50 E. Huron St., Chicago, IL 60611-2795. *Deadline for applications:* December 1, 1991. *1991 winner:* Deb Tuma Church.

ALA Whitney-Carnegie Awards. These awards are granted to individuals for preparation of guides to research resources. The aids must be aimed at a scholarly audience but have general applicability. $5,000 is the maximum amount awarded. The amounts and number of awards are at the discretion of the ALA Publishing Committee and vary from year to year. Preference is given to projects for which the American Library Association can serve as publisher. Administered by the ALA Publishing Committee. *Deadline for applications:* Accepted throughout the year. *Send nominations to:* ALA Publishing, 50 E. Huron St., Chicago, IL 60611-2795. *1990 winners:* Phyllis Van Orden; Frederick and Joann Koelln Frankena; James H. Sweetland; Lauri Johnson and Sally Smith; Julia Rholes; J. Gormly Miller; David Pfeiffer; Sharon Rush, Betty Taylor, and Robert J. Munro; Helaine Selin; Anne Dickason; Nancy O'Brien; Ellen Mazur Thomson.

ALA/AASL Frances Henne Award. An annual grant of $1,250 to enable a school library media specialist with five or fewer years in the profession to attend an AASL regional conference or ALA Annual Conference. Administered by the ALA American Association of School Librarians. *For more information:* ALA/AASL, 50 E. Huron St., Chicago, IL 60611-2795. *Donated by:* R.R. Bowker Co. *Deadline for applications:* February 1, 1992. *1991 winner:* David W. Calender.

ALA/ACRL Martinus Nijhoff International West European Specialist Study Grant. An annual grant for an ALA member to study some aspect of Western European studies, librarianship, or the book trade. The grant covers air travel to and from Europe, transportation in Europe, and lodging and board for no more than fourteen consecutive days. A maximum amount of 10,000 Dutch guilders is awarded per year. Administered by the Western European Specialists Section of the ALA Association of College and Research Libraries. *For more information:* ALA/ACRL, 50 E. Huron St., Chicago, IL 60611-2795. *Donated by:* Martinus Nijhoff International. *Deadline for applications:* December 2, 1991. *1991 winner:* Nancy S. Reinhardt.

ALA/ACRL Samuel Lazerow Fellowship for Research in Acquisitions or Technical Services. An annual award of $1,000 established to foster advances in acquisitions or technical services by providing librarians in those fields a fellowship. Administered by the ALA Association of College and Research Libraries. *For more information:* ALA/ACRL, 50 E. Huron St., Chicago, IL 60611-2795. *Donated by:* Institute for Scientific Information. *Deadline for applications:* December 2, 1991. *1990 winner:* Terence K. Huwe.

ALA/ALSC Putnam & Grosset Book Group Award. Four annual $600 awards presented to four children's librarians to enable them to attend ALA Annual Conference. The recipients must be members of ALSC, work directly with children, have one to ten years of library experience, and never have attended an ALA Annual Conference. Administered by the ALA Association for Library Service to Children. *For more information:* ALA/ALSC, 50 E. Huron St., Chicago, IL 60611-2795. *Donated by:* Putnam & Grosset Book Group. *Deadline for applications:* December 1, 1991. *1991 winners:* Eleanor A. Brust, Karen Quinn-Wisniewski, Sara Wright Ashworth, and Cathleen A. Towey.

ALA/ALTA/Gale Outstanding Trustee Conference Grant. A grant of $750 each to two trustees, enabling their first-time attendance at the ALA Annual Conference. The grant is awarded to two public library trustees who have demonstrated qualitative interests and efforts in supportive service to the local public library. Administered by the ALA American Library Trustee Association. *For more information:* ALA/ALTA, 50 E. Huron St., Chicago, IL 60611-2795. *Donated by:* Gale Research Co. *Deadline for applications:* December 1, 1991. *1991 winner:* Suzan G. Allen.

ALA/PLA CLSI International Studies Award. An award of up to $5,000 and a citation presented to a librarian with a demonstrated interest in and commitment to furthering international public library cooperation. The purpose of the award is to support a study tour abroad that will stimulate interest in the development of an international study project with public libraries outside the United States and enable a staff member of a U.S. public library to carry out an international study project that will improve international understanding among public libraries worldwide. Administered by the ALA Public Library Association. *For more information:* ALA/PLA, 50 E. Huron St., Chicago, IL 60611-2795. *Donated by:* CLSI, Inc. *Deadline for applications:* December 1, 1991. *1990 winner:* Debra J. Miller.

ALA/YASD Baker & Taylor Conference Grants. Two annual grants of $1,000 each awarded to young adult librarians who work directly with young adults in either a public library or a school library, to enable them to attend the ALA Annual Conference. Candidates must be members of YASD, have 1-10 years of library experience, and never have attended an ALA Annual Conference. Administered by the ALA Young Adult Services Division. *For more information:* ALA/YASD, 50 E. Huron St., Chicago, IL 60611-2795. *Donated by:* Baker & Taylor Books. *Deadline for applications:* December 14, 1991. *1991 winners:* Nancy E. Strong, Miriam Temsky.

ALISE Jane Anne Hannigan Research Award. An award of $500 for research on any aspect of library or information science, including children's literature or work with children and youth. Only untenured faculty or students in doctoral programs are eligible. Administered by the Association for Library and Information Science Education. *For more information:* Ilse Moon, ALISE, 5623 Palm Aire Dr., Sarasota, FL 34243. *Donated by:* Sheila Intner and Kaye Vandergrift from royalties on their festschrift, *Library Education and Leadership: Essays in Honor of Jane Anne Hannigan* (Scarecrow). *Deadline for applications:* October 1, 1991. *1991 winner:* Holly Willett.

ALISE Research Awards. A cash award of $2,500 for a project that reflects ALISE goals and objectives. Administered by the Association for Library and Information Science Education. *For more information:* Ilse Moon, ALISE, 5623 Palm Aire Dr., Sarasota, FL 34243. *Deadline for applications:* October 1, 1991. *1991 winner:* Patricia Reeling.

ARLIS/NA G.K. Hall Conference Attendance Award. A grant of $400 for committee members, group moderators, and chapter officers at the ARLIS/NA annual conference to help finance conference expenses. Administered by the Art Libraries Society of North America. *For more information:* ARLIS/NA, 3900 E. Timrod St., Tucson, AZ 85711. *Donated by:* G.K. Hall Co. *Deadline for applications:* December 15, 1991.

ARLIS/NA Léonce Laget Award. An award of $1,000 to help finance expenses associated with traveling to the ARLIS/NA Conference. All art information professionals who reside outside North America are eligible. Administered by the Art Libraries Society of North America. *For more information:* ARLIS/NA, 3900 E. Timrod St., Tucson, AZ 85711. *Donated by:* Librairie Léonce Laget. *Deadline for applications:* December 15, 1991.

ARLIS/NA Norman Ross Travel Award. A travel award of $500 to an ARLIS/NA member who has never attended an ARLIS/NA conference. Administered by the Art Libraries Society of North America. *For more information:* ARLIS/NA, 3900 E. Timrod St., Tucson, AZ 85711. *Donated by:* Norman Ross Publishing Co. *Deadline for applications:* December 15, 1991.

MLA Cunningham Memorial International Fellowship. A six-month grant of $3,500 and travel expenses in the United States and Canada for a foreign librarian. Administered by the

Medical Library Association. *For more information:* MLA, 6 N. Michigan Ave., Suite 300, Chicago, IL 60602. *1990 winner:* Sally Anne Montserin.

MLA Research, Development, and Demonstration Projects Grants. Awards of $100–$500 to support projects that will promote excellence in the field of health sciences librarianship. Grants will not be given to support an activity that is operational in nature or has only local usefulness. Administered by the Medical Library Association. *For more information:* MLA, 6 N. Michigan Ave., Suite 300, Chicago, IL 60602. *Deadline for applications:* February 1, October 1, 1992. *1990 winners:* Paul Wrynn, Van Afes, Diane Schwartz.

MLA Walter Gerboth Award. A cash award of $500 to support research in the first five years as a music librarian. Administered by the Music Library Association. *For more information:* MLA, Box 487, Canton, MA 02021. *Deadline for applications:* October 31, 1991. *1991 winner:* Alan A. Green.

SAA Colonial Dames Scholarship. Covers travel for two archivists to attend two meetings of the Modern Archives Institute. Administered by the Society of American Archivists. *For more information:* SAA, 600 S. Federal St., Suite 504, Chicago, IL 60605. *Donated by:* Colonial Dames of America. *Deadline for applications:* April 15, 1992. *1990 winners:* Donna Longo DiMichele, Sandra Macias.

SAA Oliver Wendell Holmes Award. This award allows overseas archivists, already in the United States or Canada for training, to augment their visit by traveling to other archival institutions, national or regional archival meetings, or archival institutes. Administered by the Society of American Archivists. *For more information:* SAA, 600 S. Federal St., Suite 504, Chicago, IL 60605. *1990 winner:* Samuel Njovana.

Awards

For intellectual freedom

ALA John Phillip Immroth Memorial Award for Intellectual Freedom. An annual award consisting of $500 and a citation presented to an intellectual freedom fighter who has made a notable contribution to intellectual freedom and demonstrated remarkable personal courage. Administered by the ALA Intellectual Freedom Round Table. *For more information:* ALA Office for Intellectual Freedom, 50 E. Huron St., Chicago, IL 60611-2795. *Deadline for applications:* December 1, 1991. *1991 winner:* Christopher Merrett.

ALA State Program Award. An annual award consisting of $1,000 and a citation presented to the state intellectual freedom committee that has implemented the most successful and creative state IFC project during the calendar year. Administered by the ALA Intellectual Freedom Round Table. *For more information:* ALA Office for Intellectual Freedom, 50 E. Huron St., Chicago, IL 60611-2795. *Donated by:* Social Issues Resources Series, Inc. *Deadline for applications:* December 1, 1991. *1991 winner:* Oregon Intellectual Freedom Clearinghouse.

ALA/AASL/SIRS Intellectual Freedom Award. An annual award consisting of $2,000 and an engraved plaque presented to a school library media specialist at any level who has upheld the principles of intellectual freedom as set forth in *Policies and Procedures for Selection of Instructional Materials.* The award also provides a grant of $1,000 and a framed certificate to a school library media center designated by the recipient. Administered by the ALA American Association of School Librarians. *For more information:* ALA/AASL, 50 E. Huron St., Chicago, IL 60611-2795. *Donated by:* Social Issues Resources Series, Inc. *Deadline for applications:* February 1, 1992. *1991 winner:* Neva Thompson.

For professional achievement

ALA CIS/GODORT *Documents to the People* Award. An annual award, consisting of a citation of achievement and a cash stipend of $2,000 to be used to promote professional advancement in the field of librarianship. The award is presented to the individual and/or library, organization, or other appropriate noncommercial group that has most effectively encouraged the use of government documents and information in support of library services. Administered by the ALA Government Documents Round Table. *For more information:* ALA, 50 E. Huron St., Chicago,

IL 60611-2795. *Donated by:* Congressional Information Service, Inc. *Deadline for applications:* December 15, 1991. *1991 winner:* Mary Redmond.

ALA Federal Librarians Achievement Award. An annual citation and gift for leadership or achievement in the promotion of library and information science in the federal community. Administered by the ALA Federal Librarians Round Table. *For more information:* Anne Heanue, ALA Washington Office, 110 Maryland Ave., N.E., Washington, DC 20002. *Deadline for applications:* December 15, 1991. *1990 winner:* Elisabeth S. Knauff.

ALA Gale Research Company Financial Development Award. An annual award of $2,500 and a certificate presented to a library organization that exhibited meritorious achievement in carrying out a library financial development project to secure new funding resources for a public or academic library entity. Administered by the American Library Association Awards Committee. *For more information:* JoAn S. Segal, ALA, 50 E. Huron St., Chicago, IL 60611-2795. *Donated by:* Gale Research Company. *Deadline for applications:* December 15, 1991. *1991 winner:* Bud Werner Memorial Library, Steamboat Springs, Colo.

ALA Hugh C. Atkinson Memorial Award. An annual award consisting of an unrestricted cash prize and a plaque established to honor the life and accomplishments of Hugh C. Atkinson, one of the major innovators in modern librarianship, and to recognize outstanding achievement (including risk-taking) by academic librarians that has contributed significantly to improvements in the area of library automation, library management, and/or library development or research. Nominees must be librarians employed in a university, college, or community college library in the year prior to application for the award and must have a minimum of five years of professional experience in an academic library. The award is jointly sponsored by the ALA Association of College and Research Libraries, the Library Administration and Management Association, and the Association for Library Collections and Technical Services. It is funded by an endowment created by divisional, individual, and vendor contributions given in memory of Hugh C. Atkinson. *For more information:* ALA/ACRL, 50 E. Huron St., Chicago, IL 60611-2795. *Deadline for applications:* December 1, 1991. *1991 winner:* Donald E. Riggs.

ALA James Bennett Childs Award. An annual award, consisting of an engraved plaque, presented to a librarian or other individual for distinguished contributions to documents librarianship. Administered by the ALA Government Documents Round Table. *For more information:* ALA, 50 E. Huron St., Chicago, IL 60611-2795. *Deadline for applications:* December 15, 1991. *1990 winner:* Judith S. Rowe.

ALA John Ames Humphry/Forest Press Award. The $1,000 award is made to a librarian or other person who has made significant contributions to international librarianship. Primary consideration will be given to contributions in the field of classification and subject analysis, and to work in Third World countries, but the award is not limited to these areas. Administered by the ALA International Relations Committee. *For more information:* Robert P. Doyle, ALA, 50 E. Huron St., Chicago, IL 60611-2795. *Donated by:* Forest Press, Inc. *Deadline for applications:* December 1, 1991. *1991 winner:* Hwa-Wei Lee.

ALA Kohlstedt Exhibit Award. An annual citation recognizing the best single, multiple, and island booth displays at ALA Annual Conference. The award is named after Donald W. Kohlstedt in recognition of his hard work for better library conference exhibits. Six librarians judge the exhibits on the first day they are open. Administered by a committee of the ALA Exhibits Round Table. *For more information:* Barbara A. Macikas, ALA, 50 E. Huron St., Chicago, IL 60611-2795. *1990 winners:* Storey/Garden Way Publishers, H.W. Wilson Co., Highsmith.

ALA MAGERT Honors Award. A citation and cash award of $25 to recognize outstanding contributions by a MAGERT member to map librarianship, MAGERT, or a specific MAGERT project. Administered by the ALA Map and Geography Round Table. *For more information:* ALA, 50 E. Huron St., Chicago, IL 60611-2795. *Deadline for applications:* December 1, 1991. *1990 winner:* Alice C. Hudson.

ALA Melvil Dewey Medal. An engraved medal and a citation presented annually to an individual or a group for recent creative professional achievement of a high order, particularly in those fields in which Melvil Dewey was actively interested, notably: library management, library training, cataloging and classification, and the tools and techniques of librarianship. Administered by the American Library Association Awards Committee. *For more information:* JoAn S. Segal, ALA, 50 E. Huron St., Chicago, IL 60611-2795. *Donated by:* Forest Press, Inc. *Deadline for applications:* December 1, 1991. *1991 winner:* Lucia Rather.

ALA/ACRL Academic or Research Librarian of the Year Award. An annual award of $3,000 presented to the individual who has made an outstanding national or international contribution to academic and research librarianship and library development. Administered by a committee of the ALA Association of College and Research Libraries. *For more information:* ALA/ACRL, 50 E. Huron St., Chicago, IL 60611-2795. *Donated by:* Baker & Taylor Books. *Deadline for applications:* December 2, 1991. *1991 winner:* Richard DeGennaro.

ALA/ACRL Community College Learning Resources Achievement Awards. Two annual awards to recognize significant achievement in the areas of program development and leadership or community service. Individuals or groups from two-year institutions, as well as the two-year institutions themselves, are eligible to receive the awards, which are printed citations. Administered by the Community and Junior College Libraries Section of the ALA Association of College and Research Libraries. *For more information:* ALA/ACRL, 50 E. Huron St., Chicago, IL 60611-2795. *Deadline for applications:* December 2, 1991. *1991 winners:* Jimmie Anne Nourse and Rudy Widman; James O. Wallace.

ALA/ACRL Miriam Dudley Bibliographic Instruction Librarian of the Year Award. An annual award of $1,000 presented to a librarian who has made an especially significant contribution to the advancement of bibliographic instruction. Administered by the Bibliographic Instruction Section of the ALA Association of College and Research Libraries. *For more information:* ALA/ACRL, 50 E. Huron St., Chicago, IL 60611-2795. *Donated by:* Mountainside Publishing Co., on behalf of *Research Strategies. Deadline for applications:* December 2, 1991. *1991 winner:* Carla Stoffle.

ALA/ALCTS Esther J. Piercy Award. An annual citation presented in recognition of a contribution to librarianship in the field of technical services by a librarian with not more than ten years of professional experience who has shown outstanding promise for continuing contributions and leadership in any of the fields comprising technical services through leadership, methodology, publication, or research. Administered by the ALA Association for Library Collections and Technical Services. *For more information:* ALA/ALCTS, 50 E. Huron St., Chicago, IL 60611-2795. *Deadline for applications:* December 2, 1991. *1991 winner:* Carol Pitts Hawks.

ALA/ALCTS Margaret Mann Citation. An annual citation made to a cataloger or classifier, not necessarily an American, for outstanding professional achievement in cataloging or classification, either through publication of significant professional literature, participation in professional cataloging associations, introduction of new techniques of recognized importance, or outstanding work in the area of teaching within the past five years. Administered by the Cataloging and Classification Section of the ALA Association for Library Collections and Technical Services. *For more information:* ALA/ALCTS, 50 E. Huron St., Chicago, IL 60611-2795. *Deadline for applications:* December 2, 1991. *1991 winner:* Margaret F. Maxwell.

ALA/ALCTS/Bowker/Ulrich's Serials Librarianship Award. An annual award consisting of a citation and a $1,500 cash award for distinguished contributions to serials librarianship within the previous three years, demonstrated by such activities as leadership in serials-related activities, through participation in professional associations and/or library education programs, contributions to the body of serials literature, conducting research in the area of serials, development of tools or methods to enhance access to or management of serials, or other advances leading to a better understanding of the field of serials. Administered by the Serials Section of the ALA Association for Library Collections and Technical Services. *For more information:* ALA/ALCTS, 50 E. Huron St., Chicago, IL 60611-2795. *Donated by:* R.R. Bowker Co. *Deadline for applications:* December 2, 1991. *1991 winners:* Deana L. Astle, Charles A. Hamaker.

ALA/ASCLA Exceptional Achievement Award. A citation presented to recognize leadership and achievement in the following areas of activity: consulting, multitype library cooperation, and state library development. The award recognizes sustained activity that has been characterized by professional growth and effectiveness, and has enhanced the status of these areas of activity. Administered by the ALA Association of Specialized and Cooperative Library Agencies. *For more information:* ALA/ASCLA, 50 E. Huron St., Chicago, IL 60611-2795. *Deadline for applications:* December 1, 1991. *1991 winners:* William G. Asp, Barratt Wilkins.

ALA/LAMA AIA Library Buildings Award Program. An award presented by the American Institute of Architects and the ALA Library Administration and Management Association to encourage excellence in the architectural design and planning of libraries. Awards are made to all types of libraries. Citations are presented to the winning architectural firms and to libraries. *For more information:* ALA/LAMA, 50 E. Huron St., Chicago, IL 60611-2795. *Deadline for applications:*

October 1, 1991. *1991 winners:* Las Vegas Clark County (Nev.) Library and Discovery Museum; Bucks County (Pa.) Free Library and District Center; Stillwater (Minn.) Public Library; Humboldt Library, Berlin; Headquarters Library of the Clayton County (Ga.) Library System; Buckhead Branch Library, Atlanta.

ALA/LAMA John Cotton Dana Public Relations Awards. An annual citation made to libraries or library organizations of all types submitting materials representing the year's public relations program or a special project. Sponsored jointly by the H.W. Wilson Company and the Public Relations Section of the ALA Library Administration and Management Association. *For more information:* H.W. Wilson Company, 950 University Ave., Bronx, NY 10452-9978. *Deadline for applications:* February 3, 1992. *1991 winners:* Animal Welfare Information Center, Beltsville, Md.; Cumberland County (N.C.) PL and Information Center; Harry Spence Elementary School, La Crosse, Wisc.; Atlanta-Fulton (Ga.) PL; British Columbia Library Association; Coronado (Colo.) PL; George County (Miss.) Library; Holloway Middle School, Whitehouse, Tex.; Illinois State Library; Louisiana State University Library; Metropolitan School District, Indianapolis; Multnomah County (Ore.) Library; Nappanee (Ind.) PL; Pike's Peak Library District; Prince George's County (Md.) Library System; Spokane (Wash.) PL.

ALA/RASD Gale Research Award for Excellence in Business Librarianship. An annual award of $1,000 and a citation made to an individual in the field of business librarianship. Administered by the Business Reference and Services Section of the ALA Reference and Adult Services Division. *For more information:* ALA/RASD, 50 E. Huron St., Chicago, IL 60611-2795. *Donated by:* Gale Research, Inc. *Deadline for applications:* December 15, 1991. *1991 winner:* Gerald L. Gill.

ALA/RASD Isadore Gilbert Mudge Citation. A citation to be given at ALA Annual Conference to a person who has made a distinguished contribution to reference librarianship. The contribution may take the form of an imaginative and constructive program in a particular library; the writing of a significant book or articles in the reference field; creative and inspirational teaching of reference service; active participation in professional associations; or other noteworthy activities that stimulate reference librarians to more distinguished performance. Administered by the ALA Reference and Adult Services Division. *For more information:* ALA/RASD, 50 E. Huron St., Chicago, IL 60611-2795. *Deadline for applications:* December 15, 1991. *1991 winner:* Peter Watson-Boone.

ALISE Award for Outstanding Professional Contributions to Library and Information Science Education. Administered by the Association for Library and Information Science Education. *For more information:* Ilse Moon, ALISE, 5623 Palm Aire Dr., Sarasota, FL 34243. *Deadline for applications:* June 1, 1992. *1991 winner:* Herman Totten.

ASIS Award of Merit. For an outstanding contribution to the field of information science. Administered by the American Society for Information Science. *For more information:* ASIS, 8720 Georgia Ave., Suite 501, Silver Spring, MD 20910. *Deadline for applications:* June 1, 1992. *1990 winner:* Pauline Atherton Cochrane.

CLA/CACUL Distinguished Academic Librarian Award. Administered by the Canadian Association of College and University Libraries of the Canadian Library Association. *For more information:* CLA, 200 Elgin St., Ottawa, Ontario K2P 1L5, Canada. *Donated by:* Blackwell/North America. *Deadline for applications:* February 1, 1992. *1990 winner:* Jean Weihs.

CLA/CASLIS Award for Special Librarianship in Canada. Administered by the Canadian Association of Special Libraries and Information Services of the Canadian Library Association. *For more information:* CLA, 200 Elgin St., Ottawa, Ontario K2P 1L5, Canada. *Deadline for applications:* January 15, 1992. *1990 winner:* Georgia Ellis.

MLA Award for Excellence and Achievement in Hospital Librarianship. Awarded to an MLA member who has contributed significantly to overall distinction or leadership in hospital library administration or service, production of a definitive publication, teaching, research, advocacy, or the development or application of innovative technology related to hospital librarianship. Administered by the Medical Library Association. *For more information:* MLA, 6 N. Michigan Ave., Chicago, IL 60602. *Deadline for applications:* February 1, 1992.

MLA Estelle Brodman Award. A cash award of $500 and a certificate presented to honor both significant achievement and the potential for leadership and continuing excellence at midcareer in the area of academic health sciences librarianship. Administered by the Medical Library Association. *For more information:* MLA, 6 N. Michigan Ave., Chicago, IL 60602. *Donated by:* Irwin

H. Pizer. *Deadline for applications:* December 15, 1991. *1990 winner:* Kathryn Hoffman.

MLA Louise Darling Medal. Presented to individuals, institutions, or groups of individuals who have made significant contributions to collection development in health sciences librarianship. Administered by the Medical Library Association. *For more information:* MLA, 6 N. Michigan Ave., Suite 300, Chicago, IL 60602. *Donated by:* Ballen Booksellers International. *Deadline for applications:* September 1, 1992. *1990 winner:* Virginia M. Bowden.

MLA Marcia C. Noyes Award. The award, an engraved 8-inch sterling silver Revere bowl, recognizes a career that has resulted in lasting, outstanding contributions to medical librarianship. Administered by the Medical Library Association. *For more information:* MLA, 6 N. Michigan Ave., Suite 300, Chicago, IL 60602. *Deadline for applications:* October 1, 1992. *1990 winner:* David Bishop.

SLA John Cotton Dana Award. For exceptional support and encouragement of special librarianship. Administered by the Special Libraries Association. *For more information:* SLA, 1700 18th St., N.W., Washington, DC 20009. *Deadline for applications:* December 13, 1991. *1991 winner:* Dorothy McGarry.

SLA Professional Award. Given to an individual or group in recognition of a specific major achievement in librarianship or information science, which advances the objectives of the SLA. Administered by the Special Libraries Association. *For more information:* SLA, 1700 18th St., N.W., Washington, DC 20009. *1991 winners:* James M. Matarazzo, Laurence Prusak.

For publications and research

AALL Joseph L. Andrews Bibliographical Award. Administered by the American Association of Law Libraries. *For more information:* AALL, 53 W. Jackson Blvd., Chicago, IL 60604. *Deadline for applications:* March 1, 1992. *1990 winner:* Arturo A. Flores and Thomas H. Reynolds, for *Foreign Law: Current Sources of Codes and Legislation in Jurisdictions of the World.*

AALL *Law Library Journal* Article of the Year. For the best article appearing in the *Law Library Journal* for the previous year. Selected by the *Law Library Journal* Advisory Committee and administered by the American Association of Law Libraries. *For more information:* AALL, 53 W. Jackson Blvd., Chicago, IL 60604. *1990 winner:* Bruce M. Kennedy, "Confidentiality of Library Records."

AALL Law Library Publications Award. For publications by a law library. Administered by the American Association of Law Libraries. *For more information:* AALL, 53 W. Jackson Blvd., Chicago, IL 60604. *Deadline for applications:* March 1, 1992. *1990 winner:* Emory University Law Library, for *A Guide to . . . in the Emory Law Library.*

AJL Reference Book Awards. Awards of $500 each for an outstanding book-length bibliography and a general reference book in Judaica. Administered by the Association of Jewish Libraries. *For more information:* AJL, 330 Seventh Ave., 21st Fl., New York, NY 10001. *Deadline for applications:* January 31, 1992. *1990 winner:* Rabbi Adin Steinsaltz, *The Talmud: The Steinsaltz Edition* (Random House, 1989-   ).

AJL Sydney Taylor Body of Work Award. An award of $1,000 for a lifetime of publications in the field of Jewish children's books. Administered by the Association of Jewish Libraries. *For more information:* AJL, 330 Seventh Ave., 21st Fl., New York, NY 10001. *Deadline for applications:* January 31, 1992. *1990 winner:* Yaffa Ganz.

AJL Sydney Taylor Children's Book Awards. Awards of $500 each for the best Jewish children's books for older and younger children. Administered by the Association of Jewish Libraries. *For more information:* AJL, 330 Seventh Ave., 21st Fl., New York, NY 10001. *Deadline for applications:* January 31, 1992. *1990 winners:* Esther Blanc, *Berchick—My Mother's Horse* (Volcano, 1989), for older children; Lois Lowry, *Number the Stars* (Houghton, 1989), for younger children.

AJL Sydney Taylor Manuscript Award. An award of $1,000 for a Jewish children's book (either fiction or nonfiction) by a first-time author. Administered by the Association of Jewish Libraries. *For more information:* AJL, 330 Seventh Ave., 21st Fl., New York, NY 10001. *Deadline for applications:* January 31, 1992.

ALA Coretta Scott King Award. Award(s) given to a black author and to a black illustrator for an outstandingly inspirational and educational contribution. They are designed to commemorate the life and work of Martin Luther King, Jr., and to honor Coretta Scott King for her courage and determination in continuing to work for peace and world brotherhood. Book(s) must be published one year prior to the year of the award presentation. The award consists of a plaque and a cash award of $250 to the author and $250 to the illustrator. Sets of encyclopedias are also donated: *Encyclopaedia Britannica* to the author and *World Book* to the illustrator. Administered by the ALA Social Responsibilities Round Table. *For more information:* ALA, 50 E. Huron St., Chicago, IL 60611-2795. *Donated by:* Johnson Publications. *1991 winner:* Mildred D. Taylor, *The Road to Memphis.*

ALA Eli M. Oboler Memorial Award. A biennial award of $1,500 presented to the author(s) of an article (including a review article), a series of thematically connected articles, a book, or a manual, published on the local, state, or national level, in English or in English translation. The works to be considered must have as their central concern one or more issues, events, questions, or controversies in the area of intellectual freedom. Administered by the ALA Intellectual Freedom Round Table. *For more information:* ALA Office for Intellectual Freedom, 50 E. Huron St., Chicago, IL 60611-2795. *Donated by:* HBW Associates, Inc. *Deadline for applications:* December 1, 1991. *1990 winner:* Aileen Helmick and Floyd Pentlin, eds., for Spring 1988 issue of *Media Horizons.*

ALA G.K. Hall Award for Library Literature. An award, consisting of $500 and a citation, presented to an individual who makes an outstanding contribution to library literature issued during the three years preceding the presentation. Administered by the American Library Association Awards Committee. *For more information:* JoAn S. Segal, ALA, 50 E. Huron St., Chicago, IL 60611-2795. *Donated by:* G.K. Hall & Co., Inc. *Deadline for applications:* October 1, 1991. *1991 winners:* Wayne Wiegand, *An Active Instrument for Propaganda: The American Public Library during World War I* (Greenwood, 1989).

ALA Gay and Lesbian Book Award. An annual award honoring a book or books of exceptional merit relating to the gay/lesbian experience. The form of the award is not fixed but is designated by the ALA Gay Book Award Committee each year as appropriate. Fiction and nonfiction titles, including book-length bibliographies, are eligible. Nominations must be made by any individual not affiliated by the publisher. Administered by the Gay and Lesbian Task Force of the ALA Social Responsibilities Round Table. *For more information:* ALA, 50 E. Huron St., Chicago, IL 60611-2795. *Deadline for applications:* December 15, 1991. *1991 winners:* Minnie Bruce Prat, *Crime Against Nature;* Wayne Dynes, ed., *Encyclopedia of Homosexuality.*

ALA H.W. Wilson Library Periodical Award. An annual award consisting of $500 and a certificate, presented to a periodical published by a local, state, or regional library, library group, or library association in the United States or Canada that has made an outstanding contribution to librarianship. (This excludes publications of ALA, CLA, and their divisions.) Administered by the American Library Association Awards Committee. *For more information:* JoAn S. Segal, ALA, 50 E. Huron St., Chicago, IL 60611-2795. *Donated by:* H.W. Wilson Co. *Deadline for applications:* December 1, 1991. *1991 winner: Mississippi Librarian.*

ALA Jesse H. Shera Award for Research. A $500 award presented annually to the person submitting the best completed library research paper. Submitted papers must not exceed 50 pages. The winner of the competition presents the research at one of the LRRT Research Forums at ALA Annual Conference. Administered by the ALA Library Research Round Table. *For more information:* ALA Office for Research, 50 E. Huron St., Chicago, IL 60611-2795. *Deadline for applications:* February 1, 1992. *1991 winners:* Patricia Dewdney, Roma Harris.

ALA Justin Winsor Prize Essay. An award of $500 established to encourage excellence in research in library history. The winner will be offered the privilege of being invited to submit the essay for publication in a future issue of *Libraries and Culture.* Essays should embody original historical research on a significant subject of library history, should be based on source materials and manuscripts if possible, and should use good English composition and superior style. Administered by the ALA Library History Round Table. *For more information:* Charles Harmon, ALA, 50 E. Huron St., Chicago, IL 60611-2795. *1991 winner:* Margaret F. Stieg, for "Postwar Purge of German Public Libraries, Democracy, and the American Reaction."

ALA/AASL *Emergency Librarian* Publication Award. An annual grant of $500 presented to a school library media association that is an affiliate of AASL in recognition of an outstanding publication in the field of school librarianship. The award celebrates the efforts of AASL affiliates to promote excellence in school library media programs through publications for members. Administered by the ALA American Association of School Librarians. *For more information:* ALA/ AASL, 50 E. Huron St., Chicago, IL 60611-2795. *Donated by:* The publishers of *Emergency*

Librarian. Deadline for applications: February 1, 1992. *1991 winner:* Florida Association for Media in Education.

ALA/ACRL K.G. Saur Award for Best *C&RL* Article. An annual award of $500 presented to the author(s) to recognize the most outstanding article published in *College & Research Libraries* during the preceding volume year. The winning article will be selected on the basis of originality, timeliness, scope, usefulness, format, and special features. Administered by the ALA Association of College and Research Libraries. *For more information:* ALA/ACRL, 50 E. Huron St., Chicago, IL 60611-2795. *Donated by:* K.G. Saur. *Deadline for applications*: December 1, 1991. *1991 winner:* Susan A. Cady, for "The Electronic Revolution in Libraries: Microfilm Déjà Vu?" July 1990.

ALA/ACRL Katharine Kyes Leab and Daniel J. Leab *American Book Prices Current* Award. Three annual awards for the best catalogue published by American or Canadian institutions in conjunction with exhibitions of books and/or manuscripts. Entries are divided into three budget categories: expensive, moderately expensive, and inexpensive, based on production costs of the catalogues. The awards take the form of printed citations to the institutions organizing the exhibitions. Administered by the Rare Books and Manuscripts Section of the ALA Association of College and Research Libraries. *For more information:* ALA/ACRL, 50 E. Huron St., Chicago, IL 60611-2795. *Donated by:* Katharine Kyes Leab and Daniel J. Leab. *Deadline for applications:* September 30, 1992. *1991 winners:* Houghton Library, Harvard University; Linda Hall Library; Thomas Fisher Rare Book Library, University of Toronto.

ALA/ACRL Oberly Award for Bibliography in the Agricultural Sciences. A biennial award given in odd-numbered years, consisting of a citation and a cash award, presented to an American citizen who compiles the best bibliography in the field of agriculture or one of the related sciences in the two-year period preceding the year in which the award is made. Administered by the Science and Technology Section of the ALA Association of College and Research Libraries. *For more information:* ALA/ACRL, 50 E. Huron St., Chicago, IL 60611-2795. *Donated by:* Oberly Memorial Fund. *Deadline for applications:* January 1, 1993. *1991 winner:* Michael J. Balick and Hans T. Beck, *Useful Palms of the World* (Columbia University, 1990).

ALA/ALCTS Best of *LRTS* Award. Annual citation to be given to the author(s) of the best paper published each year in the division's official journal, *Library Resources and Technical Services.* Each of the papers published in the volume for the preceding calendar year is eligible for consideration, with the exception of official reports and documents, obituaries, letters to the editor, and biographies of award winners. Administered by the ALA Association for Library Collections and Technical Services. *For more information:* ALA/ALCTS, 50 E. Huron St., Chicago, IL 60611-2795. *Deadline for applications:* December 2, 1991. *1991 winners:* Beth M. Paskell, Anna H. Perrault.

ALA/ALCTS Blackwell/North America Scholarship Award. An annual award consisting of a citation given to the winner and a $1,000 scholarship to the library school of the winner's choice. The citation is presented to the author(s) of an outstanding monograph, published article, or original paper in the field of acquisitions, collection development, and related areas of resources development in libraries. Administered by the Resources Section of the ALA Association for Library Collections and Technical Services. *For more information:* ALA/ALCTS, 50 E. Huron St., Chicago, IL 60611-2795. *Donated by:* Blackwell/North America. *Deadline for applications:* December 2, 1991. *1991 winner:* Gary D. Bird.

ALA/ALSC Andrew Carnegie Medal. A medal presented annually to an American producer for the outstanding video production for children released in the United States in the previous calendar year. Administered by the Notable Film and Video Committee of the ALA Association for Library Service to Children. *For more information:* ALA/ALSC, 50 E. Huron St., Chicago, IL 60611-2795. *Donated by:* Carnegie Corporation of New York. *1991 winners:* George McQuilkin and John Matthews, for "Ralph S. Mouse."

ALA/ALSC John Newbery Medal. A medal presented annually to the author of the most distinguished contribution to American literature for children published in the United States in the preceding year. The recipient must be a citizen or resident of the United States. Administered by the ALA Association for Library Service to Children. *For more information:* ALA/ALSC, 50 E. Huron St., Chicago, IL 60611-2795. *Donated by:* Daniel Melcher. *1991 winner:* Jerry Spinelli, *Maniac Magee* (Little, Brown, 1990).

ALA/ALSC Laura Ingalls Wilder Medal. A medal presented to an author or illustrator whose books, published in the United States, have over a period of years made a substantial and lasting contribution to children's literature. Presented every three years. Administered by the ALA

Association for Library Service to Children. *For more information:* ALA/ALSC, 50 E. Huron St., Chicago, IL 60611-2795. *Deadline for applications:* December 1, 1991. *1989 winner:* Elizabeth George Speare.

ALA/ALSC Mildred L. Batchelder Award. A citation presented to an American publisher for a children's book considered to be the most outstanding of those books originally published in a foreign language in a foreign country and subsequently published in English in the United States during the preceding year. Administered by the ALA Association for Library Service to Children. *For more information:* ALA/ALSC, 50 E. Huron St., Chicago, IL 60611-2795. *1991 winner:* Rafik Schami, *A Hand Full of Stars* (Dutton, 1990), translated from German by Rika Lesser.

ALA/ALSC Randolph Caldecott Medal. A medal presented annually to the illustrator of the most distinguished American picture book for children published in the United States in the preceding year. Administered by the ALA Association for Library Service to Children. *For more information:* ALA/ALSC, 50 E. Huron St., Chicago, IL 60611-2795. *Donated by:* Daniel Melcher. *1991 winner:* David Macaulay, *Black and White* (Houghton, 1990).

ALA/RASD Dartmouth Medal. A medal presented to honor achievement in creating reference works outstanding in quality and significance. Creating reference works may include, but not be limited to, writing, compiling, editing, or publishing books or the provision of information in other forms for reference use, e.g., a database. Administered by the ALA Reference and Adult Services Division. *For more information:* ALA/RASD, 50 E. Huron St., Chicago, IL 60611-2795. *Donated by:* Dartmouth College. *Deadline for applications:* December 15, 1991. *1991 winner: Encyclopedia of the Holocaust* (Macmillan).

ALA/RASD Denali Press Award. An annual award of $500 and a citation to recognize achievement in creating reference works, outstanding in quality and significance, that provide information specifically about ethnic and minority groups in the United States. Administered by the ALA Reference and Adult Services Division. *For more information:* ALA/RASD, 50 E. Huron St., Chicago, IL 60611-2795. *Donated by:* Denali Press. *Deadline for applications:* December 15, 1991. *1991 winner: Harlem Renaissance and Beyond,* by Lorraine Roses and Ruth Randolph (G.K. Hall).

ALA/RASD Louis Shores-Oryx Press Award. An annual award of $1,000 presented to an individual, a team of individuals, or an organization to recognize excellence in reviewing of books and other materials for libraries. The award may be given to reviewers, review editors, review media, teachers, or organizations that through their activities have furthered the quality and professionalism of reviews and the reviewing process. Administered by the ALA Reference and Adult Services Division. *For more information:* ALA/RASD, 50 E. Huron St., Chicago, IL 60611-2795. *Donated by:* Oryx Press. *Deadline for applications:* December 15, 1991. *1991 winner:* Helen K. Wright.

ALA/RASD Reference Service Press Award. An annual award of $500 presented to recognize the most outstanding article published in *RQ* during the preceding two volume years. Administered by the ALA Reference and Adult Services Division. *For more information:* ALA/RASD, 50 E. Huron St., Chicago, IL 60611-2795. *Donated by:* Reference Service Press, Inc. *1991 winner:* A. Anneli Ahtola, "In-House Databases," Fall 1989.

ALA/YASD Margaret A. Edwards Award. An award given to an author or co-author whose book(s) over a period of time have been accepted by young adults as an authentic voice that continues to illuminate their experiences and emotions, giving insight into their lives. The award consists of $1,000 cash and a citation. Administered by the ALA Young Adult Services Division. *For more information:* ALA/YASD, 50 E. Huron St., Chicago, IL 60611-2795. *Donated by:* School Library Journal. *1991 winner:* Robert Cormier.

ALISE Research Paper Competition. An award of $500 for a previously unpublished research paper concerning any aspect of librarianship or information studies by a member cf ALISE. Administered by the Association for Library and Information Science Education. *For more information:* Ilse Moon, ALISE, 5623 Palm Aire Drive, Sarasota, FL 34243. *Deadline for applications:* October 2, 1992. *1991 winner:* John Richardson.

ARLIS/NA George Wittenborn Memorial Award. Awarded to publishers for excellence in art publications produced or distributed in North America during the previous calendar year. Administered by the Art Libraries Society of North America. *For more information:* ARLIS/NA, 3900 E. Timrod St., Tucson, AZ 85711. *Deadline for applications:* December 31, 1991. *1990 winners:* Abbeville Press, Bedford Arts Publishers/The Corcoran Gallery of Art, Graphics Press, National Gallery of Canada, Yale University Press.

ARLIS/NA Gerd Muehsam Memorial Award. A $200 cash award, one-year membership in ARLIS/NA, and $300 in travel funds for the best paper by a graduate student on a subject related to art or visual resources librarianship. Administered by the Art Libraries Society of North America. *For more information:* ARLIS/NA, 3900 E. Timrod St., Tucson, AZ 85711. *Deadline for applications:* October 15, 1992. *1989 winner:* Peter P. Blank.

ASI H.W. Wilson Company Indexing Award. A cash award of $500 and a citation for excellence in indexing of an English-language monograph or other nonserial publication published in the United States during the previous calendar year. The publisher of the index also receives a citation. Administered by the American Society of Indexers. *For more information:* ASI, 1700 18th St., N.W., Washington, DC 20009. *Donated by:* H.W. Wilson Co. *Deadline for applications:* April 1, 1992. *1990 winner:* Marcia Carlson.

ASIS Best Information Science Book. For the best book published in the field of information science during the preceding year. Administered by the American Society for Information Science. *For more information:* ASIS, 8720 Georgia Ave., Suite 501, Silver Spring, MD 20910. *Deadline for applications:* June 1, 1992. *1990 winner:* Bryan Pfaffenberger, *Democratizing Information* (G.K. Hall, 1989).

ASIS Best *JASIS* Paper Award. For the outstanding paper published in the *Journal of the American Society for Information Science.* Administered by the American Society for Information Science. *For more information:* ASIS, 8720 Georgia Ave., Suite 501, Silver Spring, MD 20910. *Deadline for applications:* June 1, 1992. *1990 winner:* Gary Marchionini, "Information-Seeking Strategies of Novices Using a Full-Text Electronic Encyclopedia," January 1989.

ASIS Doctoral Forum. For outstanding achievements by information scientists in the completion of dissertation projects. Administered by the American Society for Information Science. *For more information:* ASIS, 8720 Georgia Ave., Suite 501, Silver Spring, MD 20910. *Deadline for applications:* June 1, 1992. *1990 winner:* Helen Ruth Tibbo.

ASIS Research Award. For a systematic program of research or outstanding research contributions in the field of information science. Administered by the American Society for Information Science. *For more information:* ASIS, 8720 Georgia Ave., Suite 501, Silver Spring, MD 20910. *Deadline for applications:* June 1, 1992. *1990 winners:* José-Marie Griffiths, Donald W. King.

ASIS Student Paper Award. For an outstanding student paper in information science. Administered by the American Society for Information Science. *For more information:* ASIS, 8720 Georgia Ave., Suite 501, Silver Spring, MD 20910. *Deadline for applications:* June 15, 1992. *1990 winner:* Charlotte Weise.

CLA John Brubaker Memorial Award. For the best article in *Catholic Library World* in the previous year. Administered by the *Catholic Library World* Committee of the Catholic Library Association. *For more information:* CLA, 461 W. Lancaster Ave., Haverford, PA 19041. *1991 winner:* Sr. Mary Elizabeth Gallagher.

CLA Regina Medal. A silver medal awarded to an author or illustrator for a lifetime contribution to children's books. Administered by the Catholic Library Association. *For more information:* CLA, 461 W. Lancaster Ave., Haverford, PA 19041. *1991 winner:* Leonard Everett Fisher.

CLA/CACL Amelia Frances Howard-Gibbon Award. Presented annually to the illustrator of an outstanding children's book published in Canada. Administered by the Canadian Association of Childrens' Librarians of the Canadian Library Association. *For more information:* CLA, 200 Elgin St., Ottawa, Ontario K2P 1L5, Canada. *Deadline for applications:* February 1, 1992. *1990 winner:* Kady MacDonald Denton, for *Til All the Stars Have Fallen* (Kids Can Press, 1989).

CLA/CACL Book of the Year for Children Award. Presented annually to the author of an outstanding children's book published in Canada. Administered by the Canadian Association of Childrens' Librarians of the Canadian Library Association. *For more information:* CLA, 200 Elgin St., Ottawa, Ontario K2P 1L5, Canada. *Deadline for applications:* January 1, 1992. *1990 winner:* Kit Pearson, *The Sky Is Falling* (Penguin, 1989).

CLA/CSLA CANEBSCO School Library Media Periodical Award. Recognizes a school library media periodical as a vehicle for the professional development of school library media personnel. Administered by the Canadian School Library Association of the Canadian Library Association. *For more information:* CLA, 200 Elgin St., Ottawa, Ontario K2P 1L5, Canada. *Donated by:* CANEBSCO, Inc. *Deadline for applications:* December 31, 1991. *1990 winner:* The Bookmark.

CLA/CSLA Grolier Award for Research in School Librarianship in Canada. A $1,000 award for theoretical or applied research that advances the field of school librarianship. Administered by the Canadian School Library Association of the Canadian Library Association. *For more information:* CLA, 200 Elgin St., Ottawa, Ontario K2P 1L5, Canada. *Donated by:* Grolier Corp. *Deadline for applications:* December 31, 1991. *1989 winners:* Alixe Hambleton, John Wilkinson.

CLA/YASIG Young Adult Canadian Book Award. Recognizes an author of an outstanding English-language Canadian book appealing to young adults. Administered by the Young Adult Services Interest Group of the Canadian Library Association. *For more information:* CLA, 200 Elgin St., Ottawa, Ontario K2P 1L5, Canada. *1990 winner:* Diana Wieler, *Bad Boy* (Groundwood, 1989).

CSLA Helen Keating Ott Award for Outstanding Contribution to Children's Literature. Given to a person or organization that has made a significant contribution to promoting high moral and ethical values through children's literature. Administered by the Church and Synagogue Library Association. *For more information:* CSLA, Box 19357, Portland, OR 97219. *1990 winner:* Elizabeth A. Van Steenwyk.

MLA Ida and George Eliot Prize. An award of $200 for an essay published in any journal in the preceding calendar year that has been judged most effective in furthering medical librarianship. Administered by the Medical Library Association. *For more information:* MLA, 6 N. Michigan Ave., Suite 300, Chicago, IL 60602. *Donated by:* Login Brothers Book Co. *Deadline for applications:* December 15, 1991. *1990 winners:* Joyce E.B. Backus, Sara Davidson, Roy Rada, "Searching for Patterns in the MeSH Vocabulary."

MLA Murray Gottlieb Prize. An award of $100 for the best unpublished essay written by a medical librarian on the history of medicine and allied sciences. Administered by the Medical Library Association. *For more information:* MLA, 6 N. Michigan Ave., Suite 300, Chicago, IL 60602. *Donated by:* Ralph and Jo Grimes. *Deadline for applications:* September 1, 1992. *1989 winner:* Joan Krizack.

MLA Rittenhouse Award. Given for the best unpublished paper on medical librarianship submitted by a student enrolled in a course for credit in an ALA-accredited library school, or a trainee in an internship in medical librarianship. Administered by the Medical Library Association. *For more information:* MLA, 6 N. Michigan Ave., Suite 300, Chicago, IL 60602. *Donated by:* Rittenhouse Medical Book Store. *Deadline for applications:* September 1, 1992. *1989 winner:* P.F. Anderson.

MLA Eva Judd O'Meara Award. A $250 award for the best book or score review published in the MLA journal, *Notes.* Administered by the Music Library Association. *For more information:* MLA, Box 487, Canton, MA 02021. *Deadline for applications:* November 15, 1991. *1990 winner:* William Kraft, for his review of Stravinsky's *L'Histoire du Soldat* (September 1989).

MLA Richard S. Hill Award. A $250 award for the best article-length bibliography and article on music librarianship. Administered by the Music Library Association. *For more information:* MLA, Box 487, Canton, MA 02021. *Deadline for applications:* November 15, 1991. *1990 winner:* Gillian B. Anderson, for "Putting the Experience of the World at the Nations Command: Music at the Library of Congress, 1800–1917," *Journal of the American Musicological Society* (1989).

MLA Vincent H. Duckles Award. An award of $500 for the best book-length bibliography or music reference work. Administered by the Music Library Association. *For more information:* MLA, Box 487, Canton, MA 02021. *Deadline for applications:* November 15, 1991. *1990 winner:* Hans-Joachim Schulze and Christoph Wolff, for *Bach Compendium* (Leipzig, 1985-89).

SAA C.F.W. Coker Prize. For finding aids or finding aid systems that have a substantial impact on archival descriptive practices. Administered by the Society of American Archivists. *For more information:* SAA, 600 S. Federal St., Suite 504, Chicago, IL 60605. *1990 winner:* Center for Legislative Archives of the National Archives and Records Administration.

SAA Fellows' Posner Prize. For the best article in the *American Archivist.* Administered by the Society of American Archivists. *For more information:* SAA, 600 S. Federal St., Suite 504, Chicago, IL 60605. *1990 winner:* Working Group on Standards for Archival Description.

SAA Philip M. Hamer-Elizabeth Hamer Kegan Award. For outstanding work by an editor of a documentary publication. Administered by the Society of American Archivists. *For more information:* SAA, 600 S. Federal St., Suite 504, Chicago, IL 60605. *1990 winner:* Judy Hohmann.

SAA Theodore Calvin Pease Award. For superior writing achievement by a student of archival administration. Administered by the Society of American Archivists. *For more information:* SAA, 600 S. Federal St., Suite 504, Chicago, IL 60605. *1990 winner:* Luke J. Swetland.

SAA Waldo Gifford Leland Prize. For writing of superior excellence and usefulness in the field of archival history, theory, or practice published as a monograph in North America. Administered by the Society of American Archivists. *For more information:* SAA, 600 S. Federal St., Suite 504, Chicago, IL 60605. *1990 winner:* Henry Putney Beers, *French and Spanish Records of Louisiana.*

SLA Public Relations Award. Presented to a journalist who writes the most outstanding article on special librarianship published in a general circulation magazine or newspaper. Administered by the Special Libraries Association. *For more information:* SLA, 1700 18th St., N.W., Washington, DC 20009. *Donated by:* Moody's Investor Service. *1991 winner:* Gloria Stashower.

TLA Award. For excellence in writing books about film, TV, or radio. Reference books excluded. *For more information:* Stephen Vallillo, Betty Rose Theatre Collection, New York Public Library, 111 Amsterdam Ave., New York, NY 10023. *Deadline for applications:* February 28, 1992. *1990 winner:* Charles T. Malland, *Chaplin and American Culture* (Princeton, 1989).

TLA George Freedley Award. A cash award of $250 for excellence in writing books about the theatre. Reference books excluded. Administered by the Theatre Library Association. *For more information:* Stephen Vallillo, Betty Rose Theatre Collection, New York Public Library, 111 Amsterdam Ave., New York, NY 10023. *Deadline for applications:* February 28, 1992. *1990 winner:* Martin Duberman, *Paul Robeson* (Knopf, 1989).

For service in general

AALL Marian Gould Gallagher Distinguished Service Award. Administered by the American Association of Law Libraries. *For more information:* AALL, 53 W. Jackson, Chicago, IL 60604. *Deadline for applications:* February 1, 1992. *1990 winners:* Hibernia Turbeville, Viola Bird.

ALA Beta Phi Mu Award. An annual award consisting of $500 and a citation of achievement, presented to a library school faculty member or to an individual for distinguished service to education for librarianship. Administered by the ALA Awards Committee. *For more information:* JoAn S. Segal, ALA, 50 E. Huron St., Chicago, IL 60611-2795. *Donated by:* Beta Phi Mu International Library Science Honorary Society. *Deadline for applications:* December 1, 1991. *1991 winner:* Edward P. Holley.

ALA Joseph W. Lippincott Award. An award consisting of $1,000 and a citation of achievement, presented annually to a librarian for distinguished service to the profession of librarianship, such service to include outstanding participation in the activities of professional library associations, notable published professional writing, or other significant activity on behalf of the profession and its aims. Administered by the ALA Awards Committee. *For more information:* JoAn S. Segal, ALA, 50 E. Huron St., Chicago, IL 60611-2795. *Donated by:* Joseph W. Lippincott, Jr. *Deadline for applications:* December 1, 1991. *1991 winner:* Peggy Sullivan.

ALA/ALTA Major Benefactors Honor Award. An annual award consisting of a citation to recognize benefactors to public libraries. The recipient may be any person(s), institution, agency, or organization. The significance of the gift will be measured from the point of view of the recipient library. Administered by the ALA American Library Trustee Association. *For more information:* ALA/ALTA, 50 E. Huron St., Chicago, IL 60611-2795. *Deadline for applications:* December 1, 1991. *1991 winners:* The Coit Family; Charles W. Barber and the Rapides Bank & Trust; Sioux City PL Foundation; Estate of Alvin F. and Gertrude M. Schroeder.

ALA/ALTA Trustee Citations. A citation presented to each of two outstanding trustees, in actual service during part of the calendar year preceding the presentation, for distinguished service to library development, whether on the local, state, or national level. Equal consideration is to be given trustees of small and large public libraries. Administered by the ALA American Library Trustee Association. *For more information:* ALA/ALTA, 50 E. Huron St., Chicago, IL 60611-2795. *Deadline for applications:* December 1, 1991. *1991 winners:* Roslyn S. Kurland, Renee Becker Swartz.

ALA/LAMA Recognition of Achievement Awards. Presented annually to encourage, recognize, and command excellence in service to LAMA and its sections. The awards are a certificate of appreciation for a significant contribution to the goals of LAMA over a period of several years, and a certificate of special thanks for a single, specific, significant contribution to the goals of LAMA. Administered by the ALA Library Administration and Management Association. *For more information:* ALA/LAMA, 50 E. Huron St., Chicago, IL 60611-2795. *Deadline for applications:* 1991. *1991 winners:* Nancy A. Davenport, Gary M. Shirk, John J. Vasi, Joyce G. Taylor.

ALA/PLA Allie Beth Martin Award. An award of $3,000 and a citation presented to a librarian who, in a public library setting, has demonstrated an extraordinary range and depth of knowledge about books or other library materials and has exhibited a distinguished ability to share that knowledge. Administered by the ALA Public Library Association. *For more information:* ALA/PLA, 50 E. Huron St., Chicago, IL 60611-2795. *Donated by:* Baker and Taylor Books. *Deadline for applications:* December 1, 1991. *1991 winner:* Sandra M. Neerman.

ALA/RASD Gale Research Award for Excellence in Reference and Adult Services. An annual award of $1,000 and a citation presented to a library or library system for developing an imaginative and unique library resource to meet the patrons' reference needs. Administered by the ALA Reference and Adult Services Division. *For more information:* ALA/RASD, 50 E. Huron St., Chicago, IL 60611-2795. *Donated by:* Gale Research, Inc. *Deadline for applications:* December 15, 1991. *1991 winner:* University of Arkansas Library, Fayetteville.

ALA/RASD Margaret E. Monroe Library Adult Services Award. A citation to be given to a librarian who has made significant contributions to and an impact on library adult services. The person may be a practicing librarian, a library and information science researcher or educator, or a retired librarian who has brought distinction to the profession's understanding and practice of services to adults. Administered by the ALA Reference and Adult Services Division. *For more information:* ALA/RASD, 50 E. Huron St., Chicago, IL 60611-2795. *Deadline for applications:* December 15, 1991. *1991 winner:* Kathleen M. Heim.

ALISE Service Award. For regular and sustained service to ALISE. Administered by the Association for Library and Information Science Education. *For more information:* Ilse Moon, ALISE, 5623 Palm Aire Drive, Sarasota, FL 34243. *Deadline for applications:* June 1, 1992. *1990 winner:* Norman Horrocks.

ASIS Outstanding Information Science Teacher Award. A cash award of $500 acknowledging sustained excellence in the teaching of information science. Administered by the American Society for Information Science. *For more information:* ASIS, 8720 Georgia Ave., Suite 501, Silver Spring, MD 20910. *Donated by:* Institute for Scientific Information. *Deadline for applications:* June 15, 1992. *1990 winner:* Nicholas J. Belkin.

ASIS Watson Davis Award. For a significant long-term contribution to ASIS. Administered by the American Society for Information Science. *For more information:* ASIS, 8720 Georgia Ave., Suite 501, Silver Spring, MD 20910. *Deadline for applications:* July 15, 1992. *1990 winner:* Julie A.C. Virgo.

CLA Outstanding Service to Librarianship. An award for distinguished service in the field of Canadian librarianship. Administered by the Canadian Library Association. *For more information:* CLA, 200 Elgin St., Ottawa, Ontario K2P 1L5, Canada. *Donated by:* R.R. Bowker. *Deadline for applications:* January 31, 1992. *1990 winner:* Beryl Anderson.

CLA/CAPL Outstanding Public Library Service Award. An award for outstanding service in the field of Canadian public librarianship. Administered by the Canadian Library Association. *For more information:* CLA, 200 Elgin St., Ottawa, Ontario K2P 1L5, Canada. *Deadline for applications:* January 31, 1992. *1990 winner:* Barbara Clubb.

CLA/CLTA Merit Award for Distinguished Service as a Library Trustee. For exceptional service as a trustee in the library field at local, provincial, and national levels. Administered by the Canadian Library Trustees Association of the Canadian Library Association. *For more information:* CLA, 200 Elgin St., Ottawa, Ontario K2P 1L5, Canada. *Deadline for applications:* January 31, 1992. *1990 winner:* Lorraine Williams.

MLA Distinguished Public Service Award. Presented to honor persons whose exemplary actions have served to advance the health, welfare, and intellectual freedom of the public. Awardees are selected only on occasions when the merits of a nominee clearly recommend recognition by the MLA. Administered by the Medical Library Association. *For more information:* MLA, 6 N. Michigan Ave., Suite 300, Chicago, IL 60602. *1990 winner:* Hon. William H. Natcher.

MLA President's Award. For a notable or important contribution to medical librarianship made during the past association year. Administered by the Medical Library Association. *For more information:* MLA, 6 N. Michigan Ave., Suite 300, Chicago, IL 60602. *1989 winners:* Louise Darling, Lois Ann Colaianni, David Bishop.

SAA Distinguished Service Award. To recognize an archival institution for outstanding public service and an exemplary contribution to the archival profession. Administered by the Society of American Archivists. *For more information:* SAA, 600 S. Federal St., Suite 504, Chicago, IL 60605. *1990 winner:* Arthur and Elizabeth Schlesinger Library on the History of Women in America, Radcliffe College.

SAA J. Franklin Jameson Archival Advocacy Award. To recognize an individual, institution, or organization not directly involved in archival work, that promotes greater public awareness of archival activities or programs. Administered by the Society of American Archivists. *For more information:* SAA, 600 S. Federal St., Suite 504, Chicago, IL 60605. *1990 winner:* Sen. Mark O. Hatfield.

SLA Hall of Fame Award. Granted to a member of SLA at or near the end of an active professional career for an extended period of distinguished service to the association in all spheres. Administered by the Special Libraries Association. *For more information:* SLA, 1700 18th St., N.W., Washington, DC 20009. *1991 winners:* Efren W. Gonzalez, Dorothy Kasman, Charles D. Missar, Mary Vasilakis.

SLA Member Recognition for Excellence in Public Relations. An award for outstanding contributions by an SLA member to the association's public relations goals during the previous year. Administered by the Special Libraries Association. *For more information:* SLA, 1700 18th St., N.W., Washington, DC 20009. *1991 winner:* Carol Ginsburg.

SLA President's Award. Given to an SLA member or group of members for a notable or important contribution to SLA during the past association year. Administered by the Special Libraries Association. *For more information:* SLA, 1700 18th St., N.W., Washington, DC 20009. *1991 winner:* Barbara S. Mattscheck.

For service to children and young adults

ALA Grolier Foundation Award. An annual award, consisting of $1,000 and a citation of achievement presented to a librarian who has made an unusual contribution to the stimulation and guidance of reading by children and young people. The award is given for outstanding work with children and young people through high school age, for continuing service, or in recognition of one particular contribution of lasting value. Administered by the ALA Awards Committee. *For more information:* JoAn S. Segal, ALA, 50 E. Huron St., Chicago, IL 60611-2795. *Donated by:* Grolier Foundation. *Deadline for applications:* December 1, 1991. *1991 winner:* Dorothy Broderick.

ALA/AASL Baker & Taylor Distinguished Service Award. An annual award of $3,000 presented to the individual who has demonstrated excellence and provided an outstanding national or international contribution to school librarianship and school library media development. Administered by the ALA American Association of School Librarians. *For more information:* ALA/AASL, 50 E. Huron St., Chicago, IL 60611-2795. *Donated by:* Baker and Taylor Books. *Deadline for applications:* February 1, 1992. *1991 winner:* Barbara Spriestersbach.

ALA/AASL Distinguished Library Service Award for School Administrators. An annual grant of $2,000 presented to a person directly responsible for the administration of a school or group of schools who has made an outstanding and sustained contribution toward furthering the role of the library and its development in elementary and/or secondary education. Administered by the ALA American Association of School Librarians. *For more information:* ALA/AASL, 50 E. Huron St., Chicago, IL 60611-2795. *Donated by:* Social Issues Resources Series, Inc. *Deadline for applications:* February 1, 1992. *1991 winner:* Marilyn Blakely.

ALA/AASL National School Library Media Program of the Year Award. Cash awards presented annually to school districts that display outstanding achievement in exemplary library media programs. Schools or districts representing elementary schools, secondary schools, or a combination of both may apply. Administered by the ALA American Association of School Librarians. *For more information:* ALA/AASL, 50 E. Huron St., Chicago, IL 60611-2795. *Donated by:* Encyclopaedia Brittanica Co. *Deadline for applications:* February 1, 1992. *1991 winners:* Beecher Road School, Woodbridge, Conn.; Irving Independent School District, Tex.

ALA/ALSC Econo-Clad Literature Program Award. One annual $1,000 award to help defray the cost of ALA conference attendance, presented to a member of ALSC who has developed and implemented a unique and outstanding library program for children involving reading and the use of literature with children. The recipient must be a librarian who works directly with children and whose program, targeted at and designed for children, has taken place within the past 12 months in a public library or school library media center. Administered by the ALA Association for Library Service to Children. *For more information:* ALA/ALSC, 50 E. Huron St., Chicago, IL 60611-2795. *Donated by:* Econo-Clad Literature Program. *Deadline for applications:* December 1, 1991. *1991 winner:* Ellen Fader.

ALA/YASD Econo-Clad Literature Program Award. An annual award given to a member of YASD who has developed and implemented a unique and outstanding library program for young adults involving reading and the use of literature. The $1,000 award is to be used to help defray the cost of ALA conference attendance by the winner. Administered by the ALA Young Adult Services Division. *For more information:* ALA/YASD, 50 E. Huron St., Chicago, IL 60611-2795. *Donated by:* Econo-Clad Literature Program. *Deadline for applications:* December 1, 1991. *1991 winner:* Constance Johnson.

CLA/CSLA Canadian School Executive Award. To a Canadian school executive for distinguished service to school libraries. Administered by the Canadian School Libraries Association of the Canadian Library Association. *For more information:* CLA, 200 Elgin St., Ottawa, Ontario K2P 1L5, Canada. *Deadline for applications:* December 31, 1991. *1989 winner:* Ken Haycock.

CLA/CSLA Maclean Hunter Teacher-Librarian of the Year Award. To a school-based teacher-librarian who has made an outstanding contribution to school librarianship in Canada. The award consists of a plaque and registration and travel costs to the CLA Annual Conference. Administered by the Canadian School Library Association of the Canadian Library Association. *For more information:* CLA, 200 Elgin St., Ottawa, Ontario K2P 1L5, Canada. *Donated by:* Maclean Hunter Library Services. *1990 winner:* Joyce Marie Birch.

CLA/CSLA/OLA Margaret B. Scott Memorial Award. An award of $400 for the development of school libraries at the national level in Canada. Administered by the Canadian School Libraries Association of the Canadian Library Association and the Ontario Library Association. *For more information:* CLA, 200 Elgin St., Ottawa, Ontario K2P 1L5, Canada. *Deadline for applications:* December 30, 1991. *1990 winner:* Warren Grabinsky.

CLA/HSLS Certificate of Merit. For an outstanding contribution to high school librarianship. Administered by the High School Library Section of the Catholic Library Association. *For more information:* CLA, 461 W. Lancaster Ave., Haverford, PA 19041. *Deadline for applications:* February 1, 1992. *1991 winner:* U.S. Catholic Conference.

For service to special populations

ALA Bessie Boehm Moore Award. An annual award consisting of $1,000 and a citation of achievement, presented to a library organization that has developed an outstanding and creative program for public library service to the aging. Administered by the ALA Awards Committee. *For more information:* JoAn S. Segal, ALA, 50 E. Huron St., Chicago, IL 60611-2795. *Donated by:* Bessie Boehm Moore. *Deadline for applications:* December 1, 1991. *1991 winner:* Rochester Hills (Mich.) PL.

ALA/ASCLA Exceptional Service Award. A citation presented to recognize exceptional service to patients, to the homebound, to medical, nursing, and other professional staff in hospitals, and to inmates, as well as to recognize professional leadership, effective interpretation of programs, pioneering activity, and significant research of experimental projects. Administered by the ALA Association of Specialized and Cooperative Library Agencies. *For more information:* ALA/ASCLA, 50 E. Huron St., Chicago, IL 60611-2795. *Deadline for applications:* December 1, 1991. *1991 winner:* Kathleen Mayo.

ALA/ASCLA Francis Joseph Campbell Citation. An annual award consisting of a citation and a medal, presented to a person who has made an outstanding contribution to the advancement of library service for the blind and physically handicapped. Administered by the Libraries Serving Special Populations Section of the ALA Association of Specialized and Cooperative Library Agencies. *For more information:* ALA/ASCLA, 50 E. Huron St., Chicago, IL 60611-2795. *Deadline for applications:* December 1, 1991. *1991 winner:* Stuart Carothers.

ALA/ASCLA National Organization on the Disabled. An annual award of $1,000 and a certificate are given to a library organization in recognition of either a specific innovative, creative, and well-organized program of services for persons who are disabled or for a library that has made its total services more accessible through changing physical and/or attitudinal barriers. Administered by the ALA Association of Specialized and Cooperative Library Agencies. *For more information:* ALA/ASCLA, 50 E. Huron St., Chicago, IL 60611-2795. *Donated by:* J.C. Penney Co., through the National Organization on the Disabled. *Deadline for applications:* December 1, 1991. *1991 winner:* King County Library System, Seattle.

ALA/PLA Leonard Wertheimer Multilingual Award. An award presented to a person, group, or organization in recognition of work that enhances and promotes multilingual public library service. Administered by the ALA Public Library Association. *For more information:* ALA/PLA, 50 E. Huron St., Chicago, IL 60611-2795. *Donated by:* National Textbook Co. *Deadline for applications:* December 1, 1991. *1991 winner:* Adriana Acauan Tandler.

ALA/RASD John Sessions Memorial Award. A plaque to be presented to a library or a library system in recognition of significant efforts to work with the labor community. Such efforts may include outreach projects to local labor unions; the establishment of, or significant expansion of, special labor collections; or other library activities that serve the labor community. Administered by the ALA Reference and Adult Services Division. *For more information:* ALA/RASD, 50 E. Huron St., Chicago, IL 60611-2795. *Donated by:* AFL/CIO. *Deadline for applications:* December 15, 1991. *1991 winner:* Department of Archives and Special Collections, Ohio University Libraries, Athens.

APALA Distinguished Service Award. For significant contributions to Asian/Pacific society in the field of library and information science. Administered by the Asian/Pacific American Library Association. *For more information:* Charlotte Kim, Chicago Public Library, 1224 W. Van Buren St., Chicago, IL 60607. *Deadline for applications:* April 15, 1992. *1990 winner:* Betty Lee Sung.

CALA Distinguished Service Award. To a member of CALA. Administered by the Chinese-American Librarians Association. *For more information:* CALA, Auraria Library, Lawrence at 11 St., Denver, CO 80204. *1990 winners:* Harris Seng, Ming Ku.

CSLA Pat Tabler Memorial Scholarship Award. Presented to a librarian who has shown initiative and creativity in starting a new, or renewing, a congregational library. Administered by the Church and Synagogue Library Association. *For more information:* CSLA, Box 19357, Portland, OR 97219. *1990 winner:* Cheri Grout.

For social responsibility

ALA Equality Award. A certificate and a cash award of $500 given to an individual or group for an outstanding contribution towards promoting equality between women and men in the library profession. The contribution may be either a sustained one or a single outstanding accomplishment. The award may be given for an activist or scholarly contribution in such areas as pay equity, affirmative action, legislative work, and nonsexist education. Administered by the ALA Awards Committee. *For more information:* JoAn S. Segal, ALA, 50 E. Huron St., Chicago, IL 60611-2795. *Donated by:* Scarecrow Press, Inc. *Deadline for applications:* December 1, 1991. *1991 winner:* E. J. Josey.

ALA Peace Award. An annual award given to a library, which in the course of its educational and social mission, or to a librarian, who in the course of professional activities, has contributed significantly to the advancement of knowledge related to issues of international peace and security. The contribution may be in the form of, but not limited to, a bibliographical compilation, research and publication of an original historical nature, or a nonprint media creation, display, or distribution. Administered by the ALA Social Responsibilities Round Table. *For more information:* ALA, 50 E. Huron St., Chicago, IL 60611-2795. *Donated by:* Social Issues Resources Series, Inc. *Deadline for applications:* January 6, 1992. *1991 winner:* Faye A. Lander.

ALA/ALTA Literacy Award. An annual award given to that individual who has done an outstanding job in making contributions toward the extirpation of illiteracy. Administered by the ALA American Library Trustee Association. *For more information:* ALA/ALTA, 50 E. Huron St., Chicago, IL 60611-2795. *Deadline for applications:* December 1, 1991. *1991 winner:* Helen S. Kohlman.

ALA/PLA Advancement of Literacy Award. An award presented to an American publisher or bookseller who has made a significant contribution to the advancement of literacy. Administered by the Adult Lifelong Learning Section of the ALA Public Library Association. *For more information:* ALA/PLA, 50 E. Huron St., Chicago, IL 60611-2795. *Donated by:* RHC Spacemaster Corporation. *Deadline for applications:* December 1, 1991. *1991 winner:* Baker & Taylor Books.

CLA/CLTA Achievement in Literacy Award. To recognize a public library board that has initiated an innovative program that has made a significant contribution to the advancement of literacy in its community. Administered by the Canadian Library Trustee Association of the Canadian Library Association. *For more information:* CLA, 200 Elgin St., Ottawa, Ontario K2P 1L5, Canada. *1990 winner:* Thunder Bay (Ont.) PL Board.

For specialized military and congregational libraries

ALA Armed Forces Library Achievement Citation. An annual citation presented to members of the Armed Forces Library Round Table who have made significant contributions to the development of armed forces library service, and to organizations encouraging an interest in libraries and reading. Administered by the Armed Forces Library Round Table. *For more information:* JoAn S. Segal, ALA, 50 E. Huron St., Chicago, IL 60611-2795. *Deadline for applications:* December 1, 1991. *1990 winner:* Elizabeth R. Snoke.

ALA Armed Forces Library Certificate of Merit. This award is presented in recognition of special contributions to Armed Forces Libraries. Recipients need not be librarians or members of ALA. Administered by the Armed Forces Library Round Table. *For more information:* JoAn S. Segal, ALA, 50 E. Huron St., Chicago, IL 60611-2795. *Deadline for applications:* December 1, 1991.

ALA Armed Forces Library Newsbank Scholarship Award. This award recognizes members of the Armed Forces Library Round Table who have given exemplary service in the area of library support for off-duty education programs in the armed forces. Administered by the ALA Armed Forces Library Round Table. *For more information:* JoAn S. Segal, ALA, 50 E. Huron St., Chicago, IL 60611-2795. *Deadline for applications:* December 1, 1991. *1990 winner:* Margaret Ono.

CLA Aggiornamento Award. For an outstanding contribution to the growth of parish librarianship. Administered by the Parish Library Section of the Catholic Library Association. *For more information:* CLA, 461 W. Lancaster Ave., Haverford, PA 19041. *Deadline for applications:* February 1, 1992. *1991 winner:* Twenty-Third Publications.

CSLA Award for Outstanding Congregational Librarian. For distinguished service to the congregation and/or community through devotion to the congregational library. Administered by the Church and Synagogue Library Association. *For more information:* CSLA, Box 19357, Portland, OR 92719. *1990 winner:* Dorothy Lofton.

CSLA Award for Outstanding Congregational Library. For responding in creative and innovative ways to the library's mission of reaching and serving the congregation and/or the wider community. Administered by the Church and Synagogue Library Association. *For more information:* CSLA, Box 19357, Portland, OR 92719. *1990 winner:* Esther Ayres, Mesa, Arizona.

CSLA Award for Outstanding Contribution to Congregational Libraries. For providing inspiration, guidance, leadership, or resources to enrich the field of church or synagogue librarianship. Administered by the Church and Synagogue Library Association. *For more information:* CSLA, Box 19357, Portland, OR 92719. *1990 winner:* Jennifer Pritchett.

SAA Sister M. Claude Lane Award. For significant contribution to the field of religious archives. Administered by the Society of American Archivists. *For more information:* SAA, 600 S. Federal St., Suite 504, Chicago, IL 60605. *Donated by:* Society of Southwest Archivists. *1990 winner:* Thomas Wilsted.

For technology

ALA/AASL Follett Software Company Microcomputer in the Media Center Award. This award is designed to recognize and honor library media specialists who have demonstrated innovative approaches to microcomputer applications in their respective libraries or media centers. There are two award categories: 1) for the innovative use of the microcomputer in the school library media center in an elementary (K-6) setting; 2) for the innovative use of the microcomputer in the school library media center in a secondary (7-12) setting. Two national winners may be recommended, one in each category. Each recipient librarian will receive a $1,000 cash award and travel to the award ceremony; and each recipient library will receive a $500 cash award. Administered by the ALA American Association of School Librarians. *For more information:* ALA/AASL, 50 E. Huron St., Chicago, IL 60611-2795. *Donated by:* Follett Software Co. *Deadline for applications:* February 1, 1992. *1991 winners:* David J. Henderson, Bonnie Fish.

ALA/LITA Gaylord Award for Achievement in Library and Information Technology. An annual award of $1,000 presented to recognize distinguished leadership, notable development or application of technology, superior accomplishments in research or education, or original contributions to the literature of the field. Administered by the ALA Library and Information Technology

Association. *For more information:* ALA/LITA, 50 E. Huron St., Chicago, IL 60611-2795. *Donated by:* Gaylord Bros., Inc. *Deadline for applications:* December 15, 1991. *1991 winner:* Clifford A. Lynch.

ALA/LITA Meckler Award for Technological Innovation in Libraries. An annual award of a citation and $500 intended to recognize outstanding instances of the innovative use of technology in a library. It may be awarded to either an individual or a library. Administered by the ALA Library and Information Technology Association. *For more information:* ALA/LITA, 50 E. Huron St., Chicago, IL 60611-2795. *Donated by:* Meckler Corporation. *Deadline for applications:* October 1, 1991.

ALA/PLA Library Video Award. A recognition and a $1,000 honorarium to a public library demonstrating excellence and innovation in library programming with video and the ability to market and promote the use of these services to library users. Administered by the ALA Public Library Association. *For more information:* ALA/PLA, 50 E. Huron St., Chicago, IL 60611-2795. *Donated by:* Baker and Taylor Video. *Deadline for applications:* December 1, 1991. *1991 winner:* Dixon (Ill.) PL.

MLA Frank Bradway Rogers Information Advancement Award. A cash award of $500 for an outstanding contribution to the application of technology to the delivery of health sciences information, to the science of information, or to the facilitation of information delivery. Administered by the Medical Library Association. *For more information:* MLA, 6 N. Michigan Ave., Suite 300, Chicago, IL 60602. *Donated by:* Institute for Scientific Information. *Deadline for applications:* September 1, 1992. *1990 winners:* John E. Anderson, Davis B. McCarn, Rose Marie Woodsmall.

Library education: A mini-history

by Haynes McMullen

MORE THAN A CENTURY AGO, the first library school in North America opened at Columbia University because one person, Melvil Dewey, felt the best way to prepare librarians was through classroom instruction combined with practical work in a library. The Columbia School of Library Economy accomplished its aim soon after it opened on January 5, 1887; but its director, although intelligent and imaginative, had no gift for following the rules and regulations of the trustees. Few tears were shed by that group when Dewey moved the school to the State Library in Albany in 1889, and soon after he became secretary of the New York Board of Regents and state librarian.

The curriculum in Dewey's school and in others that were soon started by his graduates emphasized technical subjects such as bibliography and cataloging; nonetheless, his students became enthusiastic missionaries who went forth to preach the value of libraries in American life. They must have been much like library school students today who learn to apply computer technology to library processes and then go out to show the library world how it should transform itself through automation.

Prominent librarians in the early days of library education were not as happy about the schools as were the students. Beginning around 1900, various committees and individual librarians investigated the work of the schools, never hesitating to make recommendations for improvement.

In 1923 a document appeared that had much more impact than any before it: *Training for Library Service,* a report prepared for the Carnegie Corporation by C.C. Williamson, a department head in the New York Public Library. Most of his recommendations were accepted by the schools, partly because what he wrote made sense to the library profession generally, and partly, perhaps, because the Carnegie Corporation had already shown an interest in providing financial support for the improvement of library education.

From 1923 to the mid-1930s, library education made considerable progress, encouraged by the corporation's generous gifts to the schools and its gifts to the American Library Association to support the ALA Board of Education for Librarianship, established in 1924. Part of the board's duty was to keep an eye on the schools to insure that they did a good job, so it was not always popular with library school officials.

One kind of library education, beginning in the late 1920s, went its own way with little encouragement from the library profession. The Graduate Library School was opened at the University of Chicago in 1926, largely because Frederick P. Keppel, who had become president of the Carnegie Corporation in 1923, thought that an advanced, research-oriented library school was needed. The corporation offered $1 million, later increased to about $1.6 million, as an endowment. The school turned out a few graduates, well-trained in research methods, who took responsible library positions mainly in academic libraries and as library school teachers and deans. Also, the school's publications were well respected. However, many librarians were slow to see the need for this kind of education; doctoral programs were not started at other universities until Illinois and Michigan began to offer the Ph.D. in 1948.

During the decade from 1936 to 1946, a half-dozen critical volumes by librarians and library school faculty were published on library education; from 1940 to 1948, seven conferences were held on the subject. Partly as a result of the opinions expressed in these books and conferences, it came to be felt that a professional librarian needed a graduate-level education with a greater emphasis than before on principles, theory, and problem solving; the student should be rewarded by the granting of a master's degree. Until ALA revised its standards in 1951, some schools that offered only a bachelor's degree or an undergraduate major had been approved.

The decade of the 1950s was a good one for library education; curricula were considered satisfactory and enrollments increased. In the mid-1950s the federal government, in line with its increasing concern for the welfare of less privileged Americans, began to give more financial aid to libraries than ever before. Demand for librarians grew, and recruiters descended on library schools, whose graduates often had the pleasant task of deciding among several job offers.

This increase in the need for librarians resulted in the federal government coming to the aid of library schools as well. Beginning in the mid-1960s, it supplied money to support students at both the master's and the doctoral levels. One reason for federal support of doctoral programs was that instruction at the master's level required more well-trained teachers than doctoral-level schools could produce.

In the 1970s, however, things did not go so well. A less favorable political climate in Washington and reduced employment opportunities in libraries occurred while library schools were expanding and new schools were opening. By the mid-1970s, qualified graduates were scrambling for jobs. In the last few years, a number of library schools have closed (see list on page 143). But the employment situation has improved somewhat, and the supply of library school graduates now corresponds more closely to the number needed.

In the years since World War II, debate about new directions for library education has continued. For example, the increasing importance of library automation and the need for libraries to enter the world of electronic information systems have caused major changes in curricula. To accommodate these new elements, a few schools have increased the requirements for the master's degree; several have added such terms as "information science" or "information studies" to their name. Also, librarians now need additional schooling to keep up with advances in information science; the library school is one of the agencies providing continuing education.

Over the years, education for librarianship in America, like education for other professions, has shown uneven progress. It has changed, sometimes in

New York State Library School, 1915

response to criticism from the library field, sometimes as a result of experimentation by the schools themselves, and sometimes because of stimulation provided by foundations or government agencies. This kind of development is to be expected in the education for any profession that exists in a free society that does not have an all-powerful government to hand down directives.

Source: "Library Education: A Mini-History," *American Libraries,* June 1986, pp. 406–8

Accredited library programs

THE FOLLOWING GRADUATE LIBRARY education programs are accredited (as of mid-1991) by the American Library Association under its 1972 *Standards for Accreditation.* All programs offer a master's-level degree; those marked with an asterisk (*) offer a doctorate or post-master's specialist or certificate program.

Brigham Young University, School of Library and Information Sciences, Provo, UT 84602; (801) 378-2977. Nathan M. Smith, director.

*Catholic University of America, School of Library and Information Science, Washington, DC 20064; (202) 319-5085. Deanna B. Marcum, dean.

*Clarion University of Pennsylvania, College of Communication, Computer Information Science and Library Science, Clarion, PA 16214; (814) 226-2271. Ahmad Gamaluddin, director.

*Clark Atlanta University, School of Library and Information Studies, Atlanta, GA 30314; (404) 880-8696. Charles D. Churchwell, dean.

Dalhousie University, School of Library and Information Studies, Halifax, NS, Canada B3H 4H8. Mary Dykstra, director.

*Drexel University, College of Information Studies, Philadelphia, PA 19104; (215) 895-2474. Richard H. Lytle, dean.

*Emporia State University, School of Library and Information Management, Emporia, KS 66801; (316) 343-5203. Martha L. Hale, dean.

*Florida State University, School of Library and Information Studies, R106,

Tallahassee, FL 32306; (904) 644-5775. F. William Summers, dean.

*Indiana University, School of Library and Information Science, Bloomington, IN 47405; (812) 855-2848. Daniel J. Callison, acting dean.

*Kent State University, School of Library Science, Kent, OH 44242; (216) 672-2782. Rosemary R. DuMont, dean.

*Louisiana State University, School of Library and Information Science, Baton Rouge, LA 70803; (504) 388-3158. Bert R. Boyce, dean.

McGill University, Graduate School of Library and Information Studies, Montreal, PQ, Canada H3A 1Y1; (514) 398-4204. J. Andrew Large, director.

North Carolina Central University, School of Library and Information Sciences, Durham, NC 27707; (919) 560-6485. Benjamin F. Speller Jr., dean.

Northern Illinois University, Department of Library and Information Studies, DeKalb, IL 60115; (815) 753-1733. Cosette N. Kies, chair.

*Pratt Institute, School of Information and Library Science, Brooklyn, NY 11205; (718) 636-3702. Rhoda Garoogian, dean.

*Queens College, City University of New York, Graduate School of Library and Information Studies, Rosenthall Room 254, Flushing, NY 11367; (718) 520-7194. Thomas Surprenant, director.

*Rosary College, Graduate School of Library and Information Science, River Forest, IL 60305; (708) 366-2490. Michael E.D. Koenig, dean.

*Rutgers University, School of Communication, Information and Library Studies, 4 Huntingdon St., New Brunswick, NJ 08903; (201) 932-7917. Betty J. Turock, chair and program director.

*St. John's University, Division of Library and Information Science, Jamaica, NY 11439; (718) 990-6200. Emmett Corry, director.

San Jose State University, Division of Library and Information Science, San Jose, CA 95192-0029; (408) 924-2490. James S. Healey, director.

*Simmons College, Graduate School of Library and Information Science, Boston, MA 02115-5898; (617) 738-2225. Robert D. Stueart, dean.

*Southern Connecticut State University, School of Library Science and Instructional Technology, New Haven, CT 06515; (203) 397-4532. Emanuel T. Prostano, dean.

*State University of New York at Albany, School of Information Science and Policy, Albany, NY 12222; (518) 442-5115. Richard S. Halsey, dean.

*State University of New York at Buffalo, School of Information and Library Studies, Buffalo, NY 14260; (716) 636-2412. George S. Bobinski, dean.

*Syracuse University, School of Information Studies, 4-206 Center for Science and Technology, Syracuse, NY 13244-2340; (315) 443-2736.

*Texas Woman's University, School of Library and Information Studies, Denton, TX 76204; (817) 898-2602. Keith Swigger, interim dean.

Université de Montréal, École de bibliothéconomie et des sciences de l'information, Montréal, PQ, Canada H3C 3J7; (514) 343-6044. Marcel Lajeunesse, directeur.

*University of Alabama, School of Library and Information Studies, Tuscaloosa, AL 35487-0252; (205) 348-4610. Philip M. Turner, dean.

University of Alberta, Faculty of Library and Information Studies, Edmonton, Alberta, Canada T6G 2J4; (403) 492-4578. Sheila Bertram, dean.

University of Arizona, Graduate Library School, Tucson, AZ 85719; (602) 621-3565. Charlie D. Hurt, director.

University of British Columbia, School of Library, Archival and Information Studies, Vancouver, BC, Canada V6T 1Y3; (604) 228-2404. Basil Stuart-Stubbs, director.

*University of California, Berkeley, School of Library and Information Studies, Berkeley, CA 94720; (415) 642-1464. Patrick Wilson, acting dean.

*University of California, Los Angeles, Graduate School of Library and Information Science, Los Angeles, CA 90024-1520; (213) 825-4351. Beverly P. Lynch, dean.

*University of Hawaii, School of Library and Information Studies, Honolulu, HI 96822; (808) 948-7321. Miles M. Jackson, dean.

*University of Illinois, Graduate School of Library and Information Science, 1407 W. Gregory, 410 DKH, Urbana, IL 61801-3680; (217) 333-3280. Leigh Estabrook, dean.

University of Iowa, School of Library and Information Science, Iowa City, IA 52242; (319) 335-5707. Carl F. Orgren, director.

University of Kentucky, College of Library and Information Science, Lexington, KY 40506-0039; (606) 257-8876. Thomas J. Waldhart, dean.

*University of Maryland, College of Library and Information Services, College Park, MD 20742; (301) 405-2033. Claude E. Walston, dean.

*University of Michigan, School of Information and Library Studies, Ann Arbor, MI 48109-1092; (313) 764-9376. Robert M. Warner, dean.

University of Missouri, Columbia, School of Library and Informational Science, Columbia, MO 65211; (314) 882-4546. Mary F. Lenox, dean.

*University of North Carolina, School of Information and Library Science, Chapel Hill, NC 27599-3360; (919) 962-8366. Barbara B. Moran, dean.

University of North Carolina at Greensboro, Department of Library and Information Studies, Greensboro, NC 27412; (919) 334-5100. Marilyn L. Miller, chair.

*University of North Texas, School of Library and Information Sciences, Denton, TX 76203; (817) 565-2445. Raymond F. Vondran, dean.

*University of Oklahoma, School of Library and Information Studies, Norman, OK 73019; (405) 325-3921. Robert D. Swisher, director.

*University of Pittsburgh, School of Library and Information Science, Pittsburgh, PA 15260; (412) 624-5230. Toni Carbo Bearman, dean.

University of Puerto Rico, Escuela Graduada de Bibliotecologia y Ciencias de la Información, Rio Piedras, PR 00931; (809) 763-6199. Annie F. Thompson, director.

Closings of ALA-accredited programs since 1978

1978	University of Oregon
1981	Alabama A&M
1983	Western Michigan University
1984	SUNY Geneseo
1984	University of Mississippi
1985	University of Minnesota
1985	University of Denver
1985	Ball State University
1986	Case Western Reserve University
1986	University of Southern California
1988	Emory University
1988	Vanderbilt University
1990	University of Chicago
1992	Columbia University

In 1970 there were 50 accredited programs; in 1980 there were 68, and in 1990 there were 60. The highest number was 70 programs, in March 1982. Since 1978 there has been a 7.8% reduction in the number of accredited programs.

In the past decade, only three programs have been accredited for the first time: University of Southern Mississippi, 1980; University of North Carolina at Greensboro, 1982; and University of Puerto Rico, 1990.

Source: Wilson Library Bulletin, January 1991, p. 49

University of Rhode Island, Graduate School of Library and Information Studies, Rodman Hall, Kingston, RI 02881; (401) 792-2947. Elizabeth Futas, director.

*University of South Carolina, College of Library and Information Science, Columbia, SC 29208; (803) 777-3858. Fred W. Roper, dean.

*University of South Florida, School of Library and Information Science, Tampa, FL 33620-8300; (813) 974-3520. John A. McCrossan, interim director.

University of Southern Mississippi, School of Library Science, Hattiesburg, MS 39406; (601) 266-4228. Jeannine Laughlin-Porter, director.

University of Tennessee, Knoxville, Graduate School of Library and Information Science, Knoxville, TN 37996-4330; (615) 974-2148. Glenn E. Estes, director.

*University of Texas at Austin, Graduate School of Library and Information Science, Austin, TX 78712-1276; (512) 471-3821. Brooke E. Sheldon, dean.

*University of Toronto, Faculty of Library and Information Science, Toronto, ON, Canada M5S 1A1; (416) 978-3202. Adele M. Fasick, dean.

University of Washington, Graduate School of Library and Information Science, Seattle, WA 98195; (206) 543-1794. Margaret Chisholm, director.

*University of Western Ontario, School of Library and Information Science, London, ON, Canada N6G 1H1; (519) 661-3542. Jean M. Tague, dean.

*University of Wisconsin-Madison, School of Library and Information Studies, Madison, WI 53706; (608) 263-2900. Jane B. Robbins, director.

*University of Wisconsin-Milwaukee, School of Library and Information Science, Milwaukee, WI 53201; (414) 229-4707. Mohammed M. Aman, director.

*Wayne State University, Library Science Program, Detroit, MI 48202; (313) 577-1825. Joseph J. Mika, director.

Source: Graduate Library Education Programs (Chicago: ALA, March 1991)

How to choose a library school

A PROSPECTIVE STUDENT should consider several factors in choosing a graduate program to obtain the master's in library/information studies. These factors may include both personal and professional considerations, such as the student's career plans, interest in various specifications, geographical mobility, and financial and other resources available. The following guidelines discuss program aspects and information gathering techniques that may assist the prospective student in making an informed decision.

Considerations in making a decision

ALA-accredited programs

The American Library Association accredits U.S. and Canadian master's programs in library and information studies that meet the ALA *Standards for Accreditation*. ALA considers the master's degree from an ALA-accredited library education program as the appropriate professional degree for librarians.

There are some non-accredited graduate programs of education for librarianship that are recognized in their geographical areas as providing sound programs for the preparation of librarians, but the reputation of these schools is not usually national. An individual has more geographical mobility and flexibility with a master's degree from an ALA-accredited program. Many institutions' hiring policies require that professional positions be filled by persons with a degree from an ALA-accredited program.

Norm's Library Levity

Like all true professions, librarianship has a language all of its own and one that, at present, is filled with both acronyms and cryptic words. A famous Rutgers dissertation alleged that the language of information science had a finite limit, which was fast approaching, on the number of terms it could devise—but we all know better than that. When an old idea is reborn, we will find a new name for it. Standard professional dictionaries, glossaries, and thesauri may tell us what normal words mean; the wonderful alternative definitions that so many librarians have been able to come up with tell us what the library meaning is. The following is a short, random selection of such definitions carefully stolen from a variety of authors and sources.

Assistant librarian. There is only one head librarian; the other 11 librarians on the staff are all assistant librarians. (Dale N. Bentz)

Authority file. A sort of master key to all the problems of the cat(alogue) burglar. (M. Hutton)

Bermanize. To assign access points to information based on acceptable contemporary social usage rather than an outmoded set of terminology codified in official formats. (Norman D. Stevens)

Cooperation. A term, with many variants, used to describe a range of library activities allegedly designed to enable libraries to work with each other in the sharing of resources to provide better service to all users, but which, in effect, are a means whereby individual libraries seek to provide the best service to their own users with the least direct expenditure of funds, while making the maximum use, at the least cost, of the resources and services of other libraries. (Norman D. Stevens)

DeGennaro. The minimal royalty payment usually made to an author by the Copyright Clearance Center, thus giving us the popular phrase, "This article isn't worth a DeGennaro!" *See also* Gennaro. (Barbara E. Markuson)

Faculty status. This usually means that an academic librarian is an instructor whom the rest of the faculty consider one notch higher than a clerk. (Dale N. Bentz)

Gennaro. The average royalty payment per use made to an author by the Copyright Clearance Center. *See also* DeGennaro. (Barbara E. Markuson)

Indicator digit. Look up these words separately in a dictionary and you will come to the conclusion that this means a finger-breadth instrument showing pressure. You will not be far wrong. The Moving Finger writes, and having writ moves on, but if we could have cancelled it, we would have done so, substituting the simple English word "pointer." (M. Hutton)

Libraryese. Any language used by a librarian or information scientist that is characterized by one or more of the following faults: inappropriate or unnecessary use of abstraction; euphemism; redundancy; circumlocution; the passive voice; or unnecessarily complicated or pretentious diction and syntax. (David Isaacson)

Page. Youngischer madchen vas ist buchen upsidedownen geshelven und all der time on Saturdaydate gedreamen. (Alice Payne)

Patron. Stubbornischer herren und frauen demanden readen *Peyton Place* und/oder sexlicher buchen instead *Moby Dick*. (Alice Payne)

Public library. The people's university. *See also* University library. (anon.)

Shelflist. The wobble in outmoded movable cabinets made of warped wood; also, an inventory of stock in which there are no embarrassing features such as analytical entries. (M. Hutton)

University library. The heart of the university. *See also* Public library. (anon.)

—Norman D. Stevens, The Molesworth Institute

ALA does not rank individual schools. Periodically, using a variety of methodologies, some researchers have compiled rankings of graduate schools in various disciplines. The validity of these rankings is questioned by some and accepted by others. Students interested in this type of listing should inquire at their local library reference department.

Generalist vs. specialist

Some students may prefer a general education in librarianship to a more specialized approach. Some may see their interests shift once they are enrolled in school and are exposed to the wide variety of settings in which librarianship and information management are practiced.

In addition to general preparation, some schools offer specialized tracks or courses that permit or encourage concentration in a specific area of library or information studies (e.g., school librarianship, art librarianship, medical librarianship, database design, serials management). The opportunity to specialize depends on the availability of special courses, on specialized class project/paper opportunities, and the availability of practicum/field site or student employment options.

Prospective students should plan a program of study and an intended career path based on an assessment of their past experiences, education, strengths and weaknesses, geographic mobility and future plans. Although students should be aware of job market opportunities, this should not necessarily dictate specializations. Faculty advisers can help greatly in the process of developing a program of study. Prospective students should recognize that the master's program is a beginning professional education level. They will need to have continuing education throughout their careers to keep up-to-date and to learn new skills applicable to different positions.

Gathering basic information

In addition to written information, prospective students can benefit from visits to schools they are considering. Most schools do not require an interview, but meetings can be arranged with an administrator or faculty member.

Curriculum

1. Catalogs. Contact the schools directly for their latest catalog and other information. The school catalogs provide much information on the curriculum available, such as the required courses, courses applicable to various specializations, and scope of electives. Also the catalogs usually include the school's mission, goals and objectives, application dates, and admission requirements and procedures (e.g., is there continuous admission or a specific deadline each year?).

2. Course schedules. Although the catalogs describe courses that are part of the curriculum, schools usually have a separate listing of courses that are being offered for the current term. Most have projected course schedules for the next academic year, and some will have projections for the next two to three years.

Students should carefully review the calendar of course offerings because not all courses will be presented each term. In some cases there may be prerequisites for certain courses or recommended "tracks" for different types of specializations. During a summer term the number of courses offered may differ from other times of the year. Summer courses are often at an accelerated pace for a shorter duration.

Flexibility

Flexibility in fulfilling course requirements is often available and is quite important to persons who are working or live some distance from a campus. Because correspondence courses are not counted for academic credit in ALA-accredited programs, it is important to determine what other options are available. Most programs allow limited credits to be taken in other schools or graduate departments on campus or in other universities to count towards the master's in library/information studies. Most schools will offer some type of independent study credits, but the number of these applicable to the degree is usually limited. Some schools will allow individuals to obtain a degree through a summers-only program; however, most have a time limit for completing a degree. Some schools emphasize full-time studies, while others have a larger percentage of part-time students. Many schools offer off-campus extension programs in their state or region, but may limit the number of courses that can be taken off-campus. Some offer courses through telecommunications at sites away from the main campus. In the future there may be more development of telecommunication courses, but for now only a few schools offer a limited number of credits in this fashion.

3

Faculty

The catalog for each school will list names of faculty, often with their degrees and specialization, and will indicate whether they are full-time or part-time. Additional biographical information may be reviewed in the *Directory of Library and Information Professionals,* available in some local library reference sections. The dean, director, or department chairperson of the school can provide information on the unavailability of faculty due to sabbaticals or other reasons during the projected enrollment period. Students might wish to check the professional affiliations, publications of faculty members, their areas of research and particularly those who teach in the specialized areas of interest.

Financial aid

Although financial aid varies from school to school, it is usually in the form of scholarships, teaching and researching assistantships, grants, work-study, loans and tuition assistance. Some financial aid opportunities are administered by the library school and others through the general university financial aid office. Higher tuition costs in some schools may be offset by larger scholarships or other financial aid amounts; determining the actual net cost of a program should be done with knowledge of the true bottom line cost, not just on the basis of one cost factor (tuition). Foreign students may be required to pay a differential fee in addition to the regular tuition fee. There may be reciprocal tuition agreements between states that can reduce tuition or tuition waivers with assistantship jobs.

Prospective students should describe their specific circumstances to the dean or director of admissions of a school in which they are interested, since many schools try to help individuals develop the best financial support package available. In addition to work-study and other part-time positions through the university, many local area libraries or other information agencies send to the schools notices of part- or full-time job opportunities. Some libraries or companies have tuition assistance as a fringe benefit. Work in an information agency such as a library not only helps finance an education; it provides valuable experience as well. Listings of aid from a variety of sources are provided in *Financial Assistance for Library Education,* an annual compilation available from the American Library Association in late October or early November for the following academic year. In Canada, prospective students should also write to the Canadian Library Association, Scholarship and Awards Committee, 200 Elgin St., Suite 602, Ottawa, Ontario, Canada K2P 1L5. Scholarship application deadlines vary and may be as early as a year in advance of the term of enrollment. Prospective students need to start the application process early if relying on financial assistance.

Placement services

Most schools offer some type of placement service for their current students as well as alumni. Many provide job-hunting and resume-writing seminars. Some have a designated placement officer, while others use faculty for job search advising. Placement credentials may be sent from the school or a central university office. Prospective students may wish to inquire about placement statistics of recent graduates. Some schools are better able to help graduates find jobs in the geographical area in which the school is located, but many receive job listings from around the country.

The institution

In addition to course offerings in the library school, prospective students may wish to check course offerings in other academic departments of the institution. Some schools offer the opportunity to obtain an interdisciplinary degree, namely, the library/information studies degree in addition to a degree in another discipline (e.g., joint MLS/MBA; MLS/M.Ed.). Prospective students should investigate other facilities such as computer and library resources, special collections (e.g., is there a special children's book collection for students interested in children's librarianship?), and various support services. Some schools have their own library while others cooperate with the university library to provide materials in support of the school curriculum. The general campus environment, availability of affordable on-campus housing or housing near the university, child care facilities, and certain types of extracurricular activities (e.g., student association, foreign student support group) may be important to some students.

Other sources of information

Employers in the local area and students and alumni of the school may be able to provide additional information about the school. Prospective students may know someone in the profession they admire who can provide general advice.

The Association for Library and Information Science Education (ALISE), 5623 Palm Aire Dr., Sarasota, FL 34243-3702, publishes an annual *Library and Information Science Education Statistical Report,* which compiles information on faculty, students, curriculum, income and expenditures, and continuing education for each school. ALISE also issues, as part of its *Journal of Education for Library and Information Science,* an annual directory of faculty with their subject area interests. Check a local library reference department for these publications.

The annual listing of "Placements and Salaries" in *Library Journal* (usually an October issue) provides information on the placements and salaries of the previous year's graduates from ALA-accredited master's degree programs (reprint available from ALA Office for Library Personnel Resources). The Canadian Library Association also has information on placements in Canada.

Students who plan to work in a school or public library should check state or provincial certification requirements prior to planning a curriculum. Library schools usually have this information or addresses of state library agencies, and state school library media supervisors to contact for this information are listed in the *Bowker Annual of Library and Book Trade Information,* available in most libraries. In Canada it is advisable to contact the provincial Departments of Education if one is interested in working in school libraries. These addresses and the provincial library associations can be found in the *Canadian Almanac and Directory.*

Job listings in professional journals, such as *American Libraries, Library Journal, Canadian Library Journal* and *Feliciter,* offer brief information on the types of qualifications desired for entry-level positions; these might be considered in selecting a school for the most appropriate master's program for particular career goals. The "Guide to Library Placement Sources" available from the ALA Office for Library Personnel Resources lists other sources of job listings. Other specialized national library and information science associations can provide career information in their area of interest.

Source: Guidelines for Choosing a Library and Information Studies Graduate Program
(Chicago: ALA Office for Library Personnel Resources, 1989)

Library students: Attitudes and aspirations

by Kathleen M. Heim and William E. Moen

THE LIBRARY AND INFORMATION SCIENCE Students' Attitudes, Demographics and Aspirations Survey (LISSADA) was designed to gather information on the population of master's students enrolled in U.S. ALA-accredited programs of library and information science in the spring of 1988. The top two tables on this page analyze the educational background of respondents to the survey, while the bottom table summarizes the influences that persuaded the students to pursue a career in library and information science.

3

Undergraduate majors ranked

Major	Number	%
English	625	18.5%
Education	553	16.4%
Social sciences	529	15.7%
Arts & humanities	527	15.6%
History	354	10.5%
Language	174	5.1%
Library & information science	131	3.9%
Biological sciences	129	3.8%
Business	107	3.2%
Physical sciences	91	2.7%
Law & medicine	43	1.3%
Engineering	13	0.4%

Master's subjects ranked

Subject	Number	%
Education	202	26.9%
Arts & humanities	175	23.3%
Social sciences	75	10.0%
English literature	68	9.0%
History	62	8.2%
Library & information science	39	5.2%
Biological sciences	32	4.3%
Business	29	3.9%
Physical sciences	21	2.8%
Law & medicine	6	0.8%
Engineering	2	0.3%
Other	15	2.0%

Influences to pursue library and information science work by enrollment status

	Part-time N	Part-time %	Full-time N	Full-time %
Brochure	80	4.3%	66	4.5%
Brother	14	0.8%	6	0.4%
Sister	19	1.0%	27	1.8%
Spouse/partner	110	6.0%	90	6.1%
Parent	76	4.1%	81	5.5%
Career counselor	31	1.7%	49	3.3%
Clergy	9	0.5%	11	0.8%
College librarian	138	7.5%	151	10.2%
Friend	247	13.4%	189	12.9%
Newspaper/magazine article	17	0.9%	18	1.2%
Occupational Outlook Handbook	28	1.5%	31	2.1%
Public librarian	197	10.6%	165	11.3%
School librarian	203	11.0%	125	8.6%
Special librarian	119	6.5%	92	6.3%
Teacher/faculty member	192	10.4%	171	11.6%

Type of position ranked most desirable upon graduation

Position	Number	% *
Reference services	968	28.9%
Youth services	874	26.0%
Education/research	605	18.1%
Computer systems/automation	543	16.2%
Adult services	513	15.4%
Collection development	505	15.1%
Administration	413	12.3%
Public relations	302	9.0%
Archival work	272	8.1%
Further graduate study	260	7.8%
Technical services	260	7.8%
Cataloging	254	7.6%
Service to minorities	246	7.4%
Bibliographic instruction	240	7.2%
Independent librarian/consultant	228	6.8%
Information broker	186	5.6%
Network/cooperative systems coordinator	175	5.3%
Government documents	148	4.4%
Abstracting/indexing	79	2.4%

* Categories were ranked separately, thus totals are not 100% overall but reflect high percentage for each category.

The table above shows what jobs students wanted to have after graduation, while the table below shows what type of library they wanted to work in. All of the data collected for the survey has been used to develop recruitment strategies to bring a more diverse group of highly qualified people into the profession.

Source: Kathleen M. Heim and William E. Moen, *Occupational Entry: Library and Information Science Students' Attitudes, Demographics and Aspirations Survey* (Chicago: ALA Office for Library Personnel Resources, 1989)

Type of library setting ranked most desirable upon graduation

Type of Library	Number	%
Large college or university	763	22.7%
School library media center	664	19.8%
Moderate-to-large public	610	18.2%
Non-corporate special	562	16.8%
Small college	550	16.4%
Library of Congress	325	9.8%
Community college	271	8.0%
Rural public	264	7.9%
Archives	263	7.9%
State	253	7.6%
Government	238	7.1%
Medical	213	6.4%
Law	196	5.9%
Computer industry	196	5.9%

* Categories were ranked separately, thus totals are not 100% overall but reflect high percentage for each category.

Writing books for the library profession

by Art Plotnik

WHAT WE USUALLY ASSOCIATE with shades of immortality is the book format. No other format provides quite the same durability, physical singularity, room for self-expression, and professional stature. At the same time, nothing can yield more frustration, trepidation, anxiety, and angst than a book project.

Even a modest 250-page survey-type of book can drag itself through four or five years of your life. Unless it's an easy spinoff of the work you do every day, or you have summers and sabbaticals to concentrate on it, such a book could take two years to put together, a year before you find the right publisher, another year for editing and manufacturing, and a year of helping the publisher get the thing reviewed and purchased. By that time, if the book isn't out of date, it may sell 1,500 copies, a fairly decent total for most library publishers. Your earnings will be about 10%, or some $3,000, or an average of $11.50 a week for the time you put into it. You'd be much better off with a paper-delivery route.

Earnings aside, there are at least the general rewards of publishing. If the book gets you tenure, a raise, or a new job offer, then your investment looks better. But don't forget, it can also bomb and embarrass you profoundly. What if every time you pick up a journal you find yourself being called a fatuous know-nothing?

Why are the anxieties of preparing a book so great? First of all, because the book format demands the highest standards of accuracy, which makes checking and rechecking seem endless. Second, the long stretch between completed manuscript and publication constantly threatens to render the work outdated.

Every librarian I know who has written a book has a horror story. Yet they'd all do it again. In addition to the traditional rewards, there are some special ones in this profession. Who else but librarians could thrill to seeing their titles come up for the first time on an OCLC terminal? And get excited watching the location symbols multiply over the next few months? ("Look, Maude—BHS! They've bought my book at the Black Hills State College in Spearfish, South Dakota!")

But writing a book is more than a series of little highs and lows. For many professionals trapped in one of the more mundane and tedious areas of library work—like being the library director—a book is a handle on something larger. It's a risk, a quest, that you can be proud of—even if it fails. The three-to-five years you're involved in a book give you that wonderful feeling of building something. Life becomes more than simply getting through each day without crying.

Books are one format available to people who don't write very well, but who do know their field. For, say, a book of readings, one can be merely a compiler, yet experience all the colorful agonies of an author. Actually, most library book publishers aren't terribly concerned about the quality of your prose, as long as it can be edited. What count most in the publishing decision are usually the following five factors; these are the items to address in a book "proposal"—the letter to a publisher that explains your project.

- The timeliness the topic will enjoy when it appears two or three years hence.
- The size and buying motivation of your market.
- Your authority to write on the subject—your credibility.
- The unique value of your particular approach to the subject.
- The cost of producing and marketing the book vs. the return that can be expected.

How well you write is not paramount in many types of projects. Of course, it always helps if you can write like an angel; but one reason it seems so impossible in this field—and why we have such a phobia for our literature—is the very nature of the library language. The nominatives and verbs we're encumbered with would challenge the very titans of American literature.

What if, instead of *The Old Man and the Sea*, Hemingway had called his book *The Aging End User and the Sea?* Nothing would have worked for Ernest in library language. I can just hear his macho characters saying, "It is good to access the online author catalog with you, my brother. But I spit upon your collection management and bibliographic control, and I obscenity your problem patron!"

Do not, my brother and sister writers, obscenity the professional library literature any further. It needs your help.

I think the overall best reason to publish is to share some unique insights on significant matters with as many colleagues as possible. This is why you might also consider writing a popular article for a general library magazine: because what you've come up with is so urgent, so useful to your colleagues, that it can't wait for a two-year scholarly cycle and then reach a handful of skeptics at best. We all do something in the course of our work that would be intriguing and timely to others. All we need is the perspective to recognize it and the motivation to spread the word. The motivation can come from any of these reasons, then, or a combination: to gain tenure, to become known, to add to the literature, or to share something hot while it's still hot.

Source: Art Plotnik, "Secrets of Writing for the Professional Literature of Librarianship without Losing Your Self-Esteem," in Betty-Carol Sellen, ed., *Librarian/Author: A Practical Guide on How to Get Published* (New York: Neal-Schuman, 1985), pp. 79–90

How to convert a dissertation or thesis into a book

A MANUSCRIPT DESIGNED to communicate mastery of the research process to an examining committee frequently fails to satisfy the requirements of a publisher. Authors submitting theses and dissertations to a publisher may anticipate requests for extensive modifications of their manuscript if it is accepted for publication. Indeed, some effort at revision prior to submission will enhance the likelihood of acceptance.

A book is addressed to an audience that is very different from the audience to whom a thesis, dissertation, or other research report is addressed. These differences include level of interest, prior knowledge of the subject, and objectives in reading the work. Major revisions are usually necessary, even to the most effective works.

Revisions that are often required include deletions, reorganization, and the writing of additional material. Some examples:

- The style of a dissertation frequently requires the repetition of material from section to section. In many cases this redundancy can be eliminated. Tables often should be deleted or converted into an explanatory narrative.
- Many of the fine points concerning prior research or methodology on the subject should be placed in appendices or footnotes.
- Abstractions must be carefully related to the concrete world through more extensive interpretation than would be necessary in a dissertation or thesis.

Source: College & Research Libraries News, April 1986, p. 277

Research tips

by Natalie L. Sproull

Ways to increase the response rate of mailed questionnaires

1. Include a cover letter which appeals to respondent's affiliation such as "as a graduate of Michigan State University, you may want to . . . "
2. Mail a reminder postcard about 10 days after the first mailing. Every respondent will have to receive this postcard unless subjects who have returned questionnaires are identified.
3. Mail a second questionnaire about one week after the postcard.
4. Contact nonrespondents by telephone.
5. Enclose a token, such as a pencil, pen or coin, with the questionnaire.
6. Write clear directions.
7. Mention how little time is required to complete the questionnaire.
8. Avoid open-ended items, if possible. People are more likely to respond to a format in which they can check items rather than generate responses.
9. Structure item responses so respondent can answer quickly and easily.
10. Structure the entire questionnaire so respondent can complete it easily and quickly. Make placement and sequencing of items logical and easy to follow.
11. Ensure that the questionnaire is professionally typed and printed so that its appearance gives the impression of credibility and professionalism.

Reasons to avoid questioning people*

1. **Lying.** People sometimes lie, particularly with sensitive items such as income, age, frequency of sex, and if they are ashamed of doing or not doing something. Items such as "have you ever stolen anything from a retail store?" or "did you vote in the last presidential election?" inevitably elicit some lying. Some people lie on all items because they resent being questioned.
2. **Omission.** People will often omit or refuse to answer sensitive items like those in #1. If too many people omit the same item, which is likely to occur with sensitive items, the item cannot be analyzed and important data will be missing.
3. **Inaccurate recall.** What did you eat for lunch last Thursday? What clothing did you wear to work Monday? With whom did you speak at work last week? The responses to questions like these depend on how well the respondent remembers. Memory deteriorates rather rapidly over time, particularly with items which are not significant to the respondent.
4. **Insufficient information.** Some people do not know and never knew the answer to a question, or they may have only pieces of information but not the whole. What corporations do you feel have the best environmental policies? People who are unfamiliar with organizations' environmental policies will tend to either omit the item or lie rather than admit insufficient information.
5. **Interviewer bias.** The interviewer might "lead" the subject to a certain response, either consciously or unconsciously.
6. **Interviewer-respondent interaction.** Sometimes the respondent and interviewer clash, creating respondent resentment which affects responses.
7. **Item bias.** Sometimes questionnaire items are worded so that they "lead" the respondent to specific responses.

---

*All of these reasons greatly lower the validity of the data. The best way to overcome these problems is to avoid questioning people and use other data collection methods.

Source: Natalie L. Sproull, *Handbook of Research Methods* (Metuchen, N.J.: Scarecrow, 1988)

MATERIALS 4

How to identify a first edition

by Bill McBride

Editing, printing, impression

AN EDITION IS the number of books printed before a certain percentage of the contents is revised. A **printing** is the number of copies produced when the printing plates or type are on the press. An **impression** is the same thing as a printing.

To the book collector, a **first edition** means a copy from the first printing of the first edition. To the publisher, a first edition may mean any copy of a title before it was substantially revised.

When a book says on the copyright page, "First and second printings before publication," it means that before the book was actually released for sale (publication), orders from booksellers exceeded the quantity of the first printing and the book had to be reprinted. Such a copy is not a book collector's first edition.

For a publisher-by-publisher guide to identifying first editions, see my *Pocket Guide to the Identification of First Editions* (4th ed. rev., 1989), available from McBride/Publisher, 161 S. Whitney St., Hartford, CT 06105.

Numbers and letters

Since the late 1940s, some publishers have adopted a new method of identifying their first editions. A series of letters (abcde . . .) or numbers (123456789 or 987654321 or 135798642) appears somewhere on the copyright page. If the "a" or the "1" is present, the copy in hand is from the first printing of the first edition. If this method were used by all publishers, there would be few identification problems.

Some questions have been raised about numbers and letters when they are used in conjunction with "first edition" or "first printing." A copyright page might show "FIRST EDITION B C D E" or "FIRST PRINTING 23456789." These are usually first editions because on second printings, the words "first edition" or "first printing" are removed, leaving the letters or numbers only.

Unfortunately, some publishers have used the system of numbers and letters in conjunction with FIRST EDITION, but leave the FIRST EDITION on the copyright page and remove the number "1" or letter "a" to indicate the second printing.

Identifying Book Club editions

Many titles of 20th-century fiction and nonfiction were published in Book Club editions. These editions often resemble the true first trade editions. Here are some ways to identify Book Club editions:

1. **No price** on the dust jacket. In the last few years some publishers, notably Vanguard, have taken to printing dust jackets without prices so that individual retail booksellers can affix their own price stickers. This is confounding to the collector, but typically the Book Club versions are lighter, smaller, and do not

carry the standard first edition identifier on the copyright page. In addition, university publishers usually do not print prices on their dust jackets.

2. **Book Club Edition** printed on the dust jacket's lower inner front flap. If this portion of the jacket is cut off, be wary and look further.

3. **Back cover debossing** at the bottom near the spine. A debossed (indented) star, circle, dot, crown, or other geometric device, colored or uncolored, indicates a Book Club edition, even when all other first edition indicators check out. This practice began about 1947, primarily by the Book-of-the-Month Club. Occasionally, the debossed symbol is found at the top of the back cover or somewhere in between the bottom and top edges of the back cover along the spine.

4. **"A Selection of the Book-of-the-Month Club"** printed on the dust jacket where the price is usually printed (upper front dust jacket flap). This practice was common in the 1960s and early 1970s. In the later 1970s and up, the same phrase was used as a promotional line on the jacket, and you may need to compare Book Club editions side by side with trade editions to determine firsts from Book Club editions, especially if there is no debossing on the back cover.

5. **Reprints from original plates.** Many books printed by such publishers as A. L. Burt, Grosset & Dunlap, Tower Books, The Book League, The Literary Guild, and others, often used the printing plates of the true first edition and neglected to alter the copyright page. Thus, some books may appear to be first editions, when in fact they are actually reprints by another company.

6. **Switched dust jackets: a caution.** Some Book Club editions so closely resemble true first editions that the mere substitution of a second trade edition dust jacket for the Book Club jacket can fool even veteran collectors and dealers. It is therefore wise to check *all* points of Book Club identification before purchase or sale. Many of these books are termed *false firsts*, Book Club editions that masquerade as true firsts.

4

Source: Bill McBride, comp., *A Pocket Guide to the Identification of First Editions* (Hartford, Conn.: The author, 1989)

Book sizes

THERE IS MUCH CONFUSION about the definition of book sizes and little consistency in usage. The common book trade designation of sizes was based originally on the relation to a sheet of paper measuring approximately 19 by 25 inches. When folded once to make two leaves (4 pages), it was a **folio**; when folded twice to make four leaves (8 pages), it was a **quarto**; when folded to eight leaves (16 pages), an **octavo**; when folded to 12 leaves (24 pages), a **duodecimo** or **twelvemo**; when folded to 16 leaves (32 pages), a **sixteenmo**, etc.

This is the historical background of book sizes and is the basis for terms still used in the rare book trade. In exact bibliographical descriptions, as in describing rare books, the historical definition applies.

However, present trade practice almost invariably refers to a measurement of the height of the binding, not the size of the leaf. Usual library practice calls for the use of centimeters, the measurement again referring to the height of the binding.

With the present variety of paper sizes, all dimensions are approximate:

Folio, F or 2o, over 30 cm (approx. 15 inches) high.
Quarto, 4to, 30 cm (approx. 12 inches) high.
Octavo, 8vo, 25 cm (approx. $9^3/4$ inches) high.
Duodecimo or **twelvemo,** 12mo, 20 cm (approx. $7^3/4$ inches) high.
Sixteenmo, 16mo, $17^1/2$ cm (approx. $6^3/4$ inches) high.
Twentyfourmo, 24mo, 15 cm (approx. $5^3/4$ inches) high.
Thirtytwomo, 32mo, approx. 5 inches high.

Fortyeightmo, 48mo, approx. 4 inches high.
Sixtyfourmo, 64mo, approx. 3 inches high.

Other sizes include:

Double elephant folio, approx. 50 inches high.
Atlas folio, approx. 25 inches high.
Elephant folio, approx. 23 inches high.

Any book wider than it is high is designated as oblong and such descriptive note is abbreviated "obl." or "ob." and precedes such terms as quarto, octavo, etc. If the width of the book is less than three-fifths of its height, it is designated narrow, abbreviated "nar." If the width of a book exceeds three-fourths of its height, but is no greater than its height, it is designated square.

Source: Heartsill Young, ed., *The ALA Glossary of Library and Information Science*
(Chicago: American Library Association, 1983)

Colophons and curses

by Leila Avrin

colophon. 1. In early printed books, the statement given at the end of the text proper which provides some or all of the following particulars: author, title, subject, printer, publisher, place, and date. 2. In modern books, a statement given at the end of the text proper or on the verso of the title lead which provides some or all of the following particulars: printer, typeface, type of paper, the materials used in binding, the printing equipment employed, the names of the personnel engaged in the production of the item.—*The ALA Glossary of Library and Information Science*

In the literature found in Mesopotamian libraries there was often a colophon in the last column. The tradition of the colophon is much older than its Greek name implies; it flourished in ancient Mesopotamia and Egypt. The colophon's information and composition varied. It gave the standard title, that is, the book's opening words, and the name of the scribe, at times with his patronym. Seldom  was the book's author named. Sometimes the colophon verified that this edition was a true copy of the original book, giving the name of the scribe of the prototype and its date and owner. Then the date of the copy would be given along with the name of the patron who commissioned the book and the nature of the work. If the book was composed of several tablets, each one would be numbered and identified by the work's title. Catchlines were also used, that is, the first line of each tablet was written at the bottom of the preceding one. At times the total number of lines on the following tablet would be recorded as well. Other books-in-series would be subdivided into parts and numbered, so that books using both catchlines and numbered sections were doubly protected against the loss of their pages. The longest clay book found has seventy-one tablets containing eight thousand lines, which would make it less convenient bedtime reading than the fifteen-board, wax-tablet book of a similar text, where twice as much could be written on each page. Another aspect of the Mesopotamian colophon was the blessing upon the reader who preserves the text and a curse upon the one who would try to alter it, burn it, dissolve it in water, lose it, lend it, or allow anyone to steal it. Neo-

Babylonian books have curses in them. The curse continued to be the custom in colophons of Hebrew and Arabic books into the Middle Ages, and the practice continued in European manuscripts as well. One is reminded of these when one reads the words of caution against copyright infringement in contemporary books, although these are mild in comparison to a good Near Eastern book curse.

The note found at the end of Greek scrolls eventually came to be called *colophon*, believed to mean "summit" or "finishing stroke" in Greek, although no one is sure of the term's origin and it may not have been used until the Renaissance. It has been attributed to Erasmus. (Colophon was the name of a town off the coast of Asia Minor.) No Hellenistic colophon with a scribe's name has yet come to light. The major purpose of the Greek colophon in the Hellenistic and Roman periods seems to have been to prove the authenticity of the text copied, not only for its own validity but to emphasize the authority and quality of the text that served as its model. The archives or library or temple in which the original was housed was identified.

Some Hellenistic scribes and Greek-writing scribes of the Roman and Byzantine periods, in their colophons, counted the lines that they wrote, for poetry at first and then for prose as well, and recorded the total. The practice originated as an assurance to the reader or the purchaser of the scroll that the text was copied properly and in its entirety. But line-counting also served a more practical purpose—it determined the scribe's fee for transcribing the book.

The colophons left to us by Latin scribes of the Middle Ages number in the thousands. Here are a few quoted by Falconer Madan in *Books in Manuscript*, translated by Peter Gulewich:

"Let the copyist be permitted to put an end to his labor."

"Now I've written the whole thing: for Christ's sake give me a drink."

"Let the reader's voice honor the writer's pen."

The European writer of the colophon usually recorded his name, the date, and the place of writing. Sometimes he left a curse against the unauthorized borrower or destroyer of the book, in Near Eastern fashion. Here is one from Barcelona, which may have been influenced by its Jewish or Muslim counterparts:

"For him that stealeth, or borroweth and returneth not, this book from its owner, let it change into a serpent in his hand and rend him. Let him be struck with palsy, and all his members blasted. Let him languish in pain crying aloud for mercy, and let there be no surcease to his agony till he sing in dissolution. Let bookworms gnaw his entrails in token of the Worm that dieth not, and when at last he goeth to his final punishment, let the flames of Hell consume him forever."

Source: Leila Avrin, Scribes, Script and Books: The Book Arts from Antiquity to the Renaissance (Chicago and London: American Library Association/British Library, 1991)

Book production costs

The American Booksellers Association reports that costs for a typical $19.95 book are:

Manufacturing	$1.75
Composition/typesetting/design	$1.50
Overhead	$2.65
Promotion	$ .60
Royalties	$2.00
Retailer profit	$9.35
Publisher profit	$2.10

Source: American Libraries, November 1990, p. 942

Booklist's best of the 1980s

AT THE END OF THE DECADE, the editors of *Booklist* (an ALA review magazine) chose the best books and nonprint materials reviewed by the magazine in the past 10 years. These are the adult nonfiction and fiction titles they selected. If you are searching for a good book and don't quite know what you want, this is a good place to start. You may want to read the original reviews, too.

Nonfiction

Baker, Russell. *Growing Up* (Congdon & Weed, 1982).

Bloom, Allan. *The Closing of the American Mind* (Simon & Schuster, 1987).

Brundvand, Jan Harold. *The Vanishing Hitchhiker* (Norton, 1981).

Callahan, Daniel. *Setting Limits: Medical Goals in an Aging Society* (Simon & Schuster, 1987).

Calvino, Italo. *Italian Folktales* (HBJ, 1980).

Carruth, Hayden. *Tell Me Again How the White Heron Rises and Flies across the Nacreous River at Twilight toward the Distant Islands* (New Directions, 1989).

Child, Julia. *The Way to Cook* (Knopf, 1989).

Clampitt, Amy. *The Kingfisher* (Knopf, 1983).

Collier, James Lincoln. *Louis Armstrong: An American Genius* (Oxford, 1983).

Gage, Nicholas. *Eleni* (Random, 1983).

Gay, Peter. *Freud: A Life for Our Time* (Norton, 1988).

Gonzalez-Crussi, F. *The Five Senses* (HBJ, 1989).

Hamilton, Ian. *Robert Lowell* (Random, 1983).

Hughes, Robert. *The Fatal Shore* (Knopf, 1987).

Hyde, Dayton O. *Don Coyote* (American Original, 1986).

Jackman, Brian. *The Marsh Lions: The Story of an African Pride* (Godine, 1983).

Johnson, Paul. *Modern Times* (Harper, 1983).

Kazan, Elia. *Elia Kazan: A Life* (Knopf, 1988).

Kidder, Tracy. *Among Schoolchildren* (Houghton, 1989).

Kingston, Maxine Hong. *China Men* (Knopf, 1980).

Lane, Harlan. *When the Mind Hears: A History of the Deaf* (Random, 1984).

Lovell, Mary S. *Straight on Till Morning: The Biography of Beryl Markham* (St. Martin's, 1987).

Lukas, J. Anthony. *Common Ground* (Knopf, 1985).

Luker, Kristin. *Abortion and the Politics of Motherhood* (Univ. of California, 1984).

McPherson, James. *Battle Cry of Freedom: The Era of the Civil War* (Oxford, 1988).

Manchester, William. *Goodbye, Darkness: A Memoir of the Pacific War* (Little, Brown, 1980).

Milosz, Czeslaw. *The Collected Poems, 1931-1987* (Ecco, 1988).

Morris, Jan. *Journeys* (Oxford, 1985).

Pagels, Elaine. *Adam, Eve and the Serpent* (Random, 1988).

Plowden, David. *An American Chronology* (Viking/Studio, 1982).

Rhodes, Richard. *The Making of the Atomic Bomb* (Simon & Schuster, 1987).

Rodriguez, Richard. *Hunger of Memory* (Godine, 1982).

Sherry, Norman. *The Life of Graham Greene* (Viking, 1989).

Shilts, Randy. *And the Band Played On: Politics, People, and the AIDS Epidemic* (St. Martin's, 1987).

Timerman, Jacobo. *Prisoner without a Name, Cell without a Number* (Knopf, 1981).

Truitt, Ann. *Turn: The Journal of an Artist* (Viking, 1986).

Wideman, John Edgar. *Brothers and Keepers* (Holt, 1984).

Wilford, John Noble. *The Riddle of the Dinosaur* (Knopf, 1986).

Winn, Marie. *Children without Childhood* (Pantheon, 1983).

Fiction

Allende, Isabel. *The House of the Spirits* (Knopf, 1985).
Ariyoshi, Sawako. *The Twilight Years* (Kodansha, 1984).
Atwood, Margaret. *Cat's Eye* (Doubleday, 1989).
Benford, Gregory. *Great Sky River* (Bantam/Spectra, 1987).
Carver, Raymond. *What We Talk about When We Talk about Love* (Knopf, 1981).
Coetzee, J. M. *Waiting for the Barbarians* (Penguin, 1982).
DeLillo, Don. *White Noise* (Viking, 1985).
Erdrich, Louise. *Love Medicine* (Holt, 1984).
García Márquez, Gabriel. *Love in the Time of Cholera* (Knopf, 1988).
Helprin, Mark. *Winter's Tale* (HBJ, 1983).
James, P. D. *A Taste of Death* (Knopf, 1986).
le Carré, John. *Smiley's People* (Knopf, 1980).
Leonard, Elmore. *Stick* (Arbor House, 1983).
McCarthy, Cormac. *Blood Meridian* (Random, 1985).
McMurtry, Larry. *Lonesome Dove* (Simon & Schuster, 1985).
Malamud, Bernard. *The Stories of Bernard Malamud* (Farrar, 1983).
Mason, Bobbie Ann. *In Country* (Harper, 1985).
Morrison, Toni. *Beloved* (Knopf, 1987).
Ozick, Cynthia. *The Messiah of Stockholm* (Knopf, 1987).
Phillips, Jayne Anne. *Machine Dreams* (Dutton, 1984).
Powers, J. F. *Wheat That Springeth Green* (Knopf, 1988).
Price, Reynolds. *Kate Vaiden* (Atheneum, 1986).
Toole, John Kennedy. *A Confederacy of Dunces* (Louisiana State Univ., 1980).
Tyler, Anne. *Dinner at the Homesick Restaurant* (Knopf, 1982).
Updike, John. *Rabbit Is Rich* (Knopf, 1981).
Walker, Alice. *The Color Purple* (HBJ, 1982).
Welty, Eudora. *Collected Stories* (Harcourt, 1980).

4

Source: Booklist, December 15, 1989

Norm's Library Levity

Originally published in the January 22, 1982, issue of *The Innocent Bystander* at the University of Connecticut Libraries, and reprinted in the famous "Marginalia" column of *The Chronicle of Higher Education* on February 17, 1982, this gentle spoof of the quality of that year's best sellers still retains a certain accuracy.

101 Things to Do with a Dead Rubik's Cube. An imaginative guide, lavishly illustrated in cartoon fashion, that demonstrates the many and varied uses that can be made of a Rubik's cube once the owner has given up trying to solve it.

Rubik's Cat. The story of, and possible solutions to, a new puzzle in which you are challenged to reassemble Rubik's disassembled calico cat, with all colors exactly as they were originally, as quickly as possible and before the cat dies from a loss of blood.

The Official Preppy Cat and Cube Handbook. A guide to the proper preppy attitudes toward, and selection of, cats as pets, strays, cartoons, and posters as well as to the variety of cube type games and puzzles.

Garfield Solves Rubik's Cube. America's most popular cat's solution to the world's most popular puzzle.

Lincoln's Doctor's Dog Challenges Garfield's Solutions to Rubik's Cube. An all-time classic best seller meets a combination of contemporary best sellers in an all-out effort to climb to the top of the best-seller list.

—*Norman D. Stevens, The Molesworth Institute*

Outstanding reference sources

EACH YEAR THE ALA Reference and Adult Services Division's Reference Sources Committee examines hundreds of reference works to identify those that are essential for small and medium-sized public or academic libraries. The following are their picks for 1990 and 1991, incorporating reference sources published between 1988 and 1990.

General

Barnow, Erik, ed. *International Encyclopedia of Communications* (Oxford University, 1989).

Breen, Walter. *Walter Breen's Complete Encyclopedia of U.S. and Colonial Coins* (Doubleday, 1988).

Callis, Scott, ed. *The Sports Address Book* (Pocket, 1988).

Compton's Multimedia Encyclopedia [CD-ROM] (Britannica Software, 1990).

Dickson, Paul. *The Dickson Baseball Dictionary* (Facts on File, 1989).

Sader, Marion, ed. *General Reference Books for Adults: Authoritative Evaluations of Encyclopedias, Atlases, and Dictionaries* (Bowker, 1988).

Shatzkin, Mike, ed. *The Ballplayers: Baseball's Ultimate Biographical Reference* (Arbor House, 1990).

Shea, Peter, and others. *Across America: An Atlas and Guide to the National Parks for Visitors with Disabilities* (Northern Cartographic, 1988).

Science and medicine

Asimov, Isaac. *Asimov's Chronology of Science and Discovery* (Harper and Row, 1989).

Bruce, Katherine, and others. *Science Experiments on File: Experiments, Demonstrations and Projects for School and Home* (Facts on File, 1989).

Burgess, Warren E., and others. *Dr. Burgess's Atlas of Marine Aquarium Fishes* (T.F.H., 1988).

Clayman, Charles B. *The American Medical Association Encyclopedia of Medicine* (Random House, 1989).

Goldsmith, Edward, and Nicholas Hildyard. *The Earth Report: The Essential Guide to Global Ecological Issues* (Price Stern Sloan, 1988).

Immelmann, Klaus, and Colin Beer. *A Dictionary of Ethology* (Harvard University, 1989).

Moore, David M., ed. *Marshall Cavendish Illustrated Encyclopedia of Plants and Earth Sciences* (Marshall Cavendish, 1988).

Netter, Frank H. *Atlas of Human Anatomy* (CIBA-GEIGY, 1989).

Sammons, Vivian Ovelton. *Blacks in Science and Medicine* (Hemisphere, 1989).

Wilcox, Bonnie, and Chris Walkowicz. *Atlas of Dog Breeds of the World* (T.F.H., 1989).

Humanities and the arts

Banham, Martin, ed. *Cambridge Guide to World Theatre* (Cambridge University, 1988).

Blain, Virginia, and others. *The Feminist Companion to Literature in English: Women Writers from the Middle Ages to the Present* (Yale University, 1990).

Clark, Gregory R., comp. *Words of the Vietnam War* (McFarland, 1990).

Denvir, Bernard. *The Thames and Hudson Dictionary of Impressionism* (Thames and Hudson, 1990).

Gänzl, Kurt, and Andrew Lamb. *Gänzl's Book of Musical Theatre* (Schirmer, 1989).

Hanks, Patrick, and Flavia Hodges. *A Dictionary of Surnames* (Oxford University, 1988).

Hodgson, Terry. *The Drama Dictionary* (New Amsterdam Books, 1988).

Kernfeld, Barry, ed. *New Grove Dictionary of Jazz* (Grove's Dictionaries of Music, 1988).

Leo, John R., comp. *Guide to American Poetry Explication, Vol. 2* (G.K. Hall, 1989).

Magill, Frank, ed. *Critical Survey of Mystery and Detective Fiction* (Salem Press, 1989).

Ruppert, James, comp. *Guide to American Poetry Explication, Vol. 1* (G.K. Hall, 1989).

Sadie, Stanley, and Alison Latham, eds. *The Norton/Grove Concise Encyclopedia of Music* (Norton, 1988).

Solé, Carlos A., and Maria Isabel Abrev, eds. *Latin American Writers* (Scribners, 1989).

Stockdale, Freddie, and Martin Dreyer. *The International Opera Guide* (Trafalgar Square, 1990).

Vinson, James, ed. *International Directory of Art and Artists, Vol. 1* (St. James, 1990).

Webster's Dictionary of English Usage (Merriam-Webster, 1989).

Culture and civilization

Abrams, Irwin. *The Nobel Peace Prize and the Laureates: 1901-1987* (G.K. Hall, 1988).

Charney, Israel W., ed. *Genocide: A Critical Bibliographic Review* (Facts on File, 1988).

Congress A to Z: CQ's Ready Reference Encyclopedia (Congressional Quarterly, 1988).

Darnay, Arsen J., ed. *Manufacturing USA: Industry Analyses, Statistics, and Leading Companies* (Gale, 1989).

Eichholz, Alice, ed. *Ancestry's Red Book: American State, County and Town Resources* (Ancestry, 1989).

Frumkin, Norman. *Guide to Economic Indicators* (M.E. Sharpe, 1990).

Gutman, Israel, ed. *The Encyclopedia of the Holocaust* (Macmillan, 1990).

Herbst, Sharon Tyler. *The Food Lover's Companion: Comprehensive Definitions of over 3,000 Food, Wine and Culinary Terms* (Barron's, 1990).

Magel, Charles R. *Keyguide to Information Sources in Animal Rights* (McFarland, 1989).

Miller, Randall M., and John David Smith, eds. *The Dictionary of Afro-American Slavery* (Greenwood, 1988).

Mitchell, Sally, ed. *Victorian Britain: An Encyclopedia* (Garland, 1988).

Nelson, Michael, ed. *Congressional Quarterly's Guide to the Presidency* (Congressional Quarterly, 1989).

Shafritz, Jay M. *The Dorsey Dictionary of American Government and Politics* (Dorsey, 1988).

Watson, Bruce W., and others, eds. *United States Intelligence: An Encyclopedia* (Garland, 1990).

Wilson, Charles Reagan, and William Ferris, eds. *Encyclopedia of Southern Culture* (University of North Carolina, 1989).

Zophy, Angela Howard, ed. *Handbook of American Women's History* (Garland, 1990).

Social sciences

Brooklyn Public Library, Business Library Staff. *Business Rankings Annual* (Gale, 1989-).

Cordasco, Francesco, ed. *Dictionary of American Immigration History* (Scarecrow, 1990).

Derdak, Thomas, and others, eds. *International Directory of Company Histories*, vol. 1 (St. James, 1988).

Doctor, Ronald M., and Ada P. Kahn. *The Encyclopedia of Phobias, Fears, and Anxieties* (Facts on File, 1989).

Dynes, Wayne R., ed. *Encyclopedia of Homosexuality* (Garland, 1990).

Kastenbaum, Robert, and Beatrice Kastenbaum. *Encyclopedia of Death* (Oryx, 1989).

Strauss, Diane Wheeler. *Handbook of Business Information: A Guide for Librarians, Students, and Researchers* (Libraries Unlimited, 1988).

Religion

Guiley, Rosemary Ellen. *The Encyclopedia of Witches and Witchcraft* (Facts on File, 1989).

Melton, J. Gordon, Jerome Clark, and Aidan A. Kelley. *New Age Encyclopedia* (Gale, 1990).

Mills, Watson E., and others, eds. *Mercer Dictionary of the Bible* (Mercer University, 1990).

Reid, Daniel G. *Dictionary of Christianity in America: A Comprehensive Resource on the Religious Impulse that Shaped a Continent* (InterVarsity, 1990).

Wigoder, Geoffrey, ed. *The Encyclopedia of Judaism* (Macmillan, 1989).

Source: Reference Sources Committee, ALA Reference and Adult Services Division

Notable books, 1988–1990

THE FOLLOWING BOOKS, all published between 1987 and 1990, have been chosen for their significant contribution to the expansion of knowledge or for the pleasure they can provide to adult readers. Each year the Notable Books Council of the ALA Reference and Adult Services Division makes the selections, based on the criteria of wide general appeal and literary merit. More information on the books can be found by consulting *Booklist*, *Choice*, or other book-review journals.

Fiction

Allende, Isabel. *Eva Luna* (Knopf, 1988).

Atwood, Margaret. *Cat's Eye* (Doubleday, 1989).

Bausch, Richard. *Mr. Field's Daughter* (Simon & Schuster, 1990).

Bell, Christine. *Perez Family* (Norton, 1990).

Boyle, T. Coraghessan. *East Is East* (Viking, 1990).

Boyle, T. Coraghessan. *If the River Was Whiskey* (Viking, 1989).

Burgess, Anthony. *Any Old Iron* (Random House, 1989).

Busch, Frederick. *Absent Friends* (Knopf, 1989).

Byatt, A. S. *Possession: A Romance* (Random House, 1990).

Carver, Raymond. *Where I'm Calling From: New and Selected Stories* (Atlantic Monthly, 1988).

Casey, John. *Spartina* (Knopf, 1989).
Coetzee, J. M. *Age of Iron* (Random House, 1990).
DeLillo, Don. *Libra* (Viking, 1989).
Desai, Anita. *Baumgartner's Bombay* (Knopf, 1989).
Dexter, Pete. *Paris Trout* (Random House, 1988).
Dubus, Andre. *Selected Stories* (Godine, 1988).
Erdrich, Louise. *Tracks* (Henry Holt, 1988).
Garciá Márquez, Gabriel. *Love in the Time of Cholera* (Knopf, 1988).
Gordon, Mary. *The Other Side* (Viking, 1989).
Greenberg, Joanne. *Of Such Small Differences* (Henry Holt, 1988).
Hamill, Pete. *Loving Women: A Novel of the Fifties* (Random House, 1989).
Hoffman, Alice. *Seventh Heaven* (Putnam, 1990).
Irving, John. *A Prayer for Owen Meany* (Morrow, 1989).
Ishiguro, Kazuo. *The Remains of the Day* (Knopf, 1989).
Kingsolver, Barbara. *Animal Dreams* (Harper Collins, 1990).
Kingsolver, Barbara. *Homeland* (Harper, 1989).
Lessing, Doris. *The Fifth Child* (Knopf, 1989).
Lively, Penelope. *Passing On* (Grove Weidenfeld, 1989).
Mahfuz, Najib. *Palace Walk* (Doubleday, 1990).
Miller, Sue. *Family Pictures* (Harper, 1990).
Mukherjee, Bharati. *The Middleman and Other Stories* (Grove, 1989).
Munro, Alice. *Friend of My Youth* (Knopf, 1990).
Naylor, Gloria. *Mama Day* (Ticknor & Fields, 1988).
O'Brien, Tim. *The Things They Carried* (Houghton Mifflin, 1990).
Ozick, Cynthia. *The Shawl* (Knopf, 1989).
Popham, Melinda. *Sky Water* (Graywolf, 1990).
Powers, J. F. *Wheat That Springeth Green* (Knopf, 1988).
Schaeffer, Susan Fromberg. *Buffalo Afternoon* (Knopf, 1989).
Sexton, Linda Gray. *Points of Light* (Little, Brown, 1988).
Smith, Lee. *Fair and Tender Ladies* (Putnam, 1988).
Smith, Lee. *Me and My Baby View the Eclipse* (Putnam, 1990).
Spark, Muriel. *A Far Cry from Kensington* (Houghton, 1988).
Stegner, Wallace. *Collected Stories of Wallace Stegner* (Random House, 1990).
Tan, Amy. *The Joy Luck Club* (Putnam, 1989).
Tilghman, Christopher. *In a Father's Place* (Farrar, 1990).
Tyler, Anne. *Breathing Lessons* (Knopf, 1988).
Wilson, Robley. *Terrible Kisses* (Simon & Schuster, 1989).
Yehoshua, A. B. *Five Seasons* (Doubleday, 1989).

Poetry

Carver, Raymond. *A New Path to the Waterfall* (Atlantic Monthly, 1989).

Harris, Marie, and Kathleen Aguero, eds. *An Ear to the Ground: An Anthology of Contemporary American Poetry* (University of Georgia, 1989).

Klein, Michael, ed. *Poets for Life: Seventy-six Poets Respond to AIDS* (Crown, 1989).

Wright, James. *Above the River: The Complete Poems* (Farrar, 1990).

Nonfiction

Ackerman, Diane. *Natural History of the Senses* (Random House, 1990).

Bentsen, Cheryl. *Maasai Days* (Summit, 1989).

Berton, Pierre. *The Arctic Grail: The Quest for the North-West Passage and the North Pole, 1818-1909* (Viking, 1988).

Bishop, Jerry E., and Michael Waldholz. *Genome: The Story of the Most Astonishing Adventure of Our Time—The Attempt to Map All the Genes in the Human Body* (Simon & Schuster, 1990).

Branch, Taylor. *Parting the Waters: America in the King Years, 1954-1963* (Simon & Schuster, 1989).

Cagin, Seth, and Philip Dray. *We Are Not Afraid: The Story of Goodman, Schwerner, and Chaney and the Civil Rights Campaign for Mississippi* (Macmillan, 1988).

Chestnut, J. L., Jr., and Julia Cass. *Black in Selma* (Farrar, 1990).

Conway, Jill Kerr. *The Road from Coorain* (Knopf, 1989).

Dorris, Michael. *The Broken Card* (Harper, 1989).

Duberman, Martin Bauml. *Paul Robeson* (Knopf, 1989).

Ellmann, Richard. *Oscar Wilde* (Knopf, 1988).

Freedman, Samuel. *Small Victories* (Harper, 1990).

Friedman, Thomas L. *From Beirut to Jerusalem* (Farrar, 1989).

Gay, Peter. *Freud: A Life for Our Times* (Norton, 1988).

Goodall, Jane. *Through a Window: My Thirty Years with the Chimpanzees of Gombe* (Houghton Mifflin, 1990).

Goodwin, Richard N. *Remembering America: A Voice from the Sixties* (Little, Brown, 1988).

Hansen, Eric. *Stranger in the Forest: On Foot across Borneo* (Houghton, 1988).

Hirsch, Kathleen. *Songs from the Alley* (Ticknor & Fields, 1989).

Kidder, Tracy. *Among Schoolchildren* (Houghton, 1989).

Klüver, Billy, and Julie Martin. *KiKi's Paris: Artists and Lovers, 1900-1930* (Abrams, 1989).

Lester, Julius. *Lovesong: Becoming a Jew* (Henry Holt, 1988).

Lord, Bette Bao. *Legacies: A Chinese Mosaic* (Knopf, 1990).

McPherson, James M. *Battle Cry of Freedom: The Civil War Era* (Oxford University, 1988).

Maddox, Brenda. *Nora: The Real Life of Molly Bloom* (Houghton, 1988).

Malan, Rian. *My Traitor's Heart: A South African Exile Returns to Face His Country, His Tribe and His Conscience* (Atlantic Monthly, 1990).

Pagels, Elaine. *Adam, Eve, and the Serpent* (Random House, 1988).

Sharansky, Natan. *Fear No Evil* (Random House, 1988).

Szarkowski, John. *Photography until Now* (Museum of Modern Art, 1989).

Takaki, Ronald. *Strangers from a Different Shore: A History of Asian Americans* (Little, Brown, 1989).

Wills, Garry. *Under God: Religion and American Politics* (Simon & Schuster, 1990).

Source: Notable Books Council, ALA Reference and Adult Services Division

Coretta Scott King Awards

THE CORETTA SCOTT KING AWARD is presented annually by the Coretta Scott King Task Force of the ALA's Social Responsibilities Round Table. Recipients are African American authors and illustrators whose distinguished books promote an understanding and appreciation of the culture and contribution of all people to the realization of the "American dream." The award commemorates the life and work of Martin Luther King, Jr., and honors his widow, Coretta Scott King, for her courage and determination in continuing the work for peace and world brotherhood.

The award was founded in 1969 by the late Glyndon Flynt Greer, a distinguished African American school librarian, and it became an official ALA unit award in 1982. The following are the award-winning authors and illustrators since 1970.

Authors

1991—Mildred D. Taylor, *The Road to Memphis* (Dial, 1990).
1990—Patricia and Frederick McKissack, *A Long Hard Journey: The Story of the Pullman Porter* (Walker, 1989).
1989—Walter Dean Myers, *Fallen Angels* (Scholastic, 1988).
1988—Mildred D. Taylor, *The Friendship* (Dial, 1987).
1987—Mildred Pitts Walter, *Justin and the Best Biscuits in the World* (Lothrop, 1986).
1986—Virginia Hamilton, *The People Could Fly: American Black Folktales* (Knopf, 1985).
1985—Walter Dean Myers, *Motown and Didi* (Viking, 1984).
1984—Lucille Clifton, *Everett Anderson's Goodbye* (Holt, 1983).
1983—Virginia Hamilton, *Sweet Whispers, Brother Rush* (Philomel, 1982).
1982—Mildred D. Taylor, *Let the Circle Be Unbroken* (Dial, 1981).
1981—Sidney Poitier, *This Life* (Knopf, 1980).
1980—Walter Dean Myers, *The Young Landlords* (Viking, 1979).
1979—Ossie Davis, *Escape to Freedom: A Play about Young Frederick Douglass* (Viking, 1977).
1978—Eloise Greenfield, *Africa Dream* (Crowell, 1977).
1977—James Haskins, *The Story of Stevie Wonder* (Lothrop, 1976).
1976—Pearl Bailey, *Duey's Tale* (Harcourt, 1975).
1975—Dorothy Robinson, *The Legend of Africania* (Johnson, 1974).
1974—Sharon Bell Mathis, *Ray Charles* (Crowell, 1973),
1973—Alfred Duckett, *I Never Had It Made: The Autobiography of Jackie Robinson* (Putnam, 1972).
1972—Elton C. Fax, *17 Black Artists* (Dodd, 1971).
1971—Charlemae Rollins, *Black Troubadour: Langston Hughes* (Rand McNally, 1970).
1970—Lillie Patterson, *Dr. Martin Luther King, Jr., Man of Peace* (Garrard, 1969).

Illustrators

1991—Leo and Diane Dillon, for *Aida,* by Leontyne Price (HBJ, 1990).
1990—Jan Spivey Gilchrist, for *Nathaniel Talking,* by Eloise Greenfield (Black Butterfly, 1988).
1989—Jerry Pinkney, for *Mirandy and Brother Wind,* by Patricia C. McKissack (Knopf, 1988).
1988—John Steptoe, for *Mufaro's Beautiful Daughters* (Lothrop, 1987).
1987—Jerry Pinkney, for *Half a Moon and One Whole Star,* by Crescent Dragonwagon (Macmillan, 1986).
1986—Jerry Pinkney, for *The Patchwork Quilt,* by Valerie Flournoy (Dial, 1985).
1984—Pat Cummings, for *My Mama Needs Me,* by Mildred Pitts Walter (Lothrop, 1983).
1983—Peter Magubane, for *Black Child* (Knopf, 1982).
1982—John Steptoe, for *Mother Crocodile: An Uncle Amadou Tale from Senegal,* translated by Rosa Guy (Delacorte, 1981).
1981—Ashley Bryan, for *Beat the Story Drum Pum-Pum* (Atheneum, 1980).
1980—Carole Byard, for *Cornrows,* by Camille Yarbrough (Coward-McCann, 1979).
1979—Tom Feelings, for *Something on My Mind,* by Nikki Grimes (Dial, 1978).
1974—George Ford, for *Ray Charles,* by Sharon Bell Mathis (Crowell, 1973).

Source: ALA Social Responsibilities Round Table and ALA Office for Library Outreach Services

Famous librarians' favorite books

WHAT DO PROMINENT LIBRARIANS have to say about their favorite books? In late 1990 a group of library leaders was polled on their preferences—those publications that have given them great enjoyment or have significantly affected their professional or personal lives and philosophies. We defined the term "book" as loosely as possible, so that they could have the widest latitude to include such widely disparate media as 15th-century incunabula, audiovisual materials, Ph.D. dissertations, oral histories, dramatic performances, or entire runs of periodicals. Here are the results, in their own words.

Toni Carbo Bearman, Dean and Professor, University of Pittsburgh School of Library and Information Science

1) *The Dead* (1987), a film directed by John Huston and based on the short story by James Joyce. Its images are locked in my mind.

2) National Commission on Libraries and Information Science, *National Information Policy: Report to the President of the United States* (1976). As pertinent today as it was then.

3) A. D. Little, *Into the Information Age* (ALA, 1978). This deserves to be read widely and discussed by all of us.

4) Martha E. Williams, ed., *Annual Review of Information Science and Technology.* I learn from each of these volumes, published on behalf of the American Society for Information Science.

5) S. I. Hayakawa, *Language in Thought and Action* (5th ed., 1989). I read this early in my teens and have gone back to it frequently for its simple and clear reminders of the complexities of thought and communication.

Gordon Conable, Director, Monroe County (Mich.) Library System

1) Gershon Legman, *The Rationale of the Dirty Joke* (1975).
2) Lynd Ward, *God's Man* (1929).
3) Austin Tappan Wright, *Islandia* (1942).
4) Knut Hamsun, *Growth of the Soil* (1917).
5) Christo, *Christo: Surrounded Islands* (1985).
6) Norma Klein, *The Swap* (1983).
7) Olive Schreiner, *The Story of an African Farm* (1883).
8) Eadweard Muybridge, *Animal Locomotion* (1887).
9) Milton H. Erickson, *Collected Papers* (1980).
10) Walt Kelly, *The Pogo Stepmother Goose* (1954).

Ann H. Eastman, Executive Director, Virginia Center for the Book

The books in the field that have most affected me are those projects on which I have worked with ALA and other groups:

1) Walter C. Allen, Eleanor Blum, and Ann Eastman, "The Quality of Trade Book Publishing in the 1980s," *Library Trends,* Fall 1984.

2) Ann Eastman and Roger Parent, *Great Library Promotion Ideas* (ALA, 1984).

3) Peter S. Jennison and Robert N. Sheridan, *The Future of General Adult Books and Reading in America* (ALA, 1970).

4) Dan Lacy, *Freedom and Equality of Access to Information* (ALA, 1986).

5) Nancy Larrick, *A Parent's Guide to Children's Reading* (1983).

6) Daniel Melcher and Margaret Saul, *Melcher on Acquisition* (ALA, 1971).

7) Donald E. Riggs and Gordon A. Sabine, *Libraries in the '90s: What the Leaders Expect* (1988).

Barbara J. Ford, Associate Director, Trinity University Library, San Antonio

1) Jesse H. Shera, *The Foundations of Education for Librarianship* (1972). Shera's classic exploration of the role of the library and library profession offers inspiration and ideas.

2) Alan Lakein, *How to Get Control of Your Time and Your Life* (1973). An important book for those who need to make the best use of their time. Return to it periodically and be reminded of good approaches.

3) Donald W. Krummel, ed., *A Librarian's Collacon: An Anthology of Quotations and Aphorisms Reflecting the Moral Philosophy of the Library Profession* (1971). Delightful, though dated, collection of quotations of interest to librarians.

4) Betty-Carol Sellen, ed., *The Librarian's Cookbook* (1989). Mouth-watering collection of recipes from librarians.

5) Wisconsin Women Library Workers, *Murial Fuller Memorial Series*. Postcards celebrating women librarians, including Minnie Earl Sears, May Massee, Agnes Inglis, Eliza Atkins Gleason, and Margaret E. Monroe.

6) *REFORMA Newsletter*, quarterly, edited by Elena Tscherny, Washington, D.C. A good way to stay current on library services to the Spanish-speaking population.

7) Kathleen Weibel and Kathleen M. Heim, *The Role of Women in Librarianship, 1876-1976* (1979). A sourcebook that documents the ongoing struggle of women librarians to achieve full opportunities and recognition.

8) *SRRT Newsletter*, quarterly, edited by Chris Sokol, Chicago. A good forum for issues of social responsibility.

9) *WLW Newsletter*, quarterly, edited by Audrey Eaglen, Jefferson, N.C. Founded over ten years ago by Women Library Workers in Berkeley, California, to provide a forum to evaluate library materials and share information on the empowerment of women.

10) Committee on the Status of Women in Librarianship, *Your Library: A Feminist Resource* (ALA, 1985). Brief bibliographies on women's issues.

4

Norman Horrocks, Vice President, Scarecrow Press

1) *The Oxford English Dictionary* (2d ed., 1989). Words and their meanings have always held a fascination for me, so the *OED* has to be the top of my list. Now that the University of Waterloo has online searching capabilities, the potential for browsing is enormous.

2) William Shakespeare, *The Complete Works*. To read, to declaim, and—above all—to enjoy, there really is none to place ahead of him.

3) Of all the sports with which I have been associated as player or spectator, cricket remains supreme. It has inspired a literature beyond any other, and the writings of Neville Cardus are still a joy to turn to. He puts the flesh on the bones of the games he describes, all of which are recorded in the pages of *Wisden's Cricketer's Almanack* from 1864 onwards.

4) Sir Arthur Conan Doyle created the world's greatest detective in Sherlock Holmes; the Holmes stories are fascinating to read and re-read.

5) Having served in Britain's Army Intelligence Corps, I find books on espionage appealing. James Bamford's *The Puzzle Palace* (1983) is superb in dealing with codes and ciphers.

Winona Jones, Librarian, East Lake High School, Tarpon Springs, Fla.

1) Margaret Mitchell, *Gone with the Wind* (1936). This became a favorite when I was very young. Only years later did I see the movie. Scarlett's return to Tara is *still* my very favorite literary passage.

2) Robert Frost, *Poems*. Each has had a very special memory for me, especially "The Road Not Taken."

3) Robert Louis Stevenson, *A Child's Garden of Verses* (1885). The only gift I ever

received from my father. I was shocked but happily surprised. I spent countless hours reading it over and over again, and I can still quote some of them from memory.

4) William Cullen Bryant, "Thanatopsis" (1817). I first learned of this piece as the Worthy Matron of my Eastern Star chapter. I have made the final section my life guide.

5) *The Declaration of Independence* (1776). Nothing can compare with this document. It is the epitome of the rights of *all* persons.

Patrick O'Brien, Director of Libraries, Dallas Public Library

1) Herman Hesse, *Journey to the East* (1932).
2) Richard Wright, *Black Boy* (1945).
3) J. P. Donleavy, *The Ginger Man* (1955).
4) Marshall McLuhan, *Understanding Media* (1964).
5) Richard Brautigan, *Trout Fishing in America* (1967).
6) John McPhee, *Levels of the Game* (1969).
7) Pauline Wilson, *Community Elite and the Public Library* (1977).
8) Mary Gordon, *Final Payments* (1978).
9) Pat Conroy, *Prince of Tides* (1986).
10) Alvin Kernan, *The Death of Literature* (1990).

Amy Owen, Director, State Library Division, State of Utah, Salt Lake City

1) Ivan Doig, *Dancing at the Rascal Fair* (1987). It's always Doig's language that captures me. He writes words that almost force me to read aloud in order to savor their flavor and hear their rhythms. This novel dissects the tangled web of friendship and betrayal between two young Scottish immigrants in frontier Montana.

2) Gary Zukav, *The Dancing Wu Li Masters: An Overview of the New Physics* (1979). A fascinating, nonchemical path to an altered state of consciousness.

3) Natalie Babbit, *The Devil's Storybook* (1974). It's sly, it's funny, it's short. It deserves to be read aloud, slowly, to an appreciative audience. I don't think I could ever like anyone who can't find something to smile about in this book.

4) Orson Scott Card, *Ender's Game* (1985). One of Card's best. Through the story of a game that proves to be no game, it probes the human heart and human values.

5) Roger Tory Peterson, *A Field Guide to Western Birds* (1969). Watching birds has been one of the greatest pleasures of my adult life, and this field guide is an absolute classic.

6) Tony Hillerman, *Listening Woman* (1978). This mystery captures the haunting beauty of the Southwestern desert and the rich interplay of Anglo, Hispanic, and Native American cultures in the Four Corners region. I dare anyone to read past the first page and put it (or any other Hillerman mystery) down.

Charles Robinson, Director, Baltimore County Public Library

1) Rex Roberts, *Your Engineered House* (1964). Questions the conventional wisdom in house construction. It inspired me to build my summer house in Maine and a Victorian garage, updated by post-and-beam construction, in Maryland. Great fun. Carpenters seldom need psychiatrists. Must be the hammering.

2) Robert H. Waterman, Jr., *The Renewal Factor: How the Best Get and Keep the Competitive Edge* (1988). I hate long-range planning, but if I don't do it, the library will go, like many others, to hell in a handbasket. This book helped enormously. Don't knock pop management: it's better than bad management.

3) *Skinned Knuckles: A Journal of Car Restoration*, monthly, Monrovia, Calif.; and *The Antique Studebaker Review*, bi-monthly, Dallas, Tex. Self-explanatory. I have been skinning my knuckles on a 1938 Studebaker coupe since 1982. Like house construction, great fun—and the project is never finished!

4) *Library Journal*, bimonthly, New York. Over the years, editor in chief John

Berry has goaded me into thinking about public libraries. My philosophy has developed diametrically opposed to his, but we share the same enthusiasm and commitment. He's nuts, but I owe him a lot.

5) Thomas H. Ballard, *The Failure of Resource Sharing in Public Libraries and Alternative Strategies for Service* (ALA, 1986). Ballard knocks the conventional wisdom in libraries, and he's at least 86.83% right. An important and pragmatic book. I'm one of only 20 people who have read it.

6) C. S. Forester, *Captain Horatio Hornblower* (1939). I read it first in 1941, and it started me on a lifelong love affair with British naval history. I've since read about 1,862 books in this area of interest. Naturally, I served two years in the U.S. Army.

Patricia Glass Schuman, President, Neal-Schuman Publishers, Inc.

1) Albert Camus, *The Stranger* (1942).
2) Saul Alinsky, *Reveille for Radicals* (1989).
3) Robert Heinlein, *Stranger in a Strange Land* (1963).
4) Dan W. Dodson, *Power Conflict and Community Organizations* (Council for American Unity).
5) *Chin P'ing Mei: The Adventurous History of Hsi Men and His Six Wives* (1960).
6) John Kenneth Galbraith, *The Anatomy of Power* (1983).
7) Shoshanna Zuboff, *In the Age of the Smart Machine* (1988).
8) Elizabeth Janeway, *Man's World, Women's Place: A Study in Social Mythology* (1971).

Elliot L. Shelkrot, President and Director, The Free Library of Philadelphia

1) Thomas North Gilmore, *Making a Leadership Change* (1988). Tom Gilmore's ability to give an organizational leader a sense of options and perspective has been of great use. I recommend it highly for new leaders in any organization.

2) A. Wolf, *The True Story of the 3 Little Pigs* (1989). I knew there was something wrong with the Three Little Pigs story. This myth has finally been retold and the true villains and victims are sorted out for all time.

Phyllis Van Orden, Professor, Florida State University School of Library and Information Science

1) Esther Forbes, *Johnny Tremain* (1941). For introducing me, as a child, to the world of historical fiction based on thorough research.

2) Jella Lepman, *A Bridge of Children's Books* (ALA, 1969). For inspiration about the difference one individual can make in the world through introducing children to books.

3) Hilda Taba, *Curriculum Development: Theory and Practice* (1962). For her informative synthesis and analysis of the many theories that influence education, and for Taba's ability to relate these to practice.

4) Lillian Gerhardt, editor of *School Library Journal.* For timely, thought-provoking editorials and coverage.

5) Austin Tappan Wright, *Islandia* (1942). For a novel that withstands many readings, as one explores with the hero one's own values and dreams.

6) "The Year's Work in . . ." articles in *Library Resources and Technical Services.* For their thoughtful and comprehensive review of the year's literature and the identification of current issues and concerns.

Government documents

Federal archives and records

THE NATIONAL ARCHIVES and Records Administration (NARA) establishes policies and procedures for managing the records of the U.S. government. It was established in 1984 as an independent agency to replace the National Archives and Records Service, which was an office of the General Services Administration. The NARA makes original documents and records available for use by researchers, answers requests for information, and provides copies of documents for a fee. The office also publishes the daily *Federal Register*, the *Code of Federal Regulations*, the *U.S. Government Manual*, and many other public documents.

How to locate an unpublished government record

First, contact the Records Clerk or Records Manager for the Federal agency in question. They should be able to tell you the location and accessibility of the document. If it is available at a Federal Records Center or the National Archives, they can give you the reference and box numbers you will need when you contact the appropriate records center or archive.

Second, if the agency cannot provide satisfactory information, contact the Federal Records Center or archives office directly.

Third, if the document is classified or otherwise unfindable, you have the option of issuing a Freedom of Information Act request to the appropriate Federal agency (see the next section for details).

National and regional archives offices

Each archives office receives records from Federal agencies in the region it serves. Roughly 3% of all Federal records are eventually retained in the national or regional archives offices. The other 97% are destroyed after 10–75 years, according to schedules set by statute. When documents are transferred to the National Archives, they become public property and available to researchers.

National Archives, 8th and Pennsylvania Ave., N.W., Washington, DC 20408; (202) 501-5400.

National Archives—New England Region, 380 Trapelo Road, Waltham, MA 02154; (617) 647-8100.

National Archives—Northeast Region, Building 22, Military Ocean Terminal, Bayonne, NJ 07002-5388; (201) 823-7252.

National Archives—Mid-Atlantic Region, 9th and Market Streets, Room 1350, Philadelphia, PA 19107; (215) 597-3000.

National Archives—Southeast Region, 1557 St. Joseph Ave., East Point, GA 30344; (404) 763-7477.

National Archives—Great Lakes Region, 7358 S. Pulaski Rd., Chicago, IL 60629; (312) 581-7816.

National Archives—Central Plains Region, 2312 E. Bannister Road, Kansas City, MO 64131; (816) 926-6272.

National Archives—Southwest Region, 501 W. Felix St., P.O. Box 6216, Fort

Worth, TX 76115; (817) 334-5525.

National Archives—Rocky Mountain Region, Building 48, Denver Federal Center, P.O. Box 25307, Denver, CO 80225; (303) 236-0818.

National Archives—Pacific Southwest Region, 24000 Avila Road, P.O. Box 6719, Laguna Niguel, CA 92677-6719; (714) 643-4241.

National Archives—Pacific Sierra Region, 1000 Commodore Drive, San Bruno, CA 94066; (415) 876-9009.

National Archives—Pacific Northwest Region, 6125 Sand Point Way, NE, Seattle, WA 98115; (206) 526-6507.

National Archives—Alaska Region, 654 W. Third Ave., Room 012, Anchorage, AK 99501; (907) 271-2441.

Federal records centers

The National Archives and Records Administration also manages fifteen Federal Records Centers. Federal agencies retire certain noncurrent public records to these centers in accordance with established disposition schedules. These records are still controlled by the originating agencies, but stored at the centers until they are either destroyed or sent to the national or regional archives. The Federal Records Centers provide reference services and furnish information from the records they hold.

Federal Records Center—Atlanta, 1557 St. Joseph Ave., East Point, GA 30344; (404) 763-7476.

Federal Records Center—Boston, 380 Trapelo Rd., Waltham, MA 02154; (617) 647-8745.

Federal Records Center—Chicago, 7358 S. Pulaski Rd., Chicago, IL 60629; (312) 581-7816.

Federal Records Center—Dayton, 3150 Springboro Rd., Dayton, OH 45439; (513) 225-2878.

Federal Records Center—Denver, Building 48, Denver Federal Center, P.O. Box 25307, Denver, CO 80225; (303) 236-0804.

Federal Records Center—Fort Worth, Box 6216, Fort Worth, TX 76115; (817) 334-5515.

Federal Records Center—Kansas City, 2312 E. Bannister Rd., Kansas City, MO 64131; (816) 926-7271.

Federal Records Center—Los Angeles, 24000 Avila Rd., Laguna Niguel, CA 92677; (714) 643-4220.

Federal Records Center—New York, Building 22, Military Ocean Terminal, Bayonne, NJ 07002; (201) 823-7161.

Federal Records Center—Philadelphia, 5000 Wissahickon Ave., Philadelphia, PA 19144; (215) 951-5588.

Federal Records Center—San Francisco, 1000 Commodore Dr., San Bruno, CA 94066; (415) 876-9003.

Federal Records Center—Seattle, 6125 Sand Point Way, NE, Seattle, WA 98115; (206) 526-6501.

National Personnel Records Center, Civilian Personnel Records, 111 Winnebago St., St. Louis, MO 63118; (314) 425-5722.

National Personnel Records Center, Military Personnel Records, 9700 Page Blvd., St. Louis, MO 63132-5100; (314) 263-7201.

Washington National Records Center, 4205 Suitland Rd., Suitland, MD 20409; (301) 763-7000.

Source: National Archives and Records Administration; Federal Records Center—Chicago

How to file a Freedom of Information Act request

by Don Schmitt and Paul Jeffries

WHETHER YOU ARE requesting information about a UFO sighting or about FBI surveillance of library patron records, you might have a need to use the Freedom of Information Act (FOIA). The FOIA is a federal law which provides that all records of agencies of the federal government are open to the public unless there is a specific exemption from disclosure. The FOIA permits any person to request agency records. What follows is a brief outline of the best way to seek records from federal agencies under the Freedom of Information Act.

1. **Determine first which agency has the records.** If you aren't sure which agency has the records you seek, consult the *United States Government Manual* or the *Federal Legal Directory* (Oryx, 1990), which describe the various agencies and their functions. If in doubt, contact each potentially relevant agency, talk with the "Freedom of Information Officer" of the agency, and ask whether the agency has the records you seek, and if not, which agency does.

2. **Write to the "Freedom of Information Officer."** Each agency has an employee or department that handles FOIA requests. Correspond with that employee or department.

3. **Make your request pursuant to the Freedom of Information Act.** "I am writing to request agency records pursuant to the Freedom of Information Act, 5 U.S.C. 552."

4. **Arrange to pay the agency search and copying fees.** Ask the agency what it charges to search for and copy requested records. Tell the agency in writing you will pay all fees or will pay all fees up to a certain specified dollar amount, to comply with your request. For example: "I agree to pay search and copying fees required to satisfy this request up to $25. If you anticipate the total fees will exceed $25, please expend $25 to retrieve those records which are most responsive and readily available, and advise me as to the amount of any additional fees necessary to comply with this request."

5. **Describe precisely which records you want.** Give the agency as much specific information as possible to identify the documents whose disclosure you seek, such as subject matter, relevant dates or time periods, and authors and recipients of the records. The more detailed and specific identifying information you give the agency, the greater the likelihood the agency will promptly locate and retrieve the records you seek.

6. **Use "and" and "or."** Ask for all records that concern "inquiry no. 1" or that relate to "inquiry no. 2" or that have to do with both "1" and "2." Don't let the agency play grammatical games with you.

7. **Ask for the "disclosure of all reasonably segregable portions of records which are in whole or in part exempt from disclosure."** Tell the agency to give you those portions of a document not exempt from disclosure, even if other parts of the document cannot be released. Otherwise the agency might withhold the entire document just because a part of it is exempt from disclosure.

8. **Tell the agency you expect a written reply within the statutory time limits of the FOIA.** The agency must make a "determination" on any request under the FOIA within 10 days of the agency's receipt of your request. In unusual circumstances, the agency can take an additional 10 days to respond. Hold the agency to the time limits.

The 10 days for agency determination on a request and the 20 days for agency determination on an appeal do not include Saturdays, Sundays, and legal public holidays. Also, the 10-day extension for agency determinations under "unusual circumstances" applies to both initial agency determinations and agency appeal determinations. Therefore, in "unusual circumstances" an agency can take 20 days to issue a determination on a request and 30 days to decide an appeal.

9. **If the agency does not answer your request on time, appeal immediately.** If the agency denies your request, you can appeal. Treat a delay as a denial of your request. Appeal the denial right away. Find out from the agency to whom you should appeal. Appeal in writing. Attach copies of all relevant correspondence, e.g., your initial FOIA request letter. The agency must respond to your appeal within 20 days.

10. **If the agency denies your request on the merits, appeal immediately.** Most agencies have a 30-day time limit on appeals. Appeal sooner rather than later.

11. **If the agency denies your appeal, you can sue.** Consult legal counsel before suing. If counsel advises you that you have a good case, consider suing in federal district court to compel the agency to release the requested records to you. Federal district courts give some priority to FOIA cases. If you win your case, the court may award you attorney's fees and court costs.

12. **Be aware of the FOIA's exemptions.** One exemption protects national security from disclosure. Another exempts certain intra-agency memoranda. Seek legal counsel when faced with claims of exemption. But do not let mere claims by the agency that the records you seek are exempt deter you. Federal courts interpret narrowly the FOIA's exemptions, in favor of disclosure and against agency secrecy. And the FOIA provides that any reasonably segregable portion of a record shall be disclosed to any person requesting it after deletion of the exempted portions. Although you should expect agencies to claim exemptions, FOIA researchers have had some success in the courts in securing release of certain documents.

Today it is more important than ever to pressure government agencies to release federal records. In these times of encroaching restrictions on free access to government information, let's make full use of the powerful FOIA research tool.

Source: Don Schmitt and Paul Jeffries, "How to Use the Freedom of Information Act," *International UFO Reporter* 12 (May/June 1987): 22–23

Reference sources for U.S. government publications

by Julia Schwartz

FINDING SPECIFIC DOCUMENTS can be complicated, even when you have an accurate citation. This list, modified from Julia Schwartz's *Easy Access to Information in United States Government Documents* (ALA, 1986), gives a likely reference source for the types of document you might be searching for. Consult her book for more detailed instructions.

Bills, current
    CCH Congressional Index; access by subject and author. Gives latest status, summary of contents.

Bills, digest
    Digest of Public General Bills and Resolutions, 1936–present; access by subject, short title. Indexed by sponsor, cosponsor, identical bills.

Bills on microfiche

Superintendent of Documents Microfiche User's Guide for Congressional House and Senate Bills, 1980–present; access by bill number. Provides identifying microfiche number and grid coordinates.

Committee prints

CIS/Annual, 1970–present; access by subject, name, title. Has index of Senate print numbers.

Congress, members of

CCH Congressional Index, 1937–present; access by name. Biographies, lists of committee assignments, state delegations, officers, addresses, and telephone numbers.

Congressional reports and documents

CIS U.S. Serial Set Index, 1789–1969; access by subject, keyword. Indexes 1st–91st Congress, 1st Session. Includes American State Papers.

CCH Congressional Index, 1937–present; access by report number. Found in Committee hearings section.

CIS/Annual, 1970–present; access by subject and title. Has index of report and document numbers.

Monthly Catalog of U.S. Government Publications, 1981–present; access by author, title, subject. Title keyword, series/report, stock, bill number index.

Contract reports

Government Reports Announcements and Index, 1945–present; access by keyword, personal and corporate author. Has contract/grant number, NTIS order/report number index.

Documents

Cumulative Subject Index to the Monthly Catalog of U.S. Government Publications, 1895–1899; access by subject. Cites *Monthly Catalog* year and page.

Cumulative Subject Index to the Monthly Catalog of U.S. Government Publications, 1900–1971; access by subject. Cites *Monthly Catalog* year, page, or entry number.

Cumulative Title Index to U.S. Public Documents, 1789–1976; access by title. Provides SuDoc number and date, reel code reference to *Checklist '76*.

Monthly Catalog of U.S. Government Publications, 1895–present; access by author, title, subject. Indexes by title keyword, series/report, contract, stock, classification numbers.

Documents for sale

Publications Reference File (PRF), 1979–present; access by author, title, subject. Gives stock and catalog numbers, keyword, series index, prices.

Government Reports Announcements and Index, 1945–present; access by keyword, personal and corporate author. Has contract/grant number, NTIS order/report number index, price code.

NTIS Title Index, 1964–present; access by keyword and author. Has report/accession number index, price code.

Hearings

CIS U.S. Congressional Committee Hearings Index, 1800s–1969; access by subject, organization, name, title. Indexes by bill, SuDoc, and report number.

CIS/Annual, 1970–present; access by subject, name, title. Index of Senate hearing numbers.

Hearings, current

CCH Congressional Index; access by name of committee or subcommittee. Provides subject, date of hearing.

Laws

United States Code, 1926–present; access by subject and popular name of law. Cites the text of the law in *United States Statutes*.

United States Statutes at Large, 1873–present; access by subject, title, names of individuals. Gives the number of the bill, date, and citations to the *United States Code.*

Laws, current
CCH Congressional Index; access by subject and author. Listed by public law number and bill number in "Enactment" section.

Laws, digests
Digest of Public General Bills and Resolutions, 1936–present; access by public law number, subject, short title.

Legislative history
CCH Congressional Index, 1937–present; access by subject and author. See "Status of Bills" and "Enactments" sections.

CIS/Annual, 1970–present; access by subject and title. Found in "Legislative Histories" section.

Digest of Public General Bills and Resolutions, 1936–present; access by subject and short title. Found in "Public Laws" section.

Periodicals
Index to U.S. Government Periodicals, 1970–present; access by author and subject. Gives title of periodical; SuDoc numbers listed in front of each issue.

Monthly Catalog of U.S. Government Publications—Periodicals Supplement, 1985–present; access by author, title, subject. Title keyword, series/report, stock numbers index.

Presidential documents
Weekly Compilation of Presidential Documents, 1965–present; access by subject and name. Material is also contained in *Public Papers of the Presidents.*

Rules
Index to the Code of Federal Regulations, 1977–present; access by subject, geographic region.

CIS Federal Register Index, 1984–present; access by subject and name. Has indexes to CFR number and agency docket number.

Statistics
American Statistics Index, 1974–present; access by subject, name, title, report number. Indexed within categories: geographic, economic, demographic.

Supreme Court decisions
Digest of U.S. Supreme Court Reports, Lawyers' Edition, 1969–present; access by subject, case name.

CCH United States Supreme Court Bulletin; access by subject, case name. Gives status of docket.

Treaties
CIS/Annual, 1970–present; access by subject and title. Has index of document numbers.

CCH Congressional Index; access by subject. Summarizes treaties.

Vetoes
CCH Congressional Index; access by subject, author. Found in "Enactments—Vetoes" section.

Voting records
CCH Congressional Index; access by subject, author. Roll call votes in "Voting Records" section; voice votes in "Status" section.

Rare books

What to do with your old books

by Peter Van Wingen

THESE ARE SOME frequently asked questions about rare books and book values. The answers are meant only as general responses to these questions, and the many possible exceptions are not described. A pamphlet containing the following questions and answers, and suitable for distributing to library patrons, is available from ALA Graphics, 50 E. Huron St., Chicago, IL 60611, at a cost of $20 for fifty copies.

What makes a book rare?

Over the past 500 years, millions and millions of books, pamphlets, magazines, newspapers, and broadsides have come off of printing presses. Only a small portion of these items, however, would be considered "rare" by specialists. In simple terms, a book achieves some degree of rarity only when the demand for it is greater than the supply.

Such a broad definition suggests that rarity is very subjective. Indeed it is, and this fact keeps collectors, dealers, and librarians constantly on the lookout for books previously neglected but now seen as important. Unfortunately, there are no easy formulas or unequivocal guides to rarity. In fact, there is often no one distinctive feature that will set a rare book apart from other books.

In the final analysis, the most essential factor is the book's *intrinsic* importance, for only books with some acknowledged importance will have a consumer demand that creates market value and a sense of rarity.

What makes a book important?

"Of the making of books there is no end"— and the topics books cover are equally infinite. The books that are most sought are the significant editions of major works in the arts and sciences. These include early reports of discoveries or inventions, early texts of important literary or historical works, and books with illustrations that give a new interpretation of a text or are the work of a fine artist.

Books may have added interest if the text was originally suppressed or little acknowledged in its own day, with the result that few copies survive today. A book also can have physical characteristics that lend importance—a special binding, first use of a new printing process, an innovative design, an autograph or inscription.

Where are rare books found?

Because books are portable they turn up everywhere, from well-ordered private libraries to attics, basements, and barns. Books found in out-of-the-way places, however, often show signs of neglect. Given the importance of condition for collectors, librarians, and dealers, the book that has been well cared for has a much better chance of being valuable than a book treated poorly.

Are all old books rare?

The age of a book has very little to do with its value. Dealers, collectors, and librarians, however, do use some broad time spans to establish dates of likely importance: e.g., all books printed before 1501, English books printed before 1641, and books printed in the Americas before 1801. These dates are rough guidelines at best and are always subject to the overriding factors of intrinsic importance, condition, and demand.

What is the difference between a rare book and a secondhand book?

Books found in attics, basements, and yard sales often appear to be old, interesting, or valuable to people unfamiliar with the vast numbers of books that survive from earlier centuries. While it is always possible to find a rare book in any setting, the secondhand book is more likely to be encountered than the rare book. A gray area exists between these two categories, but for the most part a secondhand book is a used book that is not distinguished by its edition, provenance, binding, or overall condition; its retail price generally is quite modest.

Does scarcity mean rarity?

A book known to exist in only a few copies may have value if it has importance and is in demand. A book without importance or demand has little value regardless of how few copies survive. The *National Union Catalogue: Pre-1956 Imprints,* available in most large libraries, will give you some idea of the number of surviving copies in major institutional libraries in North America. Determining the number of copies of a book in private hands is virtually impossible.

Does the number of copies printed determine a book's value?

The production figures for print runs are seldom available. Even if the number of original copies is known, this information seldom provides an idea of current worth.

Exceptions occur in the case of works by noted authors that made their first appearances in editions of very small quantities. Also, some books printed in the 20th century are finely produced on handpresses in very limited editions. A limitation statement alone does not make a book valuable, but the fact the edition is limited will be one of the factors that determines its value.

What about condition?

Condition is a major factor in determining a book's value along with intrinsic importance, supply, and demand. Condition refers to both the book's external physical appearance and to the completeness of its contents.

4

A book in "fine" condition is complete in all respects, has no tears or other signs of misuse or overuse, and is in an original or appropriate and intact binding. A book that has been rebound or is in less than fine condition must be very important or in high demand to be of substantial value. Loose pages are a defect, and missing pages or illustrations are a major fault that will make most books almost valueless.

Will someone want my single volume of a set?

Single volumes of sets or incomplete sets have little appeal to booksellers, collectors, and librarians. The chance of finding a buyer with a set missing the exact volume or volumes is very remote.

What kinds of books are usually not rare?

Bibles. No single work has been printed more often than the Bible; therefore, an extremely small percentage of the total number has any monetary value at all. Bibles are treasured by their owners and have considerable sentimental value. Sentimental value, however, does not translate into importance or demand.

Certain important editions of the Bible have long been collected. Generally recognized as important are: the first Bibles written in several languages; the first authorized English (King James) version; and a variety of 16th- and 17th-century oddities such as the "Breeches" Bible, the "Vinegar" Bible, and the "Wicked" Bible, which are sought because of some important misprint or peculiar wording.

Sermons and religious instruction. The principles set down above for printed Bibles generally apply to other religious books as well. Much of this material was intended for wide circulation, and great quantities were printed. Moreover, the owners of the books often treasured them with the result that substantial numbers survive today. Religious texts often are printed cheaply and distributed as inexpensively as possible, which, combined with the size of the field and restricted present-day demand, give them a low monetary value. Religious tracts or sermons written by major figures in the history of religion or those that relate to historic events or significant people are possible exceptions.

Collected editions of an author's works. After authors have become firmly established, publishers often take advantage of their success by putting out collected editions of their works. These editions are often fancy and may even be limited, but they are seldom rare. Most frequently, collected editions were prepared without the author's immediate attention and consequently have little textual importance. If splendidly bound in high-quality leather and preserved in fine condition, they on occasion can bring considerable sums.

Recently, certain scholarly editions of authors' collected works have been produced that incorporate the results of careful textual comparisons. In these cases the texts are important and the published price of the full set may be high, but the volumes are scholarly texts rather than rare books.

Encyclopedias. In general, encyclopedias are bought for their current information. Obsolete editions of encyclopedias have little monetary value whatever the historical interest of their articles. Sets of the first edition (1768–1771) and the eleventh edition (1911) of the *Encyclopaedia Britannica* are exceptions. The former is in considerable demand, and the latter has a modest but steady sales record when in fine condition.

Textbooks. An old schoolbook rarely has any monetary value. Depending on their condition, American primers before 1800 may have interest to collectors and libraries. Values for the Eclectic Readers of William Holmes McGuffey vary considerably depending on the edition. The first six McGuffey Readers, published between 1836 and 1856, are in particular demand. Illustrated textbooks printed before 1850 are also sought.

Reprints and facsimiles. Reprinting important texts in typographic or photographic facsimile is an inexpensive means of producing a previously printed text and is a common publishing practice. Except for extremely high-quality reproductions of medieval and renaissance manuscripts and early printed books, facsimile reprints seldom have much value in the rare book market.

Newspapers, magazines, and comic books. While certain titles, years, and individual issues within these categories are sought by collectors and dealers, a great deal of this material has little or no interest. In the case of newspapers, a few single issues have great significance, but these have been reprinted so often that the chance of having an original is slight.

The Library of Congress Serial and Government Publications Division (Washington, DC 20540) has free circulars that give detailed information on how to distinguish facsimiles and originals of sixteen newspaper issues. These include: *The Ulster County Gazette,* January 4, 1800; *The New York Herald,* April 15, 1865; and the wallpaper editions of *The Daily Citizen* of Vicksburg, Mississippi.

Are old letters, scrapbooks, and documents of interest to collectors, librarians, and dealers?

In general, letters, cards, documents, and manuscripts written by or signed by figures who have made significant contributions in their fields are of particular interest to collectors. Letters or diaries of unknown writers can be of interest if they give new information about important historical events, places, or trends. The value of manuscripts, documents, and photographs, like that of printed books, depends on the interest and condition of the individual pieces.

More information on such papers can be found in a brochure distributed by the Society of American Archivists: *A Donor's Guide to the Preservation of Personal and Family Papers and the Records of Organizations.*

What is a first edition?

In the strictest sense, "first edition" refers to a copy of a book printed from the first setting of type, constituting the first public appearance of the text in that form. Subsequent changes to the printed text through corrections of the original typesetting produces different "states" and "issues" but not a new edition.

The liberal use of the term "first edition" has made it seem synonymous with "scarce" and "valuable." This is by no means the case. Most books appear in only one edition. Determining if a book is a true first edition takes considerable experience or substantial work with reference books.

Collectors of literary works especially are interested in first editions, and there is a lively and well-documented market for these books. Condition plays an even greater role than usual in determining the monetary value of literary first editions. If an author revises the text for a later edition, it may be of interest too.

Is a book signed or marked up by a previous owner or autographed by the author more valuable?

The association of a book with a previous owner can add to its value, depending on how well-known the previous owner is and how important the book was in relation to this person. Indication of previous ownership may be in the form of a bookplate, signature, inscription, or other distinctive mark. All need to be authenticated before a positive statement of association can be made.

Finding a 20th-century book signed by its author is quite common. Authors routinely make publicity tours across the country signing copies of their books, and their signatures alone do not have much importance. Still, autographed copies carry more value for collectors than unsigned copies.

When trying to determine the worth of an author's autograph, remember that books are signed for different reasons. In ascending level of interest these are: books signed as part of a publicity event, copies inscribed by request of the owner, copies of a book inscribed and presented by the author. The autographs of certain authors are always more desirable than others, and fads and fancies change so that only someone familiar with the market will be able to give a precise idea of the value of a signed or inscribed copy.

Should I have my books rebound before selling them?

Few books are worth the cost of rebinding. Rebinding also may destroy or alter some special aspect of the book that might have given it value—e.g., original covers, an autograph or bookplate on the inside cover, or original sewing construction.

Books in poor condition may need to be repaired to lessen the chance of further damage, but the cost should be judged according to the book's worth—this would include, of course, the sentimental value of those books that the author intends to keep. Conservators can construct tailor-made boxes as an alternative to expensive rebinding. A well-made box will protect a fragile book and will help keep all of the parts together. Your local library may have a list of binders in your area.

How can I keep my books in good condition?

Books are very sensitive to temperature and humidity. A cool, dry environment is best. This usually rules out storing books in the basement or attic. Sunlight, especially direct sunlight, is detrimental to books.

Sometimes people go to the opposite extreme and store their books in cardboard boxes, first wrapping them in newspaper or plastic. Both materials can cause damage. Newspapers are printed on highly acidic paper, and this acid will enter the book and stain it. Plastic tends to be airtight, allowing mold to develop with the slightest moisture, and some plastics, like newsprint, are acidic.

Books kept in bookcases under conditions comfortable to humans will survive for years, but even a solid book placed in hot or damp conditions will soon deteriorate. Very large books need extra care. If at all possible they should lie horizontally on the shelves rather than stand vertically. Under no circumstances should self-adhesive, plastic tape be used to repair torn pages. As the tape ages it will make a sticky mess that will seal and stain the pages and become almost impossible to remove.

Do I need to insure my books?

Generally, your regular householder's insurance policy will cover the value of your book collection. If a book in your collection has been professionally appraised at a substantial amount, you may want to have your insurance agent draw up a rider policy.

To be safe you may want to compile a list of your books—include author, title, and date for hardbacks, and the total number of your paperbacks—so that in case of fire, flood, or other disaster you will have a record of your holdings. Only in the case of quite valuable items, however, will your books make a significant contribution to your total household worth.

Can I sell or give my books to a library?

Libraries are obvious places to go to sell old books, but most public libraries concentrate on materials that circulate frequently. Moreover, libraries are chronically short of money and must often depend on the generosity of supporters.

Before adding an old or rare book through purchase, the library will consider the importance of the book, the reader demand for it, and the book's condition. Research libraries may want to have materials on certain subjects regardless of current demand but will nevertheless insist on long-term scholarly importance and good condition for anything they purchase.

All libraries buy books, but some find the administrative details of buying books from individuals difficult and on occasion impossible. If the library wants a book and is willing to pay for it, the person offering it probably will have to set the price, since many libraries are not permitted to make offers for materials. This could mean that the potential donor has to pay an appraiser's fee. The cost of the appraisal must always be weighed against the value of the item.

The fair market value of books given to tax-exempt libraries may be claimed as a charitable donation on income tax returns. Again, a professional appraisal may be called for. This is the donor's responsibility. The free IRS publication, *Valuation of Donated Property*, no. 561, is helpful.

Where else can I give my books?

Many organizations receive books as donations and hold book sales to sell them at moderate prices. Volunteer thrift shops, charitable organizations, and church and school bazaars often are eager to receive book donations.

Who will appraise books for me?

Professional book appraisers and most booksellers appraise and evaluate book materials. Individuals who have been in the business for some years know market trends and have often handled the book or books in question. They are well aware of the criteria that give books value. The charge for an appraisal should be based on the time the appraisal takes. Expenses, such as travel, normally will be added to these charges.

How do I find a bookseller or appraiser?

Booksellers and appraisers are listed in various directories, although none is comprehensive. The Antiquarian Booksellers Association of America publishes an annual membership directory that lists addresses, phone numbers, and specialties (available from ABAA, 50 Rockefeller Plaza, New York, NY 10020). A listing of ABAA members and smaller dealers across the country can be found in *Rare Books 1983-84: Trends, Collections, Sources*, edited by Alice D. Schreyer (New York: Bowker, 1984). Local yellow pages or business directories often carry listings under "Book Dealers" or "Book Dealers: Used and Rare." Be careful to find someone who truly has some idea of the marketplace, particularly in areas of specialization such as modern first editions, early printed books, or music.

How can I be sure that a dealer will give me a fair price?

Booksellers, like other business people, depend on maintaining a reputation of trust, good service, and dependability. People who sell books often have no idea of their actual worth and must depend to a great extent on the trustworthiness and professional behavior of the dealer. Also keep in mind that many books that owners believe have great value are not necessarily salable. It costs money to keep books on shelves, and the dealer must figure into an offer the possibility that it may take a long time to find a buyer. Dealers may also buy a whole box of books even though only one or two will readily sell. Often they do this as a favor to sellers interested in clearing out things quickly.

How do I describe my books?

Frequently dealers or librarians will want to see a list of the books being offered to give them a quick idea of the kinds of books available and to help them determine if the books fall in to the areas in which they normally buy. Any listing of books should include for them the name of the author, the exact title, the name of the publisher, and the place and date of publication. This information should come from the title page, not from the binding or dust jacket. If the date does not appear on the title page, the back of the title page may carry a copyright date. The description also should include some brief comment on the book's condition.

Source: Peter Van Wingen, *Your Old Books* (Chicago: American Library Association, 1988)

Unfamiliar genres

MANY RARE BOOK LIBRARIES maintain files of certain categories, or genres, of works found in their collections. These files are especially useful when a researcher cares more about the genre than the author, title, or topic. Here are some odd ones.

Artillery election sermons	Jestbooks
Begging poems	Mazarinades
Bills of mortality	Newscarriers' addresses
Captivity narratives	Orders in council
Celestial atlases	Pasquinades
Chrestomathies	Penny dreadfuls
Farces	Promptbooks
Fast day proclamations	Robinsonades
Fourth of July sermons	Spirit communications
Fraternity rituals	Three deckers
Imaginary voyages	Yellowbooks

Source: ALA Rare Books and Manuscripts Section, Standards Committee,
Genre Terms: A Thesaurus for Use in Rare Book and Special Collections Cataloguing (1983)

Paper defects

THESE ARE TERMS used by special collections catalogers to describe "below par" qualities of paper. The defects might be the result of the manufacturing process, handling, storage, treatment, or they might be flaws in the original material.

Air bells	tiny, circular, thin spots
Baggy papers	papers with thicker middles than edges
Blackening	papers showing burn marks on the surface
Bleach scale	pearly, light brown, brittle spots
Blisters	bubble-like raised areas
Bristle marks	indentations in the surface of coated papers in the shape of brush bristles

Brush marks	streaks in the surface of coated papers made by brushes
Calendar cuts	small wrinkles parallel to one of the sides
Cloudy papers	papers with unevenness in look-through
Cockle	wrinkles
Contraries	any foreign substance in paper, such as sand, feathers, string
Couch marks	long, thin area parallel to one of the sides where fibers have clumped together thickly, causing adjacent thinner areas in look-through
Cracking	cracks in the surface of coated papers
Craters	small pits in coated papers
Crocking	papers with surface dyes rubbed off
Crush marks	areas in which the pulp is pressed so tightly that it produces a mottled or "crowded" appearance in the fibers
Curl	papers that curl up when placed on a flat surface
Dog-eared papers	page corners are folded over
Dusting papers	papers that flake or powder from loose fibers on the surface
Feathered papers	papers whose deckled edges are quite large and thin
Foul papers	paper with dirt specks
Foxing	discoloration
Fur	small bits of paper, usually detached from the edges, that are attached to the surface of the sheet
Grainy edges	edges that are clumpy or rough
Grit	scratchy or abrasive substances in papers
Haircuts	hair-thin cuts in the surface where it appears that hairs or long fibers have been pulled out of the surface
Lumps	swellings
Phozy	featherweight paper with fibers too loosely pressed, yielding a light, weak sheet easy to tear
Pinholes	tiny holes
Plucking	spots on coated papers that have been rubbed or pulled off in the paper's manufacture
Retree	any defective hand-made papers
Roping	longitudinal wrinkles in coated papers
Shiners	tiny, hard, light-reflective particles that leave pinholes when they are removed
Skipped coating	sheets where the coating is lacking in places
Slaps	ruptured spots at the edges of machine-made papers
Slivers	small splinters of wood in paper
Snailing	streaks or snail-like marks on the surface
Specks	particles of foreign matter such as bronze, carbon, iron, or rosin
Spongy papers	paper that is too compressible or ink too absorbent
Spots	small discolorations caused by alum, dye, grease, oil, or other foreign substances
Vatman's tears	small, circular, thin spots, thicker around the circular edges, where a drop of water has dispersed the fibers in the hand papermaking process
Wild papers	sheets with uneven, random distribution of fibers, yielding a mottled appearance on look-through
Winder welts	long, grain-direction ridges in the surface
Woody papers	translucent, hard, brittle papers
Wrinkles	small creases or ridges

4

Source: ALA/ACRL Rare Books and Manuscripts Section, Bibliographic Standards Committee, *Paper Terms: A Thesaurus for Use in Rare Book and Special Collections Cataloguing* (Chicago: ALA, 1990); Heartsill Young, ed., *The ALA Glossary of Library and Information Science* (Chicago: ALA, 1983)

Children's books

Early children's collections

AS EARLY AS 1810, a public library had been established in Salisbury, Conn., with the gift of 150 books from noted educator Caleb Bingham, for the use of all children from 9 to 16 years of age. Lexington, Mass., followed in 1827 when the town voted to establish a juvenile library. Other early youth libraries were the Brooklyn Youth Library (1823), the West Cambridge (now Arlington, Mass.) Juvenile Library (1835), and the Hartford (Conn.) Young Men's Institute (1875). Until the 1870s most public libraries denied access to readers under the age of 12 or 14. Possibly the first children's rooms in public libraries were in the Aguilar Free Library at 624 Fifth Street in New York in 1886, and on the third floor of the George Bruce Library in 1888, a branch of the New York Free Circulating System.

Twenty U.S. libraries started service to children by establishing a children's room in the 1890s.

1890	Brookline, Mass.		Cambridge, Mass.
	Minneapolis, Minn.		Kalamazoo, Mich.
1892	Circleville, Ohio		Seattle, Wash.
1893	San Francisco, Calif.	1897	Brooklyn, N.Y.
	Buffalo, N.Y.	1898	Milwaukee, Wisc.
1894	Denver, Colo.		New York State Library,
1895	Boston, Mass.		Albany
	New Haven, Conn.	After 1897	(exact year not known):
1896	Pittsburgh, Pa.		Everett, Mass.
	Detroit, Mich.		Cleveland, Ohio
	Omaha, Nebr.		Helena, Mont.

Children's Room, Cleveland Public Library, West Side Branch, ca. 1898

The first children's room to be included in architectural plans for a new library building and brought to completion was at the Pratt Institute Free Library in Brooklyn, New York, in 1897. The first library school course devoted to children's librarianship was at the New York State Library School in 1898, followed by the Pratt Institute in 1899.

Source: Kalamazoo Public Library; Elizabeth W. Stone, *American Library Development, 1600–1899* (New York: H. W. Wilson, 1977)

Early predictors of reading success

FACTORS SUCH AS MENTAL AGE, IQ, parental education, affluence, left- and right-handedness, perceptual motor skills, and oral language characteristics are all poor predictors of how preschoolers will eventually read. Instead, *Beginning to Read: Thinking and Learning About Print—A Summary,* a recently released study sponsored by OERI's Office of Research, identifies three powerful predictors of reading success:

4

- Preschoolers' ability to recognize and name letters of the alphabet;
- Their general knowledge about text (i.e., which is the front of the book and which is the back, whether the story is told by the pictures or the print, and which way to turn pages), and
- Their awareness of phonemes—speech sounds that correspond roughly to individual letters.

The report notes that the third factor—awareness of phonemes—is the most powerful predictor of all, accounting for as much as half of the variance in children's reading ability at the end of first grade. But it also points out that preschoolers' awareness of phonemes is closely linked to how much exposure to reading they receive in their homes, and that reading aloud to children is the most important thing parents can do to build the knowledge and skills eventually required for learning to read.

Frequent reading is equally important for children who have learned the basics. In fact, the single most effective activity for improving students' reading is having them read as often, broadly, and thoughtfully as possible. This is also the most important factor in promoting vocabulary development, writing skills, and conceptual growth.

Directed at teachers, administrators, and others involved with the education of young children, *Beginning to Read* contends, "Isn't it time that we recognize that written text has both form and function? To read, children must learn to deal with both, and we must help them."

The 160-page summary was produced by the Reading Research and Education Center, through a cooperative agreement between the Office of Research and the University of Illinois at Urbana-Champaign's Center for the Study of Reading.

Beginning to Read is available for $5.00 by writing to the Center for the Study of Reading, University of Illinois, P.O. Box 2276, Station A, Champaign, IL 61825-2276.

Source: Office of Educational Research and Improvement Bulletin, Summer 1990, pp. 3–4

How to raise a reader

SHARING BOOKS WITH CHILDREN is a gift you can give infants from the time they are born. Chanting nursery rhymes, singing songs, and reading stories can comfort and entertain even the youngest child. Parents, child-care providers, teachers, and other adults interested in the development of young children have a wealth of good books to choose from. Here is a list of some of the best with easy-to-do tips developed by members of the ALA Association for Library Service to Children.

Sharing books . . .

- Helps create a special bond between parents and children.
- Introduces children to art through the illustrations.
- Enhances children's listening skills and develops language skills.
- Introduces children to a wide variety of experiences.
- Helps prepare children to learn to read.
- Improves and enriches the quality of children's lives.
- Provides fun and enjoyment for children and adults.

When to share books

- Begin when your child is born.
- Set aside a special time each day, such as nap time, bedtime, or after meals.
- Share books when you and your child are in a relaxed mood.
- Limit sharing time if your child becomes fussy or restless.
- Take advantage of "waiting" times to share books—on trips, at the doctor's office, in line at the grocery store.
- Soothe your child when sick or cranky.

How to share books

- Find a comfortable place to sit (a rocking chair is wonderful).
- Recite or sing rhymes from your favorite books.
- Turn off other distractions—television, radio, or stereo.
- Hold the book so your child can see the pages clearly.
- Involve your child by having him or her point out objects, talk about the pictures, or repeat common words.
- Read with expression.
- Vary the pace of your reading—slow or fast.
- Have your child select books to read.
- Reread your child's favorite books whenever asked.

And remember . . .

- Be enthusiastic about books.
- Be an example for your child—let her or him see you read books, too.
- Keep a wide selection of reading materials at home.
- Be aware of your child's reading interests.
- Give books as presents.
- Begin to build a child's home library.
- Use your local library regularly and register your child for a library card.

Some good books to share

Bang, Molly. *Ten, Nine, Eight* (Greenwillow, 1983).
Barton, Byron. *Trucks* (Harper, 1986).
Brown, Marc. *Play Rhymes* (Dutton, 1985).
Brown, Margaret Wise. *Goodnight, Moon* (Harper, 1947).
Burningham, John. *The Blanket* (Harper, 1976).
Campbell, Rod. *Buster's Bedtime* (Bedrick Books, 1987).
Carle, Eric. *The Very Hungry Caterpillar* (Putnam, 1981).
Chorao, Kay. *The Baby's Lap Book* (Dutton, 1977).
Crews, Donald. *Freight Train* (Greenwillow, 1978).
dePaola, Tomie. *Tomie dePaola's Mother Goose* (Putnam, 1985).
Hill, Eric. *Where's Spot?* (Putnam, 1987).
Isadora, Rachel. *I See* (Greenwillow, 1985).
Jonas, Ann. *Holes & Peeks* (Greenwillow, 1984).
Keats, Ezra Jack. *Peter's Chair* (Harper, 1967).
Martin, Bill, Jr. *Brown Bear, Brown Bear, What Do You See?* (Holt, 1985).
Ormerod, Jan. *Reading* (Lothrop, 1985).
Oxenbury, Helen. *Clap Hands* (Macmillan, 1987).
Pooley, Sarah. *A Day of Rhymes* (Knopf, 1988).
Songs from Dreamland (Random, 1989).
Steptoe, John. *Baby Says* (Lothrop, 1988).
Tafuri, Nancy. *Have You Seen My Duckling?* (Greenwillow, 1984).
Watanabe, Shigeo. *How Do I Put It On?* (Putnam, 1984).
Wells, Rosemary. *Max's Bath* (Dial, 1985).
Yolen, Jane. *Lap-Time Song and Play Book* (Harcourt, 1989).

Source: ALA Association for Library Service to Children, *How to Raise a Reader* (Chicago: ALA,1990)

Books to match children's developmental stages

by Maralita L. Freeny

Infants

PUBLISHERS HAVE BEEN SLOW to realize that babies constitute an audience for books. For example, the excellent Brimax series of books is appropriate for infants, but according to the covers of the books, its publisher is promoting it for two- to four-year-olds.

Developing a sense of hearing. In the earliest months, read anything aloud— newspapers, your favorite magazines, a professional journal.

In the earliest months, the sound of a voice is more important than the sense of what is being read. Therefore, Mother Goose books are among the best first books for babies. The rhymes are melodic and easily memorized, and they can be used anywhere by parents who want to amuse their children. Later, as children learn to talk, they will be able to memorize and recite the rhymes easily, giving themselves a sense of accomplishment. Raymond Briggs' *Mother Goose Treasury* (Putnam, 1966) is a good collection of rhymes and a good first book.

Song books, poetry, and the so-called sound or noise books are also appropriate for infants. Aliki, *Hush Little Baby* (Prentice-Hall, 1968); Sally Kilroy, *Animal Noises* (Four Winds, 1983); and Peter Spier, *Crash! Bang! Boom!* (Doubleday, 1972), present interesting songs and sounds for babies.

Sharon, Lois and Bram's Mother Goose (Atlantic Monthly, 1986) includes both rhymes and songs and makes an excellent gift for a new baby.

Developing a sense of touch. Board books lend themselves to use by babies. They are nearly indestructible. Babies can pull or chew on them. Good choices among the many board books available are Patricia Wynne, *Animal ABC* (Random, 1977); Ethel and Len Kessler, *Are There Hippos on the Farm?* (Simon & Schuster, 1987); and Helen Oxenbury, *All Fall Down* (Macmillan, 1987).

Texture or "touch and feel" books are appropriate when children are developing their sense of touch. Dorothy Kunhardt's *Pat the Bunny* (Western, 1942), now a classic, provides a variety of textures for baby to experience.

Developing clearer vision when the eyes begin to focus. Books with large, clear, uncluttered illustrations in bright, primary colors provide the best visual experience when baby's eyes first begin to focus. Naming books, alphabet books, and color and number books, such as Brian Wildsmith's *ABC* (Watts, 1962) and Lucille Ogle's *I Spy* (American Heritage, 1970), are examples.

Identifying objects. In their earliest experiences with books, children especially delight in finding objects on a page. *Baby's Catalogue*, by Janet and Allan Ahlberg (Little, 1983), is a naming book that is appropriate.

Number, alphabet, and color books also lend themselves to point and name activities with a parent. *Colors* by Jan Pienkowski (Simon & Schuster, 1981) and Helen Oxenbury's *Numbers of Things* (Watts, 1968) are good choices to use.

Naming objects. In order to enhance language development, use the books cited earlier, but instead of having the child point to the object and the parent name it, the parent should point and have the child do the naming. Feodor Rojankovsky, *Great Big Animal Book* (Golden, 1950); Richard Scarry, *Early Words* (Random House, 1976); and John Burningham, *Mr. Gumpy's Outing* (Holt, 1971), are illustrated with pictures of items children can easily learn to identify.

Toddlers

The books you use during these years will depend on whether or not you read to the child during her infancy. It is not necessary to limit books to those with vocabularies within the immediate experience of the child.

Developing manual dexterity. Use books that are small, "little books for little hands." Small board books, such as *You Do It Too*; Sesame Street, *Muppets in My Neighborhood* (Random, 1977); and Rosemary Wells, *Max's New Suit* (Dial, 1979), are appropriate for toddlers to handle even without supervision.

Little books with paper pages, such as Jan Ormerod, *Young Joe* (Lothrop, 1985), and John Burningham, *The Rabbit* (Harper, 1975), are also easily handled by toddlers, but adults must supervise their use more closely.

More advanced language usage. More complicated alphabet, naming, sound, and number books can be used to enhance the toddler's rapidly developing language. Try Brian Wildsmith, *Wild Animals* (Oxford University, 1976), and Janet Beller, *A-B-Cing* (Crown, 1985).

Descriptive books, such as Chiyoko Nakatani, *My Day on the Farm* (Crowell, 1976); Ruth Brown, *Our Cat Flossie* (Dutton, 1986); and Douglas Florian, *A Winter Day* (Greenwillow, 1987), are excellent books to use for language development while a child's attention span is too short to use picture stories effectively.

Negativism. Books which ask questions, especially when the appropriate answers are negative, are ideal for a stage when the toddler's favorite word is "no."

Shigeo Watanabe, *How Do I Put It On?* (Putnam, 1980); and Eric Hill, *Where's Spot?* (Putnam, 1987), are two favorite books with questions answered in the negative.

Sense of accomplishment. Flap books, such as Rod Campbell's *Dear Zoo* (Macmillan, 1984), and the Spot series, provide a sense of accomplishment to toddlers, who quickly learn how and when to lift the flap.

When children can independently know when to turn the page, they feel a sense of accomplishment. Simple stories are good to use as is a good collection of Mother Goose rhymes, for example, Tomie dePaola's *Mother Goose* (Putnam, 1985).

Learning simple concepts, such as numbers, letters, colors, and days of the week. Simple concepts can be taught through a good book. Donald Crews, *Freight Train* (Greenwillow, 1978); Bill Martin, Jr., *Brown Bear, Brown Bear, What Do You See?* (Holt, 1983); and Robert Kalan, *Rain* (Greenwillow, 1978), introduce colors within a lively and appealing context.

Good books to use to teach counting and number recognition are Pat Hutchins, *One Hunter* (Greenwillow, 1982), and Nancy Tafuri, *Who's Counting?* (Greenwillow, 1986).

Increased attention spans. Simple descriptive books can be followed by short, simple stories with believable situations. The story is all important; the text must be good. Look for books by Eve Rice, Pat Hutchins, Ann Jonas, and Eric Carle. *Benny Bakes a Cake* by Rice (Greenwillow, 1981), *Titch* by Hutchins (Macmillan, 1971), *Two Bear Cubs* by Jonas (Greenwillow, 1982), and *The Very Hungry Caterpillar* by Carle (Putnam, 1981), are among my favorites.

It's okay for animals to act like children in these stories. *Wide-Awake Timothy*, by Joyce Wakefield (Childrens Press, 1981), is a good example of a short, simple story in which an animal, in this case a koala bear, is very childlike.

Three-year-olds

I can't emphasize enough how important it is to remember that children develop at different rates. Some three-year-olds will be ready for the books listed in this section; some will have devoured them during their toddler years. The following are merely loose guidelines to help you in your selections.

Increased interest in the use of words. Poetry provides richness of language and rhythm which enhances a child's interest in language. Frank Josette, ed., *Poems to Read to the Very Young* (Random, 1982); Jack Prelutsky, ed., *Read-Aloud Rhymes for the Very Young* (Knopf, 1986); and David McCord, *Every Time I Climb a Tree* (Little, 1967), are collections that are personal favorites of mine. "Mary Had a Little Lamb" and "Three Little Kittens" are examples of single rhymes that are often illustrated and published as whole books.

Nonsense books present new words to youngsters who are becoming really interested in language. These same books also demonstrate rhythm and cadence. In addition to books by the well-known Dr. Seuss, Bruce Degen's *Jamberry* (Harper, 1983) is a good choice.

The repetition in cumulative stories also provides a rich experience for the preschooler who has an increased interest in language. Good cumulative stories are Audrey Woods, *Napping House* (Harcourt, 1984); Kaj Beckman, *Lisa Cannot Sleep* (Watts, 1969); and Rose Robart, *The Cake That Mack Ate* (Little, 1987).

Growing independence and sense of accomplishment. Books that allow the child to participate in the telling are ideal for three-year-olds. Children respond to the hidden pictures and shapes in Janet and Allan Ahlberg, *Each Peach Pear Plum* (Viking, 1979), and Charles G. Shaw, *It Looked Like Spilt Milk* (Harper, 1988). Robert Crowther's *The Most Amazing Hide-and-Seek Alphabet Book* (Viking, 1978) is an unusually fine tab book which also invites participation by the child.

Singing is another way to involve children in books. Songs illustrated and published as whole books can be used to accomplish this. Raffi, *Wheels on the Bus* (Crown, 1988); Merle Peek, *Mary Wore Her Red Dress* (Ticknor & Fields, 1985); Nadine Westcott, *The Lady with the Alligator Purse* (Little, 1988); and Paul Galdone, *The Cat Goes Fiddle-i-fee* (Ticknor & Fields, 1985), are always popular.

Development of self-esteem. As children develop personality and accept themselves, they respond to books with characters with whom they can identify. Ezra Jack Keats, *Whistle for Willie* (Viking, 1964); Shirley Hughes, *Alfie's Feet*

(Lothrop, 1983); and Rosemary Wells, *Noisy Nora* (Dial, 1973), are some good authors to use. While Wells' characters are usually animals, children will have no trouble identifying with them.

Comfort with familiar things. Preschoolers are curious about the world around them, but they are most comfortable with the familiar. Read books about their everyday life, about their pets, their toys, their experiences in the community. Try Gene Zion, *Harry the Dirty Dog* (Harper, 1956), or Keiki Kanao, *Kitten up a Tree* (Knopf, 1987), excellent stories about pets; or try *My Barber* (Macmillan, 1981) and *The Supermarket* (Macmillan, 1979), both by Anne and Harlow Rockwell, who have written about a variety of everyday experiences.

Advanced concept-learning. Books can encourage a child's understanding of concepts. Shapes, spatial relationships, and time are within the grasp of a three-year-old.

Leonard Everett Fisher, *Look Around!* (Viking, 1987); Betsy Maestro, *Where Is My Friend?* (Crown, 1976); and Robert Kalan, *Blue Sea* (Greenwillow, 1979), introduce shapes, spatial relationships, and contrasting sizes respectively.

Developing imagination. Read books that appeal to the child's imagination. Books that personify animals, toys, and other things are well-liked by three-year-olds.

Look for books by Don Freeman; his *Corduroy* (Viking, 1968) and *Dandelion* (Viking, 1964) are sure-fire hits.

Virginia Lee Burton's *Mike Mulligan and His Steam Shovel* (Houghton, 1939), in which a steam shovel has a personality, has become a classic.

Need for parental love and security. Mood books, or books that help children settle down are appropriate for this age. Books like Molly Bang, *Ten, Nine, Eight* (Greenwillow, 1983); Robert Kraus, *Whose Mouse Are You?* (Macmillan, 1970); Nancy Carlstrom, *The Moon Came Too* (Macmillan, 1987); and Margaret Wise Brown, *Goodnight, Moon* (Harper, 1949), are perfect for sharing at nap time or bedtime.

Read books that reflect parental love, for instance, Ann Herbert Scott, *On Mother's Lap* (McGraw, 1972); and Dick Gackenback, *Claude and Pepper* (Houghton, 1976).

Four- and five-year-olds

Desire for fairness. Older preschoolers have a strong feeling about what is and isn't fair. They like and want poetic justice of the kind that is present in Beatrix Potter's *The Tale of Peter Rabbit* (Warne, 1987). They also like happy endings in books in which a character has been in danger. Wilhelmina Harper, *Gunniwolf* (Dutton, 1967), and Leo Lionni, *Swimmy* (Pantheon, 1966), are prime examples.

Beast fairy tales are appropriate at this stage. Preread fairy tales so that you are not disappointed with unfamiliar variations. For example, in some versions of "The Three Little Pigs," the pigs are eaten by the wolf; in others, all three escape unharmed. Determine which version you have before reading it aloud to the child. Many versions of traditional fairy tales are nicely illustrated. Paul Galdone's *The Three Bears* (Houghton, 1972) comes to mind, as does *Red Riding Hood* by James Marshall (Dial, 1987).

Modern nontraditional fairy tales are popular with four- and five-year-olds. Anita Lobel, *The Straw Maid* (Greenwillow, 1983), and Joanna Galdone, *The Little Girl and the Big Bear* (Houghton, 1980), are personal favorites of my family.

Curiosity about the world at large. Older preschoolers become interested in the world outside their own everyday experiences. They yearn to find out about science, religion, history, famous people, other lands, and more. Factual picture books are now in plentiful supply on this level. Gail Gibbons is a prolific author to remember. Her nonfiction books are brief, precise, and quite interesting. *Boat Book* (Holiday, 1983) is just one example.

The world of science is widely represented in preschool books. Kate Petty, *Snakes* (Watts, 1985); Helen and Kelly Oechsli, *In My Garden* (Macmillan, 1985); and Franklyn M. Branley, *The Sky Is Full of Stars* (Harper, 1983), are just three examples of the many excellent books available.

To introduce history, you can read stories based on truth as well as traditional nonfiction books. Riki Levinson, *Watch the Stars Come Out* (Dutton, 1985), is an appealing historical picture story; Betsy Maestro, *The Story of the Statue of Liberty* (Lothrop, 1986), is an example of a factual historical picture book.

Advanced verbal skills. Wordless books encourage children to be creative and expressive by allowing them to tell stories in their own words. Nonny Hogrogian, *Apples* (Macmillan, 1972), and John S. Goodall, *Creepy Castle* (Atheneum, 1975), are two such wordless picture books.

Panorama books, such as those made popular by Richard Scarry, provide detailed illustrations just waiting for children with advanced verbal skills to describe. *Richard Scarry's Best Word Book Ever* (Western, 1963) is one of the author's best.

Increased attention span. There is less need for illustrations in the stories you share with four- and five-year-olds. You will now be able to read the many excellent, longer picture book stories, especially folk stories. Try Arlene Mosel, *Tikki Tikki Tembo* (Holt, 1968), and Jakob Grimm's *Snow White and the Seven Dwarfs* (Farrar, 1972).

Collections of stories are suitable for this age. Anne Rockwell's *Three Bears and Fifteen Other Stories* (Harper, 1975) is a good choice, as is *Tomie dePaola's Favorite Nursery Tales* (Putnam, 1986).

Adventurous nature. Four- and five-year-olds love adventure and suspense in their books; many children this age enjoy being scared.

Adventure books to read are Chris Van Allsburg, *Jumanji* (Houghton, 1981); Tomi Ungerer, *Crictor* (Harper, 1958); David McPhail, *Pig Pig Grows Up* (Dutton, 1980); and Tan Koide, *May We Sleep Here Tonight?* (Macmillan, 1983).

Advanced sense of humor. Children at this stage begin to understand the humor in many situations. Jack Kent writes wonderfully funny books for this age. *Round Robin* (Prentice-Hall, 1982) and *The Once-upon-a-Time Dragon* (Harcourt, 1982) are examples of his best work.

You will laugh along with your child when you read Raymond Briggs, *Jim and the Beanstalk* (Putnam, 1980), and Marc Brown, *Pickle Things* (Parents, 1980).

Source: Nell Colburn and Maralita L. Freeny, *First Steps to Literacy* (Chicago: American Library Association, 1990)

Children's services

CHILDREN ARE BIG USERS of public library services. In fact, 37% of public library users in the fall of 1988 were children 14 years and younger, according to a survey recently released by the National Center for Education Statistics.

Conducted at the request of OERI's Office of Library Programs, this was the first national survey of public library services and resources for children. The results are timely, as many of the public library services for children that were surveyed relate to issues named in the president's national education goals for the year 2000, especially those involving school readiness and improving student achievement. Included in the survey are some of the ways in which public libraries can help to achieve those goals, such as reading readiness programs for toddlers, summer reading programs for school-age children, and cooperative activities with school libraries, preschools, and day-care centers. There are data on the availability and usage of these and other library resources and services for children, as well as data on the number and educational level of children's librarians in public libraries.

Among the survey's findings:

- Almost all libraries provide study space for children (94%), summer reading programs (95%), story hours (89%), reading lists (87%), and reader advisory services (93%).
- Between 86% and 92% of libraries allowed all children to use foreign language materials, interlibrary loan services, and audio recordings. Five percent or less denied use of these services or resources to any children.
- Libraries were somewhat more restrictive about books in the adult collection: while 71% of libraries allowed all children access to these books, 25% limited access to only some children, and 4% of libraries did not allow any children to use these books.
- Access to personal computers and computer software was more restricted, with only about half (56%) of libraries allowing all children to use these resources and services, and 12% denying access to all children.
- Over half (58%) of public libraries did not have any librarians on staff whose primary job was serving children; 34% of libraries had only one children's librarian, and 8% had two or more children's librarians on staff.

Source: National Center for Education Statistics Announcement, May 1990

Newbery Medal Awards

THE NEWBERY MEDAL, named for 18th-century British bookseller John Newbery, is awarded annually by the ALA Association for Library Service to Children to the author of the most distinguished contribution to American literature for children. Here are the award winners since the award's inception in 1922.

1991—Jerry Spinelli, *Maniac Magee* (Little, Brown, 1990)
1990—Lois Lowry, *Number the Stars* (Houghton, 1989).
1989—Paul Fleischman, *Joyful Noise: Poems for Two Voices* (Harper, 1988).
1988—Russell Freedman, *Lincoln: A Photobiography* (Houghton, 1987).
1987—Sid Fleischman, *The Whipping Boy* (Greenwillow, 1986).
1986—Patricia MacLachlan, *Sarah, Plain and Tall* (Harper, 1985).
1985—Robin McKinley, *The Hero and the Crown* (Greenwillow, 1984).
1984—Beverly Cleary, *Dear Mr. Henshaw* (Morrow, 1983).
1983—Cynthia Voigt, *Dicey's Song* (Atheneum, 1982).
1982—Nancy Willard, *A Visit to William Blake's Inn: Poems for Innocent and Experienced Travelers* (Harcourt, 1981).
1981—Katherine Paterson, *Jacob Have I Loved* (Crowell, 1980).
1980—Joan W. Blos, *A Gathering of Days* (Scribner, 1979).
1979—Ellen Raskin, *The Westing Game* (Dutton, 1978).
1978—Katherine Paterson, *Bridge to Treblinka* (Crowell, 1977).
1977—Mildred D. Taylor, *Roll of Thunder, Hear My Cry* (Dial, 1976).
1976—Susan Cooper, *The Grey King* (Atheneum, 1975).
1975—Virginia Hamilton, *M.C. Higgins, the Great* (Macmillan, 1974).
1974—Paula Fox, *The Slave Dancer* (Bradbury, 1973).
1973—Jean Craighead George, *Julie of the Wolves* (Harper, 1972).
1972—Robert C. O'Brien, *Mrs. Frisby and the Rats of NIMH* (Atheneum, 1971).
1971—Betsy Byars, *Summer of the Swans* (Viking, 1970).
1970—William H. Armstrong, *Sounder* (Harper, 1969).
1969—Lloyd Alexander, *The High King* (Holt, 1968).
1968—E. L. Konigsburg, *From the Mixed-Up Files of Mrs. Basil E. Frankweiler* (Atheneum, 1967).

1967—Irene Hunt, *Up a Road Slowly* (Follett, 1966).
1966—Elizabeth Borton de Trevino, *I, Juan de Pareja* (Farrar, 1965).
1965—Maia Wojciechowska, *Shadow of a Bull* (Atheneum, 1964).
1964—Emily Neville, *It's Like This, Cat* (Harper, 1963).
1963—Madeleine L'Engle, *A Wrinkle in Time* (Farrar, 1962).
1962—Elizabeth George Speare, *The Bronze Bow* (Houghton, 1961).
1961—Scott O'Dell, *Island of the Blue Dolphins* (Houghton, 1960).
1960—Joseph Krumgold, *Onion John* (Crowell, 1959).
1959—Elizabeth George Speare, *The Witch of Blackbird Pond* (Houghton, 1958).
1958—Harold Keith, *Rifles for Watie* (Crowell, 1957).
1957—Virginia Sorensen, *Miracles on Maple Hill* (Harcourt, 1956).
1956—Jean Lee Latham, *Carry On, Mr. Bowditch* (Houghton, 1955).
1955—Meindert DeJong, *The Wheel of the School* (Harper, 1954).
1954—Joseph Krumgold, *. . . And Now Miguel* (Crowell, 1953).
1953—Ann Nolan Clark, *Secret of the Andes* (Viking, 1952).
1952—Eleanor Estes, *Ginger Pye* (Harcourt, 1951).
1951—Elizabeth Yates, *Amos Fortune, Free Man* (Dutton, 1950).
1950—Marguerite de Angeli, *The Door in the Wall* (Doubleday, 1949).
1949—Marguerite Henry, *King of the Wind* (Rand McNally, 1948).
1948—William Pène du Bois, *The Twenty-One Balloons* (Viking, 1947).
1947—Carolyn Bailey, *Miss Hickory* (Viking, 1946).
1946—Lois Lenski, *Strawberry Girl* (Lippincott, 1945).
1945—Robert Lawson, *Rabbit Hill* (Viking, 1944).
1944—Esther Forbes, *Johnny Tremain* (Houghton, 1943).
1943—Elizabeth Gray, *Adam of the Road* (Viking, 1942).
1942—Walter Edmonds, *The Matchlock Gun* (Dodd, 1941).
1941—Armstrong Sperry, *Call It Courage* (Macmillan, 1940).
1940—James Daugherty, *Daniel Boone* (Viking, 1939).
1939—Elizabeth Enright, *Thimble Summer* (Rinehart, 1938).
1938—Kate Seredy, *The White Stag* (Viking, 1937).
1937—Ruth Sawyer, *Roller Skates* (Viking, 1936).
1936—Carol Brink, *Caddie Woodlawn* (Macmillan, 1935).
1935—Monica Shannon, *Dobry* (Viking, 1934).
1934—Cornelia Meigs, *Invincible Louisa* (Little, Brown, 1933).
1933—Elizabeth Lewis, *Young Fu of the Upper Yangtze* (Winston, 1932).
1932—Laura Armer, *Waterless Mountain* (Longmans, 1931).
1931—Elizabeth Coatsworth, *The Cat Who Went to Heaven* (Macmillan, 1930).
1930—Rachel Field, *Hitty, Her First Hundred Years* (Macmillan, 1929).
1929—Eric P. Kelly, *The Trumpeter of Krakow* (Macmillan, 1928).
1928—Dhan Mukerji, *Gay Neck, the Story of a Pigeon* (Dutton, 1927).
1927—Will James, *Smoky, the Cowhorse* (Scribner, 1926).
1926—Arthur Chrisman, *Shen of the Sea* (Dutton, 1925).
1925—Charles Finger, *Tales from Silver Lands* (Doubleday, 1924).
1924—Charles Hawes, *The Dark Frigate* (Atlantic/Little, 1923).
1923—Hugh Lofting, *The Voyages of Doctor Dolittle* (Lippincott, 1922).
1922—Henrik Van Loon, *The Story of Mankind* (Liveright, 1921).

Source: ALA Association for Library Service to Children

Caldecott Medal winners

THE CALDECOTT MEDAL, named in honor of 19th-century English illustrator Randolph Caldecott, is awarded annually by the ALA Association for Library Service to Children to the artist of the most distinguished American picture book for children. Here are the award winners since the award's inception in 1938.

1991—David Macaulay, *Black and White* (Houghton, 1990).

1990—Ed Young, *Lon Po Po* (Philomel, 1989).

1989—Karen Ackerman, *Song and Dance Man* (Knopf, 1988); illustrated by Stephen Gammell.

1988—Jane Yolen, *Owl Moon* (Philomel, 1987); illustrated by John Schoenherr.

1987—Arthur Yorinks, *Hey, Al* (Farrar, 1986); illustrated by Richard Egielski.

1986—Chris Van Allsburg, *The Polar Express* (Houghton, 1985).

1985—Margaret Hodges, *Saint George and the Dragon* (Little, Brown, 1984); illustrated by Trina Schart Hyman.

1984—Alice and Martin Provensen, *The Glorious Flight: Across the Channel with Louis Blériot* (Viking, 1983).

1983—Blaise Cendrars, *Shadow* (Scribner, 1982); illustrated by Marcia Brown.

1982—Chris Van Allsburg, *Jumanji* (Houghton, 1981).

1981—Arnold Lobel, *Fables* (Harper, 1980).

1980—Donald Hall, *Ox-Cart Man* (Viking, 1979); illustrated by Barbara Cooney.

1979—Paul Goble, *The Girl Who Loved Wild Horses* (Bradbury, 1978).

1978—Peter Spier, *Noah's Ark* (Doubleday, 1977).

1977—Margaret Musgrove, *Ashanti to Zulu* (Dial, 1976); illustrated by Leo and Diane Dillon.

1976—Verna Aardema, *Why Mosquitoes Buzz in People's Ears* (Dial, 1975); illustrated by Leo and Diane Dillon.

1975—Gerald McDermott, *Arrow to the Sun* (Viking, 1974).

1974—Harve Zemach, *Duffy and the Devil* (Farrar, 1973); illustrated by Margot Zemach.

1973—Lafcadio Hearn, retold by Arlene Mosel, *The Funny Little Woman* (Dutton, 1972); illustrated by Blair Lent.

1972—Nonny Hogrogian, *One Fine Day* (Macmillan, 1971).

1971—Gail E. Haley, *A Story A Story* (Atheneum, 1970).

1970—William Steig, *Sylvester and the Magic Pebble* (Windmill, 1969).

1969—Arthur Ransome, *The Fool of the World and the Flying Ship* (Farrar, 1968); illustrated by Uri Shulevitz.

1968—Barbara Emberley, *Drummer Hoff* (Prentice-Hall, 1967); illustrated by Ed Emberley.

1967—Evaline Ness, *Sam, Bangs & Moonshine* (Holt, 1966).

1966—Sorche Nic Leodhas, *Always Room for One More* (Holt, 1965); illustrated by Nonny Hogrogian.

1965—Beatrice Schenk de Regniers, *May I Bring a Friend?* (Atheneum, 1964); illustrated by Beni Montresor.

1964—Maurice Sendak, *Where the Wild Things Are* (Harper, 1963).

1963—Ezra Jack Keats, *The Snowy Day* (Viking, 1962).

1962—Marcia Brown, *Once a Mouse* (Scribner, 1961).

1961—Ruth Robbins, *Baboushka and the Three Kings* (Parnassus, 1960); illustrated by Nicolas Sidjakov.

1960—Marie Hall Ets and Aurora Labastida, *Nine Days to Christmas* (Viking, 1959).

1959—Barbara Clooney, *Chanticleer and the Fox* (Crowell, 1958).

1958—Robert McCloskey, *Time of Wonder* (Viking, 1957).

1957—Janice Udry, *A Tree Is Nice* (Harper, 1956); illustrated by Marc Simont.
1956—John Langstaff, *Frog Went A-Courtin'* (Harcourt, 1955); illustrated by Feodor Rojankovsky.
1955—Marcia Brown, *Cinderella* (Scribner, 1954).
1954—Ludwig Bemelmans, *Madeline's Rescue* (Viking, 1953).
1953—Lynd Ward, *The Biggest Bear* (Houghton, 1952).
1952—Will Lipkind, *Finders Keepers* (Harcourt, 1951); illustrated by Nicolas Mordvinoff.
1951—Katherine Milhous, *The Egg Tree* (Scribner, 1950).
1950—Leo Politi, *Song of the Swallows* (Scribner, 1949).
1949—Berta and Elmer Hader, *The Big Snow* (Macmillan, 1948).
1948—Alvin Tresselt, *White Snow, Bright Snow* (Lothrop, 1947); illustrated by Roger Duvoisin.
1947—Golden McDonald, *The Little Island* (Doubleday, 1946); illustrated by Leonard Weisgard.
1946—Maude and Miska Petersham, *The Rooster Crows* (Macmillan, 1945).
1945—Rachel Field, *Prayer for a Child* (Macmillan, 1944); illustrated by Elizabeth Orton Jones.
1944—James Thurber, *Many Moons* (Harcourt, 1943); illustrated by Louis Slobodkin.
1943—Virginia Lee Burton, *The Little House* (Houghton, 1942).
1942—Robert McCloskey, *Make Way for Ducklings* (Viking, 1941).
1941—Robert Lawson, *They Were Strong and Good* (Viking, 1940).
1940—Ingri and Edgar Parin d'Aulaire, *Abraham Lincoln* (Doubleday, 1939).
1939—Thomas Handforth, *Mei Li* (Doubleday, 1938).
1938—Helen Dean Fish, *Animals of the Bible* (Lippincott, 1937); illustrated by Dorothy P. Lathrop.

Batchelder Award winners

THE MILDRED L. BATCHELDER AWARD is given each year to an American publisher for the most outstanding children's book originally published in a foreign language or in another country. The ALA Association for Library Service to Children gives the award to encourage American publishers to seek out superior children's books abroad and to promote communication between the peoples of the world. The award is named for Mildred L. Batchelder, a children's librarian whose work over three decades has had an international influence. Here are the award winners since the award's inception in 1968.

1991—Rafik Schami, *A Hand Full of Stars* (Dutton, 1990); translated from German by Rika Lesser.
1990—Bjarne Reuter, *Buster's World* (Dutton, 1989); translated from Danish by Anthea Bell.
1989—Peter Härtling, *Crutches* (Lothrop, 1988); translated from German by Elizabeth D. Crawford.
1988—Ulf Nilsson, *If You Didn't Have Me* (Macmillan, 1987); translated from Swedish by George Blecher and Lone Thygesen-Blecher.
1987—Rudolph Frank, *No Hero for the Kaiser* (Lothrop, 1986); translated from German by Patricia Crampton.
1986—Christophe Gallaz and Roberto Innocenti, *Rose Blanche* (Creative Education, 1986); translated from French by Martha Coventry and Richard Graglia.
1985—Uri Orlev, *The Island on Bird Street* (Houghton, 1984); translated from Hebrew by Hillel Halkin.
1984—Astrid Lindgren, *Ronia, the Robber's Daughter* (Viking, 1983); translated from Swedish by Patricia Crampton.

1983—Toshi Maruki, *Hiroshima No Pika* (Lothrop, 1982); translated from Japanese through the Kurita-Bando Literary Agency.

1982—Harry Kullman, Jr., *The Battle Horse* (Bradbury, 1981); translated from Swedish by George Blecher and Lone Thygesen-Blecher.

1981—Els Pelgrom, *The Winter When Time Was Frozen* (Morrow, 1980); translated from Dutch by Maryka and Raphael Rudnik.

1980—Aliki Zei, *The Sound of the Dragon's Feet* (Dutton, 1979); translated from Greek by Edward Fenton.

1979—Jörg Steiner, *Rabbit Island* (Harcourt, 1978); translated from German by Ann Conrad Lammers.

1978—Christine Nöstlinger, *Konrad* (Watts, 1977); translated from German by Anthea Bell.

1977—Cecil Bødker, *The Leopard* (Atheneum, 1977); translated from Danish by Gunnar Poulsen.

1976—Ruth Hürlimann, *The Cat and the Mouse Who Shared a House* (Walck, 1974); translated from German by Anthea Bell.

1975—Aleksandr Linevskii, *An Old Tale Carved out of Stone* (Crown, 1973); translated from Russian by Maria Polushkin.

1974—Aliki Zei, *Petros' War* (Dutton, 1972); translated from Greek by Edward Fenton.

1973—S. R. van Iterson, *Pulga* (Morrow, 1971); translated from Dutch by Alexander and Alison Gode.

1972—Hans Peter Richter, *Friedrich* (Holt, 1970); translated from German by Edite Kroll.

1971—Hans Baumann, *In the Land of Ur: The Discovery of Ancient Mesopotamia* (Pantheon, 1969); translated from German by Stella Humphries.

1970—Aliki Zei, *Wildcat under Glass* (Holt, 1968); translated from Greek by Edward Fenton.

1969—Babbis Friis-Baastad, *Don't Take Teddy* (Scribner, 1967); translated from Norwegian by Lise Sømme McKinnon.

1968—Erich Kästner, *The Little Man* (Knopf, 1966); translated from German by James Kirkup.

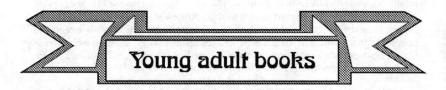

Young adult books

Young adult services

A 1987 SURVEY of public libraries commissioned by the National Center for Education Statistics made these findings about young adult services.

- One out of every four public library patrons in 1986–87 was a young adult (between the ages of 12 and 18).
- Only 11% of the nation's public libraries have the services of a young adult librarian.
- 84% of libraries offer a section or collection of materials specially designated for young adults. In 74% of these libraries, the young adult section or collection was moderately or heavily used.
- Libraries that employ a young adult services librarian were more likely to report moderate or heavy use of library services by young adults, includ-

ing: use of the library after school, evenings, and on weekends; use of the reference, adult circulation, and children's sections of the library; and use of readers advisory services for both school and independent needs, study space, and college and career information.

- In libraries without a young adult librarian on staff, young adults are served primarily by generalists. Only 16% of libraries that do not employ a young adult librarian require continuing in-service training in young adult services and materials.

Source: "Services and Resources for Young Adults in Public Libraries,"
National Center for Education Statistics Survey Report, July 1988

Quick picks: books for young adults

WHAT BOOKS MAKE GREAT READING? Books with exciting stories and interesting characters—books about real-life heroes and fantastic adventures—books that tell you how to fix up your car and help you deal with day-to-day problems. The following recent books are recommended by the ALA Young Adult Services Division's Recommended Books for Reluctant Young Readers Committee for young adults who, for whatever reason, do not like to read. The books chosen demonstrate high appeal in terms of content, format, and artwork. All titles are sixth-grade reading level or below, demonstrate simplicity of plot or organization of information, contain short sentences and short paragraphs, and have uncomplicated dialogue and vocabulary.

Agard, John. *Life Doesn't Frighten Me at All* (Henry Holt, 1990).
Angell, Judie. *Leave the Cooking to Me* (Bantam, 1990).
Baczewski, Paul. *Just for Kicks* (Lippincott, 1990).
Baird, Thomas. *Smart Rats* (Harper, 1990).
Beckelman, Laurie. *Alzheimer's Disease (The Facts About series)* (Crestwood, 1989).
Bennett, Jay. *Sing Me a Death Song* (Watts, 1990).
Blake, Jeanne. *Risky Times: How to Be AIDS-Smart and Stay Healthy* (Workman, 1990).
Clements, Bruce. *Tom Loves Anna Loves Tom* (Farrar, Straus, Giroux, 1990).
Cooney, Caroline B. *The Face on the Milk Carton* (Bantam, 1990).
Emert, Phyllis. *Monsters, Strange Dreams and UFOs* (Tor, 1990).
Emert, Phyllis. *Mysteries of Ships and Planes* (Tor, 1990).
George, Nelson. *Stop the Violence* (Pantheon, 1990).
Grant, Cynthia. *Phoenix Rising* (Atheneum, 1989).
Gutman, Paul. *Smitty II: The Olympia* (Turman, 1990).
Hahn, Mary Downing. *The Dead Man in Indian Creek* (Clarion, 1990).
Hall, Lynn. *Halsey's Pride* (Scribners, 1990).
Hamanaka, Sheila. *The Journey: Japanese Americans, Racism and Renewal* (Orchard, 1990).
Hamm, Diane. *Bunkhouse Journal* (Scribners, 1990).
Johnson, Linda C. *Barbara Jordan: Congresswoman* (Blackbirch, 1990).
Klause, Annette Curtis. *The Silver Kiss* (Delacorte, 1990).
Korman, Gordon. *Losing Joe's Place* (Scholastic, 1990).
Landau, Elaine. *We Have AIDS* (Watts, 1990).
Lauber, Patricia. *Seeing Earth from Space* (Orchard, 1990).
Lyons, Mary E. *Sorrow's Kitchen: The Life Folklore of Zora Neale Hurston* (Scribners, 1990).

Paulsen, Gary. *Woodsong* (Bradbury, 1990).
Pevsner, Stella. *How Could You Do It, Diane?* (Clarion, 1989).
Schenker, Dona. *Throw a Hungry Loop* (Knopf, 1990).
Schwandt, Stephen. *Guilt Trip* (Atheneum, 1990).
Shuker-Haines, Frances. *Everything You Need to Know about Date Rape* (Rosen, 1989).
Sonnermark, Laura. *Something's Rotten in the State of Maryland* (Scholastic, 1990).
Steiner, Barbara. *Puppy Love* (Willowisp, 1990).
Stine, R. L. *How I Broke Up with Ernie* (Archway, 1990).
Thesman, Jean. *The Whitney Cousins: Erin* (Avon, 1990).
Wardlaw, Lee. *Corey's Fire* (Avon, 1990).
Wersba, Barbara. *The Farewell Kid* (Harper, 1990).
Willey, Margaret. *Saving Lenny* (Bantam, 1990).

Source: ALA Young Adult Services Division

Best books for young adults, 1991

EACH YEAR THE ALA Young Adult Services Division compiles a list of fiction and nonfiction titles that have potential appeal to young adults and exhibit either high literacy standards or technical accuracy. The following 1991 list encompasses 51 fiction and 34 nonfiction titles.

Abdul-Jabbar, Kareem, and Mignon McCarthy. *Kareem* (Random, 1990).
Agard, John. *Life Doesn't Frighten Me at All* (Holt, 1990).
Anderson, Scott. *Distant Fires* (Pfeifer-Hamilton, 1990).
Ansa, Tina McElroy. *Baby of the Family* (Harcourt, 1989).
Appel, Allen. *Till the End of Time* (Doubleday, 1990).
Avi. *The True Confessions of Charlotte Doyle* (Orchard, 1990).
Baldwin, J., ed. *The Whole Earth Ecolog: The Best Environmental Tools and Ideas* (Harmony, 1990).
Bell, Clare. *Ratha and the Thistle-Chaser* (Atheneum, 1990).
Bennett, James. *I Can Hear the Mourning Dove* (Houghton, 1990).
Blake, Jeanne. *Risky Times: How to Be AIDS-Smart and Stay Healthy* (Workman, 1990).
Bode, Janet. *The Voices of Rape* (Watts, 1990).
Brooks, Polly Schoyer. *Beyond the Myth: The Story of Joan of Arc* (Lippincott, 1990).
Cannon, A. E. *The Shadow Brothers* (Doubleday, 1990).
Carter, Peter. *Borderlands* (Farrar, Straus, Giroux, 1990).
Caseley, Judith. *Kisses* (McKay, 1990).
Chestnut, J. L. *Black in Selma: The Uncommon Life of J. L. Chestnut Jr.* (Farrar, Straus, Giroux, 1990).
Chetwin, Grace. *Collidescope* (Bradbury, 1990).
Clarke, J. *The Heroic Life of Al Capsella* (Holt, 1990).
Clements, Bruce. *Tom Loves Anna Loves Tom* (Farrar, Straus, Giroux, 1990).
Crispin, A. C. *Starbridge* (Ace, 1989).
Cushman, Kathleen, and Montana Miller. *Circus Dreams: The Making of a Circus Artist* (Little, 1990).
Doherty, Berlie. *White Peak Arm* (Orchard, 1990).

Donofrio, Beverly. *Riding in Cars with Boys: Confessions of a Bad Girl Who Makes Good* (Morrow, 1990).

Embury, Barbara, and Tom D. Crouch. *The Dream Is Alive: A Flight of Discovery Aboard the Space Shuttle* (Harper, 1990).

Ferris, Jean. *Across the Grain* (Farrar, Straus, Giroux, 1990).

Feuer, Elizabeth. *Paper Doll* (Farrar, Straus, Giroux, 1990).

Freedman, Russell. *Franklin Delano Roosevelt* (Clarion, 1990).

Freedman, Samuel G. *Small Victories: The Real World of a Teacher, Her Students and Their High School* (Harper, 1990).

Friedman, Ina R. *The Other Victims* (Houghton, 1990).

Gallo, Donald R., comp. *Speaking for Ourselves* (National Council of Teachers of English, 1990).

Gilmore, Kate. *Enter Three Witches* (Houghton, 1990).

Hall, Barbara. *Dixie Storms* (Harcourt, 1990).

Hamanaka, Sheila. *The Journey: Japanese Americans, Racism and Renewal* (Orchard, 1990).

Hamilton, Virginia. *Cousins* (Putnam, 1990).

Harrison, Sue. *Mother Earth, Father Sky* (Doubleday, 1990).

Haskins, James. *Black Dance in America: A History through Its People* (Crowell, 1990).

Hendry, Frances Mary. *Quest for a Maid* (Farrar, Straus, Giroux, 1990).

Ho, Minfong. *Rice without Rain* (Lothrop, 1990).

Hudson, Jan. *Dawn Rider* (Philomel, 1990).

Human Rights in China staff. *Children of the Dragon: The Story of Tiananmen Square* (Macmillan, 1990).

James, J. Alison. *Sing for a Gentle Rain* (Atheneum, 1990).

Janeczko, Paul B. *The Place My Words Are Looking for* (Bradbury, 1990).

Jordan, Robert. *The Eye of the World* (Tor, 1990).

Katz, William L. *Breaking the Chains: African-American Slave Resistance* (Atheneum, 1990).

Kilworth, Garry. *The Foxes of Firstdark* (Doubleday, 1990).

Kisor, Henry. *What's That Pig Outdoors? A Memoir of Deafness* (Farrar, Straus, Giroux, 1990).

Klause, Annette Curtis. *The Silver Kiss* (Delacorte, 1990).

Koertge, Ron. *The Boy in the Moon* (Joy Street, 1990).

Korman, Gordon. *Losing Joe's Place* (Scholastic, 1990).

Larson, Gary. *PreHistory of the Far Side* (Andrews & McMeel, 1989).

Lauber, Patricia. *Seeing Earth from Space* (Orchard, 1990).

Levin, Betty. *Brother Moose* (Greenwillow, 1990).

Lord, Bette Bao. *Legacies: A Chinese Mosaic* (Knopf, 1990).

McCorkle, Jill. *Ferris Beach* (Algonquin, 1990).

Martin, Valerie. *Mary Reilly* (Doubleday, 1990).

Meltzer, Milton. *Columbus and the World around Him* (Watts, 1990).

Myers, Walter Dean. *The Mouse Rap* (Harper, 1990).

Naar, Jon. *Design for a Livable Planet* (Harper, 1990).

Naidoo, Beverley. *Chain of Fire* (Harper, 1990).

Naylor, Phyllis Reynolds. *Send No Blessings* (Atheneum, 1990).

O'Brien, Tim. *The Things They Carried* (Houghton, 1990).

Parks, Gordon. *Voices in the Mirror* (Doubleday, 1990).

Paulsen, Gary. *Woodsong* (Bradbury, 1990).

Pershall, Mary K. *You Take the High Road* (Dial, 1990).

Pierce, Meredith Ann. *The Pearl of the Soul of the World* (Joy Street, 1990).

Popham, Melinda Worth. *Skywater* (Graywolf, 1990).

Pullman, Philip. *The Tiger in the Well* (Knopf, 1990).

Ray, Delia. *A Nation Torn* (Lodestar/Dutton, 1990).

Rylant, Cynthia. *A Couple of Kooks: And Other Stories about Love* (Orchard, 1990).

Rylant, Cynthia. *Soda Jerk* (Orchard, 1990).
Sanders, Dori. *Clover* (Algonquin, 1990).
Schami, Rafik. *A Hand Full of Stars* (Dutton, 1990).
Sleator, William. *Strange Attractors* (Dutton, 1990).
Snyder, Zilpha Keatley. *Libby on Wednesday* (Delacorte, 1990).
Soto, Gary. *Baseball in April: And Other Stories* (Harcourt, 1990).
Spinelli, Jerry. *Maniac Magee* (Little, Brown, 1990).
Stoll, Clifford. *The Cuckoo's Egg: Tracking a Spy through the Maze of Computer Espionage* (Doubleday, 1989).
Strauss, Gwen. *Trail of Stones* (Knopf, 1990).
Taylor, Mildred. *Road to Memphis* (Dial, 1990).
Van Raven, Pieter. *Pickle and Price* (Scribners, 1990).
Voigt, Cynthia. *On Fortune's Wheel* (Atheneum, 1990).
Weiss, Ann E. *Who's to Know? Information, the Media and Public Awareness* (Houghton, 1990).
Willey, Margaret. *Saving Lenny* (Bantam, 1990).
Woolley, Persia. *Queen of the Summer Stars* (Poseidon, 1990).
Wrede, Patricia C. *Dealing with Dragons* (Harcourt, 1990).

Source: ALA Young Adult Services Division

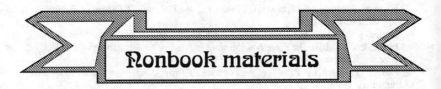

ℜonbook materials

Artifacts

WITHIN MOST LIBRARIES are small collections of freak objects—nonbook, non-AV, non-anything but artifacts oddly acquired or inherited. Some have research value; others are held because no one knew what else to do with them. Here are a few we've heard about:

- **Library of Congress:** The contents of Abe Lincoln's pockets the night of his assassination; also, a brooch picturing James Madison and containing a lock of his hair.
- **Boston Public Library:** The ashes of radicals Nicola Sacco and Bartolomeo Vanzetti, executed in 1927.
- **Hoover Institution Archives and Library:** X-rays of Adolf Hitler's head.
- **Metropolitan Toronto Reference Library:** Sherlock Holmes-type pipes and other realia in the Arthur Conan Doyle Room collection; clothing labels in the Arts Department.
- **Northwestern University Dental School Library:** Collection of Tooth Fairy artifacts, including coins and pillows; 18th-century Dutch carving in ivory and pear wood entitled, "Peasant Dental Treatment."
- **Yale University's Beinecke Rare Book and Manuscript Library:** 500 years' worth of playing cards, with a four-volume catalog.

Source: "Nonbook indeed!" *American Libraries*, June 1989, p. 483

Some AV definitions

by Nancy B. Olson

WHENEVER MOST OF US hear the term "audiovisual" or "nonbook" materials, we think of films, microforms, and sound recordings. However, as nonbook librarians know, these terms encompass much, much more. Here are definitions for some that are sometimes overlooked.

Architectural rendering. A pictorial representation of a building intended to show, before it has been built, how the building will look when completed.

Bathymetric map. A relief map of the ocean floor or a lake bed.

Cel. A transparent, plastic sheet used for animation.

Cradle. The holder for a globe.

Diorama. A three-dimensional representation of a scene created by placing objects, figures, etc., in front of a two-dimensional painted background.

EIAJ (Electrical Industries Association of Japan). The most common type of black-and-white $1/2$-inch open-reel videotape. Represents the industry's first attempt at standardization of videotape formats.

Filmslip. A short length of film containing a succession of images, without sound accompaniment, designed to be viewed frame by frame, sometimes mounted in a rigid format.

Firmware. A computer program that is permanently fixed inside a chip, for example, a program in ROM (read-only memory).

Graticule. An imaginary network of meridians and parallels on the surface of the earth or other celestial body. A network of lines, on the face of a map, which represents meridians and parallels.

Inaudible signal. The pulse on sound recordings designed to accompany synchronized filmstrips and slide sets that activates the mechanism to advance the material through the projector.

Lantern slide. The hand-drawn, painted, or photographic images on glass intended for viewing by projection; often made in sets. Phototransparency lantern slides were introduced in the United States by 1850 and remained popular through World War I. They are commonly $3^1/2$ by 4 in. with a black paper mask, a cover glass, and taped edges, although they may also be found in circular and novelty shapes. The emulsion may be albumen, collodion, or silver gelatin.

Manipulative. Any item designed to aid in development of hand-eye coordination, motor skills, etc.; includes sets of blocks, toys designed to be taken apart and reassembled, beads to be strung, etc.

Realia. Real items; tangible objects (artifacts, specimens) as opposed to replicas or pictorial representations. Examples of realia include sea shells, rocks, chairs, and tools.

Serigraphy. A printing technique in which ink is forced directly onto paper or canvas through a stencil containing the image.

Sound page. A flexible sheet of plastic with a sound disc on one side and pictures and/or printed material on the other side. The sound page is inserted in a specially designed player in which the playing mechanism rather than the disc revolves while the printed material can be read or the picture examined.

Ultrafiche. A microfiche containing images with a reduction ratio of 90x or more.

Wire recording. A magnetized wire capable of recording and playing back sound. Wire was a popular sound recording medium in the United States during the 1940s and early 1950s, but tape generally had replaced wire by the mid-1950s.

Source: Nancy B. Olson, *Audiovisual Material Glossary* (Dublin, O.: OCLC, 1988)

Notable nonbook materials for children

THE NOTABLE CHILDREN'S Films/Videos, Filmstrips, Recordings and (new this year!) Computer Software list is compiled annually by three (now four) committees of the ALA Association for Library Service to Children to highlight nonbook materials released in 1990. For a full description of the items described, see the April 1991 issue of *School Library Journal*.

Films/Videos

Alexander Who Used to Be Rich Last Sunday (Aims). Alexander relates how he squandered, lost, and flushed the $5 he was "absolutely, positively" going to save. This well-acted film is based on the book by Judith Viorst. Preschool through Intermediate.

Buy Me That. "Buyer beware!" advises this video for young consumers. Entertaining demonstrations explain that what is seen in a commercial is not always what you get. Primary through Junior High.

The Emperor's New Clothes (Weston Woods). This witty and whimsical adaptation of Hans Christian Andersen's story with Nadine Wescott's illustrations uses brilliantly colored animation and jazzy music to update the tale of the clothes-loving emperor. Preschool through Adult.

Jacob Have I Loved (Films, Inc.). Fifteen-year-old Louise Bradshaw wants to leave her island home to escape the shadow of her beautiful, talented twin, Caroline. This adaptation of Katherine Peterson's Newbery Award-winning novel features outstanding acting and the backdrop of Chesapeake Bay. Intermediate through Adult.

Joyful Noise (American School Publishers). The insect world is celebrated through a variety of film techniques in this creative presentation of Paul Fleischman's Newbery Award-winning poetry. Intermediate through Adult.

Juke Bar (National Film Board of Canada). Hordes of pesky cockroaches in a greasy spoon diner dance to the sounds of a brightly lit juke box. Live action sequences are mixed with puppet animation in this imaginative, wacky film. Primary through Adult.

Meet the Newbery Author: Cynthia Rylant (American School Publishers). Rylant provides insight into her writing through candid discussion of her life. Warm and witty, her honesty will inspire beginning writers. Intermediate through Junior High.

Ralph S. Mouse (Churchill). In his third film adventure, based on Beverly Cleary's book, Ralph is taken to school where his rollicking adventures begin. Live action mixed with puppet animation. 1991 Carnegie Video Medal Winner. Primary through Intermediate.

Sacajawea. The moving tale of Sacajawea's life is told with dazzling animation and eloquent narration through the voice of a childhood friend. Primary through Junior High.

Sadako and the Thousand Paper Cranes (Informed Democracy). This story of a spirited Japanese girl whose life was cut short by the "atomic bomb sickness" features Ed Young's impressionist artwork and Liv Ullman's expressive narration and translates Eleanor Coerr's poignant, hope-filled story into a moving film presentation. Intermediate through Adult.

Snowballs and Sandcastles (Bullfrog). This wordless film contrasts the images of summer and winter, deftly intercut to show the fun and frustration of the two seasons.

Truman (Direct Cinema). A young boy reluctantly faces the dreaded, stomach-churning task of rope-climbing in gym class, with unexpected results. This is every clumsy child's revenge fantasy. Intermediate through Adult.

Filmstrips

Follow the Drinking Gourd (American School Publishers, 1990). Based on the book by Jeanette Winter. 87 fr., 11 min.

Fox's Dream (Random House Media/Miller Brody, 1989). Based on the book by Tejima. 57 fr., 6 min. Original score by John Guth.

Meet the Author: Robert Louis Stevenson (Random House Media/Miller Brody, 1989). 138 fr., 18:15 min.

Mushroom in the Rain (Weston Woods, 1989). Based on the book by Mirra Ginsburg, illustrated by Ariane Dewey. 41 fr., 6:30 min.

Song and Dance Man (Miller Brody, 1990). Based on the book by Karen Ackerman, illustrated by Stephen Gammell. 80 fr., 8 min.

Titch (Weston Woods, 1989). Based on the book by Pat Hutchins. 30 fr., 3:30 min.

Recordings

4

Bill Wellington Presents WOOF Radio. By Bill Wellington (Well-In-Tune Productions, 1990). 42 min. cassette.

The Birthday Burglar and a Very Wicked Headmistress. By Margaret Mahy (Chivers Audio Books, 1990). 90 min. 2 cassettes.

Chickens in the Garden. By Phil Rosenthal (American Melody, 1990). 36 min. cassette.

Dave Van Ronk Presents Peter and the Wolf (Alacazam, 1990). 38 min. cassette; phonodisc.

The Demon Headmaster. By Gillian Cross (Chivers Audio Books, 1990). 3 cassettes.

Doc Watson Sings Songs for Little Pickers. By Doc Watson (Alacazam, 1990). 36 min. cassette; CD.

Evergreen, Everblue. By Raffi (Troubadour, 1990). 40 min. cassette; phonodisc; CD.

A Fish That's a Song (Smithsonian/Folkways, 1990). 43 min. cassette with booklet.

Follow the Drinking Gourd. By Jeanette Winter (American School Publishers, 1990). 11 min. read-along book and cassette.

Granny, Will Your Dog Bite? By Gerald Milnes, illustrated by Kimberly Bulcken Root (Knopf, 1990). 40 min. cassette and book.

Holiday Memories of a Shtetl Childhood. By Roslyn Bresnick-Perry (Global Villlage Music, 1990). 53 min. cassette.

King Arthur and His Knights. Told by Jim Weiss (Greathall Productions, 1990). 60 min. cassette.

Lullaby Berceuse. By Connie Kaldor and Carmen Campagne (Music for Little People, 1990). 38 min. cassette.

Mother Earth. By Tom Chapin (A&M Records, 1990). 36 min. cassette; CD.

Mozart's Magic Fantasy: A Journey through "The Magic Flute" (Classical Kids, 1990). 47 min. cassette; CD.

The Night-Watchmen. By Helen Cresswell (Chivers Audio Books, 1990). 190 min. 3 cassettes.

Oh, the Animals: Songs for Kids. By David Williams (Trapdoor Records, 1990). 42 min. cassette.

Prince Ivan and the Frog Princess (DELOS International, 1990). 58 min. cassette; CD.

Shake It to the One That You Love the Best: Play Songs and Lullabies from Black Musical Traditions. Collected and adapted by Cheryl Warren Mattox (Warren-Mattox Productions, 1990). 43 min. cassette and book.

Sharon, Lois and Bram Sing A to Z. By Sharon, Lois, and Bram (A&M Records, 1990). 65 min. cassette; CD.

Sing a Song of Seasons: A Musical Celebration for the Whole Family. By Judith Minogue and the Mill Creek Ramblers (Rosewood Records, 1990). 19 min. cassette.

The Snow Queen (DELOS International, 1990). 63 min. cassette; CD.

Song and Dance Man. By Karen Ackerman (American School Publishers, 1990). 8 min. cassette with book.

Three Hairs from the Devil's Beard and Other Tales. By Rosalind Hinman (American Melody, 1990). 46 min. cassette.

'Twas on a Night Like This: A Christmas Legacy. By Cathy Barton, Dave Para, and the Paton Family (Folk-Legacy Records, 1990). 62 min. cassette; CD; lyric booklet.

Zlateh the Goat and Other Stories. By Isaac Bashevis Singer (Caedmon Audio, 1990). 60 min. cassette.

Computer software

Hyperstudio, ver. 2.1. El Cajon, Calif.: Robert Wagner Publishing, 1989–1990. Apple IIGS. At least 1 MB. 3.5-inch disk drive. Allows user to create original programs (stacks) and to access and modify stacks created by others.

Math Blaster Mystery. Torrance, Calif.: Davidson and Associates, 1989. Apple II series/IBM/Mac. 128K and extended 80-column card. Follow steps to solve story problems, weigh evidence on scales, work to break numerical codes, and search for clues to solve math problems. Grades 5-12.

The Playroom. San Rafael, Calif.: Broderbund. Apple II series/IBM/Mac. 128K. Color monitor recommended. Pepper Mouse leads the way as preschoolers explore letters and numbers, telling time, and creating picture stories.

Where in Time Is Carmen San Diego? San Rafael, Calif.: Broderbund. Apple II series/IBM/Mac. 128K. Grades 5 and up.

Source: ALA Association for Library Service to Children

Selected films for young adults, 1991

THESE FILMS FOR young adults were chosen by a committee of the Young Adult Services Division on the basis of young adult appeal, technical quality, subject content, and use for different age levels.

Ashpet: An American Cinderella (Tom Davenport, 1990). A humorously touching version of the classic fairy tale "Cinderella." It is set in the rural South during the early years of World War II.

Baby Blues (National Film Board of Canada, 1989). Pregnant after unprotected sex, Kristen—a graduating senior with a coveted music scholarship—and Jason, her boyfriend, must face difficult questions about their future.

Black Magic (Varied Directions, 1988). Double dutch jump rope is shown through the experiences of the world champions Black Magic. Their trip to London and the thrill of competition are blended to create a unique view of a popular sport.

Choices (AIMS, 1989). Running away brings immediate relief from a sexually abusive father, but life on the street brings a new set of choices for a young woman.

Just for the Summer (Churchill, 1990). A high school track star must come to terms with Alzheimer's disease when his grandmother comes to live with his family just for the summer.

Life of Sojourner Truth (Coronet/MTI, 1990). A dramatization that chronicles the major events that led Sojourner Truth to become a famous orator and spokeswoman against slavery and for the rights of women.

Perfect Date (Filmfair, 1990). Sports hero Stephen arranges the perfect date with the most popular girl at school. With dad's new sports car, tickets to the "hot ticket" concert, and a party with the in crowd, what can go wrong? Almost everything!

Right to Be Mohawk (West Glen Films, 1989). A contemporary look at the Mohawk tribe in Akwesasne, New York. We see how they are continually adapting, evolving, and trying to live in harmony with Mother Earth, and how they are trying to retain their traditional culture in a modern world.

Road to Brown (California Newsreel, 1990). This documentary chronicles the heroic efforts of lawyer Charles Houston to overturn the Jim Crow laws that resulted from the U.S. Supreme Court's *Plessey v. Ferguson* decision. These efforts led to the *Brown v. Board of Education* decision.

Skin (Landmark Films, 1990). A stylized theatre piece that looks at subtle forms of racism through the eyes of three teens, one from India, one from Vietnam, and one African American. This film is humorous, sensitive, and creative.

Wild Women Don't Have the Blues (California Newsreel, 1990). A celebration of female blues singers from Ma Rainey and Bessie Smith to Koko Taylor. This documentary uses interviews interspersed with performance and archival footage to place the blues in a cultural and historical context.

Source: ALA, Selected Films for Young Adults Committee, Young Adult Services Division

Resources

Useful addresses

YOUR UNANSWERED QUESTIONS on library matters might be directed to one of the following organizations. See also other lists of addresses and telephone numbers on pages 49–50 (job placement sources), 96–97 (support staff networks), 116–39 (grants, scholarships, and awards), 141–44 (accredited library school programs), 172–73 (federal archives and records offices), and 409–11 (state library literacy contacts).

American Association of Law Libraries, 53 W. Jackson Blvd., Suite 940, Chicago, IL 60604; (312) 939-4764.

American Booksellers Association, 137 W. 25th St., New York, NY; (212) 463-8450.

American Film and Video Association, 920 Barnsdale Rd., Suite 152, La Grange Park, IL 60525; (708) 482-4000.

American Library Association, 50 E. Huron St., Chicago, IL 60611-2795; (800) 545-2433.

American Library Association, Washington Office, 110 Maryland Ave., N.E., Washington, DC 20002; (202) 547-4440.

American Society for Information Science, 8720 Georgia Ave., Suite 501, Silver Spring, MD 20910-3602.

American Society of Indexers, 1700 18th St., N.W., Washington, DC 20009; (202) 328-7110.

Art Libraries Society of North America, 3900 E. Timrod St., Tucson, AZ 85711; (602) 881-8479.

Association for Educational Communications and Technology, 1126 16th St., N.W., Washington, DC 20036; (202) 466-4780.

Association for Information and Image Management, 1100 Wayne Ave., Silver Spring, MD 20910; (301) 587-8202.

Association for Library and Information Science Education, 5623 Palm Aire Dr., Sarasota, FL 34243; (813) 355-1795.

Association of American Colleges, 1818 R St., N.W., Washington, DC 20009; (202) 387-3760.

Association of Records Managers and Administrators International, 4200 Somerset Dr., Suite 215, Prairie Village, KS 66208; (913) 341-3808.

Association of Research Libraries, 1527 New Hampshire Ave., N.W., Washington, DC 20036; (202) 232-2466.

Association of Research Libraries, Office of Managment Services, 1527 New Hampshire Ave., N.W., Washington, DC 20036; (202) 232-8656.

Beta Phi Mu International Library Science Honor Society, School of Library and Information Science, University of Pittsburgh, 135 N. Bellefield Ave., Pittsburgh, PA 15260; (412) 624-5230.

Bibliographical Society of America, Box 397, Grand Central Station, New York, NY 10163; (718) 832-1060.

Canadian Library Association, 200 Elgin St., Ottawa, Ontario, Canada K2P 1L5; (613) 232-9625.

Catholic Library Association, 461 W. Lancaster Ave., Haverford, PA 19041; (215) 649-5250.

Center for the Study of Reading, University of Illinois, P.O. Box 2276, Station A, Champaign, IL 61825-2276.

Choice, 100 Riverview Center, Middletown, CT 06457; (203) 347-6933.

Council on Library Resources, 1785 Massachusetts Ave., Suite 313, Washington, DC 20036; (202) 483-7474.

Library of Congress, 10 First St., S.E., Washington, DC 20540; (202) 707-5000.

Literacy Volunteers of America, Inc., 5795 Widewaters Parkway, Syracuse, NY 13214; (315) 445-8000.

Medical Library Association, 6 N. Michigan Ave., Suite 300, Chicago, IL 60602; (312) 419-9094.

Music Library Association, Box 487, Canton, MA 02021; (617) 828-8450.

National Committee on Pay Equity, 1201 16th St., N.W., Suite 420, Washington, DC 20036; (202) 822-7304.

National Council of Teachers of Mathematics, 1906 Association Dr., Reston, VA 22091-1593; (703) 620-9840.

OCLC, Inc., 6565 Frantz Road, Dublin, OH 43017-3395; (614) 764-6000.

Office of Educational Research and Improvement, National Center for Education Statistics, 550 New Jersey Ave., N.W., Washington, DC 20208-1404; (202) 357-6642.

Oral History Association, 1093 Broxton Ave., #720, Los Angeles, CA 90024.

Sociedad de Bibliotecarios de Puerto Rico, University of Puerto Rico Station, P.O. Box 28988, Rio Piedras, PR 00931.

Society of American Archivists, 600 S. Federal St., Suite 504, Chicago, IL 60605; (312) 922-0140.

Special Libraries Association, 1700 18th St., N.W., Washington, DC 20009; (202) 234-4700.

OPERATIONS 5

Bibliography

International Standard Book Numbers (ISBNs)

ISBNs ARE SPECIALLY DESIGNED and computed, ten-digit numbers that are supposed to be printed on the back cover and the reverse side of the title page of every book published in the world. The ISBN numbering system was designed in the late 1960s and is followed by essentially all publishers in the industrialized, wealthy nations, but is largely ignored by publishers in poorer countries. Each publisher is assigned special ISBN numbers by its nation's ISBN agency. To begin to understand the intricacies of the ISBN, let's look at the example below—the number for Anthony Browne's book, *Willy the Wimp*, published by Knopf.

> This last number is the "secret" **check digit**, to make sure this is an authentic ISBN.

ISBN 0–394–87061–1

This first number tells the **place of publication**; books published in the United States and the United Kingdom begin with either 0 or 1; books published in France, 2; Germany, 3; Japan, 4; the Soviet Union, 5; and so on.	This group of numbers, which can be up to 7 digits long, is the **publisher's number.** For example, all books published by Random House are 394; all books published by Scholastic Books are printed with the numbers 590.	This group of numbers identifies each specific book **title and binding**; a different binding for the same book receives a different number; for example, the library (heavy duty) binding of *Willy the Wimp* is 97061.

The last number, the **check digit,** is computed by taking the first nine numbers of the ISBN and multiplying, adding, dividing, and then subtracting. See the sidebar on the next page for instructions on computing the check digit; it's fun—try it! The check digit is designed to identify any ISBNs that might be incorrectly printed. The fact is that an average of only one of every eleven ten-digit numbers qualifies as an authentic ISBN.

What needs an ISBN?

General. A separate ISBN must be assigned to every different edition of a book, but *not* to an unchanged impression or unchanged reprint of the same book in the same format and by the same publisher. Price changes do not need a new ISBN.

Facsimile reprints. A separate ISBN must be assigned to a facsimile reprint produced by a different publisher.

Books in different formats. A separate ISBN must be assigned to the different formats in which a particular title is published. For example, a hardback edition

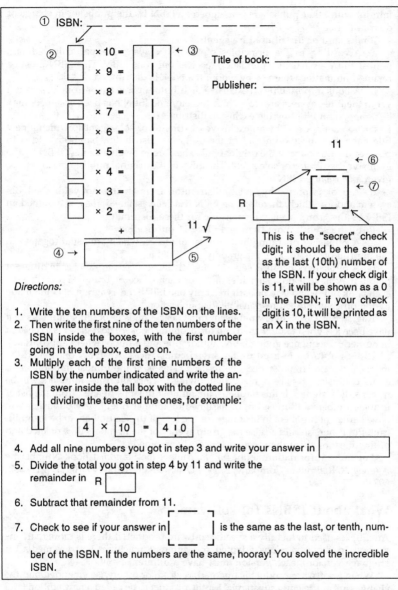

① ISBN: _ _ _ _ _ _ _ _ _ _

② ☐ × 10 = ← ③

Title of book: _____

☐ × 9 =

Publisher: _____

☐ × 8 =

☐ × 7 =

☐ × 6 =

☐ × 5 =

11

☐ × 4 =

— ← ⑥

☐ × 3 =

← ⑦

☐ × 2 =

R

+

11 √

④ →

⑤

This is the "secret" check digit; it should be the same as the last (10th) number of the ISBN. If your check digit is 11, it will be shown as a 0 in the ISBN; if your check digit is 10, it will be printed as an X in the ISBN.

Directions:

1. Write the ten numbers of the ISBN on the lines.
2. Then write the first nine of the ten numbers of the ISBN inside the boxes, with the first number going in the top box, and so on.
3. Multiply each of the first nine numbers of the ISBN by the number indicated and write the answer inside the tall box with the dotted line dividing the tens and the ones, for example:

4 × ☐10 = 4 ┆ 0

4. Add all nine numbers you got in step 3 and write your answer in ☐
5. Divide the total you got in step 4 by 11 and write the remainder in R ☐
6. Subtract that remainder from 11.
7. Check to see if your answer in ☐ is the same as the last, or tenth, number of the ISBN. If the numbers are the same, hooray! You solved the incredible ISBN.

5

and a paperback edition each receives a separate ISBN. On the same principle, a microform edition receives a separate ISBN.

Looseleaf publications. If a publication appears in looseleaf form, an ISBN is allocated to identify an edition at a given time. Individual issues of additions or replacement sheets will likewise be given an ISBN.

Multivolume works. An ISBN must be assigned to the whole set of volumes of a multivolume work as well as to each individual volume in the set.

Back stock. Publishers are required to number their back stocks and publish the ISBN in their catalogs. They must also print the ISBN in the first available reprint of an item from back stock.

Collaborative publications. A publication issued as a co-edition or joint imprint with other publishers is assigned an ISBN by the publisher in charge of distribution.

Books sold or distributed by agents.

a. According to the principles of the ISBN system, a particular edition, published by a particular publisher, receives only one ISBN. This ISBN must be retained no matter where or by whom the book is distributed or sold.

b. A book imported by an exclusive distributor or sole agent from an area not yet in the ISBN system and for which therefore no ISBN has been assigned, may be assigned an ISBN by the exclusive distributor.

c. Books imported by an exclusive distributor or sole agent to which a new title page, bearing the imprint of the exclusive distributor, has been added in place of the title page of the original publisher, are to be given a new ISBN by the exclusive distributor or sole agent. The ISBN of the original publisher is also to be given as a related ISBN.

d. A book imported by several distributors from an area not yet in the ISBN system and for which, therefore, no ISBN has been assigned, may be assigned an ISBN by the group agency responsible for these distributors.

Publishers with more than one place of publication.

a. A publisher operating in a number of places, which are listed together in the imprint of a book, will assign only one ISBN to the book.

b. A publisher operating separate and distinct offices or branches in different places may have a publisher identifier for each office or branch. Nevertheless, each book published is to be assigned only one ISBN, the assignment being made by the office or branch responsible for publication.

Register of ISBN. Every publisher must keep a register of ISBN numbers that have been assigned to published and forthcoming books. The register is to be kept in numerical sequence giving ISBN, author, title and edition (where appropriate).

ISBN not to be re-used under any circumstances. An ISBN once allocated must, under no circumstances, be re-used. This is of the utmost importance to avoid confusion. It is recognized that, owing to clerical errors, numbers will be incorrectly assigned. If this happens, the number must be deleted from the list of usable numbers and must not be assigned to another title. Every publisher will have sufficient numbers in his range for the loss of these numbers to be insignificant. Publishers should advise the group agency of the numbers thus deleted and of the titles to which they were erroneously assigned.

For more information about ISBNs, contact the Standard Book Numbering Agency, R. R. Bowker Company, 245 W. 17th St., New York, NY 10011; (212) 337-6971.

What about ISBNs for software?

An ISBN is used to identify a specific software product. If there is more than one version (perhaps versions adapted for different machines, carrier media, or language version), each version must have a different ISBN.

When a software product is updated, revised, or otherwise amended and the changes are sufficiently substantial for the product to be called a new edition (and thus probably the subject of a new launch, or marketing push), then a new ISBN must be allocated.

A relaunch of an existing product, even in new packaging where there is no basic difference in the performance of the new and the old product, does *not* justify a new ISBN, and the original ISBN must be used.

When software is accompanied by a manual, useful only as an adjunct to the software, and the software needs the manual before it can be operated, and the two items are always sold as a package, one ISBN must be used to cover both items.

When two or more items in a software package (as above) can be used separately, or are sold separately as well as together, then:

a. The package as a whole must have an ISBN.
b. Each item in the package must have its own ISBN.

ISBNs should be allocated to a software product independent of its physical form, e.g., if software is only available from a remote database whence it is downloaded to the customer.

As well as identifying the product itself, an ISBN identifies the publisher or manufacturer; it should not be used to identify a distributor or wholesaler.

Sources: Warren A. Hatch, "An Explanation of the ISBN System," *Arithmetic Teacher,* April 1989, pp.2–3; *The ISBN System Users' Manual* (Berlin: International ISBN Agency, 1986)

International Standard Serial Numbers (ISSNs)

IF YOU PUBLISH A SERIAL you will want to obtain an ISSN (International Standard Serial Number) for your publication. The ISSN is the essential element in an international system designed to improve bibliographic control over serial publications.

The ISSN usually appears in very small type on the table of contents page. The last number, the **check digit,** can be computed by the following method. No special meaning is attached to the first seven digits of the ISSN.

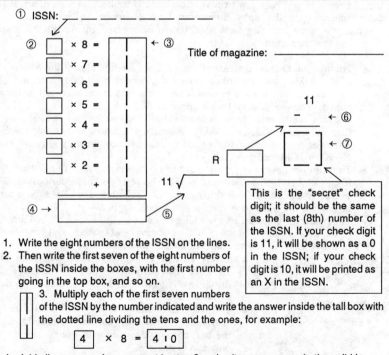

1. Write the eight numbers of the ISSN on the lines.
2. Then write the first seven of the eight numbers of the ISSN inside the boxes, with the first number going in the top box, and so on.

   This is the "secret" check digit; it should be the same as the last (8th) number of the ISSN. If your check digit is 11, it will be shown as a 0 in the ISSN; if your check digit is 10, it will be printed as an X in the ISSN.

   3. Multiply each of the first seven numbers of the ISSN by the number indicated and write the answer inside the tall box with the dotted line dividing the tens and the ones, for example:

   | 4 | × 8 = | 4 | 0 |

4. Add all seven numbers you got in step 3 and write your answer in the solid box.
5. Divide the total you got in step 4 by 11 and write the remainder in the dashed box.
6. Subtract that remainder from 11.
7. Check to see if your answer is the same as the last.

The ISSN is suitable to many management functions applied to serials—from invoicing and inventory control to checking in issues and citing articles. Acknowledged as an invaluable identification number for serials, particularly in a computer environment, the ISSN is being used by groups such as the Copyright Clearance Center, Inc., and the U.S. Postal Service.

For further information and ISSN assignments, write to the Library of Congress, National Serials Data Program, Washington, DC 20540; (202) 707–6452. The assignment of ISSNs is a free service.

Sources: Warren A. Hatch, "An Explanation of the ISSN System," *Arithmetic Teacher*, April 1989, pp.2–3; The Library of Congress

The National Union Catalog, Pre-1956 Imprints

THE MONUMENTAL, 754-VOLUME *National Union Catalog, Pre-1956 Imprints*, completed in 1981 after 14 years of cooperative endeavor, is a cumulative author list representing Library of Congress printed cards for books, pamphlets, maps, atlases, music, and periodicals reported by North American libraries and published before 1956. These pre-1956 volumes greatly assist librarians in acquisitions, cataloging, bibliography, interlibrary loan, reference, and research.

Here are some amazing facts and figures discovered by Art Plotnik that pertain to this mammoth set.—*GME.*

- Theft-proof! One set consists of 754 volumes totaling almost three tons. A thief sneaking out one volume every day would need two years and 24 days to complete the job, by which time he would suffer excruciating back pain and be well known by his grimace.
- The number of author entries exceeds 11 million—at the time, in 1981, more than the OCLC, RLIN, and WLN databases combined, discounting duplicated network records. This is also more than the combined populations of New York City and Los Angeles.
- The volumes have been published at an average rate of about 4.8 per month from October 1968 to December 1981. The total gestation period was 13 years and 2 months, a span during which 7$^1/_2$ elephants or 2,054 rabbits can be born to the same busy elephant or rabbit mother.
- The peak number of editors working together on the catalog at the Library of Congress equals the total of all the starters, head coaches, and governors of the Atlantic Division, National Basketball Division, or 35.
  - Given a large enough set of scales, with all 1,131,000 volumes on one tray, it would take 45 full-grown blue whales, 100 tons each, to tip the balance.
  - The volumes of one set take up 125 linear feet of shelving. Thrown from the first volume toward the last, the world-record shot-put would reach only to volume 458.
  - The total cost of the project, excluding financing expenses, was some $34 million, more than it cost to build the five-story, 364,000-square-foot Metropolitan Toronto Library.

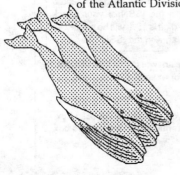

- One set contains some 528,000 pages. *American Libraries,* at its present rate of page output and with 50,000 pages in the bank, will need 679 years to catch up.
- Laid end to end, the total number of volumes manufactured by the publisher—1,131,000—would stretch 243 miles.
- Balanced one upon the other, the 13.6-inch-tall volumes in a single set would be higher than the Pan Am Building in New York, though less suitable as a helicopter pad.
- If all the pages of all the sets manufactured were spread over Manhattan Island, every inch of space from the Staten Island Ferry to Central Park would be littered with scholarly bibliography.

Source: Art Plotnik, "Amazing, Incredible, Astounding Facts and Figures,"
American Libraries, September 1981, pp. 456–57

OCLC facts and figures

IN 1967 THE PRESIDENTS of the colleges and universities in Ohio founded the Ohio College Library Center (OCLC) to develop a computerized system in which the libraries of Ohio academic institutions could share resources and reduce costs. In 1977 changes were adopted to allow libraries outside Ohio to become members. In 1981 the legal name of the corporation became OCLC Online Computer Library Center, and in 1990 OCLC served more than 11,000 libraries of all types in the United States and 36 other countries and territories.

OCLC members include the following libraries: 1,271 academic; 88 research; 608 public; 45 state; 74 state/municipal government; 80 processing centers; 335 law; 298 medical; 422 corporate; 120 theological; 482 federal; 82 school; 383 community or junior college; and 323 others.

OCLC's bibliographic database, the Online Union Catalog, began operation in 1971. Initially supporting only online computerized cataloging, the Online Union Catalog now supports more than 60 related services ranging from reference databases on CD-ROM to telecommunications services.

As of July 1990, the OCLC cooperative database held more than 22 million records with 365 million location listings attached. It grows at a rate of 31,000 records a week.

Most bibliographic records are in English (14.8 million), followed by German (1.4 million), French (1.2 million), Spanish (960,500), Russian (429,900), Italian (376,900), Portuguese (205,700), Latin (194,100), Chinese (189,000), and Japanese (176,800).

Member libraries used the OCLC Interlibrary Loan Subsystem to transact 4.9 million loans in 1989/90. They used the OCLC Online System to catalog approximately 425,000 books and other materials per week.

OCLC systems are housed in a specially designed, 44,400-square-foot, three-story computer room at OCLC's headquarters in Dublin, Ohio. As of June 1990, the Online System comprised 10,940 terminals or workstations online; 300,000 miles of telephone lines; and a large central system of 17 mainframes, 101 minicomputers, and 106.6 gigabytes of storage.

The system currently processes more than 3 million messages during normal operating hours. Overall, the system is available 99.8% of scheduled time, and users enjoy an average response time of under six seconds.

Source: OCLC Online Computer Library Center

Glossary of database terms

Authority list. A set of records establishing the forms of headings to be used in a set of bibliographic records and the references to be made to and from the headings. Categories of authority files include name authority file, series authority file, and subject authority file.

Basic index. Generally, those fields that are searched automatically unless terms are qualified with one or more field indicators. The basic index of most bibliographic databases includes title, descriptors, identifiers, section headings, and note words, when they are available.

Data conversion. The process of converting data from one form to another, usually from a human-readable form to a machine-readable form, or from one recording medium to another.

Database. A collection or file of bibliographic citations or unit records representing original items or published literature or other recorded material.

Descriptor. In indexing, a term, notation, or other string of symbols used to designate the subject of a work.

Downloading. The ability to capture information in an online search and store it in a nonprint format or the recording of information received from a host computer during an online search.

Field. A portion of a citation or unit record representing a specific item of information, e.g., author, title, abstract.

File conversion. The transfer of all or part of records in a file from one medium to another, usually from a non-machine-readable to a machine-readable form.

Identifier. A word or phrase supplied by an indexer to describe the subject matter in a citation when standardized lists are not sufficient to provide access to new terminology.

Machine-readable data file. A body of information coded by methods that require the use of a machine (typically but not always a computer) for processing. Examples include files stored on magnetic tape, punched cards, aperture cards, disks, etc.

Offline. Non-direct communications with a computer. For example, offline printing of bibliographic citations is done when a user is not communicating directly through a terminal and telecommunications network.

Online. Direct communication between a terminal or computer with modem and a computer through the use of telecommunications.

Record. A bibliographic or descriptive record of an item of published literature or other recorded material.

Rotated descriptor. An alphabetical index to all words found in a descriptor list where each subject word is rearranged into filing position in the context of all other words within the string of subject headings.

Selective Dissemination of Information (SDI). A service provided whereby its users are periodically notified of new publications, report literature, or other sources of information in subjects based on a profile of specific interests.

Sorting. To arrange output into a chosen sequence for either online or offline printing. For example, a set of retrieved items can be sorted in order by author, journal name, geographical area, amount of sales, or product classification.

Updates. Most recent additions to a database. Databases are typically updated on a regular basis as part of normal file maintenance.

Vendor. An organization that makes one or more databases available on a time-sharing computer system for interactive retrieval.

Source: "Guidelines for a Database Search Guide," *RQ*, Summer 1987, pp. 441–43; Heartsill Young, ed., *The ALA Glossary of Library and Information Science* (Chicago: ALA, 1983)

How to prepare a bibliography

THE BIBLIOGRAPHY COMMITTEE of the ALA Reference and Adult Services Division (RASD) has prepared these guidelines intended for bibliographers, publishers, and evaluators. They are concerned with the quality and character of the elements included in a bibliography; the purpose and place of a given bibliography vis-a-vis other available resources; and its accessibility, its availability, its durability, and its readability. The elements of a good bibliography are the same whether they are produced online or printed on paper.

Purpose

The bibliography should fill a significant need in order to justify its compilation. The subject should fit into the general scheme of available bibliographical sources, without unnecessary duplication. If similar bibliographies exist, they should be reviewed and the unique contribution of this new one should be stated explicitly.

The subject should be clearly stated in the title and defined in a preliminary statement.

Scope

Scope should be clearly defined.

The work should strive for completeness within its stated limitations (period, geographical area, form, language, library holdings, best books only, intended audience, etc.).

Formats, where different, should be identified and each described appropriately.

Methodology

Sources consulted and information on the method of compilation should be provided.

The compiler should work with the bibliographic units. A bibliographic unit is any entity in a bibliography: book; chapters of a book; journal articles; reports; manuscripts; sound and video recordings; computer programs or printouts; films; charts; etc. All items not personally examined by the compiler should be so identified.

Organization

Principles of organization. The organization of material should be suitable for the subject.

The main arrangement should make it possible to use the bibliography from at least one approach without consulting the index.

Multiple means of access should be provided.

The scheme for a classified bibliography should be logical and easy for users to understand.

Necessary components. Every bibliography should have a statement of scope and purpose.

An explanation of how to use the bibliography should be given.

Every bibliography should have a key to all abbreviations used.

A table of contents should be provided.

An index or indexes should be provided.

Indexes should be sufficiently detailed to provide acceptable levels of recall and precision.

Terminology should be appropriate to both subject and intended users.

Cross-references should be adequate for normal reference purposes.

Desirable features. Entry numbers for bibliographic units should be considered.

Location of copies of bibliographical units, if not readily available, is helpful.

Multiple means of access is desirable.

Annotations—Access

These may be at one of three levels:

1. Informative notes, used chiefly when the title is not clear; these should show the reason for including questionable titles.

2. Abstracts should give enough of the contents to enable users to decide whether they want to read the original.

3. Critical evaluations should be discriminating and should be written by someone knowledgeable in the field.

In each case the annotations should be succinct, informative, and on a suitable level for the intended users.

Bibliographic form

There should be sufficient information to identify the bibliographic unit easily for the purpose of the bibliography and needs of the intended user.

The bibliographic form should follow a recognized standard.

The bibliographic form should be followed consistently.

Timeliness

Retrospective bibliographies should keep the time lag between closing the bibliography and its publication to a minimum.

Those bibliographies intended to be current should be issued as closely as possible after the publication of the bibliographical units listed.

Accuracy

Citations should be correct and free from typographical errors.

Information provided in annotations and elsewhere should be factually accurate and grammatically correct.

Provision for corrections after publication should be considered.

Format

Format and typeface should be clear and appropriate.

The volume should be sturdy enough to withstand anticipated use.

The bibliography should be designed to keep its price within the means of potential users without sacrificing important features that facilitate its use.

Cumulation of ongoing bibliographies is strongly recommended.

Distribution

Published bibliographies should be properly advertised and distributed.

Notice of the bibliography should be sent to a standard national bibliography.

Source: "Guidelines for the Preparation of a Bibliography," *RQ*, Fall 1982, pp. 31–32

How to evaluate an index

THIS CHECKLIST WAS PREPARED by the American Society of Indexers chiefly for publishers and editors who are about to hire an indexer and wish to examine an applicant's previous work. However, it is also very useful to librarians or book reviewers for rating the usefulness of an index in a reference or nonfiction book.—*GME.*

Indexing scheme

Is it appropriate to the material indexed?

Does it permit easy and quick scanning and ready pinpointing of the desired references?

Are the main entries easily differentiated from subentries?

Is the arrangement of subentries self-evident?

Do subentries bear a logical and grammatical relationship to main entries?

If any explanations are required, are they easily spotted and lucid?

Are page references clear? When a reference covers several consecutive pages, has the indexer indicated clearly the beginning and the end of the reference, e.g., 35-43, not 35ff?

Do page references differentiate between principal discussion and cursory mention of the topic?

If there are deviations from the normal alphabetical order, or if some other order (e.g., chronological) is employed, is this necessary and is it obvious to the user?

Depth of indexing

Are all important topics (concepts, subjects, proper names) and pertinent statements represented in the index? Check several.

Are entries sufficiently specific to permit ready access to the desired material yet sufficiently comprehensive to prevent the scattering of related items? Headings chosen should be concise, each referring to one particular subject.

Are there adequate cross-references to guide the user to main entries or other entries offering additional information?

Are there duplicate entries instead of cross-references where space permits?

Test the index for depth in two ways:

1. Choose a few passages from the work and check in the index the terms representing the major topics discussed. If the index fails to locate the selected passages through the terms chosen in more than 5% of the attempts, something is wrong. A further test should be made: attempt to locate the selected passages through more general or broader terms than those originally chosen; if this succeeds, then the terms in the index are not sufficiently specific.

2. Scan the index for terms having a noticeably large number of page references. Good indexers try to give no more than 10–12 references for any one term, avoiding strings of page numbers.

Accuracy

Are the index terms used accurate?

Are the spelling, capitalization, italicization, and punctuation used in the book followed? Is the alphabetizing accurate, either word-by-word or letter-by-letter?

Check a sample of references to be sure the material indexed is actually on the page cited. (The indexer is responsible for the original compilation of the page references, though the publisher's proofreader must catch typographical errors.)

Accuracy in the choice of index terms may be tested by checking some technical and some ambiguous terms in the index against the passages they refer to in order to make sure the terms chosen are appropriate. (In one such check, "meteors" was found to be the term used to index a passage on meteorological research!)

Consistency

Are terms used consistently in the index? (If "sodium chloride" is used, "table salt" cannot also be used.)

Is a topic indexed by a specific term in one passage indexed by the same term (not a broader or narrower one) in another passage? (If a recipe on lamb stew is indexed in a cookbook under "lamb," then a recipe on leg of lamb must also be indexed under "lamb," not under "meat.")

*Source: Guidelines for Publishers & Editors on Index Evaluation
(Washington, D.C.: American Society of Indexers)*

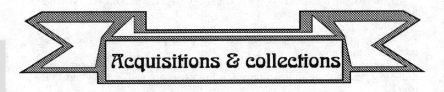

Acquisitions & collections

Acquisitions statistics

THE ACQUISITIONS MANAGER has at his or her disposal a wealth of information concerning the processes, practices, and trends in their materials-gathering activities. Most institutions keep some kind of records relating to these processes. Often the type of records kept is mandated by a higher administrative office's need for measures of collection growth, budget performance, materials costs, etc. The frequency of these reports may be governed by fiscal year reporting schedules, grant reporting requirements, contracts, or other factors. Generally, a second level of statistic is maintained to take the pulse of the local operation. These statistics may coincide with the needs of the higher administrative unit or simply meet the needs of departmental management. The acquisitions manager frequently has little control over the first kind of data, but may enjoy wide latitude in developing the second.

Quantifying load and demand

Managing the workload of an acquisitions department can be facilitated by some formal measure of items processed. That is, not just counting items acquired, but counting, for instance, the total number of order requests received, purchase orders generated, approval titles or forms handled, etc., all of which require labor without necessarily resulting in a receipt. Such measures are very useful in predicting and justifying changes in staffing levels. They are also very effective in planning for new systems and procedures. The acquisitions librarian should confer with library administrators to determine in advance any data needed to fulfill internal and external reporting requirements so that appropriate measures may be incorporated into the data-gathering process.

In addition to a gross count, the acquisitions manager may be interested in some of the characteristics of the raw requests for materials coming into the work flow. In particular, he or she may wish to identify those categories of requests which require special handling or processing priorities and those with special levels of urgency attached to them. Any work outside of the routine is more costly to handle, may require special equipment or staff capabilities to complete, and can lead to delays in processing the more routine requests. Therefore, the librarian may choose to establish counts such as the following for types of requests received:

a. number of new title requests received
b. number of rush requests received
c. number of course reserve requests received
d. number of out-of-print searches initiated

Identifying characteristics of order requests

The volume of requests indicates the level of demand placed upon the department. The tracking of other characteristics of the order requests received may reveal useful information about the interests of the library's clientele, the complexity of its acquisitions program, and the special skills staff must have to fulfill the department's mission successfully. It will also provide useful information for collection development staff on the current collecting interests of patrons and patterns of growth in the collection.

This category of data affords unlimited potential for creativity. The cautions noted earlier apply here in particular. If additional information on order requests is desired, the ordering process will have to have built-in mechanisms for recording them. In a manual system this may require special forms for requesting additions to the collection or special filing schemes to isolate the data. An automated system will require that fields in the order record be dedicated to recording this data. With this in mind, however, the manager may want to consider tracking order requests by the following criteria:

a. foreign-language materials
b. the foreign languages represented in the requests
c. material type (serial, monograph)
d. subject category
e. media or format
f. readership level (adult, young adult, juvenile, non-native English-language speaking, undergraduate, research, etc.)
g. multiple copy requests
h. requests originating in each branch or division
i. requests originating in each academic department, program, or special collection
j. requests originating with librarians and selectors
k. requests originating with the patrons
l. requests originating with the teaching faculty
m. requests originating with local government offices or agencies, boards of trustees, mayor's office, etc.
n. orders generated to support special library programs or projects
o. orders supported by special grant funding.

Source: Eileen D. Hardy, ed., *Statistics for Managing Library Acquisitions* (Chicago: ALA, 1989)

Survival tips for the auction-goer

by Frank W. Hoffmann

1. Before going to any auction, do your homework. Find out the conditions of the sale. If a catalog is available, obtain it and become familiar with its contents.

2. If possible, attend the presale exhibition and inspect items of interest, noting damage, repairs, or anything else that might affect the price.

3. Ask the auction staff for estimates of the selling price, but do not regard this as gospel; it should only serve as a guideline.

4. Employ a simple and direct bidding strategy; holding back when a desired object appears on the podium may destroy any chances of obtaining it.

5. Decide upon your top bid beforehand and stick to it, no matter what course the auction takes.

6. Get to know the competition. Make a point of meeting face-to-face any bidders revealing similar interests. Benefits will include new friends and contacts.

Source: Frank W. Hoffmann, *Popular Culture and Libraries* (Hamden, Conn.: Shoe String Press, 1984)

Collection terms

Collection policy. A written document defining the scope and nature of a library's existing collections and the policies and plans for continuing development of resources, with precise designation of present collection strengths and current collecting intensity in relevant subject fields and a statement of selection philosophy as related to institutional goals, general selection criteria, and intellectual freedom.

Quality. Utility to the user. Utility implies program-related economy and careful management to maintain responsive, minimally redundant or superfluous collections.

Source: Lenore Clark, ed., *Guide to Review of Library Collections* (Chicago: ALA, 1991)

Norm's Library Levity

Oversize

It was a tall librarian
  Who wished to travel far,
So paid for a whole section
  In a Pullman sleeping car.
But the porter saw him sitting
  On his berth's soft-cushioned edge,
And yelled: "Get down! You're oversize!
  You go below the ledge!"

—William Fitch Smyth, *Little Lyrics for Librarians* (1910)

How to start a local history collection

BEFORE MAKING THE COMMITMENT. A local history program should be developed only after a careful assessment has been made of the services currently or potentially being provided by other institutions and libraries within the community. The institution seeking to develop a local history collection must determine what is presently being collected and what is not being collected; what services are needed and what services are not; and to what depth such collections will be developed.

Coat of Arms, City of Chicago

Institutions developing a local history collection should make certain that such materials are placed in the most suitable collection for their best use, dissemination, and preservation.

Identification of collection limits. A major factor in the successful development of the collection is to identify its emphasis. By definition this could be geography, format, or whatever the institution desires.

Identify those materials which are to be acquired and maintained exclusively by the institution and those to be acquired cooperatively.

Acquisitions. Write an acquisitions policy for local history materials.

a. State the intended geographic collection area.

b. Describe those materials desired by the institution and the extent to which they will be collected.

c. Identify the types of materials which will definitely *not* be collected by the institution. Bear in mind that there may be other institutions which are better equipped to handle a given type of material.

d. Identify subject areas which will be acquired only on a cooperative basis.

The institution should process promptly and make available all materials collected.

Collection location and security. Local history collections should be established in an identifiable place, separate from the other collections of the library. The space so designated for local history collections should be an area secure from theft with proper provisions for monitoring the materials.

An environment which is conducive to the preservation of the materials should be provided.

Fiscal considerations. The local history collection should be processed and maintained by trained staff. Professionals can be assisted by properly trained volunteers to provide service to the patrons. A budget sufficient to acquire, process, and maintain the basic collection must be provided.

Consideration must be given for the cost of reproducing local history materials. Rare and fragile items must be protected from constant use by the patrons; copies will usually suffice to make the information available.

Much has been written about the organization and care of local materials. Items of particular usefulness are: Sam A. Suhler, *Local History Collection and Services in a Small Public Library* (ALA, 1970); technical leaflets published by the American Association for State and Local History; Enid T. Thompson, *Local History Collections: A Manual for Librarians* (American Association for State and Local History, 1978); and James H. Conrad, *Developing Local History Programs in Community Libraries* (Chicago: ALA, 1989).

Source: Local History Committee, Reference and Adult Services Division, *Guidelines for Establishing Local History Collections* (Chicago: ALA, 1979)

Current awareness profiles for collection development

by Daniel T. Law

IF THE BASIS OF collection development (CD) is the identification and procurement of resources in support of current and anticipated patron needs, then it is the primary responsibility of the CD librarian to first assess those needs, and then to select and acquire resources for the meeting of those needs. However, CD librarians are often met with distrust, particularly from faculty colleagues who often are mildly suspicious of their qualifications as book selectors ("Are they really qualified?"), or their methods of selection ("How do they choose their books anyway?"). The problem stems largely from the imprecise nature of their work. Granted, CD is not an exact science; but it need not become an entirely subjective and arbitrary undertaking either.

Perhaps what is needed is a heightened awareness on the part of collection developers to put CD on a more objective and scientific foundation. Such a feat is not as impossible as it may appear. Collection development has at least two attributes which qualify it as scientific. They are: *controllability* and *quantifiability*. Collection development is controllable, to the extent that its activities can be efficiently directed towards the attainment of desired objectives. It is quantifiable, because such directed activities can be monitored numerically, and the attainment of collection objectives can be measured quantitatively.

As an attempt to put CD on a more controlled and quantitative basis, the Research and Development Library of Smith Kline & French Laboratories has adopted an innovative approach. Key words and key phrases from in-house current awareness profiles are structured into hierarchical subject categories reflecting the research emphases of the company. The resultant Collection Development Guide serves the dual function of: 1) an empirical guide for the selection of books, and 2) an Acquisition Record for keeping track of collection activities.

Description of the CD Guide

The current awareness program at Smith Kline & French Laboratories consists of, in large part, a contracted service with the Institute for Scientific Information (ISI) in Philadelphia. Over 76 ASCA (Automated Subject Citation Alert) and ASCA Topic profiles are now being maintained, covering all areas of interest to research and development. In constructing the CD Guide, key words and key phrases from these profiles are compiled and classified into a somewhat hierarchical scheme, consisting of 13 major subjects, such as molecular biology, tumor, gastrointestinal, anti-infectives, etc. Under each major subject, key words and key phrases from various profiles are further grouped together into sub-categories.

In actual practice, a fresh copy of this Guide is used each month to record acquisition transactions for the month. Whenever a title is ordered under a particular subject, its listed price is entered in the space provided next to the appropriate category. If the title happens to be a reference work, its cost is then circled in red. At the end of each month, expenditure by subjects and types of books ordered (i.e., reference vs. non-reference) can then be readily tallied and obtained.

By using this simple Guide, we have found the following purposes served:

1. With the use of this instrument, CD has become to us a purposeful and targeted activity guided by parameters derived from the objective analysis of research directions and interests of the company.

2. The use of this Guide as an acquisition record also permits the tracking of monthly expenditure by subjects and types of books ordered. This in turn provides us with the basis for program monitoring, since collection efforts are now traceable by subjects and costs.

3. Furthermore, the adoption of this approach to CD has successfully allowed us to put an essentially subjective activity as CD on a more objective and scientific foundation, thus making the selling of the CD concept to our research/scientific community a much easier task.

Source: Daniel T. Law, "Innovative Use of In-house Current Awareness Profiles as a Guide for Collection Development in a Pharmaceutical Library," *College & Research Libraries News,* May 1989, pp. 372–74

Cataloging

The most concise AACR2

by Michael Gorman

5

HAVING COMPLETED A CONCISE edition of AACR2 (*The Concise AACR2,* ALA, 1981), Michael Gorman, unable to suppress the urge to condense the code even further, sent *American Libraries* this version shortly thereafter. In a heroic effort, he has squeezed the 677-page 1988 edition into the following few pithy rules.—*GME.*

Rule 1. Describe the item you have in hand. Record the following details in this order and with this punctuation:

Title : subtitle / author's name as given; names of other persons or bodies named on the title page, label, container, title frame, etc. — Edition (abbreviated). — Place of publication : Publisher, Year of publication.
Number of pages, volumes, discs, reels, objects, etc. ; Dimensions of the object (metric). — (Name of series)
Descriptive notes

Examples

i) His last bow : some reminiscences of Sherlock Holmes / A. Conan Doyle. — London : Murray, 1917.
305 p. ; 20 cm. — (Murray's fiction library)

ii) A white sport coat and a pink crustacean / Jimmy Buffett. — New York : ABC, 1973.
1 sound disc ; 12 in.
Backing by the Coral Reefer Band.

iii) Little Ernie's big day / by Norma Eustace ; designed by Doris Manier. — 2d ed. — Chicago : Little Folks, 1980.
1 filmstrip ; 35 mm. — (Big day filmstrips)

If the item is a serial (periodical, etc.), add the numbering of the first issue before the place of publication and leave the date and number of volumes "open" as in this example:

Circulation systems review. — Vol. 1, no. 1–   . — New Orleans : Borax Press, 1980-

v. ; 25 cm.

Rule 2. Make as many copies of the description as are necessary and add to each the name of the author and of other persons or bodies associated with the work.

Rule 2A. Give the names of people in their best known form.

Wodehouse, P. G.
Buffett, Jimmy
Harris, Emmylou
Suess, Dr.

Rule 2B. Give the names of corporate bodies in their best known form.

Yale University
Coral Reefer Band
Newberry Library

If a corporate body is part of another body, give it as a subheading *only if* it has an indistinct (blah) name.

United States. Department of the Interior
F.W. Woolworth Company. Personnel Division
University of Michigan. Library

Source: Michael Gorman, "The Most Concise AACR2," *American Libraries,* September 1981, p. 499

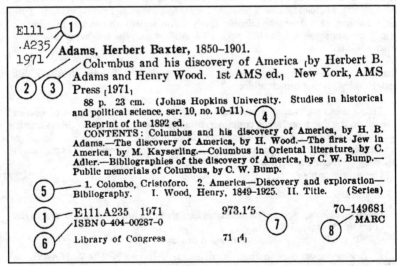

Catalog card

1. Call number.
2. Author (or main entry).
3. Title and publication information.
4. Series note.
5. Record of other headings under which the card is filed.
6. International Standard Book Number.
7. Decimal Classification Number (for other libraries using this system).
8. Library of Congress card number for ordering MARC cards.

Fun with AACR2: Articles and prepositions in surnames

THE *ANGLO-AMERICAN CATALOGUING RULES* have uses beyond the immediate needs of catalogers. I often turn to the section on people's names (chapter 22) to find out how non-English, historical, or compound surnames should be alphabetized in an index or bibliography. The rules for sacred scriptures and liturgical works (chapter 25) and the appendices on capitalization, abbreviations, and numerals are similarly fascinating and most instructive. Here's how AACR2 recommends that articles and prepositions in surnames be placed.—*GME*.

22.5D1. Articles and prepositions. If a surname includes an article or preposition or combination of the two, enter under the element most commonly used as entry element in alphabetically arranged directories, etc., in the person's language or country of residence or activity. The rules listed under languages and language groups below summarize entry element practice.

If such a name is listed in a nonstandard fashion in reference sources in the person's language or country of residence, enter under the entry element used in those sources.

If a person has used two or more languages, enter the name according to the language of most of that person's works. In case of doubt, follow the rules for English if English is one of the languages. Otherwise, if the person is known to have changed his or her country of residence, follow the rules for the language of the adopted country. As a last resort, follow the rules for the language of the name.

Afrikaans. Enter under the prefix.

> De Villiers, Anna Johanna Dorothea
> Du Toit, Stephanus Johannes
> Van der Post, Christiaan Willem Hendrik
> Von Wielligh, Gideon Retief

Czech and Slovak. If the surname consists of a place name in the genitive case preceded by *z*, enter under the part following the prefix. Refer from the place name in the nominative case. Omit the *z* from the reference.

> Zerotína, Karel z
> × Zerotín, Karel

Danish. *See* Scandinavian languages.

Dutch. If the surname is Dutch, enter under the part following the prefix unless the prefix is *ver*. In that case, enter under the prefix.

> Aa, Pieter van der
> Beeck, Leo op de
> Braak, Menno ter
> Brink, Jan ten
> Driessche, Albert van
> Hertog, Ary den
> Hoff, Jacobus Henricus van 't
> Wijngaert, Frank van den
> Winter, Karel de
> Ver Boven, Daisy

If the surname is not Dutch, enter the name of a Netherlander under the part following the prefix and the name of a Belgian according to the rules for the language of the name.

> Faille, Jacob Baart de la
>   *(Netherlander)*
> Long, Isaäc le
>   *(Netherlander)*

5

Du Jardin, Thomas
(Belgian; French name)

English. Enter under the prefix.

D'Anvers, Knightley
De Morgan, Augustus
De la Mare, Walter
Du Maurier, Daphne
Le Gailienne, Richard
Van Buren, Martin
Von Braun, Wernher

Flemish. *See* Dutch.

French. If the prefix consists of an article or of a contraction of an article and a preposition, enter under the prefix.

Le Rouge, Gustave
La Bruyère, René
Du Méril, Édélestand Pontas
Des Granges, Charles-Marc

Otherwise, enter under the part of the name following the preposition.

Aubigné, Théodore Agrippa d'
Musset, Alfred de
La Fontaine, Jean de

German. If the name is German and the prefix consists of an article or a contraction of an article and a preposition, enter under the prefix.

Am Thym, August
Aus'm Weerth, Ernst
Vom Ende, Erich
Zum Busch, Josef Paul
Zur Linde, Otto

Follow the same rule for Dutch names with a prefix consisting of an article or of a contraction of an article and a preposition.

De Boor, Hans Otto
(Name of Dutch origin)
Ten Bruggencate, Paul
(Name of Dutch origin)

Enter other German and Dutch names under the part of the name following the prefix.

Goethe, Johann Wolfgang von
Mühll, Peter von der
Urff, Georg Ludwig von und zu

Enter names that are neither German nor Dutch according to the rules for the language of the name.

Du Bois-Raymond, Emil
Le Fort, Gertrud

Italian. Enter modern names under the prefix.

A Prato, Giovanni
D'Arienzo, Nicola
Da Ponte, Lorenzo
De Amicis, Pietro Maria
Del Lungo, Isidoro
Della Volpaia, Eufrosino
Di Costanzo, Angelo
Li Greci, Gioacchino
Lo Savio, Niccolò

For medieval and early modern names, consult reference sources about whether a prefix is part of a name. If a preposition is sometimes omitted from the name, enter under the part following the preposition. *De, de', degli, dei,* and *de li* occurring in names of the period are rarely part of the surname.

Alberti, Antonio degli

Anghiera, Pietro Martire d'

Medici, Lorenzo de'

Do not treat the preposition in an Italian title of nobility used as an entry element as a prefix.

Norwegian. *See* Scandinavian languages.

Portuguese. Enter under the part of the name following the prefix.

Fonseca, Martinho Augusto da

Santos, João Adolpho dos

Romanian. Enter under the prefix unless it is *de*. In that case, enter under the part of the name following the prefix.

A Mariei, Vasile

Puşcariu, Emil de

Scandinavian languages. Enter under the part of the name following the prefix if the prefix is of Scandinavian, German, or Dutch origin (except for the Dutch *de*). If the prefix is the Dutch *de* or is of another origin, enter under the prefix.

Hallström, Gunnar Johannes af

Linné, Carl von

De Geer, Gerard

De la Gardie, Magnus Gabriel

La Cour, Jens Lassen

Slovak. *See* Czech and Slovak.

Spanish. If the prefix consists of an article only, enter under it.

Las Heras, Manuel Antonio

Enter all other names under the part following the prefix.

Figueroa, Francisco de

Casas, Bartolomé de las

Rio, Antonio del

Swedish. *See* Scandinavian languages.

22.5D2. Other prefixes. If the prefix is neither an article, nor a preposition, nor a combination of the two, enter under the prefix.

'Abd al-Ḥamid, Ahmad

A'Beckett, Gilbert Abbott

Abū Zahrah, Muḥammad

Al Yāsîn, Muhammad Ḥasan

Ap Rhys Price, Henry Edward

Ben Maÿr, Berl

Ó Faoláin, Seán

Mac Muireadach, Niall Mór

5

Source: Michael Gorman and Paul Winkler, eds., *Anglo-American Cataloguing Rules*, 2d ed. (American Library Association, Canadian Library Association, Library Association, 1988)

Cataloging in Publication (CIP)

THE CATALOGING IN PUBLICATION (CIP) program serves both publishers of U.S. monographs and American libraries by preparing cataloging data for new titles before publication. The publisher prints the CIP data in the publications, thereby reducing libraries' cataloging costs, and making new books available to readers more quickly. The service benefits publishers because the cataloging records for CIP titles are entered onto Library of Congress MARC computer tapes, which alert librarians to forthcoming publications and enable them to select and order new publications promptly and accurately.

Under this program, publishers submit nonreturnable galleys or manuscripts of forthcoming books to the CIP Division. Soon after this material is received, CIP cataloging data are returned to the publisher to be printed on the copyright page. Since the data include an LC catalog card number, it is not necessary for publishers to request a preassigned card number in addition to requesting CIP data.

There is no charge for this service, but the publisher is obliged to send the CIP Division one advance complimentary copy of each publication containing CIP information so that a final cataloging record can be produced. This record is supplied to libraries who use LC cataloging records in card form or from the computer tapes. The advance copy, which is in addition to any copies necessary for copyright compliance, should be sent to the address below.

More information about the CIP program, which has recently undergone some procedural changes, is available from the Library of Congress, Cataloging in Publication Division, Washington, DC 20540.

LC catalog card numbers

A unique Library of Congress catalog card number is assigned to each individual catalog record prepared by the Library of Congress. Librarians use this number to order printed catalog cards and to locate specific catalog records in automated databases. The card number is also often cited when placing book orders with dealers or publishers. Each number consists of two digits, a hyphen, and one to six digits; for example, 78-1 or 78-123456. The first two digits indicate the year that the number is issued, not the publication date of the title to which it has been assigned.

LC catalog card numbers are assigned in one of two ways:

1. A card number is routinely assigned to each published book that has been selected for the Library's collections and for which full cataloging will be done. To obtain a number for a published book, the publisher should donate a copy to the Library so that it can be considered for LC's collections. Complimentary copies should be addressed to the Library of Congress, Gift Section, Exchange and Gift Division, Washington, DC 20540. A letter should be enclosed, asking to be informed of the selection decision and of the card number assigned if the book is selected for Library cataloging.

2. A card number may also be preassigned to a title in advance of publication, for the purpose of printing it on the copyright page, as an aid to librarians. To request a preassigned LC catalog card number for a forthcoming title, publishers should submit an application form to the CIP Division, as early as possible in the publication cycle. Application forms and printed instructions may be obtained from the address below. There is no charge for this service, but the publisher is obliged to send LC one advance complimentary copy of each finished publication to which a card number has been preassigned. This copy, which is additional to any copies required by the Copyright Office for copyright compliance, should be sent to the address below. If, after a final review, it is determined that the title is needed for the Library's collections, catalog cards are prepared.

Publications being submitted for Cataloging in Publication (CIP) data need not be submitted separately for a preassigned LC card number. The number will be assigned automatically when the CIP data are created.

Certain types of material are not eligible to receive a preassigned card number; for example, publications under fifty pages, periodicals and other serial publications, foreign publications, and workbooks.

For further information about preassigned LC catalog card numbers and the eligibility of certain materials, contact the Library of Congress, Cataloging in Publication Division, Washington, DC 20540; (202) 287-6372.

Source: The Library of Congress

Fun with AACR2: Rule for spirit communications

21.26A. Enter a communication presented as having been received from a spirit under the heading for the spirit (see 22.14). Make an added entry under the heading for the medium or other person recording the communication.

Food for the million, or, Thoughts from beyond the borders of the material / by Theodore Parker ; through the hand of Sarah A. Ramsdell

Main entry under the heading for the spirit of Parker

Added entry under the heading for Ramsdell

Source: Anglo-American Cataloguing Rules, 2d ed., 1988 revision

Norm's Library Levity

Of the making of jokes about catalogers there is no end.

How many catalogers does it take to catalog a book? One—except at the Library of Congress where it has taken four, until recent experiments with "whole book" cataloging. Now it may only take two working together as a team. In prose and poetry, catalogers and their arcane practices have probably been the chief target of the humorists of our profession. Certainly Edmund Lester Pearson, our most noted library humorist, regularly attacked catalogers, as he did in the following piece from his column, "The Librarian," from the *Boston Evening Transcript* of January 3, 1912.

"It is a fact to be lamented, but the Amalgamated Brotherhood and Sisterhood of Bibliographic Catalogers have removed Mr. D. N. Way from membership, and passed a vote of censure against him. Mr. Way is well known as the assistant librarian of the Ezra Beesly Free Public Library. A few weeks ago he was passing through the catalogue department of that library, when he saw the chief cataloguer and her assistants engaged in an animated discussion. The debated question was whether a certain technical drawing in a book should be described as a 'plan' or a 'diagram.'

"They appealed to Mr. Way for a decision. He took a cent out of his pocket and tossed it in the air, remarking: 'Heads, a plan; tails, a diagram.' Then he picked up the cent and said: 'Tails. It's a diagram—put it so on the card, Miss Carey,' and walked out of the room.

"Two or three cataloguers swooned, and Miss Carey was incapacitated for any more work that day. Of course, the matter was reported to the chief librarian, who reproved his assistant, and informed the Amalgamated Bibliographic Cataloguers. They took the matter under consideration, and finally referred it to the Sub-Committee on the Promotion of Fiddle-Faddle. The committee reported last week, and the removal of Mr. Way and the vote of censure followed promptly."

—*Norman D. Stevens, The Molesworth Institute*

5

Name that catalog!

FEW LIBRARIES EVER gave a name to their hulking card catalogs other than "That !@#'! Mess of a Catalog!" But in promoting new online catalogs, librarians have come up with catchy names that stimulate interest and use. Some names are acronyms, and some incorporate key initials in the library's name. Let's see how many institutions you can identify as proprietors of the following catalogs.

1.	ACORN	11.	JIM
2.	CAROLINE	12.	LUMINA
3.	BISON	13.	OASYS
4.	UNLOC	14.	MIRLYN
5.	BYLINE	15.	MAGGIE
6.	QLINE	16.	MUSE
7.	CATALYST	17.	VIRGO
8.	PITTCAT	18.	HOLLIS
9.	DELCAT	19.	CODA
10.	LOVE YOUR CAT	20.	MAUD

Answers are on page 234

50 years of LC cataloging

by Sigrid P. Milner

WHEN ARCHIBALD MACLEISH became Librarian of Congress in 1939, he electrified some employees by announcing that they must awaken from their "enchanted lethargy." He began a reorganization of the entire Library. An internal management committee learned that of 5.8 million volumes, about 1.5 million were not fully processed. The arrearage at that time was growing by 30,000 a year. Each cataloging assistant produced 400 titles a year, or 1.5 per workday.

Since LC created separate Descriptive and Subject Cataloging Divisions 50 years ago, these divisions have produced almost 8 million cataloging records that are used by libraries throughout the country and around the world.

Selected highlights of five decades of LC cataloging follow:

1943–44: The work week increased to 48 hours. Personnel turnover in Descriptive Cataloging was an extraordinary 38.6%. Descriptive cataloging took between 84 and 131 minutes per title, and revising between 29 and 38 minutes per title.

1949–50: The priority system had four categories: *rush*, to be processed within a day; *hasten*, to be processsed within a week; *regular*, completed within a year; and *Priority 4*. Russian materials got the highest priority.

1954–55: LC classification schedules were said to be seriously ossified and in urgent need of revision.

1960–61: The 6th edition of *Library of Congress Subject Headings* went out of print, provoking public astonishment that the Superintendent of Documents had allowed this to happen. An 11,000-card arrearage to be reprinted due to new and changed headings required one employee-year to eliminate.

1963–64: At then-current production levels, the department estimated it would require 132 work-years to search the arrearage, 80 work-years to perform preliminary processing, and 280 work-years to catalog them.

1968–69: President Johnson forwarded a letter written to him that requested Subject Cataloging to change the subject heading of Negro to Black.

1970–71: LC developed the Cataloging in Publication (CIP) program.

1975–76: The heading Negroes became Afro-Americans, Maize changed to Corn, and Salesman and Salesmanship "desexed" to Sales Personnel and Selling. "Insurance, Social" and "Hygiene, Public" changed to "Social Security" and "Public Health." Corpulence updated to Obesity.

1978–79: LC changed the subject heading Water-Closets to Toilets.

1982–83: Two pigeons attempted to nest on a fifth floor window ledge. The Library installed the falling books sculpture to no one's approval.

1984: A committee to study see-also references met 18 times.

1984–85: Because of vacancies, arrearages climbed 45.9% to 67,070 items.

1985–86: The first microcomputer arrived in Subject Cataloging.

1987: On April 10 Subject Cataloging cataloged the first book online, a volume on memorial cremation in Thai. A Working Group on Job Satisfaction was established, which made an early recommendation to permit personal headsets at work.

1988–89: Subject Cataloging reduced its arrearages by 42.8%; Descriptive Cataloging, despite a vacancy rate of 24%, was able to reduce its arrearages slightly.

Source: Sigrid P. Milner, "Library Observes 50 Years of Cataloging for the Nation," *LC Information Bulletin,* December 17, 1990, pp. 444–47

LC's arrearage

ARE YOU LOSING GROUND to your workload? Are the piles on your desk threatening to bury you? If misery really does love company, take heart.

The Library of Congress backlog of unprocessed acquisitions, subject of a comprehensive census in 1989, totaled **38,069,000** items. These included:

- 1,178,000 books (3.1% of the total);
- 2,543,000 serials (6.7%);
- 34,348,000 items in other formats (90.2%).

These other formats included pictorial materials and manuscripts—more than 12,000,000 of each!

Perhaps more daunting, the arrearage grew by some 1,820,000 items in 1989—a growth rate of some 4.8%. In 1990, although the arrearage expanded to a record total of **40,000,000** items, the annual growth rate slowed to 3.4%.

LC estimates that using current processing techniques, the labor cost of stopping further growth and reducing the current backlog by 80% would be $616 million through the end of the year 2000.

As anyone with an overflowing worksite knows, backlogs also cause space problems. For LC, the cost of space adequate to cope with the arrearage, plus attendant expenses for preservation, automation support, supplies, equipment, and furniture, is estimated to be at least equal to the labor costs.

LC believes that as many as 20% of the items in the existing arrearage, especially manuscript and graphic materials, may not require processing; their limited research value may not justify processing costs.

In 1990, the number of unprocessed print materials actually decreased by 4.3%, from 4.31 million items in 1989 to 4.13 million. The big decrease was for serials, which declined by 6.5%; a large part of the serials decrease was attributable to the Law Library, which filed an arrearage of nearly 500,000 looseleaf materials during the year. The number of unprocessed sound recordings increased by 7.5% and unprocessed manuscripts increased by 5.1%.

In 1991, some funds were allocated to help reduce the backlog and new staff was hired, so the prognosis is good for the year 2000.

Source: "LC's Arrearage," *American Libraries,* October 1990, p. 841

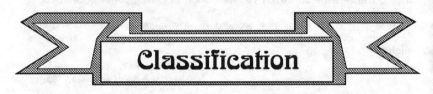

Classification

Basic shelving techniques

WHEN FACED WITH instructing new library assistants for the first time on the finer points of shelving (or when confronted with having to appear knowledgeable on the subject, even though you've avoided actually doing it ever since you got your MLS 15 years ago), it helps to be prepared. These instructions for library pages might come in handy in such a situation!—*GME.*

We expect you will build up speed and be able to meet the satisfactory performance standard for numbers of books shelved, but *accuracy is more important than speed.* Keep this general principle in mind while you're shelving: Items should be in order, be lined up neatly, and positioned so patrons can remove and/or replace an item easily. Be sure the materials you're planning to shelve have been properly discharged. Carts at your library may be labeled "To be shelved," or their mere placement may indicate their readiness for shelving.

Sorting. When shelving cataloged materials from carts, first you'll need to put the materials in order upon the cart. It's not easy to reorganize a whole cart jam-packed with different sized books. You'll probably work out your own special way of doing it, but you might try this method to begin with. Scan the cart and identify several books that fall at the beginning of the range you'll be shelving. For

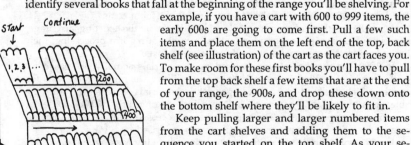

example, if you have a cart with 600 to 999 items, the early 600s are going to come first. Pull a few such items and place them on the left end of the top, back shelf (see illustration) of the cart as the cart faces you. To make room for these first books you'll have to pull from the top back shelf a few items that are at the end of your range, the 900s, and drop these down onto the bottom shelf where they'll be likely to fit in.

Keep pulling larger and larger numbered items from the cart shelves and adding them to the sequence you started on the top shelf. As your sequence expands, taking up more room, you'll continue onto the top near shelf, then the shelf directly below it, then the back lower shelf. Unlike the top shelves of the cart where both rows of books face the same direction, the lower shelves demand that you place the books with the call number or spine label sticking outward so that it can be read.

An alternate method of putting a cart in order might be to order the top near shelf first, then the shelf under it, then the top back shelf, then the shelf under that. Do what works best for you. But remember, the order of books on the real shelves runs from left to right, and downward, the same way you read a page of a book. It may take you almost half as much time to put your cart in order as it does to shelve it!

Shelving. When you get out into the stacks and begin shelving, glance over the shelf where you're about to put a book. Glance over the whole shelf to make sure you're not misplacing the book by putting it next to another misplaced book. Reshelve books which you notice are out of place. Stray books, which are completely out of place, should be returned to the circulation desk when you return your cart. And if a whole section is really out of order, consult with your supervisor. There may not be time to correct the whole section at the moment.

Don't try to handle too many books at a time, but if you can't get your cart down an aisle (patrons browsing the shelves?), carry 5 or 10 books to the shelves at a time so you won't waste steps. Don't leave books or records near a heat source because heat damages materials. Be on the alert for items in need of repair. Always shelve by the pocket, since the spine information can be erroneous. Check for classification, due date card (if the card is in the pocket it may not have been discharged), and branch ownership.

Library shelves all have some type of bookend. It may be freestanding or it may be a wire fixture that hangs from the shelf above. Bookends help hold books upright on the slippery, metal shelves. One mistake many pages make is to tighten the bookend too much. If books are too tightly packed, the patron who removes a book (and even this may be difficult to do) will not be able to replace it. The patron might leave the book anywhere, or what's worse, they may try to cram it back onto the shelf, pushing several books which fall off the back of the shelf. Patrons get very frustrated and so would you, if you didn't know how the bookends worked. So push the bookend in only as far as it needs to go to hold the books vertically.

Books loosely shelved are an invitation to disaster. A book loosely shelved may easily be pushed to the back of the shelf, eventually fall behind and not be found for some time. Or it may fall off the front of the shelf and land on someone's head (yours?). When books are properly shelved, there's always the hope that the patron will replace a book correctly. If there are too many gaps between books, the patron will not be able to readily choose the one where the book was taken from. The spines should be even with the front edge of the shelf. (Sometimes our "helpers" push rows and rows of books back from the front edge of the shelf.) This makes them easier to see and easier to pull off the shelf.

Shelving adult fiction. In many public libraries books are shelved alphabetically by the author's last name, first name, and then by title. Exceptions to this rule in some libraries are Mysteries, Science Fiction, Westerns, and Large Print, which are shelved in their own separate sections, so patrons looking exclusively for those genres can find what they want more easily. Collections of these genres which have been cataloged with a literature call number (808.83—non-fiction) may be grouped together following all the titles that are shelved as fiction. In other libraries they are kept with the non-fiction.

You may want to arrange a fiction cart in rough order by the first letter of the last name, and then begin shelving, putting each letter in order as you come to it, and eliminating the frustration of reorganizing when patrons browse through the cart.

If two authors have the same last name, arrange by the first name or initials so that all books by the same person will be found together on the shelf. For example, novels by Angela Brooks precede novels by Clarissa Brooks. If there is more than

5

one book by the same author, the books are arranged alphabetically by title; for example, *Graffiti* by Angela Brooks would follow *Destitute* by Angela Brooks. If your library has an extremely high page workload, these rules may be modified, such as no organization by title within the same author's work, but even if your library cuts corners, remember that these procedures are the ideal to strive for when time allows.

All abbreviations must be treated as though they were spelled out:

St. is Saint.

Mr. is Mister.

Names beginning with "Mc" and "Mac" are shelved as though they were both spelled "Mac." "MacDougall" would follow "McBain."

If the first word of the title is "A," "An," or "The," shelve alphabetically by the second word in the title.

Source: Fairfax County (Va.) Public Library, *Page Package: A Training Manual* (Chicago: ALA Public Library Association, 1988)

Dewey Decimal Classification: The hundred divisions

MOST LIBRARY USERS KNOW the general structure of Melvil Dewey's decimal classification. First published in 1876, the Dewey Decimal Classification divides knowledge into ten main classes, with further subdivisions. Here is an outline of its 100 major subdivisions.

000 (Generalities)

010	Bibliography
020	Library and information sciences
030	General encyclopedic works
040	[not assigned]
050	General serials and their indexes
060	General organizations and museology
070	News media, journalism, publishing
080	General collections
090	Manuscripts and rare books

100 (Philosophy and psychology)

110	Metaphysics
120	Epistemology, causation, humankind
130	Paranormal phenomena
140	Specific philosophical schools
150	Psychology
160	Logic
170	Ethics (Moral philosophy)
180	Ancient, medieval, Oriental philosophy
190	Modern Western philosophy

200 (Religion)

210   Natural theology
220   Bible
230   Christian theology
240   Christian moral and devotional theology
250   Christian orders and local church
260   Christian social theology
270   Christian church history
280   Christian denominations and sects
290   Other and comparative religions

300 (Social sciences)

310   General statistics
320   Political science
330   Economics
340   Law
350   Public administration
360   Social services; association
370   Education
380   Commerce, communications, transport
390   Customs, etiquette, folklore

5

400 (Language)

410   Linguistics
420   English and Old English
430   Germanic languages
440   Romance languages; French
450   Italian, Romanian, Rhaeto-Romanic
460   Spanish and Portuguese languages
470   Italic languages; Latin
480   Hellenic languages; classical Greek
490   Other languages

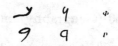

500 (Natural sciences and mathematics)

510   Mathematics
520   Astronomy and allied sciences
530   Physics
540   Chemistry and allied sciences
550   Earth sciences
560   Paleontology, paleozoology
570   Life sciences
580   Botanical sciences
590   Zoological sciences

600 (Technology and applied sciences)

610   Medical sciences; medicine
620   Engineering and allied operations
630   Agriculture
640   Home economics and family living
650   Management and auxiliary services

660   Chemical engineering
670   Manufacturing
680   Manufacture for specific uses
690   Buildings

700 (The arts)

710   Civic and landscape art
720   Architecture
730   Plastic arts, sculpture
740   Drawing and decorative arts
750   Painting and paintings
760   Graphic arts; printmaking and prints
770   Photography and photographs
780   Music
790   Recreational and performing arts

800 (Literature and rhetoric)

810   American literature in English
820   English and Old English literature
830   Literatures of Germanic languages
840   Literatures of Romance languages
850   Italian, Romanian, Rhaeto-Romanic
860   Spanish and Portuguese literatures
870   Italic literatures; Latin
880   Hellenic literatures; classical Greek
890   Literatures of other languages

900 (Geography and history)

910   Geography and travel
920   Biography, genealogy, insignia
930   History of the ancient world
940   General history of Europe
950   General history of Asia
960   General history of Africa
970   General history of North America
980   General history of South America
990   General history of other areas

Source: Dewey Decimal Classification Summaries, DDC 20 (Albany, N.Y.: Forest Press, 1989)

The Dewey and LC classes

More than 200,000 libraries in 135 countries use the Dewey Decimal Classification (DDC) to organize their collections. Its simple and logical framework is based on the principle of decimal fractions as class marks, which are expandable to make further subdivisions. DDC also has auxiliary tables for forms, areas, literatures, languages, racial, ethnic, and national groups, and persons, which are applicable for most of the class marks. In the United States, 95% of all school and public libraries, 25% of all academic libraries, and 25% of all special libraries use DDC.

The Library of Congress (LC) scheme is in fact a loosely coordinated system of 21 special classifications, each with its own tables and structure. It was developed to reflect the actualities of published materials, rather than to encompass a logical framework for all knowledge. It does tend to avoid the long notations that DDC is prone to in science and technology especially.—*GME.*

LC classification outline

THE LC CLASSIFICATION was developed and used at the Library of Congress beginning in 1899. It has become the system of choice for many large research libraries. This list gives the scope for most one- or two-letter designators, which may serve as an aid in learning the classification schedules in more detail.

A (General works)

AC   Collections, series, collected works
AE   Encyclopedias (general)
AG   Dictionaries and other general reference books
AI   Indexes (general)
AM   Museums (general), collectors and collecting
AN   Newspapers
AP   Periodicals (general)
AS   Academies and learned societies (general)
AY   Yearbooks, almanacs, directories
AZ   History of scholarship and learning

B (Philosophy, psychology, religion)

5

B   Philosophy (general)
BC   Logic
BD   Speculative philosophy
BF   Psychology, parapsychology, occult sciences
BH   Aesthetics
BJ   Ethics, social usages, etiquette
BL   Religions, mythology, rationalism
BM   Judaism
BP   Islam, Bahaism, theosophy
BQ   Buddhism
BR   Christianity
BS   The Bible
BT   Doctrinal theology
BV   Practical theology
BX   Christian denominations

C (Auxiliary sciences of history)

C   Auxiliary sciences of history (general)
CB   History of civilization
CC   Archaeology (general)
CD   Diplomatics, archives, seals
CE   Technical chronology, calendars
CJ   Numismatics
CN   Inscriptions, epigraphy
CR   Heraldry
CS   Genealogy
CT   Biography (general)

D (History, general and Old World)

D   History (general)
DA   Great Britain

DB Austria, Liechtenstein, Hungary, Czechoslovakia
DC France
DD Germany
DE The Mediterranean region, the Greco-Roman world
DF Greece
DG Italy
DH The Low Countries
DJ Holland
DJK Eastern Europe
DK Soviet Union, Poland
DL Scandinavia
DP Spain, Portugal
DQ Switzerland
DR Balkan Peninsula
DS Asia
DT Africa
DU Australia, Oceania
DX Gypsies

E-F (History, America)

E Indians, United States (general)
F U.S. local history, Canada, Mexico,
     Central and South America

G (Geography, anthropology, recreation)

G Geography (general), atlases, maps
GA Mathematical geography, cartography
GB Physical geography
GC Oceanography
GF Human ecology, anthropogeography
GN Anthropology
GR Folklore, manners and customs
GV Recreation, sports, leisure

H (Social sciences)

H Social sciences (general)
HA Statistics
HB Economic theory, demography
HC Economic history and conditions (by region or country)
HD Production, land use, agriculture, industry, labor
HE Transportation, communications
HF Commerce, accounting
HG Finance
HJ Public finance
HM Sociology (general and theoretical)
HN Social history, social problems,
     social reform
HQ The family, marriage, woman
HS Societies (secret, benevolent), clubs
HT Communities, classes, races
HV Social pathology, social and public
     welfare, criminology
HX Socialism, communism, anarchism

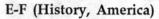

J (Political science)

- **J**   General legislative and executive papers
- **JA** Collections and general works
- **JC** Political theory, theory of the state
- **JF** Constitutional history and administration (general and comparative)
- **JK** United States government (federal and state)
- **JL** British America, Latin America
- **JN** Europe
- **JQ** Asia, Africa, Australia, Oceania
- **JS** Local government
- **JV** Colonies and colonization, emigration and immigration
- **JX** International law and international relations

K (Law)

- **K**   Law (general)
- **KD-KDK** United Kingdom and Ireland
- **KDZ**   America, North America
- **KE-KEZ** Canada
- **KF-KFZ** United States
- **KG-KGZ** Mexico, Central America, West Indies
- **KH-KHW** South America
- **KJ-KKZ** Europe

5

L (Education)

- **L**   Education (general)
- **LA** History of education
- **LB** Theory and practice of education
- **LC** Special aspects of education
- **LD** United States
- **LE** America, except United States
- **LF** Europe
- **LG** Asia, Africa, Oceania
- **LH** College and school magazines and papers
- **LJ** Student fraternities and societies, U.S.
- **LT** Textbooks

M (Music and books on music)

- **M**   Music
- **ML** Literature of music
- **MT** Musical instruction and study

N (Fine arts)

- **N**   Visual arts (general)
- **NA** Architecture
- **NB** Sculpture
- **NC** Drawing, design, illustration
- **ND** Painting
- **NE** Print media
- **NK** Decorative arts, applied arts, antiques, other arts
- **NX** Arts in general

P (Language and literature)

P	Philology and linguistics (general)
PA	Classical languages and literature
PB	General European languages, Celtic language and literature
PC	Romance languages
PD	Old Germanic, Scandinavian
PE	English
PF	Dutch, Flemish, Frisian, German
PG	Slavic, Baltic, Albanian
PH	Finno-Ugrian, Basque
PJ	Egyptian, Libyan, Berber, Cushitic, Semitic languages
PK	Indo-Iranian, Armenian, Caucasian
PL	East Asian, African, Oceanic languages
PM	Hyperborean, Indian, and artificial languages
PN	Literary history and collections, drama, journalism, collections
PQ	Romance literatures
PR	English literature
PT	Germanic literatures
PZ	Juvenile belles lettres, miscellaneous literature

Q (Science)

Q	Science (general), information theory
QA	Mathematics
QB	Astronomy
QC	Physics
QD	Chemistry
QE	Geology
QH	Natural history, biology
QK	Botany
QL	Zoology
QM	Human anatomy
QP	Physiology
QR	Microbiology

R (Medicine)

R	Medicine (general)
RA	Public aspects of medicine
RB	Pathology
RC	Internal medicine, medical practice
RD	Surgery
RE	Ophthalmology
RF	Otorhinolaryngology
RG	Gynecology and obstetrics
RJ	Pediatrics
RK	Dentistry
RL	Dermatology
RM	Therapeutics, pharmacology
RS	Pharmacy and materia medica
RT	Nursing
RV	Eclectic medicine
RX	Homeopathy
RZ	Other systems of medicine

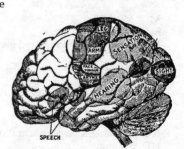

S (Agriculture)

S	Agriculture (general)
SB	Plant culture
SD	Forestry
SF	Animal culture
SH	Aquaculture, fisheries, angling
SK	Hunting, wildlife management

T (Technology)

T	Technology (general)
TA	Engineering (general), civil engineering (general)
TC	Hydraulic engineering
TD	Environmental technology, sanitary engineering
TE	Highway engineering, roads and pavements
TF	Railroad engineering and operation
TG	Bridge engineering
TH	Building construction
TJ	Mechanical engineering and machinery
TK	Electrical engineering, electronics
TL	Motor vehicles, aeronautics, UFOs
TN	Mining engineering, metallurgy
TP	Chemical technology
TR	Photography
TS	Manufactures
TT	Handicrafts, arts and crafts
TX	Home economics

5

U (Military science)

U	Military science (general)
UA	Armies
UB	Military administration
UC	Maintenance and transportation
UD	Infantry
UE	Cavalry, armored and mechanized cavalry
UF	Artillery
UG	Military engineering, air forces, air warfare
UH	Other services

V (Naval science)

V	Naval science (general)
VA	Navies
VB	Naval administration
VC	Naval maintenance
VD	Naval seamen
VE	Marines
VF	Naval ordnance
VG	Minor services of navies
VK	Navigation, merchant marine
VM	Naval architecture, shipbuilding, diving

Z (Bibliography, library science)

Z	History of books, booktrade, libraries, bibliography

Source: LC Classification Outline (Washington: Library of Congress, 1986)

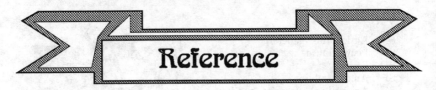

Reference

Choosing an encyclopedia

by Sandy Whiteley

AFTER NARROWING DOWN the field based on the appropriateness of the sets for the intended age group, there are 12 criteria that can be used in evaluating an encyclopedia. Each characteristic is briefly explained below. Prospective purchasers should visit their local public library and compare encyclopedias, looking up topics on which they are already knowledgeable to assess the relative strengths of the sets.

Authority. Authority derives from the credentials of contributors and editors and the general reputation of the publisher. While distinguished contributors may be listed as the authors of articles, the editors determine what information to include as well as the format in which it will appear. Sets differ in the extent to which they use outside experts to draft articles. *New Standard Encyclopedia* and *Children's Britannica* articles are written by staff and are thus unsigned. Many sets have long articles signed by outside authors and unsigned short articles, while *World Book* has authors' signatures at the ends of even the briefest articles. Potential purchasers of an encyclopedia can find the credentials of its contributors listed, usually in either the first or last volume of the set. An examination of the lists of contributors to all encyclopedias shows that some of them are dead or long-retired. For instance, one of the authors of "Botany" in one encyclopedia taught at Oberlin College from 1898 to 1933. A contributor of articles on the history of science to another set retired from Harvard in 1951.

Arrangement. Most encyclopedias are arranged alphabetically, either word by word or letter by letter. (For example, a word-by-word arrangement is *ice cream, ice hockey, iceboating, Iceland*. A letter-by-letter arrangement is *iceboating, ice cream, ice hockey, Iceland*.) A word-by-word arrangement is easier for most children to use. It is helpful for younger readers if the alphabet is divided so that all of one letter (or all of a combination of letters like WXYZ) is in one volume.

To assist readers in finding related information, encyclopedias provide indexes, cross-references, and tables of contents and boxed summaries at the beginnings of long articles. A detailed index is particularly helpful in drawing together information that may be scattered throughout the set. Artists, for example, may have articles of their own but may also be discussed in broader articles on painting or sculpture. To test an encyclopedia's indexing and cross-referencing system, pick four or five topics and see how the various keys lead to related information. Compare the same topics in similar encyclopedias.

Subject coverage. To determine appropriateness of subject coverage to your own needs, consider the type and range of topics included in the encyclopedia and the relative space allotted to various subjects. Are "hot" topics and contemporary issues covered or only those items that have been proven by the passage of time to be part of our cultural heritage? Does the allocation of space to various subjects meet the purchaser's requirements? A purchaser interested in such practical topics as careers or nutrition or how-to-do-it information, for example, should not purchase a set that covers strictly academic topics. Encyclopedias for children will, of course, devote more attention to such topics as pets, hobbies, and sports than will adult encyclopedias.

Accuracy. Readers often take for granted that information in an encyclopedia is accurate, but outdated statistics and erroneous dates can be found. Generally, however, editors take special care to make articles as accurate as possible, and all copy goes through a lengthy checking procedure. Before investing in an encyclopedia, prospective buyers should inspect topics with which they are familiar to see if articles on them are precise and accurate.

Objectivity. Space limitations in general encyclopedias make lengthy representation of all views on controversial topics an impossibility. Readers therefore depend on the editorial judgment of encyclopedia editors to present a balanced picture. Consumers should examine specific articles to see to what extent opposing doctrines are given fair and balanced consideration. Encyclopedias are written to sell to the widest possible audience, and therefore most articles represent mainstream thinking. Users looking for articles that propound unorthodox views on health, for instance, will not find them in these sets. Readers should also be on the alert for the presence of racial and sexual biases. Attempts to counter racial bias in encyclopedias have included adding biographies and articles on minority history and eliminating denigrating language. Similar steps have been taken to eliminate sexual bias; however, it lingers in some sets. The reader should be wary of the stereotyping of women, overuse of the pronoun *he,* and single-gender characterizations of various vocations, for example, exclusively male airline pilots or female secretaries. Encyclopedias that have revised their texts on these topics may still be using older photographs that reflect stereotypes.

Recency. There are facts that do not "date." Much of the information on the humanities—art, music, philosophy—does not change dramatically over time. However, population statistics, election results, important scientific breakthroughs, and sports records are among the many topics on which out-of-date information is misleading. Just because an encyclopedia undergoes an annual revision does not mean that *all* facts are updated. All encyclopedia editors have a page budget that limits the number of pages they are able to change in any one revision, with most sets making changes in about 10% of the pages. Before investing in an encyclopedia, a would-be purchaser should check the currency of information on topics with which he or she is familiar.

Quality. Items that determine the quality of individual articles in an encyclopedia include many of the characteristics discussed under other headings here. Another factor, however, is the length of articles, which should vary with the importance and complexity of the subject. Encyclopedias differ in the degree to which they present information on specific topics or subsume material on related topics into broad articles. *The Encyclopedia Americana,* for instance, tends to have articles on specific subjects. *Collier's,* on the other hand, has fewer, longer articles on broader topics. *The New Encyclopaedia Britannica* uses both approaches, with long articles on broad topics in the *Macropaedia* and shorter articles on narrower topics in the *Micropaedia.* None of these procedures is necessarily better than the others; each appeals to some individuals.

Within each article, data should be presented in logical fashion without ambiguity or oversimplification. The information selected for inclusion should be relevant to the needs of the reader. For instance, biographies should provide summaries of persons' contributions rather than focusing on dates and degrees. The treatment of such complex topics as the Middle East or nuclear energy will help indicate the quality of the encyclopedia as a whole.

Style. The hallmarks of effective encyclopedia style are simplicity and directness. Even though the subject matter of an encyclopedia is largely factual, an encyclopedia article should be a pleasure to read. The language should be appropriate to the subject and to the intended audience. Some publishers of encyclopedias for children sometimes use controlled vocabularies or test the reading level of their articles using various readability formulas in order to guarantee that children will be able to understand them. In sets for all age levels,

5

technical and advanced terms should be defined when they first appear. Difficult topics should be introduced gradually and with sufficient explanation, so that they do not confuse or overwhelm the reader.

Bibliographies. Many encyclopedias include with their articles bibliographies of suggested readings as guides to further study. Lists of books, magazines, or other items that are grouped on the basis of difficulty are particularly useful. The works listed should be current and generally available. Bibliographies are most useful when they appear at the ends of articles instead of being segregated in a separate volume. Teachers sometimes discourage students from using encyclopedias because they suspect that they rely too much on them when writing term papers, but the encyclopedia article provides an excellent introduction to the term-paper topic, and its bibliography will provide titles of materials for further research.

Illustrations. Drawings, maps, portraits, photographs, diagrams, and other graphics are an interesting and often instructional component of encyclopedias. Illustrations should be clear, informative, attractive, and placed in proper relation to the articles on the subjects they depict, with captions complete enough to avoid confusion. The size should be appropriate to their subject matter; paintings, for instance, should not be reduced to the size of postage stamps. The use of color enhances the attractiveness of an encyclopedia, and encyclopedia publishers are increasingly using more color. Some sets are printed on four-color presses, which means that color can appear on any page. Some publishers still print only selected sections on a four-color press, which means the decision of where to use color is partially determined by where the article appears in the set rather than its subject.

Physical format. First, the buyer should notice whether the encyclopedia is durably and attractively bound. Is the binding strong enough in relation to the weight of the volumes? Some encyclopedias have more than one binding available at different prices. For home use, the most inexpensive binding should be suitable. Test a volume to see whether it lies flat when opened. The centers of double-page maps and illustrations should not disappear into the binding. The paper should be opaque so that the print on one side of a page does not bleed through on the reverse. Type should be clear and legible, and a variety of sizes and spacing should be used to avoid monotony. Encyclopedias for young children are usually set in a large typeface that is easier to read.

Special attributes. Some encyclopedias have extra features sold as part of a package, such as reference services, separate atlases, dictionaries, or other materials, that are intended to lure hesitant buyers. Consumers should weigh very carefully the added value of such features and not let their presence distract them from assessing the encyclopedia's main objectives and quality.

Source: Sandy Whiteley, ed., *Purchasing an Encyclopedia: 12 Points to Consider* (Chicago: ALA *Booklist*, 1989)

Stump your librarian

Reference service hit the airwaves at Saginaw (Mich.) Public Library in 1988 when local radio station WSGW invited librarians to field questions on "Open Line," a popular morning talk show. Library director Catherine O'Connell and disk jockey Art Lewis chatted about library services and encouraged listeners to call in and challenge the research skills of librarians Lorri Lea and Kate Tesdell, who responded on the air via two phone lines to the library.

Saginaw librarians offer radio reference service twice a year, and on one occasion they did the broadcast live from the reference room. Tesdell, head of public services, said the reference librarians are almost never stumped and usually deliver the answer while the caller is still on the line. Asked if anyone managed to stump a professional this time, Tesdell said, "One caller wanted to know if a B-52 bomber has ever done a loop-the-loop. We had a little trouble with that one."—*American Libraries*, May 1989.

Four ways to keep a dictionary on its stand

UNTIL RECENTLY, libraries could purchase dictionary stands with screwed-on metal strips that held the covers of the dictionary flat against the stand and kept the volumes from disappearing. However, since these stands are no longer available and since our dictionaries had a way of disappearing, I came up with an alternative solution in my home workshop. I cut and bent simple metal strips to serve the same function with our wooden dictionary stands. These strips are about two inches longer than the dictionary cover height. Width is not critical. Strips that are half an inch to an inch wide will do. Likewise, thickness can be one-sixteenth to one-eighth of an inch depending on the type of metal used. Either steel or aluminum may be used, although steel strips should be properly cleaned and painted with a quality enamel to prevent rust stains on the book. The strips are bent slightly less than one inch from each end into an offset of about one-eighth of an inch to allow for the cover thickness, and a hole is drilled in each end for an ordinary roundhead wood screw. Each book requires two strips, one each for the front and back covers of the volume. The dictionary is placed open on the stand, the strips are placed across the inside covers about halfway from hinge to edge, and the screws are driven into pre-drilled starter holes in the stand through the holes in the ends of each strip. Made properly, the strips will hold the dictionary snugly without damaging the covers and without allowing patrons to slip the covers out from underneath.—*Thomas R. Harrington, Gallaudet University Library, Washington, D.C.*

We have five dictionary stands in the library. Each holds an unabridged dictionary. We place a desk-sized abridged dictionary on the shelf below. We label each stand, each unabridged dictionary, and each abridged dictionary with a number ("Dictionary Stand #1," "Dictionary Stand #2," etc.). For the cost of several abridged dictionaries, we have been able to satisfy the need for portable dictionaries around the library and still keep the unabridged dictionaries available. When the dictionaries are found elsewhere, the labels get them back in the right place.—*Cynthia M. Dyer, Simpson College, Indianola, Iowa.*

The Language and Literature Division of the Brooklyn Public Library fastens the front and back covers of unabridged dictionaries to wooden dictionary stands at the top and bottom corners with large screws driven in very tightly through the covers and the wood.—*Lillian Tudiver, Borough of Manhattan Community and Brooklyn College.*

To combat the problem of wandering dictionaries, we have put the following sign just above our unabridged dictionaries: "Please do not remove. Dictionaries for room use are available at the circulation desk." These signs have been very effective mostly because our students tend to use abridged rather than unabridged dictionaries. We do keep old editions of unabridged dictionaries in the reference collection in case patrons need to use them at the reference study tables. Before we arrived at this solution, we did find that holes could be drilled through the front and back covers of the dictionary. Fortunately, we have not had to resort to this method.—*Jan Keller, College of the Canyons Instructional Center, Santa Clarita (Calif.).*

Source: "Action Exchange," *American Libraries*, February 1990, March 1990

Vicki Young as "Ify," the Information Fairy

User instruction as theatre

THIS IS HOW ONE LIBRARIAN handled an age-old problem: how to make talks about the library interesting to freshmen college students.

At Xavier University in Cincinnati, Vicki Young, head of reader services, used her theatrical background to get students interested. During freshman orientation in 1987, the library was the last item on a two-hour agenda held on a Saturday morning, which included academic policies, bookstore policies, and ROTC. Realizing that the students would be at an information overload, Vicki wanted to present the library in a positive light and reduce students' anxiety. Dressed as "Ify" the Information Fairy, Vicki talked about six major misconceptions about librarians and libraries.

Misconception #1: Librarians are boring, stern, old, with their hair in buns and chains on their glasses.

Wrong! Librarians at Xavier are just the opposite of this stereotype. They are helpful, friendly, and they have a sense of humor.

Misconception #2: Everyone who works in a library is a librarian.

Wrong! Everyone who works in a hospital isn't a doctor. Only half of the people you see working in libraries are librarians. Librarians have a master's degree in library science.

Misconception #3: You should know how to use a library by the time you get to college, and people will think you are stupid if you ask for help.

Wrong! Just because you've used a high school library doesn't mean you'll know everything about a university library. Librarians don't expect you to. One of the duties of a reference librarian is to sit at the reference desk and answer questions. So please ask questions.

Misconception #4: All librarians do is order books, read books, and check out books.

Wrong! Actually this is only a small part of a librarian's job. The main duty of a librarian is to help people find information.

Misconception #5: Libraries only have books.

Wrong! Libraries have: microfilm, journals, records, microfiche, periodicals, videos, magazines, newspapers, and CD-ROM reference sources.

Misconception #6: The main purpose of a library is to provide study space.

Wrong! While the 3rd floor of the library is devoted to quiet study and has study carrels, the library is also a place to do research and find information.

The presentation was a big hit, and she has repeated it many times.

In 1988, Vicki wore a safari outfit and used the theme on an ALA poster: "It's an information jungle out there. Let your librarian be your guide."

Source: "BI as Theatre," College & Research Libraries News, January 1989, p. 30

Encouraging words

WHAT ARE THE BEST WAYS for reference librarians to approach a bewildered patron? Two suggestions appeared in the *American Libraries* "Action Exchange."

We haven't compiled a phrase book, but we frequently discuss with staff members phrases to use, such as, "Is there any way that I can help you this evening?" After the PA system announces closing time, it's tactful to say, "Is there anything I might help you with before we close?" We also encourage librarians to simply smile and say, "Good morning" or "Hello."

We find that library patrons are much more receptive if librarians move around and approach people, rather than waiting for a patron to come to a desk. We also find it beneficial to suggest titles other than those that users are specifically looking for.—*Marijean Zahorski, Brown County (Wisc.) Library, Green Bay.*

I scrupulously avoid the question, "May I help you?" which is so wrong for so many reasons. When I'm behind the reference desk and a user approaches, I think that person intends to ask a question, so I ask, "What is your question?" Ninety-nine percent of the time, the user then puts the question. When I approach someone away from the desk, I say, "Do you have a question?" Both phrases are neutral in tone as well as substance and quite logical in context.

The most difficult problem is to approach someone already searching the catalog or index in a neutral or encouraging manner. Marvin Scilken has suggested "Are you finding something?" or "Are you finding what you want?" All I can add is a variant, "Are you finding the books (or articles) you are looking for?" The experienced user will probably answer "Yes," while the person who needs help will often respond with "Yes, but . . ." or "Not really," and the librarian has an entrée.—*Fred W. Oser, Monmouth County (N.J.) Library, Manalapan.*

Source: "Action Exchange," American Libraries, July/August 1987, pp. 567–68

How to evaluate information

by Hannelore Rader, Billie Reinhart, and Gary Thompson

CRITICAL THINKING IS A SKILL that is rarely taught in school. Some people are born with this talent, some learn from enlightened parents, but many others have only minimal critical facilities. Evaluating information is central to living a successful and healthy life. It should also be second nature to reference librarians who have to gauge the quality of the answers they provide, and who may have opportunities to encourage information literacy in the users they serve.

Copies of a brochure featuring the checklist on the following pages (suitable for giving to your library patrons) are available from ALA Graphics, 50 E. Huron St., Chicago, IL 60611, at a cost of $20 for 100.—*GME.*

Why do you need to evaluate information?

We have entered the Information Age and are inundated daily with data from many sources in a variety of forms.

- Each year the number of books and journals published increases. In 1989, 45,718 books were published in the United States alone.
- A daily edition of *The New York Times* includes more information than a person in the 17th century would come across in a lifetime.
- People can watch television 24 hours a day on more than 1,064 stations. In addition to 500 new movies produced each year, thousands of videotapes are released of old movies and on any topic imaginable.
- Thousands of radio stations broadcast nonstop worldwide and modern communication technology allows immediate news everywhere.
- Last but not least, electronic publishing assaults computer users with a never-ending array of information.

In this data-rich environment, information consumers must learn to cope with information anxiety and to sift through the information for sensible decision making. The following checklist of questions can be used as a guide to evaluating information you find in its many forms.

Identify your information need

- What information do you need?
- What do you already know about the subject?
- Do you have any preconceived ideas or biases on the topic?
- Do you want general or specialized information?
- What is the central focus of your information need?
- How much information do you want to gather?

Evaluate the source of the information

- How did you find the source of information? Did you use an index, a review, or references from other works?
- What type of source is it? Is it scholarly, popular, governmental, private?
- What are the author's or producer's qualifications for this topic: education, experience, occupation, position, affiliation, publications?
- When was the information published? Is it a first edition, a revision, a reprint, or a rerun?
- In which country was it published or produced?
- What is the reputation of the publisher, producer, or distributor? Is it a university, an alternative press, or a private/political organization?
- Was the material reviewed or edited for publication?
- Does the source show political or cultural biases?
- Is a bibliography or another form of documentation included?
- What is the best format for accessing the information, considering cost, time, ease of use?
- Is it organized so you can easily access the information you require?

Determine if the source is suitable for your needs

- What is the scope and purpose of the work?
- For what audience is it intended: general public, students, professionals?
- Is the information in the most appropriate format for your topic: print, slide, film, sound?

- Is it presented clearly and objectively?
- Is it suitable for your level of understanding of the subject, or is it too simple or too difficult?
- Are you able to retrieve the information needed through tables of contents, indexes, or other locaters?
- Does it have the features you need: graphs, charts, tables, glossaries, maps, illustrations?
- Does it contain the information you need?
- Is the information current enough for your topic or do you need historical information? What is the geographical coverage or orientation?

Evaluate the information content

- What is the author's thesis or purpose?
- What are the main points or concepts?
- What facts and opinions are presented?
- Are various points of view represented?
- Is this a report of primary research: surveys, experiments, observations?
- Is it a compilation of information gathered from other sources?
- Is the source organized in a logical manner for the subject?
- What are the major findings?
- Are the conclusions justified by the information presented?
- Is there adequate documentation: bibliography, notes, credits, quotations?
- Does this work update, substantiate, or add to the knowledge on the subject?
- Is this information verified in other sources in the discipline?
- Do experts in the field agree on the findings?
- Can the data be transferred or manipulated electronically?
- Do the findings support or refute your original ideas on the topic?

In this information age, we are all information processors. Whenever we listen to a news report, talk to another student, read a magazine, look out over a crowd of faces in classes and lectures, we are perceiving and processing information. Once we have accepted this, then we can set about improving our skills as processors of information at all levels in our lives. (Based on Richard Wurman's *Information Anxiety*, New York: Doubleday, 1989.)

Source: Evaluating Information: A Basic Checklist (Chicago: ALA, 1990)

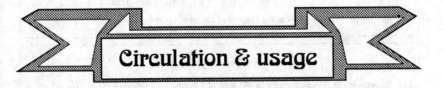

Circulation & usage

Circulation figures

by Katy Sherlock

PUBLIC LIBRARY CIRCULATION continued its modest growth pattern in 1989, while expenditures grew at a less dramatic pace than in 1988. The 1989 Index of American Public Library Circulation was 124, up three points since 1988 for an increase of 2.5%. The 1989 Index of American Public Library Expenditures was up four points for an increase of 2%. However, in 1980 dollars the 1989 expenditure index decreased 2.1%, from 140 in 1988 to 137 in 1989. The modest decrease in the expenditure index in constant 1980 dollars follows a constant-dollar increase of 6.9% in 1988.

Annual Indexes for a sample of American public libraries: 1978–1989
(with 1980 = 100; for 1980–88, N* = 53; for 1989, N = 51)

	1978	'79	'80	'81	'82	'83	'84	'85	'86	'87	'88	'89
Circulation	99	97	100	104	107	107	109	111	111	118	121	124
Expenditures	85	89	100	110	121	130	145	159	176	181	196	200
In 1980 dollars	107	101	100	100	104	108	115	121	133	131	140	137

Circulation percentages

	1980 (N = 34)	1988 (N = 41)	1989 (N = 41)
Adult	69%	65%	65%
Juvenile	31%	35%	35%

Expenditure percentages

	1980 (N = 53)	1988 (N = 51)	1989 (N = 50)
Salaries	63%	60%	62%
Materials	16%	16%	16%
Other	21%	24%	23%

Annual Indexes for circulation and expenditure categories
(for 1989, N = 32)

Medians	1980	'81	'82	'83	'84	'85	'86	'87	'88	'89
Adult circulation	100	95	108	111	114	112	109	108	108	110
Juvenile circulation	100	96	106	108	112	117	120	133	140	154

(for 1989, N = 51)

	1980	'81	'82	'83	'84	'85	'86	'87	'88	'89
Exp. for salaries	100	112	123	137	147	154	162	183	191	207
Exp. for materials	100	108	123	123	141	149	174	187	197	220
Exp. for other	100	113	117	120	149	150	178	177	207	205

Other measures:

Medians	1980	'81	'82	'83	'84	'85	'86	'87	'88	'89
Circulation per capita	4.7	5.2	5.2	5.4	5.3	5.4	5.6	5.7	5.7	6.1
Exp. per capita	7.39	8.26	9.49	9.78	10.73	11.14	11.61	12.09	13.15	15.30
Exp. per circulation	1.42	1.56	1.57	1.65	1.81	1.84	2.04	2.10	2.28	2.50
Exp. per capita, library materials	1.10	1.17	1.18	1.27	1.49	1.57	1.99	1.85	2.32	2.60

*N is the number of libraries reporting

In previous years

The University of Illinois Graduate School of Library and Information Science index shows a steady increase in circulation since 1950 (1980 = 100):

1950	45	1970	89
1955	54	1975	98
1960	71	1980	100
1965	83	1985	111

In his autobiography, Robert Downs stated that library circulation has expanded at twice the rate of population growth for the past four decades.

Source: George S. Bobinski, "New Year's Cheer," *American Libraries,* January 1988, p. 65

Index values are based on reports from a sample of 53 public libraries representative of circulation and current expenditures for all U.S. public libraries serving over 25,000 people each. For 1989, 51 libraries responded to the annual survey. The sample, drawn based on changes in circulation and expenditures from 1975 to 1980, has been surveyed annually since 1980.

The score for each library is computed by dividing each library's reported 1989 circulation and expenditures by its corresponding 1980 figures and multiplying by 100. The resulting scores are ranked from highest to lowest, and the median is the index value for circulation or expenditures. To calculate spending in 1980 dollars, the 1989 expenditures index is divided by the change in the U.S. Consumer Price Index for All Urban Consumers from 1980 to 1989.

The average percent of expenditures spent on salaries showed a slight increase from 60% in 1988 to 62% in 1989. The average percent spent on materials stayed the same (16%), while that spent on "other" decreased from 24% to 23%. While the index for "other" decreased 1% (from 207 to 205), indexes for salaries and materials increased by 8.4% and 12% respectively.

Adult/juvenile circulation

As in previous years, 41 libraries, comprising 77% of the sample, also reported adult and juvenile circulation figures. For this group of libraries, average adult circulation is 65% of total circulation and average juvenile circulation is 35% of total circulation. This breakdown has remained constant since 1987. The index of adult circulation increased from 108 in 1988 to 110 in 1989 (a 1.9% increase), while the index of juvenile circulation increased 10% (from 140 to 154). For this group of libraries, the Index of Circulation is slightly higher than for the entire sample (128), while the Index of Expenditures is the same as for the entire sample (200).

For 1989, 21 libraries reported adult fiction and nonfiction circulation totals. Once again, adult fiction represented the largest percent of adult circulation totals (33%), while the average percent of adult nonfiction accounted for 30%. Both figures represent an increase from 1988; adult fiction is up from 31% and adult nonfiction increased from 25%. Libraries reporting these figures showed a higher expenditure index (207) than for the whole sample. The circulation index for this group of libraries is 115, which is slightly less than that reported for the whole sample.

All of the median values for "other measures" increased in 1989. Circulation per capita increased 70% (up to 6.1), which is the highest percent increase since 1980-81. Expenditures per circulation increased 9.6% from 1988—which, in constant 1980 dollars, is a 4.3% rise, up a total of 28.4% since 1980. Expenditures per capita for library materials are up 12%—to $1.78 in constant 1980 dollars, an increase of 7.2%.

Since 1980, circulation per capita has risen 30%. In current dollars expenditures per capita more than doubled since 1980, from $7.39 to $15.30, and expenditures per capita rose 42%, from $7.39 to $10.47. Total U.S. population rose 9.1% from 1980 to 1989, while the Index of Circulation rose 24% and the Index of Expenditures 37% in 1980 dollars.

Sources: Katy Sherlock, "Public Library Circulation, Expenditures Edge Upward," *American Libraries*, September 1990, p. 740

Sunday hours

NATIONAL DATA ON WEEKEND library hours are unavailable, but perhaps the state of Colorado is representative. The 20 largest Colorado libraries (in terms of budget) were polled in 1990 on Sunday open hours and public use. The survey found that:

- More than half of the libraries surveyed were open Sundays, all of them between 1:00 and 5:00 p.m. (though some opened earlier or closed later).
- Of those open Sundays, almost half were closed Sundays during the summer months.
- Sunday library hours are universally popular with users, but get only a so-so (three on a five-point scale) overall rating from library staff.
- Sunday hours were no more popular with staff who were paid extra for working Sundays than with staff who did not receive extra pay.
- Of those libraries that compared Sunday with weekday use, all indicated having the same or more general use, and half indicated more general users than on weekdays.
- Among selected user groups, Sunday hours were rated most popular with young adults; followed by children, college students, and families; and finally, new users and older adults.
- The only libraries that report extra compensation to staff who worked Sundays were those where Sunday hours are covered by regular staff on a rotating basis.
- Of the three methods for scheduling Sunday staffing, rotating regular staff to cover the hours was the most popular (six responses), followed by having some staff work Sundays routinely (four responses), and finally, hiring special staff to work Sundays (two responses).

Source: First Facts (Colorado State Library), July 16, 1990, pp. 1–2

Your library's handbook

by Paul Heller and Betsey Brenneman

BETSEY BRENNEMAN OF Worcester State College's Learning Resources Center has developed an instrument for judging library handbooks that can serve as an aid in self-evaluation or as a checklist for grading a set of materials. The checklist was compiled at the request of Paul Heller, public services librarian at Norwich University, to evaluate entries in the Vermont Library Association Handbook Contest in which all entrants received an individualized critique.— *GME.*

Generally speaking, the library handbook orients the patron to the library building and locates, usually by map or floorplan, "specific services and collections, elevators, handicapped access, drinking fountains, telephones and other patron aids. It may in addition take the user on a tour of the building, identifying each noteworthy location." The narrative portion describes each service, giving rules and regulations as well as hours for service. In order to facilitate its use the guide should be indexed and the index should have multiple entry points and be as free of jargon as possible.

The library handbook has been around since 1905 when Cambridge University introduced *Notes for Readers.* Since then the concept has prevailed and the handbook has become an important public relations tool. Its omission is noted by accrediting agencies and it is often used entirely or in part by development officials, architects, academic administrators, and new faculty members.

Criteria for library handbooks

Content
- *Essential information:* full identification of the school and library; location (street address, room number); days and hours of service; date of hand-

book's publication (if frequent revision is not expected, this is often coded, as its usefulness is primarily internal).

- *Services provided:* circulation; interlibrary loan; reference; online searching; bibliographic instruction; regulations regarding use, including eligibility.
- *Means of contacting departments:* telephone numbers; names, if turnover is infrequent or revision will be easy.
- *Methods of access to collections:* catalogs; indexes & abstracts; staff assistance (role of the librarian and encouragement for users to seek assistance).

Useful additional information
- Information about other related information and research sources.
- Floor plans or other simple directions to guide users to desired information.
- Table of contents or index (determined by size and complexity of handbook).
- History of the library (also special architectural features).
- Special collections or related services.

Order of presentation
- Most basic information (identification, location, etc.) must be given most prominence (cover, or at beginning).
- Constantly needed information (hours, telephone numbers, etc.) should be placed to facilitate access (beginning, end, cover, or insert).
- Bulk of descriptive information should be arranged in order of decreasing importance to the user (since readers are unlikely to read the handbook from cover to cover—the earlier information is presented, the more likely the reader can absorb it).
- Information presented in a logical manner; related items grouped.

Style of writing
- Narrative should be brief and concise as possible.
- Terminology should be explained from the *reader's* point of view; avoid technical jargon whenever possible.
- The tone should be positive and should invite interest in reading the handbook and using the library.
- Headings should be made with the reader's interest in mind and should be written to facilitate scanning. This is important when a handbook is too brief to require an index.
- An index depends on the size and complexity of the guide's contents.

Format and design

- Attractive in appearance.
- Easy to understand.
- Handy to use.
- Easy to obtain.
- Designed for retention.
- Economical to revise.
- Typeface (gives character to a page, resulting in a streamlined appearance).
- Illustrations: add, do not detract from the guide's attractiveness and usefulness; serve a purpose; placement with related passages of text; conform to limitations of the printing process; are of high quality; well produced; color (for emphasis and liveliness, ease in reading).

Source: Paul Heller & Betsey Brenneman, "A Checklist for Evaluating Your Library's Handbook," *College & Research Libraries News,* February 1988, pp. 78–79

Every child . . . a library card

THEY VISITED THOUSANDS of classrooms and told countless stories. They resorted to contests, drawings, and bribes. They turned to pizza and teddy bears and rap music.

"They" are America's librarians. And they were responding to the challenge presented by former U.S. Secretary of Education William J. Bennett, when he wrote in his report "First Lessons" that: "Children should belong to the public library. There is one within striking distance of practically everybody. Let's have a national campaign: Every child should obtain a library card—and use it."

In October 1987 the National Commission on Libraries and Information Science and the American Library Association (ALA) launched such a campaign on the Mall in Washington, D.C., with Bennett, more than 500 area school children, their teachers, and librarians on hand.

"You'll be getting many cards in your life," Bennett told his young audience. "Social security, driver's license, charge cards—but none will be more important than your library card. Don't leave home without it."

Phase one of the campaign featured the parent-directed message, "The Best Gift You'll Ever Give Your Child," on campaign promotional materials published by the ALA and a national "Why I Love My Library Card" creative writing contest.

Phase two focused on young adults with posters and radio spots telling teens they can get "straight information" at the library, and an MTV-style television public service announcement advising, "Be cool on the inside, too. Use the library." Phase three started in fall 1989 and featured the "Wee Pals" characters of cartoonist Morrie Turner telling elementary children that "Libraries Make Good Pals."

The first Library Card Sign-up Month in September 1988 provided the focus for editorial items about library card sign-up in *Better Homes and Gardens, Woman's Day,* the Sunday *Parade Magazine* and other national publications. *Rolling Stone* magazine contributed two full-page public service announcements valued at $40,000 each. *Teen Beat* magazine ran a full page for Library Card Sign-up Month featuring a drawing for ALA's Michael J. Fox "Read" poster.

Sears, Macy's, and The Company Store catalogs all carried library card messages, as did some 25 million "Happy Meals" boxes distributed by McDonald's restaurants.

The director of the Davenport (Iowa) Public Library, said the "Best Gift" television spot produced by the ALA was aired during prime time on a local station. In Roanoke, Va., the cable station aired the spot more than 300 times in a one-month period during ESPN, CNN, USA, and other programming.

These promotional activities at the national level set the stage for aggressive efforts by school and public local librarians throughout the country.

Evaluations turned into ALA's Public Information Office indicated that many hundreds of thousands—probably millions—of children and adults have received library cards as a result of similar efforts.

The Cape Girardeau (Mo.) Public Library increased card registration by 42% among children in grades K-6. In noticing the campaign's success, the local newspaper reported that 700 children were registered at one elementary school. Before the campaign, 7.5% of the students owned library cards; afterward, 60%.

The responses came from as far away as Guam where the territorial librarian Frank R. San Agustin reported a 30% increase in card registration: "Even though the active promotion is over, a heightened awareness of the library contributes to the continued rise in patron registration."

A Vista volunteer, in Milton, Fla., reported that library card sign-up is an important part of the Literacy Volunteers efforts there. She said the program used the campaign posters and bookmarks to encourage adult learners to sign up their children.

Some libraries successfully combined library card promotion with the introduction of new automation systems or summer reading programs. In some communities, the campaign prompted new alliances among public libraries, schools, business and community groups.

And it frequently generated favorable response from the media. After the Chicago Public Library announced its "A-Card-A-Kid," campaign, the *Chicago Sun-Times* carried an editorial commenting: "What better way to encourage reading for pleasure or for information than to open up the treasures of the local library? What better key than a library card?"

For some, the campaign proved a learning experience.

In Clovis, New Mexico, the local Pizza Hut agreed to give a pizza party to each elementary school classroom with 100% library card registration. The offer worked so well that midway through the campaign, the Pizza Hut district manager halted the program due to the higher-than-anticipated response. All ended happily when the Pizza Hut National Franchise stepped in and resumed deliveries of pizzas. Today, 95% of the local children in this community of 33,000 have library cards.

The sign-up campaign is ongoing. Working with ALA's Public Information Office, you can boost library use by young people in your community. Here's how:

Library card round-up

1. Announce the campaign during National Library Card Sign-up Month in September. Run through National Library Week in April.

2. Ask the mayor and chairman of the County Commission to proclaim Library Card Sign-up Month.

3. Provide press release and "Best Gift" public service ads directed at parents to local newspapers, newsletters of schools, and community groups.

4. Provide press release and "Best Gift" public service announcement to radio station.

5. Ask local grocery store to print "Best Gift" message on grocery bags.

6. Arrange to have a letter and "Best Gift" bookmark sent home to parents of elementary children early in the school year, reminding them to make sure their children have the most important school supply of all.

7. Ask schools to give every child who registers, a "Dear Parent" letter and fact sheet about the library, library card registration form, and colorful bookmark from ALA.

8. Sponsor a library card sign-up competition for schools. Ask a community service group to sponsor prizes for every school with 100% library card sign up. Publicize winners in newspapers and on radio.

9. Provide press releases about what the library offers teens and "teen" public service ads to high school newspapers.

10. Have a banner hung downtown: "Say yes and know. Get a library card."

11. Provide all schools with ALA youth posters promoting libraries.

12. The library director/children's librarian should visit all day-care, pre-school and elementary programs (wearing cowboy hat) to "round up" those without library cards. Visits should include storytelling, booktalk and/or reading to entice children into borrowing the book from the library Give children who sign up for cards "I got carded" pins.

13. Sponsor a "Why I Love My Library Card" creative writing contest. Invite teachers to submit classroom entries. Have businesses/community groups sponsor prizes . . . free movie tickets, gift certificates, free pizza. Ask local newspapers to print winning entries with photos of winning students. Print bookmarks with the top winners to distribute in schools.

14. Ask high school teachers to have teens write a paragraph about their favorite book. Print a bookmark of "Teen favorites" with sample comments. Add a note: "Say yes and know. Get a library card. You can borrow these books for free from your Library."

15. Have a prize drawing in the library with ALA's Michael J. Fox, Garfield, and other posters popular with kids as prizes, also cash prizes donated by the bank or power company, record albums, books, movie tickets, other prizes for various ages donated by business people. Every time an elementary child or high school student checks out books, he/she gets to enter name in drawing. Every student who checks out books 10 times get a special prize during National Library Week.

16. Send letters to school superintendents, principals, and teachers asking them to announce the library card sign-up campaign, the school competition, "Why I Love My Library Card" contest, other activities planned. Invite their suggestions, cooperation. Tell them you will be calling to schedule a classroom visit. Offer tours of the library and other special assistance. Include a library fact sheet, contest forms, bookmarks to distribute.

17. Send letter from the chairman of the library board asking local businesses to cooperate with a "Show Us Your Library Card" campaign. Adults and children showing library cards would receive discounts on movie tickets, coffee, dry cleaning, other goods and services. Follow up with a phone call. Publish names of cooperating firms and distribute flyers in library, through schools, cooperating businesses. Ask businesses to sponsor ads in local newspapers. Project could run during National Library Week in April or any time.

18. Sponsor a regular library pizza/cookie party for older children and teens. They must show library card to attend. Ask those attending to take turns talking about their favorite books. Show a video of a popular teen film (based on a book if possible).

19. Sponsor special programs for older students on how to do a better term paper, study better.

20. Publicize campaign results. Post an "I Got Carded" poster in the library with names and Polaroid pictures of children who sign up. Send press release announcing number of children signed up and increase in library use during National Library Week to newspapers and radio stations. Send thank you letters reporting campaign results in cooperating businesses, community groups, teachers, etc.

Source: Linda K. Wallace, ed., *Every Child . . . A Library Card* (Chicago: ALA, 1989)

Interlibrary loan

National Interlibrary Loan Code

INTERLIBRARY LOAN IS ESSENTIAL to the vitality of libraries of all types and sizes and is a means by which a wide range of material can be made available to users. This code is designed primarily to regulate lending relations between research libraries and between libraries operating outside networks or consortia. It is recognized that through specific agreements, libraries organized geographically, by mutual subject interest, or other bases will have developed codes of their own. It is not the intent of this code to prescribe the nature of interlibrary lending under such arrangements. (See "Model Interlibrary Loan Code for Regional, State, Local, or Other Special Groups of Libraries," available from ALA.)

The effectiveness of a national system of interlibrary lending is directly related to the equitable distribution of costs among all the libraries involved. Interlibrary loan is an adjunct to, not a substitute for, collection development in individual libraries. Requests to national and research libraries or requests beyond networks and consortia should only be made after local, state, and regional sources have been exhausted. It is understood that every library must maintain an appropriate balance between resource sharing and responsibility to its primary clientele.

This national code contains general guidelines for the borrowing and lending of library material. Details of procedures to be used in implementing the code will be found in the *Interlibrary Loan Procedure Manual* published by the American Library Association. All libraries participating in interlibrary loan should have copies of this publication and should follow these recommendations. The manual also provides information on international interlibrary loan.

The Reference and Adult Services Division, acting for the American Library Association in its adoption of this code, recognizes that the exchange of material between libraries is an important element in the provision of library service and believes it to be in the public interest to encourage such an exchange.

Definition

An interlibrary loan is a transaction in which library material, or a copy of the material, is made available by one library to another upon request.

Purpose

The purpose of interlibrary loan as defined in this code is to obtain, for research and serious study, library material not available through local, state, or regional libraries.

Scope

A. A loan or a copy of any material may be requested from another library in accordance with the published lending policy of that library. The lending library will decide in each case whether a particular item can be provided.

B. Most libraries will not ordinarily lend the following types of materials:

1. Rare or valuable material, including manuscripts;
2. Bulky or fragile items that are difficult or expensive to ship;

3. Material in high demand at the lending library;
4. Material with local circulation restrictions;
5. Unique material that would be difficult or impossible to replace.

Responsibilities of borrowing libraries

A. Each library should provide the resources to meet the study, instructional, informational, and normal research needs of its primary clientele. This can be accomplished through its own collection or through local, state, or regional cooperative resource-sharing agreements. Material requested from another library under this code should generally be limited to those items that do not conform to the library's collection development policy and for which there is no recurring demand.

B. The interlibrary loan staff of each library should be familiar with, and use, relevant interlibrary loan documents and aids. These include this code, the *Interlibrary Loan Procedure Manual*, lending policies of the major research libraries, and standard bibliographic tools and services.

C. Each library should inform its users of the purpose of interlibrary loan and of the library's interlibrary borrowing policy.

D. The borrowing library is responsible for compliance with the copyright law (Title 17, U.S. Code) and its accompanying guidelines, and should inform its users of the applicable portions of the law. An indication of compliance must be provided with all copy requests.

E. Requested material must be described completely and accurately following accepted bibliographic practice as outlined in the current *Interlibrary Loan Procedure Manual*. If the item cannot be verified, the statement "cannot verify" should be included along with complete information as to the original source of the citation.

F. The borrowing library should carefully screen all requests for loans and reject any that do not conform to this code.

G. Standard bibliographic tools, such as union catalogs, computerized databases, and other listing services, should be used in determining the location of material. Care should be taken to avoid concentrating the burden of requests on a few libraries.

H. Standard interlibrary loan formats should be used for all requests, regardless of the means of transmission.

I. The safety of borrowed material is the responsibility of the borrowing library from the time the material leaves the lending library until it is received by the lending library. The borrowing library is responsible for packaging the material so as to ensure its return in good condition. If damage or loss occurs, the borrowing library must meet all costs of repair or replacement, in accordance with the preference of the lending library.

J. The borrowing library and its users must comply with the conditions of loan established by the lending library. Unless specifically forbidden by the lending library, copying by the borrowing library is permitted provided that it is in accordance with the copyright law and no damage to the original material will result.

K. The borrowing library should encourage library users to travel to other libraries for onsite access to material when extensive use of a collection is required or the nature of the material requires special handling. The borrowing library should assist the user in making the necessary arrangements.

Responsibilities of lending libraries

A. The decision to loan material is at the discretion of the lending library. Each library is encouraged, however, to interpret as generously as possible its own lending policy with due consideration to the interests of its primary clientele.

B. A statement of interlibrary loan policy and charges should be made available upon request.

C. The lending library should process requests promptly. Conditions of loan should be stated clearly and material should be packaged carefully. The lending library should notify the borrowing library when unable to fill a request, stating the reason for not filling the request.

D. A lending library is responsible for informing any borrowing library of its apparent failure to follow the provisions of this code.

Expenses

A. The borrowing library assumes responsibility for all costs charged by the lending library, including transportation, insurance, copying, and any service charges. The borrowing library should try to anticipate charges and authorize them on the original request.

B. It is recommended that nominal costs, such as postage, be absorbed by the lending library.

C. If the charges are more than nominal and not authorized by the borrowing library, the lending library should inform the requesting library and ask for authorization to proceed.

Duration of loan

A. The duration of loan, unless otherwise specified by the lending library, is the period of time the item may remain with the borrowing library disregarding the time spent in transit.

B. Interlibrary loan material should be returned promptly.

C. The borrowing library should ask for renewals only in unusual circumstances. The renewal request should be sent in time to reach the lending library no later than the date due. If the lending library does not respond, it will be assumed that renewal, for the same period as the original loan, is granted.

D. All material on loan is subject to immediate recall, and the borrowing library should comply promptly.

Violation of code

Continued disregard of any provision of this code is sufficient reason for suspension of borrowing privileges.

Source: ALA Reference and Adult Services Division, *National Interlibrary Loan Code* (Chicago: ALA, 1980)

Interlibrary loans criticized

by Thomas H. Ballard

THE NATIONAL CENTER FOR EDUCATION STATISTICS (NCES) has issued a series of documents containing data about the borrowing practices of public libraries. To support his dissident view of interlibrary loan (ILL) as a waste of vast resources, Ballard shows that such loans comprise a very small percentage of library circulation. He argues for more expenditure on local resources. Others respond that percentages do not account for the importance of ILL to research and patron satisfaction.—*GME*

Adding survey data of my own to the NCES statistics, I have obtained recent ILL data for all but two states and have been able to compare present levels of borrowing with an earlier year for 35 states. Because the 1988 NCES data some-

Interlibrary loan comparison

State	Early Year[1]	ILLs	Circulation	ILL%	Recent Year	ILLs	Circulation	ILL%
Ala.	FY 1983	49,661	12,139,142	0.41%	FY 1989	116,234	11,458,124	1.01%
Alaska	FY 1983	13,293	2,136,490	0.62%	FY 1989	21,388	3,093,779	0.69%
Ariz.[6]	—	—	—	—	FY 1989	49,299	20,968,079	0.24%
Ark.	—	—	—	—	FY 1988[2]	21,537	7,663,919	0.28%
Calif.	FY 1979	228,682	111,000,000	0.21%	FY 1989	310,539	141,407,548	0.22%
Colo.	—	—	—	—	1988	75,328	19,058,887	0.40%
Conn.[6]	—	—	—	—	FY 1988[9]	116,820	20,311,699	0.58%
Del.	FY 1984	14,996	2,185,094	0.69%	FY 1988[2]	6,286	2,342,619	0.27%
D.C.	—	—	—	—	FY 1988[2]	303	1,949,455	0.02%
Fla.	FY 1982	62,794	35,906,395	0.17%	FY 1988	130,043	46,442,126	0.28%
Ga.[7]	—	—	—	—	FY 1988	105,172	21,034,487	0.50%
Hawaii[6]	—	—	—	—	1989[10]	94,490	5,998,241	1.58%
Idaho	FY 1983	25,000	4,900,000	0.51%	FY 1988	23,277	6,466,376	0.36%
Ill.[8]	FY 1984	525,833	59,005,559	0.89%	—	—	—	—
Ind.	FY 1983	67,042	31,496,122	0.21%	FY 1988	67,765	39,559,830	0.17%
Iowa	FY 1986[3]	83,688	20,439,631	0.41%	FY 1989	87,384	21,947,741	0.40%
Kan.	1983	73,220	11,893,466	0.62%	1988	84,885	15,195,495	0.56%
Ky.	FY 1984	45,271	16,073,163	0.28%	FY 1989	36,550	17,496,334	0.21%
La.	FY 1983	77,896	13,678,102	0.57%	FY 1988	91,416	16,865,614	0.54%
Maine	FY 1983	45,000	5,705,869	0.78%	FY 1989	42,122	6,318,715	0.67%
Md.	FY 1983	154,930	32,164,132	0.48%	FY 1989[4]	210,000	41,969,597	0.50%
Mass.	—	—	—	—	FY 1988	156,280	33,113,039	0.47%
Mich.[6]	—	—	—	—	FY 1990	255,194	43,191,451	0.59%
Minn.	1982	157,866	26,942,875	0.59%	1988	182,390	35,019,847	0.52%
Miss.	FY 1983	26,140	7,134,008	0.37%	FY 1988	27,056	7,393,937	0.37%
Mo.	FY 1983	57,000	25,510,569	0.22%	FY 1989	55,338	29,650,269	0.19%
Mont.[6]	—	—	—	—	FY 1988	27,363	3,813,184	0.72%
Nebr.	FY 1983	66,839	8,540,460	0.78%	FY 1988	59,196	9,215,711	0.64%
Nev.	FY 1983	9,048	3,847,611	0.24%	FY 1985[5]	7,378	3,841,648	0.19%
N.H.	1982	13,167	5,486,403	0.24%	1988	29,481	6,321,962	0.47%
N.J.	1984	141,674	33,269,520	0.43%	1988	167,722	36,215,814	0.46%
N.M.	FY 1983	12,246	4,946,593	0.25%	FY 1989	18,081	6,550,532	0.28%
N.Y.	1982	1,008,214	87,147,714	1.16%	1988	987,533	104,357,213	0.95%
N.C.	FY 1983	76,380	25,064,293	0.30%	FY 1989	90,741	27,420,080	0.33%
N.D.	FY 1983	11,571	2,813,767	0.41%	FY 1989	10,230	3,602,430	0.28%
Ohio	1983	107,980	78,117,285	0.14%	1988	143,964	94,956,923	0.15%
Okla.	FY 1983	32,459	10,405,709	0.31%	FY 1988	49,460	13,957,572	0.35%
Ore.	1984	72,239	16,054,363	0.45%	1989	135,375	19,909,208	0.68%
Pa.	FY 1982	206,219	38,632,329	0.53%	FY 1988	243,986	42,857,611	0.57%
R.I.	FY 1987	26,409	4,333,192	0.61%	FY 1989	28,024	5,657,359	0.50%
S.C.	FY 1983	16,464	9,636,352	0.17%	FY 1989	26,007	11,452,215	0.23%
S.D.	—	—	—	—	1988	20,495	4,141,962	0.49%
Tenn.	FY 1983	59,294	14,432,375	0.41%	FY 1988	61,294	15,221,099	0.40%
Tex.	FY 1983	106,410	44,775,379	0.24%	FY 1988	157,928	61,635,948	0.26%
Utah	1983	7,680	10,446,200	0.07%	1988	17,883	11,740,934	0.15%
Vt.	—	—	—	—	FY 1989	22,692	2,913,722	0.78%
Va.	FY 1983	26,402	30,942,000	0.09%	FY 1988	38,822	36,563,146	0.11%
Wash.	1983	59,755	25,191,032	0.24%	1988	103,022	40,000,903	0.26%
W.Va.	—	—	—	—	FY 1989	21,441	8,231,379	0.26%
Wisc.[11]	—	—	—	—	FY 1988	544,065	35,168,941	1.55%
Wyo.	—	—	—	—	FY 1988[2]	19,050	3,801,288	0.50%
TOTALS		3,768,762	872,393,194	0.43%		5,356,019	1,225,465,992	0.44%

[1]Data obtained from state libraries in 1984.

[2]Data from National Center for Education Statistics.

[3]Earliest year for which ILL data are available.

[4]Called a "conservative estimate" for ILLs by state library.

[5]For some unexplained reason, Nevada stopped gathering ILL data.

[6]The state library specifically said that early data do not exist.

[7]No ILL data exist for Georgia. The author has arbitrarily assumed that the level of ILLs amounts to 0.50% of total circulation.

[8]Illinois was unable to provide ILL data for a recent year comparable to its 1984 data.

[9]The Interlibrary Loan Center believes there are 150,000 requests. Existing ILL agencies have a fill rate of 77.88%. Applying the fill rate to these requests produces a figure of 116,820.

[10]Hawaii is a single library system. It had only 86 actual ILLs, and the remainder is actually intrabranch loans.

[11]There are two sources of error here. First, all the ILLs are not borrowed by public libraries, but the estimate is that only about 10% go elsewhere. Second, some ILLs within automated networks are not counted as ILLs but only as circulations. The data problems are in opposite directions; to what extent they contradict each other is unknown.

times only include the majority rather than all public libraries in a given state, I have preferred to use data received in response to my January 1990 written requests, although this meant mixing FY 1988 and FY 1989 results. While this introduces possible errors, the small change from year to year does not seriously compromise the final estimate of the nation's ILLs borrowed by public libraries.

The table on the previous page compares actual numbers of ILLs as well as the percentage of total circulations. Of the 35 states for which two sets of data were available, only Alabama, Florida, New Hampshire, and Utah were able to double ILLs and, with the exception of Alabama, all started from relatively low levels. Nine states actually had fewer ILLs during the more recent year than they had in the earlier one. Overall, ILL borrowing in these 35 states failed to keep pace with circulation—if the percentage of circulation coming from ILLs in these states in recent years is calculated separately, the figure is even lower at 0.38%.

Source: Thomas H. Ballard, "The Unfulfilled Promise of Resource Sharing," *American Libraries,* November 1990, pp. 990–93 (tables have been consolidated)

Faxing your ILL requests

THE FASTEST GROWING APPLICATION of telefacsimile technology in libraries is its use as a mechanism for the rapid relay of interlibrary loan requests and/or responses to those requests when they take the form of brief journal articles, excerpts from larger works, and other easily reproduced materials that have been requested through accepted communications channels.

These guidelines address the needs of libraries that use telefacsimile transmission in the interlibrary borrowing and lending processes. They are intended to enhance other interlibrary loan codes and guidelines currently in use. These telefacsimile guidelines should be used to expedite interlibrary loan via telefacsimile when no state, regional, network, or consortium guidelines apply. The purposes for these guidelines are: 1) to establish uniformity with regard to type of equipment to be used; 2) to recommend uniform practices with regard to equipment operation and administration; 3) to establish guidelines for borrowing and the formatting of requests to be transmitted via telefacsimile; and 4) to set guidelines for the response to requests by lending libraries.

Equipment

Telefacsimile equipment should be digital equipment compatible with the Consultative Committee for International Telephone and Telegraph (CCITT) Group III standards. It should have, as a minimum, features providing automatic sending and receiving, and a document feeder that allows the transmission of multiple pages.

Each facsimile machine should have a dedicated telecommunication line to insure high quality transmission and maximum access.

General guidelines

An interlibrary loan request may be transmitted by telefacsimile to another library, and/or a telefacsimile response may be requested of that library in accordance with state, regional, or national interlibrary loan codes and the library's published lending policy.

Each telefacsimile transmission should be preceded by a cover sheet identifying the sender and the receiver, indicating the number of pages being transmitted, and including the address, telephone number, and telefacsimile number of the sender. The cover sheet may be omitted when transmitting an interlibrary loan request provided all identifying information is on the request form.

Documents that may not transmit well should not be sent via telefacsimile. These include photographs, detailed charts, maps, and graphs: text, including scientific and mathematical symbols, small print, and foreign languages with diacritical, vocalization, or other small marks; and poor quality photocopy.

Unless a telefacsimile response is specifically requested, the lending library will determine the method to be used in delivery of the requested material.

Borrowing

An interlibrary loan request for a document to be delivered via telefacsimile may be submitted through the interlibrary loan subsystem of a bibliographic utility, a local online network, or any other transmission system (including telefacsimile) acceptable to both the borrowing and the lending library.

A request transmitted by telefacsimile or other method of communication should be printed on a standard ALA interlibrary loan form or in a standard free-form format approximating the ALA form (see *American National Standard for Interlibrary Loan Data Elements*), and transmitted in accordance with policies and procedures of the lending library.

A request for a telefacsimile response should contain the note: "PLEASE FAX TO: (fax number)" in the borrowing notes field or in a conspicuous place on the request form.

A rush request should contain the note: "PLEASE RUSH, NEED BEFORE MM/DD/YY" in the borrowing notes field or in a conspicuous place on the request form. Use of telefacsimile to transmit a request will not automatically elicit a rush response. Borrowing libraries should use discretion in requesting rush service except in instances in which local guidelines have been written to accommodate the service by special arrangement.

Lending

Lending libraries should check interlibrary loan subsystems, online networks, facsimile machines, and other methods of transmission at least once per working day for incoming requests.

Telefacsimile requests should be merged into the normal workflow of the lending library and processed within a reasonable period of time.

Rush requests should be processed within one working day of their receipt.

When a telefacsimile response is requested, the lending library should attempt to comply, provided the document is of reasonable length and of a quality that will transmit well.

Any photocopy of a document produced in response to a request for telefacsimile service should be discarded after the transaction has been completed. Photocopy should not be mailed as a follow-up measure unless requested by the borrowing library.

A negative report should be made via the same network or transmission method through which the request was received.

A negative response to a rush request should be transmitted by telefacsimile or telephone within one working day.

It is recommended that no additional fees or special handling charges be levied by the lending library for a document or a response sent via telefacsimile transmission.

Source: Interlibrary Loan Committee, ALA Reference and Adult Services Division, "Guidelines and Procedures for Telefacsimile Transmission of Interlibrary Loan Requests," *RQ,* Winter 1990, pp. 266–67

Preservation

5

Binding styles

NEXT TIME YOU want to bind a run of journals, don't just ask for a "library binding," or even a calf or vellum binding. Casually mention to your binding staff that you're thinking about having the entire occult collection redone in one of the following styles.—*GME.*

Cathedral binding. Cloth and leather bindings with Gothic architectural motifs, often including a rose window, done between 1815 and 1840 in England and France.

Cottage style binding. A characteristic English binding of the late 17th century in which the top and bottom of the center panel are given a gable-like, broken-pediment design, and the spaces are filled with a variety of small patterns.

Dentelle binding. A style of toothlike or lacelike ornamentation on the borders of a binding, particularly associated with 18th-century leather bindings.

Etruscan binding. An English binding style used from the 1770s through the 1830s, characterized by an outer border of palmettes created by acid staining, and a central panel that is usually tree calf.

Fanfare binding. A style originally of 16th-century Parisian binding with interlaced ribbons, defined by a double line on one side and a single one on the other, which divide the cover into symmetrical compartments of varying sizes.

Grotesque binding. 16th-century binding decorated with grotesque figures, usually classical.

Kermes dyed binding. 15th- to 16th-century bindings dyed with a red color obtained from a Mediterranean scale insect.

Lacquered binding. 16th-century binding with scenes on the cover that are first painted and then covered with lacquer.

Masonic binding. Binding decorated with masonic motifs, primarily late 18th and early 19th centuries.

Mudéjar binding. A Spanish binding style, used in the 13th-15th centuries, with elaborate geometric interlace bands against a background filled with many small knotwork or cablework tools.

Penitential binding. Late 16th-century Parisian binding, tooled in silver on a dark brown morocco to create a somber appearance.

Retrospective binding. A conscious imitation of an earlier style.

Shagreen binding. Binding made from untanned leather prepared in Asia from the skins of horses, asses, or camels, and covered with small round granulations by pressing small seeds into the grain or hair side when moist.

Treasure binding. Bindings covered with gold and silver, ivory, enamelwork, and gems.

Sources: Binding Terms: A Thesaurus for Use in Rare Book and Special Collections Cataloguing (Chicago: ALA/ACRL Rare Books and Manuscripts Section, Standards Committee, 1988); Heartsill Young, ed., *The ALA Glossary of Library and Information Science* (Chicago: ALA, 1983)

Brittle books:
A major preservation problem

by David Weber

IN 1987 DAVID C. WEBER, director of the Stanford University Libraries, presented an eloquent statement on brittle books in our nation's libraries to the U.S. House Subcommittee on Postsecondary Education. The following is an excerpt from that presentation.—*GME*.

While you have heard of the frightful rate at which valuable cultural records are becoming embrittled, this "brittle books" challenge must be faced and corrections made over the next two to three decades or we all shall have lost a good deal of who and what we are.

To put it in a local context, I shall describe the situation in my home town, Palo Alto, California—a city of some 60,000 people, including many scientists, engineers, teachers, government officials, students and writers.

An individual interested in a current political issue and concerned with its antecedents, causes, and past corrective attempts has available the following:

• A fine public library with over 230,000 volumes.

• The nearby Stanford University Libraries and the Hoover Institution, together having 5.5 million volumes, also nearly 3 million microtext sheets and large numbers of maps, motion picture films, photographs, prints, slides, sound recordings and data sets.

• And within 20 miles there are a state university library, two private college libraries, four community college libraries, and a dozen other public libraries linked by a State Library inter-system service.

A richness for that individual pursuing a political issue? Yes and no.

The resources for study are, at 6 million volumes and upwards of 60 million manuscripts, far greater than in most communities for 60,000 people. The Hoover Institution alone has more archival records of social action than many entire states. However, over a quarter of these resources are now so fragile that use is perilous, and in little more than a decade any use will be problematic due to the rapid decay of paper. Most of those resources are housed in quarters where temperatures bake the materials several months of the year, a situation gradually being corrected at Stanford and elsewhere.

Requests for interlibrary loan increasingly result in no availability because the owning library indicates its book is too fragile to loan, and a microfilm does not exist, or by policy original letters and archival documents do not circulate outside the building, and again no film copy exists.

How frustrating for the individual researcher! How limiting if one does not live in Washington, New York, Philadelphia, or Boston! How frightening to realize that the condition is nationwide, of awesome proportions, and getting worse every year!

The production of preservation microfilm is one of long standing. Starting in the early 1930s there have been programs in some university libraries, and other research libraries such as the New York Public Library, to make archival master film copies of brittle material, copies from which public reading copies are made, thereby archivally assuring availability of the original text for future generations.

Let me use one example. In the early 1950s at the Harvard University Library, I was responsible for a foreign newspaper microfilm project that had been originated in 1938 with Rockefeller Foundation funds. One of the challenges that was undertaken was to prepare a complete master microfilm of every issue of *Pravda* and *Izvestia*. The first of these Russian newspapers began publishing March 18, 1917, and the second on February 28, 1917. The task was to complete the file for the first 20 years. This required obtaining negative film from copies of individual issues held at Columbia, the New York Public Library, the Hoover Institution, Harvard, the British Museum Library, the Bibliothèque Nationale, the Bibliothèque de Documentation Internationale Contemporaine in Paris, and a few issues found only in Moscow itself. Even so, the master archival film still lacked 24 issues from 1917, nine in 1918, one in 1919, four in 1920, and one in 1921.

One can reflect, however, on how important was that preservation effort, as just one example of this ubiquitous "brittle books" problem. Copies of that film have now been sold to many libraries here and abroad. It is the only nearly complete record of these primary sources, regardless of where in the world an individual may be working.

Brittle books reside in libraries of all sizes and types. How any one library addresses the brittle book problem depends on a number of factors including but not limited to the number of brittle books to be treated, the filming and processing equipment, trained staff, and financial support available to the library.

Smaller libraries facing this special problem might take a number of different approaches. In some cases, a nearby library that has developed an in-house facility might provide preservation services for other libraries. A few commercial firms can handle archival microfilming. In addition, regional non-profit preservation laboratories have been established as cooperative and "mutual help" projects. One regional center is the Northeast Document Conservation Center (NEDCC) in Andover, Massachusetts; developed with funds from the Council on Library Resources, the National Endowment for the Humanities, and private sources, the Center has evolved into a full-service treatment facility for preservation of research materials. Another center is the Mid-Atlantic Preservation Service, based at Lehigh University. Each of these options has its limitations.

The majority of libraries will seek services outside their own organization to treat their brittle books. They will require many of the same things as libraries with an in-house program:

- Staff trained to assess the extent of the "brittle book problem" in a library collection, to develop a strategy for addressing the problem, and to coordinate the work.
- An internal process to identify, ensure completeness of, and prioritize the material needing treatment, within the context of a national strategy.
- Management support, e.g., operational models, guidelines, instructions, manuals, public information programs, and staff workshops for continuing education.
- Bibliographic information within a national network to determine whether the brittle materials in library collections are unique, whether the item has already been reformatted and the microfilm available, or whether the item has been

selected for filming but not yet treated elsewhere.

• Funding to support staff to identify brittle materials that require reformatting and to pay for archival preservation filming, entering of the revised bibliographic data into a national database, and storage locally or elsewhere of the archival master file under archival conditions.

It was most welcome news in 1985 when the National Endowment for the Humanities expanded its response to this national need by establishing the Office of Preservation. I can hardly exaggerate how important this NEH Preservation Program has been to libraries, though the funding has yet been much too small. Grants available from the Department of Education under the Higher Education Act, Title II-C, constitute another source of funding of extreme importance to a national preservation effort. Fortunately foundations such as the Andrew W. Mellon Foundation have also provided significant support. The State of New York has budgeted an exemplary statewide preservation program, and individual libraries have also built into their basic operating budgets a substantial commitment of financial resources.

Since we know the magnitude of the problem, and since we have a methodology for selecting how and where to begin our attack, it is apparent that a solution to the problem is at hand if we act together. Let me add to its solution by providing the answers to three key questions.

1. What are the appropriate federal, state and private sector roles in efforts to address this problem? Each sector plays a key role, as I have suggested. Essential cooperative planning is provided by such organizations as the American Library Association, the Association of Research Libraries (ARL), the Research Libraries Group (RLG), and the Council on Library Resources. The National Commission on Preservation and Access can play a lead role. The Library of Congress has for years done us all a great service with its research and development work and its publicizing and proselytizing of the state of the preservation art—including international coordination work. The National Agricultural Library and the National Library of Medicine have also initiated preservation programs of value nationally and internationally. The Higher Education Act Title II-C program and the National Historical Publications and Records Commission program are modestly funded but make significant contributions to the national preservation strategies. The program of the Office of Preservation in the National Endowment for the Humanities should be greatly strengthened.

2. What procedures are necessary to ensure public access to preserved materials? Part of the answer is easy, since public, academic and independent research libraries have a long-standing commitment to access. In addition, it requires that individual institutions, professional associations, and funding agencies insist that bibliographic data be currently maintained on what is in the queue for filming, what has been completed and by whom. It requires that reading copies of the master films be readily available and publicized, and that the interlibrary services staff and users consider films as routine rather than exceptional loans. There is a role here for ALA, ARL, and consortia such as RLG.

3. And what are the costs and who should bear them? The Council on Library Resources has made fair estimates of the total cost. The total effort we face is daunting, perhaps on the order of tens of millions of dollars. While each group might like some other to pay full costs, that is patently unrealistic. A consensus exists among libraries that costs must be shared; some costs must be covered locally. Start-up costs in particular need government and foundation help. Ongoing costs require local budgeting for at least a significant share, with endowment support for preservation programs in research libraries to the extent possible.

Yet one must recognize that libraries generally are so meagerly financed that there is little budgetary potential for dealing with problems of ten or fifty years hence when current book budgets and clientele services are severely beleaguered. The brittle books problem is a national concern, and indeed worldwide.

Going,   Going,   Going,

Going,   Going,   Going,

Gone.   Gone.   Gone.

Because of poor production, poor paper and poor storage, many library books and other printed materials are literally vanishing before our eyes. With your help, we can make this problem disappear.

Because of poor production, poor paper and poor storage, many library books and other printed materials are literally falling apart at the seams. You can help. All you have to do is give a damn.

Because of poor production, poor paper and poor storage, many library books and other printed materials are literally turning to dust. Please help. Our hands are already full.

Books worth reading are books worth saving.

For a free brochure, write: The Assn. for Library Collections and Technical Services, American Library Association, 50 E. Huron St., Chicago, IL 60611

Books worth reading are books worth saving.

For a free brochure, write: The Assn. for Library Collections and Technical Services, American Library Association, 50 E. Huron St., Chicago, IL 60611

Books worth reading are books worth saving.

For a free brochure, write: The Assn. for Library Collections and Technical Services, American Library Association, 50 E. Huron St., Chicago, IL 60611

5

Recognizing that, Federal support for a few decades is essential. A major share of start-up costs should be a Federal responsibility, as should a strong portion of local operating costs.

Just as the federal highway system is financed as being in the nation's interest, for both civilian and national defense purposes, exactly so should the "brittle books" system be financed as in the nation's interest: Students, scholars, our defense structure, our very civilization demands no less protection against the now recognized seeds of cultural destruction.

Source: David C. Weber, "Brittle Books in Our Nation's Libraries," *College & Research Libraries News*, May 1987, pp. 238–44

Glossary of preservation terms

THE FOLLOWING GLOSSARY has been developed by the Library Vendors Task Force of ALA's Association for Library Collections and Technical Services to help librarians and consumers of conservation supplies choose appropriate materials for use in treating their collections. A second goal was to create an agreed-upon core of terms that all suppliers can use in their advertising.

A number of published sources have been referred to in compiling this glossary, and feedback from professional conservators, preservation specialists, vendors, and librarians has been included in an effort to make the terms both accurate and easily understood. By calling this list of terms a glossary, the Task Force intends readers to understand it as a collection of "brief explanatory notes," not a series of technical definitions. Not all of these terms have agreed-upon definitions; nor should this be considered a definitive or technical dictionary of terms.

The task of creating such a glossary is difficult. Much has been omitted, and much has been simplified in an effort to keep it short enough to be reprinted in vendors' catalogs.

Acid. In chemistry, a substance capable of forming hydrogen ions when dissolved in water. Acids can weaken *cellulose* in paper, board, and cloth, leading to embrittlement. Acids may be introduced in the manufacture of library materials and may be left in intentionally (as in certain sizings) or incidentally. Acids may also be introduced by migration from other materials or from atmospheric pollution. See also *pH* and *acid migration*.

Acid-free. In chemistry, materials that have a *pH* of 7.0 or higher. Sometimes used incorrectly as a synonym for *alkaline* or buffered. Such materials may be produced from virtually any *cellulose* fiber source (cotton and wood, among others), if measures are taken during manufacture to eliminate active acid from the pulp. However free of acid a paper or board may be immediately after manufacture, over time the presence of residual chlorine from bleaching, aluminum sulfate from sizing, or pollutants in the atmosphere may lead to the formation of acid unless the paper or board has been buffered with an alkaline substance.

Acid migration. The transfer of *acid* from an acidic material to a less acidic or *pH* or *alkaline* neutral material. This may occur directly, when the two materials are in intimate contact. For instance, acid may migrate from boards, endpapers, and protective tissues, as well as the paper covers of books and pamphlets, to less acidic paper of the text.

Acrylic. A plastic noted for transparency, lightweight, weather resistance, colorfastness, and rigidity. In addition to these qualities, acrylics are important in preservation because of their stability, or resistance to chemical change over time, a characteristic not common to all plastics. Acrylics are available in sheets, films, and resin adhesives. Some common trade names for the sheet form are: Perspex, Lucite, and Plexiglas.

Alkaline. Alkaline substances have a *pH* over 7.0. They may be added to materials to neutralize acids or as an alkaline reserve or buffer for the purpose of counteracting acids that may form in the future. A buffer may be added during manufacture or during the process of *deacidification*. While a number of chemicals may be used as buffers, the most common are magnesium carbonate and calcium carbonate.

Alpha cellulose. A form of cellulose derived from cotton. The presence of alpha cellulose in paper or board is one indication of its stability or longevity.

Archival; Archivally sound. A nontechnical term that suggests that a material or product is *permanent, durable* or chemically *stable,* and that it can therefore safely be used for *preservation* purposes. The phrase is not quantifiable; no standards exist that describe how long an "archival" or "archivally sound" material will last.

Board. See *fiber board; pressboard;* or *solid board.*

Buffer. See *alkaline.*

Calcium carbonate. An *alkaline* chemical used as a buffer in papers and boards.

Cellulose. The chief constituent of the cell walls of all plants. Also, the chief constituent of many fibrous plant products, including paper, board, and some cloth.

Chemical stability. Not easily decomposed or otherwise modified chemically. This is a desirable characteristic for materials used in *preservation,* since it suggests an ability to resist chemical degradation (such as the embrittlement of paper) over time and/or upon exposure to various conditions during use or storage. Other terms used loosely as synonyms: inert, stable, chemically inert.

Conservation. The treatment of library or archive materials, works of art, or museum objects to stabilize them chemically or strengthen them physically, sustaining their survival as long as possible in their original form. See also *preservation.*

Deacidification. A common term for a chemical treatment that neutralizes *acid* in a material such as paper and deposits an *alkaline* buffer to counteract future acid attack. Deacidification technically refers only to the neutralization of acids present at the time of treatment, not to the deposit of a buffer. For this reason, the term is being slowly replaced with the more accurate phrase "neutralization and alkalization." While deacidification increases the chemical stability of paper, it does not restore strength or flexibility to brittle materials. See also *pH.*

Durability. The degree to which a material retains its physical properties while subjected to stress, such as heavy use. To say that a material is durable suggests that it has a high initial strength.

Encapsulation; Polyester encapsulation. A form of protective enclosure for papers and other flat objects; involves placing the item between two sheets of transparent polyester film that are subsequently sealed around all edges. The object is thus physically supported and protected from the atmosphere, although it may continue to deteriorate in the capsule. Because the object is not adhered to the polyester, it can be removed simply by cutting one or more edges of the polyester.

Fiber board. Paperboard made of laminated sheets of heavily pressed fiber.

Fiber content. A statement of the types and percentages of fibers used in the manufacture of a paper, board, or cloth. Important because the quality of the fiber significantly affects both the *durability* and *chemical stability* of the material.

Inert. See *chemical stability.*

Lamination. A process of reinforcing fragile paper, usually with thin, translucent, or transparent shoots. Some forms of lamination are considered unacceptable as conservation methods because of potential damage from high heat and pressure during application, instability of the lamination materials, or difficulty in removing the lamination from the hem, especially long after the treatment was performed.

Lignin. A component of the cell walls of plants that occurs naturally, along with *cellulose*. Lignin is largely responsible for the strength and rigidity of plants, but its presence in paper and board is believed to contribute to chemical degradation. It can be, to a large extent, removed during manufacture. No standards exist for the term "lignin free," and additional research is needed to determine the precise role of lignin in the *durability* and *permanence* of paper.

Mil. Unit of thickness squalling one thousandth of an inch (.001"), usually used as a measurement of plastics.

Mylar. See *polyester.*

Neutral. Having a *pH* of 7; neither *acid* nor *alkaline.*

pH. In chemistry, pH is a measure of the concentration of hydrogen ions in a solution, which is a measure of *acidity* or *alkalinity*. The pH scale runs from 0 to 14, and each number indicates a tenfold differential. Seven is pH *neutral*, numbers below 7 indicate increasing acidity, with 1 being most acid. Numbers above 7 indicate increasing alkalinity, with 14 being most alkaline. Paper with a pH below 5 is considered highly acidic. Buffered storage materials typically have a pH between 7 and 9. See also *acid; alkaline.*

PVA. See *polyvinyl acetate.*

PVC. See *polyvinyl chloride.*

Permanence. Ability of a material to resist chemical deterioration, but not a quantifiable term. Permanent paper usually refers to a *durable alkaline* paper that is manufactured according to ANSI Standard Z39.48-1984 *Permanence of Paper for Printed Library Materials*. Even so-called permanent materials depend for their longevity upon proper storage conditions. See also *chemical stability.*

Plexiglas. Trade name for *acrylic* sheet material made by Rohm and Haas. See *acrylic* for other trade names.

Point. A unit of thickness of paper or board; one thousandth of an inch. For example, .060" equals sixty points. See also *mil.*

Polyester. A common name for the plastic polyethylene terephthalate. Its characteristics include transparency, colorlessness, and high tensile strength. In addition, it is useful in *preservation* because it is very *chemically stable*. Commonly used in sheet or film form to make folders, encapsulations, and book jackets. Its thickness is often measured in *mils*. Common trade names are Mylar by DuPont and Mellinex by ICI.

Polyethylene. A *chemically stable*, highly flexible, transparent or translucent plastic. Used in preservation to make sleeves for photographic materials, among other uses.

Polypropylene. A stiff, heat-resistant, *chemically stable* plastic. Common uses in *preservation:* sleeves for 35mm slides or films, containers.

Polyvinyl acetate. A plastic usually abbreviated as PVA. A colorless transparent solid, it is usually used in adhesives, which are themselves also referred to as PVA or PVA adhesive. There are dozens of PVA adhesives, some are "internally plasticized" and are suitable for use in conservation because of their greater *chemical stability*, among other qualities.

Polyvinyl chloride. A plastic, often abbreviated as PVC. It is not as *chemically stable* as some other plastics, since it can emit hydrochloric acid (which in turn can damage library materials) as it deteriorates. It, therefore, has limited application in the preservation of books and paper. Some plastics called *vinyl* may, in fact, be polyvinyl chloride.

Preservation. Activities associated with maintaining library, archival, or museum materials for use, either in their original physical form or in some other format. Preservation is considered a broader term than *conservation*. See *conservation.*

Pressboard. A tough, dense, highly glazed paperboard, used where strength and stiffness are required of a relatively thin (e.g., .030") board. It is almost as hard as a sheet of fiberboard, and is commonly used for the covers of notebooks. See also *solid board, fiber board.*

Reversibility. Ability to undo a process or treatment with no change to the object. Reversibility is an important goal of conservation treatment, but it must be balanced with other treatment goals and options.

Sizings. Chemicals added to paper and board that make it less absorbent, so that inks applied will not bleed. *Acidic* sizings can be harmful and can cause paper to deteriorate. Use of nonacidic sizings is expected to yield more *chemically stable* paper and board.

Solid board. A paperboard made of the same material throughout. Distinct from a combination board where two or more types of fiber stock are used, in layers. See also *fiber board, pressboard.*

Stability. See *chemical stability.*

UV filter. A material used to filter the ultraviolet (UV) rays out of visible light. Ultraviolet radiation is potentially damaging to library, archival, and museum objects. More is present in sunlight and fluorescent light than in incandescent light. Removing UV radiation from storage, use, and exhibition spaces can reduce the rate of deterioration of library materials stored there. Usually a UV filtering material is placed over windows or fluorescent light tubes or built into glass used in framing or exhibition cases. Certain *acrylic* sheet materials have UV filtering properties built in.

Vinyl. The word vinyl is imprecisely used to refer to any of a number of plastics, many of which are not appropriate for use in preservation. For specific safe plastics, see *polyester, polypropylene, polyvinyl acetate, acrylic.*

Source: Library Vendors Task Force, *Glossary of Selected Preservation Terms* (Chicago: ALA/ALCTS)

5

Preventing damage in special collections

by Anthony Amodeo

THE DESK ATTENDANT in a special collections, rare book, or archives reading room is in a unique position regarding the conservation of the collections. Both surveillance for the prevention of theft and monitoring the physical treatment of materials are obviously important responsibilities. An additional contribution which deserves attention is the desk attendant's attitude toward the collections and their handling, which is picked up by both patrons and staff. The following suggestions have been drawn up as a sample of the kinds of concerns that should be addressed in the training of special collections desk attendants. Every reading room has its own rules and procedures, but the nature of the materials stored and used in special reading rooms dictates a universal approach.

Materials

A printed list of rules and suggestions should be available for distribution to readers. These rules can be read while materials are being paged. The list might be written so as to encourage the patron to point out damage, uncut pages, and possible conservation needs to the desk attendant, thus giving the reader a conscious stake in the well-being of the collections. They can also serve as a useful, authoritative "backup" to which the desk attendant can point when a patron exhibits indifference to suggestions regarding safe handling of materials.

Some notification regarding the checking of coats, briefcases, large handbags, newspapers, etc., prior to entry into the special collections room should be clearly posted at or near the entry door; those who enter carrying such items should be politely but promptly dispatched to the checking area.

See that pencils rather than any sort of ink pens are used by readers and staff (including yourself) in the reading room. Ink that transfers to fingers will transfer to paper; modern inks are complex and very difficult to remove.

Keep an adequate supply of decent pencils on hand for patron use. Display them prominently and inform patrons of the no-ink policy verbally as a matter of course when they register.

Do your best to prevent accidents before they happen. Be conscious of situations that may lead to damage or mishandling and watch for them. Prevent pile-ups of materials. Piles of more than three or four books can lead to spills and may subject the bottom books to pressure and abrasion. Be sure to place all fragile items on the reading table separately, not in (or especially at the bottom of) piles of books.

In general it is preferable to limit the amount of material or number of volumes a reader may use at once for safe handling and security. When those special cases arise that require simultaneous use of much material or many volumes, use book-ends, bookcarts, and so forth to accommodate materials safely.

Prevent materials from hanging over the edges of tables, where they will be knocked about by passersby or leaned on by the patron. In this regard, very large books and flat, oversized paper (e.g., maps and blueprints) are very susceptible to damage. Reserve an oversized table or two for such items if possible.

Do not allow patrons to write on paper laid over library materials, whether open or closed. A variety of problems, from paper damage to the damaging of binding structures, may result. A piece of thick book board should be made available for patrons having no table space upon which to write.

Tracing library materials should not, in general, be allowed. If an exception is made, tracing (in pencil only, of course) should be done in such a way that no damage, including impressions from the tracing tool, be done to the original. A piece of stiff mylar intervening between the original and tracing layers may help prevent damage; but if the paper is brittle, this precaution itself may cause damage.

Have a supply of acid-free paper strips available for patrons to use as bookmarks. This can help prevent such harmful practices as "dog-earing," the use of pencils or other objects as bookmarks, or the laying of open books face down. Be sure that the strips you supply are taller than the books used. When dealing with materials that might scratch, chip, or flake (e.g., illuminated manuscripts), use acid-free tissue paper cut in wide strips if bookmarks are necessary.

If you notice that an item about to be given out is so fragile that any use might cause damage, have the curator, conservator, or other senior staff person examine the item before it is delivered to the patron. Also, seek approval before opening any uncut pages in books or pamphlets, in case the uncut state is bibliographically significant. Often a second, service copy is available that will satisfy the patron.

Have a sufficient number of cradles, stands, or other supportive structures available for reader use and see that they are used when necessary. Bringing a stand and booksnake to a patron who is holding a book in the air by one cover while taking notes is both damage-preventive and tactful, especially in the case of patrons with bad sight. Or better yet, anticipate the need and supply a cradle before the item is given out.

A rolled-up piece of felt or piece of plastic foam wrapped in a stable covering (felt or mylar) provides good support for heavy book covers, especially when they would otherwise flex beyond a 180-degree opening.

Some books (e.g., "perfect-bound" paperbacks) may be better off held in the hands rather than flattened on a table. However, be sure that both sides of the open book are supported at all times.

If a book has special bosses or other potentially harmful features, be sure to keep it separate from other materials. A piece of felt or binders' board placed under such a book would be appropriate.

Attitude

When bringing out materials to a reader, the desk attendant or page sets the example in the handling of the materials. Therefore, place materials carefully on the reading table or bookstand as if they were bowls of hot soup. Do not slide, toss, throw down, fling, or otherwise roughly handle library materials, many of which have value as artifacts.

If a book or pamphlet comes in a drop-spine (solander) box or a folder, take the entire package to the patron's table, and open and remove the item carefully in front of the patron. This helps to garner respect for the materials, which are probably in a container for reasons of fragility or value. When the item has been delivered to the patron, be sure to take the box, folder, or other container back to the staff desk or holding area. Items housed in slipcases or other non-conservation containers (especially those which make removal difficult) are best taken out where none can see the shameful deed.

If you know that an item is fragile, tightly bound, or brittle, be sure to tell the patron so. In many cases it is appropriate to give suggestions as to its handling, such as: "This book is tightly bound. Could you please refrain from opening it more than about ninety degrees?" Or, "This paper is somewhat brittle. Could you be sure to turn the pages slowly and carefully without bending the corners?"

A patron using boxes of manuscripts, multiple folders, or other unbound materials should be shown an appropriate method for maintaining the strict order in which these materials are found. Separation of individual sheets for photocopy orders and the like should be discouraged in advance, and the patron supplied with acid-free slips for indication of such copying needs.

Above all, if a patron is mishandling an item don't be shy about correcting the situation. Use tact, but be persistent. Remember, you are the guardian of the collections in the reading room. No amount of money or environmental control will prevent damage to the collections unless you do your part at the time of use. Be polite and courteous, be fair and reasonable. But when it comes to the physical well-being of the collections, be firm and resolute—if the collections are to last for generations, then you must do your job. A hundred years from now it will matter.

Training

Desk attendants are often students or interns, perhaps not used to correcting their elders (or professors). Therefore, the initial training in conservation awareness is very important. Ideally this training should be performed by a senior staff member, curator or conservator/conservation librarian. In any case, awareness is best raised by setting a good and consistent example.

If the librarian or support staff doing the training handles a variety of problematic situations over the course of a week or more with the trainee in tow, and if the trainee is taught to respect the materials being used by the example of careful handling of materials and attention to detail set by the instructor and other reading room staff, then the level and tone of awareness will in all probability become part of the trainee's day-to-day work.

Once "converted" and given proper support (especially with problem patrons) most students or interns will respond with a high level of proficiency in damage prevention. On the other hand (need it be said?), abandoning the new attendant after a few hours' training, and careless handling of library materials by staff, will guarantee future problems.

Source: Anthony J. Amodeo, "Special Collections Desk Duty: Preventing Damage," *College & Research Libraries News,* June 1983, pp. 177–82

Are you a book batterer?

by Jocelyn Godolphin

TO COMMEMORATE THEIR Care for Books campaign, the University of British Columbia Library published this quiz which supposedly appeared in the *Review of Bibliotension.*—GME.

Learn the truth about your attitudes to books. Do you harbor a deep resentment to printed forms of information? Do you long for a world pure and ignorant, free of all learning? Are you a pussycat in your relations with other people, but a tiger when handling books? Are you actively trying to reduce the amount of information in the world by abusing books? This short test will reveal your true attitude. Check the most appropriate response.

1. I remove books from the shelf by pulling the top of the spine and am pleased to hear the sound of tearing, especially with a new book.
   ❏ always   ❏ frequently   ❏ sometimes   ❏ never
2. I eat or drink while reading and feel better when crumbs drop into the pages or when I spill coffee on them.
   ❏ always   ❏ frequently   ❏ sometimes   ❏ never
3. I push down hard on the spine of a book when I'm photocopying in order to break its spine.
   ❏ always   ❏ frequently   ❏ sometimes   ❏ never
4. I mark my place in a book with a rusty paperclip or a wet lettuce leaf unless I have a slice of bacon handy.
   ❏ always   ❏ frequently   ❏ sometimes   ❏ never
5. I leave books on the radiator or in the sunlight, and am disappointed when the paper doesn't yellow in a day or two.
   ❏ always   ❏ frequently   ❏ sometimes   ❏ never
6. I underline and annotate books with a pen, especially library books, so that others will have the benefit of what I believe the truth to be.
   ❏ always   ❏ frequently   ❏ sometimes   ❏ never
7. I like to read while showering and store books in the bathroom because watching pages curl turns me on.
   ❏ always   ❏ frequently   ❏ sometimes   ❏ never
8. When shelving books, I fill each shelf as full as possible and am gratified when I can jam that last volume into a space obviously too small for it.
   ❏ always   ❏ frequently   ❏ sometimes   ❏ never
9. I like to stack books up in piles, putting the smallest and flimsiest books on the bottom and topping the pile up with the largest, hoping that the whole thing will go tumbling onto the floor.
   ❏ always   ❏ frequently   ❏ sometimes   ❏ never
10. I razor or tear articles, pages, pictures out of library books, especially if I think something might be useful to others.
    ❏ always   ❏ frequently   ❏ sometimes   ❏ never
11. I give my dog a book to chew whenever I run out of Gaines burgerbits and call him "Bookcruncher" for short.
    ❏ always   ❏ frequently   ❏ sometimes   ❏ never

Scoring

Give yourself 3 points for each "always," 2 for "frequently," 1 for "sometimes," 0 for "never." Add up the total.

26–33 = unhealthy attitude to books and learning. Leave university and go to work as far from all information as possible. You should consider professional treatment.

17–25 = you require immediate therapy if you intend to continue at university or work where printed information is handled. Ask your family doctor to refer you to your nearest bibliotherapist.

8–16 = your attitude to information is unhealthy and you need actively to change it.

1–7 = watch yourself. You could be developing a hostile attitude to books and learning. There is still time to redirect your potential hostility.

0 = congratulations. Your attitude towards printed information is very healthy. Stay vigilant.

Reprinted from the *University of British Columbia Library Bulletin*.

Source: Jocelyn Godolphin, "Are You a Book Batterer?" *College & Research Libraries News*, April 1983, p. 117

Salvaging water-damaged materials
by Peter Waters

CELLULOSE ABSORBS WATER at different rates depending on the age, condition, and composition of the material. Thus, some understanding of the mechanism of swelling action, as well as the development of mold, is essential to planning a successful salvage operation. In addition, when large collections are at stake, one must be able to calculate in advance the approximate amount of water which will have to be extracted in the drying process. Of equal importance is some knowledge of the length of time each type of material can be submerged in water before serious deterioration occurs.

Estimating water absorption. Generally speaking, manuscripts and books dated earlier than 1840 will absorb water to an average of 80% of their original weight. Since there is a greater concentration of proteinaceous material and receptivity to water in such early books, they are especially vulnerable to mold but will withstand longer periods of time submerged in water than will books printed on the less durable papers of more recent years. Modern books, other than those with the most brittle paper, will absorb an average of 60 percent of their original weight. Thus, in estimating the *original* weight of a collection, if one assumes an average of four pounds per book when dry for 20,000 books in each category, drying techniques must be set up to remove 64,000 pounds of water from the earlier materials and 48,000 pounds from the later.

The major part of all damage to bound volumes caused by swelling will take place within the first eight hours after they have been soaked. Since the paper in the text block and the cardboard cores of book covers have a greater capacity for swelling than the covering materials used for the bindings, the text block of a soaked book usually expands so much that the spine assumes a concave shape and the fore-edge a convex, thus forcing the case to become partially or completely detached.

Leather and vellum covers, especially those of the 15th, 16th, and 17th centuries, can usually be restored successfully if they are allowed to dry slowly. However, this should only be done under controlled environmental conditions by a trained conservator or under the supervision of a conservator. Unfortunately, modern manufacturing processes so degrade the natural structure of leather that, once water soaked, covers of these later materials are often impossible to restore. Some leather bindings will be reduced to a brown sludge, and others will shrink by as much as one-tenth of their original size.

Swelling of covering materials, such as cloth, buckram, and certain plastics is negligible. Cover cores, however, which are made of a highly absorbent cardboard, swell faster than an equivalent thickness of text block. Book covering materials which have already deteriorated will absorb water at about the same rate as the cores.

Once access to the collections is gained, the external appearance of each volume and group of volumes is a useful indication of the degree of water damage. Those volumes found, usually in heaps, in the aisles will be the most damaged. Not only will they have sustained the shock of falling, as rapid swelling caused them to burst from the shelves, but they will also have been immersed in water for a longer period than the volumes on the shelves above them. These will need the most extensive restoration. The appearance of such volumes can be a devastating shock, but one must not give way to panic; every volume can be saved, provided it is worth the cost of salvage and restoration, and provided proper methods of removal are followed.

Shelves which have been submerged will usually contain a mixture of wet and partially wet volumes. Misshapen volumes with concave spines and convex fore-edges can be immediately identified as belonging in the category of very wet. These will need to be rebound after they have been thoroughly dried. Others may still maintain their normal shape because they have absorbed less water. These stand the best chance of drying without distortion. Hand-bound volumes in this condition may only need recovering.

Coated papers *must not* be permitted to begin drying until each volume can be dealt with under carefully controlled conditions. The period between pumping out the water and the beginning of salvage efforts is critical. It may be desirable to leave these volumes under water until a few hours before they are to be removed.

Summary of emergency procedures

1. Seek the advice and help of book and paper conservators with experience in salvaging water-damaged materials as soon as possible.

2. Turn off heat and create free circulation of air.

3. Keep fans and air-conditioning on at night, except when a fungicidal fogging operation is in process, because a constant flow of air is necessary to reduce the threat of mold.

4. Brief each worker carefully before salvage operations begin, giving full information on the dangers of proceeding except as directed. Emphasize the seriousness of timing and the priorities and aims of the whole operation. Instruct workers on means of recognizing manuscripts, materials with water-soluble components, leather and vellum bindings, materials printed on coated paper stock, and photographic materials.

5. Do *not* allow workers to attempt restoration of any items on-site. (This was a common error in the first 10 days after the Florence flood, when rare and valuable leather- and vellum-bound volumes were subjected to scrubbing and processing to remove mud. This resulted in driving mud into the interstices of leather, vellum, cloth, and paper, caused extensive damage to the volumes, and made the later work of restoration more difficult, time consuming, and extremely costly.)

6. Carry out all cleaning operations, whether outside the building or in controlled-environment rooms, by washing gently with fresh, cold running water and soft cellulose sponges to aid in the release of mud and filth. Use sponges with a dabbing motion; *do not rub*. These instructions do not apply to materials with water-soluble components. Such materials should be frozen as quickly as possible.

7. Do not attempt to open a wet book. (Wet paper is very weak and will tear at a touch. *One tear costs at least one dollar to mend!*) Hold a book firmly closed

when cleaning, especially when washing or sponging. A closed book is highly resistant to impregnation and damage.

8. Do not attempt to separate single-sheet materials unless they are supported on polyester film or fabric.

9. Do not attempt to remove all mud by sponging. Mud is best removed from clothes when dry; this is also true of library materials.

10. Do not remove covers from books, as they will help to support the books during drying. When partially dry, books may be hung over nylon lines to finish drying. Do not hang books from lines while they are very wet because the weight will cause damage to the inside folds of the sections.

11. Do not press books and documents mechanically when they are water soaked. This can force mud into the paper and subject the materials to stresses which will damage their structures.

12. Use soft pencils for making notes on slips of paper but do not attempt to write on wet paper or other artifacts.

13. Clean, white blotter paper, white paper towels, *strong* toilet paper, and unprinted newsprint paper may be used for interleaving in the drying process. When nothing better is available, all but the color sections of printed newspapers may be used. Great care must be taken to avoid rubbing the inked surface of the newspaper over the material being dried; otherwise some offsetting of the ink may occur.

14. *Under no circumstance should newly dried materials be packed in boxes and left without attention for more than a few days.*

15. Do not use bleaches, detergents, water-soluble fungicides, wire staples, paper or bulldog clips, adhesive tape, or adhesives of any kind. Never use felt-tipped fiber or ballpoint pens or any marking device on wet paper. Never use colored blotting paper or colored paper of any kind to dry books and other documents.

Source: Peter Waters, *Procedures for Salvage of Water-Damaged Library Materials* (Washington, D.C.: Library of Congress, 1979)

5

Norm's Library Levity

John David Marshall took a dim view of the potential for preservation microfilm in a short piece, "The 1984 Style Library," in the *Antiquarian Bookman* (July 20, 1964). "When all the books have been reduced to microfilm copies," Marshall wrote, "it will become essential that librarians offer three new services to their patrons. On entering the library of microfilm copies, the library patron—let us call him John Q. Reader—will stop first at the office of the resident optometrist who will examine Mr. Reader's eyes and will prescribe the proper glasses for him. Next Mr. Reader will go to the resident optician's office to have the optometrist's prescription filled. A matter of moments only this will take, since every possible prescription for glasses will be in stock. Having obtained his glasses, Mr. Reader will be prepared to pursue his library reading on the microfilm projector. When he has finished his reading with the aid of his new glasses and the microfilm projector provided by the library, Mr. Reader will present himself at the office of the Director of the Library's Seeing-Eye Dog Kennel. Here he will be provided with a seeing-eye dog which will lead him all the way home."

—*Norman D. Stevens , The Molesworth Institute*

Security

"Will my disks go floo if I take them through?"

by Patricia B. M. Brennan and Joel S. Silverberg

COMPUTER DISKETTES have become as common a campus commodity as syllabi and chalk. Students and faculty think nothing of popping them in backpacks and briefcases and transporting them everywhere. Most computer users are aware that disks have certain handling and care requirements. Along with dust, fingerprints, heat and pressure, both the library and computer literatures resound with the commandment: avoid magnetic fields.

Prompted by concern expressed by colleagues that was reflected in a question to the *American Libraries* "Action Exchange"' and in reports to *Library Hotline* concerning magnetic field damage to library media (including software), a series of experiments was designed to determine the effect of a magnetic security system (Tattle Tape model #31) on a standard 5.25-inch floppy disk.

Romeo and Watstein have succinctly outlined the basic structure of the 3M Tattle Tape security system:

> The Tattle Tape system operates on an electromagnetic principle. A thin pressure-sensitive detection strip is hidden in the book spine or between the pages in the gutter of a book or periodical. An exitway is formed by a detection post and lattice-like set sensing unit, which emits an electronic detection field from the floor to the top of the screen.—Louis J. Romeo, "Electronic Theft Detection Systems," *Library & Archival Security* 2, no. 3/4 (1978): 1, 7-14.

> At the heart of the Tattle Tape Detection System is the Tattle Tape Detection Strip. This device is a small, thin, flexible, metallic strip that generates an electrical signal when stimulated by a low frequency alternating electromagnetic field.—Sarah B. Watstein, "Book Mutilation," *Library & Archival Security* 5 (Spring 1983): 11-33.

In addition to the exit gate sensor and the detection strips, the third component of the system consists of an activator/deactivator unit that magnetically sensitizes and desensitizes the detection strips as part of the circulation process.

We considered the question: Under what circumstances would the security system and any computer disks normally interact? We identified three possibilities. Repeated exposure to the exit gate sensor would be normal for any patron making frequent use of the library. Second, it is possible that disks might be exposed to sensitized or "hot" magnetic strips in the books used within the building. We also investigated an extreme case of prolonged exposure to the exit sensor, although this is unlikely to occur. Finally, the possible consequences of accidental exposure to the activator/deactivator unit were examined.

An Apple II computer was used to create a sequential text file, recorded on a Verbatim (Datalife) single-density floppy disk. The Verbatim brand was chosen because of its widespread use. The file contained 3,200 repetitions of the normal alphabetic sequence: A through Z. A verification program was then written to check that disk after each experiment to see if any data within the file had been lost, damaged, or altered. The verification program contained a "standard" alphabetic sequence against which each of the 3,200 alphabets was checked. The program recorded how many sequences matched its standard and how many failed the comparison. Thus, any deviation from the expected sequence of 83,200 characters (3200 x 26) would be detected and recorded.

Experiment I involved the help of a student assistant who carried the data disk past the sensor 100 times, as if exiting the building. The verification program showed no loss of data.

In Experiment II, a sensitized book was chosen at random from the collection. The Circulation Department checked the book to make sure the detection strip was "hot." The data disk was then placed inside the book and left undisturbed for 10 hours. As before, the verification program revealed the data to be unaltered.

Experiment III was designed to test an extreme situation: one unlikely to occur in practice. Particular concern had been expressed by some colleagues about carrying their disks past the exit sensor on a daily basis. The data disk was attached by its paper jacket to the exit gate sensor. It was left in this position seven days. The gate remained in continuous operation and continued to detect a number of sensitized books while the disk was attached to it. The verification program once again showed no alterations of the 3,200 alphabetic sequences during the 168-hour trial.

The first three experiments considered normal interactions between the disk and the security system. A less usual hazard is the accidental exposure of a computer disk to the activator/deactivator unit. The data disk was "accidentally" left as a bookmark in a book which was then passed through the activator/deactivator unit during routine check-in procedures. The verification program was unable to read the disk at all. Further examination of the disk by other programs revealed extensive damage to the operating system, disk directories, and data. For all practical purposes, the data disk was rendered unusable.

This series of practical field tests supports the statements of Gene Heltemes, 3M engineer, that the Tattle Tape system has "such a weak magnetic field that it could not possibly damage a tape being carried through it." Neither sensitized books nor the detection mechanism of the exit gate affected the type of disk used in these experiments. It appears that computer disks may be carried and used in the library without undue concern.

Accidents, of course, can still happen. The one that seemed most likely to occur (exposure to the activator/deactivator unit during check-in or check-out) constituted our fourth experiment. Such exposure did indeed render the disk unusable. It is the opinion of the authors that data disks, or in fact any magnetic media, should never be brought into close proximity with the activator/deactivator mechanism because of the demonstrated effects of its strong magnetic field.

Source: Patricia B. M. Brennan & Joel S. Silverberg, "Will My Disks Go Floo If I Take Them Through?" *College & Research Libraries News,* September 1985, pp. 423–24

Marking rare books

MUCH THOUGHTFUL DISCUSSION has taken place on the appropriateness of permanently marking rare books, manuscripts, and other special collections. Recent cases of theft have shown that the clear identification of library material is vital if the material, once recovered, is to be returned to its rightful owner. Marking is essential. The guidelines which follow are intended to aid libraries and other institutions in marking their materials and are intended primarily to provide as consistent and uniform a practice as possible, given the variety and special nature of the materials concerned. The ALA Rare Books and Manuscripts Section's Security Committee recommends that libraries and other institutions use marking as part of their overall security arrangements; and that they attempt to strike a balance between the implications of two major considerations: deterrence (visibility, permanence) and integrity of the document (both physical and aesthetic).

General recommendations

1. That a form of permanent ink be used for marking.
2. That secret marking as a primary identification device be avoided.
3. That the ownership mark be placed where it can easily be located (but not in a place that is too prominent or disfiguring).
4. That it be placed away from text or image.

For the sake of uniformity and other advantages, marking in ink has been preferred to embossing or perforating. Visible marking is meant to reduce or obviate the need for secret marking, which lacks an immediate deterrence value. Placement of the ownership mark will always be a matter of careful and trained judgment, varying according to each document. For the purposes of these guidelines, the place selected should be as close to the lower portion as possible, on the verso, at a site that is blank on both sides of the leaf and removed sufficiently from the text or image on the side of the leaf on which it is placed to avoid disfigurement or confusion. Where circumstances or peculiarities of the item do not allow the above to be readily followed, marking may be deferred until further consensus is reached.

Specific recommendations

Marks should be located as follows:

1. Medieval and Renaissance manuscripts. On the verso of the first leaf of principal text, on the inner margin, approximate to the last line of text. Additional markings may be needed when the item is a composite manuscript or otherwise has a substantial text that may be broken away without noticeable injury to the volume. The location of each subsequent marking would be the same, i.e., lower inner margin approximate to the last line of the text.

When the manuscript is too tightly bound to mark in the inner margin, alternate locations may be made in any blank area of the verso, as close to the lower portion of the text as possible. The mark should be so placed that it may not be excised without extreme cropping. (In manuscripts of double columns the mark might be located in the blank area between the two columns.)

2. Incunabula and early printed books. On the verso of the first leaf of principal text on the lower inner margin, approximate to the last line of text. Follow the same instructions as given under Medieval and Renaissance Manuscripts above, with the same precautions and alternatives.

3. Leaf books, single leaves from manuscripts, etc. On either verso or recto, at the lower portion of the text or image of each leaf. The choice may be determined by the document itself if one of the sides has more importance (owing to an illustration, manuscript annotation, etc.) The ownership mark should then be placed on the reverse side.

4. Broadsides, prints, maps, single leaf letters and documents. On the verso, in the lower margin of the area occupied by text or image or the opposite side. Care should be taken here to insure that the specific area is blank on the side opposite to that which is to carry the mark. If the back side is entirely blank, the ownership mark may be placed freely in areas other than the lower margin.

5. Multiple leaf manuscript letters, documents, newspapers, ephemera. On the verso of the first leaf in the lower margin. It may be appropriate to place an additional mark later in the work if a portion (such as a famous signature, paper seal, first appearance of a poem, etc.) would have independent value if detached or excised.

6. Modern printed books, pamphlets, serial issues. On the verso of the first leaf of the opening text, directly below the bottom line. The placement here is designed to spare the title-page, half-title, dedication page, etc., which in many valuable productions have a separate aesthetic appeal not to be disfigured even on the verso. As in the case of multiple-leaf materials (see above, no. 5) additional markings may be indicated for those internal items (illustration, maps, etc.) that may have separate marketable value.

Ink and equipment

The ink used should be permanent (i.e., sufficiently difficult to remove to act in most cases as a deterrent), inert in itself and in conservation treatment, and able to be applied in minute quantity. The ink and equipment (rubber stamp and balsa wood pad) described in the Library of Congress's *Preservation Leaflet no. 4, Marking Manuscripts,* may serve as an example.

Form and size of mark

The size should be kept to a minimum (ca. 5-point type size for lettering). The form should be made up of initials identifying the institution as succinctly as possible, based on the National Union Catalog symbols, and suitable for arranging in lists to circulate to dealers, auction houses, collectors, etc.

Cancellation of mark

Do not attempt to obliterate marks of ownership made according to these guidelines, even in the event that the material is to be deaccessioned. No system has yet been devised for canceling marks that cannot be imitated with relative ease by thieves, and there seems no alternative but to assume permanent responsibility for the fact of one's mark of ownership in a book, manuscript, or other document. Permanent records should be kept of deaccessioned material containing marks of ownership made according to these guidelines, and the material itself when released should be accompanied by a signed letter of authorization on institutional stationery.

Source: Security Committee, ALA Association of College & Research Libraries, *Guidelines for the Security of Rare Book, Manuscript, and Other Special Collections* (Chicago: ALA, 1990)

Security measures

THE FOLLOWING SAFETY SUGGESTIONS are from the University of Illinois Library Committee on Security and Safety.

Suggested opening procedures. These guidelines should be custom-designed for your particular library or unit, and should be written out for all your staff to read and discuss periodically.

1. Appoint one staff member to do an early morning rounds check of the entire library to look for anything that does not appear to be in order.

2. Check work areas for signs of missing equipment or supplies.

3. Check overnight book drop for signs of tampering or vandalism.

Suggested closing procedures. Custom-design your own.

1. Set up a procedure for clearing the library of patrons at closing time.

2. Lock all doors and windows.

3. Check all spots where people might be concealed.

4. Arrange for staff members to leave the building together after evening closings. If students are working alone until closing time, suggest that they en-

courage a friend to study in the library until it closes, so that the student does not have to leave the building unaccompanied.

5. Strongly encourage staff members without transportation to utilize a carpool.

6. Keep a written record of any irregular incidents which have occurred during closing procedures (patron refuses to leave building, etc.).

Suggested general security measures.

1. Check all doors and windows for adequate locks. Report any that do not function properly to the Library Business Office.

2. Keep an inventory of all major office equipment, including serial numbers and descriptions.

3. Keep accurate and up-to-date records of all people who have keys to the library or building. Report lost keys promptly.

4. Keep all spare keys locked up.

5. Establish a system of communicating problems and unusual incidents to supervisors. Keep a log of such problems and violations. Follow up by completing an "Incident Report Form" and sending it to the director of your service.

6. Make sure your library has the best possible physical arrangement for safety. Consider exits, visibility, etc. Keep work area well defined, and restricted to staff only.

7. One staff member should make "rounds" of the library at regular intervals, especially in the course of the evening.

8. Keep the police and fire department phone numbers by every telephone. Most library units have the police and fire department phone numbers as part of their speed call option; memorize these numbers. In case of theft, unruly patrons, or even suspicious behavior, call the police. In case of theft or vandalism, leave scene exactly as you found it until the police arrive. Follow up by completing an "Incident Report Form" and sending it to the director of your unit.

Power failure. Always keep a flashlight in a designated spot for staff to use if the power fails and lights go out.

Bomb threat. If a bomb threat is received, follow these procedures:

1. Keep the caller on the line as long as possible. Ask the caller to repeat the message. Try to write down every word spoken by the person.

2. If the caller does not indicate the location of the bomb, or the time of possible detonation, *ask for this information.*

3. Inform the caller that the building is occupied, and the bomb could result in injury or death for innocent people.

4. Listen closely to the voice (male, female), voice quality (calm, excited), accents and speech impediments.

5. Pay special attention to peculiar background noises such as: motors running, background music, and any other noises which may give a clue as to where the call is being made.

6. Immediately after the caller hangs up, contact the police and inform the person in charge. Since the police will want to talk first-hand with the person who received the call, remain available until they arrive.

7. If available, use the public intercom system, or initiate the phone tree procedure to evacuate the building. Announce, "There is an emergency and the police have requested that everyone leaves the building."

8. When evacuating the building, follow the same evacuation procedures established for fire.

Source: Building Security and Personal Safety, SPEC Kit #150
(Washington, D.C.: Office of Management Services, Association of Research Libraries, January 1989)

Dealing with disruptive behavior

THE UNIVERSITY OF CHICAGO Library has the following guidelines for library staff response to disruptive behavior, accidents, or thefts:

1. Remain calm.
2. Repeat your request if necessary.
3. Do not argue with outrageous statements.
4. Be explicit.
5. Stay in control of the situation; do not allow patron to manipulate you.
6. Avoid humor or personal remarks.
7. Alert other staff members when strange behavior occurs.
8. Be considerate; listen to whole explanation even if you have heard it a thousand times before.
9. Offer a choice of actions or alternatives if you can.
10. Be a team player when confronting a disturbed patron: get help. Do not try to handle it alone. Ask another staff member to watch the person while you call for help.
11. Give support to another staff member who has had to confront a disturbed patron.
12. Never try to restrain or detain a patron forcefully. Do not touch a disturbed patron.

> —Adapted from "Twelve Commandments" by Marianne Steinberg, social worker at the Crisis Center, San Francisco's Tenderloin.

5

The following are descriptions of types of disruptive behavior, and the steps that should be taken when each type of behavior is encountered:

Angry verbal abuse. Examples: extremely abusive and threatening argument about a bill, insistence upon special library privileges, etc. Normally calm and reasonable library patrons may be aggravated into disruptive behavior by frustration: a bill they feel is undeserved, a book that is missing, etc. Your goal is to defuse the patron's anger.

1. Acknowledge existence of problem: explain procedures, describe steps that can be taken to solve the problem. Listen supportively, with empathy and understanding. Be aware that patron is venting inner frustration; anger is probably not directed at you, especially in the early stages.

2. Enlist aid of supervisor or another staff member. If complaint seems legitimate, refer problem to supervisor.

3. Personal verbal abuse should not be tolerated. If a patron's tirade goes beyond criticism of library policy and focuses on you, particularly if this abuse is racist, sexist, or ageist in nature, retreat from the confrontation immediately.

Call your supervisor, or if that person is not available, call another staff member or campus security.

Theft of personal property from patron in library. This is somewhat different than the other types of behavior described, but the patron will probably be disturbed and approach a staff member for help.

1. Be supportive and helpful to the patron, but do not say anything which could be construed that the library has any responsibility for the loss.

2. Encourage the patron to use your telephone to call campus security.

Accident or illness of users.

1. Call security. If the person is ambulatory, security will come and transport them to a hospital.

2. If the person is not ambulatory, tell the security dispatcher to call an ambulance.

3. If other users volunteer to assist, use them in ways that do not require any decisions on their part, or put them in any jeopardy, such as waiting at the front door for security to arrive and escorting the officer directly to the area.

Destruction of library materials. Examples: writing in books, cutting out pages, damaging furniture, using library materials destructively, etc.

1. If action seems to be accidental, unintentional, or fairly minor, tell the patron to stop. If the patron is cooperative and this is a first offense, you may want to handle the problem locally (have the patron replace the material, etc.). Use your own judgment, but call for help if you have any doubts.

2. If action seems deliberate and seriously destructive, call campus security. Confront the person and ask for his or her I.D. card. Keep the card and give to the security officer when he or she arrives, and secure the damaged materials as evidence. If the person refuses to give you an I.D. card, or leaves the area, be prepared to give security a physical description and to make a formal complaint when the security officer arrives. If the person is a student, a copy of the complaint will be sent to the dean of students for disciplinary review.

3. If you observe damage to furniture or the building, but did not see someone do it, call security anyway and ask them to come and take a report of vandalism.

Suspected attempt of theft of library materials. Occasionally you will suspect that a user is trying to take library material without charging it out, or that the library markings have been removed to make an item appear to be personal property.

1. Since it may only be a suspicion on your part, *do not* accuse the person of anything. Calmly take the piece in question, *and* another properly charged library book from the same person if one is available, and tell the person that you need to have a supervisor check them.

2. If you are able to leave the area, take the pieces to a supervisor. If you cannot leave your post, call a supervisor. *Do not* get into a discussion with the user. The person may leave before the matter has been resolved, but do not try to detain him or her. If you have a book with charge evidence, that will identify the person. If the person becomes agitated, calmly hold your ground and repeat that the supervisor will talk with him or her. Never use an accusatory manner. Always state that the library records need to be checked, so that the user will not have any problems with the loan.

3. The above directions are more difficult and delicate if there is no supervisor available. Start out as above, by taking the material and saying that you will have to have a supervisor check it, and that the user can pick it up at the Circulation Desk at his or her convenience. Then put the material on the supervisor's desk with the necessary information for follow-up.

4. If the person objects strongly to #3, have the person write down the call number, piece number (bar code) and his or her patron number on a piece of paper (check these against the piece and the person's I.D. card). Also have the user write his or her name and phone number so that the supervisor can get in contact with him or her. Again, make sure it sounds like it is the library's problem with records. Then let the user take the item in question, if he or she insists, and leave the paper with the information for the supervisor. Staff will follow up on each of these—to apologize for the delay if the library cannot substantiate any problem, or to take action through the appropriate channels if there is a problem.

Refusal to abide by library rules. Examples: refusal to show I.D. card upon entry or books upon exiting library, insistence upon smoking or eating in inappropriate area, etc.

1. Advise patron of the rule. Explain the reasoning behind the rule. Provide patron with alternatives: explain where patron may go to get I.D. or to smoke or eat.

2. If behavior continues, ask the patron for his or her name and library card

number, record these, and then ask the patron to leave the library. Give name and information about incident to the head of circulation services.

3. If the patron refuses to give a name or leave, call campus security and ask them to come and make out a report of the incident, and escort the person out of the library.

Bizarre but nonthreatening behavior. Examples: random, senseless movements; erratic, inappropriate, abnormal actions that are distracting to others.

1. Approach the patron directly, and ask if patron needs assistance. Enlist aid of another staff member if possible.

2. Tell the patron the behavior is distracting and disturbing to other library users and must be stopped. Be direct and firm.

3. If behavior continues, call your supervisor or campus security.

Disruptive behavior. Examples: loud talking, singing, approaching staff or other patrons and engaging them in unwanted and inappropriate interaction.

1. Tell the patron to be quiet. Inform the patron that the behavior is disturbing to the other library users and must be stopped. Enlist the aid of another staff member.

2. Follow numbers 2 and 3 in "Refusal to Abide by Library Rules" above.

Suspicious lurking. Examples: person seems to be out of place, is not using library materials, seems to be watching other patrons or their belongings, or attempts to enter a nonpublic area.

1. Ask if the patron needs assistance.

2. Watch the person—or ask another staff member to watch while you notify your supervisor or the head of circulation.

3. If person's response is not appropriate or seems evasive, call campus security. If the person leaves the area before security arrives, be prepared to give a complete description of the person.

Sexual offenses. Examples: indecent exposure, inappropriate sexual advances.

1. Call campus security immediately. Say you are reporting a sexual offense. Give your name, your building, and room number. Give as full a description of the offender as possible, and the last place seen or direction of flight.

2. The patron or staff member to whom the behavior was directed may be very upset. Do not try to get them to give you all the details in a public area. Try to take the person to an office or an area away from others. If possible, it is best to have the victim talk directly to the security dispatcher. Be supportive of the feelings of the victimized patron or staff member.

Threats to personal safety of staff and patrons. Example: disturbed patron is armed and/or violent.

1. Call campus security immediately. Say you have a violent person in the library. If the person is armed, inform the dispatcher. Give your name, your building, and room number.

2. Keep an eye on the situation, but without risking your own safety or inflaming the situation try to get others out of the area and remain at a safe distance yourself. Security will give you directions when they arrive.

5

Source: Building Security and Personal Safety, SPEC Kit #150
(Washington, D.C.: Office of Management Services, Association of Research Libraries, January 1989)

How to move or shift books

by Anthony J. Amodeo

IN THIS ERA OF EBBING financial support for libraries, in which the costs of repair, rebinding, and replacement of even ordinary materials continue to climb, it makes perfect sense to take precautions that prevent unnecessary damage to collections, especially research collections. It will not be surprising, therefore, to see better handling procedures encouraged in libraries, through staff training and patron education, once its cost-effectiveness is realized.

The processes involved in moving or shifting a substantial number of library materials make this activity an especially important occasion for staff training and close supervision. If care is not taken, many years worth of wear and tear and accidental damage to materials can be inflicted in a matter of hours.

Marking

Instead of using pressure-sensitive tags on books for marking range or shelving order, try tall color-coded or numbered strips of paper that can be inserted either between books or in the first or final book. These slips, always taller than the books themselves, should be removed after the move is complete, since they are probably acidic.

Removal from shelf

Staff should be trained to remove books by grasping them at the middle ("waist") rather than tugging at the headcap, which causes damage. Supervisors must be watchful for this, especially as the day wears on and bad habits surface. Adjacent books may be pushed slightly toward the back of the shelf to expose enough of the desired book for grasping.

Books should be grasped securely and in small enough quantity to assure safe handling. Careful handling is cheaper than excessive speed.

All books should be supported in an upright position at all stages of handling or else laid flat. This means that when books are taken from a shelf, the remaining books are not allowed to slouch, sag, or slide. One hand can hold the unsupported book against the remainder of books on the shelf while a second person loads the book truck or cart. An alternative is the use of wrapped housebricks to hold otherwise unsupported books upright; these are easier to manipulate than book-ends, and can be slid quickly with one hand. Lacking bricks or bookends, the last three or four books in the row can be stacked flat to provide support. However, if three-person teams are used for the move (one to remove books, one to place them on the cart, a third to transport the cart), stacking is usually unnecessary.

An adequate number of stable standing kickstools or other risers should be provided for each team, so that materials on the top shelves will not be yanked off, or the remaining books fall off the shelf for lack of support.

Loading carts

Bookcarts should be loaded in a pre-scribed order to prevent both nonse-quential transfer into new locations, and any instability of the cart during transit which may cause spills. The bookcart may be loaded from the top down (see illustration), or from the bottom up (to avoid top-heaviness), or one side at a time (to increase speed), as long as it is done consistently and care-fully. If double rows of books are set on the truck, this becomes of paramount importance. Rare books should only be moved in single rows.

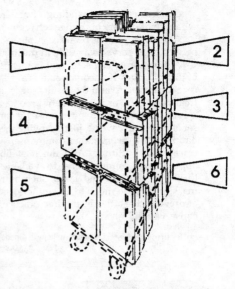

Books should be adequately sup-ported on the carts so that there will be minimum sliding and no leaning dur-ing transport. At the same time, books should not be stuffed tightly enough to cause abrasion or crushing. Wrapped bricks can be used to support books during the loading, and bricks or bookends should be used for support during transit if the truck is not filled end-to-end.

If spillage of material occurs during transit, the cause should be identified and a solution found immediately. Some causes may be: the cart was pushed too fast, especially around corners; large books were loaded in double rather than single rows; the rows were not centered on the cart; books were not adequately supported on the cart, or held too loosely; the type of cart or flooring caused excessive vibration. In the last case, single-row loading should be employed for all books, which should be constantly monitored during transit. If problems per-sist, inner tubes might be cut into large "rubber bands" about two inches wide and carefully slipped around the cart; the same could be done with lengths of non-abrasive cloth, tied at one end. The surface of the carts might also be padded securely for extra protection.

Reshelving

Materials should be carefully placed in order in their new locations; books will not then need to be slid around to accommodate out-of-sequence material. This is easily accomplished if the cart-loading procedure is consistent throughout the move. Location slips can be removed when the shelves have been read.

General guidelines

The move should be constantly supervised to avoid the reversion to habit that accompanies fatigue. Adequate break time is important.

Very thick, large, or heavy books are better moved laid flat on the truck. Flat or fragile materials should be protected by a folder or other protective enclosure before the move begins; otherwise, movers should be alerted to their existence and handling. Items in bad repair may have to be bagged, boxed, or tied to avoid loss of parts.

No books should be shelved or carted on their fore-edges; if a large book does not fit upright on the cart or shelf, it should be laid flat or set spine down.

Problems and logjams should be dealt with as they occur, and procedures modified where necessary. Planned alternatives can be useful.

Careless or rough handling of materials should not be tolerated. A worker who cannot modify his or her behavior should be reassigned to less critical work.

After the move has been accomplished, a memorandum or short report should be written to serve as a guide in future moves.

A move can be a useful tool in identifying the maintenance and repair needs of the collection. If adequate staff is available, a system for noting items that need care can be set up and the results subsequently used as resources for appropriate treatment, care, or replacement become available.

Any librarian with a good sense for conservation could compile and add to this set of rules and caveats, just by giving the matter some thought. If the recommendations above seem rather commonsensical—congratulations! You have a good conservation attitude. And much of library conservation has to do with the application of common sense to available information. Similar awareness applied to library routines and tasks, such as reshelving, circulation procedures, and marking, will do much to lower the costs of a library "doing business." This sort of preventative attitude, put into practice, is one of the best and cheapest kinds of conservation.

Source: Anthony J. Amodeo, "Helpful Hints for Moving or Shifting Collections," *College & Research Libraries News*, March 1983, pp. 82–83

Budgeting

Budget allocation

BUDGET ALLOCATION IS THE PROCESS of distributing the available financial resources at the disposal of an organization for specified purposes and functions. Allocation criteria may be objective or subjective. Objective criteria are helpful in assuring fairness, but not all factors appropriately considered in the budget process are quantifiable. The following list of allocation criteria is intended to suggest the range of possible factors, rather than present an exhaustive enumeration.

- Current collecting emphasis as described in the collection development policy
- Size and character of the user community
- Need for multiple copies
- Cost of materials
- Amount of relevant publishing
- Extent of reliance on serials, monographs, and other formats
- Need for new information formats and technologies
- Availability of other resources and services in the vicinity
- Potential for external funding
- Statistics on use
- Existence of special gift funds or endowments

Examples of allocation criteria typical of academic libraries

- Faculty size, composition, scholarly activity
- Undergraduate and graduate enrollment by major
- Credit hours offered by department or academic program

- Degree of dependence of discipline on library resources
- Degrees granted
- Prestige accorded academic or research programs
- Existence of special collections

Examples of allocation criteria typical of public libraries

- Composition of communities served (age, ethnicity, language, educational level, employment indicators, etc.)
- Special community needs influenced by changing economic, social, and political factors
- Ratio of copies per title purchases for best-sellers
- Demand for materials in high-use areas
- Level of support required for information services
- Extent of reserve, purchase, and interlibrary loan requests
- Juxtaposition of new and old formats (such as compact disks, cassette tapes, and LPs)
- Need for replacement of lost and damaged materials

Examples of allocation criteria typical of special libraries

- Role of library in assisting the parent organization to achieve its objectives
- Number of departments or clients served and their physical location
- Acceptable turnaround time for patron requests
- Whether services are charged back to users
- Degree of need for current, time-sensitive information
- Extent to which users' needs are served by the internal collection rather than interlibrary loan, document retrieval, or use of other collections
- Need for end users to access information when library staff is not present
- Need for exhaustive coverage in certain subject areas
- Need to collect and house confidential materials

5

Examples of allocation criteria typical of school libraries

- Philosophy and goals of the school district
- Intellectual content and level of the collection
- Changes in the curriculum
- Ability levels, learning styles, and social and emotional development of the students
- Attrition rate by loss, weeding, and aging of the collection
- Degree to which the collection includes professional materials for teachers

Source: Subcommittee on Budget Allocation, Resources Section,
Guide to Budget Allocation for Information Resources
(Chicago: ALA Association for Library Collections & Technical Services, 1991)

Media center budget formulas

Formula for calculating materials budget

$$MB = C \times (1 \pm V + Aw + Ad + Al) \times (1 + I)$$

This formula represents one way to calculate budgetary needs for maintenance of the current building-level media center materials allocation. The formula is not intended to take into account special needs for enhancing the budget, such as those occasioned by extensive curriculum revisions, textbook changes, lower than appropriate materials expenditures, and so on. Additional expenditure amounts should be allocated for specific nonperiodic needs.

Dollar amounts used in the formula should be based on the building allocation of funds for all forms of media, excluding equipment. Materials covered by this formula are library media center books and audiovisual materials, including microcomputer software, periodicals, reference materials, and microfilm.

Category definitions

MB	=	Materials budget for the upcoming year
C	=	Amount spent for media in the current year
V	=	Variation in student population
Aw	=	Attrition by weeding
Ad	=	Attrition by date
Al	=	Attrition by loss
I	=	Inflation rate

Criteria

V — Variation in Student Population. This is the change in the number of students served. Calculate this number using the equation below. It will be added if it represents an increase or subtracted if it represents a decrease.

$$\text{(increase or decrease) V original} \times 0.2 =$$

Aw — Attrition by Weeding. The attrition by weeding is determined using the percent of the collection that has been weeded.

% of Collection Weeded	Added to Formula
0 to 1.99%	0.00
2 to 4.99%	0.01
5 to 9.99%	0.02
10% or more	0.03

Ad — Attrition by Date. This will indicate the age of the collection. Do a systematic sampling of the collection of print and audiovisual nonfiction materials. One sampling procedure is described below.

Assume that 100 cards in the shelflist equal one inch. Select a sample of approximately 200 items using these steps.

1. Estimate the size of the nonfiction collection. First, measure the shelflist with a ruler and estimate that each inch represents 100 cards. For example, a nonfiction shelflist that measures about 40 inches suggests that the nonfiction collection includes about 4,000 items.

2. Divide the size of the nonfiction collection (in inches) by the size of the sample desired. This produces the sampling interval. Convert the resulting number to sixteenths of an inch to make measuring the shelflist easier. A 200-item sample is probably large enough to ensure that judgments based upon it will be accurate. For example, to sample 200 titles from a 40-inch nonfiction collection, divide 40 by 200. The sampling interval is 0.2, or 3/16 of an inch.

3. Using the calculated sampling interval, pull shelflist cards and note the latest copyright date of each title selected. Determine the percentage of the nonfiction collection that is 15 years old or older and then add the appropriate number to the formula.

% of Nonfiction Collection 15+ Years	Add to Formula
0 to 2.99%	0.00
3 to 4.99%	0.01
5 to 9.99%	0.02
10 to 19.99%	0.03
20% or more	0.04

Al — Attrition by Loss. Every year, a number of items cannot be accounted for and may be declared lost. Add a number to the formula based upon the percentage of the collection that has been lost.

% of Collection Lost	Add to Formula
0 to 0.99%	0.00
1 to 1.99%	0.01
2 to 2.99%	0.02
3% or more	0.03

I — Inflation. The latest inflation rate percent of change listed in the Consumer Price Index can be used in the formula. Another source is the most current edition of a world almanac.

An alternative is to identify the inflation rate for books and other media and to use those figures or an average of them. The choice is up to those using the formula. It is important to be consistent once the choice of inflation rate has been made.

For the sake of illustration, imagine a building media center collection that includes 15,000 media items of all types. Last year, the center's total materials budget was $4,800: it served 400 students.

The school enrollment increased by 23 students; 289 books were lost and 241 weeded. Sixty of 400 randomly selected items were found to be 15 years old or older. The inflation rate for the last year was 0.038.

Those using the formula above to calculate the materials budget for the coming year must first determine the numbers that will go into the formula.

C = $4,800
V = Increase of 23 students
23 V 400 = 0.0575 increase in student population
0.0575 × 0.2 = 0.0115, so add 0.0115
Aw = 242 items weeded from a collection of 15,000 items
242 V 15,000 = 0.016
This is less than 2%, so add nothing.
Ad = For a collection of 12,000 nonfiction books (15,000 items minus 3000 fiction titles), 320 cards were checked and 60 found to be for items 15 years old or older.
60 V 320 = 0.1875
18.75% is over 10%, so add 0.03.
Al = 289 books were unaccounted for out of the 15,000-item collection
289 V 15,000 = 0.019
1.9% is between 1% and 2% of the collection, so add 0.01.
I = The inflation rate listed was 0.038.

Now the variables can be used in the formula.

MB = $C \times (1 \pm V + Aw + Ad + Al) \times (1 + I)$
= $4,800 × (1 + 0.0115 + 0.00 + 0.03 + 0.01) × (1 + 0.038)$
= ($4,800 × 1.0515) × (1.038)
= $5,047.20 × 1.038
MB = $5,238.99

For justification purposes, the new materials budget should be $5,238.99.

Formula for calculating equipment budget

$$EB = C \times AA + R(V)(I)$$

Category definitions

EB = Equipment budget
C = Current inventory replacement value
AA = Average age of equipment
R = Replacement value for lost, stolen, or damaged items
I = Inflation rate

Example: Value of the current inventory is $100,000 and the average age is seven years. One VCR was damaged beyond repair during the year, replacement cost is $315. Rate of inflation is figured at 1.2%.

$100,000 × 7 = $700,000 × .012 = $8400 + $315 = $8715 EB

For a new school with the same inventory, the budget would be

$100,000 × .012 = $1200 EB.

Quoted with permission from: Dianne M. Hopkins, Leslyn Shires, M. Elaine Anderson, and Richard J. Sorenson. *School Library Media Programs: A Resource and Planning Guide*, pp. 65-66. Wisconsin Department of Public Instruction, 1987.

Source: Information Power: Guidelines for School Library Media Programs
(Chicago: American Library Association;
Washington: Association for Educational Communications and Technology, 1988)

SPECIAL POPULATIONS

6

Library services to Hispanics

PROVIDING LIBRARY SERVICES to Hispanics can be complex; nationality, regional differences, and culture provide myriad combinations for that single community. For example, there are significant linguistic and cultural differences reflected in the varieties of Spanish spoken by Mexicans, Puerto Ricans, Cubans, and other Hispanic groups. Recognizing these differences and responding correctly to them are major themes.

REFORMA, the National Association to Promote Library Services to the Spanish Speaking, has taken an active role in the production of these guidelines. They were written consciously for all librarians who may need to initiate service to this population. In that sense, they are a beginner's manual intended for a hypothetical librarian serving as an administrator of a medium-to-small institution newly aware of the needs of a Hispanic community within its service area.

Collection and selection of materials

Persons in the Hispanic communities in the United States do not all speak and read only Spanish; they do not all speak and read only English; nor are they all bilingual. The members of these communities have diverse needs and are entitled to access to materials diverse enough to meet those needs.

Relevancy. The selection of library materials for Hispanics should meet the educational and recreational needs of the community by providing relevant and culturally sensitive materials. Stereotypes should be avoided.

Language. The collection should contain materials in Spanish, materials in English, and bilingual materials. Materials selected should reflect the particular linguistic characteristics of the community served. They should also include standard Spanish-language titles from Spain and other Hispanic cultures.

Physical access. If a separate collection of materials for Hispanics is maintained by the library, it should be visible and accessible to the community. In libraries that do not separate these materials, adherence to bibliographic access is strongly recommended.

Bibliographic access to the library's collection should include Spanish-language subject headings in the public catalog when appropriate for the population served. Locally produced access and identification aids, including lists, bibliographies, and point-of-use bibliographic instructional materials, should be in Spanish when appropriate.

Formats. Print and nonprint materials, whether educational or recreational, should be included.

Programs, services, and community relations

Programming, both traditional and nontraditional, is an effective vehicle to attract and meet the needs of the members of the Hispanic community. This is particularly true for those who have recently immigrated and who are unfamiliar with the library services available in the United States. As a result of the potentially limited resources available for service to Hispanics within any given institution, cooperation among all libraries serving the target population is encouraged. Such cooperation may manifest itself in the sharing of program costs, cooperative acquisitions, or joint borrowing privileges, to name but a few.

Diversity of culture. Because the population served may comprise several different Hispanic cultures, each specific culture must be considered in the development of programming and should be accurately reflected in its content.

Outreach services. In order to aid in the planning and delivery of library services to meet community needs, there should be an ongoing process of community analysis and assessment. To further these aims:

1. the library should participate in the work of local community organizations of Hispanics; and

2. the library should work with such organizations in the development and presentation of library programs and services.

Intercultural understanding. As part of its activities in working with local populations in which a multiplicity of cultures is represented, the library should actively promote intercultural communication and cooperation among them.

Service to nonusers. Attention should be paid to the library nonuser. Programs, literature, and publicity should be used in nontraditional ways and in settings designed to attract those for whom libraries are not part of the experience of life.

Bibliographic instruction. Bibliographic instruction should be offered in Spanish when necessary.

Language. In keeping with the ALA policy in support of multilingual services, the language used for programming and services (Spanish or English, bilingual or monolingual) as well as vocabulary, accent, and nuance must be carefully selected. Choices should be based upon characteristics of the local community.

Personnel

Librarians serving Hispanic communities should be actively recruited. Contact should be made with Hispanic graduates of library education programs accredited by the American Library Association, and extensive use should be made of hotlines, minority recruiting services, and services provided by Hispanic library organizations. Professional staff should be recruited from library education programs accredited by the American Library Association. Written personnel procedures and affirmative action programs should be established and fully implemented. See the *ALA Policy Manual* for amplification of these.

Qualification—professional and support staff. In addition to the required standards for librarians and support staff, bilingualism and biculturalism are qualities that should be sought; these qualities will ensure sensitivity to the library and information needs of the Hispanic community and enhance service delivery.

Bilingual and bicultural librarians and support staff should be adequately compensated in positions where job specifications or actual conditions require the knowledge of Spanish.

Staff development. Librarians and support staff should be provided opportunities to exchange information and ideas as well as to participate in continuing education programs that would enhance the services provided to libraries in Hispanic communities. Examples of programs that could be explored include training in teaching English as a second language, acquisition of Spanish-language materials, citizenship requirements, and community information services.

Opportunities for advancement should be provided and encouraged by the library administration.

Buildings

The library building, through its location, architecture, and appearance, should be an attraction, not a barrier, to members of the Hispanic community.

Interior and exterior. While the structure may not be able to be altered in any significant way, interior and exterior decor can be modified by choosing decorations and graphics to create an ambience suitable to the clientele served. Care must be taken that the alterations made will conform to the culture of the community.

Signage. In any library serving a bilingual community, signs should be bilingual. Attention must be paid to the particular dialect of Spanish used so that the wording, phraseology, and connotation of the language conform to the culture of the community. Signage should be both prominent and visible.

Location. When it is possible to control the location of the library within the community to be served, a location should be considered that will induce the target population into the library. When space is allocated within existing structures, it should be both visible and accessible.

Source: Library Services to the Spanish Speaking Committee, *Guidelines for Library Services to Hispanics* (Chicago: ALA Reference and Adult Services Division, 1988)

Spanish library phrases

by Patricia Promis and Maria Segura Hoopes

THESE ARE BASIC STRUCTURES that can be used to build dialogues, followed by lists of terms to fill in the phrase according to specific needs. Optional terms are provided when more than one is appropriate:

Directional questions

— ¿Dónde está? / ¿Dónde queda . . .? Where is . . . ?
— ¿Cuál es? / ¿Cuáles son . . . ? Which is . . . ?
— ¿Quién es? / ¿Quiénes son . . . ? Who is . . . who are . . . ?

(el) ascensor / elevador	elevator
(el) asiento	seat
(el) autor / (la) autora	author/authoress
(el) baño / lavatorios	bath/restrooms
(la) biblioteca de ciencias / central	SEL/Main
(el) buzón para libros	bookdrop
(el) cajón	drawer
(el) clip	(paper) clip
(la) grapadora / corchetera	stapler
(el) escritorio	desk
(el) edificio	building
(la) editorial	publisher
(la) entrada	entrance
(el) estante / (la) estanteria	bookshelf
(las) fotocopiadoras	copiers
(el) guión / manuscrito / original	manuscript
(el) letrero	sign
(la) librería	bookstore
(el) manual	handbook
(la) máquina para cambiar billetes	change machine
(la) mesa	table
(el) mesón / mostrador	counter
(el) mesón de préstamos	loan desk
(el) perforador	hole puncher
(el) papelero	wastebasket
(el) poste / pilar	pillar
(la) puerta	door
(la) referencia recíproca	cross reference

(el) reloj	clock/watch
(el) sacapuntas	pencil sharpener
(la) sala de lectura	reading room
(la) sala de reservas	reserve book room
(la) sección multas	fines office
(la) sala de préstamos interbibliotecas	interlibrary loan
(la) sala / oficina de objetos perdidos	lost & found
(la) salida	exit
(la) silla	chair
(la) sucursal	branch
(la) ventana	window

— ¿Puede repetir la pregunta más despacio, por favor?
— Would you please repeat the question more slowly?

Directional answers

— El / la ... queda / está ...
— The ... is ...

a la derecha de	to the right of ...
a la izquierda de	to the left of ...
derecho al fondo	straight ahead
cerca de	close to
lejos de	far from
arriba	up or above
abajo	down or under
junto a	next to
al lado de	next to
al norte de	north of ...
al sur de	south of ...
al este de	east of ...
al oeste de	west of ...
en la planta baja / subterráneo	in the basement
primer piso	first floor
segundo piso	second floor
tercer piso	third floor
cuarto piso	fourth floor
quinto piso	fifth floor
sala de clases	classroom
vestíbulo	lobby

6

The reference interview

Question:
— I need information about ...
— I'm doing research on ...

— Busco / necesito / quiero información / material sobre ...
— Estoy haciendo una investigación sobre ...

Response:
— Are you looking for information in Spanish and English?
— ¿Quiere información en inglés y en español?

Follow-up questions:
— Can you read English?
— ¿Puede leer en inglés?

— Do you need books or articles or both?
— ¿Necesita libros, artículos o ambos?

— Are you looking for current material?
— ¿Necesita información publicada recientemente?

To look for books:
— You look for books by subject in the subject catalog.
— Monografías o libros sobre el tema se buscan en el fichero de materias.

— You can also look for books in the online catalog. Follow the instructions screen by screen.
— Usted también puede consultar el catálogo computarizado. Siga paso a paso las instrucciones que aparecen el la pantalla.

by subject	por materia / tema
by author	por autor / autor corporativo
by title	por título

To look for articles:
— You look for articles in the appropriate indexes.
— Artículos publicados en revistas se buscan en los indices correspondientes.

— How do you look . . .
— ¿Cómo se buscan?

— For example, this is a citation for one article.
— Por ejemplo, esta cita corresponde a un artículo.

— This is the title of the article.
— Este es el título del artículo.

— This is the author.
— Este es el autor.

— Here, in italics, is the title of the journal.
— Aquí, en cursiva, está el título de la revista.

— This is an abbreviation for the title of the journal.
— Esta es la abreviatura del título de la revista.

Spanish Garfield poster is available from ALA Graphics

— This is an acronym.
— Esta es una sigla.

— If you need really current articles, which will usually be in English, you can do a computer search.
— Si Usted necesita artículos más nuevos, que generalmente estarán en inglés, puede hacer una búsqueda computarizada.

— I'd like to do a computerized literature search on . . .
— Necesito / quiero / ¿puedo? hacer una búsqueda computarizada de material / literatura en / sobre.

Please note that local or regional terms may differ slightly.

Source: Patricia Promis and Maria Segura Hoopes, *¿Habla Español? Practical Spanish for the Reference Desk* (ALA Reference and Adult Services Division, 1991)

Multilingual materials

TRADITIONALLY, THE UNITED STATES has been a country that attracts large numbers of immigrants from all over the globe. While some libraries have established collections and programs to serve the needs of library users whose native language is not English, nothing has been done on a national scale to systematically address these needs. In addition, the multilingual needs of library patrons who are language students, foreign students, or bilingual citizens have been underserved by traditional library service.

The ALA Reference and Adult Services Multilingual Materials Subcommittee, in conjunction with the Public Library Association's Multilingual Material and Library Service Committee, has written these guidelines to promote the development and maintenance of multilingual library services and collections.

It is assumed that it is the responsibility of libraries to provide an equitable level of service to all members of their communities regardless of ethnic, cultural, or linguistic background. Access to library materials for ethnic, cultural, and linguistic groups should not be seen as "additional" or "extra" services, but as an integral part of every library's services.

Collection and selection of materials

Libraries should provide an effective, balanced, and substantial collection for each ethnic, cultural, or linguistic group in the community.

In the case of small or widely scattered groups, a central or cooperative library effort is the best means to provide materials and services in order to maximize efficiency, reduce costs, and still provide adequate materials and services.

Levels for selection. Provision of library materials should be related primarily to the size of the group in the community. Demand and availability of materials are important factors to be considered in establishing a level of collection development. The low volume of publishing in some languages, or difficulty in obtaining what is published, may make it impossible to provide the same amount of material in all languages.

Demand may not correspond to the population size of an ethnic, linguistic, or cultural group in the community. Low demand could be the result of situations where inadequate or no service has been previously provided, or because of low expectations or unfamiliarity with library services on the part of some potential users. In addition, demand may be affected by the educational level or reading interest level of the target community. Therefore, the library must make every effort to determine the potential need for service as a preliminary step for collection development.

In general, the amount of materials provided should be at least at the same level as for the general population. However, it may be necessary in the case of smaller and widely scattered groups, to provide a proportionally higher level in order to establish a minimally effective collection.

Types of formats of materials. Materials should be acquired in a variety of formats, including print, audiovisual, and computer software. Where there is a shortage of materials in one format, the increased provision of circulating materials in another format should be considered as an alternative. Where there is a lack of written materials in a language, libraries should encourage the recording of materials from the oral tradition in appropriate formats.

Libraries should acquire materials to service the diverse needs of the community including children, the physically challenged, and all educational and reading levels.

Multilingual collections should represent a cross section of subjects, literary

6

genres, and time periods. This should specifically include materials by authors from each particular national and linguistic group, published within and without the country of origin. Works of important world literature should be available in other languages in addition to the original language.

In order to provide information and to promote intercultural awareness and understanding, it is desirable that library materials reflecting the interests and experiences of the ethnic groups be available in English.

Libraries should provide language-learning materials to encourage heritage language retention and to provide Americans with an opportunity to learn or review other languages.

Libraries should provide materials to aid in learning English as a second language. English-learning materials oriented toward learners of specific language backgrounds should be available. In addition, English-language learning materials suitable for all language backgrounds should be available.

Libraries should facilitate, encourage, and sponsor the preservation of original materials that relate to the heritage of local ethnic, linguistic, and cultural groups.

Bibliographic access. Libraries should catalog all materials in the original language and script. They should provide subject access both in English and in the original language. Bibliographic information must be transliterated for staff use.

Physical access. Multilingual collections housed separately should be visible and accessible to the community.

Directional signage should be highly visible and in the languages of the major linguistic groups that use the library's multilingual collection.

Library registration forms, overdue notices, and other forms used by the library should be available in targeted languages.

Collection maintenance. Collections should be maintained so that they contain current and relevant materials as well as classic literature.

Out-of-date and worn-out materials should be evaluated, then discarded or offered to community organizations' archives or special collections, or other appropriate groups.

Programs, services, and community relations

Libraries should provide and actively promote multilingual services and provide programming for the various ethnic groups in the community.

Library multilingual services should be provided at the same levels according to the same standards as for the general public.

Cultural diversity. Because the population served comprises various cultures, each specific culture must be considered in the development of programming and services.

The degree of bilingualism and the retention of linguistic cultural identity by particular groups, as well as the level of social integration or assimilation will also be important in determining the level of service to a particular ethnic group. Some members of these groups may wish to be regarded as Americans only, rather than as members of an ethnic group.

Programming and marketing. Social and cultural community activities organized by the library should be directed toward the targeted ethnic, linguistic, and cultural groups. Programs such as concerts of ethnic music, exhibitions, and demonstrations of traditional arts and crafts may be considered appropriate examples.

Programming and publicity should be in the preferred languages of the ethnic groups. Care also should be taken that the means of communication for publicity be appropriate for the sensibilities and expectations of the targeted group.

Libraries should provide facilities, promote, and offer English-as-a-second-language, literacy classes, and programs for English learners.

In addition to programs within the library, libraries and librarians should also participate in the life of the community, by becoming involved with, and initiating local events such as festivals, commemorations, and other cultural activities related to the various ethnic, linguistic, and cultural groups in the area.

Outreach services. Libraries should provide multilingual services and materials to those patrons not able to use the library personally, including the homebound, and those in correctional institutions and hospitals.

Libraries should carry out outreach activities in nonlibrary, but familiar, alternative locations, such as factories, meeting rooms of ethnic organizations, churches, etc.

Information and reference services. Libraries should provide reference and information services in the most commonly used languages. In addition, special effort must be made to provide service to recently arrived immigrant groups.

Libraries should provide the same level of service for interlibrary loan in all languages, by title or subject, as for the English-speaking patrons.

Libraries should provide reference and referral services about multicultural and multilingual local resources.

Libraries should provide bibliographic instruction in appropriate languages as necessary.

Staffing

Library staff working with multilingual patrons should be multilingual in order to provide effective service. In addition, they should possess relevant cultural knowledge to ensure sensitivity to the community.

Libraries should offer continuing education or staff development programs that promote the cultural, ethnic, and linguistic awareness of the staff and enhance their abilities in dealing with ethnically different patrons.

Library staff with expertise in languages and cultures should share their expertise with other staff and other libraries and be recognized for these abilities.

Schools of library science should advertise the need for multicultural and multilingual librarians and actively recruit people of linguistic and ethnic minorities. They should offer courses that deal with the issues involved in serving an ethnically, culturally, and linguistically diverse society.

6

Source: Guidelines for Multilingual Materials Collection and Development and Library Services
(Chicago: ALA Reference and Adult Services Division, 1990)

Native American patrons

KNOW YOUR PATRONS. Know both the general tribal groups to which they belong (e.g., Plains Indians) and something about Indian Nations across the country.

Locate someone who can act as liaison between your library and the patrons you wish to serve.

If you are near a reservation, attempt to make a contact through your liaison with a member of the tribal council. Ask for an opportunity to explain library services.

Never promise anything you cannot deliver.

Ask the tribal council to appoint a consultant whose responsibility would be to advise on types of materials and services the tribe might need.

For Indian people away from their reservations, your first contact might be through an Indian center.

Build your collection to include items on American Indian history and culture.

Be prepared to furnish services of a nontraditional nature; for example, space for classes in arts and crafts, storytelling, cooking, languages, tutoring for high school equivalency exams.

Hire Native Americans.

Remember that it took a long time to alienate Indian people. It will take a long time to regain their trust.

Source: Factors in Serving American Indian Patrons
(Chicago: ALA Subcommittee on Library Service for American Indians)

Martin Luther King, Jr., Day activities

THE BIRTHDAY OF MARTIN LUTHER KING, JR. (January 15, but observed on the third Monday in January) and Black History Month (February) offer special opportunities to become involved with your community.

Your participation will:

- Highlight the key role played by libraries in preserving and sharing the record of African-American history.
- Show librarians as leaders in actively promoting community awareness of this heritage.
- Celebrate diversity and promote appreciation of all people and all cultures.
- Strengthen the library's relationships within a multicultural community.
- Attract new library users through innovative activities for all ages.
- Build partnerships with community organizations and individuals with special talents and knowledge to share
- Focus attention on the principles of racial equality and nonviolent social change taught by Martin Luther King, Jr.

Libraries across the country have offered a vast array of programs to celebrate the Martin Luther King, Jr. holiday and Black History Month. Here's a sampling of activities:

Celebrate

> *"I find, in being black, a thing of beauty; a joy; a strength;*
> *a secret cup of gladness—a native land in neither time nor place*
> *—a native land in every negro face!"*—Ossie Davis

- Host a concert of African-American music. The Chicago Public Library offered a series that combined readings and performances of gospel, blues, and jazz. Or, offer a tribute to a single composer—Scott Joplin, Duke Ellington, and W.C. Handy are only a few possibilities.
- Offer a program for families exploring African and African-American contributions to science, literature, and other aspects of our nation's culture. Set the mood by inviting all who attend to wear something from an African or African-American culture.
- Offer a taste of something special. The Metropolitan Library System in Oklahoma City sponsored a Soul Food Luncheon featuring African-American, Caribbean, and African food. Ask restaurants to donate their specialty. Hold a cooking demonstration.
- Celebrate the creativity of contemporary African Americans. Invite nationally or locally known writers, musicians, and other artists to participate in a series of programs. Famed actor Ossie Davis is among those who have made appearances as part of the St. Louis (Mo.) Public Library's Black

History Month celebration.

- Work with a local school or drama group to commission a short play written and produced by African Americans. Present the play at the library.
- Organize a festival of African and African-American art, crafts, and collectibles. Set up tables where local artists, crafts people, and collectors can demonstrate or display their special interests. Your local art guild, antiques club, or college may be able to assist.

Spread the word

> *"Truth is proper and beautiful in all times and in all places."*
> —Frederick Douglass

- Work with a local TV or radio station to sponsor a "Black History Question of the Day" contest. Award books, videotapes, and recordings featuring African Americans.
- Promote the library as a central clearing house for information on events of interest to the African-American community. Set up a single location to highlight activities. Post notices of lectures, workshops, performances, radio and television programs of special interest.
- Extend a program experience by publishing a booklist. Encourage your audience to explore the library's resources with a listing printed conveniently on the back of a program flyer.
- Work with your local TV or radio station to produce a "read more about it" tag line to follow their Black History Month programs.
- Use visual impact to convey your message. Feature pictures of Dr. King in January library publications. Create bulletin board displays using relevant quotations during February.
- Send a black history fact sheet to local radio disc jockeys for use during Black History Month, compliments of your library.

6

Remember

> *"Know from whence you came. If you know whence you came, there is really no limit to where you can go."*—James Baldwin

- Organize a commemorative program to honor Dr. King's birthday.
- Host an open house and provide an opportunity for local residents to share their experiences in the Civil Rights Movement. These memories may be the beginning of a local oral history project.
- Work with a local genealogical society or archive to present a workshop on "Tracing Your Roots," such as the one sponsored by the L.S. Navarre Branch of the Monroe (Mich.) Public Library.
- Sponsor a community sing-along of traditional hymns and freedom songs used during the Civil Rights Movement. Provide copies of words and music for the audience. The New Orleans Public Library sponsors an annual Gospel festival.
- Offer a trip into the past using slides, photographs, and memorabilia from other eras. "The Black Experience in the West" was the theme for a Black History Month celebration featuring exhibits and programming at the Pikes Peak (Colo.) Library District.

- Stage a tribute to a famous African American. With poetry and music, the Harlem Branch of the New York Public Library sponsored a tribute to Malcolm X.

Share

> *"Education is our passport to the future, for tomorrow belongs to the people who prepare for it today."*—Malcolm X

- Hold a discussion of Dr. King's ideas, such as his philosophy of nonviolence and its significance in confronting contemporary problems. Show films depicting King's life and the history of the Civil Rights Movement.
- Offer a multimedia learning experience.
- The Harlem Renaissance is a rich source of inspiration. Contact your local college or speaker's bureau for a lecturer. Recordings or a performance of the music of the period, documentary films, and selections of readings can introduce the audience to this memorable era.
- Sponsor an African dance workshop. New York Public Library's Harlem Branch invited a dancer to instruct the audience in the dance movements of Africa, Haiti, and Brazil.
- Present a film festival. Feature African-American directors or a theme highlighting the contributions of African Americans. "Artistry in Black," presented by the Boston Public Library, focused on prominent black artists.
- Offer a hands-on exploration of African musical instruments and the American instruments they inspired. The Hamilton Grange Branch of the New York Public Library offered a lecture and live demonstration of African-American drum rhythms.
- Present a lecture/discussion series on African-American literature featuring local scholars or authors. The Flint (Mich.) Public Library received a grant from the Michigan Council for the Humanities for such a program. Or, launch a year-round Black Literature Discussion Group beginning in February.
- Use a special exhibit as the focal point for panel discussions, films, and other programming. "Ethnic Images in Comics and Advertising" was the theme for Black History Month activities offered at the St. Louis Public Library in cooperation with the Anti-Defamation League of B'nai B'rith, the Junior League, and other community groups.

Recognize achievement

> *"Bring me all of your dreams / You dreamers / Bring me all of your / Heart melodies . . ."*—Langston Hughes

- Recognize local citizens who exemplify Dr. King's principles. Involve local civic groups in selecting honorees. Spotlight community heroes.
- Sponsor a contest honoring achievements by African Americans. Essays, short stories, art, and rapping are among the possibilities. Include local schools in your planning and promotion. Donations for prizes can come from local businesses. Hold an awards ceremony featuring readings, performances, or displays of the winning entries. The Ypsilanti (Mich.) District Library compiled a 16-page booklet featuring the winners of a creative writing contest.
- Encourage budding African-American poets by organizing a poetry recital. Send invitations to local writers' workshops, area schools, and colleges.
- Organize a competition among schools. African-American history can be turned into a fun and informative challenge with an interscholastic quiz. Arrange to have the final round of competition broadcast on radio or TV. Contact the Prince George's County (Md.) Memorial Library System for information on its "Black Pursuits" contest.

- Display Coretta Scott King Award-winning books. Sponsored annually by the Social Responsibilities Round Table of the American Library Association (ALA), the award honors outstanding African-American authors and illustrators of children's books.

Special for kids

*"Our children may learn about heroes of the past.
Our task is to make ourselves architects of the future."*—Jomo Kenyatta

- Have an "unbirthday party" honoring a famous African American. Provide cake, ice cream, balloons and party favors, such as photographs or buttons featuring the person being honored. Appropriate songs can be sung, a story told. Have each child read aloud a fact about the honoree.
- Present a special story hour focusing on Dr. King's life and writing.
- Offer performances by folksingers, storytellers, dancers, and theater groups based on African folklore and music.
- Help children visualize the big picture. The Fairmount Heights Branch of Prince George's County Memorial Library System invited children to color in large drawings of people and events in African-American history. The colorful posters were displayed throughout the year. Children at the Newark (N.J.) Public Library created a mural in honor of Dr. King.
- Bring history to life with portrayals of African-American heros. The Beta Gamma Xino sorority provided the performances at a "Positive Images for Black Youth in the 1990s" program at the Kent branch of the Toledo-Lucas County (Ohio) Public Library.

Source: A Time to Celebrate! (Chicago: ALA Public Information Office, 1990)

Library instruction for the print-handicapped

6

by Margaret Currie and Dallas McLean-Howe

ENCOURAGED BY "MAINSTREAMING" in primary and secondary schools and by the establishment of support services at post-secondary institutions, more handicapped students are applying to universities and colleges.

University libraries have responded with a new sensitivity to the special needs of such students. Wheelchair access ramps and elevators have been added, washrooms made easier to use, automatic doors installed. And we, as bibliographic instruction librarians, have modified our classes and tours.

Most difficult of all, however, is the challenge of instructing the print-handicapped. University libraries are print resources. Most of the new technologies, such as online services, CD-ROM databases, and fax document delivery are only new ways of accessing knowledge available in printed form. Voice-activated, computer-controlled equipment is available at a cost prohibitive for most academic libraries at present, although obviously acquisition of such equipment should become a priority wherever possible.

But in general, to be print-handicapped while attending a university is the most serious challenge a student can face. What useful form can bibliographic instruction take for such students?

Working together with Larry Booth, the coordinator for the Toronto-area Pre-University Skills Program of the Canadian National Institute for the Blind (CNIB), our library has arranged several introductory sessions for print-handicapped students. We are ready to make a few suggestions for those librarians who are about to embark on a similar venture.

Library staff

The first recommendation: sensitize your staff. Months before you hold sessions for the print-handicapped, arrange staff sessions. These special students will require extra staff attention. Most library staff are willing to provide this help if they know what form that extra effort should take.

One promising option involves hiring students to assist their handicapped fellows in the library, making the necessary photocopies, fetching books and journals, and reading the results to the print-handicapped student. These helpers could be volunteers, carefully trained by the library staff in the research process, training that would undoubtedly benefit them as well as enabling them to become useful helpers.

For our full-time staff, we arranged a tour of local CNIB facilities, viewing the library, talking to CNIB staff, and seeing some of the equipment available to help the visually impaired. Then, we arranged an in-depth workshop at our library. CNIB staff spent half a day with our staff, fielding their questions and allaying any apprehensions. They also gave us a demonstration of our newly received Visualtek reader and our 8-track tape player, both useful aids for the print-handicapped.

The result? We had so many volunteers that each print-handicapped potential student has a staff helper.

Institutional context

Our second recommendation: coordinate your proposed introductory session with other sections of your college or university, such as labs, student center, and so on. If your institution has a coordinator for handicapped students, you can work through that office and arrange, as we did, for the students to have a tour of other areas. As well as being fun for the students, it helps to place the library in context.

Degree of handicap

Third, before your students arrive for their initial tour, certainly before they arrive as registered students, determine the degree of their handicaps. Some will be able to read print with the assistance of magnifying aids such as a Visualtek reader; some will be able to find their own way around part of your print resources if signs, call numbers, etc., are in large enough letters. Others have fluctuating degrees of handicap (e.g., dyslexia).

Again, a central coordinator for handicapped students would be helpful here. If all else fails, you can, as we were forced to do, ask the students themselves.

Tailor your session to these varying degrees of visual acuity, as well as to the different levels of library and educational experiences, as you would with any group. Such an adjustment is particularly important for this group as print-handicapped students tend to be older than the average undergraduate and some may have recently lost their sight and have considerable previous experience in libraries.

Space needs

A fourth suggestion is that you be aware of the special space needs of such students. Some will have human helpers, some will have guide dogs, and all will need to have clearly defined paths mapped out for them in order for them to travel with ease from one library resource to another.

If possible, the establishment of a special room, set aside for print-handicapped students, placed near the entrance to the library, will minimize transit difficulties. Guide dogs can have their water dishes here, special equipment can be safely stored, and the door can be closed for the quiet needed to tape essays and listen to recorded notes.

An initial valuable aid would be a taped "map" of the library for students to have in their portable tape players.

Introductory session

Try to schedule your session when your library is at its quietest. Seat students and helpers in a quiet room or area and spend 5-10 minutes setting the group at ease. Ask about their college plans. Introduce each staff volunteer, by name and position in the library; student volunteers by year and course plans. All participants should wear name tags in extra-large letters.

The instruction session itself should start with a general discussion of the library and the types of material to be found there, from required readings through to the most advanced research materials; then continue with an overview of the research process usually required for undergraduate courses.

As with any group, carefully question them to find out what they already know about libraries. Expect a number of questions; these students are realistically apprehensive. Prompt such questions if necessary or prod some of the staff volunteers to ask them.

Follow the initial discussion with a tour, using a route checked for hazards and obstacles. With a little imagination, depart from your usual visual approach to the teaching process and give copious, detailed verbal descriptions of those library features that may be unfamiliar to most of the students. (They may not know what a photocopier is, for instance.) Encourage them to participate. They might be invited to feel the weight of a bound journal or run their hands along a shelf of *Psychological Abstracts* and then compare the size of a CD-ROM version. Encourage questions and relate everything possible to courses you know the students might take to complete their degrees.

Assignment

Next, we very much recommend following another standard practice in bibliographic instruction, even though you may at first think it dubious. Give an assignment to be completed in the library. It need not be overly complicated—to find a book on a certain subject or an encyclopedia article—but its successful completion (and your staff or student helpers will ensure that it will be completed successfully) will build confidence, not only for your handicapped students, but for their helpers as well. A final benefit is that an assignment serves to alert you to difficulties you may or may not have anticipated, either in the arrangement of your library or deficiencies in your instruction.

In our case, the assignment was to find a journal article on a certain subject and to make a photocopy. Successful completion required using a periodical index, our list of serial holdings, call numbers, the stacks, and the photocopiers.

Problems arose. Our Visualtek reader was necessarily, but inconveniently, located in the print-handicapped room, away from the indexes and from the stacks. Making their way around our library was difficult for the students due to our crowded conditions. Setbacks normal for any students, such as a particular volume not being on the shelf, or having to select a new topic due to an absence of references, were particularly formidable for these students. We were torn between the advisability of "cooking" the assignment to ensure that everything would run smoothly or leaving things "natural" to give a realistic idea of library research process.

At some point, what the library staff can and cannot do for print-handicapped students should be spelled out. Extra help may involve fetching, photocopying, telephoning, but must never involve usurping the student's right to an education. The research decisions—which information to select or use—should be left to the student. Helpers should not preselect or decide.

If the effort to instruct the print-handicapped in library techniques seems formidable, we can assure you that it is worth it. To see our print-handicapped students now in their second or third year, using the library confidently on a regular basis, knowing that you have been a part of the process that has made it possible, is truly gratifying. No instruction librarian could ask for anything more satisfying and, at the same time, of more service to "equality of opportunity" for all students.

Source: Margaret Currie and Dallas McLean-Howe, "Bibliographic Instruction for the Print-Handicapped," *College & Research Libraries News,* November 1988, pp. 672–74

Library service to the deaf and hard of hearing

THE FOLLOWING REPORT was presented by the ALA Association of Specialized and Cooperative Library Agencies' Standards for Library Service to the Deaf Subcommittee early in 1981 in response to many inquiries about how libraries can and should serve the deaf and hard of hearing. It provides guidance to all types of libraries in the areas of communications, resources, publicity, programs, participation, and staffing.

Deafness affects people of every race, age, and educational background. There are eight general categories of deaf people: oralists, American Sign Language users, users of both American Sign Language and English, deafened adults, minimal language users, hard-of-hearing individuals, hearing impaired elderly, and hearing people with deaf or hard-of-hearing members in the family. Each category includes persons with varying degrees of hearing loss. Some may have additional handicaps, such as blindness. Reading skills and skills in using speech vary from highly gifted to no skills at all. Some deaf people can understand speech and gain information aurally through the use of amplification devices or auditory training.

Libraries must conform to all laws and regulations prohibiting discrimination and mandating the *reasonable* availability of a library's services to handicapped as well as non-handicapped persons. Deaf and hard-of-hearing persons are part of every community served by libraries. The following ideas are intended to help libraries make all of their resources, programs, and services available to these persons.

Communication

1. Communication with deaf persons will take various forms, such as sign language, lip reading, or note writing. The means of communication used should be appropriate to the individual and to the community. All available methods of communication should be used.

2. For many deaf persons, English is a second language and sign language is recognized as their primary means of communication.

3. Communication in the library will be facilitated by:

- directional and informational signs which use the international symbol code as well as English;
- the availability of interpreters at all public programs or classes offered by the library;
- library staff who are trained in communicating with deaf persons.

4. Deaf and hard-of-hearing persons increasingly make use of the telephone by means of telecommunications devices for the deaf (TDD). These devices, commonly called TTYs, allow deaf persons to type out two-way messages on a keyboard. Libraries should utilize TDDs in a variety of ways.

- Libraries should have at least one TDD for the delivery of reference and information and referral services and for access to all regular telephone services offered to patrons.
- Public access TDDs may be made available for use by patrons needing to make calls to other TDDS. In some cases the location of the TDD helps the library provide both reference and public access services.
- Additional TDDs may be required in other locations within the library system in order to adequately serve the deaf and hard-of-hearing population.

5. Auditory aids may be helpful to hard-of-hearing persons. Libraries that offer listening stations for phonograph records, audiocassettes, and other audio formats should take into consideration the need for amplification for hard-of-hearing persons having enough residual hearing to enjoy music or foreign language lessons. Audio equipment, particularly headphones, should be capable of the heavier loads imposed by amplification well above "normal" levels. Amplification for at least one public telephone should be considered.

6. Video is an important format from which deaf persons can obtain information. To receive closed captioned programs, libraries should supplement their television sets with a decoder.

7. Library assembly and meeting rooms should be suitably illuminated for persons using interpreters and for those depending upon lip reading. Meeting rooms may need raised platforms for speakers and interpreters. Circular or semicircular conference tables facilitate communication when interpreters are present.

8. Library facilities should be set up so that they do not present safety hazards to deaf and hard-of-hearing persons. In case of fire or other emergency, library staff should be sure to alert everyone in the building. Visible warning signals such as blinking lights should be considered.

Resources

1. The information needs of deaf persons are much the same as everyone else's. For deaf adults the library collection should provide a broad range of reading interests and a variety of reading materials in different formats.

2. Because the levels of English reading skills vary considerably among deaf and hard-of-hearing persons, the library's collection should include such materials as these:

- high-interest, low-level materials;
- heavily illustrated print materials;
- film and electronic video formats, both captioned and non-captioned;
- and materials developed especially for deaf children and adults.

3. Libraries should collect and display up-to-date information on deafness and hearing impairment, such as medical, legal, and educational materials and the cultural and life experiences of deaf persons and their families. Such collections should include materials for both adults and children.

4. The library's information and referral files should contain a complete and up-to-date file of speakers, agencies, organizations, institutions, and individuals who provide services for deaf persons.

5. Libraries with special services for the deaf should attempt to provide open access to their resources and services for deaf persons residing outside their jurisdictions.

Publicity and programs

1. All programs, services, or classes sponsored by the library should be publicized to deaf and hard-of-hearing persons. Local and state organizations serving the deaf and hard of hearing should be included in the library's promotional efforts.

2. Regular library publications should include information on services for deaf persons. Special publications and the TDD may also be used as promotional tools.

3. TDD numbers should be included on press releases, library stationery, and appropriate announcements.

4. Where library programs are promoted on television, the promotion should be captioned or interpreted for deaf persons.

5. The availability of interpreters' services for library programs should be advertised as part of the regular promotion for such programs. Interpreters should be provided upon request for all programs.

6. Non-narrated films and captioned films should be included as a regular part of the library's film program.

7. Special efforts should be made to make the library's services and programs accessible and available to deaf persons with multiple handicaps.

Participation and staffing

1. The library should recruit representatives of deaf and hard-of-hearing populations for advisory boards, administrative boards, and voluntary groups.

2. Programs and classes about or for deaf persons and deafness should involve the deaf in planning and implementation.

3. Library staff members trained to communicate with the deaf should be available to work with deaf patrons and to coordinate services to them.

4. Through ongoing deaf awareness, libraries should consider the contributions that the deaf can make as employees.

Source: Techniques for Library Service to the Deaf and Hard of Hearing (Chicago: ALA Association of Specialized and Cooperative Library Agencies, 1981)

Disabled students

A SURVEY OF DISABLED STUDENTS who use the Florida State University libraries shows some little-known needs and problems pertaining to library use. For example, wheelchair-bound and other motor-disabled students are concerned about library evacuation procedures during emergencies, and visually and hearing impaired students need bibliographic instruction in various formats, including braille and audiocassettes. Also, students in all disabled groups prefer individual to group instruction.

Marsha D. Broadway and Sharon W. Self report on their survey in the Winter 1986 issue of *Southeastern Librarian*. Based upon data gathered in a questionnaire and 53 personal interviews (22% of the disabled population on campus), the authors recommended ten actions to improve library service to disabled students. Among them: provide double-swinging or automatic doors; formulate evacuation procedures for disabled students and tell the students about them;

modify a number of study tables and carrels on each floor for wheelchair-bound students; appoint a resource librarian to coordinate library services for the disabled; increase the size of library signs and put them at eye level; use in-service training to instruct library staff about types and levels of disabilities and about assisting disabled patrons in a sensitive manner; offer special library orientation tours for visually and hearing impaired students; and offer bibliographic instruction in print and on audio-cassette.

Fifty percent of disabled students participating in the survey gave library staff a favorable rating—only four said staff was unhelpful. Several students said librarians were not sensitive to "invisible" disabilities, and a hearing-impaired student said the staff "made me feel conspicuous by talking loud and in elementary words." Another student suggested that librarians "be on the lookout for disabled students in need and not wait to be asked for assistance."

Source: "Disabled Students," *American Libraries*, May 1987, p. 330

Services to the mentally ill

THE QUALITY OF LIBRARY SERVICES in residential mental health facilities is determined by the interplay of many factors: the facility's clients, staff, budget, collection, physical space, and ease of access.

Service policy. The library director shall develop a written service policy that reflects the clients' interests and needs and describes how the library meets them. It shall also address services to family members, facility staff, and community service providers.

Hours of service. Library staff shall provide services during the hours most convenient to clients, including evening, weekend and holiday hours as well as weekday. There shall be a minimum of 40 hours of service per week. The library shall be open 12 months per year. Adequate staff shall be available to keep the library open during staff vacations, illness, and continuing education activities. Library hours shall be clearly posted in the library and in the living areas.

User services. Library staff shall provide services in the least restrictive environment possible to encourage individual, unstructured use. All services shall be age-appropriate and include, but not be limited to:

• *Library orientation:* information on library services and policies as part of the facility's orientation process. This also includes on-site orientation to the library and its services for new clients, according to individual or group needs; and individual staff or staff groups early in their employment.

• *User guidance:* guidance for individual users in selection and use of materials and equipment. This includes motivating readers, locating appropriate resources, referring users to other sources, and, when appropriate, helping to interpret materials.

• *Reference/information and referral:* the timely response to requests for information, including using resources beyond the library's collection as needed. When appropriate, library staff shall refer the client to a convenient community library or information service when the client is being discharged.

• *Facility program support:* support of other facility programs and activities, including cooperation and consultation with other staff to facilitate their work with clients.

• *Programming:* formal and informal programs for individuals and groups. Programming done in cooperation with departments and outside agencies is encouraged.

6

1. These shall include, but not be limited to, interactive programs that encourage reading, listening, or viewing of library materials or teaching library skills, with a view to the client's reintegration into the community. Programs may include bibliotherapy, creative writing, dramatics, poetry readings, story hours, puppet shows, discussion groups, audiovisual presentations, video production, concerts, listening groups, music or art appreciation, arts and crafts activities, contests and games, guest lecturers, special displays, and field trips.

2. Formal programs shall be governed by the same standards as other education, training, or therapy programs to insure that the goals and objectives of the facility are addressed.

Talking book services. Library staff shall provide a deposit collection of talking books and machines (from the Library of Congress/National Library Service for the Blind and Physically Handicapped) for eligible clients. Services shall include registration of eligible clients for direct service, demonstration of equipment, and promotion of individual and group use.

Outreach services. The library staff shall provide alternative services to persons who are unable to visit the library. Services shall be provided to all regardless of the degree of their disability or their inability to come to the library for any reason. Services shall be comparable to those provided at the library.

Components of outreach services to living areas shall be based on local needs assessment and include activities such as the following:

1. Programming.

2. Material delivery service on a regular basis.

3. Collections in living areas of current library materials, including basic reference sources. These collections shall be rotated frequently.

4. Regular loans of audiovisual equipment and materials.

Services to living areas shall be coordinated with other departments of the facility (for example, nursing services and activity services) but remain the responsibility of the library staff.

Public library access. Library staff shall encourage clients to explore public library resources and services. This may include activities such as providing information about public libraries, taking clients to a public library, involving clients in public library programs, and helping clients acquire the skills needed to make effective use of public libraries.

Promotional activities. The library shall actively publicize its ongoing services and special activities to the entire client and staff populations. Promotional efforts may include use of the facility's newsletter, posters, fliers, banners, video production, lists of new acquisitions, and subject reading lists; pamphlets and bookmarks which give the library location and hours; and bulletin boards, exhibits, and displays.

Source: Standards & Guidelines for Client Library Services in Residential Mental Health Facilities (Chicago: ALA Association of Specialized and Cooperative Library Agencies, 1987)

Service to older adults

THE IMPORTANCE OF LIBRARY SERVICES to meet the particular needs of older adults increases along with this group's numbers. These guidelines, developed by ALA's Library Services to an Aging Population Committee, suggest means whereby librarians can meet those needs.

1. **Exhibit and promote a positive attitude toward the aging process and older adults.**

Actively seek to improve communication skills with people of all ages.

Educate the administrators, librarians, and library staff regarding physiological, psychological, social, and cultural development of people throughout the lifespan.

Participate in continuing education which will enhance skills in working with older adults.

Avoid labeling and look beyond the stereotypes and mythologies of aging.

Exhibit the same level of interest, comfort, and respect with older adults as with any other patrons.

2. **Promote information and resources on aging and its implications** not only to older adults themselves but also to family members, professionals in the field of aging, and other persons interested in the aging process.

Assess the information needs of the older population in order to build a collection that meets the real needs of:

- people interested in understanding the aging process;
- people planning for a change in lifestyle or employment;
- individuals who act as advocates for the aging;
- service providers; and
- younger people learning about the potential for growth over the lifespan.

Assure that library selection and weeding policies lead to the acquisition of current and useful materials that reflect diverse formats and information needs. Collection development should include information on:

- lifelong learning;
- older adults as consumers of aging services;
- behavioral implications;
- cultural, ethnic, economic, and regional differences;
- leisure time activities; and
- issues raised by the rapid aging of our society

Locate sources of appropriate materials including large print books, pamphlets, and audiovisual materials (e.g., talking books, tapes, films, videotapes, etc.) that are available for purchase, for loan, or at no cost.

Survey the existing gerontological resources within the community and make available the materials or information about them.

Organize information on community agencies, activities, and resources for use by older adults and those who work with them.

Provide ready access to an information and referral service which includes current information on:

- human services agencies serving older adults;
- speakers, reviewers, and other resource people available for programming; and
- publications, reports, community population profiles, funding agencies, and other research sources.

Publicize the availability of resources by:

- providing reading lists, advertisements, and exhibits of interest to the publics identified above;
- introducing the materials, demonstrating their use or cosponsoring with other agencies and organizations, discussion series and programs at the library or in the community;
- mailing informative brochures to club presidents, committee chairpersons, interested individuals, and concerned agencies and organizations; and
- attending meetings, giving presentations, and working actively towards community involvement.

3. **Assure services for older adults that reflect cultural, ethnic, and economic differences.**

Become knowledgeable about the cultural, ethnic, and economic composition of the community.

Use this information to purchase materials and arrange service, to train staff, to conduct programs, and to develop and maintain interagency cooperation.

Actively participate with existing agencies to serve the literacy needs of the older population.

4. **Provide library service appropriate to the special needs of all older**

adults, including the minority who are geographically isolated, homebound, institutionalized, or disabled.

Provide trained staff to serve older adults.

Provide special materials such as talking books or large-print books and periodicals.

Provide special equipment such as tape recorders, magnifying devices, page turners, reading machines, etc., to help in the reading process.

Provide personalized library service to meet the special needs of the individual within the institution (i.e., bed-to-bed, etc.) or the home.

Cooperate with the institutional administration in the planning and implementation of library services for the institutionalized.

Provide on-site service to the homebound and institutionalized, with training and transportation provided by the library.

5. **Utilize the potential of older adults (paid or volunteer) as liaisons to reach their peers and as a resource in intergenerational programming.**

Develop and implement well-organized training sessions for the individuals carrying out the library program.

Invite staff (including volunteers) to participate in library staff meetings so that they can be kept current about resources and policies.

Work closely with staff to solicit ideas, ensure a meaningful work experience, and provide as much autonomy as is desirable.

6. **Employ older adults at both professional and support levels** for either general library work or for programs specifically targeted to older adults.

Make certain that older adults are given serious consideration as candidates for either professional or support staff positions as available.

Request volunteer help only when funding is not available for paid positions.

7. **Involve older adults in the planning and design of library services and programs** for the entire community and for older adults in particular.

Identify representative older adults to participate in library planning.

Assure that adequate needs assessment is conducted to represent the needs and interests of the older adults of the community.

Actively plan and implement programming to meet the needs identified.

8. **Promote and develop working relationships** with other agencies and groups connected with the needs of older adults.

Identify agencies, organizations, and groups in the community that are interested in older adults. Confer with agency leadership about ways in which the library can contribute to the achievement of their goals and objectives through:

- providing resources, materials, and services for older adults and for professional and lay workers in the field;
- cooperating in programming, service delivery, and in-service training; and
- involving key persons in cooperative library and interagency planning.

Identify organizations of older adults in the community and involve them in the planning and delivery of services.

Enlist participation of area librarians in developing cooperative collection development, and in developing services, programs, continuing education, and staff training to improve library service to older adults.

Work toward comprehensive cooperative planning for older adults by:

- working with educational institutions to promote lifelong learning opportunities for older adults;
- locating and working with preretirement groups sponsored by business, industry, and other agencies;
- coordinating with other agencies to eliminate unnecessary duplication of services;
- making available a list of community resources for information and referral which would then be available to older adults and the agencies that serve them; and

- asking that professional staff and administration keep abreast of current developments in gerontology and geriatrics regionally and nationally so that informed interagency communication can be facilitated.

9. **Provide programs, services, and information for those preparing for retirement or later-life career alternatives.**

Develop a collection of materials and information on preretirement planning, retirement, and career alternatives, and provide bibliographies on these topics.

Cooperate with other community agencies to provide workshops, programs, and seminars on such topics as preretirement planning, retirement, and career alternatives.

Serve as a clearinghouse for information on retirement, alternate employment, and other career opportunities.

10. **Facilitate library use by older persons through improved library design and access to transportation.**

Make sure that both the collection and meeting rooms are physically accessible to older adults, with special regard for the impaired elderly, by providing as necessary ramps, hand bars, and other design features.

Provide or be knowledgeable about the availability of assistive devices such as audio loops, infrared listening systems, etc.

Provide furniture for use with wheelchairs.

Strategically locate large-print signage, including informational and safety guides.

Inform or assist older adults in securing transportation by utilizing public or volunteer transportation, new or existing van services, or dial-a-ride systems.

Seek and secure funding for any of the above.

11. **Incorporate as part of the library's planning and evaluation process the changing needs of an aging population.**

Conduct periodic needs assessments to determine whether library resources and programs are satisfying the changing needs of older adults.

Use the results of the needs assessments and continuing evaluation of current programs and services to assist with planning.

12. **Aggressively seek sources of funding, and commit a portion of the library budget to programs and services for older adults.**

Use these funds to acquire resources, assign or recruit staff, promote services, conduct staff development, and forge interagency cooperation.

Pursue sources of additional funds in order to provide for special or one-time-only projects.

Source: Guidelines for Library Service to Older Adults
(Chicago: ALA Reference and Adult Services Division, 1987)

Comfort level checklist

EXPRESS, A PUBLICATION OF the Ontario Library Service—Rideau, in Ottawa, offers the following points for assessing the "library comfort level" for older adults in its May 1987 issue. The publication emphasizes that improvements in the environment for older people are improvements for everyone who uses the library.

1. Be sure that ramps are short and only slightly inclined.

2. Doorsills and joints between different areas of the building should be smooth.

3. Floor surfaces should be non-slip.

4. Carpeting needs to be in good condition and firmly tacked down.

5. Handrails should be located in strategic positions, such as along ramps and staircases.

6. Edges of handrails, doorframes, and intersections of wall and floor should

be in contrasting colors for easy identification.

7. Doors, drawers, and mobile equipment should be easy to move and operate.

8. Levers, knobs, latches, and faucets should be easy to turn, move, and operate.

9. Devices that must be grasped or operated should be within easy reach and defined by color and texture.

10. Shelving, signs, and displays should not become obstacles.

11. Program and meeting rooms need bright light.

12. All instructions should be simply worded and clearly visible.

13. Shelving should be easily reached in terms of both height and depth.

14. Seating must be firm, well-padded, and easy to get in and out of.

15. There should be resting stations on staircases.

16. Individual stairsteps should be closed in rather than open at the back and sides.

17. Waiting areas should have restrooms and suitable seating.

Source: "Library Comfort Level Checklist for Serving Older Adults," *American Libraries,* September 1987, p. 690

Serving the impaired elderly

by Nancy Bolin, Sheila Carlson, Elliott Kanner, and Carol Rickert

Libraries provide programming for the impaired elderly in a wide variety of ways in order to meet the broad range of the needs of the individuals and the organizations that serve them.

The ideal program is one that takes into account the self-expressed needs and interests of the individuals involved appropriate to their age and life experience. Consider these examples:

Homebound

• Book discussion groups that link homebound individuals to one another to discuss books and topics of interest. Library service providers get individual permission and exchange participant numbers.

• Program packages which allow homebound persons, their family, neighbors and friends to share a group experience with ensuing discussion. Library staff furnish the audiovisual materials and equipment where needed for the patron, or for others to utilize at an appropriate time.

• Library program participation, when the client's condition and available transportation (e.g., volunteer, handicap van service, etc.) allow for a trip to the library. Coordination of the trip with other agencies is likely to be needed.

• Special interest visits from library volunteers who share a hobby, an interest, a career or a life experience with the homebound person. Related book materials should be sent at the time or shortly thereafter. An oral history project is an example of what can be developed for this shared experience.

Care Facilities (long-term, intermediate, and hospice)

• Discussion groups may include specific book titles, poetry, or topics of interest to provide for reminiscence, for reality orientation, needed information, or pure enjoyment. Books in large or regular print, multiple copy titles, audiovisuals materials, realia, discussion leadership training or facilitation may be provided by a library.

• Audiovisual programs using films, slide, or multi-sensory kits may be provided to facilities or used by staff for interactive programs with participants. In using audiovisual materials for group programs, special attention should be given to the quality of the sound (speakers away from projection equipment, limited overlapping of music and narrative voices) and clarity of the projected image (avoid dissolved or diffused quality of images—crisp and sharp images are easier to see). Follow-up discussion is a must for active involvement of clients!

- Talking Book/Radio Readers Listening Service groups allow three or four clients to share a listening experience as well as discussion with or without formalized leadership.
- Book talks stimulate an interest in reading or remaining in touch with what is current. They can be used as a separate program or as a part of another activity.
- Library programs can be replicated on-site through the use of videotapes of the original programs. Handouts, displays, and refreshments might be duplicated as well.
- Therapy programs may involve library materials and personnel in a structured therapeutic program (i.e., activity, poetry, laugh, reminiscence, current events, death, and dying, validation, et al.). If a program is thus identified by a facility, the library staff involved in presenting the program or selecting materials should be familiar with the objectives of the program, what the therapy entails, and any necessary documentation, reporting, or credentialing involved.

Locating clients

The most essential steps in the delivery of service to the frail or impaired older person may be the initial steps taken in identifying potential clients for library service. To identify clients for homebound and nursing home service, library staff may want to explore a variety of resources:

- Census tracts that give population densities may help in locating community organizations (i.e., churches) that would promote service availability or help in locating clients within a given area.
- State or local agencies responsible for services to the elderly receive as well as make referrals for services.
- Visiting nurses and Meals-on-Wheels organizations may assist in the initial identification of clients as well as in helping, through referral, with the continuity of service should a client be in need of long- or short-term residential care.
- Disability groups, Libraries for the Blind and Physically Handicapped, and groups dealing with the aging children of aging parents may serve as sources for referrals as well as continued publicity.
- Clients, family members, social workers, activity staff, nursing personnel, and direct service providers may be useful referral sources for themselves, their peers, or family of the clients.

Delivering service

Whether homebound, in a care facility, or impaired enough to warrant support in accessing regular library services, the client needs a range of choice in meeting his or her library and information needs. Ideally, service delivery methods should be designed to give the broadest range of choice and accessibility possible.

Homebound
- Personalized home visits by librarians or library volunteers can bring the range of choice and services the library offers into the home.
- Piggy-backed delivery with other services, such as Meals-on-Wheels, allows for the regular delivery of materials. However, a personal link between library staff and clients is necessary for the selection of materials.
- Van or bookmobile service, with portable shelving units or a lift, allows client accessibility to a variety of materials.

• Books by Mail offers the client both a choice of materials as well as delivery to the home.

• Technological access to the library is available where home computers can be used to generate requests or to gather information; TDDs connect the client to the library as well as a broader range of community services; and where programs featuring library resources are available on cable television.

Care facilities

• Bed-to-bed delivery can personalize service and facilitate access to information and resources. Delivery is best when provided by librarians and scheduled at a time when the client is able to participate fully in the process of selection.

• The use of librarian surrogates (i.e., trained facility staff or volunteers) to provide for individual client needs allows for the delivery of the service at a time when the client may be better able to enjoy both the interaction as well as the resources (i.e., talking book service in the evening when there is little ambient or background noise).

• In-house library stations with rotating materials from the library should be staffed by the library, and might with library supervision use trained volunteers or clients to actively meet the needs of residents, including those confined to their beds.

• Vans or bookmobiles with portable shelving units or a lift allow client accessibility to a variety of materials.

Don't forget

• Alternative transportation services may bring the impaired older adult into the library.

• Between visits or service delivery clients should be encouraged to use the phone to call the library to meet their information needs.

• Aids and appliances such as magnifiers and telecaption devices may be loaned as well.

• Library accessibility for those who can come in ramps, automatic doors, doors wide enough for wheelchairs and walkers, accessible fountains and toilets; visible signage, tactile signage, and large-print listings in large print, availability of aids and appliances, and handicapped parking need to be considered if service is to be fully accessible.

Source: 101 Ideas for Serving the Impaired Elderly
(Chicago: ALA Association of Specialized and Cooperative Library Agencies, 1989)

Libraries and the homeless

MANY LIBRARIES PLAY a leadership role in addressing the problem of homelessness in their communities by working in cooperation with other agencies and by providing direct services such as special reading collections in shelters for the homeless, literacy programs, and information and referral services.

At its 1990 Annual Conference, the ALA's 200-member governing Council endorsed a proposed "Poor People's Services" policy, citing an urgent need to respond to the increasing number of poor children, adults, and families in America affected by illiteracy, illness, homelessness, hunger, and discrimination. The policy calls on libraries to assist the poor in participating fully in a democratic society by: 1) encouraging them to use the resources available in America's libraries; and 2) developing new strategies, materials, and services to help meet the special needs of these library users.

Examples of how libraries serve the homeless:

• Pat Woodrum, director of the Tulsa City-County Public Library System, called a meeting with representatives of community service agencies to focus on how to deal with the area's growing problem of homelessness. One year later, the Tulsa Day Center for the Homeless opened. The goal: to provide a haven for the homeless with "a nonjudgmental atmosphere like that found in the library." Funded by private sources, the center is a place where homeless people can find a safe refuge, take a shower, get a change of clothing, enjoy a snack, seek counseling, and get medical attention. The library provides reading materials.

• The Dallas Public Library is part of a similar effort known as Dallas Agencies Serving the Homeless (DASH) and is represented on a citywide task force on the homeless.

• The Multnomah County (Ore.) Public Library in Portland and Milwaukee (Wis.) Public Library received federal grants to create reading rooms in centers for the homeless.

• A new public library in Haverhill, Mass., includes a "community room" specifically designed for an estimated 150 of the town's homeless. It will be furnished with sofas, easy chairs, a television, and a coffee maker. Newspapers, magazines, and paperbacks will be provided, along with information on community social services. According to director Howard Curtis, the library seems to be "one of the few places in the area where the homeless are welcome."

• The San Francisco Public Library recently adopted a policy to provide library cards to the homeless as well as those with permanent addresses. The library provides extensive programming for children, including story hours and films, at city shelters for the homeless. The Free Library of Philadelphia operates a similar program.

• The Special Services and Manhattan branch offices of the New York Public Library operate five projects for the homeless in welfare hotels, motels, and day-care shelters. Services include special reading collections for children and adults, educational and cultural programs, parenting workshops, and volunteer readers who read stories to children.

• The Montgomery County (Md.) Department of Public Libraries issues "shelter cards" listing community services available to the homeless, including where to receive emergency food and shelter, as an aid both for those needing help and those trying to provide it. The cards are distributed at libraries and through fire departments, churches, and social agencies.

• The Cumberland County (N.C.) Public Library in Fayetteville operates an information and referral service, ACCESS, recognized as the central information and referral agency for the county. Many other libraries, including the San Diego Public Libraries and Memphis/Shelby County (Tenn.) Public Library and Information Center, operate referral services with up-to-date data on social service agencies that aid the homeless.

• Many libraries, including the San Francisco and Milwaukee public libraries, sponsor or participate in literacy programs that benefit the homeless.

Source: America's Libraries and the Homeless: An ALA Fact Sheet
(Chicago: ALA Public Information Office, 1991)

6

Services to adult correctional institutions

THE LATTER YEARS of the 1980s saw a tremendous growth in the number of correctional institutions constructed in the United States. With each new facility came the potential for the establishment of library service within the correctional community. The burgeoning rate of incarceration taxed already overcrowded facilities and placed greater demands on library programs. While correctional librarians struggled with the development of programs in these new facilities, the demand for services increased due to inmate population growth. The world of libraries and information science changed rapidly. The information explosion and the inmate population increase in the 1980s made the 1981 library standards document less relevant to current conditions. As a result, librarians working in correctional institutions requested a revision of this document to reflect the new technologies, the changing role of libraries, and the role of the librarian in developing library service in correctional institutions.

The correctional librarian, often a one-person manager in a community otherwise isolated from library and information science, relies heavily on professional association standards as guidance, as model, and as legitimization for program development and service delivery. Likewise, the correctional administrator using professional standards is assisted in planning for the capital investment necessary for service, the staffing requirements of the program, and short and long-term substantiation for budget requests.

[*Editor's Note:* At the time of publication, these standards have not yet been formally approved by either ASCLA or the ALA Standards Committee. Some minor modifications may still be made before they are formally adopted.]

Services

Technical services shall include planned collection management to meet the identifiable needs of users, the standardized organization of resources for the most effective use in the institution, and procedures designed for the maximum circulation of library materials.

The library shall provide resources to reflect the stated inmates' needs based on an annually updated profile of the inmate population. User services shall include:

- Reader services for materials at the appropriate reading level.
- Library orientation and instruction at appropriate levels offered on a regular basis to all inmates.
- Access to other library collections through state and regional library systems, networks, consortia, or other cooperative relationships.
- Advisory service to aid inmates in the meaningful use of library materials.
- Reference and information services to meet the inmates' needs for facts and data.
- Access to special need services (e.g., materials from the National Library Service for the Blind and Physically Handicapped).

The library shall offer programs that provide avariety of activities. These programs may be in accordance with the roles the library has selected.

The library shall regularly promote its programs and services.

Library service to individual inmates shall be restricted only for documented abuses of the library service itself.

The library shall provide services to inmates in limited access status equivalent to those provided the general population.

Library service provided to limited access unit inmates shall include one or more of the following:

- Separate access to the library facility, at least once a week for a minimum of one hour.
- A deposit collection in the unit consisting of at least 100 books or other appropriate library materials, or 2 per inmate in the unit, whichever is greater. This collection shall be changed at least once every month.
- A book cart with at least 100 items. Each inmate shall be able to browse and select at least 2 titles from this cart at least once per week.
- A list of at least 300 current titles of books and other appropriate library materials. Inmates may select from this list at least 2 items per week.

- Deliveries of requested items or suitable substitutes shall be made within seven working days. This list shall be revised at least annually.

Materials for limited access units shall be selected according to the same criteria as materials in the general collection.

Services to inmates in limited access units shall include access to circulating materials in the general collection on request, interlibrary loan, and answers to reference questions. Inmates in limited access units shall have the opportunity to suggest acquisitions and services.

The annual assessment of library and information needs shall include the limited access population(s). The periodic performance audit shall include services to inmates in limited access status.

Library materials

Library materials shall be selected to meet the informational, cultural, educational, vocational, and recreational needs of the inmate population and of the correctional institution.

The library shall have a written collectoin policy statement defining the principles and criteria for selecting and maintaining library materials, whether acquired by purchase or gift. Appended to this policy shall be the *Library Bill of Rights, Resolution on Prisoners Right to Read, Policy on Confidentiality of Library Records, Freedom to Read Statement,* and *Freedom to View.* This policy shall address:

- The ethnic composition, ages, reading levels, and languages of the inmate population.
- The need for materials helpful in preparing inmates for reentry into the community, including information on community resources, job and housing opportunities, educational, and vocational training opportunities.
- The need for reference and other materials supporting programs offered by the institution.
- A process for recommending acquisitions.
- The security requirements of the correctional institution.
- Procedures for handling requests to add or remove materials from the collection.

The materials collection shall include a variety of current print and nonprint formats similar to those found in a public or school library. The collection shall be weeded and enhanced continuously and systematically.

A full-service library shall provide the following materials. Items in heavy demand shall be provided in multiple copies.

Books. A collection of no less than 5,000 titles, selected according to policy, or 15 titles per inmate, whichever is greater.

Magazines. A minimum of 50 titles or one title per 10 inmates, whichever is greater.

Newspapers. Local, state and national newspapers, the number to be decided by the geographical areas of the state and regions most represented by the inmate population.

Audio recordings. A core collection of 100 titles, thereafter one title per 5 inmates, whichever is greater.

Video recordings. A minimum collection of 20 titles or one per 30 inmates, whichever is greater, with access to cooperative video circuits or collections.

Computer software. A representative core collection covering word processing, current business usage, academic learning, and graphic creation programs. Additions shall be chosen reflecting the library role and the interests and needs of the users and the institution.

Source: Library Standards for Adult Correctional Institutions (Draft)
(Chicago: ALA Association of Specialized and Cooperative Library Agencies, 1991)

Prison librarians

IN MID-1988 Mary Jeanne Letters, senior librarian at the Soledad (Calif.) Correctional Training Facility, sent a questionnaire to 156 prison librarians across the nation. Letters received 54 responses; results and comments are excerpted below.

Salaries ranged from $14,000 to $45,000 (earned by a 61-year-old who had been a prison librarian for 15 years).

A 20-year veteran of a Florida prison library wanted to know if anyone had "endured" longer; the answer is "no." The average age of the respondents was 49, and only one was under 30; even so, the average length of service was just 5.5 years.

Only 35 have graduate library degrees, and only 30 have been trained in legal work (none extensively, and some were self-taught).

Collections ranged from 1,150 volumes to 35,000 (nearly 10,000 more than the next largest). Nine respondents had collections of more than 20,000 volumes, and 21 had fewer than 10,000 (average size was 11,466). The legal collections ranged from 41 volumes to 13,754 (average 3,134).

A big surprise was that so many inmates use the library, especially considering their supposedly low education levels. The average usage level is 42% of the prisoners.

The most surprising answers were those concerning security for librarians: 27 librarians have an officer present, 44 have a telephone nearby, 12 have an alarm box, 9 have a whistle, and one has a beeper. Ten of the librarians have no security whatsoever.

Source: "Prison Librarians," *American Libraries*, January 1989, p. 16

PUBLIC RELATIONS 7

National Library Week

by Peggy Barber and Marcia Kuszmaul

AMERICAN LIBRARIANS AND BOOK PUBLISHERS noted an alarming trend in the mid-1950s: people were spending more money for radios, television sets, and musical instruments and less for books. To encourage reading and keep books free and widely available, the American Library Association and the American Book Publishers Council summoned a group of concerned citizens and formed the nonprofit National Book Committee in 1954.

Before long, the committee dreamed up the idea of a National Library Week. The Junior Chamber of Commerce of Youngstown, Ohio, had originated a local observance of library week in 1937, and Jackson, Miss., had successfully celebrated a "Know your library week." California had celebrated several statewide library observances.

The National Book Committee organized America's first National Library Week (NLW), March 16–22, 1958, in cooperation with ALA through local and state committees. The United States and Canada were advised to "Wake Up and Read!" President Dwight D. Eisenhower kicked off the week by a proclamation that called for "the fullest participation" by the people of the U.S. The Advertising Council approved NLW as a public service campaign, and more than 5,000 cities and towns joined in the celebration, setting library records in registration and circulation.

The following year, Canadian libraries and publishers formed the Canadian Library Week Council to celebrate the week simultaneously with the United States. The ALA Council voted to continue observing the library week annually in April.

Since the National Book Committee was formed to promote reading, its NLW campaign slogans often focused on that theme. After the National Book Committee disbanded in 1974, the American Library Association continued the tradition of National Library Week. In 1975, NLW became the framework for a Legislative Day in Washington, D.C., when librarians and trustees personally talk to their legislators about library needs.

As the first truly national program for library promotion, National Library Week gave ALA a leadership role in the previously neglected area of increasing public awareness. Using bold graph-

READ READ READ SUCCEED

NATIONAL LIBRARY WEEK

■ APRIL 14-20, 1991 ■

American Library Association

Kids
WHO
READ
SUCCEED

National Library Week
April 14-20, 1991

American Library Association

ics and messages emphasizing libraries and library services, ALA won two top public relations awards with its 1975 "Information power" campaign. The Public Relations Society of America said, "Libraries no longer looked dull, they looked alive and exciting." Recent themes (see list on next page) have stirred comment and controversy.

In addition to providing theme posters and other materials and ideas for local library celebrations, ALA publicizes National Library Week on network television and radio, national wire services, and in consumer magazines with feature stories and public service announcements.

National Library Week is a tool for getting librarians together to make the most of limited promotion resources. Whether it works depends on how realistically and enthusiastically the tool is put to work. NLW has inspired criticism as well as praise in its 26-year history.

Source: Peggy Barber and Marcia Kuszmaul, "Whither National Library Week—and Why?"
American Libraries, January 1983, p. 28

7

National Library Weeks to 2001

1992, April 5–11
1993, April 18–24
1994, April 17–23
1995, April 9–15
1996, April 14–21

1997, April 13–19
1998, April 19–25
1999, April 11–17
2000, April 9–15
2001, April 1–7

National Library Week themes and slogans

1958 Wake up and read.
1959 Wake up and read.
1960 Open wonderful new worlds . . . wake up and read.
1961 For a richer, fuller, life, read.
1962 Read and watch your world grow.
1963 Read—the fifth freedom, enjoy it.
1964 Reading is the key.
1965 1) Open your mind—read.
2) Know what you're talking about—read.
1966 1) Read—keep growing.
2) Know what you're talking about—read.
1967 1) Explore inner space.
2) Reading is what's happening.
1968 Be all you can be—read.
1969 Be all you can be—read.
1970 Reading is for everybody.
1971 You've got a right to read.
1972 1) Reading makes the world go round.
2) Books bring people together.
1973 1) Get ahead—read.
2) Widen your world.
1974 1) Grow with books.
2) Get it all together.
1975 Information Power.
1976 1) Information Power.
2) At the library? At the library.
1977 Use your library.
1978 Info to go . . . at your library.
1979 The library is filled with success stories.
1980 America's greatest bargain . . . the library.
1981 America, the library has your number.
1982 A word to the wise: library.
1983 Go for it! Use your library.
1984 Knowledge Is *Real* Power.
1985 A Nation of Readers.
1986 Get a head start at The Library.
1987 "Take time to read . . . use your library."
1988 The Card with a Charge . . . Use Your Library.
1989 Ask a Professional. Ask Your Librarian.
1990 Reach for a star—Ask a librarian.
1991 Kids who read succeed/Read, succeed.

Get Answers To All Your Little Questions Too.

Ask A Professional. Ask Your Librarian.

National Library Week
April 9-15, 1989

©1989 American Library Association

National Library Week countdown

August: Get organized

- Brainstorm with key staff. Discuss the national NLW theme, special events, and other promotion ideas. Come up with your own ideas. Come up with your own ideas to suit the needs and interests of your community.
- Outline a year-round plan with goals, target audiences, timeline, budget. Make program assignments.
- Make sure you're on the mailing list to receive ALA's Graphics Catalog, published in the fall. If you ordered ALA posters last year, you'll automatically receive the catalog. If not, see what you've been missing—write ALA Graphics, Public Information Office, for a free catalog.

September: Plan the action

- Meet with the library board and/or Friends. Explain the NLW theme. Present your ideas and invite theirs. Ask for a commitment in time and money.
- Hold a staff meeting. Outline your ideas and invite input. Aim to inspire enthusiasm and a sense of involvement. Explain your purpose, whether it's to increase public awareness of the library and its varied services or raise badly needed funds. Offer a choice of assignments where possible.
- Work with the board to organize an honorary NLW committee. Send letters of invitation to the mayor, newspaper editor, well-known figures whose support will inspire cooperation from others. Make follow-up calls. Committees should be asked to participate in special events.

October: Follow through

- Contact local chapters of NLW Partner organizations. Invite their participation in helping to organize, fund, and promote library activities, especially those of special interest to their members.
- Hold a breakfast meeting to acquaint honorary committee members and representatives with the library and your plans. Encourage suggestions on how they can best support you (also what you can do for them).
- If you plan to invite celebrity participation—local or national—now is the time to write letters inviting their cooperation.

November: Spread the word

- Finalize your calendar of events.
- Outline a publicity plan, with a timeline for contacting all media. Be sure to include newsletters—business, PTA, church, government, Partner, other community organizations.
- Announce your committee and plans. Seek support from local media. Will they create public service announcements? What kind of stories can the library develop for the newspaper?

December: Keep going

- Order posters and other publicity materials from ALA.
- Follow up unanswered letters.
- Monitor staff and volunteer progress. Send holiday greetings, an activity update, and thank you for work performed so far.

January: Full speed ahead

- Get commitments from speakers for NLW events. Collect bios and other background for NLW news releases.
- Keep making those follow-up calls.
- Attend the NLW workshop at ALA's Midwinter Meeting.
- Mail releases and public service ads early to monthly newsletters and other publications with a long lead time.

February: The heat is on

- You should have a day-by-day listing of all your NLW activities. Meet with staff. Who needs help?
- Write out drafts of news releases on NLW events. What are the photo possibilities? What would be good for television?
- Make sure your press lists are current. Start booking—or find out when you need to start trying to make placements on radio or TV talk shows.

March: No turning back

- Do you have all your materials from ALA?
- Finalize your program plans. Send letters of confirmation to speakers, other cosponsors.

April: Showtime!

- Send out releases on NLW. Follow up with phone calls.
- Distribute posters and flyers throughout the community.
- Distribute evaluations at programs.
- Clip all mentions of your activities for your scrapbook and reports.
- Send thank-you letters and/or certificates of appreciation to all involved.

Source: The Card with a Charge (Chicago: ALA Public Information Office, 1988)

Celebrities for NLW

MANY CELEBRITIES have appeared on American Library Association posters advocating reading and literacy. Here is the lineup as of early 1991:

Wally Amos	Harrison Ford	Paddington Bear
Mikhail Baryshnikov	Michael J. Fox	Miss Piggy
Ruben Blades	Gandhi	Pinocchio
David Bowie	Garfield	Ramona
Bugs Bunny	Goldie Hawn	R.E.M.
George Burns	Zora Neal Hurston	Eleanor Roosevelt
The California Raisins	William Hurt	Margaret Sanger
Kirk Cameron	Bo Jackson	The Simpsons
Diahann Carroll	Jughead	Sting
The Cat in the Hat	John F. Kennedy	Isaiah Thomas
Glenn Close	Martin Luther King, Jr.	Denzel Washington
Phil Collins	Pippi Longstocking	Jesse White Tumbling Team
Bill Cosby	Steve Martin	Billy Dee Williams
Curious George	Mickey Mouse	Oprah Winfrey
Frederick Douglass	Bette Midler	Winnie the Pooh
The Flintstones	Paul Newman	Yoda

The U.S. national library symbol

THE NATIONAL LIBRARY SYMBOL
was launched at the 1982 ALA Annual
Conference for use by libraries throughout the United States in promoting
awareness of their services. Originally developed by the Western Maryland
Public Libraries, this symbol was recommended for national use by an ALA
presidential task force.

Its purpose is to increase public awareness of libraries through widespread
use on library directional signs and promotional materials. The symbol was
designed primarily for use on exterior library signs appearing on streets, high-
ways, campuses, and buildings; but it can also be used by individual libraries on
newsletters, posters, booklists, library cards, bookmarks, letterhead, and other
promotional materials.

The impetus for adopting a national library symbol developed from a recommendation of the 1979 White House Conference on Library and Information
Services, which suggested "adopting a library symbol for the Nation" as one way
to increase public awareness.

The ALA task force chose the Western Maryland symbol because it was
designed as part of a total, coordinated sign system and because it met the
following criteria for a good library symbol:

- instantly understood by the average person without supporting text;
- easily reproduced for both large and small applications;
- universally recognized and associated with a library;
- suggestive of the active use of information by library patrons;
- aesthetically pleasing, clear, and simple in design, similar to the graphic
  style of international symbols already in widespread use;
- capable of modification if the nature of libraries should change significantly in the future.

The symbol triggers instant recognition of a library through a graphic representation that people instantly associate with libraries—the book and reader. It
does not attempt to capture the essence of the modern library or represent the
range of its resources. This would be impossible to do in a clean, easily recognized
image. Once the public is cued to the presence of a library by the basic symbol,
additional symbols, signs, and promotional materials can be used to further
educate users about the full range of library resources.

A standard shade of blue (PMS 285) is generally used as the background color
for exterior use of the symbol on directional and building signs.

Source: ALA Public Information Office

7

Library logo in the United Kingdom

As part of a campaign to raise the profile of all libraries in the
United Kingdom, the Library Association launched this
symbol at its London headquarters in 1983.

The blue-and-white symbol, designed by free-lance
graphic designer John Gibbs of Bath, won a national competition organized by the Library Association's Public Libraries
Group and the Society of Industrial Artists and Designers. It
appears on buildings, vehicles, and promotional items including sweatshirts, ties, and herb pots.

Public library trustees and public relations

by Alice Ihrig

THROUGH THE YEARS, the library trustees who differ on their powers, their relations with their directors, their planning processes, and their evaluations of the libraries and directors have been brought together on one principle: "It is the responsibility of the library trustee to relate to the public on behalf of the library."

This function is called, variously, public relations, advocacy, creating public awareness, building community support, fund-raising and, recently, elevating the image and standing of the library in the community. Now a statement on trustee involvement in relating to the many segments of the total public is likely to appear in the long-range plans as a goal, in the building plan as an integral role, and on trustee board agendas for continuing attention.

Trustees have come to accept their special ability to represent community interest; directors see how trustees enhance their activities; staff members look to trustees for their enthusiasm; the community expects its trustees to be affirmative, positive and knowledgeable about the library that so many do know is essential to the community's quality of life.

The library trustee is responsible for providing the best possible library service to the community of which the trustee is the citizen representative. Unless the trustees *relate to the public,* they will have trouble being representatives of the community and its needs for excellent library service.

Relating to the public should be a natural role for trustees, coming as they do as volunteers, usually with many social and civic roots. The library trustee finds a place in the total public relations picture and plans by:

- deliberately **mixing** with many segments and interests in the community;
- **listening** to what people are saying about the library and about the community's needs and aspirations;
- **explaining** the library and its usefulness to individuals, groups, and the political structure;
- **responding** to questions and comments with positive, accurate, and convincing information;
- **working** closely in an organized fashion with the other trustees, the library staff, and support groups (such as the Friends of the Library) for maximum impact and measurable results;
- **being open** to new ideas and suggestions and encouraging comments and questions from all parts of the community;
- **suggesting** areas of library service for discussion and consideration;
- **volunteering** to speak to groups about the library;
- **recognizing** the inadequacies of the library by planning to overcome them with community help;
- **using** the library's many resources so that trustees have information to give;
- **attending** the meetings of other groups in the community to assess attitudes and concerns and to encourage communication;
- **recruiting** members for Friends of the Library and/or for a volunteer corps, if one is in place;
- **participating** in meetings and conferences where trustees learn more about libraries and develop skills in raising the library's status;
- **exploring** the community outlook through appropriate tools, such as surveys, trial programs, and special interest projects;
- **realizing** that library growth and effectiveness are part of a continuous

process requiring ongoing vocal and financial support from many sources;

- **reading** local publications for clues to community activities and changes;
- **organizing** support for the library, its plans, its programs, and its growth; and
- **accepting** the challenge of change and the value of meeting new needs.

The library trustee can say best what library supporters need to hear: "I stand solidly behind good library service, delivered to my community by the best people we can find and in equitable and exciting ways . . . and I am willing to pay for good library service and ask you to help!"

From timid to top-notch

Trustees have to admit that they do have public relations value. Trustees are the premier volunteers to whom a library has access, and that means all the social webs that trustees have in the community. Therefore, one objective for a trustee is to move more rapidly to being seen as a spokesperson for the library, overcoming shyness and timidity to develop visibility.

An excellent example is that of the library trustees who were thrust into raising funds by some economic mishap and found they liked talking about the library, liked urging public participation, and enjoyed speaking up and out. To get money, to become bold, to express ideas and to push for success became a necessity. With success came recognition of their skills from community leaders and then, inevitably, the right to call their efforts lobbying.

Why relate?

The library is indeed an institution that flourishes with use, grows with community needs, and stands out among civic services for its desire to help everyone and its belief that this can be done somehow.

7

Libraries given trustees' attention and using public involvement have always fared better than those that do without promotion. The kinds of relations with the public exhibited by excellent trustee action have paid off: in citizen response to library needs, in funding for buildings and activities, in protection of tax rates, in heavy use and in the kinds of lobbying citizens do when aroused by any threat to a library. But all the good things that have happened as a result of trustee activity may be in danger. A "no more taxes" mentality can creep into community reaction to any plans. A library's long-term love affair with its supporters may dwindle. Failure to continue to act positively for the library can strand the best plans through benign neglect.

Trustees need always to be on the advance side of this question: what should the library be doing to anticipate and meet community needs?

Let public relations by trustees begin with an assessment of needs—not perhaps a formal study but at least a good analysis—and look at needs as perceived by library staff and trustees, assisted by those in the community "in the know." A library board which asks, "How does the community feel about the library and how well is it doing?" is evaluating comfortably and pinpointing problems so that goals and objectives can be set.

A good example of trustee activity in this phase of public relations is that of the library that periodically seeks information through some kind of survey, analyzes the results and assigns attention to those public relations activities bearing on the problem.

- Does the business community know about library services and react favorably?
- Does the community tend to use mostly the traditional services (children, light reading, references, etc.) which it expects from the library?
- Does a select group of community leaders include the library among community assets? Necessities? How?
- Are community groups naturally a part of the library's support? The Friends? The funding body? Municipal or other government? The PTA? The education community?
- Does the library have a publicity plan (using staff or volunteers), and can this impact be traced?

Trustees can make surveys all the time as they carry out public relations responsibilities to:

- talk to people about the library mostly on an informal basis in order to gain knowledge of how people feel about and use the library;
- select targets at which to direct information about the library; (try meeting in depth with media people, approaching service clubs like Rotary and Kiwanis to present programs, asking for slices of time at club meetings.)
- listen to what people say when they know that they are talking to a trustee, especially to one who makes clear that he or she is a public representative working with others to encourage development of a fine public service;
- return to the entire board with important comments that may tickle an idea or reveal a potential problem; and
- adopt goals and objectives for the trustees' public relations activities.

Sample public relations goals for trustees

Here are examples of how public relations goals can be stated.

"Within the next six months, the trustees of this library will meet individually with the following community leaders to present an update of the library."

"Over an eight-month period, the trustees will study how additional publicity can be prepared and circulated, perhaps using volunteers and reaching out to additional media such as church bulletins and organization newsletters."

"Within six months, the trustee board will arrange a meeting with members of the funding body to discuss mutual concerns and begin preparation of the budget."

Public relations goals and objectives should mesh well with those of the library in general. Goals and objectives for specific entry of trustees into the public relations arena should be manageable, and they require careful expansion to achieve objectives. In the samples, the individual library board should state some purposes which will be explicit to the current status of the library and to the desires of the trustee board.

The library's publicity program

Most libraries have a function of "releasing news" to the media. If not, the trustees ought to ask, "Why not?" If all the staff has time to do is a "press release" sent to a moderate list of media, trustees may wish to recommend expansion. Publicity is one area in which volunteers can be helpful, with proper supervision.

Starting with a written general information piece, the program can be expanded by:

- delivering the news release to the print media with suggestions for possible pictures and an offer to make a staff member available for a feature story (watch the rules of exclusives);
- providing releases earlier than the date of the event, following up with stories that add information;
- converting a written release to radio spots or television spots, if those media are available;
- developing short paragraphs that will fit neatly into the corners of a church bulletin or newsletter;
- posting the news release at the library, perhaps with supplementary pictures (for an event, give the status of a poster or display; businesses take posters, too; and young people and volunteers are creative with artwork);
- giving information on the event on a bookmark or a flyer that can be picked up at the library or other locations (some businesses will include a flyer with their bills);
- asking the schools for occasional help in distributing flyers; and
- asking volunteers to take flyers to their meetings and appointments.

Where volunteers are used in public relations activities, they can be consulted for ideas on projects on which they are willing to work. Even one poster planted in a new spot may catch the eye of a new user.

Policy and relations with the public

The decision by trustees to become more deeply involved in relating to the public may not be unanimous and may indeed ruffle a few feathers. Therefore, the board should adopt public relations as a board function as well as part of the staff's services.

But trustees and all others connected with the library must realize that not even the largest libraries stand alone. And they thrive when "library" is heard in the land. When trustees confess their trusteeship, when community leaders state flatly that the library is so important that it deserves more money, when funding bodies proudly appoint their best to work with the library board, when trustees accept the opportunity to advocate for libraries—there is evidence of the importance of spreading the word.

Public relations is, of course, convertible to lobbying, that process by which each of us tries to convince another of a desirable action. Serving as a community representative (that wonderful definition of a library trustee!) lets people speak with authority, ask for help and demand attention. The most powerful lobbying is that done in person, at home, consistently and with the friendly smile that says, "I know what our library needs. You can be the one who gets what we need."

In serving as part of the trustee crew that speaks for the library, board members should express that function in a policy statement, something like: "Trustees of this library accept responsibility for contributing to public knowledge and support for the library by developing relations with the many elements of the public making up the total community. The trustees will speak up for libraries and serve as the community representatives of a library that is responsive to needs and a source of help and a symbol of pride to the community."

Understanding and appreciating a good library are easier when its success depends partly on what trustees are willing to do for the library. Trustees are challenged to feel the responsibility, pick up the continuity, and enjoy the privilege of being a spokesperson for the library.

Motivating trustees

Because even the most enthusiastic staff and library trustees have had periods of only token support, generating more action on the part of all of the library community may be difficult. Trustees may become bored with the problem of "selling" the library when they meet ignorance, rejection, or comments such as:

Celebrating an anniversary

A staff member of the Fraser Valley Regional Library, British Columbia, designed a colorful quilt (opposite page) showing pictures of the branches and communities served by the district library system surrounding the common vista of the Fraser River Valley. Quilted by a local quilter's group, it is now on permanent display at the district library headquarters to commemorate the library's 60th anniversary. The quilt design artwork was also used for anniversary posters and notecards that were sold to the public in boxes of ten cards. Design: Sue Gale. © Fraser Valley Regional Library.

Guide to the panels (clockwise, from upper left):

1. View of Mt. Baker and F.V.R.L. Travelling Library from near headquarters.
2. Chilliwack Library.
3. Fort Langley Library.
4. White Rock Library.
5. View from near Maple Ridge.
6. Langley Library.
7. Clearbrook Library.
8. View near Agassiz.
9. Terry Fox Library, Port Coquitlam.
10. Pitt Meadows Library.
11. M.S.A. Centennial Library, Abbotsford.
12. View near Yarrow.
13. Maple Ridge Library.
14. George Mackie Library, Delta.

Center: View of Fraser River looking toward Mission Bridge from Bradner area.

Source: Charles E. Beard, Patricia H. Latshaw, and Karen Muller, eds., *Solutions to Your Public Relations Challenges* (Chicago: ALA Library Administration and Management Association, 1991)

FRASER VALLEY REGIONAL LIBRARY

7

60th Anniversary Quilt 1930-1990

"The library has enough money. Look at all the books."
"I don't use the library. Haven't for years."
"Who has time to read anymore? I get my information from TV."
"We've always had a nice little library. Why do we need to have more?"
"I can think of better things to do with taxpayers' money."
"Let people buy the books they need."

Trustees might begin by reacting, as they surely will, to the untrue. Every trustee should have an answer for negative comments, for inaccurate information, and for misunderstanding. Talking out the best responses can set trustees on the public relations path to practice "selling" the library. Trustees will motivate each other, accepting assignments to interview difficult people, laying the groundwork for an advisory committee, or planning for visibility. (This works when trustees give speeches, when they are at the library to meet patrons, when board meetings are interesting, and when every scrap of publicity is intended to reach someone.)

Yes, trustees have to care about the library to be effective with the public. Trustees should be able to say, "Our library isn't what it could be, but it's what we have; and we constantly help it to grow. How about some help from you?"

The message

. . . is that the talents of a lot of people are necessary to keep libraries in the limelight, to capture for them the spotlight they deserve, to give libraries the support that they need to do what we know they can do, and to speak to people who are ready for a caring institution in the morass of bureaucracy. The message is to take it to the streets where the people are, where public representatives can be forceful, and where the public library trustee walks tall.

Good politicians know very well that visibility is a requirement for influence, that acquiring a reputation as a library supporter helps the library, that public funds go to those who have made the public aware of needs and options and services. Perhaps a goal of relating to the public as library trustees should be to have someone say, "You're getting to be a real politician." That's a compliment because it means the trustee is getting through!

Source: Alice Ihrig, Public Relations as a Library Trustee's Responsibility: Not New—Just Different (Chicago: ALA American Library Trustee Association, 1990)

Fund-raising by direct mail

by Eileen A. Curtis

THE USE OF DIRECT MAIL to raise funds has proven successful for many organizations. Librarians around the country have used various forms of direct mail to make patrons aware of upcoming elections that will affect funding, to introduce new services, and to raise additional funds.

Direct mail is an approach to fund-raising that must be carefully planned. A successful program is based upon many components, only one of which is the actual letter sent to a prospective donor. The use of direct mail to raise funds should be considered a part of ongoing fund-raising efforts. Dramatic results should not be expected immediately from a mailing, but averaged over a course of at least three years as the donor base expands.

To receive a greater response to your appeal, you must first make prospective donors aware of the reasons for giving to the library over other organizations requesting money. Donors must be informed of the activities of the library and the benefits that people receive before they will consider giving. Any fund-raising campaign should be preceded by publicity on the organization telling why money is being raised. A donor who is informed on the activities of the library is more inclined to give when he or she receives a request through the mail than one who is unaware of the reasons behind the solicitation.

The average age of a donor is declining as more discretionary income is available to younger people. The main source of donations has been from people over the age of forty. These donors usually make larger and more frequent gifts to organizations. The library has a broad base of donors due to the diversified ages of the patrons. Donors can be segmented into groups by age, zip code area, program interest, and/or prior giving level. You may want to ask your library patrons to fill out a brief questionnaire giving basic statistics such as age, marital status, family size, reading interests, frequency of visits, etc. Use this information to develop the materials targeted toward specific groups.

Once the donor group has been identified, you can design your direct mail piece. One basic piece can be developed and then adapted to fit the donor profile.

The four main components of a direct mail piece are:

- the letter requesting the donation;
- the mailing envelope;
- the response card; and
- a brochure about the library.

The letter. The letter seeking a donation must be creative. When writing the letter, keep in mind:

- to whom you are writing;
- what needs or special interests of the donor will be met when giving to the library;
- why the library is requesting money; and
- specifically how the donor can help.

The first two paragraphs of the letter are the most important. In the opening paragraph state who you are and why you are writing. The second paragraph should focus on familiarizing the donor with the organization.

The next paragraph should give some history of the library, what program the funds are being solicited for, and specifically how they will be used.

The fourth paragraph should tell the donors how they can help. Ask for a specific amount and repeat this request several times in the letter. You may wish to give the donor a choice on the level of contribution ($10-$75-$200). Libraries

7

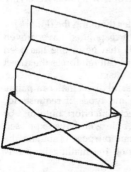

have tested sending two different letters to different groups of donors, one asking for a specific amount and the other with an option on the level of participation. Remember to record the results to determine which received the largest dollar response if you try this method.

The content of any fund-raising letter should be changed as the organization grows and objectives change. The dollar amount requested will also vary depending on the needs of the project or program. Donors want to know that their dollars aided in the completion of projects. Use examples of completed projects in your letter to illustrate how dollars donated in the past helped the library.

The letter should be signed by the director, a board member, or a peer of the donor. Letters sent to business owners would receive a better response if signed by a local businessman who supports library programs. A letter sent to alumni might generate more funds if it were signed by the alumni association president.

After the signature, the donor will most likely read the postscript (P.S.) to a letter. The purpose of the letter should be briefly restated in the P.S. As a test of the effectiveness of your P.S., you may wish to offer an alternative way to donate. Tabulate the responses to this option to determine if the method should be used again.

The mailing envelope. The envelope that contains the request for funds is the first thing the donor will see. It is necessary to make the envelope appear to be a personal letter to ensure that it is not part of the 10% of bulk mail that is thrown away unopened. The envelope should be a standard #10 business envelope. If possible, run the envelope through your library's postage meter using the bulk rate charge. A bulk rate indicia printed on the envelope may be a time saver, but it may also reduce the chances of having the envelope opened.

The response card. While an appeal for funds relies heavily on the text of the letter, the response card provides the donor with the method to designate their gift. Response cards that are printed in a certificate or coupon format aid the donors in feeling that they are giving something special to the library.

The return envelope. A return envelope (postage paid) is a must. When a donor has written the check, it is essential that sending it be as simple as possible. The size of the return envelope should coordinate with the response card.

The brochure. A brochure giving more information on the library is helpful, but not always necessary. If you feel that more background on the fund-raising project is required, then it should be included. The brochure should highlight the services the library performs and supplement the text of the letter.

Mailing lists can be developed, borrowed, and/or bought. Former and present donors, staff, board members, volunteers, and individuals affiliated with the library should be included on the mailing list. The first mailing done by a library may result in a minimum response. The primary purpose of an initial mailing is to build a donor mailing list base. Second and third mailings to the same list of donors may receive a greater response.

Lists of 500 or fewer names can be maintained on 3 x 5 cards in-house. The card may also provide a place to keep a brief donor profile. Lists of more than 500 names are easily managed on a computer. This provides more flexibility in changing addresses, etc.

When mailing your appeal for funds, have one piece sent directly to the library or a staff member who will let you know when it has arrived. Librarians have waited patiently to receive a response to their appeal to find that it was lost in the mail or delivered three weeks later than they had originally anticipated.

January, February, August, and October have proven to be the best months to mail a request for funds. It is beneficial to check with other organizations in your area to make certain that the same targeted group of people will not be receiving requests for funds at the same time.

All gifts should be acknowledged with a signed letter thanking the donors for their support. Telephone calls to donors that have not responded have proven successful in generating more funds. The donor feels that he or she has been singled out and is receiving special attention. The phone call reinforces the direct mail piece and provides the donor with one-on-one contact.

The areas noted are the basics necessary for a successful direct mail campaign. New ideas can be adapted to fit different situations and types of requests for funds. You may receive a few complaints about a direct mail effort, but don't be swayed by a few negative comments. Respond to people who have expressed concern over the mailing with an explanation of your purpose. Tabulate the results of your mailing effort in dollars before judging the mailing by a few negative replies.

How to get ideas for direct mail materials

Get on the mailing lists of other charitable organizations to obtain their mailings requesting funds.

Give $5 to diversified nonprofit organizations to get their response materials and future mailings.

Read books on marketing to gain insights on why people spend money.

Talk to professionals in the direct mail field. Ask their assistance in preparing the piece or to critique your work.

Offer to exchange your materials with librarians from other states. Adapt these ideas to use for your own targeted donor group.

Ask volunteers, family members, etc., to pass along requests for funds that they have received through the mail. Ask them to comment on their reactions to the material; would they consider donating, and if so, why.

Postage rate increases

Before beginning any direct mail effort you should contact the local post office to obtain the necessary bulk rate permits, regulations, and rates. You will also want to keep abreast of any rate increases, as the cost of sending the letter is a major expense for a direct mail fund-raising campaign.

This article has been reprinted with permission from the Michigan Library Consortium's *Development News*. The Consortium is an independent, nonprofit corporation formed in 1974 to promote resource sharing and other cost-effective projects among libraries in Michigan.

Source: Eileen A. Curtis, "Fundraising by Direct Mail," *College & Research Libraries News,* October 1984, pp. 471–73

Creativity, innovation, and risk-taking

by Joanne R. Euster

7

ONE OF THE CRITICAL QUESTIONS in thinking about creativity is how bureaucratic, highly structured organizations—our academic libraries—can encourage creative thinking and innovative behavior. We are tightly bound by policies, manuals of procedure, guidelines, standards, rules and bylaws both in our association and our jobs. Would "ALA Guidelines for Creative Thinking in Libraries" be an oxymoron? Certainly publishers and authors would like us to think otherwise. Books like *A Whack on the Side of the Head, Conceptual Blockbusting, Drawing on the Right Side of the Brain, Writing the Natural Way,* and *Winning at the Innovation Game,* as well as myriad more scholarly books and journals, promise that creativity can be taught and that innovation can be developed systematically.

"Creativity: The Human Resource" was an exhibit presented by the California Academy of Sciences in 1979. The exhibit included ideas, illustrations, mind games, and puzzles. Throughout, it illustrated how creative people do seven things:

- They challenge assumptions by daring to question what most people take as truth.
- They recognize patterns, perceiving significant similarities or differences in ideas, events or physical phenomena.
- They see the commonplace in new ways.
- They make connections between seemingly unrelated ideas.
- They take risks by trying new ways or ideas with no control over the outcome.
- They use chance, by taking advantage of the unexpected.
- They construct networks, forming associations between people for an exchange of ideas, perceptions, questions, and encouragement.

"Most Effective College Presidents are 'Risk Takers'" was the *Chronicle of Higher Education* headline for November 5, 1986, reporting on a Council for Advancement and Support of Education study. "Most effective presidents" were nominated by their colleagues, who were also asked to identify the leadership qualities that made them effective. Effective leaders were found to take more risks and to encourage others to be creative as well, among other qualities.

What is risk-taking, anyway? Words like "pilot project," "experiment," or "test" don't seem so threatening, yet they are really risks broken down into small, manageable pieces. Most of us find the risks involved in big multi-thousand or million dollar systems or projects frightening. Nevertheless, doing nothing is often the biggest risk of all, just as refusing to decide is also making a decision. Breaking down a risk into its component parts, managing it sequentially with frequent evaluations and continue/discontinue checkpoints and calling each step by a less threatening name, such as "trial project," helps to take the threat out of risks and make them more acceptable.

Similarly, if risks are depersonalized they are easier to cope with. Making the risk—the experiment—an organizational activity rather than a personal one takes much of the ego involvement out of the risk. Every experiment, by its very nature, has in it the inherent chance of failure, partial failure, or partial success as well as of success. New ideas and directions often come from failed experiments; however, when the project is managed in such a way that failure of the experiment is not equated with failure of the person.

It is essential for us to foster an atmosphere in which risk-taking and experimentation are encouraged and rewarded—not feared and punished.

Source: Joanne R. Euster, "Creativity, Innovation and Risk-Taking," *College & Research Libraries News,* July/August 1987, pp. 405–6

INNOVATIONS

Design for the "Innovations" column in *College & Research Libraries News* developed by Joanne Euster during her term as ACRL President

Your library's newsletter

by Sylverna Ford

DURING THE SPRING OF 1984, a decision was made to start a newsletter at the University Libraries of Carnegie-Mellon. The first issue of the newsletter was produced in October of that year. For nearly three years the newsletter remained under the editorship of the original editor. In the summer of 1987, I inherited the responsibility for editing *Resources: The CMU Libraries' News*. Editing a newsletter was a new experience for me and I found that I had many questions for which there were no immediate answers.

I spent several days considering the hows and whys of producing the newsletter. Turning to the professional literature for guidance I learned, to my chagrin, that there was not much available. Little has actually been written on producing a library newsletter; certainly the necessary planning process has not been addressed. The articles that have been written are primarily geared to commercially produced, for-profit publications. This dearth of information prompted me to document my own experience. Out of that grew a working guide which in time evolved into the guidelines and specifications for the newsletter of the Carnegie-Mellon University Libraries.

Purpose

Before the first word is printed, it is essential that there be a clear statement of purpose for the publication. Why should the library produce a newsletter? What does the library hope to achieve through the newsletter? In some cases the newsletter may be a public relations document, its sole purpose being to make the library look good. In a large organization with staff spread throughout a very large facility or in different locations, the purpose of the newsletter might be to foster a sense of unity. For a library dependent on outside sources for funding, the purpose of the newsletter might be to appeal to potential donors. It is possible that the newsletter will serve a number of different purposes. It is important that these purposes be considered and decided early in the process; many of your decisions on other factors will be directly affected by the overall purpose of the newsletter.

Audience

The content and style of the newsletter are often determined by the intended audience. If the newsletter is intended only for people within the library, then using library-specific terminology or examples will not be a problem. If on the other hand, this publication will be distributed to people outside of the organization, it will be important to use terminology that will be familiar to a more general group of readers. If the newsletter is to be sent to wealthy community leaders who might become donors, it will be important that it be done in a style that will be pleasing to that group. In many cases, deciding the purpose will also decide the audience at least in part. It is hard to determine what you want the document to do without also considering for whom. It is important however, to consciously identify the audience and to be sure that the stated purpose and the targeted audience are in fact compatible.

Image

As a publication of the organization, the newsletter will represent the library for many readers. Decide what image you want the newsletter to project and keep that image in mind as you make other decisions related to the content, production, and promotion of the document. Though content is the most important factor that will establish the newsletter's image, style and tone are also significant. Determining what your newsletter will do and for whom, will also set many of the parameters of style and tone. You will want your newsletter to assume a style that will fit the expectations of the audience to which it is directed. Whether the style should be formal or informal will depend upon the library's relationship with the primary audience and the image that you hope to project.

Tone too, contributes to the newsletter's image and should be in keeping with the overall goals of the publication and the desired image. Will the tone be light and airy, chatty, friendly, or businesslike? As you decide on the image that the newsletter will project, you will also have to determine whether it is a tool of management that portrays the management opinion on all issues, an employee instrument giving voice to employee concerns, an independent publication providing an open forum for all issues of concern, or an unopinionated source of facts. In order for the newsletter to be effective, it is important that the overall image be appropriate for the organization and the document. The image must also be in keeping with the established purpose of the publication.

Costs

Though a basic newsletter can be produced relatively inexpensively, there are real costs that should be carefully considered before deciding to begin a newsletter. Some costs are immediately evident while others may be hidden and thus may not be considered initially. In making the decision to start a newsletter, it is important to consider all of the cost factors that are involved in the actual production of the publication. Whether or not the newsletter is cost-effective will depend on the expense associated with these factors. Consideration must be given to such factors as the costs of equipment and technical support, writing and editing articles, the layout and design, and finally the production process including the selection of paper and ink and the printing, collating, and distribution of the final product.

For many libraries, the cost of equipment and technical support will be the single largest expense to be considered in the newsletter decision. To be most cost-effective, it is desirable to begin production using equipment that is already in use in the library. Certainly it is still possible to produce a newsletter using letter-quality type and paste-up, and many may choose to take that route. A computer can simplify the production process; however, management may not be willing to purchase desktop publishing software and a laser printer just to produce a newsletter. On the other hand, the widespread availability of desktop publishing software offers options and benefits that could make the acquisition highly desirable. Such software as Aldus PageMaker or Ventura Publisher can greatly facilitate layout and design work; these packages vary in price and capability. Since most libraries already have computer equipment, the decision in this area will be centered around selecting appropriate software or determining how to schedule time on the computer for the production of the newsletter. These factors will in turn be affected by the organization's expectations for and commitment to the newsletter.

The cost of each article is directly tied to the salary level of the person who writes it; the higher the salary, the more expensive the article. For that reason, as well as because of the opportunity for professional development, some libraries will choose to make writing of articles a responsibility for junior staff members. If, however, a higher salaried person is really the only one who has the knowledge or expertise to write the particular piece, it may be more cost-effective to have that person do it than to have someone else spend hours trying to gather the information, even at a lower salary. Whether you solicit articles from the entire staff, designate reporters, assign articles or leave it to the editor, acquiring articles for the newsletter will cost something in staff time. Remember to factor in article cost as you evaluate the factors that will affect the cost of the publication.

Layout and design

The layout and design of your newsletter will have a direct effect on the cost of its production. As you make decisions related to the overall design of the document, keep in mind that you are also making decisions that will affect how much it will cost to produce each issue. You must decide: the size of the pages, the length of the newsletter, the number and width of the columns, the width of the margins, the size of the type, any standard features to be included, how artwork and/or photographs will be handled, whether or not to print the pages back to back. Though it is necessary to maintain some flexibility in the design and layout, it is wise to have a basic plan in place before you begin.

Bimonthly newsletter of the Friends of the Reading-Berks (Pa.) Public Libraries.

Production

Decisions made in the production phase can more than double the cost of the final product. The frequency of publication, the type of paper or ink to be used, the use of color, the printing technique requested, the complexity of collating, and the amount of lead time allowed, can all affect the final cost of the newsletter. Prior to committing to producing a newsletter, it is advisable to meet with prospective printers to get some comparative data on available services and the related costs.

Distribution

Early in the decision-making process you must decide on whom you want the newsletter to reach. It is just as important that you consider how your publication will reach its target audience. The best publication is totally useless if it does not reach the people for whom it is intended. Within the organization, an internal mail system can distribute the newsletter to each employee. An alternative is a multitier distribution in which key people receive bundles of the publication and assume responsibility for distribution to staff. Placing stacks of the newsletter in the staff lounge or cafeteria is another way of getting it to library personnel. If there are regular staff meetings, the newsletter could also be distributed at some point in the meeting.

When the newsletter goes outside of the library, there are a number ways to reach the target audience. While a direct mailing may be the most precise method of distribution it is also the most expensive. If you are working with a long mailing list, first-class postage can become a major expense. You might determine that it is not necessary that the newsletter be mailed first class; a cheaper postal rate will get it to its destination a bit later but often quite a bit cheaper. Though much less precise, you might also choose to identify several places where your targeted readers gather and place copies of the newsletter there. If you want to reach library users, you can do this by placing copies in key locations throughout the library such as near the catalog, by the circulation desk, by the elevator, or in reading rooms. Distribution costs will be determined by the size and location of your audience and the level of precision that you want to achieve in your distribution.

Having determined the cost factors, you must seriously consider whether or not your library can afford such a publication. Keep in mind that the production costs will become an ongoing expense. If the newsletter is to be successful, your library must be willing to pay the necessary costs on a long-term basis. If you decide to publish a newsletter, determine in advance how much you are willing to spend on the publication and for what time period. Establish a newsletter budget and be sure to share that information with the person responsible for producing the newsletter.

Staffing

An integral part of all of the costs related to the production of a newsletter is the staffing. Just as you will pay for the time of the people who write the articles, you will also pay the cost of the production staff. The involvement of every individual in any stage of the production carries a cost, whether it is a fee paid directly to an individual or a part of the salary of someone already on the library payroll. If one of your objectives is to produce a low-cost newsletter, it is important that you pay attention to the expense of the personnel who are involved in producing the publication. Consider the level of expertise and knowledge required for a particular task and try to match that with the qualifications of the personnel. If you are doing a small in-house publication that will be published no more than three times a year, you probably don't need a person with a degree in printing and publishing to get the newsletter done. Determine if you really need to have a high-salaried executive do the job or could part or all of it be done by a lower-salaried assistant. On the other hand, be careful not to understaff as well. Successfully publishing a very large, sophisticated publication will require an individual with particular background and experience. Don't try to produce a major publication if you don't have access to the staff resources and expertise. Keep in mind also, that the startup period is likely to be quite different than the ongoing operation. You might need greater expertise to get the newsletter going than to maintain it. Know what is involved in producing your newsletter and utilize people with the appropriate levels of expertise.

Quality control

Since the newsletter invariably represents the library, it is important that attention be given to the overall quality of the publication. A shabbily done newsletter will not reflect favorably on the organization that publishes it. Be sure that your production process includes definite checkpoints that provide the opportunity for form and content to be scrutinized prior to the final printing. Include a series of proofreadings and reviews that not only check for typographical and grammatical errors but also for accuracy of facts, completeness of articles, consistency of form, coherency and overall appearance. Establish quality standards and make their enforcement a part of the production process.

Forging ahead

If after considering these production and cost factors, you determine that publishing a newsletter is right for you, the next step is to plan your document and develop guidelines for its production. While ideally your production guidelines should be in place before you begin production, often you cannot make a final decision on the guidelines until you have actually tried some of the tasks. If you are starting a new publication, it is best to begin with draft guidelines and test them through the production of a few issues. If your guidelines stand up under the test of actual application, you are then ready to adopt them, to make them official. Once you have adopted your guidelines, remember to share them with those who contribute to the newsletter as well as with the production staff. Keep in mind however, that newsletter production is not a static business; new technologies are constantly changing the field. You should be prepared to modify both your practices and your guidelines as your library changes and as you develop new expertise or acquire new technology.

Guidelines

The guidelines for the production of *Resources* were finally committed to paper during the fall of 1987. Prior to that, production was guided primarily by the memories of those who were involved in the production of the newsletter. As I began to formalize the various practices, it was both necessary and useful to consider each one on its own merit. Rather than adopting a practice because we had always done it that way, I had to determine whether or not we should continue it and if so, I had to decide upon the best way to get the job done. This review allowed me to not only document practice but to evaluate it as well.

Having written guidelines has been a tremendous boon to the production of the CMU Libraries' newsletter. Not only the members of the newsletter committee but also other interested parties including contributors can refer to the guidelines; this clarifies the production process and considerably reduces misunderstandings. It not only guarantees consistency from issue to issue but it also provides a sound basis for decision making as new situations arise. It also means that the next editor will know exactly what was done with previous issues and will have a starting point for her work. The guidelines also provide a basis for evaluating the publication over time.

While it will not be appropriate for every library, the newsletter can be an important part of the overall communications program. If well thought out and properly planned, the library newsletter can be a valued source of useful information and a good public relations tool. If you think this type of publication might have a place in your library, take the time to consider the factors that are involved in producing a newsletter. Evaluate your resources, both human and material. Decide on the level of commitment you are ready to make to this endeavor. Develop a plan for the production, distribution and control of the newsletter; prepare to do a good job.

The benefits of a well-done newsletter cannot be denied; the expense of a poorly done one must also be recognized. If it is not done for the right reason, not directed to the right audience, or not properly presented, the newsletter will simply become another addition to a growing accumulation of worthless paper and an exercise in futility for the staff members who labor over it. Worse yet, a poorly done newsletter will detract from your PR efforts and tarnish the reputation of your library. Before throwing your hat into the arena of newsletter publishers, it is important that you know what you are getting into and be sure that you want to do it. Only after considering the pros and cons can you make a sound decision. If you accept the challenge, good luck and welcome to the world of newsletter publishing!

7

Source: Sylverna Ford, "The Library Newsletter: Is It for You?"
College & Research Libraries News, November 1988, pp. 678–82

What to do if the media call

1. Ask questions. Determine the name of the publication or the network. Find out what the story is about, the reporter's angle, when the deadline is. If you do not feel qualified to address the question or are uncomfortable with the approach, say so. Suggest other angles, other sources of information.

2. Be clear about who you are representing—yourself, your library, or the American Library Association. You may want to check the ALA handbook for a policy statement.

3. Beware of manipulation. Some reporters may ask leading questions, something like, "Would you say . . .," followed by an idea for your agreement. Make your own statement.

4. Think first. Think about the subject, your audience, and what message you want to convey. Do not be pressured into responding. If you need more time, tell the reporter you'll call back.

5. Be prepared to answer the standard "who-what-when-where-how and why" questions. Have supporting facts and examples available.

6. Pause before answering questions to think about what you want to say and the best way to say it.

7. Keep your answers brief, to the point. This is even more important with broadcast media, when you may have only 20 seconds to respond. Too much information can be confusing.

8. Don't be afraid to admit you don't know. "I don't know" is a legitimate answer. Reporters do not want incorrect information. Tell them you'll get the information and call back.

Source: ALA Public Information Office

A special John Cotton Dana Award went to the Pikes Peak Library District for its "Great Pikes Peak Poetry Gathering," a partnership of cowboy poets, merchants, the media, and the library district that increased visibility and generated funds for the district's Western Book Collection

TECHNOLOGY

8

The library technology Hall of Fame

by Nancy Nelson

ALL CONFERENCE SPEAKERS at the Computers in Libraries 1990 Conference and subscribers to *Computers in Libraries* were invited to nominate founding members to CIL's Library Technology Hall of Fame (for induction during the conference general session).

Although we received hundreds of nominees, eight persons were overwhelming choices for the honor. They were, in alphabetical order:

- **Hugh Atkinson,** for the development of an early and significant campuswide automated library system at Ohio State University, which he later transported and extended throughout Illinois.
- **Henrietta Avram,** Library of Congress, for her development of MARC, the universally accepted bibliographic communications format.
- **Carlos Cuadra,** for his initial and continuing role in the development and promulgation of online database systems.
- **Miriam Drake,** for her vision and active participation in the development of the earliest campuswide, library-supported database systems.
- **Frederick Kilgour,** for the development of the Ohio College Library Consortium and its role in the subsequent evolution of library networks.
- **Allan Pratt,** for his vision in founding *Small Computers in Libraries* magazine and serving as its first editor.
- **Frank Rogers,** under whose leadership as director of the National Library of Medicine, MEDLARS was created.
- **Ralph Shaw,** for his seminal work on the earliest modern-day library technologies.

Key events

People help make events, of course, and often the events conspire to shape the course of history. So at the same time that nominees were solicited for the Hall of Fame, suggestions for the Five Key Events in Library Computing History were also invited. The top ten events listed below are ordered by their popularity among participating voters.

1. Establishment of the Ohio College Library Center, which evolved into OCLC and led to the development of rival bibliographic utilities.
2. Development of the MARC record format along with MARC record distribution services from the Library of Congress.
3. Development of personal computers (the Intel 8088-based systems), bringing computing to the staff workstation and patron workstation level. OCLC's own M300 workstation was often included as a critical part of this effort.
4. Development of public online information retrieval services and their subsequent availability via dial access to major network telecommunications systems (DIALOG, BRS).
5. Introduction of CD-ROM services and systems as a format offering inexpensive and universal access to massive databases.
6. Development of more powerful mini- and mainframe computers, extending the availability of library automated systems on the broadest scale.
7. Release of desktop publishing software for the Macintosh and subsequently the IBM PC, bringing print-shop quality into office settings.

8. Adoption of the barcode (UPC) and optical character recognition (OCR) into library circulation systems.
9. Development of mechanical and electronic "unit record" circulation systems based on the punched card in the late 1930s and beyond.
10. Introduction of the print chain for the line printer with upper- and lower-case characters and diacritical marks.

Source: Nancy Nelson, "On the Cutting Edge," *Computers in Libraries,* June 1990, p. 42

Equipment planning checklist

by William W. Sannwald

IS THE FOLLOWING EQUIPMENT and its associated manuals/software planned for use in the library, and if so, is adequate space and electrical equipment available to support it?

1. Large-print typewriter
2. Electric typewriter
3. Shield typewriter
4. Optacon
5. Kurzweil reading machine
6. Talking calculator
7. Cyberbrailler (print and braille at the same time)
8. Book and periodical holders
9. Tape duplicator
10. Speech compressor
11. Thermoform (braille duplicator)
12. Teletypewriter (TTY)
13. Braille writer
14. Magnifier
15. Tape recorders/players
16. Visualtek (or CCTV for enlargement)
17. Talking book equipment
18. Microform reader/printers
19. Microform readers
20. Microcomputers
21. Catalog terminals
22. Record players
23. Compact disk players
24. Video laser disk players
25. Video players/recorders
26. Large-screen television
27. Overhead transparency projectors
28. CD-ROM
29. Fax machines

8

Source: William W. Sannwald, ed., *Checklist of Library Building Design Considerations* (Chicago: ALA Library Administration and Management Association, 1991)

Photocopying without (much) damage

by Anthony J. Amodeo

ONE OF THE PURPOSES of having electronic photocopying machines in libraries is to provide an alternative to those selfish but unfortunately numerous souls, bereft of patience and/or moral fiber, who prefer to take pages rather than notes from library materials. Whatever inroads have been made in the fight against such obvious mutilation, the very real threat of unintentional damage by the very process of photocopying itself continues today, as it has since the introduction of those clumsy machines some three decades ago. Librarians have been aware of this problem for years; witness Richard D. Smith's warning in his article, "The Extension of Book Life" in *The Library Binder*, December 1970: "Although the ubiquitous photocopying machine has proved a boon to library patrons, the past and current generations of these machines have not been designed for copying books . . . [and the] backbones of weakened and embrittled bindings may break or be damaged when they are forced down flat into the position which single sheets naturally assume." Many years have passed, yet the problem remains.

Problems

Photocopying currently involves the turning (often, the slamming) of an open book onto a glass or plastic platen. Whether or not the book leaves get scrunched or creased, the binding is subjected to an abnormal strain. Add to this the extreme pressure often applied to the book's spine by patrons (yes, and staff) to capture the full text from the ever-narrowing gutters (inner margins) of modern book production, and you can see one reason rebinding costs form such a formidable part of library budgets. And rebinding usually narrows the gutter margin even more, produces a tighter binding, and thus assures that the new binding will serve for a relatively short while if the book is copied often.

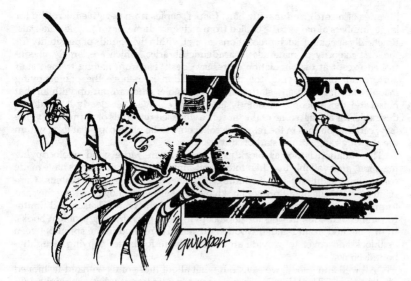

Some damage to photocopied books results from the use of an inappropriate machine. Often copy machines designed for quick single-sheet feeding have various projections to guide the originals, sense the presence of following sheets, and halt moving materials. These "teeth" can really wreak havoc with book paper, especially brittle or oversized paper. Heavy light-blocking covers meant for use with single sheets are often erroneously pressed over bindings. Some machines have mobile platens, which increase the risk of tearing and dropping materials. Even the momentary heat and intense light of some machines contribute to the further deterioration of fragile old paper.

The rapid pace and concomitant carelessness common to both hurried patrons and harried staff are a source of much unnecessary damage. So too is the excessive number of pages copied by the enthusiast in these days of unbridled (copyright law or no) reproduction. The very nature of certain paper formats makes them totally inappropriate for safe copying: sheer size and weight, tightness of binding, deteriorated condition, fragility, cultural or monetary value, or irreplaceability dictate against photocopying some books, maps, or even bound serials. One might declare, "Let them take notes!" yet that art seems to have vanished in one generation; who but a reincarnation of Marie Antoinette would chance such an anachronistic solution in this age of total access and risk a fate hardly less harsh for proposing it?

Solutions

While academic libraries are not exactly rare book libraries, they do contain a goodly percentage of very real research materials of more than passing value. The loss of these materials for any reason diminishes the library and access to research information. Easily identified rare or valuable materials may be pulled into a special collections department or treasure room, but even ordinary government documents collections of a few decades back contain some very desirable and highly priced items.

Special collections librarians and archivists have had to come up with solutions somewhat faster than their colleagues. Such policies as allowing photocopying to be done exclusively by trained staff, cognizant of the boundaries of safe copying methods and able to judge which materials ought not to be photocopied; limiting the number of openings to be copied per "healthy" volume (about 25 in libraries of record); and making hard (paper) copies from negative microfilm for large numbers of pages to be copied from a given volume, or for fragile materials. Practically speaking, such precautions are not within the bounds of possibility for the vast majority of materials in academic libraries, which are largely uncontrolled except at the circulation or reserve desk. Far from having trained staff perform all photocopying, the normal situation is to have the photocopying machines as far from any staff station as possible; who can put up with all that noise and those people constantly asking for change? Yet clearly it would be desirable, for at least some of the most heavily used materials of permanent value (say, certain volumes in the reference collection) to be photocopied at least within the viewing range of the staff on duty.

The situation is not as bleak as it might seem. More good photocopying machines are available than heretofore and some of the manufacturers have made concessions to library use, including machines with edge-flush platens. Consciousness-raising about proper bookhandling has begun, however long the road to professionwide acceptance. Some libraries use the Himmelsbach and Smith-recommended book-dowels for photocopying and microfilming problem books. In this method, round-ended wooden dowels are inserted in the spiral between textblock and cover to provide an even pressure for better copying of tightly-bound books.

"All well and good," we say, "but what about those of us with old-fashioned photocopiers?" The following is an attempt to summarize what you might do if you are restricted to flip-flop copying.

1. Select copy machines carefully. Platens should be level with the machine surface, and stable. No "teeth" should threaten paper. Special issues of *Library Technology Reports* and such publications as the *British Reprographics Quarterly* are good sources for information on photocopy machines and innovations.

2. Always fully support materials being copied. If using a machine which allows for 90°-opening copying, be sure no part of the book is allowed to hang over the edge, or damage may be as great or even greater than with ordinary flat copying; this is especially the case with heavy books and those with weak hinges. Hanging can also damage oversize flat paper.

3. Never allow a book to be flexed over 180°; some books being photocopied resemble birds in flight; sure damage will result.

4. For oversized materials, such as large atlases, maps, oversized, very thick, or heavy books, or books with fragile paper, photocopying at all may be questionable. Paper copies from microfilm (yours or someone else's) may be a solution. If copying must be done the standard way, two persons should perform the copying, preferably one of them a trained staff member. One person supports the item to be copied with both hands, while the other aims the material on the machine, steadies it with one hand, and pushes the print button with the other. If a large book overhangs the machine, or if a folded map bound into a book must be copied, the use of two persons is especially important if tears (pronounce that either way) are to be avoided.

5. Be especially vigilant, whether copying is by patrons or staff, about undue pressure being exerted on materials to "get a good copy." Use signs, posters, and word-of-mouth to educate patrons and staff in this regard. Tightly-bound books are especially liable to be damaged in this way, including bound periodicals which have been guillotined at the spine and oversewn, rather than sewn through the folds.

6. Limit the number of pages that can be copied from any one volume of irreplaceable material, especially books in heavy use. For those in good shape, 50 pages or 25 openings are certainly a reasonable cut-off point. Problematic books might have precautionary slips inserted, asking patrons to have them copied by staff, to copy with care, or not to photocopy at all. Although such controls over circulating collections may be impossible to enforce, their very existence would at least give photocopy zealots pause, and perhaps raise their consciousness.

7. Reference books of permanent value, especially those which are not easily replaced, should where possible be copied by staff rather than patrons, and a copying limit imposed fairly strictly. For materials which have very heavy use (e.g., those articles which faculty have on their reading or reserve lists year after year), having a negative microfilm on hand or a master photocopy from which paper copies can be made might be a good solution.

8. Space should always be available adjacent to photocopy machines for the safe holding of materials which have been copied. This can be in the form of an empty shelf, table or bookcart, preferably with bookends. This receiving area should be policed often, with the materials removed, or left in an orderly condition to encourage users to follow suit. The piling of books on floors or in tall or haphazard stacks should be actively discouraged.

It would be a good idea to include some pointed remarks on proper photocopying, perhaps with a demonstration, in library orientation classes or during bibliographic instruction; proper bookhandling in general would also be an appropriate topic. Such coverage would save the library much in the way of rebinding expenses and books prematurely used up, for it has been shown time and time again that, once convinced of the importance of conservation, patrons do become conscientious about photocopying, shelving, and general handling of library materials.

Source: Anthony J. Amodeo, "Photocopying without (Much) Damage," *Colllege & Research Libraries News*, November 1983, pp. 365, 368–70

Profile sheet: Edge copiers

by Debra McKern

THOUGH COMPILED IN 1989, this summary of equipment suitable for photocopying books and other bound materials was still valid as of 1991. See *Library Technology Reports*, Spring 1989, for more detailed information.

Feature	Xerox 5042	Selectec 1603	Selectec 1707	Océ 1725	Océ 1925
Angle of edge	125°	120°	135°	105°	120°
Monthly copy volume	5,000–25,000	0–20,000	0–40,000	10,000–125,000	10,000–125,000
Power voltage required	115	110	120	110	220
Platen size	17 × 17	11 × 17	11 × 17	8 1/2 × 14	11 × 17
Paper tray capacity	925 (2 trays)	500 (2 trays)	1000 (3 trays)	2200 (2 trays)	2200 (2 trays)
Paper tray sizes	8 1/2 × 11 8 1/2 × 14 11 × 17	8 1/2 × 11 8 1/2 × 14 11 × 17	8 1/2 × 11 8 1/2 × 14 11 × 17	8 1/2 × 11 8 1/2 × 14	8 1/2 × 11 8 1/2 × 14
Copy speed (per minute)	35	21	32	45	45
Warm-up time	4 1/2 min.	2 1/2 min.	3 min.	5 min.	5 min.
Lockable internal parts	✔	✔	✔	✔	✔
Lockable paper trays	available	available w/access device	available w/access device	✔	✔
Toner system	dry ink	dry ink cartridge	dry ink cartridge	dry ink cartridge	dry ink cartridge

8

Feature	Xerox 5042	Selectec 1603	Selectec 1707	Océ 1725	Océ 1925
Lid style	articulated hinges, to 2"	articulated hinges, to 9"	articulated hinges, to 9"	extended hinges, to 4" w/flaps	extended hinges, to 4" w/flaps
Book support shelf	✔	no	no	adjustable	adjustable
Overall dimensions	47" W 29" D 41" H	28 1/8" W 23 5/16" D 15 5/16" H	29 3/4" W 25 9/16" D 22 7/16" H	56" W 28" D 44" H	66" W 30" D 44" H
Overall weight	375 lbs.	162 lbs.	246 lbs.	760 lbs.	900 lbs.
Reduction	fixed; variable to 64%	no	fixed; variable to 64%	no	fixed; 75%/65%
Enlargement	fixed;	no variable to 141%	fixed or variable (non-book only)	no	no
Capable of charging user for reduction or other features	✔	✔	✔	✔	✔
Contrast control	fixed; 3 levels	variable	automatic or variable	variable	variable
Halftone setting for photographs	NA	NA	NA	✔	✔
Ability to accommodate different papers/weights:	16–32 lbs.	16–32 lbs.	16–32 lbs.	16–34 lbs.	16–34 lbs.
• alkaline paper?	✔	✔	✔	✔	✔
• transparencies?	✔	✔	✔	✔	✔
• card stock?	✔	✔	✔	✔	✔
• pre-gummed labels?	✔	✔	✔	✔	✔
Duplex copying	no	no	available	no	no
Margin shift	no	no	no	no	no
Single-sheet bypass	✔	✔	✔	✔	✔
Multicopy capability	✔	✔	✔	✔	✔
Available accessories:					
• accounting controls	✔	✔	✔	✔	✔
• sorter	no	✔	✔	✔	✔
• document feeder	no	no	✔	no	no
• added capacity paper tray	525 sheets	2500 sheets	2500 sheets	no	no
Cost of base copier (list price)	$9,470	$6,995	$8,795	$14,900	$16,900
Access device options:					
• coin	✔	✔	✔	✔	✔
• bill	✔	✔	✔	no	no
• card	✔	✔	✔	✔	✔
Cost of access device (as displayed)	NA	NA	NA	NA	NA
Does the vendor provide a service contract?	✔	Service available through authorized dealers & branches		✔	✔
Available for lease through intermediary?	✔	✔	✔	✔	✔

NA = not available

Source: Debra McKern, 1989

From Moses to megabytes: A short history of online access

MOSES WAS HAVING TROUBLE with his followers' morals. They kept on coveting their neighbors' wives, working on the seventh day, and making graven images, not to mention stealing, committing adultery and killing. He issued guidelines from time to time and introduced sanctions, but they all gave the impression of improvisation. He needed something more authoritative.

So he thought he would go and log on to the ultimate source of wisdom, the Great Online Database (GOD), sometimes also called the Grand Old Datalink. The only terminal within reasonable reach was up a mountain, where it was safer from vandalism and unofficial use. (There was another terminal, made by Bush, which caught fire and came to be remembered as the Burning Bush, but the less said about that the better). Moses was a bit rusty with the procedures, but the system was user-friendly and interactive, and Moses was soon able to say what he needed—a fairly short set of rules. One by one they were displayed on the terminal.

"Oh GOD," keyed in Moses, "I'll never remember all that, and in any case the people will need some proof. Can I have a printout?"

"Regret only form of material available at your terminal as a physical printout medium," replied GOD, "is stone."

"That will have to do," keyed in Moses.

So, with the old-fashioned chisel printers around in those days, the stones were slowly engraved with the Ten Commandments, and Moses struggled slowly down the mountain with them. The people were convinced, and felt more guilty thereafter when they coveted, worked on the seventh day, etc., etc.

The stone printout had the excellent feature of permanence but was very heavy to carry around, and as Moses had to keep moving from one place to another, he began to look around for a lighter substitute. His mind went back to his earliest infancy. The bulrushes wouldn't do, but what about the papyrus nearby? That proved to be just the thing, although the ink tended to run when they crossed the river or whenever the heavens opened. So they built a shrine (this was the first library, though it wasn't called that).

Centuries passed. The terminal on Mount Sinai became obsolete, and in their wanderings and battles the Hebrews forsook GOD—indeed, they lost all knowledge of the system. Various writing materials were tried, but they tended to be fragile like papyrus or expensive like vellum. So the Chinese invented paper. Scrolls proved a nuisance, and separate sheets kept getting out of order, so someone found a way of sewing and sticking them together and called it a CODEX (Collection Of Documents EXtremely handy). Although there wasn't exactly a labor shortage in China (or anywhere else) to produce multiple copies, the Chinese also invented printing and the Europeans went and did the same. Books proliferated. These were for the intellectuals, and to keep a more and more literate public fed with information (and gossip) newspapers were started. Authors grew in number and self-importance, and although they liked to be read they were more concerned just to see their works printed.

The world's forests began to disappear faster than new trees could be planted. Library shelves overflowed. Bibliographies were created to provide more control over the vast and increasing quantities of printed material, and these grew even faster in number and size than the printed material they tried to control. Librarians grew in number and self-importance. Microfilm was invented but served as an additional rather than alternative medium, ideal for totally unreadable material.

Users were in despair. They couldn't keep track of *what* was being produced that they ought to read, let alone find time to read it, and when they wanted something badly they couldn't always get it quickly enough, especially as their libraries failed more and more dismally to keep pace with world output. Abstracts were invented, but these whetted users' appetites still more without really satisfying them, like advertisements for unavailable goods.

Meanwhile computers were invented. They were used to produce bibliographies more quickly and with more up-to-date indexes. These consumed an ever-increasing proportion of library budgets, so that they could afford to buy even less of the literature covered by the bibliographies. So the bibliographies were made available online, which cost so much that the money available to buy literature was still further reduced. Librarians were in despair.

Publishers too were in despair, and started to make their products available online in the hope of building up a second market alongside the failing one for printed literature. Access cost so much that . . .

Alternative media were now competing for the market—various forms of sound and vision, and mixtures of sound and vision. The world was overflowing with information.

Meanwhile, up in the heavens, satellites had begun to reappear (GOD was of course accessed via satellite all those thousands of years ago). Information could be transmitted from almost anywhere instantly (although so far as I know Mount Sinai still hasn't replaced its long-lost terminal). Users were now completely confused with all the quantity, richness and variety of information available, and sought help. What we need, they cried, is a Prophet who will tell us what to access and will access it for us.

The wheel had come full circle.

Editor's Note: This essay, whose author wishes to remain anonymous, has been reprinted with permission from the *UC + R Newsletter*, published by the University, College and Research Section of the (British) Library Association.

Source: "From Moses to Megabytes: A Short History of Online Information Access," *College & Research Libraries News*, December 1983, pp. 425–26

Planning for a system: 10 tips

by Patrick R. Dewey

THE COMPUTERIZATION PROCESS includes a number of distinct steps, from the initial brainstorming sessions to a formal and written plan, and should include input from a variety of people, installation of equipment, and a system for review of ideas and feedback.

1. The plan should outline what is to be computerized, who is to do it, what hardware and software will be used, etc.

2. Set-up. A properly equipped workstation, with lighting, supplies, and quiet, should be made available. Equipment should be set up by someone with experience or by the vendor.

3. Staff training and recruitment. Staff must be trained on the software and hardware, and new staff members must be given training as old staff members leave. These are essential to the health and future life of the project.

4. Liaison with staff. Someone must provide a direct line to the administrator or project manager. Staff must feel that their wishes are important and at least being given a hearing.

5. Volunteers can be useful for certain types of computer work, especially data entry. For instance, some seniors enjoy going through old local newspapers and indexing them, a task that would otherwise require much regular staff time.

6. Backup is a crucial aspect of computing. Work that has not been saved to disk may be lost if power fails. One disk can be easily destroyed or lost. Two disks, stored in separate locations, are safer, and three safer still.

7. Programming software from scratch may also require that changes be made to accommodate new features (or "patches" may be added to solve problems). Not to do either is to invalidate many of the reasons for programming software in the first place.

8. New software (updates and changes). Many projects find that the original software, though initially adequate, may not have been the best selection after all, and then opt for new software. Upgrades are a fact of life, and when offered by the vendor, they should be ordered and installed like new software. (Make sure that the new version is compatible with the old data.)

9. New hardware (change in system or peripherals). "Add-on's" can enhance the memory, speed, or other capability of the computer. A new laser printer can produce letter- and production-quality output. As prices fall on such devices, libraries will want to update hardware configurations to reflect the changing world.

10. Feedback and refinement respond to the need to see how well the entire project is going. If there is a set of objectives, including time frame, production schedules, tasks or systems to be computerized, etc., initial evaluations should not be difficult. Later, after the system is under way, periodic checks will be needed to determine adjustments to maintain or improve it.

8

Source: Patrick R. Dewey, 101 Microcomputer Projects to Do in Your Library (Chicago: ALA, 1990)

Notes from the field

by Patrick R. Dewey

Macintosh computers for public use

Torrance Public Library, California, serves a population of nearly 133,000 with an annual budget of $2.5 million. Holdings include 175,000 book titles and nearly 400,000 total volumes.

The library's public access project featured both an IBM-compatible computer and a Macintosh. Both are in considerable demand, the IBM only slightly more than the Macintosh. There being no budget or staff assigned to the project specifically, everyone shares responsibility for the center as time allows. Use is by appointment. For security reasons, the machine is cabled and locked to the table; the keyboard and the mouse are both kept at the service desk. To use the center, patrons are required to attend an orientation session, during which a librarian explains the rules, the Macintosh and how to insert and use the diskettes, and what other services are available.

To inform patrons on an ongoing basis, the library has prepared an excellent and useful "Microcomputer Center User's Guide and Information Package." Aside from the hardware and software lists, the guide contains the rules for those contemplating such a service. A "User Agreement" also spells out the responsibilities of the users and the terms guarding against potential damage (either to the Macintosh, the software, or to the user's data or diskettes).

A grant through the state originally purchased the Macintosh for adult literacy training purposes. After the two-year grant program expired, one Macintosh was placed out for the general public to use.

Hardware: Originally the library owned a 128K Macintosh. This was finally upgraded to a Macintosh Plus.

Software: A variety of software is now available, though nearly all was given to the center by vendors as complimentary copies, since the center has no budget for acquisitions.

Microcomputer center for adults

The Chester County Library and District Center, Exton, Pa., serves a population of over 300,000, with 16 member libraries.

A genuine effort has been made to attract adults to this center and provide a wide range of services. Users must be 18 years or older, according to the terms of the grant. The center provides use of microcomputers in the building, and also allows users to check out software for home use.

In addition, the Chester County Library plays host to a PC "users group" once a month. Library patrons have a chance to learn about many aspects of microcomputers through this club and its seven special interest groups. There is no cost to use any of the equipment or software, but there is a fee charged for expendables (5 cents per sheet of paper, 3 cents per sheet when using the patron's own paper, and 10 cents per sheet for graphics printing—Print Shop, etc.). Users must bring their own data disks. For persons without prior computer experience, a special orientation program is required, held twice each month. Appointments are not required, but they are recommended.

A general disclaimer for the center reads: "The Chester County Library assumes no responsibility for any damage or loss of data, or any other consequential damage arising out of patron's use of the Library's hardware, software, or related facilities."

Hardware: Five IBM PCs, each with a printer.

Software: Eighty commercial packages, and 500 shareware and public domain programs.

Retrospective conversion on a microcomputer

Jane Beaumont is an independent library systems consultant in Toronto. Information for this project was gathered from several sources, including Jane's notes in the proceedings of the *Small Computers in Libraries* conference.

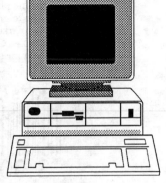

Instead of just telling the story of one library that survived retrospective conversion, it seems better to note what people who are involved with such projects have to say about a system or method for proceeding. Many libraries have now been through *retrospective conversion*—the process of converting a library's old records (usually a card catalog) to a machine-readable format that can be used in an automated circulation system or put to other uses. At a recent conference, Beaumont outlined a number of steps that determined the most efficient way in which to achieve conversion, since the method involved depends heavily upon the finished product's use, e.g., circulation or cataloging, etc. Pertinent questions include:

Will the records conform to the MARC standard or some subset of that standard?

What cataloging standards are to be used—AACR2 or a mix?

What is the approach to authority control?

If a bibliographic utility is the source of records, who owns the records and what are the library's rights in reusing the records it has created?

Once a project has been decided upon, many conversion methods utilize a microcomputer as part of the process at some point. If the conversion takes place in-house, microcomputer involvement may figure in at least one of three ways:

1. using a micro with software such as Cuadra Associates' STAR system to serve as host system when "cataloging copy from a microfiche or hard copy source, editing it as required and then keying the data into the database";

2. accessing the complete MARC database on CD-ROM using a microcomputer as an in-house online source; and

3. using an IBM or M300 to find and process records through a bibliographic utility such as OCLC, UTLAS, and WLN (i.e., using the microcomputer as a simple terminal).

A second method involves the use of a service bureau. In such cases, the service bureau takes the prepared record (done in-house) and then matches it against an established, comprehensive database. In-house staff work involves the generation of a "search key" (ISBN, ISSN, LCCN, etc.) and such other information (brief title, author, publisher, date) as required to ascertain the match. Once correctly matched, the library has a complete record for its database.

A third way to proceed is to have the service bureau do the entire job, working from the library shelflist.

Hardware: IBM or M300.

Source: Patrick R. Dewey, *101 Microcomputer Projects to Do in Your Library* (Chicago: ALA, 1990)

8

How barcodes work

by Michael Schuyler and Elliott Swanson

WE SUSPECT MOST OF YOU have an intuitive idea of how barcodes work. Those black-and-white zebra stripes must be a code for numbers. When a wand rushes across the code, it picks up the changes between light and dark and translates these to numbers. There are many different kinds of barcodes. The Universal Product Code used on a box of Cheerios is fundamentally different from the barcode used in most libraries: Codabar.

Actually, Codabar was once proposed for use as the grocery barcode. It was also proposed for several POS (Point of Sale) applications. Some department stores still use Codabar, but this type of barcode is most often used in non-retail operations. This includes such operations as Federal Express, blood banks, medical operations, and photo finishing envelopes. It also includes most libraries.

Why? We venture to guess it is because CLSI chose Codabar a long time ago. Anyone new on the market used Codabar in hopes of wooing away customers. The vendors even copied CLSI's format of "2" for a patron and "3" for a book. The next four digits stand for the institution, followed by an actual item number and a check digit. This is one of many forms that can be used.

The code

The code for these critters is composed of bars and spaces, in both narrow and wide widths. Each character has four bars and three spaces. The usual numbers 1 to 9 all have one wide bar and one wide space. Some of the other characters such as the plus sign have a slightly different configuration.

In addition to the characters themselves, there are start and stop bits at either end of the barcode. Our barcodes have a small "a" at the beginning and a small "t" at the end. Not only do the bits inform the reader that the beginning or end of the barcode has been scanned, they also allow barcodes to be read from either direction. If a small "t" shows up first, the entire sequence is reversed by the reading program to figure out the actual code.

The start and stop bits are also important because the program you have must be able to read them appropriately. When we first automated, we ordered barcodes directly from our vendor in advance. We placed 25,000 barcodes on our books before our automated circulation system actually walked through the door. The first time we wanded a barcode—it didn't work.

After a few minutes of sheer panic, the programmer on site figured out that the vendor's program expected a different sequence of start and stop bits. He changed the program to accommodate our difference, and suddenly we became a custom site. Other start/stop combinations for Codabar are b/n, c/* and d/e.

When ordering barcodes it is crucial to make sure the vendor understands precisely what you need. We always include a sample barcode, draw an arrow to it, and say, "We want this kind." In addition, we ask for a proof sheet which we run through the scanners to ensure "wandability." This takes a little more time, but spending several thousand dollars on barcodes which won't work is too gut-wrenching a thought to allow otherwise. Since we almost got caught once on this, we are really careful.

The check-digit is the last character in the code. It is mathematically related to all the other characters with a formula. If the rest of the characters are read incorrectly, chances are nine out of ten that the check digit will catch the error. The single-digit mistake will throw the formula off so that the check digit rejects the wanding. Codabar does not require a specific number of characters in the code, therefore the check digit calculation will vary.

Codabar is somewhat complicated because there are 18 different potential width combinations. According to industry sources, this makes Codabar printing equipment more expensive than it would need to be if there were fewer combinations. Nevertheless, the error rate is impressive. Codabar is one of only two barcode types that has independent test data to back up a claim of 1 error in 9.1 million digits read. With data like this, it is fair to say that Codabar works pretty well.

Codabar, like all barcodes, uses a cipher system to represent numbers and a few characters. Unlike some codes capable of the entire ASCII character set, Codabar prints numbers, a few special characters, and a few small letters for start and stop bits: 24 characters (or ciphers) in all. Here they are:

0	10101000111	:	1110101110111
1	10101110001	/	1110111010111
2	10100010111	.	1110111011101
3	11100010101	+	1011101110111
4	10111010001	a	1011100010001
5	11101010001	b	1000100010111
6	10001010111	c	1010001000111
7	10001011101	d	1010001110001
8	10001110101	t	1011100010001
9	11101000101	n	1000100010111
-	10100011101	*	1010001000111
$	10111000101	e	1010001110001

Close scrutiny of these ciphers will reveal there are two different overall patterns. The ciphers on the left are coded in "2/7" and the ciphers on the right are coded in "3/7." A "2/7" code means that two out of the seven discrete elements of the code are wide, either wide bars or wide spaces. Here the wide elements are represented by three bits, either ON (1) or OFF (0). The narrow elements, of course, have only one bit. The number "9" is coded as follows:

1. wide bar
2. narrow space
3. narrow bar
4. wide space
5. narrow bar
6. narrow space
7. narrow bar

Two out of seven elements are wide. This holds throughout the column. The right-hand column is composed of ciphers which are coded in "3/7" which have three wide elements per character. They have 13 bits altogether, contrasted with eleven bits for the 2/7 codes.

There are all kinds of ciphers for barcodes. The UPC set has both left-hand and right-hand ciphers. If a given number appears on the left of the code, it is represented one way; if it appears on the right, a different cipher is used. Code 128 has (surprise) the first 128 ASCII codes.

Check digit in depth

The check digit is the last character cipher before the stop bit in a complete barcode. As stated above, it is mathematically related to the other numbers in the code. Here's how it works with an example from one of our patron barcodes (mine). The barcode sample without the check digit is:

2-9068-00075060

Step 1: Multiply every other digit, starting with the first, by two, then total the digits in any multi-digit product. Sum this series.

Original barcode:

2-9-0-6-8-0-0-0-7-5-0-6-0

Multiply every other digit:

4 0 16 0 14 0 0

Sum multiple digit products:

- - 7 - 5 - -

The resulting series is:

4 0 7 0 5 0 0

Add these numbers together:

$4 + 0 + 7 + 0 + 5 + 0 + 0 = 16$

Step 2: Now sum the digits that were not included in Step 1. Start with the second digit:

Original barcode:

2-9-0-6-8-0-0-0-7-5-0-6-0

Sum every other digit:

$9 + 6 + 0 + 0 + 5 + 6 = 26$

Step 3: Add the results of steps 1 and 2, then subtract the rightmost digit from ten. Voila: Check digit. 26 + 16 = 42. Rightmost digit is 2. Then, 10 - 2 = 8. Eight is the check digit.

The finished barcode is:

2-9068-00075060-8

Source: Michael Schuyler and Elliott Swanson, *The Systems Librarian Guide to Computers* (Westport, Conn.: Meckler, 1991)

I WANT YOU

TO GET YOUR BARCODE TODAY

Choosing CD-ROM products

by John Haar, Juleigh Clark,
Sally Jacobs, and Frank Campbell

DECIDING WHICH CD-ROM products are most appropriate to purchase for a library can be a much more complex process than it may appear. In fact, any purchase decision arrived at too easily may well be one that should be reconsidered. Recognizing the complexities of the task can be the first step in making a sound decision, one that weighs the impact of each CD-ROM product throughout the library. Although the most popular CD packages are reference tools, a thorough evaluation will reveal that their acquisition affects far more than reference service alone.

Most CD-ROM products, particularly those that require annual updates, represent a major investment. A purchase decision means obligating thousands of budget dollars for initial acquisition and assuming yearly commitments of thousands more for renewal charges, which like serial renewals can be expected to increase steadily.

This fiscal implication is all too evident, and its consideration is basic to any purchase decision. But other factors, some involving hidden costs, may be less noticeable in a cursory review. Among them are the provision of hardware and the availability of staff necessary for training and maintenance. Equally worthy of attention is how closely the CD product relates to academic programs the library supports and whether it provides information at an intellectual level consistent with those programs. The best decisions can be made only when all the potential outcomes of any purchase can be identified and fully investigated.

At Virginia Commonwealth University we developed guidelines for CD-ROM selection in the form of questions that selectors must answer in a written proposal requesting funds for a CD purchase. Our intent was to encourage all selectors to ask themselves questions about a proposed purchase that involves the library-wide consequences of a CD's acquisition and use.

The questions range from the philosophical to the practical. Some require selectors to reflect upon whether the library and its patrons are best served by CD tools of a general or highly subject-specific nature. Others necessitate a review of lease terms and long-term costs. Most are not designed to elicit "correct" answers. Rather, their intent is that selectors gather all relevant information and compare the potential advantages and disadvantages of each proposed acquisition. In this way the staff is guided toward recommending a purchase that best addresses the entire library's needs by providing information relative to local programs at an affordable cost and with potential hardware and service demands that the library can meet.

These guidelines should continue to be useful even as the library moves toward loading databases into its online system. Questions pertinent to CD-ROM purchases will also apply to decisions about databases made available through public access terminals.

VCU is an urban university of more than 20,000 students. It includes a major medical school and extensive programs in business, education, the arts, and social work. The checklist that follows was, of course, developed in this context. But it can easily be modified to apply to academic communities of any kind.

CD-ROM selection checklist

Name of product:
Preferred vendor:
Brief description of product:

Acquisition. What is the initial subscription cost of the product?

What, if any, are the costs for current disks and archival disks?

What are the ongoing costs, if any, for regular updates?

Is a discount applied to the cost if the product is already being purchased in a different format (print, microfiche, etc.)?

Is the product available through purchase (i.e., will the data be owned) or lease (i.e., will the data be rented)? For example, if the library cancels the product subscription, will the library keep or have to return the software and data disks?

Is this or similar information available from vendors other than the preferred vendor in electronic or other formats (compact disk, computer tape for a PAC)? What are the vendors, and what are their costs?

If the product is available from more than one vendor, why is the preferred vendor recommended?

Are there licensing requirements—i.e., site or hardware restrictions, limits on access to and use of data?

Can the product be networked?

If the product can be networked, what is the additional cost?

Coverage. What subject area(s) does the product cover?

What is the scope of coverage?

How accurate are the data?

How thorough is the indexing?

Why is the intellectual level of the product appropriate for an academic library?

How will the product fill a curriculum support need?

Is the content suitable for ready reference, basic inquiry, or in-depth research?

Will the product assist us in responding to a demonstrated patron demand for information?

What other sources now available in the library cover this subject? How is the CD-ROM different?

What sources could it replace? What are the cost comparisons?

How frequently is it updated?

How does the content compare with similar products available from other vendors?

Software considerations. Describe the quality of the searching software. (Consider multiple searchable fields; Boolean capability; online thesauri; online help screens; ability to interrupt the search process; variety of display, print, and download options; ability to replicate search strategies after changing disks; truncation; response time; ability to download data.)

Are the searching software's commands and protocols similar to those of the software we presently own?

Is there a commitment by the producer to make software compatible with all years/disks available, including archival disks?

Does the software meet High Sierra Group/NISO standards for the CD-ROM drive?

Why is the product easy for patrons and staff to use?

Hardware considerations. Does the product run on hardware that we presently own?

If the product will not run on hardware that we presently own, what additional hardware is needed and what is its approximate cost?

Will the product's operating system be compatible with those systems already loaded on the same machine?

Based on current demand (online searches and/or referrals to print or microform sources) for the information available in this product, estimate the potential use of the product in terms of half-hour sessions per day or week.

Are the number of workstations currently available sufficient to support the projected use of the product? If not, what additional hardware will be necessary, and what is its approximate cost?

How many compact disks will be received with this product and how many additional disks will be added to the library's permanent collection each year?

Are present disk storage facilities adequate to store disk(s) acquired for this product? (This is particularly relevant to full-text databases.)

Vendor support and documentation. What user documentation is available? Describe its quality.

Is there a toll-free hotline and/or other forms of user support?

Service considerations. What staff is available to provide services for the product (training, loading software, troubleshooting, repair, etc.)?

What impact will the purchase have on online searching costs and staff time?

How will library policies rewarding CD-ROM usage (fees, restricted availability to certain patron tapes, etc.) affect patron access to the product?

This checklist has been used as a guide for compact disk purchase proposals since its inception. Librarians have found the questions helpful in conversations with vendors, both in covering all aspects of a product and in leading the vendor into relating information not in the usual sales promotion. In some cases the questions were divided among a selection committee; thus several librarians could call one company. Often we got all the information we needed, and more. During several conversations with one company's salespeople, we received conflicting replies about whether we would own or lease the product. At the time of this writing negotiations were still in progress.

In another instance, the reference department discussed and tested a product over a period of months and had come to believe that completing the checklist was merely a formality. However, new information came to light in response to the question on compatibility. We were surprised to learn that the software updates were not necessarily compatible with earlier disks. This caused a great deal of discussion, contrasting the strong desire to own the information in compact disk format with the practical problems of using different versions of software for different years of information. After these experiences, we face our future in CD-ROM with enthusiasm tempered by realism.

The process of using this checklist reinforced our initial feeling that it is an essential tool. It has proven to be highly useful in sorting out both the complex issues involved in CD-ROM selection and the variety of claims made by vendors. We would now be reluctant to make a CD-ROM product purchase without it.

Source: John Haar, Juleigh Clark, Sally Jacobs, and Frank Campbell, "Choosing CD-ROM Products," *College & Research Libraries News,* October 1990, pp. 839–41

The Internet

8

THE PROPOSED NATIONAL RESEARCH and Education Network (NREN), a high-speed "information highway" for the United States, is a hot topic with uncertain funding as of mid-1991—but the predecessor and basis for the NREN is alive, healthy and growing. The Internet is an international collaboration, a web of computer networks spanning thirty-five countries, possibly 250,000 computers and between one and three million users. The Internet will evolve toward the NREN; funding and other issues will affect the speed and shape of that evolution.

The basic model for the Internet is that individual host computers (mainframes or workstations) should connect to networks, and that networks should interconnect through gateways or routers. Internet packets or datagrams provide a standard means for packaging chunks (packets) of information with the address to which that information must be sent. Network-specific transport routines encapsulate Internet packets; the gateway "decapsulates" the packets, examines them, determines the appropriate route, and moves them along their way. In this way, each network uses its own transport protocols, but can carry packets that will wind up on very different networks.

The Internet is an offshoot of work done beginning in 1969 for ARPANET, the computer network supporting the Defense Department's Advanced Research Projects Agency (DARPA). In 1973, DARPA began looking at several ways to communicate information packets, including radio and the newly emerging local area networks; they saw the need to interconnect. The first Internet gateways appeared in 1975; the first commercial routers in 1984.

The basic protocol model for the Internet is layered and similar to the Open System Interconnect (OSI), but began five or six years earlier and breaks the OSI network layer into multiple layers: the Internet layer is part of the network layer. TCP/IP has become the generic name for the collection of roughly a hundred different protocols used in the Internet.

The U.S. backbones (or high-speed network links) for the Internet are NSFNet, the Energy Sciences Network and others; ARPANET no longer exists. Those backbones connect a group of mid-level networks such as NYSERNET, NEARNET, BARRNET and PREPNET, each of which connects institutions. The mid-level networks, in turn, connect to thousands of campus networks, business networks, and networks within government laboratories. Interconnections also link the Internet to networks such as UUNET, PSINET, and the Finnish PTT.

It's really not possible to measure the size of the Internet. One estimate is that some 5,000 networks are attached to the Internet. Additionally, 13,000 or more registered Internet addresses represent local networks and potential networks that are not yet connected to the Internet. (For example, every UNIX system includes the facilities that make a registered Internet address appropriate.)

At the National Information Standards Organization (NISO) annual meeting in 1990, Dr. Vinton G. Cerf, Corporation for National Research Initiatives, introduced some of the transport and other protocols that make the Internet work, including the User Datagram Protocol, the Simple Network Management Protocol, and many others. One important aspect of the Internet's growth is the Domain Name System, the link between the alphabetic string that "names" a network and the actual Internet address.

Higher-level protocols include TELNET (a terminal-to-host protocol that allows a user to use a remote computer over the Internet), FTP (file transfer protocol) and the Simple Mail Transfer Protocol.

There's a strong sense of pragmatism within the Internet community. It is not entirely devoted to TCP/IP; in fact, they can now layer OSI transport over TCP, and are carrying out other OSI integration plans. The Internet needs to be a multi-protocol platform for high-speed data transmission.

The Internet approach to standards always begins with experimentation. A proposal becomes a draft, and the draft is reviewed by the community at large and approved by the Internet Activities Board as a signal of acceptance. These documents are called "Requests for Comment" (RFCs). Not all RFCs are standards; many are nothing more than commentary. The Internet community never adopts a standard until the approach has been implemented and thus proved.

Knowbots

Through digital technology, we can now build a system that will accommodate both traditional library use and many other forms of information access. Cerf is fascinated by the problem of getting information databases to yield disparate contents in a uniform manner, and is particularly interested in an active paradigm that he calls the "knowbot."

A knowbot is a piece of software, possibly generated within a user's own computer or through some combination of techniques, that "understands" a request for information. The user launches the knowbot into the Internet and goes on to do other work; the knowbot goes from system to system, locating the desired information and reporting back when it is done. A knowbot may also remain in the system permanently, retrieving "interesting" new chunks of information and passing them along to the user. A knowbot may also replicate itself, spreading multiple agents within the network space to retrieve information more effectively.

The knowbot approach raises some alarms. First, how do you stop the knowbot from over-replication, avoiding the possibility of launching a plague of knowbots? Second, how do you control resource consumption—how do you assure that your innocent query doesn't result in a literal "$64,000 question"? How can limits to research be stated intelligently?

The Internet feeds the drive toward distributed information systems; knowbots and similar techniques can make sense of these distributed systems. Already, more than sixty library systems can be used over the Internet. Cerf sees a tremendous opportunity for experimentation and collaboration in the library field using the Internet, with currently available systems representing a good start.

What goes into the digital library? Anything you can digitize, at a first level. That includes scanned page images, which yield in fixed presentation, one that may be appropriate for some material. It also leads toward compound documents, with more flexible means of presentation. "Documents" can include databases with their own programs, so that users can replicate experiments; they can include images and sound.

We need to establish generalized means of dealing with "knowledge objects." Object-oriented or "objectified" data should be stored as self-controlling documents. A document should control its own use: that is, it should be able to consider the authorization for a request, the nature of the request, any constraints on use, and so on. Some chunks of information will be public domain, but some will not. In a way, the digital library may be the equivalent of a bookstore; users will be buying documents over the Internet.

Some experimental knowbotic systems are already running, such as a "knowbot information service" to search the Internet "white pages" (the Internet equivalent of telephone directories), and a National Library of Medicine experiment to provide access to forty-odd NLM databases. A knowbot interface has also been developed for the Mendelian Inheritance in Man database at Johns Hopkins.

The digital library raises many concerns, including issues of intellectual property; the need for standard access protocols (such as Z39.50); standard object representation; and user interfaces. Experimenters need to achieve a critical mass involving many parties; in the Internet tradition, they intend to experiment before preparing standards. They also need to pursue the infrastructure, the High-Performance Computing Initiative.

NISO may be able to make critical contributions toward the Digital Library. Joint work involving NISO and the Internet research community could be extremely effective.

Source: Information Standards Quarterly, October 1990, pp. 3–6

8

What is the NREN?

by Carol C. Henderson

THE PROPOSED NATIONAL RESEARCH and Education Network (or NREN, pronounced en-ren) is a high-capacity, high-quality computer network which supports a broad set of applications and network services for the research and education community. The NREN will be an expansion and upgrading of the existing interconnected array of mostly scientific research networks, such as the nationwide NSFNET (the backbone) and regional networks such as NYSERNET and SURANET, and local area networks on campuses and elsewhere, known collectively as the Internet. The aim is to reach gigabit-per-second capacity over several years. A gigabit is one billion bits, and a 3 gigabit/second network could move 100,000 typed pages or 1,000 satellite photos every second.

The concept of the NREN originated as a means to connect supercomputer centers and to accommodate the massive amounts of data produced by high-performance computer projects. Reports over the past several years by a number of organizations—the White House Office of Science and Technology Policy and its Federal Coordinating Council for Science, Engineering, and Technology (FCCSET), the National Research Council, the Congressional Office of Technology Assessment, EDUCOM, and others—have shaped the concept and moved it forward.

Supercomputers and supernetworks are needed to address "grand challenges" such as global climate change and the mapping of the human genome, but such advanced computing and communications capacity also makes possible the transmission of unprecedented volumes of other kinds of electronic data and information—from electronic mail to electronic journals to entire digital library collections including audio and visual components. Educational needs are now part of the NREN plan, although it is undecided how wide the range of users and institutions will be. However, the ability of a researcher to connect to computerized tools is becoming a necessity for scholars in all fields, students at all levels, and information seekers—wherever they are located.

Administration plan

Development of the NREN is part of a Presidential initiative described in a 1991 report from the Office of Science and Technology Policy (OSTP), "Grand Challenges: High-Performance Computing and Communications." This multiagency initiative calls for $638 million in President Bush's FY 1992 budget, an increase of about 30% over similar activities in FY 1991. These funds would support activities in four program areas: high-performance computing systems, advanced software technology and algorithms, the NREN, and basic research and human resources. The OSTP report calls the FY 1992 network under this plan the "Interagency Interim NREN."

Legislation

Legislation to establish the NREN was first introduced by Sen. Albert Gore Jr. (D-Tenn.) in 1988. He introduced the bill again in the 101st Congress, and a revised version of S.1067 passed the Senate in October 1990, but the House did not act on HR 3131, the companion bill.

Sen. Gore again introduced legislation in 1991 (S. 272, the High-Performance Computing Act of 1991) on which his Science, Technology, and Space Subcommittee held a hearing on March 5. A revised version of S. 272 was approved by the parent Commerce, Science, and Transportation Committee on March 19, 1991.

A companion bill (HR 656) was introduced by Rep. George Brown (D-Calif.), Chairman of the Science, Space, and Technology Committee. Two subcommittees held a hearing March 7, 1991, on HR 656. Rep. Rick Boucher (D-Va.) presided as Chairman of the Science Subcommittee at the hearing cosponsored by the Technology and Competitiveness Subcommittee, chaired by Rep. Tim Valentine (D-N.C.). HR 656.

A third bill is also pending (as of April 1991). S. 343, the Department of Energy High-Performance Computing Act of 1991, introduced by Sen. J. Bennett Johnston (D-La.), Chairman of the Energy and Natural Resources Committee, would have the Energy Department establish a Federal High-Performance Computer Network to serve many of the same purposes envisioned for the NREN.

Provisions of the bills

S. 272 and HR 656 assign a lead role to FCCSET, which is to develop a National High-Performance Computing Plan involving multiagency collaboration. The long list of agencies includes the Library of Congress, the National Agricultural Library, the National Library of Medicine, and the Department of Education. The National Science Foundation is designated as the lead agency to coordinate NREN development among the various agencies.

In the Committee-approved version of S. 272, the NREN is to link research and educational institutions, government, and industry in every state. Federal agencies are to work with state and local agencies, libraries, educational institutions and organizations, and private network service providers in order to ensure that researchers, educators, and students have access to the network. Within the federal government, NSF is to have primary responsibility for connecting colleges, universities, and libraries to the network. To the extent practicable, the network is to provide access to electronic information resources maintained by libraries, research facilities, publishers, and affiliated organizations.

The bills call for various agency activities and/or FCCSET reports to address such issues as standards to provide interoperability, common user interfaces, network security and user privacy, protection of copyrights, pricing policies, and plans for eventual commercialization of the network.

Library interest

The Senate bill includes some improvements suggested by the American Library Association and the Association of Research Libraries in testimony and recommended amendments, as well as some elements suggested by a Partnership for the NREN (20 education, library, and computing organizations, including ALA, ARL, the American Association of Law Libraries, the Chief Officers of State Library Agencies, the Coalition for Networked Information, EDUCOM, and the Special Libraries Association).

These improvements include the idea of NREN connections to all 50 states, additional references to education as a whole and to libraries, collaboration with potential users, the possibility of using the network as a dissemination vehicle for federal databases and information, and specifying library and information science in research, education, and training components.

S. 272 and HR 656 call for development of a mechanism to coordinate and manage the network, but are not very specific about the governance structure. This is probably the most important unresolved issue as far as Partnership for the NREN organizations are concerned. Also of concern to library and education organizations is the issue of how S. 272 and S. 343 may be reconciled, particularly with regard to governance issues and the ability of the network to serve education, broadly defined.

EDUCOM estimates that federal funding of the current Internet amounts to only about 10% of the total investment, with the remainder coming from universities, states, and industry. The bills should provide more explicitly for a governance structure with balanced participation by users of the network (including government, the private sector, educational institutions, and libraries) in establishing policy and in developing standards. Among all the reports and studies should be one on progress in connecting the broad education and library communities to the network, and on possible mechanisms for ensuring long-term, low-cost communications for educational institutions and libraries.

The American Library Association has endorsed the concept of a National Research and Education Network with library participation for the following reasons listed in ALA testimony in March 1991 on S. 272 and HR 656:

8

- The NREN has the potential to revolutionize the conduct of research, education, and information transfer.
- Current Internet users want library-like services, and libraries have responded with everything from online catalogs to electronic journals.
- Libraries provide access points for users without an institutional fee.
- With libraries and their networks, the support structure to make good use of the NREN already exists.
- NREN development should build on existing federal investments in the sharing of library and information resources and the dissemination of government information.
- The NREN's higher capacity will enable the sharing of full-text and nontextual library and archival resources.
- Libraries provide a useful laboratory for exploration of what services and what user interfaces might stimulate a mass marketplace.
- Public, school, and college libraries are appropriate institutions to bridge the growing gap between the information poor and the information rich.

Libraries of all types linked to the NREN would enhance the national investment in the network, spread its benefits more widely, and increase access to the resources available over it through an institution already established to assist users with information needs.

Source: Carol C. Henderson, *National Research and Education Network Fact Sheet* (Washington, D.C.: ALA Washington Office, April 1991)

A network glossary

by R. Bruce Miller

ADVANCED RESEARCH PROJECTS AGENCY (ARPA) An agency of the Department of Defense.

ALANET Electronic mail system provided by the American Library Association.

American Library Association (ALA) An organization to provide leadership for the development, promotion, and improvement of library and information services and the profession of librarianship in order to enhance learning and ensure access to information for all.

AppleLink An electronic mail, databank, and bulletin board system for use by employees, dealers, customers, and consultants of Apple Computer, Inc.

ARPA Advanced Research Projects Agency (old name for DARPA).

ARPANET A wide area network that began as an experiment to connect hosts and terminal servers together; the first packet network on the Internet.

Asian Shared Information & Access (ASIA) Commercial venture to provide machine-readable catalog records for Asian-language materials.

Association of Research Libraries (ARL) A group of more than 100 university, public, private, and national research libraries working together to strengthen research library resources and services.

BARRNet Bay Area Regional Research Network; a mid-level component of NSFNET.

BITNET Because It's Time Network; a network connecting academic and research organizations; run by EDUCOM.

CAUSE (non-acronym) An association for the management of information technology in higher education.

CAVIX An electronic bulletin board devoted to teachers in the vocational education field.

CLSA California Library Services Act.

Coalition for Networked Information (CNI) Formed by the Association of Research Libraries, EDUCOM, and CAUSE to promote the provision of information resources on existing networks and on proposed interconnected networks; not to be confused with the Coalition for the National Research and Education Network.

Coalition for the National Research and Education Network (CNREN) Formed to articulate the network challenge, to describe the NREN's benefits and beneficiaries, to propose a plan for the NREN's growth, to focus the issue of its funding and by whom, and to propose the next steps; not to be confused with the Coalition for Networked Information.

Colorado Alliance for Research Libraries (CARL) A consortium of academic and public libraries to provide computer-based library services.

CompuServe An electronic home and business information service provided by CompuServe, Inc.

CSNET Computer and Science Network.

Cybercasting A trademarked service of the National Public Telecomputing Network whereby a wide variety of news and information features are delivered to affiliates.

DARPA Defense Advanced Research Projects Agency.

Davis Senior High School (DSHS) A high school in California involved in an experimental data link with the University of California, Davis.

Dialog An online information retrieval service provided by Dialog Information Services, Inc.

Distance learning Learning in remote classrooms or at home via linkage to a remote school or a larger school or university.

EDUCOM (non-acronym) A coalition of several hundred colleges and universities to promote the use of information technology in higher education.

FARNET Federation of American Research Networks.

FCC Federal Communications Commission.

FCCSET (pronounced "fix it") Federal Coordinating Council for Science, Engineering, and Technology.

Federal Networking Council (FNC) Joint U.S. government body which oversees U.S. federal policy on networking.

FidoNet Made up mostly of MS/PC-DOS personal computers linked over public dial-up telephone lines.

Free-Net A free, open-access, community computer system.

Gigabit One billion bits, a measure of quantity of machine-encoded data.

Internet A sprawling composite of many hundreds of local and wide area networks united by the same transmission protocols and primarily connected by the cross-country electronic backbone provided by the NSFNET; it is estimated that far in excess of 100,000 computers are connected to the Internet; usage of the term began following the split of MILNET from ARPANET.

Internet Protocol (IP) One set of rules at the network level that controls routing and switching operations that allow different networks to pass data.

Library Administration and Management Association (LAMA) A division of the American Library Association; provides an organizational framework for encouraging the study of administrative theory, for improving the practice of administration in libraries, and for identifying and fostering administrative skills.

Library and Information Technology Association (LITA) A division of the American Library Association; concerned with the planning, development, design, application, and integration of technologies within the library and information environment, with the impact of emerging technologies on library service, and with the effect of automated technologies on people.

Library without walls The concept of remote access to the contents and services of libraries and other information resources; combines an on-site collec-

8

tion of current and heavily used materials, in both print and electronic form, with an electronic network which provides access to, and delivery from, external worldwide library and commercial information sources; also "virtual library."

Linked Systems Protocol (LSP) Standard for computer-to-computer communication for bibliographic information retrieval; NISO Z39.50.

Local Area Network (LAN) A computer network for a limited geographical area that allows each node to communicate with every other node.

LSCA Library Services and Construction Act; funding source for a variety of library-related projects.

MARC MAchine Readable Cataloging; standard for communication of machine readable cataloging data.

Medieval Early Modern Data Bank (MEMDB) Created by scholars at Rutgers University to serve as an online reference system; an example of the type of information that can be made available electronically.

MEDLINE (non-acronym) Biomedical and health sciences database supported by the National Library of Medicine.

MELVYL (non-acronym) Online union catalog of the University of California System.

Merit Computer Network A consortium of state-supported universities in Michigan; the Merit organization manages the NSFNET.

MILNET The military network that resulted from the split for security purposes of the research and military use of ARPANET.

NAC Library of Congress Network Advisory Committee.

NASA National Air and Space Administration.

National Commission on Libraries and Information Science (NCLIS) Advises the President and the Congress on the nation's library and information needs.

National digital library Senator Gore's vision of the access to national resources to be provided by NREN; related to the concept of "library without walls" and "virtual library."

National Information Standards Organization (NISO-Z39) Develops and promotes the use of voluntary standards for libraries, the information sciences, and the publishing industries; "Z39" is due to the former name, American National Standards Committee Z39.

National Public Telecomputing Network (NPTN) A nonprofit organization devoted to disseminating community computer service.

National Research and Education Network (NREN) A proposed telecommunications infrastructure which would expand and upgrade the existing interconnected array of research networks.

National Science Foundation (NSF) Agency for the support of basic and applied research and education in science and engineering.

National Telecommunications and Information Administration (NTIA) An agency of the Commerce Department.

NISO-Z39 National Information Standards Organization; "Z39" is due to the former name, American National Standards Committee Z39.

NISO Z39.50 Linked Systems Protocol.

NSFNET National Science Foundation Network; forms the "backbone" of the Internet.

NTTF EDUCOM Networking and Telecommunications Task Force.

NYSERNET New York State Education and Research Network; a mid-level component of NSFNET.

OCLC Online Computer Library Center A not-for-profit computer library services and research membership organization.

Open System Interconnect (OSI) A theoretical framework by which networking issues are separated into primary components that are amenable to standards; an emerging set of standards that presumably will replace the TCP/IP suite of protocols over time.

OSTP Office of Science and Technology Policy.

Research Libraries Group (RLG) A partnership of major universities and other research institutions dedicated to improving the management of the information resources necessary for the advancement of scholarship.

Research Libraries Information Network (RLIN) Supports the cooperative efforts of The Research Libraries Group in collection management and development, preservation, shared resources, technical systems, and bibliographic control.

SURANET Southeastern Universities Research Network; a mid-level component of NSFNET.

TCP/IP Transmission Control Protocol and Internet Protocol.

Transmission Control Protocol (TCP) One set of rules that formats the packaging of data for transmission between computers.

UUCP Unix-to-Unix Copy Program; a protocol for data communications.

University of California, Davis (UCD) A university involved in an experimental data link with a high school.

Virtual library The concept of remote access to the contents and services of libraries and other information resources; combines an on-site collection of current and heavily used materials, in both print and electronic form, with an electronic network which provides access to, and delivery from, external worldwide library and commercial information sources; also "library without walls."

The WELL Regional computer teleconference system in the San Francisco area.

Z39 see National Information Standards Organization.

Source: Carol A. Parkhurst, ed., *Library Perspectives on NREN*
(Chicago: ALA/Library and Information Technology Association, 1990)

Understanding MARC

by Betty Furrie

WHAT IS A MARC RECORD? A MARC record is a **MA**chine-**R**eadable **C**ataloging record.

Machine-readable: By "machine-readable" we mean that one particular type of machine, a computer, can read and interpret the data in the cataloging record.

Cataloging record: By "cataloging record" we mean a bibliographic record, or the information shown on a catalog card. This includes (not necessarily in this order): 1) a description of the item; 2) main entry and added entries; 3) subject headings; 4) the call number; and 5) shelflist information, such as the source of the book and its price. (MARC records often contain additional information).

MARC terms and their definitions

To recognize what people are talking about when they discuss MARC records, you need to know what is meant by these terms: fields, tags, subfields, subfield codes, indicators, and content designators.

1. Fields are marked by tags.

A field: The bibliographic data has been divided logically into fields: a field for the author, a field for title information, and so on. These fields are subdivided into one or more "subfields."

A tag: Each field is preceded by a 3-digit number called a "tag." A tag identifies the field—the kind of data—that follows. Even though a printout or screen display may show the tag immediately followed by indicators (making it appear to be a 4- or 5-digit number), the tag is always the first 3 digits.

8

Main Entry, personal name with a single surname, not to be used as a subject heading as well: *The name:*	Arnosky, Jim.

Title and Statement of Responsibility Area, pick up title for a title added entry, file under "ra..."
    Title proper:
    Statement of responsibility:
	Raccoons and ripe corn/
	Jim Arnosky.

Edition Area: *Edition statement*	1st ed.

Publication, Distribution, Etc., Area,
    Place of publication . . .
    Name of publisher . . .
    Date of publication . . .
	New York:
	Lothrop, Lee & Shepard Books,
	c1987.

Physical Description Area,
    Pagination:
    Illustrative matter:
    Size:
	[25] p.
	col. ill.;
	26 cm.

Note Area, *Summary:*	Hungry raccoons feast at night in a field of ripe corn.
Subject Added Entries, from Library of Congress subject heading list, *Topical subject:*	Raccoons.
Local Call Number:	599.74 ARN
Local Barcode Number:	8009
Local Price:	p15.07usd

Record with textual "signposts"

100	1	_a	Arnosky, Jim.
245	10	_a	Raccoons and ripe corn/
		_c	Jim Arnosky.
250		_a	1st ed.
260		_a	New York:
		_b	Lathrop, Lee & Shepard Books,
		_c	1987.
300		_a	[25] p. :
		_b	col. ill. ;
		_c	26 cm.
520		_a	Hungry raccoons feast at night in a field of ripe corn.
650	1	_a	Raccoons.
852		_h	599.74 ARN
		_p	8009
		_9	p15.07usd

Same record with MARC tags

The tags used most frequently are:

010	tag marks the **LCCN** field
020	tag marks the **ISBN** field
100	tag marks a **personal name main entry (author)** field
245	tag marks the **title information** field
	(which includes the title, other title information, and the statement of responsibility)
250	tag marks the **edition** field
260	tag marks the field for **publication information**
300	tag marks the **physical description** field
	(often referred to as the "collation" when describing books)
440	tag marks the **series** field
520	tag marks the **annotation** or summary field
650	tag marks the **topical subject heading** field
700	tag marks a **personal name added entry** field
	(joint author, editor, or illustrator)
	a **locally- or system-defined tag** (or the USMARC Holdings Format tag 852) is used for the **local call number**

2. Subfields are marked by subfield codes.

A subfield: Most fields contain several related pieces of data. Each type of data within the field is called a subfield, and each subfield is preceded by a subfield code.

For example, in the field for the physical description (defined by the tag 300) you will usually see a subfield for the extent (number of pages), a subfield for other physical details (illustration information), and a subfield for dimensions (centimeters):

> 300   _a675 p.   :_bill.   ;_c24 cm.

In this example, the subfield codes are **-a** for the extent, **-b** for other physical details, and **-c** for dimensions.

3. Some fields are further defined by indicators.

Indicators: Two spaces follow each tag. One or both of these spaces may be used for indicators. In some fields, only the second space is used; sometimes only the first is used; and sometimes both are assigned. (Sometimes neither is used—as in the 020 and 300 fields we have just studied. The rules are all spelled out in MARC format guides.)

Each indicator is a number from 0 to 9. (Though the rules say it can be a letter, letters are uncommon.) Even though two indicators together may look like a 2-digit number, they really are two single-digit numbers. In this example, the first 3 digits are the tag (245 defines this as a title field) and the next 2 digits (a 1 and a 4) are indicators. The 1 is the first indicator; 4 is the second indicator.

> 24514_aThe emperor's new clothes /_cadapted from Hans Christian Andersen and illustrated by Janet Stevens.

A **first indicator of 1** in the title field indicates that there should be a separate title entry in the catalog. In the card catalog environment, this means that a title card should be printed for this item. A 0 as the first indicator means that this is a title main entry and that the cards are to be printed with the traditional hanging indention.

Non-filing characters: One of the more interesting indicators is the second indicator for the title field. It displays the number of nonfiling characters at the beginning of the field (counting spaces). For the title, "The emperor's new clothes," the second indicator is set at "4" so the first four characters (the "T," the "h," the "e," and the space) will be skipped and the title will be filed under "emperor's."

4. Content designator is an inclusive term used to refer to tags, subfield codes, and indicators.

The three kinds of content designators—tags, subfield codes, and indicators—are the keys to the MARC notation system. In his book, *MARC for Library Use: Understanding the USMARC Formats,* Walt Crawford calls the MARC system a "shorthand notation" system. The three types of content designators are the shorthand symbols that label and explain the bibliographic record.

Source: Betty Furrie, *Understanding MARC* (McHenry, Ill.: Follett Software Co., 1991)

ISSUES

9

The Library Bill of Rights

THE AMERICAN LIBRARY ASSOCIATION affirms that all libraries are forums for information and ideas, and that the following basic policies should guide their services.

1. Books and other library resources should be provided for the interest, information, and enlightenment of all people of the community the library serves. Materials should not be excluded because of the origin, background, or views of those contributing to their creation.

2. Libraries should provide materials and information presenting all points of view on current and historical issues. Materials should not be proscribed or removed because of partisan or doctrinal disapproval.

3. Libraries should challenge censorship in the fulfillment of their responsibility to provide information and enlightenment.

4. Libraries should cooperate with all persons and groups concerned with resisting abridgment of free expression and free access to ideas.

5. A person's right to use a library should not be denied or abridged because of origin, age, background, or views.

6. Libraries which make exhibit spaces and meeting rooms available to the public they serve should make such facilities available on an equitable basis, regardless of the beliefs or affiliations of individuals or groups requesting their use.

Interpretations

Challenged materials which meet the criteria for selection in the materials selection policy of the library should not be removed under any legal or extralegal pressure.

Expurgation of library materials. Expurgation of any parts of books or other library resources by the library, its agent, or its parent institution is a violation of the Library Bill of Rights because it denies access to the complete work, and, therefore, to the entire spectrum of ideas that the work was intended to express.

Access to resources and services in the school library media program. Members of the school community involved in the collection development process employ educational criteria to select resources unfettered by their personal, social, or religious views. Students and educators served by the school library media program have access to resources and services free of constraints resulting from personal, partisan, or doctrinal disapproval and which reflect the linguistic pluralism of the community. School library media professionals resist efforts by individuals to define what is appropriate for all students or teachers to read, view, or hear.

Free access to libraries for minors. Denying minors access to certain library materials and services available to adults is a violation of the Library Bill of Rights since it is the parents—and only the parents—who may restrict their children—and only their children—from access to library materials and services.

Evaluating library collections. Evaluation of library materials is not to be used as a convenient means to remove materials presumed to be controversial or disapproved of by segments of the community.

Restricted access. Restricting access to certain titles and classes of library materials for protection and/or controlled use is a form of censorship.

Labeling certain library materials by affixing a prejudicial label to them or segregating by a prejudicial system is a practice that seeks to close paths to knowledge; such practices violate the Library Bill of Rights.

Meeting rooms, exhibit spaces, and bulletin boards. Libraries maintaining meeting rooms, exhibit spaces, and bulletin boards for outside groups and individuals should develop and publish statements governing their use. These statements can properly define and restrict eligibility for use as long as the qualifications do not pertain to the content of a meeting or exhibit or to the beliefs or affiliations of the sponsors, and are applied on an equitable basis.

Library-sponsored programs. A policy on library-initiated programming should reflect the library's philosophy regarding free access to information and ideas. Selection of library program topics, speakers, courses, classes, and resource materials should be made by library staff on the basis of the interests and needs of library users and the community.

Administrative policies and procedures affecting access to library resources and services. Restricted access to rare and special collections is solely for the protection of the materials, and must in no way limit access to the information or ideas contained in the materials. Library administration policies on interlibrary loan, library cards, reference services, use of meeting rooms and exhibit spaces should be examined for conformance to the Library Bill of Rights.

Diversity in collection development. Librarians have a professional responsibility to be inclusive, not exclusive, in collection development and in the provision of interlibrary loan. Access to all materials legally obtainable should be assured to the user and policies should not unjustly exclude materials even if offensive to the librarian or user.

Libraries cannot act in *loco parentis*. Nevertheless, ALA acknowledges and supports the exercise by parents of their responsibility to guide their own children's viewing, using published reviews of films and videotapes and/or reference works that provide information about the content, subject matter, and recommended audiences.

Source: ALA Office for Intellectual Freedom

The freedom to read

THE FREEDOM TO READ is essential to our democracy. It is continuously under attack. Private groups and public authorities in various parts of the country are working to remove books from sale, to censor textbooks, to label "controversial" books, to distribute lists of "objectionable" books or authors, and to purge libraries. These actions apparently rise from a view that our national tradition of free expression is no longer valid; that censorship and suppression are needed to avoid the subversion of politics and the corruption of morals. We, as citizens devoted to the use of books and as librarians and publishers responsible for disseminating them, wish to assert the public interest in the preservation of the freedom to read.

We are deeply concerned about these attempts at suppression. Most such attempts rest on a denial of the fundamental premise of democracy: that the ordinary citizen, by exercising his critical judgment, will accept the good and reject the bad. The censors, public and private, assume that they should determine what is good and what is bad for their fellow citizens.

We trust Americans to recognize propaganda, and to reject it. We do not

9

CAUTION!

SOME PEOPLE CONSIDER THESE BOOKS DANGEROUS

AMERICAN HERITAGE DICTIONARY • THE BIBLE • ARE YOU THERE,
GOD? IT'S ME, MARGARET • OUR BODIES, OURSELVES • TARZAN
ALICE'S ADVENTURES IN WONDERLAND • THE EXORCIST • THE
CHOCOLATE WAR • CATCH-22 • LORD OF THE FLIES • ORDINARY
PEOPLE • SOUL ON ICE • RAISIN IN THE SUN • OLIVER TWIST • A
FAREWELL TO ARMS • THE BEST SHORT STORIES OF NEGRO
WRITERS • FLOWERS FOR ALGERNON • ULYSSES • TO KILL A
MOCKINGBIRD • ROSEMARY'S BABY • THE FIXER • DEATH OF A
SALESMAN • MOTHER GOOSE • CATCHER IN THE RYE • THE
MERCHANT OF VENICE   •   ONE DAY IN THE LIFE OF IVAN
DENISOVICH • GRAPES OF WRATH • THE ADVENTURES OF
HUCKLEBERRY FINN • SLAUGHTERHOUSE-FIVE • GO ASK ALICE

BANNED BOOKS WEEK—CELEBRATING THE FREEDOM TO READ

believe they need the help of censors to assist them in this task. We do not believe they are prepared to sacrifice their heritage of a free press in order to be "protected" against what others think may be bad for them. We believe they still favor free enterprise in ideas and expression.

We are aware, of course, that books are not alone in being subjected to efforts at suppression. We are aware that these efforts are related to a larger pattern of pressures brought against education, the press, films, radio and television. The problem is not only one of actual censorship. The shadow of fear cast by these pressures leads, we suspect, to an even larger voluntary curtailment of expression by those who seek to avoid controversy.

Such pressure toward conformity is perhaps natural to a time of uneasy change and pervading fear. Especially when so many of our apprehensions are directed against an ideology, the expression of a dissident idea becomes a thing feared in itself, and we tend to move against it as against a hostile deed, with suppression.

And yet suppression is never more dangerous than in such a time of social tension. Freedom has given the United States the elasticity to endure strain. Freedom keeps open the path of novel and creative solutions, and enables change to come by choice. Every silencing of a heresy, every enforcement of an orthodoxy, diminishes the toughness and resilience of our society and leaves it the less able to deal with stress.

Now as always in our history, books are among our greatest instruments of freedom. They are almost the only means for making generally available ideas or manners of expression that can initially command only a small audience. They are the natural medium for the new idea and the untried voice from which come the original contributions to social growth. They are essential to the extended discussion which serious thought requires, and to the accumulation of knowledge and ideas into organized collections.

We believe that free communication is essential to the preservation of a free society and a creative culture. We believe that these pressures towards conformity present the danger of limiting the range and variety of inquiry and expression on which our democracy and our culture depend. We believe that every American community must jealously guard the freedom to publish and to circulate, in order to preserve its own freedom to read. We believe that publishers and librarians have a profound responsibility to give validity to that freedom to read by making it possible for the readers to choose freely from a variety of offerings.

The freedom to read is guaranteed by the Constitution. Those with faith in free men will stand firm on these constitutional guarantees of essential rights and will exercise the responsibilities that accompany these rights.

We therefore affirm these propositions:

1. It is in the public interest for publishers and librarians to make available the widest diversity of views and expressions, including those which are unorthodox or unpopular with the majority.

Creative thought is by definition new, and what is new is different. The bearer of every new thought is a rebel until his idea is refined and tested. Totalitarian systems attempt to maintain themselves in power by the ruthless suppression of any concept which challenges the established orthodoxy. The power of a democratic system to adapt to change is vastly strengthened by the freedom of its citizens to choose widely from among conflicting opinions offered freely to them. To stifle every nonconformist idea at birth would mark the end of the democratic process. Furthermore, only through the constant activity of weighing and selecting can the democratic mind attain the strength demanded by times like these. We need to know not only what we believe but why we believe it.

2. Publishers, librarians, and booksellers do not need to endorse every idea or presentation contained in the books they make available. It would conflict with the public interest for them to establish their own political, moral, or aesthetic views as a standard for determining what books should be published or circulated.

Publishers and librarians serve the educational process by helping to make available knowledge and ideas required for the growth of the mind and the increase of learning. They do not foster education by imposing as mentors the patterns of their own thought. The people should have the freedom to read and consider a broader range of ideas than those that may be held by any single librarian or publisher or government or church. It is wrong that what one man can read should be confined to what another thinks proper.

3. It is contrary to the public interest for publishers or librarians to determine the acceptability of a book on the basis of the personal history or political affiliations of the author.

A book should be judged as a book. No art or literature can flourish if it is to be measured by the political views or private lives of its creators. No society of free men can flourish which draws up lists of writers to whom it will not listen, whatever they may have to say.

4. There is no place in our society for efforts to coerce the taste of others, to confine adults to the reading matter deemed suitable for adolescents, or to inhibit the efforts of writers to achieve artistic expression.

To some, much of modern literature is shocking. But is not much of life itself shocking? We cut off literature at the source if we prevent writers from dealing with the stuff of life. Parents and teachers have a responsibility to prepare the young to meet the diversity of experiences in life to which they will be exposed, as they have a responsibility to help them learn to think critically for themselves. These are affirmative responsibilities, not to be discharged simply by preventing them from reading works for which they are not yet prepared. In these matters taste differs, and taste cannot be legislated; nor can machinery be devised which will suit the demands of one group without limiting the freedom of others.

5. It is not in the public interest to force a reader to accept with any book the prejudgment of a label characterizing the book or author as subversive or dangerous.

The ideal of labeling presupposes the existence of individuals or groups with wisdom to determine by authority what is good or bad for the citizen. It presupposes that each individual must be directed in making up his mind about the ideas he examines. But Americans do not need others to do their thinking for them.

6. It is the responsibility of publishers and librarians, as guardians of the people's freedom to read, to contest encroachments upon that freedom by

individuals or groups seeking to impose their own standards or tastes upon the community at large.

It is inevitable in the give and take of the democratic process that the political, the moral, or the aesthetic concepts of an individual or group will occasionally collide with those of another individual or group. In a free society each individual is free to determine for himself what he wishes to read, and each group is free to determine what it will recommend to its freely associated members. But no group has the right to take the law into its own hands, and to impose its own concept of politics or morality upon other members of a democratic society. Freedom is no freedom if it is accorded only to the accepted and the inoffensive.

7. It is the responsibility of publishers and librarians to give full meaning to the freedom to read by providing books that enrich the duality and diversity of thought and expression. By the exercise of this affirmative responsibility, bookmen can demonstrate that the answer to a bad book is a good one, the answer to a bad idea is a good one.

The freedom to read is of little consequence when expended on the trivial; it is frustrated when the reader cannot obtain matter fit for his purpose. What is needed is not only the absence of restraint, but the positive provision of opportunity for the people to read the best that has been thought and said. Books are the major channel by which the intellectual inheritance is handed down, and the principal means of its testing and growth. The defense of their freedom and integrity and the enlargement of their service to society require of all bookmen the utmost of their faculties, and deserve of all citizens the fullest of their support.

We state these propositions neither lightly nor as easy generalizations. We here stake out a lofty claim for the value of books. We do so because we believe that they are good, possessed of enormous variety and usefulness, worthy of cherishing and keeping free. We realize that the application of these propositions may mean the dissemination of ideas and manners of expression that are repugnant to many persons. We do not state these propositions in the comfortable belief that what people read is unimportant. We believe rather that what people read is deeply important; that ideas can be dangerous; but that the suppression of ideas is fatal to a democratic society. Freedom itself is a dangerous way of life, but it is ours.

Source: American Library Association and the Association of American Publishers

Defending the freedom to read

CREATED IN 1959 through the leadership of the American Library Association, the Freedom to Read Foundation

- promotes and protects freedom of speech and freedom of the press;
- protects the public's right of access to information and materials stored in the nation's libraries;
- safeguards libraries' right to disseminate all materials contained in their collections; and
- supports libraries and librarians in their defense of First Amendment rights by supplying them with legal counsel or the means to secure it.

The Foundation assists groups or individuals in litigation by securing counsel, or providing funding, and by participating directly or as a "friend of the court" in important and possibly precedent-setting litigation. Some of the litigation that the Foundation has participated in is listed below.

1970, T. Ellis Hodgin: Grant to aid Hodgin in challenging his dismissal as city librarian of Martinsville, Virginia, for exercising his right of free speech.

1971, **Todd v. Rochester Community Schools:** Grant to Rochester, Michigan, school system to support an appeal to overturn the state circuit court decision removing *Slaughterhouse Five* from the school library.

1972, **Moore v. Younger:** Suit filed in U.S. District Court in Los Angeles to challenge the constitutionality of California's newly enacted "harmful matter" act restricting the dissemination of communicative materials, including library materials, to minors.

1973, **Pentagon Papers Fund:** Grant to aid the defense of Daniel Ellsberg and Anthony J. Russo, Jr.

1974, **Jenkins v. Georgia:** Friend-of-the-court brief filed with the U.S. Supreme Court urging the Court to overturn "obscenity" convictions—upheld by Georgia's highest court—for showings of the movie *Carnal Knowledge.*

1975, **Knopf v. Colby:** Friend-of-the-court brief filed with U.S. Supreme Court urging the Court to review the holding of the U.S. Court of Appeals for the Fourth Circuit requiring deletions from the published text of *The CIA and the Cult of Intelligence.*

1976, **Smith v. U.S.:** Appeal taken to the U.S. Supreme Court seeking a reversal of the ruling of the Eighth Circuit bench that community standards on obscenity are "inborn and often undefinable."

1977, **Flynt v. Ohio:** Friend-of-the-court brief filed with Ohio Court of Appeal to protest the use of Ohio's organized crime law to chill freedom of expression.

1978, **Pico v. Board of Education:** Friend-of-the-court brief filed in U.S. District Court to assist student plaintiffs in protesting the removal of *The Fixer, Slaughterhouse Five, Soul on Ice, The Naked Ape,* and other works from the Island Trees, New York, school district libraries by the school board.

1979, **U.S. v. Progressive Magazine:** Friend-of-the-court brief filed with the U.S. Court of Appeals for the Seventh Circuit to assist the *Progressive* in efforts to overturn the prior restraint imposed by the U.S. District Court order permanently barring publication of an article on the H-bomb.

1980, **Jeanne Layton v. Morris F. Swapp, Sharon Shumway, and Robert Arbucle:** Grant to Davis County, Utah, librarian Layton to help defray the legal expenses incurred in her fight for reinstatement as library director. Layton had been dismissed for keeping on the shelves Don DeLillo's *Americana* despite a county commissioner's complaint. Challenge grant to match, $2 for $1, gifts made to the Layton defense fund by members of the library and education community between June 27 and December 31.

1981, **McKamey, et al., v. Mt. Diablo, Calif., Unified School District, et al.:** Grant to the plaintiffs protesting restrictions on use of *Ms.* magazine in the Ygnacio High School library.

1982, **Tattered Cover Bookstore v. Tooley:** Friend-of-the-court brief filed to challenge Colorado "minors access" law.

1983, **Peterzell et al. v. Faurer:** Support of American Civil Liberties Union National Security Project case opposing the U.S. National Security Agency's withdrawal of William Friedman's personal documents from the open shelves at the George C. Marshall Research Library at Virginia Military Institute in Lexington. Cryptologist Friedman's letters had been used in James Bamford's *The Puzzle Palace.*

1984, **Bullfrog Films, Inc. v. Charles Z. Wick, director of the United States**

9

Information Agency: Grant to the Center of Constitutional Rights to support litigation against USIA's denial of export certificates to films judged misrepresentative of the United States. Friend-of-the-court brief filed.

1985, American Council of the Blind, et al. v. Daniel Boorstin, Librarian of Congress: Friend-of-the-court brief filed in suit against the Library of Congress for ceasing publication of *Playboy* in braille.

1986, Lee McCarthy v. Douglas Fletcher: Grant to the ACLU Foundation of Southern California in support of Wasco Union High School English teacher Lee McCarthy who challenged school board prohibition against using John Gardner's *Grendel* in a senior English class without the consent of every parent.

1987, Edwin Meese III, et al. v. Keene: Friend-of-the-court brief filed in U.S. Supreme Court protesting Foreign Agents Registration Act requirement to label National Film Board of Canada films about acid rain as political propaganda.

1988, Virgil v. The School Board of Columbia County, Florida: Friend-of-the-court brief filed in U.S. District Court protesting the school board's removal of *Humanities: Cultural Roots and Continuities, Vol. 1,* because parents objected to the language in Aristophanes' *Lysistrata* and Chaucer's *The Miller's Tale* included in the work.

1989, William L. Webster, et al. v. Reproductive Health Services, et al.: Friend-of-the-court brief filed challenging the constitutionality of a Missouri statute that prohibits spending public funds to "encourage or counsel" a woman about abortion.

1990, ALA v. Thornburgh: Lawsuit filed by the Foundation, ALA, and several media trade associations challenging the Child Protection and Obscenity Enforcement Act of 1988. After a nearly total victory at the district court level, the case went to the U.S. Circuit Court of Appeals for the District of Columbia. However, the 101st Congress adopted the Child Protection Restoration and Penalties Act of 1990, designed to correct the constitutional flaws identified in this lawsuit.

Source: Twentieth Anniversary Program, Dallas 1989 (Chicago: Freedom to Read Foundation, 1989); Newsletter on Intellectual Freedom, March 1991

Freedom to view

THE FREEDOM TO VIEW, along with the freedom to speak, to hear, and to read, is protected by the First Amendment to the Constitution of the United States. In a free society, there is no place for censorship of any medium of expression. Therefore these principles are affirmed:

1. To provide the broadest possible access to film, video, and other audiovisual materials because they are a means for the communication of ideas. Liberty of circulation is essential to insure the constitutional guarantee of freedom of expression.

2. To protect the confidentiality of all individuals and institutions using film, video, and other audiovisual materials.

3. To provide film, video, and other audiovisual materials that represent a diversity of views and expression. Selection of a work does not constitute or imply agreement with or approval of the content.

4. To provide a diversity of viewpoints without the constraint of labeling or prejudging film, video, and other audiovisual materials on the basis of the moral, religious, or political beliefs of the producer or filmmaker or on the basis of controversial content.

5. To contest vigorously, by all lawful means, every encroachment upon the public's freedom to view.

Source: American Film and Video Association, 1989

Case study of a challenged book

DEENIE, BY JUDY BLUME. (Scarsdale, N.Y.: Bradbury Press, 1973.) LC: 73-80197. ISBN 0-87888061-5.

Annotation. Beautiful twelve-year-old Deenie Fenner has a hard time coping with her desire to be liked and liked by everybody else in her crowd and her mother's ambition for her to pursue a successful modeling career. But when she is diagnosed as having adolescent idiopathic scoliosis (curvature of the spine) and finds out that she will have to wear a back brace for four years to correct it, life as she has known it comes to an abrupt halt. Deenie is panic-stricken at the thought of becoming a "handicapped" person. After so many years of emphasizing the absolute importance of physical beauty, her mother doesn't know how to cope with the idea of a "deformed" daughter either, and cannot believe that this is happening to them. Her parents, who have been so supportive, are suddenly "not there" for Deenie.

Deenie must look inside herself for the strength to face this situation. In spite of many difficulties, she learns to come to terms with herself and her disability. She also learns that she does not have to be "perfect" to survive.

Masturbation is mentioned twice, as Deenie casts about for ways to comfort herself and counteract the stress she is feeling. At one point Deenie touches herself and finds that it makes her feel better. "Myths" about masturbation and its effects are explained through the character of an understanding gym teacher. Deenie is surprised and relieved to discover that her feelings and actions are normal and part of growing up.

Examples of challenges. Removed from the Utah State Library bookmobile (1980) because the book contains "the vilest sexual descriptions" and if given to "the wrong kid at the wrong time (would) ruin his life."

Removed from the Gilbert, Arizona, elementary school libraries (1980), and ordered that parental consent would be required for students to check out this title from the junior high school library.

Challenged in Orlando, Florida (1982); challenged in the Cotati-Rohnert Park, California, school district (1982) because the novel allegedly undermines parental moral values.

After the Minnesota Civil Liberties Union sued the Elk River, Minnesota, School Board (1983), the board reversed its decision to restrict this title to students who have written permission from their parents.

Banned, but later restricted to students with parental permission at the Peoria, Illinois, school district libraries (1984), because of its strong sexual content and language, and alleged lack of social or literary value.

Removed from the Hanover, Pennsylvania, school district's elementary and secondary school libraries (1984) but later placed on a "restricted shelf" at middle school libraries because the book was "indecent and inappropriate."

Challenged at the Casper, Wyoming, school libraries (1984). Challenged as profane, immoral, and offensive, but retained in the Bozeman, Montana, school libraries (1985).

9

Banned from district elementary school libraries in Gwinnett County, Georgia (1985), as "inappropriate."

Returned to the elementary and junior high school library shelves in Clayton County, Georgia (1985), after school officials determined that the book is appropriate for young readers.

Source: Hit List: Frequently Challenged Young Adult Titles
(Chicago: ALA Young Adult Services Division, 1989)

What to do about censorship in the public schools

"DEMOCRACY IS DEPENDENT upon the right of people to study and discuss issues freely . . . it is dependent upon the citizenry . . . which keeps well informed, searches actively for divergent points of view, evaluates courses of action in the light of available evidence and basic democratic values. . . . Such behaviors do not develop by accident; they are learned in the schools within the context of societal problems, many of which are controversial in nature." (National Association of Secondary School Principals, *The Bulletin*, September 1961).

One of the objectives of universal free public education is to develop in children the intellectual capacities required for the effective exercise of the rights of citizenship. This is accomplished in an atmosphere of free inquiry and discussion, supported by effective selection and use of instructional materials/educational resources.

Instructional materials (e.g., textbooks, films, magazines, newspapers and speakers) should make available to students, in classes and in school libraries, a wide range of ideas and viewpoints.

Censorship and the law

Public school districts are an example of our government working at the grassroots level. Each public school board is responsible for administering the public schools within its political jurisdiction, subject to state and federal laws and constitutions.

School boards are composed of elected public officials who set specific goals and objective policies and statements for the school district.

1. **School boards,** which receive input from the community regarding the courses to be made available in the district, have the right and responsibility to set specific guidelines for adopting school courses, reevaluating the content of those courses, and formulating a due process procedure for handling complaints from the community. The school board ultimately has the responsibility to resolve controversial matters that cannot be worked out between the professional staff and the community. However, legal precedents have clearly been established that school board members do not have the right to impose personal, political, religious, social, or aesthetic beliefs and biases on the district.

2. **Parents and other citizens** living in the school district have the rights to vote in elections for school board members, to attend school board meetings and voice opinions, to serve on school advisory boards, to observe their school district in operation, and to make specific objections to the choice of instructional materials, educational resources, and teaching methods used in the schools.

3. The **professional staff** has the responsibility to determine the content of courses offered by the school district and to select appropriate teaching methods and educational resources to be used in their classes and libraries. They do not have the right to impose personal, political, religious, social or aesthetic beliefs or biases on their students. At the superintendent's or principal's request, the professional staff has the responsibility to explain and clarify to the public any courses offered by the school district, and educational resources or teaching methods used. The professional staff has the responsibility to respond to complaints and to justify their choices of educational resources and teaching methods. The professional staff should work with the school board's established committees responsible for reconsidering choices of educational resources and teaching methods.

4. **Students** have the right to study, to be taught, and to be exposed to a wide variety of issues appropriate to their age and maturity, including controversial issues. They have the right to their own opinions and to voice those opinions in appropriate settings (e.g., class discussions and school newspapers.)

Written policies

In order to insure that there is a consistent and fair procedure for teachers selecting educational resources and teaching methods, each school board should develop a written policy that should include:

1. A statement of the philosophy and objectives for the selection of educational resources for the district.

2. A statement that delineates specific criteria to be used in selection of educational resources and teaching methods.

3. A statement delegating responsibility for the selection of educational resources to appropriate professional school personnel (i.e., teachers representing various departments and grade levels and librarians.)

Decisions of the Educational Resource Selection Committees, composed of teachers, subject areas specialists, and librarians, are subject to the approval of the principal, superintendent, and the school board. Only administrative reasons (e.g., costs) and educational judgments should be used as the basis for rejecting teachers' choices of educational resources and teaching methods, never the personal, political, religious, social or aesthetic beliefs and biases of principals, superintendents, or school board members or the worry that some members of the community will complain or think that the content of the educational resources is controversial.

In a democratic society, where it is natural for parents and others to have concern for the education of children, it is reasonable to expect that there will be questions and complaints regarding content of educational resources, class programs, and teaching methods. Such complaints are allowable in our society and should never he labeled as inappropriate or harmful in and of themselves. Rather, each school district should establish policies under which a Reconsideration Committee should receive, review, and evaluate complaints regarding school instructional material/educational resources. Such a written policy should include statements regarding the Reconsideration Committee:

1. Being appointed at the beginning of each school year rather than waiting for a specific complaint to be made.

2. Having at least teachers, librarians, and academic area specialists as members of the committee.

3. Having clearly defined procedures for functioning and indicating to whom the decision is to be referred.

4. Indicating that complainants should be given an opportunity to present their specific charges orally as well as being required to present them in writing and indicating the names of complainants.

5. Affirming that during the reconsideration reviewing, no resources will be removed.

What parents and other citizens can do

If you hear of a threat of censorship in your school district, don't immediately assume what you hear is fact. Instead, investigate all rumors to ascertain what is fact and what is fiction. When the facts have been established, do not feel helpless or intimidated because you are only one person. Remember, school board members and school administrators are public servants, and YOU are the public!

After you have established as fact that your school district has been threatened by censorship, check the written policy regarding the selection of educational resources. If there is not a written policy in your school district, call your school board members and ask them why not. Then determine if a Request for Reconsideration Form (a form formally requesting reconsideration of use of challenged material) has been filled out and submitted properly, and if the controversial material has been removed. If the material has been removed, find out whether the procedure for reconsideration was properly followed.

By talking with librarians and teachers, you will be able to find like-minded individuals and can build a support group regarding the censorship issue in your community. Throughout the country censorship threats have been opposed and eventually stopped by such support groups and networks of people coming together using well-planned and intelligent action, and by persevering.

You are entitled to a copy of the written minutes of your school board meetings. You may also go over tapes of each meeting in order to know precisely what is going on and what was said.

Find out from the school district office the proper procedure for speaking out at school board meetings. Speaking up slows down the opposition and also acts as an educational tool for the public. Writing brief, concise letters to the editor of your local newspaper, calling radio station talk shows, and contacting reporters in your school district's area help generate publicity so that others become aware of censorship issues. Talk about censorship with your friends and neighbors. By bringing together as many people as possible you add strength to your cause.

The integrity of the process of professional teachers making professional judgments in the selection of educational resources is protected against threats of censorship by having a school board that believes in resisting censorship and in supporting the Bill of Rights. Help elect school board members who support our Bill of Rights and help them to stay in office.

Source: Minnesota Civil Liberties Union

Dealing with concerns about library resources

AS WITH ANY PUBLIC SERVICE, libraries receive complaints and expressions of concern. One of the librarian's responsibilities is to handle these complaints in a respectful and fair manner. The complaints that librarians often worry about the most are those dealing with library resources or free access policies. The key to successfully handling these complaints is to be sure the library staff and the governing authorities are all knowledgeable about the complaint procedures and their implementation. As normal operating procedure each library should:

1. **Maintain a materials selection policy.** It should be in written form and approved by the appropriate governing authority. It should apply to all library materials equally.

2. **Maintain a library service policy.** This should cover registration policies, programming, and services in the library that involve access issues.

3. **Maintain a clearly defined method for handling complaints.** The complaint must be filed in writing and the complainant must be properly identified before action is taken. A decision should be deferred until fully considered by appropriate administrative authority. The process should be followed, whether the complaint originates internally or externally.

4. **Maintain in-service training.** Conduct periodic in-service training to acquaint staff, administration, and the governing authority with the materials selection policy and library service policy and procedures for handling complaints.

5. **Maintain lines of communication with civic, religious, educational, and political bodies of the community.** Library board and staff participation in local

civic organizations and presentations to these organizations should emphasize the library's selection process and intellectual freedom principles.

6. Maintain a vigorous public information program on behalf of intellectual freedom. Newspapers, radio, and television should be informed of policies governing resource selection and use, and of any special activities pertaining to intellectual freedom.

7. Maintain familiarity with any local municipal and state legislation pertaining to intellectual freedom and First Amendment rights.

Following these practices will not preclude receiving complaints from pressure groups or individuals but should provide a base from which to operate when these concerns are expressed. When a complaint is made, follow one or more of the steps listed below:

- Listen calmly and courteously to the complaint. Remember the person has a right to express a concern. Use of good communication skills helps many people understand the need for diversity in library collections and the use of library resources. In the event the person is not satisfied, advise the complainant of the library policy and procedures for handling library resource statements of concern. If a person does fill out a form about their concern, make sure a prompt written reply related to the concern is sent.
- It is essential to notify the administration and/or the governing authority (library board, etc.) of the complaint and assure them that the library's procedures are being followed. Present full, written information giving the nature of the complaint and identifying the source.
- When appropriate, seek the support of the local media. Freedom to read and freedom of the press go hand in hand.
- When appropriate, inform local civic organizations of the facts and enlist their support. Meet negative pressure with positive pressure.
- Assert the principles of the *Library Bill of Rights* as a professional responsibility. Laws governing obscenity, subversive material, and other questionable matter are subject to interpretation by courts. Library materials found to meet the standards set in the materials selection policy should not be removed from public access until after an adversary hearing resulting in a final judicial determination.
- Contact the ALA Office for Intellectual Freedom and your state intellectual freedom committee to inform them of the complaint and to enlist their support and the assistance of other agencies.

The principles and procedures discussed above apply to all kinds of resource-related complaints or attempts to censor and are supported by groups such as the National Education Association, the American Civil Liberties Union, and the National Council of Teachers of English, as well as the American Library Association. While the practices provide positive means for preparing for and meeting pressure group complaints, they serve the more general purpose of supporting the *Library Bill of Rights*, particularly Article 3 which states that: "Libraries should challenge censorship in the fulfillment of their responsibility to provide information and enlightenment."

Source: ALA Office for Intellectual Freedom, 1983

9

What to do when the censor comes

1. Remain calm.
2. Make no commitments, admissions of guilt, or threats.
3. Treat the group or individual who complains with dignity, courtesy, and humor.
4. If a complainant telephones, listen courteously and refer the person to the teacher or media person involved.
5. Try to resolve the issue informally by explaining to the complainant the school's selection procedures, criteria for selecting materials, and the educational purposes of the item.
6. Remember there is a reconsideration procedure for the purpose of considering the opinions of those persons in the school and community who are not directly involved in the selection process.
7. If the complainant is not satisfied, invite the person to file the complaint in writing on the proper form.
8. Do not remove the item (unless your policy specifically says that you must).
9. Contact the Intellectual Freedom Committee of your state organization.
10. Don't be hateful.

Source: Intellectual Freedom Committee, ALA American Association of School Librarians

Coping with law enforcement inquiries

VISITS TO LIBRARIES BY LAW ENFORCEMENT AGENTS, including FBI, state, county, and municipal police, have reached a high level of public awareness and concern, particularly as a result of revelations about the FBI Library Awareness Program. Prompted by inquiries about how to respond to visits by law enforcement officials, the ALA Intellectual Freedom Committee has developed the following guidelines for the library administrator. These guidelines should be used with ALA's Policy on Confidentiality of Library Records and Statement on Professional Ethics to assist libraries and library employees in dealing with law enforcement inquiries.

Fundamental principles

• Librarians' professional ethics require that personally identifiable information about library users be kept confidential. This principle is reflected in Article III of the Code of Ethics which ALA adopted in 1981. This includes borrower registration information.

• All state library associations have adopted the "Statement on Professional Ethics," which includes the Code of Ethics.

• Moreover, as of August 1, 1989, such library records are protected by state law in 41 states and the District of Columbia, and by attorney-general opinions in two additional states.

• Confidential records should not be made available to any agency of state, federal, or local government or any other person (outside the minimum necessary access by library staff), unless a court order requiring disclosure has been entered by a court of competent jurisdiction, after a showing of good cause by the person or agency requesting the records.

General guidelines

Confidentiality of library records is a basic principle of librarianship. As a matter of policy or procedure, the library administrator should insure that:

• The library staff and governing board are familiar with the ALA Policy on Confidentiality.

• The library staff and governing board are familiar with the state's library confidentiality statute (or attorney general's opinion) if one exists.

• The library adopts a policy on confidentiality.

• The library consults legal counsel to make counsel aware of these guidelines.

• The staff is familiar with the specific guidelines that follow.

Specific guidelines

Library procedures affect confidentiality. Law enforcement visits aside, be aware that library operating procedures have an impact on confidentiality. The following are recommendations to bring library procedures into compliance with ALA's Statement on Professional Ethics and Policy on Confidentiality, and internal library confidentiality policies.

Confidentiality statutes vary from state to state, but these suggestions may also assist in compliance with the requirements of such statutes: For example:

• Avoid unnecessary records. Think twice before committing a name to a written record.

• Check with your local governing body to see if the city, county, school board, or other agencies set a time limit on record keeping, then determine what it should be for the library, and destroy records as soon as possible.

• If your library uses names on borrower cards, consider using numbers or blacking out the names.

• Be aware of information on public view owing to library procedure; e.g., overdue notices or filled-request notices mailed on postcards, names of patrons with overdues posted by the circulation desk, or titles of interlibrary loan or reserve requests provided over the telephone to family members.

Law enforcement visits. Recommended steps to take when law enforcement agents visit:

• If a library staff person is approached by a law enforcement agent requesting information on a library user, he or she should immediately ask for identification and refer the agent to the library administrator or responsible officer of the institution.

• The library administrator should explain the library's policy or, if lacking an internal one, ALA's confidentiality policy, and the state confidentiality law where applicable. Most important, the library administrator should state that personally identifiable information about library users is not available under any circumstances, except when a proper court order has been presented.

• In response to appeals to patriotism (e.g., "a good American wants to help us"), explain that as patriotic, good citizens, library administrators and library staff value First Amendment freedoms and the corresponding privacy rights of library users.

• Compliance with FBI requests made without a warrant or court order is strictly voluntary. *The library administrator must stress to agents that maintaining*

9

professional ethics and complying with state law are principles which are not "voluntarily" surrendered.

• It is illegal to lie to a federal law enforcement officer. Without a court order, however, the FBI has no independent authority to compel cooperation with an investigation or to require answers to questions (other than name and address of the person to whom the agent is speaking). The best thing to say to an agent who has asked for confidential information is, "I'm sorry, but my professional ethics (and state law where applicable) prohibit me from responding to your request."

• Notify the American Library Association's Office for Intellectual Freedom, 50 East Huron Street, Chicago, IL 60611; (312) 280-4222.

Procedure. The library administrator should:

• Meet with the law enforcement agent and a library colleague in the library.

• Be cordial, and explain that libraries support the work of law enforcement agencies and their ethical standards are not intended to be obstructionist; rather, affirm the importance of confidentiality of personally identifiable information in the context of First Amendment rights. Should an agent be persistent, state again that information is disclosed only subject to a proper court order, and that the library's governing body firmly supports this policy, and terminate the interview.

• Report any threats or coercion to legal counsel. Repeated visits by law enforcement agents who have been informed that records will be released only upon receipt of a proper court order may constitute harassment or other grounds for legal action. Seek the advice of legal counsel on whether relief from such action should be requested from the appropriate court.

• Immediately refer any subpoena received to the appropriate legal officer for review. If there is any defect in the subpoena, including its form, the manner in which it was served upon the library, the breadth of its request for documents, or insufficient evidence that a showing of good cause has been made to a court, legal counsel will advise on the proper manner to resist the subpoena.

• Repeat the entire process, should the party requesting the information be required to submit a new subpoena.

• Through legal counsel, insist that any defects in the subpoena be cured before records are released. Insist that the subpoena be limited strictly to require release of only specifically identified records or documents.

• Together with the library's legal counsel, review any information that may be produced in response to such a subpoena prior to the release of the information. Construe the subpoena strictly and exclude any information that is arguably not covered by a proper subpoena.

• Ask the court, if disclosure is required, for an order that any information produced be kept strictly confidential and that it be used only for the limited purpose of the particular case at hand. Ask that access to it be restricted to the agents working on the case. Sometimes these terms may be agreed to informally by the party seeking the information, but even if such an agreement is reached, ALA strongly recommends that this agreement be entered as a formal order of the court. If there is such a formal order, anyone breaking the terms of the protective order might be subject to a sanction for contempt of court.

Keep in mind that a polite but firm response is the best way to deflect attempts at persuasion, coercion, or misguided appeals to patriotism. When a law enforcement officer realizes that he or she simply will not succeed by such methods, most likely he or she will abandon the effort and take the appropriate course of action by proving to the proper court that he or she has good cause to receive access to such confidential information.

• Be prepared to communicate with local news media. Develop a public information statement that may be distributed to interested members of the public and law enforcement officers detailing the principles behind confidentiality. Such a statement should include an explanation of the chilling effect on First Amendment rights which public access to personally identifiable information about library users would cause. Emphasize that the First Amendment protections of free speech and a free press guarantee the corresponding freedom to read what is written, hear what is spoken, and view other forms of expression. The protection of privacy preserves these rights. An individual's reading habits cannot be equated with his or her character or beliefs. The First Amendment does not apply only to preapproved or popular beliefs. The First Amendment guarantees the right to hold and espouse *unpopular* beliefs and ideas. The First Amendment protects dissent. The First Amendment protects against the imposition of a state or community-approved orthodoxy as well as an enforced conformity of expression and belief. The First Amendment protects all Americans' rights to read and view information and decide for themselves their points of view and opinions.

The freedom to read and to consider all types of information without fear of government or community reprisal or ostracism is crucial to the preservation of a free democratic society. The freedom to read fosters and encourages responsible citizenship and open debate in the marketplace of ideas.

The library is a central resource where information and differing points of view are available. Library users must be free to use the library, its resources and services without government interference.

Source: ALA Intellectual Freedom Committee, 1989

Test your I.F. I.Q.

ANSWER YES OR NO to the following questions on intellectual freedom practices (answers on next page). As a librarian or school media specialist, have you ever:

1. Not purchased a popular title because parents might disapprove?
2. Checked magazines or other materials for potentially controversial content and then restricted access to the item or removed the entire item from the collection?
3. Not purchased an item because a review or publishers catalog indicates the book is "for mature readers," has explicit language or illustrations, or might be controversial?
4. Not purchased sex books from a conservative religious point of view because a staff member found them personally repugnant?
5. Skipped over words while reading to students?
6. Reviewed potentially controversial materials and decided not to purchase because of poor characterization, poorly developed plot, or other violations of the "Law of Literary Merit," even though other non-controversial materials in the collection also violate the "Law of Literary Merit"?
7. Established restricted shelves of materials that might offend parents or administrators?
8. Used MPAA ratings on videocassettes to determine circulation policies?
9. Restricted interlibrary loan services to teachers?
10. Established separate collections for specific age groups in a 7-12 media center or K-12 media center?
11. Not purchased materials concerning minorities because of people saying "We don't need that book because no one in our community is gay" (or Jewish, black, or of Hispanic origin)?
12. Not purchased publications representing diverse points of view because some might consider the viewpoint "extreme"?
13. Colored in pictures or removed pages from books?
14. Used a circulation system that allows anyone to identify who has checked out an item?
15. Removed a book when requested to do so by an administrator even though your policy says a hearing must be held before a book is removed?

9

Answers

If you answered yes to *any* of these questions, your library practices violate the Library Bill of Rights and its interpretations. The answers give the specific sections affected. See pages 380–81 for the Library Bill of Rights.

1. Library Bill of Rights (LBR), Article 2; free access to libraries for minors.
2. LBR Article 5; restricted access to library materials; free access to libraries for minors.
3. LBR Articles 1, 2, and 5; free access to libraries for minors; access to resources and services in the school library media program.
4. LBR Article 2; diversity in collection development.
5. LBR Article 2; expurgation of library materials.
6. LBR Article 3; free access to libraries for minors; access to resources and services in the school library media program.
7. LBR Article 5; restricted access to library materials; free access to libraries for minors; access to resources and services in the school library media program.
8. LBR Article 3.
9. LBR Article 3; restricted access to library materials; access to resources and services in the school library media program.
10. LBR Articles 2 and 5; labeling; access to resources and services in the school library media program.
11. LBR Article 2; diversity in collection development; free access to libraries for minors.
12. LBR Articles 1, 2, and 5; diversity in collection development; access to resources and services in the school library media program.
13. LBR Article 2; expurgation of library resources.
14. LBR Article 5; confidentiality of library records.
15. LBR Articles 1, 2, 3, 4, and 5; administrative policies and procedures; evaluating library collections; challenged materials; access to resources and services in the school library media program.

Source: ALA American Association of School Librarians, 1986

Free access to libraries for minors

LIBRARY POLICIES AND PROCEDURES that effectively deny minors equal access to all library resources available to other users violate the Library Bill of Rights. The American Library Association opposes all attempts to restrict access to library services, materials, and facilities based on the age of library users.

Article 5 of the Library Bill of Rights states, "A person's right to use a library should not be denied or abridged because of origin, age, background, or views." The "right to use a library" includes free access to, and unrestricted use of, all the services, materials, and facilities the library has to offer. Every restriction on access to, and use of, library resources, based solely on the chronological age, educational level, or legal emancipation of users violates Article 5.

Libraries are charged with the mission of developing resources to meet the diverse information needs and interests of the communities they serve. Services, materials, and facilities that fulfill the needs and interests of library users at different stages in their personal development are a necessary part of library resources. The needs and interests of each library user, and resources appropriate to meet those needs and interests, must be determined on an individual basis. Librarians cannot predict what resources will best fulfill the needs and interests of any individual user based on a single criterion such as chronological age, level of education, or legal emancipation.

The selection and development of library resources should not be diluted as a result of minors having the same access to library resources as adult users. Institutional self-censorship diminishes the credibility of the library in the community and restricts access for all library users.

Librarians and library trustees should not resort to age restrictions on access to library resources in an effort to avoid actual or anticipated objections from parents or anyone else. The mission, goals, and objectives of libraries do not authorize librarians or library trustees to assume, abrogate, or overrule the rights and responsibilities of parents or guardians. Librarians and library trustees should maintain that parents—and only parents—have the right and the responsibility to restrict the access of their children—and only their children—to library resources. Parents who not want their children to have access to certain library services, materials or facilities, should so advise their children. Librarians and library trustees cannot assume the role of parents or the functions of parental authority in the private relationship between parent and child. Librarians and library trustees have a public and professional obligation to provide equal access to all library resources for all library users.

Librarians have a professional commitment to ensure that all members of the community they serve have free and equal access to the entire range of library resources regardless of content, approach, format, or amount of detail. This principle of library service applies equally to all users, minors as well as adults. Librarians and library trustees must uphold this principle in order to provide adequate and effective service to minors.

Specific examples of denial of equal access include, but are not limited to:

• restricting access to reading or reference rooms, or to otherwise open stack areas, based on the age or school grade level of the user;

• issuing limited access library cards, or otherwise restricting the circulation of materials, based on the age or school grade level of the user;

• assigning materials to special collections, such as parenting, teacher/ professional, historical/genealogical collections, and restricting access to these collections, based on the age or school grade level of the user;

• using manual or computerized registration or circulation systems that restrict access to materials, based on the age or school grade level of the user;

• sequestering or otherwise restricting access to material because of their content, based on the age or school grade level of the user;

• requiring or soliciting written permission from parent or guardian to access or restrict materials because of their content, based on the age or school grade level of the user;

• restricting access to interlibrary loan, fax, and electronic reference services, based on the age or school grade level of the user;

• restricting access to materials because of their format and/or their cost, such as computer software, compact disks, periodicals, microfilm/fiche, and videocassettes, based on the age or school grade level of the user;

• charging fees or requiring deposits to access services, materials, or facilities, based on the age or school grade level of the user;

• refusing to process interlibrary loans, reserves, or reference requests for materials classified as juvenile;

• assigning professional/nonprofessional staff to reference searches, based on the age or school grade level of the user;

• restricting access to library-sponsored programs or events otherwise designed for general audiences, based on the age or school grade level of the user;

• restricting access to public facilities, such as meeting rooms, display cases, and notice boards, based on the age or school grade level of the user.

9

Source: ALA Intellectual Freedom Committee, 1991

Exhibit spaces and bulletin boards

LIBRARIES OFTEN PROVIDE exhibit spaces and bulletin boards. The uses made of these spaces should conform to the Library Bill of Rights: Article I states, "Materials should not be excluded because of the origin, background, or views of those contributing to their creation." Article II states, "Materials should not be proscribed or removed because of partisan or doctrinal disapproval." Article VI maintains that exhibit space should be made available "on an equitable basis, regardless of the beliefs or affiliations of individuals or groups requesting their use."

In developing library exhibits, staff members should endeavor to present a broad spectrum of opinion and a variety of viewpoints. Libraries should not shrink from developing exhibits because of controversial content or because of the beliefs or affiliations of those whose work is represented. Just as libraries do not endorse the viewpoints of those whose works are represented in their collections, libraries also do not endorse the beliefs or viewpoints of topics that may be the subject of library exhibits.

Exhibit areas often are made available for use by community groups. Libraries should formulate a written policy for the use of these exhibit areas to assure that space is provided on an equitable basis to all groups that request it.

Written policies for exhibit space use should be stated in inclusive rather than exclusive terms. For example, a policy that the library's exhibit space is open "only to organizations engaged in educational, cultural, intellectual, or charitable activities" is an inclusive statement of the limited uses of the exhibit space. This defined limitation would permit religious groups to use the exhibit space because they engage in intellectual activities, but would exclude most commercial uses of the exhibit space.

A publicly supported library may limit use of its exhibit space to strictly "library-related" activities, provided that the limitation is clearly circumscribed and is viewpoint neutral.

Libraries may include in this policy rules regarding the time, place, and manner of use of the exhibit space, so long as the rules are content-neutral and are applied in the same manner to all groups wishing to use the space. A library may wish to limit access to exhibit space to groups within the community served by the library. This practice is acceptable provided that the same rules and regulations apply to everyone, and that exclusion is not made on the basis of the doctrinal, religious, or political beliefs of the potential users.

The library should not censor or remove an exhibit because some members of the community may disagree with its content. Those who object to the content of any exhibit held at the library should be able to submit their complaint and/or their own exhibit proposal to be judged according to the policies established by the library.

Libraries may wish to post a permanent notice near the exhibit area stating that the library does not advocate or endorse the viewpoints of exhibits or exhibitors.

Libraries that make bulletin boards available to public groups for posting notices of public interest should develop criteria for the use of these spaces based on the same considerations as those outlined above. Libraries may wish to develop criteria regarding the size of material to be displayed, the length of time materials may remain on the bulletin board, the frequency with which material may be posted for the same group, and the geographic area from which notices will be accepted.

Source: ALA Intellectual Freedom Committee, 1991

Meeting rooms

MANY LIBRARIES PROVIDE meeting rooms for individuals and groups as part of a program of service. Article VI of the Library Bill of Rights states that such facilities should be made available to the public served by the given library "on an equitable basis, regardless of the beliefs or affiliations of individuals or groups requesting their use."

Libraries maintaining meeting room facilities should develop and publish policy statements governing use. These statements can properly define time, place, or manner of use; such qualifications should not pertain to the content of a meeting or to the beliefs or affiliations of the sponsors. These statements should be made available in any commonly used language within the community served.

If meeting rooms in libraries supported by public funds are made available to the general public for nonlibrary-sponsored events, the library may not exclude any group based on the subject matter to be discussed or based on the ideas that the group advocates. For example, if a library allows charities and sports clubs to discuss their activities in library meeting rooms, then the library should not exclude partisan political or religious groups from discussing their activities in the same facilities. If a library opens its meeting rooms to a wide variety of civic organizations, then the library may not deny access to a religious organization. Libraries may wish to post a permanent notice near the meeting room stating that the library does not advocate or endorse the viewpoints of meetings or meeting room users.

Written policies for meeting room use should be stated in inclusive rather than exclusive terms. For example, a policy that the library's facilities are open "only to organizations engaged in educational, cultural, intellectual, or charitable activities" is an inclusive statement of the limited uses to which the facilities may be put. This defined limitation would permit religious groups to use the facilities because they engage in intellectual activities, but would exclude most commercial uses of the facility.

A publicly supported library may limit use of its meeting rooms to strictly "library-related" activities, provided that the limitation is clearly circumscribed and is viewpoint neutral.

Written policies may include limitations on frequency of use, and whether or not meetings held in library meeting rooms must be open to the public. If state and local laws permit private as well as public sessions of meetings in libraries, may choose to offer both options. The same standard should be applicable to all.

If meetings are open to the public, libraries should include in their meeting room policy statement a section which addresses admission fees. If admission fees are permitted, libraries shall seek to make it possible that these fees do not limit access to individuals who may be unable to pay, but who wish to attend the meeting. Article V of the Library Bill of Rights states that "a person's right to use a library should not be denied or abridged because of origin, age, background, or views." It is inconsistent with Article V to restrict indirectly access to library meeting rooms based on an individual's or group's ability to pay for that access.

9

Source: ALA Intellectual Freedom Committee, 1991

Principles of public information

AT ITS JUNE 29, 1990, MEETING, the National Commission on Library and Information Science adopted a major federal policy statement. The "Principles of Public Information," which followed two years of task force work and two open public hearings, assert that "public information is information owned by the people and held in trust by their government."

An introduction to the principles states that "With the coming of the Information Age and its many new technologies . . . public information has expanded so quickly that basic principles regarding its creation, use, and dissemination are in danger of being neglected and even forgotten."

The brief statement consists of eight major points:

- The public has the right of access to government information.
- The Federal government should guarantee the integrity and preservation of public information, regardless of its format.
- The Federal government should guarantee the availability to the public of public information.
- The Federal government should safeguard the privacy of persons who request information, as well as persons about whom information exists in government records.
- The Federal government should ensure a wide diversity of sources of access, private as well as governmental, to public information.
- The Federal government should not allow cost to obstruct the people's access to public information.
- The Federal government should ensure that information about government information is easily available and in a single index accessible in a variety of formats.
- The Federal government should guarantee the public's access to public information, regardless of where they live and work, through national networks and programs like the Depository Library Program.

The statement concludes by urging all branches of the federal government, as well as state and local governments and the private sector, to utilize the principles in the development of information policies and in the creation, use, dissemination, and preservation of public information.

What is NCLIS?

The National Commission on Libraries and Information Science (NCLIS) is a permanent, independent federal agency created by Public Law 91-345, signed by President Richard Nixon on July 20, 1970.

Drafted by the ALA Washington Office, P.L. 91-345 affirms that library and information services adequate to meet Americans' needs are essential to achieve national goals. The law charges the commission to advise Congress and the President as well as federal, state, local, and private agencies on library matters; conduct surveys and studies; and promote research and developmental activities to "extend and improve the nation's library and information-handling capacity."

The President appoints the commission chair and 14 other commissioners with the approval of the Senate. They must include the Librarian of Congress, five librarians or information specialists, one specialist in library technology, and an expert on the needs of older Americans. The commissioners serve five years and are compensated for attending business meetings. The commission usually meets four times a year.

Jean M. Curtis is the executive director. For more information, write NCLIS Headquarters, 1111 18th St., Suite 302, Washington, DC 20036.

Source: American Libraries, July/August 1990, p. 625; June 1988, p. 422

Legislation

How to contact your legislator

Personal visits. Face-to-face discussion is the most effective means of communication, and essential to the establishment of a solid working relationship if you do not already know each other. A meeting is more easily arranged early in a session, before pressures build up.

All legislators have one or more district offices. Visits there will often be more convenient for you than in Washington. Members of Congress return periodically (check with the district office), during Congressional recesses, and between sessions.

Constituents are always welcome in Washington. Be sure you have a firm appointment. Use the district office to make local or capitol appointments. (Get to know district staffs: secretaries and administrative assistants. Close working relationships will benefit in many ways.)

Take along others—library director, trustee, Friend, representative of a community organization, citizen activist. Keep the delegation small enough for an easy exchange of viewpoints with the legislator. Leave your card and any written information you may have prepared. Follow up with a letter of appreciation for the time given to you, and include any additional information suggested by the visit.

Telephone calls. Once you have the acquaintance of your representative, telephone calls are appropriate and easy. Make them sparingly to the legislator, whose time is heavily occupied. (Regular contact with staff is possible and desirable.) Telephone to ask support before a hearing or floor vote; to ask for help with legislative colleagues; or to convey urgent local concern. Judge how far to pursue by the reaction. Remember that it is more difficult for a legislator to temporize in a conversation than by letter.

Letters, letters, letters. These are the chief fuel powering any legislative vehicle. They are read. They elicit responses. They represent votes. (Each letter-writer is deemed to represent several like-minded if less highly motivated constituents.) Letters may be formal or informal, typewritten or handwritten. They should be composed by you, giving your reasons for your position (and giving the legislator reasons to support it). If you are asking support for a particular bill, cite it by number and author, and give its title or subject matter.

Telegrams, mailgrams, and fax. These are fast, easy ways to communicate with legislators when the need for action is critical: just prior to a committee or floor vote. Use Western Union's nationwide toll-free telephone number: (800) 325-6000. Various low rates are available.

Five basic rules for effective communication

1. **Be brief.** A legislator's time is limited. So is yours.
2. **Be appreciative.** Acknowledge past support, and convey thanks for current action.
3. **Be specific.** Refer to local library and district needs.
4. **Be informative.** Give reasons why a measure should be supported.
5. **Be courteous.** Ask; do not demand or threaten. Be positive but polite.

Source: ALA Washington Office

9

How to write a letter to your legislator

THE MOST FREQUENTLY USED, correct forms of address are:

To Your Senator:
The Honorable (full name)
United States Senate
Washington, D.C. 20510

To Your Representative:
The Honorable (full name)
U.S. House of Representatives
Washington, D.C. 20515

"Sincerely yours" is in good taste as a complimentary close. Remember to sign your given name and surname. If you use a title in your signature, be sure to enclose it in parentheses.

Forms similar to the above, addressed to your state capital, are appropriate for your state representatives and senators.

Where possible use your official letterhead. If this is not in order, and you write as an individual, use plain white bond paper, and give your official title following your signature as a means of identification and to indicate your competency to speak on the subject.

Do's

1. Your legislators like to hear opinions from home and want to be kept informed of conditions in the district. Base your letter on your own pertinent experiences and observations.

2. If writing about a specific bill, describe it by number or its popular name. Your legislators have thousands of bills before them in the course of a year, and cannot always take time to figure out to which one you are referring.

3. They appreciate intelligent, well-thought-out letters that present a definite position, even if they do not agree.

4. Even more important and valuable to them is a concrete statement of the reasons for your position—particularly if you are writing about a field in which you have specialized knowledge. Representatives have to vote on many matters with which they have had little or no first-hand experience. Some of the most valuable information they receive comes from facts presented in letters from people who have knowledge in the field.

5. Short letters are almost always best. Members of Congress receive many, many letters each day, and a long one may not get as prompt a reading as a brief statement.

6. Letters should be timed to arrive while the issue is alive. Members of the committee considering the bill will appreciate having your views while the bill is ripe for study and action.

7. Don't forget to follow through with a thank-you letter.

Don'ts

1. Avoid letters that merely demand or insist on votes for or against a certain bill; or that say what vote you want but not why. A letter with no reasoning, good or bad, is not very influential.

2. Threats of defeat at the next election are not effective.

3. Boasts of how influential the writer is are not helpful.

4. Do not ask for a vote commitment on a particular bill before the committee in charge of the subject has had a chance to hear the evidence and make its report.

5. Form letters or letters that include excerpts from other letters on the same

subject are not as influential as a simple letter drawing on your own experience.

6. Congressional courtesy requires legislators to refer letters from non-constituents to the proper offices, so you should generally confine your letter-writing to members of your state's delegation or members of the committee specifically considering the bill.

7. Do not engage in letter-writing overkill. Quality, not quantity, is what counts.

Source: ALA Washington Office

The White House Conferences

THE WHITE HOUSE CONFERENCE on Libraries and Information Services (WHCLIS) was initially conceived some 33 years ago when Channing Bete, a library trustee from Greenfield, Massachusetts, initially proposed the idea. However, four different U.S. Presidents (Johnson, Nixon, Ford, and Carter) were to preside over this nation before the first Conference was held in November 1979. More than 100,000 people participated in preconference activities including those held in each of the 57 states and territories. These preconferences elected more than 600 official delegates. An additional 4,000 attendees, including alternate delegates, observers, volunteers, and staff, made it the largest White House Conference ever held.

The 1979 Conference focused on five themes:

1. Meeting personal needs.
2. Enhancing lifelong learning.
3. Improving organizations and professions.
4. Effectively governing our society.
5. Increasing international understanding and cooperation.

By the end of the conference 49 resolutions had been considered, 25 of which passed. Among other things, the resolutions called for greater library visibility within the Department of Education, broader information access for all Americans, library services without charge in publicly supported institutions, network sharing, more national coordination, increased funding, and the convening of a White House Conference on Library and Information Services every decade.

Assessment regarding the success of the Conference was mixed. Noteworthy resolutions related to the five themes and other critical issues were passed. Political leaders at all levels, including the President of the United States, were involved in one way or another. Leaders from "information organizations," including ALA, the Information Industry Association, the Association of American Publishers, the Association of Research Libraries, and others were present. Some have suggested, however, that while the Conference underscored the importance of what the library world was already working on, it failed to develop any creative new concepts, and that while major news magazines provided moderate coverage, the coverage did not focus world attention on libraries.

The success of the Conference was also mixed so far as academic libraries were concerned. Much of the discussion was in the context of public libraries. The Conference did mention college and university libraries, but there were no academic library issues discussed per se. Only 33 academic librarians were included in the more than 900 delegates and alternates.

The 1979 Conference passed a resolution recommending that a White House Conference be held each decade "to establish national information goals and priorities for the next decade." To that end a law was passed that authorized the President to call a second Conference, which was scheduled for July 9-13, 1991.

9

The second White House Conference

At this writing, delegates were expected to gather to develop recommendations for the improvement of the library and information services of the nation and their use by the public. Likely to be adopted by the official delegates were resolutions on the federal role in expanding literacy, increasing productivity, and strengthening democracy through changes and improvements in library and information services.

The final report of the Conference, including its findings and recommendations, was to be forwarded to the President, and by him to Congress, for consideration in the development of policies and future legislation concerning library and information services for the nation. The report will be widely disseminated to raise public awareness of libraries and their services for the individual, the economy, and the nation.

The three overall themes of the second Conference were library and information services for productivity, for literacy, and for democracy. The following issues were among those to be considered as of this writing:

• How library and information services can provide business and industry improved access to information.

• How the information needs of senior citizens, the disabled, the disadvantaged, the functionally illiterate, and those whose primary language is not English can be met.

• How access to new information technologies can be assured.

• How new technology can be applied to the educational process in penal institutions.

• How library and information services can be improved through cooperation with the private sector.

• How technology can be used to store, analyze, and transmit information needed by the public and by government decision makers.

• How information users can be helped in their efforts to sift through an ever-expanding information supply, extracting what is useful, reliable, and timely.

Key organizations

National Commission on Library and Information Science (NCLIS). The Commission is a permanent, independent federal agency created to advise the government on national library and information policies and plans. It is the parent organization for the White House Conference.

White House Conference Advisory Committee (WHCAC). This Committee is composed of 30 members who are appointed (eight by the chair of NCLIS, five by the Speaker of the House, five by the President pro tem of the Senate, ten by the President; the Secretary of Education and Librarian of Congress are members by statute). The purpose of the Committee is to assist and advise NCLIS in planning and conducting the Conference.

Preconferences

Each state and territory, the District of Columbia, the American Indian Tribes, and the federal library community held preconference activities to identify library and information science issues that need to be addressed. These preconferences generated a broad grassroots involvement that assumed consideration of a wide range of library and information needs. Many of these involve issues at the state and territorial level and provide a future agenda for local consideration. Others had a national thrust and were taken to the White House Conference for further discussion and debate.

Delegates

More than 600 official voting delegates to the Conference were chosen by their respective states and territories. Twenty-five percent represented library and information professionals; 25% represented government officials at all levels; 25% represented friends, trustees, and other library supporters; and 25% represented the general public.

Source: David B. Walch, "A White House Conference primer for academic libraries," *College & Research Libraries News*, October 1990, pp. 849–50; National Commission on Libraries and Information Science, *The White House Conference on Library and Information Services, 1991* (Washington, D.C.: NCLIS, 1991)

Literacy

The American eighth-grader

WHY DO SOME CHILDREN SUCCEED in school while others do not? The answer to this question may become more evident as data collected through the National Education Longitudinal Study of 1988 (NELS:88) are analyzed over time.

NELS:88 was the first nationally representative longitudinal sample of eighth grade students in public and private schools. The data provide measures of student performance and allow for the examination of attitudes and activities of eighth graders as they pass through the education system.

At-risk issues

Early analysis of NELS:88 data examined information on six commonly used indicators of "at risk" status. Overall, 53% of the students had none of these risk factors, 27% had one, and 20% had two or more.

The at-risk indicators and the percentage of eighth graders identified in each category are

- Single parent family (22%)
- Family income less than $15,000 (21%)
- Home alone more than 3 hours a day (14%)
- Parents have no high school diploma (11%)
- Sibling dropped out (10%)
- Limited English proficiency (2%)

9

Students with several risk factors tended to have more educational problems, including lower grades and higher absenteeism, than students with none. Students with two or more risk factors were six times as likely as those with none to report that they did not expect to graduate from high school; they were twice as likely to score in the lowest 25% on achievement tests and to receive the lowest 25% of grades.

High school and college plans

Although a majority of the eighth graders had high educational aspirations, many were not planning to enter high school programs that would lead them to realize their goals.

- While two-thirds planned to finish college or attain higher degrees, only about one-third planned to enroll in a college-preparatory program. In fact, 25% of the eighth graders did not know which high school program they would enter.
- Hispanics and American Indians were the most likely to report that they did not expect to complete high school.

School safety and school climate

More than two-thirds of eighth graders reported positive feelings about school. Some subgroups were more likely than others to report negative experiences.

- Overall, 10% of students reported that someone had offered to sell them drugs at school;
- Blacks and American Indians were nearly twice as likely as whites to report that they did not feel safe at school (18% versus 9.9%).

Math and reading performance

Nineteen percent of all eighth graders and 30% of Hispanics, blacks, and American Indians were not proficient in the basic math skills considered necessary to perform everyday tasks. Fourteen percent of all eighth graders and about 30% of students who usually speak a language other than English were unable to perform basic reading tasks, such as finding information in a text or identifying the author's main thought.

To explore the connection between socioeconomic status (SES) and achievement, several family factors were taken into account—income, educational levels, and occupations of both mother and father.

- Students in the top 25% of SES were eight times as likely as those in the bottom 25% to be proficient at the advanced mathematics level (conceptual understanding).
- Among low SES students, 18% of Asians, but fewer than 8% of whites, Hispanics, and blacks performed at the advanced mathematics level.
- Among low SES students, about one-quarter of Asians, Hispanics, and blacks, and 17% of whites failed to show basic reading skills.

Other findings

Overall, 18% of the students reported that they had repeated at least one grade and about 2%, two or more. Those most likely to be repeaters are from low SES; male; black, Hispanic, or American Indian; have low grades or limited-English proficiency.

Typical eighth graders reported spending four times more hours per week watching television than doing homework (21.4 hours versus 5.6 hours); they spend about 2 hours of leisure time reading.

Source: Office of Educational Research and Improvement, *Research in Brief,* August 1990

How to develop a family literacy program in your library

1. Identify literacy programs operating in your community and find out what family literacy or general educational services are currently offered. Ask staff in these programs for their ideas about new services that are most needed (see pages 409–11 for state literacy contacts).

2. Determine the purpose, goals, and objectives for starting a family literacy program. Librarians, staff, and literacy workers should work together to articulate what a family literacy program will accomplish.

3. Identify who will administer the program and who will provide the direct service. Create an advisory committee with representatives of cooperating agencies. You may also wish to involve a member of the library board or the library Friends as well as other community groups.

4. Describe who will be served by your family literacy program. Establish guidelines or qualifications. These may include reading level of adults in the program, age of the children, or the relationship of adults and children (parent, grandparent, babysitter).

5. Work with your advisory committee to determine your program. This might include special collections of books and videos, space in library, fund-raising, and program administration, tutoring programs, field trips, story times or other activities.

6. Determine what staff is needed to implement your program. Decide if tutor training for adult literacy volunteers is needed. Decide if program staff or adult literacy staff will need special training to become familiar with materials particularly suited to family literacy, such as high-low materials, or children's literature for new adult readers.

7. Set a realistic budget and seek funding to cover start-up costs. Plan how the library will provide ongoing support for the program if it is successful or needs to expand.

8. Plan your publicity. Be sure to include radio, television, and the nonprint media.

9. Develop strategies to recruit and retain participants. Work with other educational and service agencies. Try to anticipate barriers to participation such as transportation, day care, or discomfort with new surroundings. Establishing special telephone instructions may be important because learners have preferences about when, where, and how they are contacted.

10. Plan to evaluate the program. Know how you will measure success. Be realistic about how many families will be involved in the first year and what benefits are anticipated.

Source: ALA Office for Library Outreach Services

How to start a Dial-A-Story

DIAL-A-STORY IS A LIBRARY OUTREACH PROGRAM which takes stories into homes. Callers hear a recorded story at any time of day or night. This service is free within a given calling area.

What equipment is needed?

- An answering machine adapted with a counter to log the number of calls
- Leaderless audiocassette tape (tapes with no blank space at the start)
- Phone line installed by the phone company

How much does it cost?

The equipment and installation (above) should be less than $2,000. This is a one-time investment.

Ongoing costs include monthly phone line charge and staff time needed to record stories. Cost of periodic maintenance will vary.

What is recorded on Dial-A-Story?

Folk literature (fables, tales, etc.) is a ready source of short and appealing material. Print versions of folktales can be found easily in most libraries. They need little editing. Folktales are often in the public domain.

When you're ready to start

1. Keep the tales short—no longer than 3 1/2 minutes.
2. Time the length of the stories and practice them before recording.
3. Record stories at a normal pace using a clear voice. Don't read too slowly or too fast. Avoid dialects.
4. Change stories at least weekly.
5. Advertise this service.
6. Include a welcoming message from the library inviting listeners to come to the library and get stories to take home.

Dial this number to hear a Dial-a-Story: (202) 638-5717.

Source: ALA Office for Library Outreach Services

The Bell Atlantic/ALA Family Literacy Project

The American Library Association believes that a child without family encouragement for reading and without access to educational opportunities—and all that libraries have to offer—is handicapped for life. To help fight illiteracy, ALA and Bell Atlantic have formed a partnership to encourage libraries to develop or enhance library-based family literacy projects. Twenty-five public libraries in the mid-Atlantic states received $5,000 grants, which have provided funding for a cooperative effort between the library, adult education specialists, or literacy providers, and a Bell Atlantic representative. For more information, contact ALA/OLOS, 50 E. Huron, Chicago, IL 60611-2795.

State library literacy contacts

Alabama: Mary Alice Fields, Library Consultant, Library Development Division, Alabama Public Library Service, 6030 Monticello Drive, Montgomery, AL 36130; (205) 277-7330.

Alaska: Karen R. Crane, State Librarian, Alaska State Library, P.O. Box G, Juneau, AK 99811; (907) 465-2910.

Arizona: Beth Ellen Woodard, Program Consultant, Library Extension Division, Arizona State Department of Library, Archives, and Public Records, 1700 West Washington, Phoenix, AZ 85007; (602) 542-5841.

Arkansas: Jack C. Mulkey, Associate Director for Library Development Library Development Unit, Arkansas State Library, One Capitol Mall, Little Rock, AR 72201; (501) 682-2159.

California: Al Bennett, Literacy Specialist, Library Development Services Bureau, California State Library, 1001 Sixth Street, Suite 300, Sacramento, CA 95814; (916) 322-0377.

Paul Keilly, Community Organizations/Communications Specialist, Library Development Services Bureau, California State Library, 1001 Sixth Street, Suite 300, Sacramento, CA 95814; (916) 324-7358.

Colorado: Mary Willoughby, Program Manager, Colorado Literacy Action, Office of Library and Adult Services, Colorado Department of Education, 201 E. Colfax Avenue, Room 100, Denver, CO 80203; (303) 866-6743.

Connecticut: Ilene Tobey, Outreach Consultant Division of Library Services, Connecticut State Library, 231 Capitol Avenue, Hartford, CT 06106; (203) 566-2712.

Delaware: Richard Meldrom, Senior Librarian, Delaware Division of Libraries, 33-43 South DuPont Highway, P.O. Box 1401, Dover, DE 19901; (302) 736-4748.

District of Columbia: Marcia Harrington, Adult Basic Education Specialist, Adult Services Department, Martin Luther King Jr. Memorial Library, Room 426, 909 G St., N.W., Washington, DC 20001; (202) 727-1616.

Florida: Betty Ann Scott, Library Consultant for Literacy and the Elderly, Bureau of Library Development, State Library of Florida, R. A. Gray Building, Tallahassee, FL 32399-0250; (904) 487-2651.

Georgia: Joellen Ostendorf, Consultant, Readers Services, Georgia Division of Public Library Services, 156 Trinity Avenue, SW, Atlanta, GA 30303-3692; (404) 656-2461.

Diana Tope, Deputy Director, Georgia Division of Public Library Services, 156 Trinity Avenue, SW, Atlanta, GA 30303-3692; (404) 656-2461.

Hawaii: Nyla Fujii, Statewide Young Adult Coordinator, Materials Evaluation and Programming Section, Office of the State Librarian, Hawaii State Public Library System, 465 South King St. B1, Honolulu, HI 96813; (808) 548-5593.

Idaho: Peggy McClendon, Special Projects Coordinator, Library Development Division, Idaho State Library, 325 West State Street, Boise, ID 83702; (208) 334-2153.

Illinois: Joan Seamon, Illinois Literacy Coordinator, Literacy Office of the Illinois State Library, Illinois State Library, 4th and Jackson Street, Springfield, IL 62756; (217) 785-6926.

Indiana: Suzannah Walker, Consultant for Special Services, Extension Division, Indiana State Library, 140 North Senate Avenue, Indianapolis, IN 46204; (317) 232-3717.

Iowa: William Cochran, Director of Library Development, Bureau of Library Development, State Library of Iowa, East 12th and Grand, Des Moines, IA 50319; (515) 281-4400.

Kansas: Vicki Stewart, Literacy Program Coordinator, Library Development Division, Kansas State Library, P.O. Box 2, Andover, KS 67002; (316) 733-4864.

9

Kentucky: Sara Calloway, Adult Services Coordinator, Kentucky Department for Libraries and Archives, P.O. Box 537, Frankfort, KY 40602; (502) 875-7000.

Louisiana: Ben Brady, Associate State Librarian, Library Development Division, Louisiana State Library, P.O. Box 131, Baton Rouge, LA 70821; (504) 342-4931.

Maine: Jack Boynton, Director, Library Development Services Division, Maine State Library, State House Station #64, Augusta, ME 04333; (207) 289-5620.

Maryland: Sue Courson, Branch Chief, Public Libraries, Division of Library Development and Services, Maryland State Department of Education, 200 West Baltimore Street, Baltimore, MD 21201; (301) 333-2117.

Massachusetts: Shelly Quezada, Consultant, Library Services to the Unserved, Library Development Unit, Massachusetts Board of Library Commissioners, 648 Beacon Street, Boston, MA 02215; (617) 267-9400.

Michigan: Sharon Rothenberger, Director, Library Development Division, 717 West Allegan Avenue, Lansing, MI 48909; (517) 373-1580.

Minnesota: Noell Leitzke, Public Library Specialist, Minnesota Library Development and Services, 440 Capitol Square Building, 550 Cedar Street, St. Paul, MN 55101; (612) 296-2821.

Mississippi: Ruth Ann Gibson, General Consultant, Library Development Division, Mississippi Library Commission, P.O. Box 10700, 1221 Ellis Avenue, Jackson, MS 39289-0700; (601) 359-1036.

Missouri: William Davis, Senior Associate for Library Networks and Resource Sharing, Missouri State Library, 2002 Missouri Blvd., Jefferson City, MO 65102-0387; (314) 751-3033.

Montana: Chloe Fessler, Literacy Coordinator, Montana State Library, 1515 East 6th Avenue, Helena, MT 59620; (406) 543-4135.

Nebraska: Richard Allen, Library Services Coordinator, Department of Library Development, Nebraska Library Commission, 1420 P Street, Lincoln, NE 68508; (402) 471-3216.

Nevada: Meg Kochendorfer, Director of Nevada Literacy Coalition, Nevada State Library and Archives, Capitol Complex, Carson City, NV 89710; (702) 887-2627.

Bonnie Buckley, Library Consultant and Grants Administrator, Library Development Division, Nevada State Library and Archives, Capitol Complex, Carson City, NV 89710; (702) 887-2623.

New Hampshire: Rebecca Albert, Literacy Coordinator, Bureau of Development Services, New Hampshire State Library, 20 Park Street, Concord, NH 03301; (603) 271-2425.

New Jersey: Doreitha Madden, Director, Library Literacy Programs, New Jersey State Library, 3535 Quaker Bridge Rd., Trenton, NJ 08625; (609) 588-3153, 588-6153.

New Mexico: Scott Sheldon, Program Manager for Library Development, Library Development Unit, New Mexico State Library, 325 Don Gasper, Santa Fe, NM 87503; (505) 827-3808.

New York: Carol Sheffer, Outreach Consultant, Division of Library Development, New York State Library, Room 10C50, Cultural Education Center, Albany, NY 12230; (518) 474-6971.

North Carolina: Charles Montouri, Business/Adult Services Consultant, Public Library Development Section, North Carolina Department of Cultural Resources, Division of State Library, 109 E. Jones Street, Raleigh, NC 27611; (919) 733-2570.

North Dakota: Eric Halverson, Public Library Consultant, Library Development Division, North Dakota State Library, Liberty Memorial Building, Capitol Grounds, Bismarck, ND 58505; (701) 224-4655.

Ohio: Tom Szudz, Special Services Consultant, Library Development Division, State Library of Ohio, 65 S. Front Street, Columbus, OH 43266-0334; (800) 686-1532, (614) 466-1062.

Oklahoma: Marilyn Vesely, Public Information Officer, Public Information Office, Oklahoma Department of Libraries, 200 N.E. 18th Street, Oklahoma City, OK 73105; (405) 521-2502.

Oregon: Ann Beckom, Project Manager, Oregon Literacy Initiative, Library Development Services Unit, Oregon State Library, State Library Building, Salem, OR 97310; (503) 378-2112.

Pennsylvania: Elizabeth A. Funk, Acting Coordinator, Advisory Services, Library Development Division, State Library of Pennsylvania, Box 1601, Harrisburg, PA 17105; (717) 783-5737.

Puerto Rico: Nadia Roque Lerdo, LSCA Coordinator, Public Library Division, Department of Education, P.O. Box 759, Hato Rey, PR 00919; (809) 754-7227.

Rhode Island: Sheila Carlson, Supervisor of Institutional Library Services, Division of Library Planning, Development, and Information Services, Rhode Island Department of State Library Services, 95 Davis Street, Providence, RI 02908; (401) 277-2726.

South Carolina: Mark Pumphrey, Institutional Library Consultant, Library Development Division, South Carolina State Library, 1500 Senate Street, Box 11469, Columbia, SC 29211; (803) 734-8666.

South Dakota: Dan Boyd, Director, Regional Libraries for the Handicapped and Coordinator for State Literacy Projects, Library Development Division, South Dakota State Library and Archives, 800 Governors Drive, Pierre, SD 57501; (605) 773-3131.

Tennessee: Nancy Weatherman, Special Library Services Coordinator, Planning and Development Section, Tennessee State Library and Archives, 403 Seventh Avenue, North, Nashville, TN 37219; (615) 741-3158.

Texas: Barbara Crosby, Special Services Consultant, Library Development Division, Texas State Library, Box 12927, Capitol Station, Austin, TX 78711; (512) 463-5460.

Utah: Douglas Hindmarsh, Grants Coordinator/Public Library Consultant, Development Services Program, Utah State Library Division, 2150 S. 300 West, Suite 16, Salt Lake City, UT 84115; (801) 466-5888.

Vermont: Marianne Cassell, Development and Adult Services Consultant, Library Development Division, Vermont Department of Libraries, Pavillion Office Building, Montpelier, VT 05602; (802) 828-3261.

Virginia: Dudley Colbert, Literacy Consultant, Public Library Development Division, Virginia State Library and Archives, 11th Street at Capitol Square, Richmond, VA 23219; (804) 786-2975.

Washington: Marie Zimmerman, LSCA Administrator, Library Planning and Development Division, Washington State Library, AJ-11, Olympia, WA 98504-0111; (206) 753-2114.

Karen Goettling, Literacy Project Coordinator, Library Planning and Development Division, Washington State Library, AJ-11, Olympia, WA 98504-0111; (206) 753-2114.

West Virginia: Donna Calvert, Direct Services Consultant, Direct Services Department, West Virginia Library Commission, Science and Cultural Center, Charleston, WV 25305; (304) 348-2531.

Shirley Smith, Field Services Consultant, Field Services Department, West Virginia Library Commission, Science and Cultural Center, Charleston, WV 25305; (304) 348-2041.

Wisconsin: Frances de Usabel, Consultant, Library Services for Special Users, Bureau for Library Development, Division for Library Services, Wisconsin Department of Public Instruction, P.O. Box 7841, Madison, WI 53707; (608) 266-0419.

Wyoming: Judith L. Yeo, Literacy Coordinator, Wyoming Alliance for Literacy, Wyoming State Library, Supreme Court and State Library Building, Cheyenne, WY 82002-0650; (307) 777-7281.

9

Source: ALA Office for Library Outreach Services

Copyright

Photocopying for classroom and library reserve use

THIS MODEL POLICY, still valid for academic institutions in the early 1990s, was prepared by Mary Hutchings, ALA legal counsel, in March 1982.

The Copyright Act and photocopying

From time to time, the faculty and staff of this University [College] may use photocopied materials to supplement research and teaching. In many cases, photocopying can facilitate the University's [College's] mission; that is, the development and transmission of information. However, the photocopying of copyrighted materials is a right granted under the copyright law's doctrine of "fair use" which must not be abused. This report will explain the University's [College's] policy concerning the photocopying of copyrighted materials by faculty and library staff. Please note that this policy does not address other library photocopying that may be permitted under other sections of the copyright law, e.g., 17 U.S.C. § 108.

Copyright is a constitutionally conceived property right that is designed to promote the progress of science and the useful arts by securing for an author the benefits of his or her original work of authorship for a limited time. U.S. Constitution, Art. 1, Sec. 8. The Copyright statute, 17 U.S.C. § 101 et seq., implements this policy by balancing the author's interest against the public interest in the dissemination of information affecting areas of universal concern, such as art, science, history, and business. The grand design of this delicate balance is to foster the creation and dissemination of intellectual works for the general public.

The Copyright Act defines the rights of a copyright holder and how they may be enforced against an infringer. Included within the Copyright Act is the "fair use" doctrine which allows, under certain conditions, the copying of copyrighted material. While the Act lists general factors under the heading of "fair use," it provides little in the way of specific directions for what constitutes fair use. The law states:

Limitations on exclusive rights: Fair use. Notwithstanding the provisions of section 106, the fair use of a copyrighted work, including such use by reproduction in copies or phonorecords or by any other means specified by that section, for purposes such as criticism, comment, news reporting, teaching (including multiple copies for classroom use), scholarship, or research, is not an infringement of copyright. In determining whether the use made of a work in any particular case is a fair use the factors to be considered shall include—

1. the purpose and character of the use, including whether such use is of a commercial nature or is for nonprofit educational purposes;

2. the nature of the copyrighted work;

3. the amount and substantiality of the portion used in relation to the copyrighted work as a whole; and

4. the effect of the use upon the potential market for or value of the copyrighted work. (17 U.S.C. § 107.)

The purpose of this report is to provide you, the faculty and staff of this University [College], with an explanation of when the photocopying of copyrighted material in our opinion is permitted under the fair use doctrine. Where possible, common examples of research, classroom, and library reserve photocopying have been included to illustrate what we believe to be the reach and limits of fair use.

Please note that the copyright law applies to all forms of photocopying whether it is undertaken at a commercial copying center, at the University's [College's] central or departmental copying facilities or at a self-service machine. While you are free to use the services of a commercial establishment, you should be prepared to provide documentation of permission from the publisher (if such permission is necessary under this policy), since many commercial copiers will require such proof.

We hope this report will give you an appreciation of the factors that weigh in favor of fair use and those factors that weigh against fair use, but faculty members must determine for themselves which works will be photocopied. This University [College] does not condone a policy of photocopying instead of purchasing copyrighted works where such photocopying would constitute an infringement under the Copyright law, but it does encourage faculty members to exercise good judgment in serving the best interests of students in an efficient manner. This University [College] and its faculty and staff will make a conscientious effort to comply with these guidelines.

Instructions for securing permission to photocopy copyrighted works when such copying is beyond the limits of fair use appear at the end of this report. It is the policy of this University that the user (faculty, staff or librarian) secure such permission whenever it is legally necessary.

Unrestricted photocopying

Uncopyrighted published works. Writings published before January 1, 1978, which have never been copyrighted, may be photocopied without restriction. Copies of works protected by copyright must bear a copyright notice, which consists of the letter "c" in a circle, or the word "Copyright," or the abbreviation "Copr.," plus the year of first publication, plus the name of the copyright owner. (17 U.S.C. § 401.) As to works published before January 1, 1978, in the case of a book, the notice must be placed on the title page or the reverse side of the title page. In the case of a periodical the notice must be placed either on the title page, the first page of text, or in the masthead. A pre-1978 failure to comply with the notice requirements resulted in the work being injected into the public domain, i.e., unprotected. Copyright notice requirements have been relaxed since 1978, so that the absence of notice on copies of a work published after January 1, 1978, does not necessarily mean the work is in the public domain. (17 U.S.C. § 405(a) and (c).) However, you will not be liable for damages for copyright infringement of works published after that date, if, after normal inspection, you photocopy a work on which you cannot find a copyright symbol and you have not received actual notice of the fact the work is copyrighted. (17 U.S.C. § 405(b).) However, a copyright owner who found out about your photocopying would have the right to prevent further distribution of the copies if in fact the work were copyrighted and the copies are infringing. (17 U.S.C. § 405(b).)

Published works with expired copyrights. Writings with expired copyrights may be photocopied without restriction. In 1992, all copyrights prior to 1916 have expired. (17 U.S.C. § 304(b).) Copyrights granted after 1916 may have been renewed; however the writing will probably not contain notice of the renewal. Therefore, it should be assumed all writings dated 1916 or later are covered by a valid copyright, unless information to the contrary is obtained from the owner or the U.S. Copyright Office (see Copyright Office Circular 15t).

9

Copyright Office Circular R22 explains how to investigate the copyright status of a work. One way is to use the *Catalog of Copyright Entries* published by the Copyright Office and available in [the University Library] many libraries. Alternatively you may request the Copyright Office to conduct a search of its registration and/or assignment records. The Office charges an hourly fee for this service. You will need to submit as much information as you have concerning the work in which you are interested, such as the title, author, approximate date of publication, the type of work or any available copyright data. The Copyright Office does caution that its searches are not conclusive; for instance, if a work obtained copyright less than 28 years ago, it may be fully protected although there has been no registration or deposit.

Unpublished works. Unpublished works, such as theses and dissertations, may be protected by copyright. If such a work was created before January 1, 1978, and has not been copyrighted or published without copyright notice, the work is protected under the new Act for the life of the author plus fifty years, 17 U.S.C. § 303, but in no case earlier than December 31, 2002. If such a work is published on or before that date, the copyright will not expire before December 31, 2027. Works created after January 1, 1978, and not published enjoy copyright protection for the life of the author plus fifty years. (17 U.S.C. § 302.)

U.S. government publications. All U.S. government publications with the possible exception of some National Technical Information Service publications less than five years old may be photocopied without restrictions, except to the extent they contain copyrighted materials from other sources. (17 U.S.C. § 105.) U.S. government publications are documents prepared by an official or employee of the government in an official capacity. (17 U.S.C. § 101.) Government publications include the opinions of courts in legal cases, congressional reports on proposed bills, testimony offered at congressional hearings and the works of government employees in their official capacities. Works prepared by outside authors on contract to the government may or may not be protected by copyright, depending on the specifics of the contract. In the absence of copyright notice on such works, it would be reasonable to assume they are government works in the public domain. It should be noted that state government works may be protected by copyright. (See 17 U.S.C. § 105.) However, the opinions of state courts are not protected.

Permissible photocopying of copyrighted works

The Copyright Act allows anyone to photocopy copyrighted works without securing permission from the copyright owner when the photocopying amounts to a "fair use" of the material. (17 U.S.C. § 107.) The guidelines in this report discuss the boundaries for fair use of photocopied material used in research or the classroom or in a library reserve operation. Fair use cannot always be expressed in numbers—either the number of pages copied or the number of copies distributed. Therefore, you should weigh the various factors listed in the Act and judge whether the intended use of photocopied, copyrighted material is within the spirit of the fair use doctrine. Any serious questions concerning whether a particular photocopying constitutes fair use should be directed to University [College] counsel.

Research uses. At the very least, instructors may make a single copy of any of the following for scholarly research or use in teaching or preparing to teach a class:

1. a chapter from a book;
2. an article from a periodical or newspaper;
3. a short story, short essay, or short poem, whether or not from a collective work;

4. a chart, diagram, graph, drawing, cartoon or picture from a book, periodical, or newspaper.

These examples reflect the most conservative guidelines for fair use. They do not represent inviolate ceilings for the amount of copyrighted material that can be photocopied within the boundaries of fair use. When exceeding these minimum levels, however, you again should consider the four factors listed in Section 107 of the Copyright Act to make sure that any additional photocopying is justified. The following demonstrate situations where increased levels of photocopying would continue to remain within the ambit of fair use:

1. the inability to obtain another copy of the work because it is not available from another library or source or cannot be obtained within your time constraints;

2. the intention to photocopy the material only once and not to distribute the material to others;

3. the ability to keep the amount of material photocopied within a reasonable proportion to the entire work (the larger the work, the greater amount of material which may be photocopied).

Most single-copy photocopying for your personal use in research—even when it involves a substantial portion of a work—may well constitute fair use.

Classroom uses. Primary and secondary school educators have, with publishers, developed the following guidelines, which allow a teacher to distribute photocopied material to students in a class without the publisher's prior permission, under the following conditions:

1. the distribution of the same photocopied material does not occur every semester;

2. only one copy is distributed for each student, which copy must become the student's property;

3. the material includes a copyright notice on the first page of the portion of material photocopied;

4. the students are not assessed any fee beyond the actual cost of the photocopying.

In addition, the educators agreed that the amount of material distributed should not exceed certain brevity standards. Under those guidelines, a prose work may be reproduced in its entirety if it is less than 2,500 words in length. If the work exceeds such length, the excerpt reproduced may not exceed 1,000 words, or 10% of the work, whichever is less. In the case of poetry, 250 words is the maximum permitted.

These minimum standards normally would not be realistic in the University setting. Faculty members needing to exceed these limits for college education should not feel hampered by these guidelines, although they should attempt a "selective and sparing" use of photocopied, copyrighted material.

The photocopying practices of an instructor should not have a significant detrimental impact on the market for the copyrighted work. (17 U.S.C. § 107(4).) To guard against this effect, you usually should restrict use of an item of photocopied material to one course and you should not repeatedly photocopy excerpts from one periodical or author without the permission of the copyright owner.

9

Library reserve uses. At the request of a faculty member, a library may photocopy and place on reserve excerpts from copyrighted works in its collection in accordance with guidelines similar to those governing formal classroom distribution for face-to-face teaching discussed above. This University [College] believes that these guidelines apply to the library reserve shelf to the extent it functions as an extension of classroom readings or reflects an individual student's right to photocopy for personal scholastic use under the doctrine of fair use. In general, librarians may photocopy materials for reserve room use for the convenience of students both in preparing class assignments and in pursuing informal educational activities that higher education requires, such as advanced independent study and research.

If the request calls for only *one* copy to be placed on reserve, the library may photocopy an entire article, or an entire chapter from a book, or an entire poem. Requests for *multiple* copies on reserve should meet the following guidelines:

1. the amount of material should be reasonable in relation to the total amount of material assigned for one term of a course taking into account the nature of the course, its subject matter and level (17 U.S.C. § 107(1) and (3));

2. the number of copies should be reasonable in light of the number of students enrolled, the difficulty and timing of assignments, and the number of other courses that may assign the same material (17 U.S.C. § 107(1) and (3));

3. the material should contain a notice of copyright (see 17 U.S.C. § 401);

4. the effect of photocopying the material should not be detrimental to the market for the work. (In general, the library should own at least one copy of the work.) (17 U.S.C. § 107(4).)

For example, a professor may place on reserve as a supplement to the course textbook a reasonable number of copies of articles from academic journals or chapters from trade books. A reasonable number of copies will in most instances be less than six, but factors such as the length or difficulty of the assignment, the number of enrolled students, and the length of time allowed for completion of the assignment may permit more in unusual circumstances.

In addition, a faculty member may also request that multiple copies of photocopied, copyrighted material be placed on the reserve shelf if there is insufficient time to obtain permission from the copyright owner. For example, a professor may place on reserve several photocopies of an entire article from a recent issue of *Time* magazine or the *New York Times* in lieu of distributing a copy to each member of the class. If you are in doubt as to whether a particular instance of photocopying is fair use in the reserve reading room, you should seek the publisher's permission. Most publishers will be cooperative and will waive any fee for such a use.

Uses of photocopied material requiring permission.

1. *Repetitive copying.* The classroom or reserve use of photocopied materials in multiple courses or successive years will normally require advance permission from the owner of the copyright (17 U.S.C. § 107(3)).

2. *Copying for profit.* Faculty should not charge students more than the actual cost of photocopying the material (17 U.S.C. § 107(1)).

3. *Consumable works.* The duplication of works that are consumed in the classroom, such as standardized tests, exercises, and workbooks, normally requires permission from the copyright owner (17 U.S.C. § 107(4).)

4. *Creation of anthologies as basic text material for a course.* Creation of a collective work or anthology by photocopying a number of copyrighted articles and excerpts to be purchased and used together as the basic text for a course will in most instances require the permission of the copyright owners. Such photocopying is more likely to be considered as a substitute for purchase of a book and thus less likely to be deemed fair use (17 U.S.C. § 107(4).)

How to obtain permission. When a use of photocopied material requires that you request permission, you should communicate complete and accurate information to the copyright owner. The American Association of Publishers suggests that the following information be included in a permission request letter in order to expedite the process:

1. Title, author and/or editor, and edition of materials to be duplicated.
2. Exact material to be used, giving amount, page numbers, chapters and, if possible, a photocopy of the material.
3. Number of copies to be made.
4. Use to be made of duplicated materials.
5. Form of distribution (classroom, newsletter, etc.).
6. Whether or not the material is to be sold.
7. Type of reprint (ditto, photography, offset, typeset).

The request should be sent, together with a self-addressed return envelope, to the permissions department of the publisher in question. If the address of the publisher does not appear at the front of the material, it may be readily obtained in a publication entitled *The Literary Marketplace*, published by the R. R. Bowker Company and available in all libraries.

The process of granting permission requires time for the publisher to check the status of the copyright and to evaluate the nature of the request. It is advisable, therefore, to allow enough lead time to obtain permission before the materials are needed. In some instances, the publisher may assess a fee for the permission. It is not inappropriate to pass this fee on to the students who receive copies of the photocopied material.

The Copyright Clearance Center also has the right to grant permission and collect fees for photocopying rights for certain publications. Libraries may copy from any journal that is registered with the CCC and report the copying beyond fair use to CCC and pay the set fee. A list of publications for which the CCC handles fees and permissions is available from the CCC, 21 Congress St., Salem, MA 01970; (508) 744-3350.

Sample letter to copyright owner (publisher) requesting permission to copy

March 1, 1992

Material Permissions Department
Hypothetical Book Company
500 East Avenue
Chicago, IL 60601

Dear Sir or Madam:

I would like permission to copy the following for continued use in my classes in future semesters:
Title: *Learning Is Good*, Second Edition
Copyright: Hypothetical Book Co., 1965, 1971
Author: Frank Jones
Material to be duplicated: Chapters 10, 11, and 14 (photocopy enclosed).
Number of copies: 500
Distribution: The material will be distributed to students in my classes and they will pay only the cost of the photocopying.
Type of reprint: Photocopy.
Use: The chapter will be used as supplementary teaching materials.

I have enclosed a self-addressed envelope for your convenience in replying to this request.

Sincerely,
Faculty Member

Infringement. Courts and legal scholars alike have commented that the fair use provisions in the Copyright Act are among the most vague and difficult that can be found anywhere in the law. In amending the Copyright Act in 1976, Congress anticipated the problem this would pose for users of copyrighted materials who wished to stay under the umbrella of protection offered by fair use.

9

For this reason, the Copyright Act contains specific provisions that grant additional rights to libraries and insulate employees of a non-profit educational institution, library, or archives from statutory damages for infringement where the infringer believed or had reasonable grounds to believe the photocopying was a fair use of the material (17 U.S.C. § 504(c)(2)).

Normally, an infringer is liable to the copyright owner for the actual losses sustained because of the photocopying and any additional profits of the infringor (17 U.S.C. § 504(a)(1) and (b)). Where the monetary losses are nominal, the copyright owner usually will claim statutory damages instead of the actual losses (17 U.S.C. § 504(a)(2) and (c)). The statutory damages may reach as high as $10,000 (or up to $50,000 if the infringement is willful). In addition to suing for money damages, a copyright owner can usually prevent future infringement through a court injunction (17 U.S.C. § 502).

The Copyright Act specifically exempts from statutory damages any employee of a nonprofit educational institution, library, or archives, who "believed and had reasonable grounds for believing that his or her use of the copyrighted work was a fair use under Section 107." (17 U.S.C. § 504(c)(2).) While the fair use provisions are admittedly ambiguous, any employee who attempts to stay within the guidelines contained in this report should have an adequate good faith defense in the case of an innocently committed infringement.

If the criteria contained in this report are followed, it is our view that no copyright infringement will occur and that there will be no adverse affect on the market for copyrighted works.

(Many educational institutions will provide their employees legal counsel without charge if an infringement suit is brought against the employee for photocopying performed in the course of employment. If so, this should be noted here.)

Source: "Model Policy Concerning College and University Photocopying for Classroom, Research, and Library Reserve Use," *College & Research Libraries News,* April 1982, pp. 127–131

Using videotapes and computer software

by Mary Hutchings Reed and Debra Stanek

Videotapes

The Copyright Revision Act of 1976 clearly protects audiovisual works such as films and videotapes. The rights of copyright include the rights of reproduction, adaptation, distribution, public performance and display. All of these rights are subject, however, to "fair use," depending on the purpose of the use, the nature of the work, the amount of the work used, and the effect the use has on the market for the copyrighted work.

Libraries purchase a wide range of educational and entertainment videotapes for in-library use and for lending to patrons. Since ownership of a physical object is different from ownership of the copyright therein, guidelines are necessary to define what libraries can do with the videotapes they own without infringing the copyrights they don't. If a particular use would be an infringement, permission can always be sought from the copyright owner.

In-classroom use. In-classroom performance of a copyrighted videotape is permissible under the following conditions:

1. The performance must be by instructors (including guest lecturers) or by pupils; and

2. the performance is in connection with face-to-face teaching activities; and

3. the entire audience is involved in the teaching activity; and

4. the entire audience is in the same room or same general area;

5. the teaching activities are conducted by a nonprofit education institution; and

6. the performance takes place in a classroom or similar place devoted to instruction, such as a school library, gym, auditorium, or workshop;

7. the videotape is lawfully made; the person responsible had no reason to believe that the videotape was unlawfully made.

In-library use in public libraries.

1. Most performances of a videotape in a public room as part of an entertainment or cultural program, whether a fee is charged or not, would be infringing and a performance license is required from the copyright owner.

2. To the extent a videotape is used in an educational program conducted in a library's public room, the performance will not be infringing if the requirements for classroom use are met.

3. Libraries that allow groups to use or rent their public meeting rooms should, as part of their rental agreement, require the group to warrant that it will secure all necessary performance licenses and indemnify the library for any failure on their part to do so.

4. If patrons are allowed to view videotapes on library-owned equipment, they should be limited to private performances, i.e. one person, or no more than one family, at a time.

5. User charges for private viewings should be nominal and directly related to the cost of maintenance of the videotape.

6. Even if a videotape is labelled "For Home Use Only," private viewing in the library should be considered to be authorized by the vendor's sale to the library with imputed knowledge of the library's intended use of the videotape.

7. Notices may be posted on videorecorders or players used in the library to educate and warn patrons about the existence of the copyright laws, such as: "Many videotaped materials are protected by copyright (17 U.S.C. § 101). Unauthorized copying may be prohibited by law."

Loan of videotapes.

1. Videotapes labelled "For Home Use Only" may be loaned to patrons for their personal use. They should not knowingly be loaned to groups for public performances.

2. Copyright notice as it appears on the label of a videotape should not be obscured.

3. Nominal user fees may be charged.

4. If a patron inquires about a planned performance of a videotape, he or she should be informed that only private uses of it are lawful.

5. Videorecorders may be loaned to a patron without fear of liability even if the patron uses the recorder to infringe a copyright. However, it may be a good idea to post notices on equipment that may be used for copying (even if an additional machine would be required) to assist copyright owners in preventing unauthorized reproduction.

Duplication of videotapes.

1. Under limited circumstances libraries may dupe a videotape or a part thereof, but the rules of § 108 of the Copyright Revision Act of 1976 that librarians routinely utilize with respect to photocopying, apply to the reproduction.

9

Computer software

Purchase conditions generally. Most computer software purports to be licensed rather than sold. Frequently the package containing the software is wrapped in clear plastic through which legends similar to the following appear:
"You should carefully read the following terms and conditions before opening

this diskette package. Opening this diskette package indicates your acceptance of these terms and conditions. If you do not agree with them you should promptly return the package unopened and your money will be refunded."

"Read this agreement carefully. Use of this product constitutes your acceptance of the terms and conditions of this agreement."

"This program is licensed on the condition that you agree to the terms and conditions of this license agreement. If you do not agree to them, return the package with the diskette still sealed and your purchase price will be refunded. Opening this diskette package indicates your acceptance of these terms and conditions."

While there is at present no case law concerning the validity of such agreements (which are unilaterally imposed by producers), in the absence of authority to the contrary, one should assume that such licenses are in fact binding contracts.

Therefore by opening and using the software the library or classroom may become contractually bound by the terms of the agreement wholly apart from the rights granted the copyright owner under the copyright laws.

Following such legends are the terms and conditions of the license agreement. The terms vary greatly between software producers and sometimes between programs produced by the same producer. Many explicitly prohibit rental or lending; some limit the program to use on one identified computer or to one user's personal use.

Avoiding license restrictions. Loans of software may violate the standard license terms imposed by the copyright owner. To avoid the inconsistencies between sale to a library and the standard license restriction, libraries should note on their purchase orders the intended use of software meant to circulate. Such a legend should read:

"Purchase is ordered for library circulation and patron use."

Then, if the order is filled, the library is in a good position to argue that its terms, rather than the standard license restrictions, apply.

Loaning software.

1. Copyright notice placed on a software label should not be obscured.

2. License terms, if any, should be circulated with the software package.

3. An additional notice may be added by the library to assist copyright owners in preventing theft. It might read: "Software protected by copyright, 17 U.S.C. § 101. Unauthorized copying is prohibited by law."

4. Libraries generally will not be liable for infringement committed by borrowers.

Archival copies.

1. Libraries may lawfully make one archival copy of a copyrighted program under the following conditions
- one copy is made;
- the archival copy is stored;
- if possession of the original ceases to be lawful, the archival copy must be destroyed or transferred along with the original program;
- copyright notice should appear on the copy.

2. The original may be kept for archival purposes and the "archival copy" circulated. Only one copy—either the original or the archival—may be used or circulated at any given time.

3. If the circulating copy is destroyed, another "archival" copy may be made.

4. If the circulating copy is stolen, the copyright owner should be consulted before circulating or using the "archival" copy.

In-library and in-classroom use.

1. License restrictions, if any, should be observed.

2. If only one program is owned under license, ordinarily it may only be used on one machine at a time.

3. Most licenses do not permit a single program to be loaded into a computer which can be accessed by several different terminals or into several computers for

simultaneous use.

4. If the machine is capable of being used by a patron to make a copy of a program, a warning should be posted on the machine, such as: "Many computer programs are protected by copyright, 17 U.S.C. § 101. Unauthorized copying may be prohibited by law."

Source: "Library and Classroom Use of Copyrighted Videotapes and Computer Software," *American Libraries,* February 1986

Ethics

Professional ethics

SINCE 1939, the American Library Association has recognized the importance of codifying and making known to the public and the profession the principles that guide librarians in action. This latest revision of the Code of Ethics reflects changes in the nature of the profession and in its social and institutional environment. It should be revised and augmented as necessary.

Librarians significantly influence or control the selection, organization, preservation, and dissemination of information. In a political system grounded in an informed citizenry, librarians are members of a profession explicitly committed to intellectual freedom and the freedom of access to information. We have a special obligation to ensure the free flow of information and ideas to present and future generations.

Librarians are dependent upon one another for the bibliographical resources that enable us to provide information services, and have obligations for maintaining the highest level of personal integrity and competence.

Code of ethics

1. Librarians must provide the highest level of service through appropriate and usefully organized collections, fair and equitable circulation and service policies, and skillful, accurate, unbiased, and courteous responses to all requests for assistance.

2. Librarians must resist all efforts by groups or individuals to censor library materials.

3. Librarians must protect each user's right to privacy with respect to information sought or received, and materials consulted, borrowed, or acquired.

4. Librarians must adhere to the principles of due process and equality of opportunity in peer relationships and personnel actions.

5. Librarians must distinguish clearly in their actions and statements between their personal philosophies and attitudes and those of an institution or professional body.

6. Librarians must avoid situations in which personal interests might be served or financial benefits gained at the expense of library users, colleagues, or the employing institution.

Source: American Library Association, 1981

Ethical standards for special collections librarians

THESE STANDARDS WERE DEVELOPED by the Committee on Developing Guidelines for Professional Ethics of the Rare Books and Manuscripts Section of the Association of College and Research Libraries and approved as policy in January 1987.

Rare book, manuscript, and special collections librarians hold positions of trust, involving special responsibilities for promoting scholarship by preserving and providing access to the records of knowledge in their care. Such librarians, in implementing the policies of their institutions, shall accept and discharge these responsibilities to the best of their abilities for the benefit of their institutions and the publics those institutions serve. In all their activities, they shall act with integrity, assiduously avoiding activities that could in any way compromise them or the institutions for which they work.

Appropriate supervisors should give a copy of these standards to all currently employed and newly employed rare book, manuscript, and special collections librarians in their institutions.

Access

Rare book, manuscript, and special collections librarians should be familiar with the most recent edition of "Joint Statement on Access to Original Research Materials," first approved as policy by the Association of College and Research Libraries Board of Directors in July 1976; this statement appears in the April 1979 issue of *College & Research Libraries News*. Rare book, manuscript, and special collections librarians shall respect the privacy of individuals who created or are the subject of records and papers, especially those who had no voice in the disposition of the materials. Rare book, manuscript, and special collections librarians shall neither reveal, nor profit from, information gained through work with materials to which they have access but to which others have restricted access.

Deaccession

Rare book, manuscript, and special collections librarians shall deaccession materials in their care only in accordance with the established policies of their institutions. Further safeguards, such as the advice of scholars in the field of the materials to be deaccessioned, might well be established. The procedure for the deaccession or disposal of materials shall be at least as rigorous as that for purchasing materials.

Appraisals

Rare book, manuscript, and special collections librarians should be familiar with the most recent edition of "Statement on Appraisal of Gifts," first approved as policy by the Association of College and Research Libraries Board of Directors in February 1973; this statement appeared in the March 1973 issue of *College & Research Libraries News* and is reprinted in the compilation of policy statements, "Guidelines on Manuscripts and Archives" (1977). Rare book, manuscript, and special collections librarians shall not give for a fee or on a retainer, any certificate or statement as to the authenticity or authorship or monetary value of rare books, manuscripts, and other special materials in their institution's collections or in the possession of a potential donor, except where authorized by and in accordance with the established purposes of their own or other nonprofit institutions concerned, and with the knowledge of their supervisors. Rare book, manuscript, and special collections librarians shall not appraise for personal profit any rare book, manuscript, or special collections materials except with the knowledge of their supervisors.

Preservation

Rare book, manuscript, and special collections librarians shall protect the physical integrity of the materials in their custody, guarding them against defacement, alterations, and physical damage. They shall (so far as is economically and technologically feasible) insure that their evidentiary value is not impaired in the work of restoration, arrangement, and use.

Theft

Rare book, manuscript, and special collections librarians shall not knowingly acquire nor allow to be recommended for acquisition any materials that have been stolen, or materials that have been imported in contravention of the applicable laws of the countries of origin or exporting countries. Rare book, manuscript, and special collections librarians should be familiar with the most recent edition of "Guidelines for the Security of Rare Book, Manuscript, and Other Special Collections," first approved as policy by the ACRL Board of Directors In January 1982; these Guidelines appeared in *College & Research Libraries News* in March 1982.

Personal research

Rare book, manuscript, and special collections librarians may use their institutions' holdings for personal research, publication, and profit if such practices are made known to their immediate supervisor and conveyed to the appropriate senior administrator of their institution, and if such work is done on the same terms as others using the same holdings. Because the possibility of conflict exists, the matter shall be fully discussed by rare book, manuscript, and special collections librarians with their supervisors and clear guidelines developed.

Personal collecting

Private collecting of books, manuscripts, and other materials by rare book, manuscript, and special collections librarians is not to be discouraged. However, such collecting shall not conflict, either in fact or in appearance, with the best interests of an employing institution and its collecting programs. Because the possibility of conflict exists, the matter shall be fully discussed by rare book, manuscript, and special collections librarians with their supervisors and clear guidelines developed.

Personal dealing

Rare book, manuscript, and special collections librarians shall not deal in rare books, manuscripts, and special collections materials for personal monetary profit without the knowledge of their supervisors; nor shall they be party to the recommending of materials for purchase by institutions or by collectors, if they have any undisclosed financial interest in these materials; nor shall they accept any commission, or undisclosed or otherwise compromising gift from any seller or buyer of such materials. Upgrading a private collection through occasional sales or purchases is not considered dealing in rare books, manuscript, and special collections. Because the possibility of conflict exists, the matter shall be fully discussed by rare book, manuscript, and special collections librarians with their supervisors and clear guidelines developed.

Source (Chicago: ALA/ACRL Rare Books and Manuscripts Section, 1987)

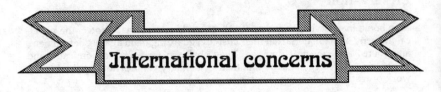

International concerns

Librarianship in the USSR

by Helen Teplitskaia

THE PROCESS OF *PERESTROIKA* started in 1985 and has considerably influenced political, economic, and cultural life in the USSR. This essay, specially written for *The Whole Library Handbook* by Helen Teplitskaia, former Council member of the Leningrad Library Society responsible for the Division of Library Management, takes a look at the major principles and significant changes in Soviet librarianship during the recent period of reconstruction.—*GME.*

The Soviet Library System was established in 1920 when the Soviet government ratified the decree, "On Centralization of Librarianship in the RSFSR" (Russian Soviet Federated Socialist Republic). The fundamental concepts of the decree were developed by V. I. Lenin and later promoted by his wife, N. K. Krupskaia, an eminent library theoretician. As a leader of the Communist party and the Soviet state, Lenin attached great significance to the evolution of librarianship. On his initiative, the promotion of Communist ideas through education and political enlightenment became the primary and permanent responsibility of Soviet libraries. A collection of Lenin's writings about libraries, compiled after his death by his wife, became the library bible for Soviet librarians.

The current library law, issued in 1984, further developed Lenin's ideas and outlined the following major principles of librarianship in the USSR:

- Consolidation of libraries into a single system;
- Planning of network development and placement;
- Guaranteed unity of library administration and leadership;
- Government planning of library education;
- Free library services accessible to all citizens;
- Participation of social institutions, work collectives, and citizens in library work.

Types of libraries

The All-Union Library System is composed of library networks belonging to all ministries and state committees of the USSR and its republics, trade unions, the Soviet Academy of Sciences, state and cooperative enterprises, and social organizations. Libraries are categorized by responsibility (from All-Union and Republican to district) and by user population, library holdings, and type of activity (universal or special).

Of all the libraries of the All-Union Library System, public libraries are the most widespread. Very much like American public libraries, Soviet public libraries are linked to the central system. However, unlike American public libraries, Soviet public libraries serve specific age groups—there are libraries for children, adolescents, and adults.

Special libraries in both countries are nearly identical. For example, there are science, health science, agriculture, school, and academic libraries in both the U.S. and the USSR.

The Soviet Union is the world leader in the average number of books, libraries, and librarians per citizen. In 1990, 326,000 libraries of the All-Union Library System held 5.6 billion items. The library system employs 480,000 librarians and other staff. On the other hand, the quality of public and technical services, the frequency of library use, and the quality of acquisitions have declined considerably in recent years.

The current crisis in Soviet libraries was caused by the overcentralization of library operations, inadequate funding, and too much emphasis on political propaganda. Forced priorities, the lack of automation, and inadequate benefits have diminished the prestige of the library profession. Many librarians, especially those working in the public and trade union libraries, have migrated to special libraries or information agencies with higher salaries and more convenient work schedules or have left the profession entirely.

In the first quarter of 1989, the average salary for all workers in the USSR was about 234 rubles per month. The average monthly salary of librarians was only 100 rubles, close to the Soviet poverty level. The vigorous activity of the professional library associations and numerous appeals and protest demonstrations in Moscow helped to achieve long-overdue salary raises in 1990. Despite low housing costs and free medical treatment and education, the standard of living for Soviet librarians is still very low.

The Lenin State Library

The same political, financial, and social pressures that affect many Soviet libraries, also apply to the Lenin State Library (LSL), the national library of the USSR. Founded in 1862, LSL houses one of the largest collections in the world. In 1989 it held 37 million items and served nearly 7,000 patrons daily. In 1974, because of the limited seating capacity of its 22 reading rooms, eligibility for membership in the library was restricted to readers at a certain level of education. As the national library, LSL is designated as the center for bibliography, interlibrary loan, research in library science, and administration for the All-Union Library System.

LSL is often compared to the Library of Congress (LC). Although many features are very similar, the differences are even greater. The Library of Congress was established to function without political interference. All U.S. citizens and visitors have access to LC, and passes or permission for entry are not required. In 1990, LC's budget was $266.7 million, while the budget of LSL was only 11 million rubles. In the same year, LC subscribed to 40,000 foreign journals, LSL to 2,000. LC is one of the few libraries in the world collecting literature in every world language. Furthermore, LC is not the central professional association and research facility for librarianship like the Lenin State Library—in the United States the American Library Association, other professional associations, and library schools share these functions.

Besides its positive contributions to Soviet cultural life, the Lenin State Library has also served as the official censor by controlling reading through recommended bibliographies and instructions to librarians, and vigorously supervising what people should and should not read. Through its acquisitions and cataloging policies, the LSL sought to protect its readers from the decaying influence of bourgeois books about religion, business, marketing, sexuality, the works of foreign Soviet scholars, and *samizdat* (underground literature).

9

Changes in the Soviet system

Today, neither librarians nor library patrons want to preserve the old order. Responding to frequent complaints about the lack of free access to the library and its resources, the decreasing quality of library service, the lack of automation, poor working conditions, and lack of space, the USSR Council of Ministers established the Extra-Ministerial Expert Commission in December 1989. After a thorough investigation, the Commission recognized the poor condition of the LSL and recommended developing a long-range plan for the rejuvenation and reconstruction of LSL and other libraries in the Soviet Library System. The conclusions and suggestions of the Commission were approved, LSL director N. S. Kartashov resigned, but as of early 1991 little else had been implemented.

In June 1990, in an attempt to accelerate the reconstruction process, librarians and Moscow friends of the Lenin State Library held a public demonstration and addressed an appeal to the USSR Supreme Soviet and many other government organizations to "Save the Book, Save Libraries, Save Culture!" Three other Moscow library institutions have also joined the reconstruction effort: the All-Union Library of Foreign Literature, the State Public Historical Library, and the N. A. Nekrasov Central Municipal Library. In addition, the disastrous 1988 fire in Leningrad's Library of the Academy of Sciences focused international attention on the plight of Soviet libraries.

Clearly, *perestroika* has significantly influenced the philosophy and professional activities of Soviet librarians in last few years. Tired of playing the role of silent conductors of the official will, librarians want to return to the democratic traditions of Russian library societies, which were abolished after the Revolution of 1917.

In 1990, the new and reestablished library societies and associations began the process of forming an All-Union Library Association that would be a national and international generalist library association like the American Library Association. Unfortunately, the uncertainty of the future of the Soviet federation has postponed. In 1991 only a regional association for the RSFSR has been formed, although it has links to other republics, including the Baltic republics.

In order to promote the development of librarianship, several official and alternative concepts have been widely discussed across the country. Humanism and democratization quickly emerged as the top priorities for librarianship, as well as new models for funding, administration, and collection development. Although the basic organization of the All-Union Library System—as a network of libraries—will probably not go through any major changes, the new approach will increase the system's problem-solving capability.

Until quite recently, only the Ministry of Culture and the State Interagency Library Commission administered the All-Union Library System. Libraries also reported to their local agencies and Soviet councils. Now library associations are demanding recognition of their right to active and equal participation in the administration and management of librarianship in the USSR.

The radical economic reforms conducted in the Soviet Union have also involved cultural and educational institutions. The current transition to new management and funding allows for economic incentive and expands the range of available library services, especially fee-based services. Some libraries have expanded their traditional services to include flowergardening and showing adult-oriented films, though this is uncommon. With the adoption of a new financial system, many libraries are now able to buy new equipment and furniture, and can offer staff salary increases.

On the other hand, libraries have been unable to improve their acquisitions budgets. With the exception of libraries receiving "depository" materials (the large All-Union, republican, and regional libraries), most other libraries suffer from the lack of materials provided to them by the publishing trade. In 1989, libraries received only 15% of the 1.5 billion copies of books published annually

in the Soviet Union. Only 45% of user-requested fiction and poetry titles, 7%-10% of nonfiction and popular literature, and 33% of children's books are carried by the designated library book vendors who provide 90% of all books purchased by Soviet libraries. Consequently, 30%-40% of all user requests for historical literature, and 55%-60% of all requests for fiction were not found in the public libraries. In order to attract users back into the library, Soviet librarians are asking for changes in the Soviet publishing system to guarantee the priority of purchasing books for libraries.

Despite these difficulties, librarians are attempting to evaluate the quality and variety of user services. Soviet public libraries are now functioning not only as information and education centers, but also as centers for social support and entertainment. Much as in American public libraries, librarians deliver books and journals to the elderly, handicapped, and veterans, and establish reading clubs for those interested in special areas, such as literature, theater, cinema, art, politics, gardening, and sewing. They organize libraries for family reading, street festivals, concerts, lectures, and quiz shows in schools and colleges. Personal invitations to join libraries are sent to socially maladjusted children and adolescents. Finally, librarians are now able to protect the freedom to read, and to return censored materials from the *spetzkhrans* (closed stacks) to readers.

Without automation, public libraries are networking with all other types of libraries through interlibrary loan, cooperative programs on information services, and continuing library education. Currently, only 4,200 of the 120,000 public libraries of the USSR Ministry of Culture are designated to participate in the developing automated information system, *Informcultura*. Only a few other information systems are in the process of expanding into a national network.

9

The library profession

To eliminate the gap between library education and current professional requirements, Soviet library schools are now providing curricula appropriate for changing information needs. The amount of time library students train as library interns has expanded from four to sixth months. Courses have been developed for specialized training in bookbinding, psychology, and computer science.

In the 1988/89 academic year, 11,693 undergraduate students graduated from the library departments of 135 Soviet colleges. In the same year, 1,812 graduate students graduated from 35 Soviet universities, teachers' institutes, and specialized institutes of culture with degrees in library science.

A well-established tradition in Soviet librarianship is its broad international orientation. For many years, Soviet librarians participated in numerous international programs on information and bibliography, standards, interlibrary loan, book exchanges, and exhibitions. Since 1959, the Soviet Union has been a member of the International Federation of Library Associations and Institutions (IFLA). Instead of being represented by a library association, the USSR was one of a very few countries represented by a State Interagency Library Commission. The reestablished library associations from the Baltic republics and the regional association for the RSFSR have had the opportunity to join IFLA. The IFLA meeting was scheduled to be held in Moscow in August 1991.

The American Library Association (ALA) has been very supportive of the democratization of Soviet librarianship. The 1917 ALA Annual Conference in Louisville, Kentucky, addressed the first greetings to the librarians of the newly established Soviet Republic.

At present, Soviet-American library cooperation is coordinated by the Commission on Library Cooperation and involves the American Council of Learned Societies and the Library Council of the USSR. The significant contribution to cooperation is also provided by the Library/Book Fellows Program of the American Library Association and the U.S. Information Agency (USIA). An Agreement and Protocol developed by the Commission outlines collaborative efforts in art and museum librarianship, access to library resources through technology and preservation, and the development of library services to children.

Other programs developed by the Commission have provided special assistance to Soviet libraries damaged by the Armenian earthquake in 1988 and to the Library of the USSR Academy of Sciences in Leningrad after the disastrous 1988 fire.

The State V. I. Lenin Library, the State Scientific/Technical Library of the Siberian Branch of the USSR Academy of Sciences, and the Moscow and Leningrad Library Associations have sent letters to their American counterparts indicating their willingness to establish direct contacts and extend existing cooperation. In response, the American Library Association recently established a Subcommittee on U.S.-U.S.S.R. Library Cooperation which will serve as a liaison to librarians in both countries.

The time is right to initiate a joint project to create an international library system and build a true "Library Without Walls"—our primary mission for the sake of better understanding and world peace.

Sources

S. Basov, *Organizatzia Dobrovolnykh Objedinenii/Obshestv i Assotziatzii v sfere bibliotechnogo dela* (Moscow: Nauchnaia Biblioteka VTZSPS, 1989).

S. Basov and A. Zonin, "Vozrodim traditzii," *Bibliotekar'*, August 1989, 10-13.

N. Blohina and V. Pudov, "Diktujut ekonomicheskie realnosti," *Bibliotekar'*, August 1990, 37-41.

Robert P. Doyle, *Fact Sheet: U.S.-U.S.S.R. Exchanges* (Chicago: ALA, 1990).

"Chistka razuma," *Sovetskaia kultura* 23 (March 10, 1990): 1.

L. Gudkov, B. Dubin, and A. Reinblat, "Preobrazovanie—ne usovershenstvovanie," *Bibliotekar'*, August 1990, 2-6.

N. Kartashov, "Ekonomicheskie metodui v praktiky bibliotek," *Bibliotekar'*, July 1989, 2-7.

"Kontzeptzia razvitia bibliotekhnogo dela v RSFSR do 2005 goda," *Bibliotekar'*, November 1989, 1-16.

E. Kuzmin, "Blesk i Nischeta Natzionalnyikh Bibliotek [Sad Commentary of the conversation with James Billington, Director, The U.S. Library of Congress],"

Literaturnaia gazeta , 28 February 1990, 3.

S. Lininja, "Ne zagruzshat chuzshimi zabotami," *Bibliotekar'* , December 1989, 6.

I. Morozova and T. Vlasenko, "Gosudarstvennaia Biblioteka imeni V.I.Lenina v sisteme bibliotek Moskvui," *Sovetskoie bibliotekovedenie* , July 1989, 38-44.

"Pervyie shagi professionalnyikh Bibliotekhnuikh Objedinenii," *Sovetskoie bibliotekovedenie* , March 1990, 3-11.

E. Ponomareva, "Na trudnom puti peremen," *Bibliotekar'* , January 1990, 4-8.

"Proekt Ustava Sovetskoi Bibliotekhnoi Assotziatzii," *Bibliotekar'* , June 1989, 4-5.

A. Sokolov, "Obojudoostryi printzip partiinosti," *Sovetskaia bibliografia* , January 1990, 44-45.

Spravochnik bibliotekarja (Moscow: Kniga, 1985).

"V zaschitu Kulturyi," *Bibliotekar'* , August 1990, 64-65.

The American Library in Paris

by Robert P. Doyle

THE AMERICAN LIBRARY IN PARIS is a private, nonprofit organization, founded in 1920 through the initiative of the American Library Association. The library was established to service the large community of expatriate Americans, which included Ernest Hemingway, Gertrude Stein, Thornton Wilder, and Steven Vincent Benét (who is said to have researched "John Brown's Body" in the library), living in Paris between the two World Wars. It was also hoped that the library would also become a cultural embassy to spread American ideas abroad and serve as a model of American library service.

Today, it is the largest English-language library in continental Europe and it has 2,000 members. 42% of the members are French, 38% American, and 20% other nationalities. With a collection of over 80,000 volumes and 350 periodicals, the American Library in Paris provides a "home away from home" to all Americans in Paris, an invaluable English-language source for French people, and the services and spirit of an American library to all English-reading people in Paris. It is funded by donations and bequests and by modest membership fees.

History

The Library War Service, established in 1917 by the American Library Association, was created to supply reading materials to the American Expeditionary Forces during World War I. Following the war, 10,000 of the more than a million volumes were carefully selected to remain in the Paris headquarters for use by soldiers before demobilization. Plans to close the library once the American troops were sent home were met with disappointment by the many nonmilitary patrons who also had been using the collection. In response, the ALA announced that it would donate the books and equipment and provide a $25,000 endowment if there was sufficient interest on the part of local residents to provide continued support. There was, and on May 20, 1920, the American Library in Paris was incorporated.

Many of its staff members in the early years were prominent U.S. librarians. Burton Stevenson was its first librarian, and Constance Winchell served as cataloger in the late twenties.

In these early years, there was briefly an American library school in Paris—the Paris Library School or École de bibliothécaires de la rue de L'Elysée. Miss Sara Bogle, assistant secretary of the American Library Association, became its direc-

9

tor, with Miss Jennie Parsons serving as resident director. First conducted as a 6-week course in 1923, the program was expanded to a 36-week session, fueled by a $50,000 gift from ALA. By the time the school was forced to close in 1929, one more victim of the worldwide economic depression, it had granted 103 diplomas, 47 to French students and the remainder to students from other countries. Richard K. Gardner in his historical study of *Education for Librarianship in France* claims that the school "certainly did lay the groundwork for a modern public library movement" in France and that "its influence was probably as great, if not greater, outside France." Its Alumni Association was an influential and distinguished group who had a major impact on library development in Europe.

While the school had to close, the library managed to survive not only the Great Depression, but also the German occupation during the Second World War. The library never closed, despite the heavy hand of Nazi officials. Although the staff pretended to follow the demand of the German authorities that "certain books" not be allowed to circulate, they secretly carried books, including proscribed books, to the homes of Jewish subscribers who were not allowed to enter the library. After the war, the former French Ambassador to the United States, Georges Bonnet, pointed to the American Library as "an open window on the free world."

After World War II, the demand for the library's services, especially by French readers, who in the mid-1940s constituted 80% of the subscribers, led to an optimistic expansion of scope and function. In 1947, an out-of-town mail service was instituted that reached even beyond the borders of France. In 1950 the U.S. State Department, recognizing success in the provision of information abroad, proposed that provincial branches be set up, primarily at universities. Officials of the library undertook this venturesome task with U.S. government funds, but they insisted that the provincial branches be independent of the U.S. government in order to avoid any suggestion of involvement with official government propaganda. Thus, beginning in 1951 ten branches, including a few in public libraries, were established.

In the beginning these collections were quite small: about 1,000 volumes, mostly French translations of American books intended primarily to serve the needs of American Studies programs in the universities. Fifteen years later when Franco-American relations chilled under Charles de Gaulle, the U.S. Information Agency support was withdrawn and the library was left with four branches and no support. The French provincial universities, however, felt the American Library branches were so useful that they assumed the operating costs, and the service continues today at universities in Toulouse, Grenoble, Montpellier, Nantes, and Nancy.

Current projects

The popularity of the branch libraries and the increasing demands of French patrons, coupled with the gradual dwindling of the American population in France, has forced the library's trustees to take a new look at the institution's long-term role in France and its potential sources of support. In the process, the library has requested assistance from the American Library Association. In 1967, the board invited David Clift, executive director of ALA, and Emerson Greenaway, director of the Free Library of Philadelphia and one-time president of ALA, to survey the library. In addition to making a number of important recommendations for more professional operation of the library and the promotion of its services, the surveyors came to the conclusion that a $4 million endowment was needed to provide an adequate annual operations budget, and to provide an assured future for the library. Though that ambitious goal has not been reached, today the endowment stands at $1.3 million and long-range development efforts are under way.

While ALA has provided financial and educational support for the library in the past and until 1973 appointed five members to the Board of Trustees, the relationship between ALA and the library today is informal and without authority. The ALA Executive Board, however, has affirmed "ALA's continuing interest and willingness to be of assistance."

An example of that continued interest is the ALA Library/Book Fellow working at the library on a 12-month assignment. Randall Barry, MARC standards specialist from the Library of Congress, started working at the library in the fall of 1988 to develop and oversee the retrospective conversion of the library's manual catalog. He has also spent time analyzing the work patterns at the library and has drawn up procedures to facilitate the transition to the integrated VTLS library system. Part of his assignment has included training staff at the library and American University of Paris Library and preparing procedural manuals in English and French to aid in creating and maintaining the library's database.

Another example: ALA Publishing Services is providing a copy of all new ALA publications to the library. The books initially will be used for a special exhibition of professional publications for librarians and eventually will become part of the library's collection.

Structure and organization

The library is governed by an independent Board of Trustees, representing leaders of the American and French communities in Paris and long-term friends of the library who now reside in the United States. The board determines the policies and priorities of the library and, through the appointment of the head librarian, delegates responsibility for the activities of the library. The head librarian is responsible, in turn, for staffing operations and daily management. The trustees and head librarian work on new subscriptions and fund-raising programs, assisted by the development officer, a newly created staff position.

Source: Robert P. Doyle, *Fact Sheet: The American Library in Paris* (Chicago: ALA, 1989)

Giving books to needy libraries

THE BEST WAY TO HELP needy libraries is by sending them unrestricted contributions for acquiring those materials they need the most. In this way libraries can save contributions to buy expensive items they otherwise could not afford or develop specific areas of their collections.

The American Library Association does not collect books for shipment to needy libraries in the United States. We are not aware of specific organizations that do. Most public libraries accept gift books with the proviso that the library is free to decide whether to keep the book in the library's collection, put it in a book sale to raise funds for the library, or discard it. Persons seeking to donate books to libraries are encouraged to call their local library and ask about donating books to it.

The American Library Association's Disaster Relief Committee in 1990 began coordinating a book donation drive to aid the University of Bucharest Library. In the 1989 Rumanian revolution, an estimated 500,000 books at the Library were destroyed. Persons who wish to help should contact Disaster Relief Committee member Oprista Popa, Business Librarian, Humanities/Social Sciences Department, University of California, Shields Library, Davis, CA 95616. Popa will schedule shipments to a warehouse in Brooklyn. The United States Information Agency has allocated $35,000 to fund the shipments to Rumania. Donors will be asked to pay for domestic postage.

There are several organizations that distribute books to other countries. Many

9

of these such as the Brother's Brother Foundation (824 Grandview Ave., Pittsburgh, PA 15211; (412) 431-1600) distribute books overseas at no cost to the donating library or person. Most of these are listed in *American Donated Books Abroad: A Guide to Distributing Organizations* by William M. Childs (American International Book Development Council (AIBDC), 1989). Publishers interested in donating books may want to consult a book written by Donald E. McNeil and published by AIBDC in 1989, *American Donated Books Abroad: The Publisher's Guide to Tax Deduction.*

The ALA International Relations Committee has a subcommittee on book donations. The subcommittee is an excellent resource for additional suggestions on this topic and would also welcome and greatly appreciate your suggestions for future development.

Source: ALA Headquarters Library

Preparing for an international exchange

ONCE YOU HAVE FOUND an exchange partner and administrative approval has been secured, you are faced with a number of questions that need to be resolved. This brief checklist, representing the collective wisdom of librarians who have planned and carried out international job exchanges, is a starting point.

Who will pay your salary? It might be your host institution if you and your partner switch salaries as well as jobs. It might be your home institution if you and your partner are granted paid leaves of absence to work abroad. Note: this plan would probably make it easier for your host institution and your host country's government to allow you to enter a work situation there; it should also reduce complications for your home institution. It might be a sponsoring agency if you have received a grant to work abroad.

Will you need a special visa or work permit? Inquire into this well ahead of your proposed departure date.

How will your exchange affect any benefits offered through your home institution? You may need to make special arrangements for either continuing or discontinuing medical insurance, life insurance, retirement funds, etc. during your absence.

Will your income be enough to meet your expenses? You will want to gather information about costs of living in your host country. You should plan for extra expenses at the start of your visit, for travel while you are overseas, etc.

What kinds of bank accounts and credit cards will you need both at home and in your host country?

Who will handle your business affairs while you're away from home? If possible, appoint an agent to take care of your banking, to pay regular bills, and to handle mail coming to your home.

Where will you live while abroad? Perhaps your host institution will assist you in renting a home. Perhaps you'll exchange residences with your partner. If so, you'll want to be sure your insurance coverage is adequate; you'll want to come to an agreement about who pays the various household bills (water, electricity, heating fuel, trash collection, etc.), about how yard work will be taken care of, and about looking after pets, if any. Instruction booklets for appliances, and a list of service people to call on in case of emergencies would be useful for your partner.

Will you exchange automobiles? If so, be sure to check your insurance policy for coverage of your car with your exchange partner as driver, and coverage of you as the driver of your exchange partner's car. You'll want to come to agreement on who is responsible for routine maintenance of the car, registration/licensing, parking stickers, paying damages in case of an accident, etc.

Will you need to get a driving license in your host country? You may be able to use your home license. You may want to obtain an International Driving Permit. You might want to get a driving license in your host country, especially as it may be a useful means of identification.

What will you need in the way of medical insurance while you are abroad?

Does your host country require any special vaccines or inoculations? Look into these well ahead of time!

How will your exchange affect your tax situation, both at home and abroad? Check into this carefully, as it could affect your plans for the length of your exchange.

Source: ALA's IRC/IRRT Joint Committee on International Exchange of Librarians and Information Professionals, with special assistance from Linda Williamson, 1986

International Federation of Library Associations and Institutions (IFLA)

by Robert P. Doyle

FOUNDED IN EDINBURGH, SCOTLAND, on September 30, 1927, the International Federation of Library Associations and Institutions (IFLA) was created to provide librarians throughout the world with a forum for exchanging ideas, promoting international cooperation, unifying library practices, and advancing the cause of librarianship. It is an independent, nongovernmental association headquartered in The Hague, Netherlands. Its membership covers 123 countries and consists of 180 associations, 903 institutional members and affiliates, and 182 personal affiliates. The main objectives of IFLA are to initiate or coordinate research and studies, publish and disseminate information, organize meetings and conferences, and collaborate with other international organizations in the fields of information, documentation, and archives.

Organization

The Federation's highest authority is the Council, the general assembly of all voting members. Council convenes every other year (in odd-numbered years) during IFLA's annual conference. IFLA's main steering bodies are the Executive and Professional Boards; the first has full powers of administration and management and the second deals with coordinating and planning professional activities. Executive Board members are elected for a four-year term and are subsequently eligible for an additional two-year term. The Board consists of an elected President and seven elected members, with the chairperson of the Professional Board serving as an ex-officio member. The Professional Board is composed of the chairpersons of the eight divisions.

The basic professional units of IFLA are the thirty-two sections, grouped in eight divisions. All members can register for sections. Some sections are concerned with type of library (e.g., public libraries, school libraries, etc.); others address type of library activities (e.g., cataloging, conservation, etc.). Each section conducts its own program and these programs are reviewed by the division's

9

coordinating board (consisting of the elected officers of all sections in the division). The sections are grouped into the divisions for coordination and the division's programs are reviewed by the Professional Board. More than 450 experts, nominated and elected by the members of the applicable section, work on the sections' standing committees.

Round tables and working groups offer two less formal avenues of professional involvement within IFLA.

IFLA's core programs

In addition to the divisions, sections, and round tables, five core programs have been established whose activities intersect the interests and concerns of all of IFLA's units, and of all libraries and their users, wherever located. Although IFLA concentrates much of its efforts on the core programs, they are entirely financed from extraordinary sources. With the exception of the Advancement of Librarianship in the Third World (ALP), which falls under the jurisdiction of the Executive Board, the Programme Management Committee coordinates and manages IFLA's core programs, including their objectives, financing, and functions, and also facilitates the liaison of those programs with the work of the sections and divisions.

The five core programs are:

Universal Availability of Publications (UAP) promotes access and availability of library materials to all categories of users by encouraging and improving policies and procedures for the production and distribution, acquisition, retention and interlibrary supply of publications within and between countries. Among other activities, a contract was signed with UNESCO for the preparation of a document on *Measuring the Performance of Document Supply Systems.* The focal point for this program is in Boston Spa in England.

Universal Bibliographic Control International MARC (UBCIM) promotes the production of a single bibliographic record for each publication, thus eliminating the duplication of effort in bibliographic recording, and providing records which are internationally compatible and available. The focal point for this program is at the British Library in London.

Universal Dataflow and Telecommunications (UDT) promotes the electronic transfer of data among libraries across national borders, thus ensuring that the vital interest of the library community in resource sharing is preserved. One of their projects aims to demonstrate the ability to interconnect library computer systems internationally using OSI standards, to demonstrate the service benefits and constraints of such an interconnection, and to provide data needed for coordinating and planning of future ILL implementations and other OSI application protocols. This program is located at the National Library of Canada.

Preservation and Conservation (PAC) promotes the search for solutions to the serious problems of physical deterioration of library and information materials, thus helping to preserve and conserve publications of the past, present, and future. This program is located at the Library of Congress in Washington, D.C.

Advancement of Librarianship in the Third World (ALP) aims to set up a focal point to provide logistic and financial support for regional cooperation, especially in Africa, Asia and Oceania, and Latin America and the Caribbean. IFLA is committed to strengthening the advancement of librarianship in the Third World and established ALP as its fifth core program in Nairobi in 1984.

At each IFLA conference, the U.S. caucus meets to orient the U.S. delegates to IFLA and to discuss the issues and concerns that may be raised at the conference. In Council years, the discussion generally centers around the elections, and official endorsements are solicited.

Source: Robert P. Doyle, *Fact Sheet: International Federation of Library Associations and Institutions (IFLA)* (Chicago: ALA, 1989)

LIBRARIANA

Words beginning with "bibl-"

THE FOLLOWING LIST consists of words deriving from the Greek words *biblion* (papyrus reed) and *biblos* (book). Egypt exported papyrus for writing material to Greece and other regions through the Phoenician port of Byblos (modern Jubail, Lebanon), from which comes the root word *bibl-*, the source of both Bible and bibliography.—*GME.*

Bible, n. The sacred scripture of Christians, comprising the Old Testament and the New Testament.

bible, n. Any book or reference work accepted as authoritative, informative, and reliable.

bible, n., v.t. In TV series production, the general outline of plots and character development prepared before the first program of the season. *Webster's New World Dictionary of Media and Communications.*

Bible paper, n. Thin, lightweight, bright, opaque, durable paper for Bibles or reference books. Originally made from vegetable fiber in China and Japan, though erroneously thought to come from India.

Bible style, n. A flexible, round-cornered, leather binding.

Bibler, n. A student or reader of the Bible.

biblet, n. (Obsolete.) A book or library. *OED.*

biblia abiblia, n. Books that are of no humanist interest; irrelevant materials brought together in one volume, simply to make a book.

Biblia pauperum, n. Medieval picture books containing illustrations of scriptural subjects.

Biblián, n. Town in Ecuador, northeast of Cuenca.

Bibliander, n. Greek surname of Theodor Buchmann, 1500?–1564, Swiss theologian and Oriental scholar.

biblic, adj. biblical. *OED.*

biblical, adj. Pertaining to the Bible or the era and region in which events of the Bible took place.

biblicism, n. Adherence to the letter of the Bible.

biblicist, n. One who so adheres.

biblioclasm, n. Destruction of books.

biblioclast, n. A person who mutilates or destroys books.

bibliofilm, n. A microfilm used to photograph the pages of valuable books.

bibliogenesis, n. Production of books.

bibliognost, n. One versed in knowledge about books.

bibliogony, n. The art of producing and publishing books.

bibliograph, v.t. To put in a bibliography.

bibliographer, n. An expert in bibliography.

bibliographic, bibliographical, adj. Pertaining to bibliography.

Bibliographic Classification, n. A classification system devised by Henry Evelyn Bliss, first published in outline form in 1910, characterized by the organization of knowledge in consistency with the scientific and educational consensus.

bibliographic control, n. Complete bibliographic records of all bibliographic items published; standardization of bibliographic description; providing physical access through consortia, networks, or other cooperative endeavors; or providing bibliographic access through compiling and distributing union lists and subject bibliographies and through bibliographic service centers.

bibliographic coupling, n. The theory that if any two scientific papers contain a citation in common, they are bibliographically related.

bibliographic database, n. A database consisting of computer records that represent works, documents, or bibliographic items.

bibliographic description, n. The description of a bibliographic item, divided into specific areas, such as title, edition, publication, etc.

bibliographic instruction, n. An information service to a group, which is designed to teach library users how to locate information efficiently.

bibliographic item, n. A document or set of documents in any physical form, forming the basis for a single bibliographic description.

bibliographic network, n. A network established and maintained for the sharing of bibliographic data through the use of a standard communication format and authority control.

bibliographic record, n. A record of a bibliographic item that comprises all data contained in or accommodated by a bibliographic format such as MARC.

bibliographic reference, n. A set of bibliographic elements essential to the identification of a work.

bibliographic search, n. The process of identifying a work and obtaining bibliographic data about it through a systematic search of bibliographic tools and other sources.

bibliographic service center, n. An organization that serves as a distributor of computer-based bibliographic processing services.

bibliographic utility, n. An organization that maintains online bibliographic databases, enabling it to offer computer-based support to any interested user.

bibliographical ghost, n. A work or edition of a work, recorded in bibliographies or otherwise mentioned, of whose existence there is no reasonable proof.

bibliographical note, n. Text set apart from the text of a document, which contains a reference to one or more works used as sources.

bibliographize, v.t. To make a bibliography of.

bibliography, n. The study of books as physical objects; the art of correctly describing books; or, a list of works, documents, or bibliographic items, usually by author, subject, or place of publication.

biblioklept, n. A person who steals books.

bibliokleptomania, n. Obsessive stealing of books.

bibliolater, n. A book worshiper.

bibliolatry, n. Extravagant devotion to or dependence upon books.

bibliologist, n. One versed in bibliology.

bibliology, n. The study of books, embracing knowledge of the physical book in all its aspects, such as paper, printing, typography, illustration, and binding.

bibliomancy, n. Divination by means of a book, especially the Bible, opened at random to some verse or passage, which is then interpreted.

bibliomania, n. Excessive fondness for acquiring and possessing books.

bibliomaniac, n., adj. Characterized by bibliomania.

bibliomanian, bibliomane, n., adj. Bibliomaniac.

bibliometrics, n. The use of statistical methods in the analysis of a body of literature to reveal the historical development of subject fields and patterns of authorship, publication, and use.

bibliopegic, adj. Related to the binding of books.

bibliopegist, n. A bookbinder.

bibliopegy, n. The art of binding books.

bibliophage, n. An ardent reader.

bibliophilately, n. The study of books and libraries on postage stamps.

bibliophile, n. A person who loves or collects books.

Bibliophile de la vieille roche, n. (French.) A book collector of the old school whose interests ranged widely and who did not specialize.

Bibliophile Jacob, n. Pseudonym of Paul Lacroix, 1806-1884, French scholar.

bibliophilism, bibliophily, n. A love of books.

bibliophobe, n. A person who hates, fears, or distrusts books.

bibliophobia, n. Dislike of books.

bibliopoesy, n. The making of books. *OED.*

bibliopole, n. A bookseller, especially a dealer in rare or used books.

10

bibliopolic, bibliopolar, adj. Pertaining to booksellers.

bibliopolism, n. The trade or art of selling books.

bibliopoly, bibliopolery, n. The selling of books.

bibliopsychology, n. Study of authors, books, and readers, as well as their interrelationships.

bibliort, n. Something other than a bookmark used by people to mark a place in a book—ticket stub, laundry list, etc. Paul Dickson.

bibliosoph, n. One who knows about books.

bibliotaph, n. A person who caches or hoards books.

bibliothec, n. A library.

bibliotheca, n. A library or collection of books.

bibliothecal classification, n. A classification system devised for arranging library materials.

bibliothecary, n. A librarian.

bibliotheke, n. A library.

Bibliothèque bleu, n. (French) Popular pamphlets with blue wrappers.

bibliotherapist, n. One who practices bibliotherapy.

bibliotherapy, n. The use of reading materials in a program of directed reading that is planned and conducted as an auxiliary in the treatment of mental and emotional disorders and social maladjustment.

bibliothetic, adj. Pertaining to or based on the placing or arrangement of books.

bibliotics, n. The analysis of handwriting and documents for authentication of authorship.

bibliotrain, n. Railroad car converted into a mobile library. De Sola.

Biblis, n. Town in Germany, north of Mannheim.

Byblia, n. A woman who fell in love with her brother Caunus and was changed into a fountain near Miletus. Ovid, *Metamorphoses.*

Byblos, n. Ancient Phoenician city known for exporting Egyptian papyrus; modern Jubail in Lebanon, 20 miles north of Beirut.

Sources: Random House Dictionary of the English Language; Webster's Unabridged Dictionary; Paul Dickson, Words (New York: Delacorte, 1982); Oxford English Dictionary; Heartsill Young, ed., The ALA Glossary of Library and Information Science (ALA, 1983);The Times Atlas of the World; Ralph De Sola, Abbreviations Dictionary (New York: Elsevier, 1981);Richard Weiner, Webster's New World Dictionary of Media and Communications (New York: Simon & Schuster, 1990)

Most mutilated journals

THE UNIVERSITY OF NEBRASKA, Omaha, in a campaign against journal mutilation, identified the ten most mutilated runs of journals in its library, September 1982–May 1983.

1. *Personnel Psychology*
2. *Journal of Conflict Resolution*
3. *Journal of Politics*
4. *Judicature*
5. *Education and Urban Society*
6. *ASCE Journal of Hydraulics*
7. *Phylon*
8. *Journal of Humanistic Philosophy*
9. *Journal of Marriage and the Family*
10. *Journal of Experimental Social Psychology*

Source: "Saving and Securing Library Materials," American Libraries, November 1983, p. 651

The Sibelius saga

AS WE APPROACH the 21st century, let us reflect on what librarians have accomplished over the past years. One minor achievement, announced by the Sibley Library of the Eastman School of Music at the University of Rochester, New York, was the return of a doctoral thesis on the Finnish composer Jean Sibelius, which had been missing from the library since 1937. Imagine the surprise of the Sibley library staff when they received the following letter (accompanied by the missing thesis) in July 1988.—*GME.*

"Dear Keepers of the Tomes:

"In honor of the Fourth of July and the 50th Reunion of the Class of 1939, October next, I am returning a long-lost gift to the Sibley Library. This gift disappeared mysteriously in February 1937, approximately 51.42 years ago. Before revealing the sparse knowledge I have, a large part of which is conjecture, I shall state that I had no official connection with the misdemeanor involved. Neither did [Professor X], the last signer of the library card.

"Apparently the thesis enclosed was mislaid and reported lost. At some time later, when it was found by a graduate student, it was not returned to the library. Rather, because it was so accurately tabulated, it became a Sibelius handbook passed around quietly, to whomever needed it most. This process continued from February 1937 to June 1940 when I was asked by a departing student to return 'a book' to the library which was then closed. Since I was not leaving until mid-morning on the following day, I promised to return the book. It so happened, however, that my folks came to pick me up on that same evening—twelve hours ahead of schedule. With five years worth of souvenirs to stow in the car, I stuffed extra goodies—including 'the book'—into my trunk to be shipped.

"By strange chance the trunk was lost in transit and finally delivered in late August 1940.

"At that time, my brother, a student at [a university in Canada], needed an extra trunk. When I finished unpacking mine for him to use, I looked inside the Sibelius for the first time and discovered that it was 3.5 years overdue! What a surprise! So—in exchange for the use of the trunk, I asked a serious favor of my brother: to mail the book back to Rochester pronto, from Canada, as anonymously as possible.

"Several years later, after finishing medical school in [an American city], my brother returned the trunk—empty except for the Sibelius.

"Since that long-ago time, at yearly inventory I have greeted this thesis with chicken-hearted regret; and, although I have become particularly enlightened in the field it treats, the pressure of unpardonable procrastination is reaching quasi-psychotic proportions.

"Please accept this belated offering with as cheerful grace as possible. Thanks a million, close to a thousand dollars of which would cover the overdue fine. Keep the change for good luck!"

The letter was signed by a 1939 graduate of the Eastman School of Music, who had also enclosed a million-dollar "Special Issue Note" in play money to amuse the library staff.—*Reprinted, with the author's permission, from* The Sibley Muse 11, *no.3/4 (September/November 1988). All references to particular persons have been removed.*

10

The word "library" in 82 different languages

Afrikaans	biblioteek	Tagalog	aklatan
Albanian	bibliothekë	Tahitian	paepae buka
Arabic	ḥizâna-t kutub	Tibetan	kun-dga-ra-ba
Armenian	qradun	Turkish	kütüphane
Basque	liburutegi	Ukrainian	biblioteka
Breton	levraoueg, fem.	Vietnamese	thư viện
Bulgarian	biblioteka	Visayan	pamasahonan
Catalan	biblioteca	Welsh	llyfrgell
Cornish	lyverjy, -ow, masc.	Xhosa	indlu yeencwadi
Czech	knihovna	Zulu	iqoqo lamabhuku
Danish	bibliotek, neut.		
Dutch	bibliotheek, com.		—GME
Egyptian (ancient)	às-t na shāu		
Esperanto	biblioteko		
Estonian	biblioteek		
Fijian	vale ni wilívola		
Finnish	kirjasto		
French	bibliothèque, fem.		
German	Bibliothek, fem.		
Greek	βιβλιοθηκα		
Hausa	lābuřařè, masc.		
Hawaiian	he waihona puke		
Hmong	tsev khaws ntawv		
Hungarian	könyvtár		
Icelandic	bókasafn, neut.		
Ido	biblioteko		
Indonesian	perpustakaan		
Italian	biblioteca, fem.		
Kikuyu	mabuku mongañi-tio gĩkundi		
Konkani	pustakañsāl, neut.		
Lao	hohng sai muit		
Latin	bibliotheca, -ae, fem.		
Latvian	biblioteka		
Lithuanian	knygynas		
Malay	khizanah kitab		
Marshallese	ḷāibrāre		
Moroccan Arabic	mektaba		
Norwegian	bibliotek		
Polish	biblioteka, fem.		
Portuguese	biblioteca, fem.		
Romanian	bibliotecǎ		
Russian	bibliotéka, fem.		
Serbo-Croatian	knjižnica, fem.		
Slovak	knižnica, fem.		
Slovenian	knjižnica		
Spanish	biblioteca, fem.		
Swahili	maktaba		
Swedish	bibliotek, neut.		
Syrian Arabic	maktabe		

The Rosetta stone.

But could they shelve?

Persian vizier Abdul Kassem Ismail (938–995) traveled with 400 camels that bore his 117,000-volume library everywhere he went. The animals were trained to walk in an order that ensured the books' alphabetical arrangement.

Source: *Adlibs*, June 1990, Metropolitan Library System of Oklahoma City

ቤተ ፡ መጻሕፍት **Amharic**

Khmer បណ្ណាល័យ

مَكْتَبَة، دار الكُتُب؛ مجموعة **Arabic**
كُتُب؛ سِلْسِلة كُتُب

Korean 도 서 관

ԳՐԱՏՈՒՆ **Armenian**

Marathi ग्रन्थालय

পুস্তকসমূহ **Bengali**

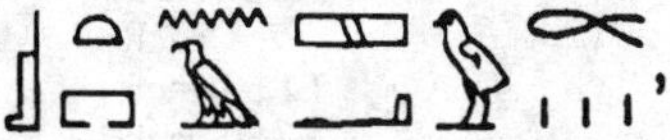

Persian مجموعة كتاب ـ

စာကြည့်တိုက် **Burmese**

Punjabi ਲਾਇਬ੍ਰੇਰੀ

大学图书馆 **Chinese**

библиотéка
Russian

Egyptian

Sanskrit पुस्तकसङ्ग्रह

पुस्तकालय **Gujarati**

Sindhi

סְפָרִים **Hebrew**

Tamil புத்தகசாலை

पुस्तक संग्रह **Hindi**

Thai ห้องสมุด

leabarlann **Irish**

די ביבליאָטעק
Yiddish

大学図書館 **Japanese**

10

New fees for library services

by Carol Hole

AS YOU MAY have noticed, inflation has increased in the past few years. Governing bodies have responded to the increase with an orgy of budget cutting. Some say this shows statesmanlike concern for responsible use of the taxpayer's dollar. Others say politicians are chicken to raise taxes because taxpayers will vote them out of office.

In any case, libraries across the land are under pressure to bring in revenue. The move to user fees is on.

Your Public Library, always on the cutting edge of new developments in library science, has moved rapidly to meet this demand for revenue. Encouraged by its beloved governing bodies and by loyal patrons who frequently snarl, "Why the heck don't y'all charge fines and make those bozos pay?" YPL has instituted fees for nearly all library services.

Our goal is to become the first profit-making public library in history. Our new motto is, "CH-A-A-ARGE!" For everything. You, our patrons, can help us achieve a resounding victory over inflation.

Bring money.

YPL fee schedule

Circulation Department	
Book checkout	
Juvenile books	10¢ each
Adult fiction	75¢ each
Best sellers	$1.50 each
Dirty books	$2.50 each
pointing out good parts	75¢/good part
Nonfiction	
Sex manuals	$5.00/day
Computer manuals	$5.00/hour
How-to books	$1.00 + $15.00 deposit
Car-repair manuals	$10.00 + car title
(title held until book returned)	
Self-help books	$2.00
(money back if personality does not improve)	
Keeping book under counter for favored patron	$1.00 each
Keeping new record under counter:	
Rock, soul, country	$3.50
All other records	$2.50
Not letting your kid check out dirty books	$10.00
Overdue books	
First 15 minutes	50¢
Each half-hour thereafter	25¢
Clearing delinquent's record	50¢/$1.00 owed
Damaged or lost books	
Total charges equal cost of replacement book + fee for searching out-of-print book dealers, if necessary + the following:	
Withdrawing card set	$1.99
Reordering	$7.50
Shipping and handling	$2.50

Recataloging	$6.85
Reprocessing	$3.50
Reshelving	10¢
Refiling card set	$1.99

Copier

Use copier	25¢/page
Explain how to use copier	10¢/minute
Give change for copier	10% of amount changed

Off-track betting

The Circulation Department makes book on the following daily totals:

Circulation	Story hour attendance
Reserves called for	Books cataloged
Books stolen	Staff on diets

Bets must be down by noon each day. Payoffs at 5 p.m. Odds and previous day's winners posted at main desk 9 a.m. to noon.

Outreach Department

Bookmobile stop at your door

1–30 circulations	$150.00/year
30–60 circulations	$100.00/year
60–100 circulations	$50.00/year
Mileage charge, all stops	25¢/mile

No bookmobile stop at your door $200.00/year

Advertising on sides of bookmobile

30-foot Gerstenslager	$150.00 per month
12-foot step van	$75.00 per month

Children's Department

Babysitting (while there's space)

If toilet-trained	$2.00/hour
If not	$5.00/hour

Supervision of teenagers $50.00/hour

Homework

Locating shortest book on reading list	$2.00
Reading book and writing report	$5.00
Translating assignment sheet and explaining what teacher wants	$1.98
Looking up subject in *World Book*	75¢
Copying *World Book* article in longhand	$3.00/page
Doing math (all levels)	$10.00/page

Reader guidance

Locating books on football, snakes, or video games	$1.50
(Video game tokens not accepted in lieu of U.S. coinage)	
Inside dope on where babies come from	$5.00

Story hours

Movies	$2.00
Picture book read aloud	$3.50
with finger plays	$4.50
Storytelling	$5.50

10

Puppet shows:

orchestra	$6.50
balcony	$5.50

Reference Department

Telephone reference

Ready reference	25¢/3 min.
If staff must get up to answer	50¢/3 min.
Singing answer	$5.00
in rhyme	$6.00
with musical backup	$7.50
Guaranteed correct answer	$10.00

Reference materials

Books

first half-hour	35¢
succeeding half-hours	50¢

Periodicals

Back issues	25¢
Current issue, per half-hour	75¢

(*Note: Magazine binder locks when time is up*)

Reader guidance

Looking in card catalog for patron

per author/title	35¢
per subject	50¢

(*Penalty of .25 for each incorrect author or title given to librarian*)

Explaining Dewey system	$2.98
Explaining LC system	$5.98
Explaining AACR2	$1,000.00

Reference questions

Directional questions	5¢
Research questions (general)	50¢/3 min.
Switching subject in mid-question	$1.50
Municipal or government documents	$2.00
Looking up symptoms in *Merck Manual*	$5.00
Genealogy questions	$10.00
repairing microfilm reader	$20.00

(*Note: Contracts for the following reference questions available at reference desk. Notary on duty at all times.*)

Business questions	10% of profits
Explaining tax form	30% of refund
Explaining how to get divorce	20% of alimony
Looking up nonpayers in city directory	
for collection agency	50% of recovery

(*Note: 20% discount on reference questions if you know what you want and can explain it in plain English.*)

Information and referral questions

Cop who fixes tickets	$1.98
Honest mechanic	$24.50

General fees

Bathrooms

Soap, towels, or running water	10¢ each
Toilet paper	Free

Directions to bathroom	$1.00
Use of drinking fountain	5¢
Use of drinking fountain w/cold water	25¢

Problem patrons

Verbal abuse of staff	$10.00/5 min.
Shouting obscenities	$20.00/5 min.
Sleepers (deposit coin in slot in chair)	50¢/hour
Flashers	$5.00, or we won't look
Book thieves	30 days and $100.00 fine

Additional attractions for discerning patrons

Video games

Available in all departments. Buy tokens at main desk.

Door prizes

Given daily at closing time. Prized by local merchants and are truly tacky. Sign up for drawing at main desk.

Overdue lounge

Take a study break in the swinging atmosphere of our mezzanine lounge. Happy Hour 5–7 daily. Live music. Free drinks if your sports reference question stumps our bartender.

A final word

Every penny you spend in Your Library is a penny saved on your taxes, so don't hold back! And remember—

THERE'S NO SUCH THING AS A FREE LUNCH!

—Your Library Staff

Source: Carol Hole, "Fees for Library Services," *American Libraries*, December 1983, pp. 716–17

First rare books in space

Auburn University's rare first edition (1770) of Oliver Goldsmith's *The Deserted Village* (from which the line, "Sweet Auburn, loveliest village of the Plain," was taken) orbited the earth with astronauts Ken Mattingly and Hank Hartsfield, both Auburn alumni, aboard the space shuttle *Columbia* on June 27, 1982.

The record for earliest imprint in space goes to the University of California, Los Angeles, Biomedical Library. A 1765 Greek and Latin edition of Hippocrates' *Aphorisms* belonging to the library's History and Special Collections Division traveled in space with Anna Fisher, one of the astronauts who flew aboard the space shuttle *Discovery*, launched on November 8, 1984. Fisher, a UCLA undergraduate and medical school alumna, had asked the university to take along something that represented the UCLA School of Medicine.

Source: College & Research Libraries News, March 1985, July/August 1985

10

Worst serial title changes

WHEN A PERIODICAL ("serial") changes its name, millions of catalog records in the world's libraries must be updated and cross-referenced, and confused patrons reoriented. Thus, the serials librarians do not take such changes lightly; this is not to say they do not make light of it. The ALA Association for Library Collections and Technical Services' (ALCTS) Serials Section has a committee that each year presents facetious awards for the Worst Serial Title Change of the Year. Presented here are the award winners for 1986–1990.—*GME.*

1990

Save Our Heritage Award
A congratulatory award to the Educational Foundation for Nuclear Science for redesigning the logo and expanding the scope of the *Bulletin of the Atomic Scientists* without choosing a new name just to "sell better."

Arnold Becker Award
To the Daily Journal Corporation for changing the *California Directory of Attorneys* to *California Attorneys* and then to *California Lawyers*.

Teenage Mutant Ninja Titles Award
To Elsevier for *Mutation Research*, which has over the years mutated and multiplied. It has been producing offshoots for 15 years, the latest sample being *Mutation Research: DNAging*.

Hands across the Sea, or Merging Is Such Sweet Sorrow Award
To the Royal Astronomical Society, the Deutsche Geophysikalische Gesellschaft, and the European Geophysical Society, who merged their journals into one that they decided to call *Geophysical Journal*. But there was already a journal with that name, and its publishers filed suit for the use of that unique title. Well, to make a long story even longer, the second *Geophysical Journal* rapidly backpedaled and changed its name (again) to *Geophysical Journal of the RAS, DGG and EGS*. That was in January 1989. It seems this wasn't quite catchy enough, so in July 1989 they finally (we hope) got the unique and catchy name they wanted: *Geophysical Journal International*.

To Teach or Not to Teach Award
To Scholastic, Inc., for flip-flopping between the titles *Instructor* and *Instructor and Teacher* and *Teacher* since 1981 when *Instructor* merged with *Teacher*.

Back to the Operating Room Award
To Springer International for causing unknown amounts of trauma to a serial title by changing *Archives of Orthopaedic and Traumatic Surgery* to *Archives of Orthopaedic and Trauma Surgery*.

Snake in the Grass Award
To Karen Muller, executive director of ALCTS, for changing *RTSD Newsletter* to *ALCTS Newsletter,* after the division voted to change its name.

Worst Serial Title Change of 1990
To IEEE for changing the *IEEE Journal of Robotics and Automation* to *IEEE Transactions on Robotics and Automation.*

1989

Best Attempt Not to Change Award
To New York University's Tisch School of the Arts. In considering a new name, they thought of *That Damned Review,* or *Theatre Dance Review,* or *Theatre, Dance, Ritual.* Nothing felt right. And then there were all those libraries which, if they

changed their name, would have to re-catalog and maybe, in doing so, cancel their subscriptions. And so what they did is become *TDR, The Drama Review: A Journal of Performance Studies.* Unfortunately, librarians have called this *Drama Review* for 20 years, so yes, we did have to recatalog. But thanks for trying.

Frequent Offender Award and Cheaper by the Dozen Award

To the USDA Economic Research Service for its continual revision of the Situation and Outlook Reports. For example: *Fruit and Vegetable Situation* changed to *Fruit Situation,* changed to *Fruit Outlook & Situation,* then to *Outlook and Situation Report. Fruit,* then to *Situation and Outlook Report. Fruit and Tree Nuts.* Isn't this fruity?

Just Say No Award

To Springer Publishing for changing *Drugs in Current Use* to *Drugs in Current Use and New Drugs,* then changing in 1988 to *Modell's Drugs in Current Use and New Drugs.*

The More It Changes, the More It Stays the Same Award

To the American Management Association for changing *Management Solutions* back to *Supervisory Management.* See the 1987 awards.

I Need a PC Award

To Meckler Publishing Company for changing *Small Computers in Libraries* to *Computers in Libraries;* changing *Library Computer Equipment Review* to *Computer Equipment Review* to *Library Computer Systems and Equipment Review;* and changing *M300 and PC Report* to *Library Workstation and PC Report* to *Library Workstation Report.*

Keep Those Catalogers Well Fed Award and Hands across the Sea Award

To the John Libbey Company for merging *Human Nutrition: Applied Nutrition* and *Human Nutrition: Clinical Nutrition* into *European Journal of Clinical Nutrition.*

Snake in the Grass Award

To the International Federation of Library Associations for changing *International Cataloguing* to *International Cataloguing and Bibliographic Control.*

Worst Serial Title Change of 1989

To PSC Publications, which merged the basic and deluxe editions of *American Home Arts Needlecraft for Today* to form *Needle & Craft.* The committee wondered if they were trying to return to their roots since they started out as *Needle & Thread.*

1988

Total Confusion Award or I Can't Remember the Title Award

To the Prime National Publishing Corporation for publishing a journal with three different titles in one and a half years and after only seven issues. It was the *American Journal of Alzheimer's Care and Related Disorders* from January to October 1986, changing to the *American Journal of Alzheimer's Care and Research* in January 1987, then to *American Journal of Alzheimer's Care and Related Disorders & Research* in July 1987.

The Hurrier I Go, the Behinder I Get Award or The Running Amuck Award

To Rodale Press for *Runner's World,* which changed to *Rodale's Runner's World,* which changed to *Runner's World incorporating The Runner.* Another award goes

10

Not descriptive enough! How about "American Pictorial Revue"?

Vol. 6, No. 5 | LIFE | January 30, 1939
REG U S. PAT. OFF.

to Rodale for changing *Organic Gardening & Farming* to *Organic Gardening* to *Rodale's Organic Gardening* to *Organic Gardening*. The Committee wishes to suggest to Rodale Press that in the future they exercise *Prevention*.

"Grand" Parent Award for Spawning Four Offspring under One Cover
To the Gerontological Society of America for changing *Journal of Gerontology* to *Journals of Gerontology*. One librarian wrote: "The `s' on Journals is significant for it tells you that in place of the single authority on basic research so familiar to the aging field over the past 40 years, there now are four distinct journals within one cover. There are four field-specific editors-in-chief, four specialized editorial boards, and four individual sets of instructions to authors, guaranteed to satisfy any department or tenure committee."

Cheaper by the Dozen, Well Almost, Award
To University Microfilms International and the Japanese Technical Information Service. After only two years they split *Japanese Technical Abstracts* into ten separate titles such as: *Japan Biosciences, Japan Business, Japan Chemistry, Japan Computers,* well, you get the idea.

We've Seen the Error of Our Ways Award and **Hands across the Sea Award**
To the Royal Institute of British Architects for changing a journal known for years as *RIBA Journal* to *The Architect*. The publishers acquiesced to subscriber demands that the title be returned to its old, familiar name, and in November 1987 it again became *RIBA Journal*.

Is This Progress? Award
To Deborah Napior, who changed *Solar Age* to *Progressive Builder: Energy Efficiency and Quality Home Construction,* to *Progressive Builder: The Magazine for the Custom Builder,* to *Custom Builder,* and finally to *Custom Builder: The Monthly Magazine of Quality Home Construction*. It remains to be seen how many more unique titles this publisher will come up with.

Snake in the Grass Award
To Libraries Unlimited for changing *Library Science Annual* to *Library and Information Science Annual*.

Worst Serial Title Change of 1988 and **Globe Trotter's Award**
To North American Publishing Co., who decided to go globe trotting after 30 years of stability. Called *American Import & Export Bulletin* from 1934 to 1974, it has had seven title changes since then, six within three years, three of them occurring in 1987. It changed to *American Import Export Bulletin,* then to *American Import Export Management,* then to *American Import-Export Management's Global Trade Executive,* then to *Global Trade Executive,* then to *American Import-Export Management Global Trade Executive,* then to *American Import/Export Management's Global Trade,* and finally to *American Import/Export Global Trade*.

1987

Sign of the Times Award
To Target, Inc., for Howard Ruff's financial success report. It was previously called *The Ruff Times*, then *Howard Ruff's Financial Survival Report*, then *Howard Ruff's Financial Success Report*. Now it's back to *Ruff Times*.

Cheaper by the Dozen Award
To Fodor's for changing all of their "guides to countries" from *Fodor's Budget Guides* to *Fodor's Budget Travel Guides*. For example: *Fodor's Budget Canada* became *Fodor's Budget Travel Canada*.

Identity Crisis Award
To Gale Research Co. for changing the well-known *IMS Ayer Directory of Publications* to the *Gale Directory of Publications*. How many years will it be before librarians and library users no longer refer to it as Ayer's?

I Can't See Where It's Going Award
To Meckler Publications for *Optical Information Systems*. When this title began in 1981, it was called *Videodisc/Teletext*. Then it changed to *Videodisc, Videotex*, then to *Videodisc and Optical Disk*, and now to its more general title.

I Know All the Answers Award or Just Ask Me Award
To the American Management Association for changing *Supervisory Management* to *Supervisory Solutions*.

Why Bother to Change Award
To Williams & Wilkins for a totally useless change of adding the word "Journal." *Pediatric Infectious Disease* became the *Pediatric Infectious Disease Journal*. At the same time, the bound-in, separately paged *Pediatric Infectious Disease Newsletter* became the *Pediatric Infectious Disease Journal Newsletter*.

Snake in the Grass Award
To the International Centre for the Registration of Serials for writing a letter that merely added to the confusion. It read, in part: "Many users were confused by the fact that the *ISDS Register* and the *ISDS Bulletin*, which were regularly combined into one, bear two different titles. The title *ISDS Bulletin* has therefore disappeared. The *ISDS Register* alone continues."

Frequent Offender Award
To Chilton's, because they never fail to provide us with at least one unnecessary title change a year. This year's most nominated award goes to *Chilton's Iron Age: Manufacturing Management*, which dropped the word Chilton's to become just *Iron Age: Manufacturing Management*.

Worst Serial Title Change of 1987 and Multiple Disaster Award
To John Wiley for again changing the names of all parts of the *Journal of Polymer Science*, and to add to the disaster, also playing musical chairs with the letter designation of each part.

1986

Cheaper by the Dozen Award and Hands across the Sea Award
To the Economic Intelligence Unit for changing the 92 different country titles of the *Quarterly Economic Review* and their supplements to *EIU Country Reports* and *EIU Country Profiles*.

If You Can't Beat Them, Join Them Award
To the National Council for Families and Television for recognizing the fact that if parents want to spend time with their children, they'll have to join them around the television set. They retitled *Television & Children* as *Television & Families*.

10

Oops Award

To Marquis Who's Who for issuing the first edition of a new Who's Who as *Who's Who in Frontier Science and Technology* and correcting it in the second edition to *Who's Who in Frontiers of Science and Technology*.

Octopus Award

To Automated Office Ltd. for merging two titles: *Information Management* and *Office Administration and Automation*, to form *Administrative Management*. Twelve other titles were swallowed up in its past history.

Outstanding New Euphemism Award

To Haworth Press for retitling the *Labor-Management Alcoholism Journal* as the *Employee Assistance Quarterly*.

Leave Well Enough Alone Award

To M&T Publishing for changing *Dr. Dobb's Journal* to *Dr. Dobb's Journal of Software Tools for the Professional Programmer*.

Custody Fight Award

A joint award to the two parties in the dispute, Springer-Verlag and Karger. Springer-Verlag publishes *Child's Nervous System,* and Karger publishes *Pediatric Neuroscience,* both of which claim to be the only authorized continuation of *Child's Brain.*

Snake in the Grass Award

To the American Library Association for retitling the *ALA Handbook of Organization and Membership Directory* as the *ALA Handbook of Organization*.

Worst Serial Title Change of 1986

To the Watt Publishing Company for retitling *Animal Nutrition & Health* as *Animal Health & Nutrition*.

Source: ALA Association for Library Collections and Technical Services

Weird titles

IN 1985 RUSSELL ASH and Brian Lake published a book-length collection of unusual book titles. Here are some full citations, inspired by their selections:

Anon., *How to Boil Water in a Paper Bag* (n.p., 1891)

George John Dudycha, *An Objective Study of Punctuality in Relation to Personality and Achievement* (N.Y.: Archives of Psychology, 1936)

Thomas Cation Duncan, *How to Be Plump* (Chicago: Duncan Brothers, 1878)

Yury Petrovich Frolov, *Fish Who Answer the Telephone* (London: Kegan Paul, Trench, Trubner, 1937)

Pauline Kohler, *I Was Hitler's Maid* (Long, 1940)

Kate Marsden, *On Sledge and Horseback to Outcast Siberian Lepers* (The Record Press, 1892)

Robert and Mimi Melnick, *Manhole Covers of Los Angeles* (L.A.: Dawson's Book Shop, 1974)

Mrs. M. E. Rattray, *Cold Meat and How to Disguise It* (C. Arthur Pearson, 1904)

A. Moore [Jonathan Swift], *The Benefit of Farting Explain'd* (London, 1727)

Proceedings of the Second International Workshop on Nude Mice (Tokyo: University of Tokyo Press, 1978)

Source: Russell Ash and Brian Lake, *Bizarre Books* (New York: St. Martin's, 1986)

Uncommon authors

A QUICK BROWSE through the *National Union Catalog* and the *British National Bibliography* can turn up some very unusual author's names. However, to save you the trouble of looking through all those heavy volumes, here are some oddly named authors with a sample title from their collected works.—*GME*.

Adebóye Babalola
  Ijálá àtenudenu (Ibadan, 1960)
Pierre Jean Jacques Bacon-Tacon
  Plan patriotique (Paris, 1790)
Ludwig von Baldass
  Hieronymus Bosch (Vienna, 1943)
Ole Bang
  Rotterne (Copenhagen, 1936)
Bogoljub Biljic
  Odabrane frantsuske pesme (Belgrade, 1967)
Konrad Bitschin
  Pädagogik (Gotha, 1905)
Wallop Brabazon
  The Deep Sea and Coast Fisheries of Ireland (Dublin, 1848)
Sleeter Bull
  A Review of American Investigations on Fattening Lambs (Urbana, Ill., 1914)
Storm Bull
  Kliniske studier over aneurysma aortae (Kristiana, 1905)
Perin H. Cabinetmaker
  Government and the Displaced Persons (Bombay, 1956)
Ellsworth Prouty Conkle
  Lots of Old People Are Really Good for Something (New York, 1964)
Lucy Cherry Crisp
  Brief Testament: Verse (N. Montpelier, Vt., 1947)
Cornelius Crocus
  Comedia sacra (Strasbourg, 1537)
Lettice May Crump
  Problems in Soil Microbiology (London, 1935)
Anna Ethel Twitt De Vere
  Expert Speed Phrases Used Successfully for Twenty Years in Verbatim Shorthand Reporting (New York, 1913)
Robert Baby Buntin Dicebat
  Superman (London, 1934)
Homer Hasenpflug Dubs
  China (Oxford, 1949)
Gottfried Egg
  Adolf Schlatters kritische Position (Stuttgart, 1968)
Hurlstone Fairchild
  An Artist's Notebook (Hollywood, Calif., 1950)
Francis M. Fillerup
  Management (New York, 1963)
Stuyvesant Fish
  Peter Stuyvesant (Baltimore, 1930)
Mercedes Formica
  La hija de don Juan de Austria (Madrid, 1973)
Semen Frug
  The Undying Foe (New York, 1938)

Ole Bang

Gergely Gergely
Tolnai Lajos pályája (Budapest, 1964)
Ya. Ya. Grunt
Borba za Ural i Sibir' (Russia, 1926)
Romulus Guga
Viata postmortem (Bucharest, 1972)
O. Heck
Physiologie (Hamburg, 1901)
Virginia Fox Hunt
How to Live in the Tropics (New York, 1942)
Kah-Ge-Ga-Gah-Bowh (George Copway)
The Ojibway Conquest (New York, 1850)
Jup Kastrati
Figura të ndrituna të rilindjes kombëtare (Shkodër, 1963)
Solon Toothaker Kimball
Family and Community in Ireland (Cambridge, Mass., 1940)
Verona Butzer Knisely
The Social Concept of Money (Chicago, 1935)
Thorgny Ossian Bolivar Napoleon Krok
Bibliotheca botanica suecana (Upsala, 1918)
Gazaway Bugg Lamar
Proceedings of the Bank Convention of the Confederate States (Charleston, S.C., 1861)
Manfred Lurker
Bibliographie zur Symbolkunde (Baden-Baden, 1968)
William Dummer Northend
Lecture on the Importance of Moral and Religious Education in a Republic (Boston, 1851)
Violet Organ
Robert Henri and His Circle (Ithaca, N.Y., 1969)
Henricus Pisart
Expositio Rubricarum Missalis Romani (Köln, 1726)
Jan de Quack
Zuma (Amsterdam, 1819)
Mary Quick
Stone Walls (Burradoo, N.S.W., 1952)
Edwin Alfred Robert Rumball-Petre
What to Do with Sex Slavery in the Community (Rochester, N.Y., 1913)
James Patrick Sex
California v. Will M. Beggs; Petition for a Re-Hearing (San Jose, Calif., 1918)
I. M. Sick
Elskov (Copenhagen, 1934)
Pansey Aiken Slappey
The South and the Nation (New York, 1946)

Kingsley Bryce Speakman Smellie
A History of Local Government (London, 1946)
Negley Teeters
They Were in Prison (Chicago, 1937)
Mrs. Chase Going Woodhouse
After College—What? (Greensboro, N.C., 1932)

Source: National Union Catalog; British National Bibliography

Bibli,oddities!

by Christopher Dodge

FOR NINE YEARS the cataloging staff at Hennepin County (Minn.) Library (HCL) has gathered and posted nominees for its annual Quasi-Notable Awards. The awards document the underside of the cataloger's rock—the bizarre, ironic, and silly of the bibliographic world—the publishers' eccentricities and subject headings made in hell. The Quasis, until now, have been but a capricious by-product in the manufacturing of a user-friendly catalog. Now it's time to bring this compendium of "bibli,oddities" to light. Enjoy!

Quasi-ironic titles

The Lighter Side of Gravity.
The Boyhood of Grace Jones.
Crappie Wisdom.
Multiple Sarcasm.
Judo: The Gentle Way.
The Joy of Stress.
Everything You Wanted to Know About Phobias but Were Afraid to Ask.
How to Repair Food.
Good News About Depression.
Looking Forward to Being Attacked.
Why Fish Carp?
Reviving the Death Penalty.
Fighting a Long Nuclear War.
Having a Baby Without a Man.
A Juggler's Handbook.
Power Lunching.
Bankruptcy: Do It Yourself.
The Consumer's Guide to Death, Dying, and Bereavement.
I Left My Fat Behind.

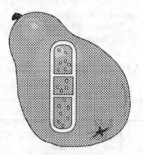

A pear repaired.

Longest Dewey

338.7678991245500977434 (Does that round up to 338.768?) [LC-assigned to: *The Motown Story,* Don Waller.]

Quasi-best dedication

"To our husbands . . . who first interested us in mating and reproduction." [*Successful Dog Breeding*]

"To my honey." [*The Simple Art of Perfect Baking*]

"To Pal and his male descendants who successfully impersonated Lassie to a generation of moviegoers." [*What a Drag: Men as Women and Women as Men in the Movies*]

Quasi-perverse subject headings

Breakfast cereals—Computer-assisted instruction—Software. [HCL]
Truth—Fiction. [HCL]
Hormones—Addresses, essays, lectures. [LC]
Hemmorhoids in the Bible. [HCL]

10

Cooking and working mothers. [HCL]
Fish pastes. [May subdivide geographically] [LC]
Graham crackers and sexuality. [HCL]
Raccoons—Biography. [LC]
Infant psychiatry. [HCL, LC]
Turkey—Operas. [HCL]
Sex aids (for canaries). [HCL]
Game and game-birds, Dressing of. [LC]

Quasi-best author blurbs

"Denise Austin is the fitness authority on NBC's *Today* show and . . . wants to meet you and let you feel her tummy."

"W. R. Philbrick was born in Boston in a building since demolished."

"Trials and tribulations cannot break Rod McKuen's heart . . . after a quarter century of verbal angst and ennui, he's still America's most understood poet."

"Marc Scott Zicree . . . currently lives in Hollywood with a marvelous wife and a vile little dog."

Quasi-success stories

The Look of Success.
A Strategy for Success.
The Art of Corporate Success.
Relax Yourself to Success.
Executive Success.
Dress for Success.
Interview for Success.
Success Is a State of Mind.
Speak the Language of Success.
The Law of Success.
Success Without Stress.
Bridges to Success.
Success: You Can Make It Happen.
Success Without Succeeding.
Market Yourself for Success.
The Success System That Never Fails.
Formula for Success.
The Success Factor.
Success Through Transactional Analysis.
Success over Sixty.
How to Achieve Total Success.
The Success Trip.
Make Your Child a Success.
Bound for Success.
Excess Success.

Quasi-library title

Managing the One-person Library. [PARTIAL CONTENTS: Personnel considerations—Further personnel considerations.]

Quasi-beloved titles

The Squat Pear Principle.
Mayonnaise and the Origin of Life.

The Brave Little Toaster: A Bedtime Story for Small Appliances.
How to Deep Freeze a Mammoth.
The Total Tomato.
More Great Pantyhose Craft.
A Red Brick Building, Ugly as Hell, in Venice, California.
The Snarkout Boys and the Avocado of Death.
Creative Chain Saw Projects.

Quasi-best publishers' warnings

"This book is sold subject on the condition that it shall not by way of trade or otherwise, be lent, re-sold, hired out, or otherwise circulated without the publisher's prior consent in any form of binding or cover other than that in which it is published and without a similar condition including this condition being imposed on the subsequent purchaser."

"Whoever Xeroxes this book calls down the curse of the seven motherless pigs."

"This paper discolors with age and was . . . selected for this quality: if the pages are yellowing, the directory is obsolete and should not be used!"

Quasi title/publisher match

Maximize Your Body Potential: 16 Weeks to a Lifetime of Effective Weight Management (Bull Publishing).

Quasi author/title matches

What to Do When the Russians Come, by Robert Conquest.
Keepers of the Sea, by Edward L. Beach.
Acne: Advice on Clearing Your Skin, by Robert Marks.
Child Protection: The Role of the Courts, by Thelma Stiffarm.
Running with Man's Best Friend, by Davia Gallup.
Tree of Paradise, by Jane Arbor.
A Quiver Full of Arrows, by Jeffrey Archer.
Seasonal Gifts from the Kitchen, by Emily Crumpacker.
Business Math Basics, by Robert E. Swindle.
The Slendernow Diet, by Richard A. Passwater.
Eggshells to Objets d'Art, by Ima Ova.

Quasi-titillating titles

Where to See Wildlife in California.
The Joy of Snacks.
Living with Llamas.
Stripper's Guide to Canoe Building.
Chickens and Their Wild Relatives.
The Secret Life of Hardware.
Dating Techniques for the Archaeologist.

Worst quasi-new editions

Your Baby's Sex. [1970]
Choose Your Baby's Sex. [1977]
How to Choose the Sex of Your Baby. [1984]
Learn How to Choose the Sex of Your Baby Today. [1991?]

10

Source: Christopher Dodge, "Biblioddities!" *American Libraries,* March 1989, pp. 264–65

Norm's Library Levity

The staff of the Boston Public Library turned up some entertaining examples in a project they conducted in the late 1970s and early 1980s that involved examining the Research Library Catalogue for both odd author-title combinations and amusing subject headings.

The author-title combinations included:

Milton Ash, *Nuclear Reactor Kinetics*
Barbara Bean, *The Crockpot Cookbook*
Edward Clodd, *A Primer of Evolution*
Sally Devore, *The Appetites of Men*
John Goodbody, *Judo*
Walter Reckless, *The Crime Problem*

Subject headings included:

Automobile houses *see* Garages
Baboons — Congresses
Celebrities *see also* Eccentrics
Infidelity *see also* Agnosticism

—*Norman D. Stevens,
The Molesworth Institute*

Funny LC subject headings

THESE LIBRARY OF CONGRESS subject headings have been selected over the years by the LC Professional Association as the funniest and most interesting.

Adult children
Beehives
   see Bee—Housing
Combustion, Spontaneous human
Crummies
   see Cabooses (Railroads)
Diving for men
Drug abuse—Programmed instruction
Errors and blunders, Literary
Feet in the Bible
Hand—Surgery—Juvenile literature
Impurity centers
Lord's supper—Admission age
Lord's supper—Reservation
Low German wit and humor
Monotone operators
Running races in rabbinical literature
Sewage—Collected works
Standing on one foot
   see One-leg resting position
Stupidity
   see Inefficiency, Intellectual
Surgery—Nutritional aspects
Thumbing the nose
   see Shanghai gesture
Urinary diversions
Venereal disease—Programmed instruction

Source: "Funny LC Subject Headings Revisited," *American Libraries*, May 1985, p. 332

Librarians on film

by Frederick Duda

LIBRARIANS ARE NOT PORTRAYED in movies as often as cowboys, detectives, soldiers, or even mad scientists, but they have made a small mark—a bookmark, perhaps—on the film industry. Frederick Duda, talking-book librarian at the Manatee County (Fla.) Public Library, Bradenton, has compiled the following cinematic summary of library-related films.—*GME.*

1932—**No Man of Her Own;** Carole Lombard as Connie Randall, public librarian
1938—**Scandal Street;** Louise Campbell as Nora Langdon, public librarian
1940—**The Philadelphia Story;** Hilda Plowright as Quaker librarian
1941—**Citizen Kane;** Georgia Backus as Bertha Anderson, manuscripts librarian, Thatcher Memorial Library
1942—**Quiet Please, Murder;** George Sanders as Fleg, library thief; Frank O'Connor as library guard
1943—**The Human Comedy;** Adeline De Walt Reynolds as children's librarian
1943—**Shadow of a Doubt;** Eily Malyon as librarian, Santa Rosa (Calif.) PL
1945—**A Tree Grows in Brooklyn;** Lillian Bronson as children's librarian
1945—**Adventure;** Greer Garson as Emily Sears, San Francisco PL
1946—**The Big Sleep;** Carole Douglas as librarian, Hollywood PL; Dorothy Malone as antiquarian bookseller
1946—**It's a Wonderful Life;** Donna Reed as Mary Hatch, Bedford Falls PL (in alternate life)
1946—**Good News;** June Allyson as Connie Lane, student library assistant, Tait College Library
1951—**Katie Did It;** Ann Blyth as Katherine Standish, librarian
1952—**The Thief;** Ray Milland as Allan Fields, atomic spy and library user
1956—**Storm Center;** Bette Davis as Alicia Hull, public librarian; Kim Hunter as Martha Lockridge, assistant, then acting librarian; Kevin Coughlin as Freddie Slater, young adult reader and arsonist
1957—**Desk Set;** Katharine Hepburn as Bunny Watson, research librarian for a communications firm; Joan Blondell as Peg Costello, and Dina Merrill as Sylvia, library support staff; Spencer Tracy as Richard Sumner, automation consultant
1961—**Breakfast at Tiffany's;** Elvia Allman as librarian, New York PL
1962—**The Music Man;** Shirley Jones as Marian Pardoo, librarian, River City (Iowa) PL
1962—**Only Two Can Play;** Peter Sellers as John Lewis, librarian, Swansea Library
1962—**Rome Adventure;** Suzanne Pleshette as Prudence Bell, assistant librarian in a girls' school
1963—**Cleopatra;** Rex Harrison as Julius Caesar, library arsonist, Alexandria, Egypt; Elizabeth Taylor as Cleopatra, intellectual freedom advocate
1964—**7 Faces of Dr. Lao;** Barbara Eden as Angela Benedict, public librarian
1966—**The Spy Who Came in from the Cold;** Claire Bloom as Nan Perry, librarian and Communist; Richard Burton as Alec Leamas, library assistant and spy
1966—**You're a Big Boy Now;** Peter Kastner as Bernard Chanticleer, library page, New York PL
1969—**Goodbye, Columbus;** Richard Benjamin as Neil Klugman, library assistant, Newark (N.J.) PL
1970—**Love Story;** Ali McGraw as student assistant, Radcliffe College Library
1974—**Mr. Sycamore;** Jean Simmons as Estelle Benbow, librarian
1976—**All the President's Men;** Jaye Stewart as library clerk, Library of Con-

10

gress; Robert Redford as Bob Woodward, and Dustin Hoffman as Carl Bernstein, LC researchers

1978—**Foul Play;** Goldie Hawn as Gloria Mundy, librarian, San Francisco

1978—**Movie Movie;** Trish Van Devere as Betsy McGuire, public librarian

1983—**Something Wicked This Way Comes;** Jason Robards Jr. as Charles Halloway, librarian, Green Town (Ill.) PL

1984—**Ghostbusters;** Alice Drummond as librarian, New York PL; John Rothman as library administrator, New York PL; Ruth Oliver as library ghost; Bill Murray as Peter Venkman, library ghost exterminator

1985—**Maxie;** Mandy Patinkin as Nick, rare book librarian, San Francisco PL; Valerie Curtin as Ophelia Sheffer, supervising librarian, San Francisco PL

1985—**Bridge Across Time** (made for TV); Adrienne Barbeau as Lynn Chandler, head librarian, Lake Havasu City PL, Arizona

1986—**The Name of the Rose;** Volker Prechtel as Malachia, monastery librarian, unnamed Benedictine abbey in Italy, 1327; Michael Habeck as Brother Berengar, assistant librarian

1986—**Off Beat;** Judge Reinhold as Joe Gower, library assistant by day, dancer by night

1989—**Major League;** Rene Russo as Lynn Westland, special collections librarian, Cleveland (Ohio) PL

1990—**Personal Ads** (made for TV); Jennifer O'Neill as killer reference librarian

1990—**It!** (made for TV); Tim Reid as Mike Hanlon, librarian, Derry (Me.) PL

Source: Frederick Duda, author of *Bib/Triv* (McFarland & Co., 1991)

Norm's Library Levity

Anne Fliotsos reports that some of the following possible movie titles appeared on the bulletin board of the School of Library and Information Science at Indiana University in 1989.

Abridged Too Far	Raiders of the Lost Archives
The ARBA Dumpling Gang	Sorry, Wrong Call Number
CD-ROMbo	stacks, lies, and microfilm
Debbie Does Dewey	The Trouble with Dewey
It Came from OCLC	
KATZ: The Musical	
M*e*S*H	
One Flew Over the Reference Desk	

—Norman D. Stevens,
The Molesworth Institute

The naming of Oscar

by Frederick Duda

ACCORDING TO MASON WILEY and Damien Bona in *Inside Oscar* (New York: Ballantine, 1987), the credit for naming the Oscar goes to Margaret Herrick, librarian of the Academy of Motion Picture Arts and Sciences, who thought that the statuette looked like her Uncle Oscar.

Bette Davis, however, credits herself with naming the Oscar after her first husband, Harmon ("Ham") Oscar Nelson, and she perpetuated this story late into her life. She contended that the statuette's fanny was a dead ringer for Ham's. "Now I couldn't call the greatest acting award in the world a *Ham*, could I?" Davis said. She dates the nickname to the time she won her first Academy Award for Best Actress for *Dangerous*, which was presented to her on March 5, 1936, several years after librarian Herrick is credited with originating the name.

Billy Wilkinson's ten favorite library postcards

by Billy R. Wilkinson

THERE ARE TENS OF THOUSANDS of library postcards in the world. Does anyone know how many? The Norman Stevens Collection contains more than twenty thousand cards. My "Favorite One Hundred Postcards" would have been less painful but the editor was adamant, so here are nine American beauties plus one wild card. Notice that I have excluded those glorious European ones, as well as postals from all other nations. As an example, you will have to see the colorful cover of the May 1989 issue of *College and Research Libraries News* for the Bodleian Library at Oxford University. I have also included only one interior view and have excluded elegant "Delivery Rooms," "Alcoves," and other interiors, such as the 1907 card of the Delivery Room at the University of Illinois, Champaign-Urbana, and the contemporary card of the Christopher Morley Alcove, Magill Library, Haverford College. In a future edition, I will campaign for Wilkinson's "Ten Favorite British Library Postcards," my "Ten Favorite Library Interiors," "Billy's Best Library Postal Exotica" (leather cards, "hold-to-the-light" postcards in which the windows "glow," metal cards, and other novelties), etc.

The following nine favorites of U.S. academic and public libraries and the Library of Congress, plus one British interior which I simply cannot exclude, are in no particular order—just the fancy of the moment.

—Billy R. Wilkinson,
Director of the Gallery,
University of Maryland,
Baltimore County

Cornell Library, Cornell University, Ithaca, N. Y.

Figure 1. Cornell University Library, Ithaca, New York. These twenty "Scenic Colored Miniatures" from the town and the university "far above Cayuga's waters" (left) were sent by George Robb to himself in Bedford, Pa. Postage was one cent without message! The top card in the packet is Goldwin Smith Hall, where there was a small departmental library on the third floor until the Cornell University Library (right), which opened in 1891, was renovated, and became the Uris Undergraduate Library in 1962.

10

Figure 2. Stanford University Library, Palo Alto, California. On April 18, 1906, this handsome, "quake proof" library collapsed during the major earthquake. It had not been quite completed and therefore not yet used by readers. I also have a "San Francisco Earthquake Pictorial" in living color, which shows the gilded dome eerily standing among the ruins of the building. It was never rebuilt.

Figure 3. Fountain, University Librarian's Court Yard, Sterling Library, Yale University, New Haven, Connecticut. Particular favorites of mine are real-photo postcards. This one represents the genre beautifully. Four figures inhabit the fountain in an interior courtyard of the Sterling Library. What an elegant cooler for champagne at a reception!

Figure 4. Handley Library, Winchester, Virginia. I have seven postcards of this magnificent building, but my favorite is the one by moonlight. Trivia from another card: When Judge John Handley of Scranton, Pa., died in 1895, he bequeathed $250,000 to Winchester for a public library. This sum was invested until $300,000 was accumulated. A monumental structure of Indiana limestone was erected in 1908 at a cost of $150,000, the balance being left for an endowment fund.

Figure 5. Exeter Public Library, Exeter, New Hampshire. This delightful card was patented in 1905. When you turn the latch and open the hinged "door," the Public Library (see insert) as well as eleven other photographs may be viewed. Even with its extra thickness, the "Postage to All Countries" was only one cent.

10

Figure 6. "Library Plaza," Columbus, Indiana. Columbus, Indiana, has many gems designed by the world's leading architects, thanks to Irwin Miller of the Cummins Engine Company. That's a Henry Moore sculpture in front of the Public Library. The whole town is a class act and the Library and its plaza (as well as its postcard) measure up.

Figure 7. Carnegie Library, Green River, Wyoming (courtesy of the Norman Stevens Collection). This is also one of Norman Stevens's favorites. It represents the more than 1,600 Carnegie libraries across the United States. We like the stark contrast between the building and the landscape. That was some edifice for Green River! Look closely and you will see a picket fence.

Figure 8. Easthampton Public Library, Easthampton, Massachusetts. "Fred" could not resist sending "Miss Nellie O'Connor" of New Britain, Conn., the Easthampton Belles (and the Public Library). Neither can I resist including them for you.

Figure 9. The Library of Congress, Washington, D.C. My collection contains 310 postals of the Library of Congress, but this is the favorite because of the sparkle that unknown hands have glued to the roof and dome (tinseling glue and special "jeweling outfits" were available to decorate postals at home). I also delight in Elizabeth's messages: "I'm having a dandy time," and "The most beautiful building I ever saw."

10

Longleat House, Warminster, Wiltshire, England. *From an Original Colour-Photograph.*

Figure 10. Longleat House, Warminster, Wiltshire, England. A gift from James Davis, special collections librarian, UCLA's Research Library, this postal of the library at Longleat House and Safari Park has to be included in any listing of all-time favorites. Trivia from the card's verso: "In the Spring of 1966, the Marquess of Bath and Mr. Jimmy Chipperfield established in the grounds of a Stately Home, the first Safari Park in Europe. . . . The lion, Marquis, was the first cub born at Longleat."

Bookplates

IN 1989 *AMERICAN LIBRARIES* issued a challenge for the best library-related personalized license plate. The editors received 16 entries from California alone. Here, for the first time anywhere, is the complete list of all the entries received.

7th KEY	LIBRARY
BA MLS	LIBRI
BK LUVR	MDM LBRN
BKWRM 3	MS INFO
BOOKD UP	PAGE 1 and PAGE 2
COPY 1 and COPY 2	READ
HIONBOOX	READ ME
HUSHHH	READER
I LVBKS	RFRR
I READ2	SERIALS
IAMSLIC	SSHHHH
INFO 2 GO	UCSD BKS
INFO DR 1	X LIBRS
INFOPRO	
INFOTOGO	
KDZ BKS	
LBRARY	
LIB TCHR	
LIBER	
LIBR CO	

Little-known facts from the New York Public Library

THE NEW YORK PUBLIC LIBRARY opened its doors to the public at Fifth Avenue and 42nd Street for the first time on May 24, 1911. On that day, 934 people used the Main Reading Room; 654 books were requested in the Public Catalog Room; and more than 50,000 people visited the new facility.

First book requested in the Public Catalog Room

On opening day, C. A. Montgomery rushed in to make sure he submitted the first call slip for a book he knew the library did not yet own—Delia Bacon's *The Philosophy of the Plays of Shakespeare Unfolded*. Montgomery, a staunch Baconian who believed Sir Francis Bacon wrote Shakespeare's works, anticipated the publicity that would accompany this "failure" to produce the first book requested, and planned to present the book to the library (which he did).

First book delivered in the Public Catalog Room

Nravstvennye idealy Nashev Vremeni (*Moral Ideas of Our Time: Friedrich Nietzsche and Lev Tolstoy*, by N. Y. Grot) was requested by A. Shub of 1699 Washington Avenue.

Famous NYPL users

E. L. Doctorow, Alfred Kazin, John Updike, Barbara Tuchman, Norman Mailer, Theodore White, Nancy Milford, Princess Grace, Rex Harrison, Jackie Onassis, Francis Ford Coppola, Marlene Dietrich, Joe Frazier, and Julie Nixon Eisenhower.

Unusual users

A Harvard doctoral candidate toiled for years, wearing a mask to fight off the dust from a million documents left by a 19th-century banker.

A man from New Jersey spent eleven years doggedly tracking down the burial places of 60,000 New Jersey soldiers who fought in the Civil War. ("I might as well be plain with you," he said, "I'm a nut.")

Invented or perfected at the library

Edwin Land formulated the concepts for his synthetic polarizer for light, which led to his invention of instant photography, the heart of the Polaroid camera.

Chester Carlson researched photoconductivity and electrostatics, leading to his invention of the Xerox copier.

DeWitt Wallace read and condensed articles in the Periodicals Room, which eventually led to his publishing *Readers' Digest*.

A close shave

Edward C. Potter, who carved the marble pair of lions at the entrance, originally gave them larger manes, but passersby wrote letters to newspapers complaining that the lions' chests were too hairy. So Potter shaved the beasts a little, and then they were completed in pink Tennessee marble.

10

Source: Daniela Weiss, ed., *Shh! Little Known Facts and Library Lore* (New York Public Library, 1986)

Rubber stamps and libraries

by Jonathan Held

A COMMON MARKING DEVICE, even one designed to aid in the most menial, repetitive office tasks, can tell a story. So it is with the lowly rubber stamp, believed to have first appeared in the 1860s and to have become a fixture in American libraries some time before the 1920s—when *Stamp Trade News* ran a series of contests focusing on library-property stamps.

The Design and Exhibits staff at the Dallas Public Library, believing that a representative collection of library rubber stamps could illustrate some of the concerns and activities of library workers, issued a call to the profession in early 1982: Send us rubber stamps no longer in use.

Inveterate collectors that they are, librarians found rubber stamps to spare— some 5,000 of them! The stamps poured in from 37 states, Canada, Japan, and Saudi Arabia.

From these contributions, Dallas staff selected 821 for a six-week fall exhibition, "Their Indelible Mark: Rubber Stamps and Libraries." Into the library's bright new Community Showcase exhibits center filed hundreds of citizens to view three categories of stamps: those having to do with Collection, Classification, and Circulation.

In general, the stamps—enhanced by an exhibit brochure, captions, and graphics—informed the public of the different tasks library workers perform, patterns of library service, and some of the ways information is categorized and disseminated. A few stamps suggested those circumstances under which information is restricted. It is an interesting historical note, for example, that this message recurred frequently enough to require a rubber stamp . . .

> THIS MATERIAL WAS PRINTED BEHIND THE
> IRON CURTAIN; THEREFORE, THE PHILOSOPHY
> EXPRESSED MAY NOT BE CONSISTENT WITH
> THAT OF WESTERN CIVILIZATION.

. . . as did this one:

> THE PASSAGE OF THE JARVIS/GANN AMENDMENT
> RESULTS IN NO FUNDING FOR THE LIBRARY, AT
> LEAST TEMPORARILY.   YOUR REQUEST CANNOT
> BE FILLED. SORRY.

These and other "indelible" impressions offered a unique and creative way to convey some historical aspects of the library institution. But will rubber stamps continue to reveal our ways? A letter sent in response to our search suggests not. The Director of the Bell Laboratories and Information Systems wrote to tell us that:

"Stamps have almost totally disappeared from our library network, which relies heavily on a complex of computer systems. The systems generate reports, messages, forms, and other inputs that do away with much of our former need for stamps."

It appears that rubber stamps may be among the first casualties of the Information Revolution, and that another facet of Americana may vanish. But they have served to remind us of how often clues to the essential nature of things are found in the most commonplace artifacts of daily life.

Source: Jonathan Held, "Their Indelible Mark: Rubber Stamps & Libraries," *American Libraries*, December 1982, pp. 680–82

THIS IS THE <u>ONLY</u> WRITTEN
NOTICE YOU WILL RECEIVE.

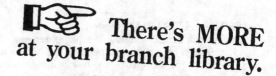

There's MORE
at your branch library.

PHOTOCOPY PERMISSION DENIED

EASY ADULT

DISCARD ALL
RECEIVED

I Read

OVERSIZE

GET IT FROM YOUR COUNTY LIBRARY

DO NOT RETURN IN CHUTE

WHITE HOUSE LIBRARY
AND
RESEARCH CENTER

Mutilation Noted

Least-understood library terms

In 1989 researchers at Carnegie-Mellon University Library measured the comprehension level of technical language used by librarians in reference interviews and handouts. Here are the terms that were least understood by students and which should probably be defined when speaking to most users.

1. Multi-volume set
2. Proceedings
3. Command search
4. Citation
5. Clearinghouse

6. Nonprint materials
7. University archives
8. Viewing carrel area
9. Primary source
10. Library rep

Source: Rachael Naismith and Joan Stein, "Library Jargon," *College & Research Libraries,*
September 1989, pp. 543–52

10

A dozen library trivia puzzlers

by George M. Eberhart

BEING A LIBRARIAN these days isn't easy. It requires nerve, cunning, omniscience, a certain amount of schizophrenia, and a pronounced talent for juggling figures on a tightrope perched high above a menacing cutback.

Perhaps the most awesome task comes at nonwork-related social gatherings and trivia-game parties, where librarians are expected to be walking encyclopedias.

Though you may feel comfortable with science, literature, entertainment, or even sports questions, how skillful are you in the trivia of your own profession?

Here is your chance to find out. Shrewdly answer the following questions, then see the answers on page 483.

1. The first woman to be employed in an American library was probably Mrs. A. B. Harnden, who was hired in 1856 at:

a. Yale University
b. Mercantile Library of San Francisco
c. Boston Athenaeum
d. Vassar College
e. Astor Library
f. Providence P.L.

2. Which pope took initial steps to transform the unorganized papal collections into the Vatican Library?

a. Boniface VIII
b. Gregory the Great
c. Innocent VIII
d. Nicholas V

3. Which U.S. academic library displays, on an outside wall adjacent to the main entrance, a limestone sculpture of a student "Nature Boy" reading a book?

a. Washington State University
b. Chaffey College
c. Lewis & Clark Community College
d. University of Delaware

4. In which Beach Boys song does the heroine go cruising in her father's car under the pretext of visiting the library?

a. Surfer Girl
b. Car Crazy Cutie
c. Lana
d. Shut Down
e. Fun, Fun, Fun
f. Little Honda

5. Which country was the first to feature a library on its postage stamps?

a. Algeria
b. Great Britain
c. Spain
d. United States
e. Iceland
f. Belgium

6. Which database vendor would you use to search for ecological literature on the Pacific islands under U.S. jurisdiction?

a. DIALOG
b. ISI
c. SDC
d. BRS

7. Where was the 1960 ALA Annual Conference held?

a. Chicago
b. Niagara Falls
c. Kansas City

d. Montreal
e. Dallas
f. Washington, D.C.

8. Which Roman consul constructed the first public library in Rome?

a. Sulpicius Gallus
b. Asinius Pollio

c. Marc Antony
d. Mucius Scaevola

9. Where would you go to see the largest U.S. collection of materials on historical witchcraft?

a. Salem State College
b. Cornell University

c. Miskatonic University
d. Columbia University

10. Which author wrote a mystery novel centering on the macabre death of the mythical "Werner-Bok" Library manuscripts librarian?

a. Charles A. Goodrum
b. Amanda Cross
c. Michael Innes

d. Jane Langton
e. Edmund Crispin
f. Robertson Davies

11. Which European capital has installed a library in its subway system to encourage, not readership, but ridership?

a. Berlin
b. London

c. Paris
d. Geneva

12. Which public library in 1980 prohibited children from checking out the Bible without parental permission?

a. Springfield, Mo.
b. Columbus Co., N.C.

c. Warsaw, Ind.
d. Wheeling, W. Va.

Answers on page 483!

Smallest American library

THE DIMINUTIVE OCRACOKE (N.C.) Library may be the smallest public library in the United States. The library is on Ocracoke Island, which can be reached only by ferrying two hours from the North Carolina mainland. The island is part of the Cape Hatteras National Seashore.

The 96-square-foot Ocracoke building was reconstructed in 1976 from a rusted-out bookmobile that still had a solid interior. It holds about 500 books and a paperback "trading post," where old titles may be exchanged for yet unread ones. A member of the Beaufort-Hyde-Martin Regional Library System, the branch is popular among the island's 500 permanent residents, whose main sources of income are commercial fishing and tourism.

The Inverness branch of the Marin County (Calif.) Free Library at one time was the smallest at 200 square feet, but in 1987 it moved into a refurbished historical house and lost its title.

10

Source: American Libraries, February 1985, June 1987

Sonata bad idea

MUSIC STUDENTS AT Ohio State University who have a gripe to air about the OSU Music/Dance Library can always "sound off" to the Johann Suggestion Box. Originally a cardboard affair, the suggestion box underwent renovation in 1981 when library staff presented a handmade, varnished, permanent version—complete with portraits of Johann Sebastian and P.D.Q. Bach on each side—to music librarian Thomas F. Heck.

Heck, who personally answers all the questions, suggestions, and complaints submitted to the box under "Johann's" signature, says it has prompted its fair share of patron interaction and is a very good public relations device.

Some of the queries are answered in verse or dialogue and all contain a fair amount of musical puns. Ever since the box was made available, student-staff relations at the library have been very "chordial."

Source: College & Research Libraries News, June 1982, p. 219

Ninety years and still trying

SOME THINGS NEVER change? In the fight against the poor quality of paper used in library materials, apparently not. The following quotation is from the Report of the Librarian of Congress, printed in the *Message from the President of the United States to the Two Houses of Congress*, published in 1899 under the McKinley administration.

"The attention of Congress has been called to the questionable quality of the paper upon which so much of the Library material is printed. The same criticism may apply to the paper used in other forms of Government records, although with that we have only a minor concern. The deleterious process in the making of modern paper, arising especially from cheapness, and the wood pulp and chemicals used, in the interests of economy, destroy its texture and durability. We have in our Library printed journals going back to the time of Charles II, over 230 years old, the paper as staunch, the ink as clear, as when they came from the press. Under modern conditions of paper manufacture, the press sending forth from day to day so much that is perishable—newspapers crumbling in the readers' hands—the question may well arise, as affecting not only our own, but all modern libraries, as to how much of our collections will become useless because of the deterioration and disintegration of the paper used in the cheaper forms of literature.

"The Prussian Government having taken up the question, so far as it affected the integrity of German records, the Library has been enabled, through the kindness of our American embassy in Berlin, to obtain a copy of the Prussian regulations. . . .

"While this important question might readily come under Government control, nothing being more essential than the physical integrity of the national archives, so far as the Library is concerned a remedy could be found under the operation of the copyright law. An amendment that no copyright should issue until articles in printed form should be printed on paper of a fixed grade would remedy the evil, so far as the important libraries are concerned. There would be no trouble to the publisher beyond the cost of a few special sheets of paper and a slight delay in the presswork; and when the value of the franchise involved in a copyright is remembered the guaranty thus exacted as to the quality of the paper would be slight return for the privilege. Extra cost of those special sheets would be cheerfully borne by the libraries, and in the end become to the publisher a profit rather than a loss."

Our great-grandparents made a bid for permanent paper in 1899; perhaps our generation can make some progress by 1999?

Source: College & Research Libraries News, March 1989, p. 223

Norman Stevens on librarians' business cards

by Norman D. Stevens

IT HAS ONLY BEEN IN RECENT YEARS that librarians have come to realize the small but important role that high-quality business cards can have in presenting themselves and/or their libraries in a positive professional manner. The rapidly changing role of libraries, along with dramatic improvements in graphic and printing technology, has made many librarians realize that a good business card is not only useful but reinforces a positive image, and that a good business card is readily and inexpensively available.

Not all librarians have yet learned that lesson. Our ancient frugality denies many of us, who should have them, business cards—unless we purchase them at our own expense—or saddles us with business cards of an inferior quality. In the only other treatment of this subject yet published, my colleague Miss Cecily Cardew analyzed at length the Molesworth Institute's collection of the business cards of librarians, as well as some of the related correspondence, and what those cards reveal about the nature of contemporary librarianship. In her typical fashion she poked fun at her colleagues and the use of those cards ("What's in a Name? A Superficial Analysis of the Business Cards of 'Librarians,'" *Wilson Library Bulletin* 63 (June 1989): 35-38, 140).

In truth there are several valuable lessons to be learned from a further more constructive analysis of that collection, which may be the largest of its kind. In today's world there are many good reasons for librarians and libraries to have business cards. Some of those are practical (so others will know who you are and how to contact you without having to write the information down on their business card) but others are intangible (the possession of a business card does convey a certain status on the bearer). The emphasis, however, must always be on developing the best quality card possible lest all of the negative old stereotypes be reinforced. A poor-quality business card is worse than no business card at all!

Institutional cards

Some business cards used by librarians have been developed within a library for the use of various members of the staff. Such cards naturally tend to feature the name of the library while adding, on an individualized basis, information about a particular staff member. Fortunately a number of libraries have moved well beyond the repetitious use of the national library symbol by producing excellent

10

cards that graphically feature the role of the library in promoting books and reading (Ames Public Library, Flathead County Library, and Jackson County Public Library) and/or graphically illustrate the library's building, geographic location, or name (DeKalb Public Library, Flathead County Library, Johnson County Library, and Uncle Remus Regional Library). The cards of those six libraries and their librarians are outstanding examples of what a good institutional card should be.

GEORGE T. LAWSON
Director

A&ES PUBLIC LIBRARY

(515) 232-4404

210 Sixth Street
Ames, Iowa 50010

FLATHEAD COUNTY LIBRARY
Georgia Lomax - Director

247 First Avenue East
Kalispell, MT 59901

(406) 752-5300, Ext 357
(406) 752-6657

Columbia Falls Branch • Whitefish Branch • Bigfork Branch

DeKalb
Public
Library

309 Oak Street
DeKalb, Illinois
60115

Telephone
(815) 756-9568

Mrs. Carol Logue
Technical Services

UNCLE REMUS REGIONAL LIBRARY

Hancock County,
Jasper County,
Morgan County

Putnam County,
Walton County

SUZANNE PAUL
Coordinator of Library Services
Walton County
(404) 267-7719

Headquarters
1131 East Avenue
Madison, GA 30650
(404) 342-1206

**JACKSON
COUNTY
PUBLIC
LIBRARY**

Connie Jo Ozinga
LIBRARY DIRECTOR

Second & Walnut Street
Seymour, Indiana 47274
(812) 522-3412

Library

Donna Lauffer
Deputy County Librarian
913/383-2042
Telefax 913/383-1243

Office address
8826 Santa Fe • Overland Park, KS • 66212

Mailing address
Box 2901 • Shawnee Mission, KS • 66201-1301

Individual cards

Other business cards used by librarians clearly have been developed through individual imagination and initiative either by individuals who are self-employed professionals, are unable to procure institutional cards, or disappointed with the quality of those cards. Here the emphasis is always on individuals and their role and sense of self-worth. Illustrations of several such cards (Leslie Chamberlin, George Eberhart, Ruth Ann Eveland, Susan P. Klement, Nel Ward, Alice Sizer Warner, and Eileen Williams) accompanied Miss Cardew's article and so have not been selected for further illustration here. Instead, newer and equally imaginative cards, which feature high-quality graphics, from Michelle Epstein, Richard Pantano, Larry A. Parsons, Doris Thibodeau, and Joan Wellander have been selected to demonstrate how well we can present ourselves when we put our minds to it. Dr. Boorstin's card, which bears the seal of the Library of Congress

Michelle Epstein
Law Library Consultant
7713 Alcove Ave.
North Hollywood, CA 91605
818-764-7731

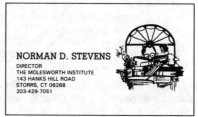

Larry A. Parsons

Library Media Specialist
W. F. West High School
342 S. W. 16th St
Chehalis, WA 98532
(206) 748-0273

Mac Hobbiist   K-9 Frisbee Enthusiast

ORIS THIBODEAU, LIBRARIAN
Institute of the History of Medicine
The Johns Hopkins University
1900 East Monument Street, Baltimore, Maryland
21205 USA   301 955-3159

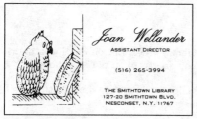

Joan Wellander
ASSISTANT DIRECTOR

(516) 265-3994

THE SMITHTOWN LIBRARY
127-20 SMITHTOWN BLVD.
NESCONSET, N.Y. 11767

DANIEL J. BOORSTIN
The Librarian of Congress

WASHINGTON, D. C. 20540

John Edward Peters
Children's Librarian

The New York Public Library

(212) 679-2645

NORMAN D. STEVENS
DIRECTOR
THE MOLESWORTH INSTITUTE
143 HANKS HILL ROAD
STORRS, CT 06268
203-429-7051

lightly and almost invisibly embossed in the upper left corner, has been included to demonstrate that even institutional cards can be given a sense of individual dignity. Mr. Peters' card has been included to demonstrate that even dignified institutional cards can, with the proper personal touch, become unique.

The electronic world

One of the joys of today's new technologies is the electronic mail systems that now enable librarians and others to communicate rapidly with colleagues across the country. The use of electronic mail has now brought with it the use of electronic business cards or signatures that offer, oddly enough, either an institutional (Kathryn S. Wright) or individual (Richard D. Hacken) sense of identity

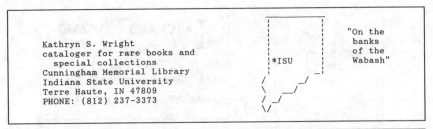

Kathryn S. Wright
cataloger for rare books and
  special collections
Cunningham Memorial Library
Indiana State University
Terre Haute, IN 47809
PHONE: (812) 237-3373

"On the
banks
of the
Wabash"

*ISU

```
*****************************************************************************
*  Richard D. Hacken              *   "WE'VE GROWN FROM SIMPLE CELLS   *
*  Germanic Studies Librarian     *        THAT FESTER . . .           *
*  Brigham Young University        *   TO WEAR OUR PANTS OF POLYESTER;  *
*  5224 HBLL, Provo, Utah  84602  *   WITH SIMPLE ACIDS NAMED "AMINO"  *
*  Humanoid: (801) 378-2374       *   WE SIT AT SLOT MACHINES          *
*  Siliconoid: LIBRDH@BYUVM.BITNET *       IN RENO . . ."      -RdH     *
*****************************************************************************
```

that parallels that found in conventional library business cards. The limits of
electronic technology results, unfortunately, in cards that may be imaginative but
lack graphic quality. The informal nature of electronic mail results in cards that
are sometimes unpolished. The development of such electronic business cards
obviously needs further work.

Source: Norman D. Stevens, The Molesworth Institute

Unusual maybe, but never stupid

FOR A COLUMN celebrating National Library Week, Detroit *Free Press* colum-
nist Robin Abcarian quizzed some Detroit librarians on "stupid" questions they'd
been asked.

"*Free Press* librarians were happy to oblige," she wrote, "since most of their
queries come from reporters." Among the questions:

- "Do you have a photo of the ozone?"
- "How many drops of water are there in a boxcar?"
- "Did Elvis die on the toilet?"
- "How many toilets are there in Moscow?"
- "Can I paint the inside of my birdcage?"
- "Did the Soviet cosmonauts see angels?"

At Detroit Public Library, librarians contacted by Abcarian refused to deni-
grate their patrons, preferring to call questions "unusual, maybe, but never
stupid."

Jeanne Salathiel, of the music and performing arts department, offered her
favorites:

- "Do you have any sound effects records with real dinosaurs on them?"
- "Do you have records of Shakespeare reading his own poetry?"
- "Do you have a record of Dristan and Isolde?"
- "How much did Beethoven's first music lesson cost?" The answer: 15
  ducats.

Jeff Tong, head of DPL's history and travel department, offered a question
concerning information on Marco Polio, and a patron who wanted to know if a
swing through West Virginia would be out of the way on a drive from Seattle to
San Francisco.

Source: American Libraries, November 1989, p. 950

Biblio-philately

by George M. Eberhart

IT WAS 1962. For over seven years Algeria had been ripped apart in bloody conflicts between the French colonial government and the Front de Libération Nationale (FLN), Algerian patriots fighting for independence. By this time it seemed likely the rebels would win, in spite of extremist measures taken by the colonialist "Secret Army," the OAS.

A desperate OAS massacre of 230 Moslems, many of them political innocents, forced the FLN to adopt sterner measures against the French. In turn, this led to intensified scorched-earth reprisals by the *pied noir* extremists.

On June 7, 1962, the OAS burned down the library of the University of Algiers, incinerating 112,500 books, and destroyed schools, laboratories, and hospital facilities. These overwhelming atrocities only sealed their fate: less than a month later in a national referendum, Algerians approved independence by a ratio of 360 to 1. France proclaimed Algeria's independence on July 3.

Many Moslem countries saw the burning of the university library as a symbol of independence and the righteousness of their cause. That is why nine of them—Algeria, Egypt, Iraq, Jordan, Kuwait, Libya, Saudi Arabia, Syria, and Yemen—commemorated the historic event on their postage stamps. The Algerian stamp shown above very strongly portrays the burning books.

Some firsts

Stamp collectors, unable to collect *every* stamp ever produced, often choose to specialize in certain topics or themes such as birds, baseball, chess, motorcycles, or nudes. Libraries, especially burning ones, are not a common theme on postage stamps, and a full set of single issues can be collected for under $150. Stamps showing books, manuscripts, maps, or other printed materials are more frequently issued, and those dealing with universities, education, or literacy are commonplace.

The U.S. Postal Service honored American libraries with a stamp in July 1982, and many other nations have handsomely commemorated libraries in their postal art. From Russia, Germany, and Spain to Greenland and the Faroe Islands have come scores of stamps on the library theme.

Earliest library stamps

Among the earliest library stamps were two nondenominational official stamps of Spain issued in 1916 and featuring the National Library in Barcelona. (Official stamps are used solely by government departments, usually as a check on the amount of mail dispatched. The United States used official stamps in 1873–1879 and 1911–1914.) The occasion was the 200th anniversary of the library's copyright depository privileges. The stamps were part of a larger series called the Cervantes Issue in honor of the novelist's death in 1616.

Another early stamp to show a library

was a 1928 Belgian 5+5 franc semi-postal issue in which the Louvain University Library appears. Semi-postals or tax stamps have a charge in addition to the postal rate which does not, strictly speaking, go to the post office, but to some other fund such as education or charity. The U.S. has never issued semi-postals. In the Belgian set, which also featured historic buildings, the surtax was used to combat tuberculosis.

The first semi-postals issued with a surtax earmarked for libraries were three stamps produced by the Philippines in 1949 to aid the restoration of war-damaged public libraries. The 4+2 centavo version depicted three former directors of the National Library in Manila; the others showed title pages of important Filipino books, including Jose Rizal's *Noli Me Tangere* (1886), which caused his exile by the Spanish government.

Stampnik

The country that has issued the greatest number of library stamps is the Soviet Union. Its first, a 30-kopeck issue of 1939 showing the Lenin State Library, was part of a series honoring the "New Moscow" of Stalinist propaganda (shown at left). Perhaps to distract attention from purges of the Trotskyites, the stamp recognized the first completed part of a new library building, the construction of which continued until 1960.

The Lenin Library, Russia's largest, owed much to the generosity of Lenin, a great admirer of libraries. The library also appears on Russian stamps of 1949, 1957, and, for its centenary, 1962. Other Soviet stamps show the Academy of Science Library in Leningrad, the Lenin University Library, the Vilnius University Library, and the Library at Erevan, Armenia.

Bulgaria has had four separate sets. One stamp commemorates the centenary of the Cyril and Methodius National Library in Sofia (1978), noted for its many Old Slavonic and Old Bulgarian manuscripts.

In 1976 East Germany issued a stamp showing the Deutsche Bücherei in Leipzig. The same library appeared on a 3-pfennig wartime stamp of 1940 issued in honor of the Leipzig Fair.

Hungary has issued two stamps commemorating the first librarian of the Budapest Municipal Library, Ervin Szabó (1877-1918), who was a leader of the doctrinaire Marxist wing of the Hungarian Socialist Party. A 1964 stamp issued in honor of Hungarian public libraries featured a portrait of Szabó, while a 1977 issue celebrated his revolutionary writings (shown at left). Szabó was responsible for translating *Das Kapital* and other writings of Marx and Engels into Magyar, introducing the decimal classification (slightly modified from Dewey) into Hungary, and almost single-handedly organizing the Budapest Library, which since 1945 has been called the Ervin Szabó Municipal Library.

Yugoslavian stamps have featured the Serbian National Library in Belgrade and the National University Library in Ljubljana. Poland and Czechoslovakia each have had library-related issues. In 1967 Romania commemorated the centenary of the Romanian Academy Library of Bucharest.

National libraries are perhaps the most obvious subjects for library postal art because they are a measure of a country's intellectual and artistic wealth.

The Scandinavians are proud of theirs. Denmark celebrated 300 years of its Royal Library in 1973 with a 120-ore stamp showing a miniature St. Mark taken from the 11th-century *Dalbybogen,* possibly the oldest book written in Scandinavia. In 1961 Sweden honored the 300th anniversary of a law enacted under Charles X whereby all Swedish printed works were to be deposited in the Royal Library at Stockholm. An Icelandic stamp of 1968 commemorated 50 years of the national library with a drawing of scholars in the reading room.

The Faroes, a group of islands in the North Atlantic between Iceland and Scotland, are a self-governing province of Denmark. The islands paid homage to both their old (shown at right) and new "national" library buildings in 1978, when the latter was completed.

Other national libraries represented on stamps are the Biblioteca Nacional de Colombia (featuring a portrait of an 18th-century Viceroy of New Grenada), the National Library of Ireland (showing a 16th-century Irish manuscript), the National Diet Library of Japan, the National Library of Vietnam (issued in 1974), and the José Marti National Library in Havana.

The Vatican's Apostolic Library, the traditional library of the popes, is essentially a national library, since Vatican City is an independent state subject to certain political restrictions under a treaty with Italy. Three stamps celebrating the 500th anniversary of the library were issued in 1975. The 100-lire version depicts Pope Sixtus IV (1471–1484), who was responsible for beautifying much of Rome; beneath his portrait are books in an old wooden press, taken from an illustration in Vatican

Codex 2044. In the same series, the 70-lire stamp shows a beautiful fresco by Melozzo di Forli in which he recalls the installation of Bartolomeo Platina as the first full-time librarian of the papal library (above).

Among other countries that have celebrated their national libraries on stamps are Austria, Belgium, Canada, Costa Rica, Dominican Republic, Egypt, Germany (Berlin), Ivory Coast, Luxembourg, and Uruguay.

Former British dependencies seem quite fond of their public libraries. To celebrate its National Day in 1975, the government of Dominica issued a set of four stamps, one of which is from a very attractive and colorful photograph of the capital's public library. Other stamps in the same set, however, featured a citrus

factory and Miss Caribbean Queen of 1975.

Barbados has one of the few stamps to feature a bookmobile (a 1984 Kenya stamp, shown at left, is another) and a visual aids truck. Both were issued in International Book Year 1972, along with stamps of Bridgetown Central Library and Codrington College. Anguilla, the Bahamas, Cyprus, and Samoa (all former British colonies) have honored their public libraries, and in 1980 Sri Lanka commemorated the opening of a new library in Colombo with a stamp.

Greenland, still a part of Denmark, in 1980 celebrated the 150th anniversary of the island's public library service by featuring the library of Godthåb's Teacher's Training College (shown at right). Prior to the establishment of true public libraries in 1905, two of

10

these college libraries served essentially the same purpose.

The University of Saarbrücken Library was featured on a 1953 stamp issued by the provisional, semi-independent state of Saar. This small territory on the Franco-German border southeast of Luxembourg was administered by France from 1944 to 1957, when it was returned to Germany.

The Elias Sourasky Library of Tel Aviv University was featured in an Israeli architectural series similar to that issued by the United States. A Portuguese stamp honored the centennial of the government's postal library in Lisbon.

The 50th anniversary Congress of the International Federation of Library Associations and Institutions (IFLA) at Brussels in 1977 was celebrated on a Belgian stamp.

The United Nations' International Year of the Child was a common stamp theme in 1979, but only Spain chose to feature children in a library. Libraries were also the focus on stamps honoring Science Day in 1980 (Algeria), the 1975 Arab Book Exhibition (Libya), and the 10th International Library Week in May 1968 (Ryukyu Islands).

Another world event commemorated in postal art was UNESCO's International Book Year. Hungary's stamp (shown at left) had a library motif.

In 1978, IFLA published a calendar that depicted many stamps commemorating library and archival organizations and events.

U.S. stamps

The first U.S. stamp honoring all of America's libraries (shown above on the right) debuted officially on July 13, 1982, at the American Library Association's annual conference in Philadelphia. Designed by graphic artist Bradbury Thompson, the library stamp features the first and last three letters from an alphabet rendered in 1523 by Geoffroy Tory of Bourges, France, whose design influenced all later Roman typefaces.

Thompson said he chose these letters for the library stamp because the "alphabet makes possible the written and printed retention and dissemination of knowledge." The particular alphabet used, which was proportioned according to the human body and face, is a variety called Sabon Antiqua.

The words "Legacies to Mankind" are adapted from a passage in Joseph Addison's *Spectator*: "Books are the legacies that a great genius leaves to mankind, which are delivered down from generation to generation as presents to the posterity of those who are yet unborn."

Thompson's original design had the words "Library of Congress" at the bottom of the stamp; but when the U.S. Postal Service and LC decided on a special stamp to commemorate the Library of Congress (shown on page 34) earlier in 1982, Addison's words were substituted.

Three earlier U.S. stamps have portrayed academic library buildings. A 1954 issue, commemorating Columbia University's bicentennial, showed Low Memorial Library. Princeton's Nassau Hall, where the first library collections were housed, appeared on a 1956 stamp—printed in black ink on orange paper to match the university's colors. The Gould Memorial Library, known as New York University Library from its opening in 1899 until it was sold to the Bronx Community College in 1973, appeared in a series on American architecture. Issued in August 1981, the stamp honors the library's architect, Stanford White.

The National Archives were honored in April 1984 on a stamp that featured profiles of George Washington and Abe Lincoln.

Source: George M. Eberhart, "Biblio-philately: Libraries and Librarians on World Postage Stamps," *American Libraries*, June 1982, pp. 382–86

Some famous librarians

ERATOSTHENES, who computed the circumference of the earth in the third century, B.C., was librarian of the Museum in Alexandria, one of the first great libraries.

Casanova (1725–1798) was librarian to Count von Waldstein for fourteen years at Dux Castle, in Bohemia, where he wrote his memoirs.

Napoleon Bonaparte (1769–1821) had a lifelong love of books. He helped organize his personal libraries and took great care in selecting librarians. As a young man he was elected librarian of the Society of the Friends of the Constitution.

August Strindberg (1849–1912) was a librarian at the Royal Library in Stockholm from 1874 until 1883.

J. Edgar Hoover worked for five years, 1912–1917, in the Exchange and Gift Division of the Library of Congress.

Boris Pasternak (1890–1960) was employed after the Bolshevik Revolution in the library of the Soviet Commissariat of Education.

The university librarian at the University of Peking, **Li Ta-chao,** was one of the founders of the Chinese Communist party. He was influential in Mao Tse-tung's becoming a Communist. **Mao Tse-tung** himself took a menial position at the university library in 1918, when he was around 25 years old, and left in 1919. He was responsible for keeping the register of library users and setting out and replacing newspapers requested by students.

Alcide de Gasperi (1881–1954), Italy's great post-war premier, was a Vatican librarian from 1931 until the end of World War II.

Jorge Luis Borges, one of the greatest living writers, was named director of the National Library of Argentina in 1955, after the fall of Perón.

Arlo Guthrie got to know Alice (of the Restaurant) when she was a librarian at the Stockbridge School.

The July 1968 *Playboy* playmate, **Melodye Prentiss,** was a librarian.

Source: Jack Womeldorf, "A Few Famous (or Infamous) Librarians," *Library of Congress Professional Association Newsletter*, December 1974

10

Library criminal justice

Shinn's last caper

JAMES R. SHINN, accused of stealing $500,000 worth of books from college and university libraries, was apprehended after he jumped bail in the summer of 1981. Spotted by Muhlenberg College librarians Dennis Phillips and Dianne Melnychuk, Shinn was arrested December 16, 1981, by FBI agents in Allentown and held in federal detention in lieu of $100,000 bail.

In January 1982 a storage operator in Bethlehem recognized Shinn as one of his customers and notified the local FBI. Agents then located 16 footlockers and 7 suitcases in a storage room that Shinn had rented, all of them containing a "mother lode" of books belonging to many university libraries, including the Universities of Illinois and Michigan.

Shinn pled guilty in July 1982 to two counts of unlawful possession and transportation of stolen property before Daniel Huyett III, a judge in the Federal District Court for Eastern Pennsylvania. Shinn's defense lawyer had initially attempted to have the evidence, 16 footlockers of books taken illegally from university libraries across the country, declared "tainted" and therefore suppressed because of Shinn's irregular arrest at Oberlin College by librarian William Moffett. However, the judge ruled that the argument lacked credibility.

Shinn was sentenced in Philadelphia on October 12, 1982, to a maximum of two consecutive 10-year federal prison terms for shipping and receiving more than $100,000 worth of rare books. Judge Huyett issued the sentences after rejecting a last-minute request by Shinn's lawyer for a delay so Shinn could help the government to identify libraries from which the books were taken. In prison, Shinn studied computer technology and corresponded with then *American Libraries* editor Art Plotnik. Released on parole in 1988, Shinn, according to Plotnik, seemed a wiser, sadder, and rehabilitated man in need of a change in luck.

Countersuit for $1 million

Former Kentucky State University philosophy professor Archibald Laud-Hammond boasted that his personal library had more philosophy books than most small college libraries. Attorney William Kirkland, a trustee of the Paul Sawyier Public Library in Frankfort, Ky., and a county sheriff proved he was right when they entered Laud-Hammond's apartment on June 21, 1988, with a civil court order to retrieve three unreturned books.

They found a sparsely furnished apartment virtually filled with books—many owned by academic and public libraries in Kentucky and Virginia. The sheriff returned with police and a search warrant and seized some 2,000 books belonging to Kentucky State University, the Kentucky Department for Libraries and Archives, Louisville Free Public Library, and the University of Virginia libraries. Many had identifying stamps and card pockets ripped out or erased. Police issued a warrant on felony theft charges.

While police were hauling away the evidence, a Cincinnati bookseller appeared at the scene and told police he'd been asked to consider purchasing the books. Laud-Hammond surrendered to police on July 12, pleading not guilty.

Full metal docket

Oscar nominee Jerry Gustave Hasford, coauthor of the screenplay for the film *Full Metal Jacket*, went to court August 18, 1988, in San Luis Obispo, Calif., on a charge of grand theft. Victimized libraries represented in the hearing included Sacramento PL, St. Louis PL, The London Library, Santa Monica PL, and Longview (Wash.) PL.

In January 1988, police opened two self-storage lockers rented by Hasford and containing 9,919 books, more than 800 of them from 62 libraries on four continents.

From a slap on the wrist to a felony charge

When arrested for trespassing and possession of burglary tools in the University of California, Riverside, library in April 1988, Stephen C. Blumberg identified himself to police as Mathew McGue, a University of Minnesota professor. Blumberg was found guilty, fined $1,000, and given three years' probation and a suspended jail sentence.

Blumberg was under investigation for library thefts totaling $1.4 million from academic libraries in California, Washington, and Oregon. As a rule, Blumberg used his forged identification to gain admittance to special collections, according to Det. Steve Huntsberry of the Washington State University police. Blumberg was also arrested for library thefts in Iowa in 1968 and in Nebraska in 1973.

Then in January 1991, the federal district court in Des Moines found Blumberg guilty on four felony counts, one of which was for possession of 21,000 rare books worth about $20 million, stolen from libraries and museums throughout the United States and Canada. Blumberg had pleaded not guilty by reason of insanity, claiming he lived in a time warp and felt driven to steal the books.

Inside job?

Ronald Redmond confessed in 1988 to the theft of some 700 books valued at $23,000 from the University of North Carolina, Greensboro Library, according to James Thompson, director. The items, now recovered, were stolen over a two-year period. Redmond, a 23-year-old UNC/G student, was arrested through the efforts of two library staffers. One learned from Redmond's roommate that his apartment was filled with library books. Associate director Doris Hulbert persuaded the roommate to cooperate with police. The only remaining mystery is whether Redmond had an accomplice on the library staff. Initially, he said that his girlfriend, who worked at circulation, aided him. He later changed his confession, saying he acted alone.

Fake librarian's career ends in court

He was an impostor, a fake librarian whose career spanned over 10 years and at least three libraries in the North Suburban (Ill.) Library System, including the directorship of Highwood Public Library.

The latest installment of Fred Lamanna's charade ended March 28, 1990, when he was placed on a year's probation in Cook County and sentenced to perform community service to atone for library thefts estimated at nearly $10,000.

With no professional credentials, Lamanna had progressed through jobs at public libraries in Northbrook, Morton Grove, and Highwood, where in 1983 he became director; he held that post until 1986, when he was exposed and fired, but never prosecuted.

The recent conviction traces back to a missing library card at the Deerfield Public Library. Deerfield Director Jack Hicks said, "The police came to me last December with lists of overdues charged to the stolen card." The card's owner had reported his driver's license and credit cards to police, but had not mentioned the library card—until he began getting overdue notices.

Hicks says word about Lamanna's past was out, and "I recognized the titles at once as being the same exact recordings and performances that every librarian in

10

this neighborhood knew about from his days as Highwood library director."

Joan Retnauer, Highwood acting director since Lamanna's dismissal in 1986, said Lamanna was fired after he used library interloan and ordering procedures to acquire materials for his own collection—"$9,000 worth of records," she said. His credentials had never been checked until it was too late.

He used the same know-how to alter the numbers on the Deerfield card so the computer linking the 46 libraries in the North Suburban system would not show the card as delinquent at checkout.

"He had some kind of Dr. Jekyll/Mr. Hyde disorder," Retnauer said. "He was a perfectly likable person, popular with the patrons. And then there was this other side of him. People just couldn't believe it."

Asked why Lamanna was not prosecuted then, Retnauer said the mayor and the library board felt there was no point in pursuing it after it was discovered that he had no money and creditors were after him.

Hicks credits Sarah Long, director, and Robert Bullin, head of administrative services, at North Suburban for pushing until Lamanna was arrested in January 1990. He also credited Deerfield detective Kevin Keel. But it was an alert clerk in Palatine who actually caught Lamanna in the act with the stolen card.

Repeated attempts by *American Libraries* to contact Lamanna, who is currently employed as an accountant, were unsuccessful, but he told the *Chicago Tribune,* "I was a good librarian. Other than the problems I got into, I really was."

15-year jail sentence for Georgia rare book thief

Robert "Skeet" Willingham, former University of Georgia rare book curator, was convicted September 8, 1988, of theft of rare library materials and sentenced to 15 years in jail. According to the *Athens Daily News,* Judge James Barrow, in pronouncing a sentence which also included 15 years' probation and $45,000 in fines, said Willingham "has breached a public trust that is irrevocable."

The paper also quoted Willingham's attorney, Ernie DePascale, who expressed "shock" at the severity of the sentence, and who immediately filed motions for sentence review and a new trial. "That kind of sentence is what we see for rape, robbery, murder, kidnapping."

Willingham, convicted of 13 counts including the theft of *Les Liliacées,* an eight-volume set of 19th-century floral prints valued at $500,000, was exonerated on one charge: Assistant District Attorney Rick Weaver failed to prove that Willingham stole a Civil War volume, purchased for $2,500, then donated it back to the University as a $3,600 partial payment of the $10,000 membership fee in The President's Club, a University booster organization.

DePascale challenged the prosecution to prove the library actually possessed the items in question. He argued that catalog cards, the only records available, were insufficient proof of ownership. He called a former UGA staffer, who testified that security had been lax enough that numerous people could have stolen the materials. According to the *Athens Observer,* DePascale would concede that only *Les Liliacées* was proved to be owned and in the possession of the Hargrett Rare Book and Manuscript Library.

"I feel good" (about the verdict), said Tom Camden, head of Hargrett. "Our collection was raped," he said. "Theft in special collections is rampant, and usually the thief gets a slap on the wrist and then opens a bookshop."

Georgia's experience may be a cautionary tale for all special collections. rooks explained that because pertinent cards had been removed from the card catalog, shelflist, and rare books shelflist, the library had difficulty proving ownership. Electronic and union list records will only serve if accompanied by additional proof of when the item was actually known to be in the collection.

A hair-raising story

In 1867, a Union Pacific railway worker named William Thompson of Omaha, Nebraska, was shot and scalped by Cheyenne Indians. He grabbed his scalp, however, and escaped on a railroad handcar. After going on tour in England with the scalp, which was billed as a medical curiosity, and lecturing on his experience, he gave his souvenir to the doctor who had treated him.

The doctor gave the scalp to the Omaha Public Library around the turn of the century, which also served as the city museum until the 1930s. Thompson's scalp is now on indefinite loan from Omaha PL to the Union Pacific Company Museum, where it can be seen today.—*Omaha Public Library.*

Answers to the trivia quiz

1. **c, Boston Athenaeum.** She was hired by William F. Poole to be his assistant, despite the warning of Poole's predecessor that "the presence of women in a library containing examples of 'the corrupter portions of the polite literature' would cause 'frequent embarrassment to modest men.'"

2. **d, Nicholas V in 1450.** A papal library or at least a collection of books had been in existence since Gregory the Great in the seventh century, and possibly earlier. Nicholas tripled the holdings by bringing manuscripts from Germany, England, and Denmark.

3. **a, Washington State University, Pullman.** The sculpture was completed in 1950 by Dudley Pratt and commemorates an early instance of "back-to-nature" living in southern California.

4. **a, Fun, Fun, Fun.** She went directly to the hamburger stand, so it "seems she forgot all about the library that she told her old man." And, of course, she had "fun, fun, fun" until her daddy took the T-Bird away. Released in February 1964.

5. **f, A 1915 Belgian stamp** shows the old Louvain University library building, destroyed a year earlier in the war. Next oldest is a 1916 official stamp of Spain that featured the National Library in Barcelona.

6. **c, SDC** offers the Pacific Islands Ecosystems database, prepared by the U.S. Fish and Wildlife Service and NTIS.

7. **d, Montreal.** This was the first and only joint ALA-CLA conference. Its theme, "Breaking Barriers," was not acknowledged by Montreal cab drivers, who were accused of stubbornly refusing to understand either French or English.

8. **b, Asinius Pollio** built the library in about 35 B.C. on the site of a temple to the goddess of liberty, Libertas, on the Aventine Hill.

9. **b, Cornell** has nearly 3,000 printed works and manuscripts in its Witchcraft Collection, begun in the 1870s by Cornell's first president, Andrew Dickson White. A catalog of the collection was published in 1977 by Kraus-Thomson. If you answered c, Miskatonic University, you must be practicing witchcraft already—for this is H. P. Lovecraft's apocryphal institution of Arkham, Mass., in whose library might be found the "monstrous and abhorred *Necronomicon* of the mad Arab Abdul Alhazrad."

10. **a, Charles A. Goodrum's** *Dewey Decimated* (1977) is also about thefts in the Werner-Bok Library. Goodrum, retired director of the Office of Planning and Development at the Library of Congress, also coauthored with Helen Dalrymple *The Library of Congress* (1982).

11. **c, Paris.** In 1984 the transit system conducted a survey to determine if further underground bibliothèques should be added.

12. **b, The Columbus County Public Library** classed the Bible as an adult book because it was considered too complex for children to understand easily.

10

Source: George M. Eberhart, "In Pursuit of Nature Boy," *American Libraries*, September 1984, pp. 585–86

ACKNOWLEDGMENTS

It is impossible to list every individual who contributed to this volume, for it is a product of many minds and much talent. Some who made a special effort to provide information and data include: Mary Jo Lynch, ALA Office for Research, who was on hand at the very inception of this project and who made absolutely certain that all the statistics were accurate; Margaret Myers, ALA Office for Library Personnel Resources, and Joey Rodger, ALA Public Library Association, who provided much material and some excellent ideas for looking at familiar data in new ways; Norman Stevens, University of Connecticut Libraries, who supplied the bits and pieces of library levity scattered throughout; Billy Wilkinson and Frederick Duda, inveterate collectors whose knowledge and wit were inspirational; Helen Teplitskaia, who went out of her way to share her insights into Soviet librarianship; all the famous librarians who examined their literary consciences for their favorite books; and all the association staff and awards committee chairs who put up with my incessant pestering about award criteria and recent winners, especially JoAn S. Segal, who had to do it on an emergency basis.

I also want to thank all those authors of articles in such journals as *College & Research Libraries News* and *American Libraries*, whose research and experiences deserve to be enshrined in a volume like this one; and everyone who served on the many committees charged with developing standards, guidelines, checklists, and tip sheets. Many hours of work go into deceptively simple documents!

My thanks also to Ed McLarin, ALA associate executive director of publishing, for his confidence and his willingness to take some chances; to copyeditor and "which-finder" extraordinaire, Sarah Guth; to Mary Frances Concepción for tracking down elusive calendar listings; to Mary Huchting, Dianne Rooney, David Epstein, and Claire DeCoster at ALA Publishing for guidance and support; and to the inventors of optical scanning hardware and software, who made my task much easier.

Last but not least, a big thank you to editor, mentor, and friend Art Plotnik, who scrutinized every line of text for error and heresy, came up with wonderful suggestions for articles from back issues of *American Libraries*, and was instrumental in crafting the content and scope of this volume.

Some final graphic credits not mentioned elsewhere: thanks to Topeka artist Greg Volpert for the excellent cartoons he drew for *College & Research Libraries News*, some of which are reprinted here (pages 341, 352–53, 357); to the Ancient and Mystical Order of the Rosae Crucis (AMORC) in San Jose for permission to use the wonderful rare book illustration (page 178) they have shown in their ads since about 1948; and to the uncredited artist who drew the silhouette on page 324 that appeared originally in *The Angolite,* the prisoner news magazine of Louisiana State Penitentiary, Angola.

AUTHOR NOTE

GEORGE M. EBERHART served for 10 years (1980–1990) as editor of *College & Research Libraries News*, the monthly news magazine of the Association of College and Research Libraries, a division of the American Library Association. He is currently managing editor of *Judges' Journal* and *Criminal Justice*, quarterly journals published by the American Bar Association. He is the author of *UFOs and the Extraterrestrial Contact Movement: A Bibliography* (Scarecrow, 1986) and *A Geo-Bibliography of Anomalies* (Greenwood, 1980), and the editor of *The Roswell Report: A Historical Perspective* (Center for UFO Studies, 1991). He holds a bachelor's degree in journalism from Ohio State University (1973) and an MLS from the University of Chicago (1976).

INDEX

Use this index to find key subject areas, bylined authors, associations and other organizations responsible for documents reprinted in this book, and people and libraries featured in illustrations.